Trusting Leviathan

Martin Daunton's major study of the [...] nineteenth century' examines the complex financial relationship between the state and its citizens. Around 1800, taxes stood at 20 per cent of national income; by the outbreak of the First World War, they had fallen to less than half of their previous level. The process of fiscal containment resulted in a high level of trust in the financial rectitude of the government and in the equity of the tax system, contributing to the political legitimacy of the British state in the second half of the nineteenth century. As a result, the state was able to fund the massive enterprises of war and welfare in the twentieth century. Combining new research with a comprehensive survey of existing knowledge, this lucid and wide-ranging book represents a major contribution to our understanding of Victorian and Edwardian Britain.

Martin Daunton is a fellow of Churchill College and professor of economic history at the University of Cambridge. He is the author of *Progress and Poverty: An Economic and Social History of Britain, 1700–1850* (1995), and editor of Volume III of *The Cambridge Urban History of Britain* (2000).

GUIDES TO TRUTH.

Frontispiece: 'Guides to truth', *Punch* 22 September 1909. The cartoon refers to the 'People's budget' of 1909. At the rear, the leader of the Conservatives, Arthur Balfour, is amending a sandwich board carried by Herbert Asquith, the Liberal prime minister. At the front, the former Liberal prime minister, Lord Rosebery, announces his opposition to the budget.

Trusting Leviathan

The Politics of Taxation in Britain, 1799–1914

Martin Daunton
University of Cambridge

9 . ii . 10

for Glen —

to celebrate the
completion of your D.Phil
with warmest best wishes,

Joshua

St. Hugh's College

CAMBRIDGE UNIVERSITY PRESS

CAMBRIDGE UNIVERSITY PRESS
Cambridge, New York, Melbourne, Madrid, Cape Town, Singapore, São Paulo

Cambridge University Press
The Edinburgh Building, Cambridge CB2 8RU, UK

Published in the United States of America by Cambridge University Press, New York

www.cambridge.org
Information on this title: www.cambridge.org/9780521803724

First published 2001
This digitally printed version 2007

A catalogue record for this publication is available from the British Library

Library of Congress Cataloguing in Publication data
Daunton, M. J. (Martin J.)
Trusting leviathan: the politics of taxation in Britain, 1799–1914 /
Martin Daunton.
       p.   cm.
Includes bibliographical references and index.
ISBN 0 521 80372 1
1. Income tax – Great Britain – History.   2. Fiscal policy – Great Britain –
History.   I. Title.
HJ4707 .D35   2001
336.2′00941 – dc21   2001025946

ISBN 978-0-521-80372-4 hardback
ISBN 978-0-521-03748-8 paperback

Contents

Illustrations

Figures

viii

Tables

Preface

The initial idea for a book on the politics of taxation in Britain, from the late eighteenth century to the present, came from David Cannadine and John Morrill. At the end of a protracted period of research and writing, I still remain grateful for their suggestion that I should tackle the subject. Their original idea expanded, for it soon became clear that a considerable amount of archival research was needed in order to make sense of the developments from the First World War through to the Thatcherite reforms. I was fortunate to obtain generous support from the Nuffield Foundation, which awarded me a Social Science Research Fellowship in 1992/3, and from the Humanities Research Board (now the Arts and Humanities Research Board) which provided an additional term of sabbatical leave in 1995/6. I was therefore able to collect a considerable amount of archival material around the country, mainly relating to the period from 1890 to the present. As a result, the initial plan for a short, single volume was abandoned, and the project migrated from Longmans to Cambridge University Press. Both Andrew McLennan and Heather McCallum at Longmans, and Elizabeth Howard and Richard Fisher at Cambridge University Press, were supportive and understanding as the project grew and developed.

The present book provides an overview of the 'long nineteenth century', from the initial introduction of the income tax in 1799 during the wars with revolutionary France when taxation amounted to about 20 per cent of the national income, through to the outbreak of the First World War when taxation was about 10 per cent of national income. It is a story of fiscal containment: the level of taxation was reduced and held down to a greater extent and for a longer period of time than in most other European countries. At the same time, the fiscal system widely came to be seen as 'fair' and equitable between interests, so helping to create the high level of legitimacy which characterised the British state in the second half of the nineteenth century and into the twentieth century. From 1914, the pattern changes: the level of fiscal extraction rose during the First World War to about 25 per cent of national income, with scarcely any fall in the 1920s and 1930s; a further increase during the Second World War took taxation to about 40 per cent of national income. The implications of this pattern will be explored in a further book, which considers in detail the demise of what may be termed the Gladstonian fiscal state whose creation is the subject of the current study.

The attempt to make sense of a new and complex topic requires more than time; it needs intellectual debate and discussion to clarify ideas and concepts. I have, again, been particularly fortunate. The intellectual stimulus for this book arose from the writings of two other historians with whom I was in close contact as I was researching and writing the book – Patrick O'Brien and Colin Matthew. Their articles on taxation in the 'long eighteenth century' and on Gladstone's budgets gave me the basis from which to start, and the present book owes much to their pioneering work. The death of Colin Matthew in 1999 shocked and saddened his many friends.

My attempt to make sense of the long-term development of the British tax system was considerably assisted by an invitation to spend three months at the Research School of Social Sciences of the Australian National University in 1994, as part of the programme on 'Administration, Governability and Compliance'. The comments on the papers I gave there in 1994 at the start of the process of writing, and again in 1996, were of great assistance in shaping my analysis. I am extremely grateful to Professor Patrick Troy of the Research School for his continued generosity and encouragement; and for providing such a congenial environment for interdisciplinary exchange. Of particular help were the comments of two others visitors: Margaret Levi of the University of Washington and Rodney Lowe of the University of Bristol.

The research and much of the writing for this book were undertaken at University College London where my students suffered from my obsession with taxation; they are spared my next obsession by my move to Cambridge. The book was completed at Cambridge, where I have been stimulated by the work of new colleagues, especially Chris Bayly, Eugenio Biagini, Peter Clarke, Boyd Hilton, Craig Muldrew, Jon Parry, Richard Smith, Gareth Stedman Jones, Simon Szreter and Adam Tooze, who have helped to bring together interests in political language, the development of welfare systems, trust, investment in public health, the finance of the empire, economic knowledge, and many other topics. I have benefitted from conversations with David Feldman, Julian Hoppit, Joanna Innes, Paul Janssens, Frank Trentmann and many others who have heard me give too many seminar papers over too long a period of time. Peter Mandler provided a thorough and extremely helpful reading. I am grateful to my Suffolk neighbour, Dave Cole, of middlegateprints.com both for finding the *Punch* cartoons and for permission to reproduce them from his collection; and to the British Museum and the Victoria and Albert Museum for permission to reproduce the cartoons of the tax eater state (Ill.1) and 'Tax land *not* food' (Ill.6). The completion of the book was greatly assisted by Chris Beauchamp who compiled the bibliography, by Linda Randall who copy-edited with her usual eye for detail, and by Auriol Griffith-Jones who produced the index.

Abbreviations

AMC	Association of Municipal Corporations
BL	British Library
BLPS	British Library of Political and Economic Science
Bod. Lib.	Bodleian Library, Oxford
DNB	*Dictionary of National Biography*
FRA	Financial Reform Association
FRU	Financial Reform Union
ILP	Independent Labour Party
LCC	London County Council
LGB	Local Government Board
LRC	Labour Representation Committee
LSE	London School of Economics
MBW	Metropolitan Board of Works
NDC	National Debt Commission
NLW	National Library of Wales
PP	Parliamentary Papers
PRO	Public Record Office
SDF	Social Democratic Federation

1 Trust, collective action and the state

When a government deals unjustly by the people with respect to taxation, that constitutes the whole matter of account between them. That has been the ground of almost all the revolutions in this country.

> Richard Cobden, 1848, quoted in H. C. G. Matthew, 'Disraeli, Gladstone and the politics of mid-Victorian budgets', *Historical Journal* 22 (1979), 616

...on the fairness of their systems of taxation the progress, the contentedness and the stability of States in large degree depends.

> Herbert Samuel, 'The taxation of the various classes of the people', *Journal of the Royal Statistical Society* 82 (1919), 181–2

The interest of the government is to tax heavily; that of the community is, to be as little taxed as the necessary expenses of good government permit.

> J. S. Mill, *Considerations on Representative Government* (London, 1861), in J. M. Robson (ed.), introduction by A. Brody, *Collected Works of John Stuart Mill*, vol. XIX: *Essays on Politics and Society* (London, 1977), p. 441

The spirit of a people, its cultural level, its social structure, the deeds its policy may prepare – all this and more is written in its fiscal history, stripped of all phrases. He who knows how to listen to its message here discerns the thunder of world history more clearly than anywhere else... The public finances are one of the best starting points for an investigation of society, especially though not exclusively of its political life.

> J. A. Schumpeter, 'The crisis of the tax state', in A. T. Peacock, R. Turvey, W. F. Stolper and E. Henderson (eds.), *International Economic Papers*, no. 4 (London and New York, 1954), p. 7

The capacity of any state to act and to realise its policy goals depends, more than anything else, on its financial resources.[1] This simple, even trite, statement is central to the formation of the state in Europe and vital

---

[1] T. Skocpol, 'Bringing the state back in: strategies of analysis in current research', in P. B. Evans, D. Rueschmeyer and T. Skocpol (eds.), *Bringing the State Back In* (Cambridge, 1985), pp. 16–18.

to its political, social and economic history, as Joseph Schumpeter was well aware. He had practical experience of the difficulties of mobilising resources as finance minister in Austria at the end of the First World War, when he pointed to a long-term shift away from a 'domain state' in the middle ages to a 'tax state' in the early modern period which he believed had reached a state of crisis.[2] The driving force for the emergence of the tax state was precisely what led to the crisis of 1918: the need of the state for resources for warfare.[3] In the middle ages, rulers relied on their own estates or domain for resources, and on the provision of goods and services by dependants. In some areas, the domain state survived into the early modern period, sometimes shifting to an entrepreneurial use of the crown's assets through exploitation of natural products such as copper and silver. Elements of the domain state survived into the nineteenth century in some European countries, where state mines and forests, or the income from railways and other services, provided a considerable income. Resources might also be obtained from outside the territory, by a process of colonial exploitation or plunder, as by Spain in the Americas or the Belgian crown in the Congo. These resources, both domestic and external, might be obtained through a process of coercion or by the use of capital in trade.[4] However, in many parts of Europe in the sixteenth and seventeenth centuries, the 'domain state' and a coercive mobilisation of resources gradually gave way to the 'tax state' as an increase in expenditure on warfare led to a search for new forms of revenue, and the development of a more complex and commercial economy created new opportunities for extracting financial resources.

The emergence of a 'tax state' was fundamental to the formation of the state in early modern Europe, and has recently been the subject of a major collaborative and comparative project.[5] The outcome differed

---

[2] J. A. Schumpeter, 'The crisis of the tax state', in A. T. Peacock, R. Turvey, W. F. Stolper and E. Henderson (eds.), *International Economic Papers*, no. 4 (London and New York, 1954), pp. 5–38. The concept is developed and applied to Denmark by E. L. Petersen, 'From domain state to tax state: synthesis and interpretation', *Scandinavian Economic History Review* 23 (1975), 116–48, and K. Krüger, 'Public finance and modernisation: the change from domain state to tax state in Hesse in the sixteenth and seventeenth centuries: a case study', in P.-C. Witt (ed.), *Wealth and Taxation in Central Europe: The History and Sociology of Public Finance* (Leamington Spa, 1987), pp. 49–62, and see table 3.1 which sets out a typology of domain and tax states.

[3] See for example C. Tilly, *Coercion, Capital, and European States, AD 990–1990* (Oxford, 1992), chapter 3; on the emergence of costly methods of warfare, see G. N. Parker, *The Military Revolution: Military Innovation and the Rise of the West, 1500–1800* (Cambridge, 1988).

[4] Tilly, *Coercion, Capital, and European States*, pp. 54–7, 99.

[5] The project was part of the European Science Foundation programme on the origins of the modern state in Europe from the thirteenth to the eighteenth centuries. The work on fiscal systems is presented in three volumes: R. Bonney (ed.), *The Origins of*

between countries, in its timing and success. The demand of the state for revenue involved a contest with other claims on resources in excess of subsistence needs – a surplus which was usually small and sometimes non-existent. The ability of any state to extract taxation depended on the power of the monarchy over groups and interests beyond its own immediate feudal tenants and estates. A demand for taxes by the crown collided with the demand of landlords for rent, and these conflicting claims on the surplus of the peasantry could provoke riot and disorder. These divergent demands had to be resolved. Agreements might be negotiated with various interests (landlords, towns, church) through assemblies in order to secure consent, possibly at the expense of exemption for particular groups such as nobles or the church. The crown might form an alliance with aristocratic lords to erode the position of small peasants to their mutual advantage; or might confirm the rights of the peasantry against their lords in order to obtain a greater share of the surplus. In Reformation Europe, the clergy might lose its exemptions and the crown might secure church lands to boost its income; in Counter-Reformation Europe, the exemptions of the church might be strengthened.[6] The outcome had major consequences for the structure of European society.

Taxation was intimately connected with the nature of the political systems of European states. The ability to extract revenue affected the capacity of the state – and the way revenue was secured, with more or less success, depended on the relationships between state and subjects. The development of assemblies, parliaments or estates varied between countries. In some cases, assemblies had more control over direct taxes and the crown might therefore opt for indirect taxes, a decision which affected the fiscal capacity of the state in different economic circumstances. In periods of recession, direct taxes might provide more revenue than indirect taxes which were sensitive to the production and sale of goods. On the

---

the *Modern State in Europe, Thirteenth to Eighteenth Centuries: Economic Systems and State Finance* (Oxford, 1995); R. Bonney (ed.), *The Rise of the Fiscal State in Europe, c. 1200–1815* (Oxford, 1999); and W. M. Ormrod, M. M. Bonney and R. J. Bonney (eds.), *Crises, Revolutions and Self-Sustained Growth: Essays in European Fiscal History, 1130–1830* (Stamford, 1999). The introduction to the final volume sets out a conceptual model of fiscal change from the middle ages to the early nineteenth century: R. Bonney and W. M. Ormrod, 'Introduction: crises, revolutions and self-sustained growth: towards a conceptual model of change in fiscal history', pp. 1–21, especially table 0.2 on pp. 4–8.

[6] For a contentious account of the allocation of the surplus, see R. Brenner, 'Agrarian class structure and economic development in pre-industrial Europe', *Past and Present* 70 (1976), 47–75; see also W. Schulze, 'The emergence and consolidation of the "tax state": the sixteenth century', in Bonney (ed.), *Economic Systems and State Finance*, pp. 267, 274–6; J. Gelabert, 'The fiscal burden', in Bonney (ed.), *Economic Systems and State Finance*, pp. 546–8, 552–7.

other hand, the yield of indirect taxes was more responsive to periods of economic growth. In some cases, the crown might secure the right to tax without future meetings of the estates; or they might sidestep control by opting for alternative methods of raising money through the sale of office. The danger of the latter course of action was the creation of a bloated, inefficient, bureaucracy and a lack of consent to taxation. The crown might well find itself incapable of securing adequate revenue, and the decision to call a meeting of the assembly to reform the fiscal system might then expose it to serious political dangers, as happened in France in 1789 when the Estates General was called for the first time since 1614/15. In other cases, the estates or parliament might make a modest grant to the crown for its ordinary spending, and retain the right to vote additional payments for extraordinary spending on war, as happened in Britain where the Commons provided a forum for compromise and consent.[7]

The emergence of a tax state could therefore be more or less successful, based on a greater or lesser degree of negotiation or duress which might expose the state to political tensions and resistance. In any case, taxes alone were not enough to meet the huge demands of war: tax revenues form an annual flow whereas the cost of war surged in periods of conflict. Taxes could only be increased to meet these pressing needs with great difficulty and political danger. The state needed to secure large amounts of money in a short period, and a number of techniques were developed in early modern Europe. The crown might sell offices or the right to collect taxes in return for a lump sum – but at the cost of creating an inefficient bureaucracy and hostility to tax farmers who were taking a private profit. The alternative was to borrow, which formed the real test of the European state by the close of the eighteenth century.[8] European states borrowed larger sums of money in relation to their annual revenues, with the risk of default and a consequent disinclination to lend to the state in the future, except on very generous terms. The tax state might therefore be unstable, liable to crisis in the face of costly wars, unless it could devise a sophisticated financial system to permit borrowing without the danger of default and loss of confidence which would make future borrowing more expensive. As Bonney and Ormrod suggest, tax states frequently collapsed before the crisis of the First World War, not least in the late eighteenth century as a result of the wars against revolutionary and Napoleonic France. By 1815, only one state in Europe

---

[7] For a detailed discussion of all these points, see Bonney (ed.), *Economic Systems and State Finance* and *Rise of the Fiscal State*.

[8] Bonney, 'The eighteenth century. II The struggle for great power status and the end of the old fiscal regime', in Bonney (ed.), *Economic Systems and State Finance*, pp. 382–6; also Bonney (ed.), *Rise of the Fiscal State, passim*, for discussion of borrowing.

had successfully mutated from a tax state to what Bonney and Ormrod term a 'fiscal state' able to combine the flow of tax revenues with large-scale borrowing – Britain. It was able to increase taxes without political and economic crisis, and at the same time borrow on an unprecedented scale as a result of a sophisticated capital market and credit network.[9]

After the settlement of 1688 and Union of 1707, England and Britain created the most successful tax state in Europe which was transformed into a fiscal state in the course of the eighteenth century. Partly, the achievement arose from a fortuitous matter of timing. Tudor and Stuart England was less affected by the military revolution and engagement in land war than most of continental Europe, so that the demands on the crown were less. Prior to 1688, taxes in England were normally in the range of 1.3 to 4.4 per cent of national income, and there was no need to resort to sale of offices, the granting of tax exemptions and privileges, or the use of tax farmers to anything like the same extent as in continental Europe. The demand of the English (and British) state for revenue rose with the accession of William III and the war with France between 1689 and 1697 to between 7.3 and 9.5 per cent, and the normal level remained between 8 and 10 per cent of national income throughout the eighteenth century. The later impact of military expenditure on the British state meant that it was able to avoid some of the difficulties encountered in the earlier stages of the shift from a domain to a tax state, which also allowed it to move more easily to a fiscal state.[10]

The creation of a British fiscal state depended on two other factors as well as the fortuitous timing of military spending. One was political, the creation of a parliamentary and administrative system which allowed the negotiation of taxes between different interests and the crown, in a way which established a high degree of consent. As Michael Braddick has argued, the tax system in England allowed individual taxpayers 'avenues of appeal and mediation', so that there was rarely a choice between paying and outright resistance which would rob the system of legitimacy. Usually, taxpayers could pay less or in a different way, and they could lobby parliament to reform and adapt the system. There was, in Braddick's

---

[9] Bonney, 'Introduction: the rise of the fiscal state in Europe, c. 1200–1815', in Bonney (ed.), *Rise of the Fiscal State*, pp. 3, 14; Bonney and Ormrod, 'Introduction', in Ormrod, Bonney and Bonney (eds.), *Crises, Revolutions and Self-Sustained Growth*, p. 20. The emergence of this combination of taxation and borrowing is explained in P. G. M. Dickson, *The Financial Revolution in England: A Study in the Development of Public Credit, 1688–1756* (London, 1967); J. Brewer, *The Sinews of Power: War, Money and the English State, 1688–1783* (London, 1989); and P. K. O'Brien and P. A. Hunt, 'England, 1485–1815', in Bonney (ed.), *Rise of the Fiscal State*, pp. 61–3, 65–6.

[10] P. K. O'Brien and P. Hunt, 'The rise of the fiscal state in England, 1485–1815', *Historical Research* 66 (1993), 129–76; O'Brien and Hunt, 'England, 1485–1815', pp. 53–100.

words, 'plenty of "give" in the system' which avoided tax revolts and allowed 'piecemeal evolution, as various strategies tested the political and administrative limits of government in order to meet escalating military costs'.[11] The English and British state was therefore able to extract more resources at less political cost, an achievement facilitated by a second factor: economic change. In the late seventeenth and eighteenth centuries, Britain's economy underwent massive change which increased the capacity of the state both to tax and to borrow. Population was released from the land and moved into industry and services, as Britain became the most urban country in Europe. The growth of traded commodities meant that it was easier to tax goods. At the same time, the economy became heavily dependent on credit which created opportunities and also risks. The dangers of business failure were moderated by a variety of means, from the growth of a culture of association and reputation to the emergence of life insurance and the creation of laws of bankruptcy. The state was both a beneficiary and an instigator of these changes, in a virtuous circle of commercialisation and financial sophistication. Parliament passed legislation to facilitate 'improvement' in transport and agriculture, and to encourage an active trade in grain. Judges developed the law of equity to allow new commercial instruments such as mortgages, life insurance and bills of exchange. Credit shifted from reliance on personal reputation and obligation to a more impersonal nexus of financial institutions – and underpinning them was the government's involvement in the financial markets of London. The reputation of the government therefore became crucial to the credit and financial system of the country.[12]

Thus taxation is intimately connected with the form of the state and the nature of the economy. Taxes varied in their responsiveness to economic growth, and the process of determining the structure and level of taxes affected the level of consent and compliance. Resistance to taxation did not simply reflect the real burden of taxes, for the way taxes were assessed and levied could produce *more* resistance in countries with *lower* levels of extraction (and vice versa). Although taxation was a higher proportion of the national income in Britain than in France in the eighteenth century, and was two to three times higher in per capita terms, resistance to taxes

[11] M. J. Braddick, *The Nerves of State: Taxation and the Financing of the English State, 1558–1714* (Manchester, 1996), especially chapter 9, pp. 180–201.
[12] I have considered these issues at length in *Progress and Poverty: An Economic and Social History of Britain, 1700–1850* (Oxford, 1995); some of the themes are discussed in C. Muldrew, *The Economy of Obligation: The Culture of Credit and Social Relations in Early Modern England* (Basingstoke and London, 1998); G. Clark, *Betting on Lives: The Culture of Life Insurance in England, 1695–1775* (Manchester, 1999); and P. Langford, *Public Life and the Propertied Englishman, 1689–1798* (Oxford, 1991).

was higher in France than in Britain. Unlike in France, there were no glaring exemptions to taxation in Britain, and taxpayers were incorporated into the fiscal regime through local machinery for assessment and collection, and participation in the negotiating of duties in parliament. The scope of excise duties was limited by the vigilance of parliament, anxious to prevent the executive from securing an independent source of revenue which would increase its power. In France, the fiscal system created greater tensions, with fewer opportunities for bargaining and resolution of conflicts. Sale of offices, use of tax farmers with a private interest in the collection of revenue, exemptions to aristocrats and church, the presence of intrusive internal duties, and the absence of an assembly to negotiate disputes between interests and with the crown, all generated tensions. French 'absolutism' was therefore constrained by a greater degree of local and sectional opposition to taxation than in Britain, and officials at the centre of the French state had less knowledge of revenues and expenditure than their British counterparts. The decision to call the Estates General to resolve the financial crisis of the *ancien régime* escalated into revolution. In Britain, constant negotiation of taxation through parliament meant a higher level of consent to taxation.[13] Consent, trust and legitimacy are crucial to the history of taxation, and these issues have been a central concern of economists, political scientists and philosophers.

A problem common to all societies is the willingness of its members to accept limits to the pursuit of individual self-interest and to opt for collective action. A simple example would be a rural community with free access to common grazing land. The individual interest of each farmer was to have as many cows and sheep as possible on the land; no single farmer could restrict the size of his neighbours' flocks, and he would be the only loser from any decision to limit his own herd. The result would be over-grazing of land, which would threaten the livelihood of every member of the community. In such a case, the community had an obvious incentive to formulate rules which imposed limits on access to the land; these rules would survive so long as each was willing to accept that his neighbours would obey the regulations, and not benefit from the restraints imposed on everyone else by himself grazing more

---

[13] Brewer, *Sinews of Power*, pp. 6–7, 15–16, 18, 22–4, 69, 73, 89–91, 127–34, 182; P. Mathias and P. K. O'Brien, 'Taxation in Britain and France, 1715–1810: a comparison of the social and economic incidence of taxes collected for the central governments', *Journal of European Economic History* 5 (1976), 610–11, 636, 640; and comments by Adam Smith, *An Inquiry into the Nature and Causes of the Wealth of Nations*, ed. R. H. Campbell, A. S. Skinner and W. B. Todd (2 vols., Oxford, 1976), vol. II, pp. 900–1, 903–5. For detailed accounts of France, see R. Bonney, 'France, 1494–1815' in Bonney (ed.), *Rise of the Fiscal State*, pp. 123–76, and J. F. Bosher, *French Finances, 1770–95: From Business to Bureaucracy* (Cambridge, 1970); on the limits to the excise, see P. Langford, *The Excise Crisis: Society and Politics in the Age of Walpole* (Oxford, 1975).

animals.[14] The basic problem is the same in a modern complex state as in a simple rural village: how is consent to collective action created, and how far will members of society agree on collective action for the provision of education, support of the elderly or investment in the infrastructure of roads, drains and water? A central issue is their willingness to pay taxes for public services rather than to retain their money for private provision through the market, philanthropy or mutual associations. How is acceptance of collective action versus private provision to be explained? Why does taxation command assent here or provoke resistance there?

One approach is associated with the Virginia school of public economics, which assumes that politicians and bureaucrats wish to maximise tax revenues and spend more, and that voters and taxpayers wish to minimise their payments and spend less. This suggests a basic conflict between a revenue-maximising state and a tax-minimising public. Much the same thought was expressed by J. S. Mill* in 1861. The important point is the creation of 'constitutional' limits through rules and procedures which fix an upper limit to the amount of tax extracted by the state. The ceiling will be reached, but the rules of the 'fiscal constitution' make it difficult to go still higher without re-negotiating the terms. In most cases, for most of the time, the 'fiscal constitution' may be taken as given, establishing the parameters within which disputes take place, much as the rules of cricket or football determine the conventions for scoring runs or goals to win a game. These rules and codes include the nature of the franchise, the powers of parliament to vary taxes or oversee expenditure and auditing procedures to control the use of funds. When the players are in agreement that they are operating within a set of rules, they can battle for advantage in order to win the game. However, at some point the 'fiscal constitution' itself becomes a matter for contestation, when the rules of the game are re-negotiated and the ceiling of taxation is raised or lowered.[15]

[14] E. Ostrom, *Governing the Commons: The Evolution of Institutions for Collective Action* (Cambridge, 1990).

[15] For a discussion of the distinction between 'constitutional' and 'in-period' choices, see G. Brennan and J. M. Buchanan, *The Power to Tax: Analytical Foundations of a Fiscal Constitution* (Cambridge, 1980), pp. 1–33, 37, and R. Hardin, 'Constitutional political economy: agreement on rules', *British Journal of Political Science* 18 (1988), 513–30. For an application of the Virginia school to the fiscal policies of William Gladstone, see B. Baysinger and R. Tollison, 'Chaining leviathan: the case of Gladstonian finance', *History of Political Economy* 12 (1980), 206–13, and C. G. Leathers, 'Gladstonian finance and the Virginia school of public finance', *History of Political Economy* 18 (1986), 515–21.

* John Stuart Mill (1806–73) was the son of James Mill; he was educated by his father and spent time in France in 1820. In 1823, he joined India House as a junior clerk, retiring with a pension in 1858 when the East India Co. was dissolved. He formed the Utilitarian Society in 1823; and contributed to the *London Review*, a journal of philosophical radicalism, from its foundation in 1835, becoming its owner from 1837 to 1840. He was

The argument suggests that expenditure reaches the maximum permitted by any particular fiscal constitution, and that the crucial issue is the periodic re-negotiation of the constitution rather than short-term manoeuvres during periods of basic agreement. The Virginia school focusses on the rules and codes which set the parameters for public expenditure, stressing the design of institutional checks on the voracious desire of the state for money.

A related approach, favoured by many social scientists in the 'public choice' school, assumes that individual taxpayers make a 'rational choice', deciding whether the payment of taxes provides a worse or better return than the purchase of services from the market. This portrays voters and taxpayers as rational economic actors who wish to maximise their utility, based on an assessment of the relative costs and efficiency of different solutions.[16] This approach has serious problems, for it assumes a particular definition of rationality rather than exploring the complex nature of motivations and the differing cultures of societies. Indeed, it can simply become a self-fulfilling, closed, explanatory system in which any action can, by some means, be portrayed as 'rational' – an approach which fails to understand the subjective understanding of action and behaviour. The 'rational choice' analysis also shares a basic assumption of the Virginia school, that the relationship between the state and the individual is essentially coercive: politicians and bureaucrats strive to take more from taxpayers than they are willing to pay, and compliance can only be achieved through fear of detection and punishment. Clearly, the extent to which taxpayers are willing to provide revenue for the state is a critical issue in politics. Richard Cobden* warned that unrest and revolution were likely outcomes of a loss of consent; individual taxpayers

MP for Westminster, 1865–8. His major publications included *Logic* (1843), *Principles of Political Economy* (1848), *On Liberty* (1859), *Representative Government* (1861), *Utilitarianism* (1863), *The Subjection of Women* (1869) and his *Autobiography* (1873). (*DNB*, vol. XXXVII, ed. S. Lee (London, 1894), pp. 390–9.)

[16] A classic statement is J. Buchanan and G. Tullock, *The Calculus of Consent: Logical Foundations of Constitutional Democracy* (Ann Arbor, 1962); see also the discussion in G. Brennan and L. Lomasky, *Democracy and Decision: The Pure Theory of Electoral Preference* (Cambridge, 1993). They develop a modified version of public choice theory, that rational actors have two personae, for the market and for the ballot box. In the latter, there is little chance of any individual voter being decisive, so electoral choice is more likely to be 'expressive' than market choice.

* Richard Cobden (1804–65) was the son of a Sussex farmer. He became a clerk and traveller for a London calico merchant, rising to a partnership in a calico warehouse in London in 1828 and in a Lancashire calico factory in 1831. He settled in Manchester, where he was one of the leaders of the Anti-Corn Law League. He was a Liberal MP from 1841 to 1857 and 1859 to 1865. He advocated international arbitration and disarmament, and negotiated the commercial treaty with France in 1859–60. (*DNB*, vol. XI, ed. L. Stephen (London, 1887), pp. 148–54.)

might engage in tax avoidance or evasion on a greater or lesser scale; or commitment to collective public action might be lost. However, the Virginia school and rational choice approaches pay little attention to the circumstances in which consent to taxation and a belief in the legitimacy of collective action might be won or lost; at most, they are concerned with the institutional structures which shape individual rational calculation.

Many social scientists now reject absolute notions of rationality and stress that decisions rest upon 'bounded rationality'. The approach of 'game theory' pays close attention to the psychology of decision making, arguing that individuals make assumptions about the trustworthiness of other actors and the extent to which a 'credible commitment' can be made. There is an obvious incentive to cheat in the payment of taxes, and to take advantage of public goods which are available to all residents of a town or nation. Why pay taxes to support a police force or school? The individual would make a considerable personal saving by evading or avoiding taxes, but the drop in local or national revenues would be minuscule, and would not affect the number of police on the beat or teachers in the classroom. There is a strong incentive for an individual taxpayer to be a 'free rider', taking advantage of facilities provided by the compliance of other taxpayers. Of course, if everyone makes the same individual calculation, revenues will collapse and collective spending will decline. Much depends upon the taxpayer's assessment of the behaviour of other taxpayers. Where the individual taxpayer believes that others *are* making their contribution, there is less temptation to evade taxation and more willingness to pay. However, if the individual taxpayer assumes that others are cheating, or that the tax system is biassed against one group in the interests of another, compliance will decline and collective action will lose its credibility and legitimacy.[17]

One answer to the 'free rider' problem might be a draconian policy of deterrence, based on fear of detection and punishment. Reliance on punishment for non-compliance could be counter-productive, for it is both costly and leads to resentment and conflict. The alternative approach is to create the conditions for co-operative solutions to problems of collective action. This rests on the creation of trust in three mutually reinforcing ways.[18] First, can the taxpayer trust other taxpayers to pay for public

---

[17] On game theory, see for example K. Binmore, *Game Theory and the Social Contract: Playing Fair* (Cambridge, Mass., and London 1994), which attempts to bring it together with political philosophy.

[18] The literature on trust is now extensive: see, for example, R. Hardin, *Collective Action* (Washington, 1982), and 'Trusting persons, trusting institution' in R. Zeckhauser (ed.), *Strategy and Choice* (Cambridge, Mass., 1991), pp. 185–209; D. Gambetta (ed.), *Trust: Making and Breaking Co-operative Relations* (Oxford, 1988); B. Barber, *The Logic and Limits of Trust* (New Brunswick, N. J., 1983); F. Fukuyama, *Trust: The Social Virtues and*

action? A lack of trust in the compliance of other taxpayers would provide a justification for non-compliance and 'free riding'. Secondly, can taxpayers trust that the state was using funds for the intended purpose, and was not diverting it to some other use? Could they be confident that revenue was not 'wasted', either through corruption and incompetence or by diverting it to the 'selfish' needs of other groups in society, whether aristocratic hangers-on at court, recipients of interest payment on the national debt or an 'underclass' of welfare scroungers? Thirdly, can the state trust taxpayers to make their payments? A lack of trust that taxpayers were 'voluntarily' compliant would lead to an increasingly complex, intrusive and deterrent system of compliance which imposed administrative, legal and accountancy costs on the taxpayer and led to resentment and hostility. The result might be a downward spiral of mutual suspicion. By their very nature, these calculations rested on guesses or gambles about the behaviour of others, and depended on social and political structures and institutions rather than individual economic rationality. The related concept of 'social capital' is helpful: the extension of networks of social interaction in civil society, through voluntary associations, clubs, commercial bodies and sociability which created a sense of reputation and mutual interdependence. A high level of social capital entails trust and a greater willingness to participate in collective action.[19]

Taxpayers have little incentive to pay their taxes in the absence of a high degree of 'trust' that other taxpayers and the government were fulfilling their obligations. The alternative approach is to create constant fear of detection for non-payment. Without trust, co-operation and 'voluntary' compliance would be impossible; the problem of 'free riding' would be endemic; and deterrence would become necessary. The presence of a high degree of mutual trust, and a willingness to make 'credible commitments', reduced the costs of collective action and so permitted the state to deal with problems which would be too expensive or politically disruptive if it were necessary to rely upon deterrence alone. Such an approach therefore moves away from the assumption that the relationship between the state and the individual is necessarily one of conflict and coercion. Rather, it points to the importance of institutional procedures and social norms which sustained co-operative solutions to the problems

the Creation of Prosperity (New York, 1995); V. Braithwaite and M. Levi (eds.), *Trust and Governance* (New York, 1998), and especially M. Levi, 'A state of trust', pp. 77–101.

[19] J. S. Coleman, 'Social capital in the creation of human capital', *American Journal of Sociology* 94 (1988), supplement 95–120; R. D. Putnam, *Making Democracy Work: Civic Traditions in Modern Italy* (Princeton, 1993) and *Bowling Alone: The Collapse and Revival of American Community Life* (New York, 2000); for a critique, see B. Fine, 'The developmental state is dead – long live social capital?', *Development and Change* 30 (1999), 1–19.

of collective action, and provided some assurance that fellow taxpayers and the government may be trusted. Like the Virginia school of public economics, the approach gives considerable weight to institutional design; unlike the Virginia school, it adopts a more complex set of attitudes and assumptions about collective action. The question becomes: what factors affected the changing willingness of taxpayers to trust each other and to trust the state, and for the state to trust taxpayers? The answer depended upon a shifting balance between four different variables.

The first important consideration was the institutional and administrative processes for collecting revenue. The design of these institutions was a technical administrative matter, but had much wider significance in exacerbating or mitigating social and political tensions. Institutional design could, at least in part, explain why a high level of extraction in one country or period led to fewer problems than a much lower level in another country or period. The design of institutions for the assessment and collection of tax was central to the creation of a co-operative rather than deterrent system of taxation. Reliance on tax farmers who took a private profit by guaranteeing a fixed sum to the state and then extracting as much as possible from the public would generate hostility and avoidance. By contrast, reliance on the taxpayers themselves to assess and collect taxes might lead to under-assessment but would also create a greater sense of fairness and consent.[20] For example, a system of assessment of liability to income tax based on lay commissioners drawn from the local business community might help to secure compliance from industrialists and merchants who had some stake in the administrative system. But if workers were to come within the reach of the income tax, they would be less well disposed to a system giving power to their employers.[21] There was a danger that institutional design might become inflexible in the face of changes in the social and political structure. A system that seemed fair in one set of circumstances might be seen as arbitrary and unreasonable as the context altered. A shift from a limited electorate to a mass democracy, from an economy based on small, family, businesses to a corporate economy or from a low to a high proportion of income taxpayers, would impose strain on institutions, and lags in adapting to change might well call into question the taxpayers' trust in the state.

---

[20] Mathias and O'Brien, 'Taxation in Britain and France', 636–40; and Brewer, *Sinews of Power*, pp. 126–34.

[21] See the problems during the First World War: R. Whiting, 'Taxation and the working class, 1915–24', *Historical Journal* 33 (1990), 895–916; and M. J. Daunton, 'How to pay for the war: state, society and taxation in Britain, 1917–24', *English Historical Review* 111 (1996), 889.

Institutional devices for the assessment and collection of taxes influenced the level of trust between taxpayers and in the government, and also had implications for a second variable: the relationship between revenue and economic change. Any tax system attaches a 'handle' to different forms of income or types of economic activity, such as rent from agricultural land, profits from trade or the consumption of goods and services which provide some external indication of wealth. The way 'handles' were attached to the tax base affected the buoyancy of revenue, and so influenced the ease with which government expenditure could be increased. Where the tax system produced an increase in revenue in line with economic growth, the government would have more room for manoeuvre in offering tax concessions and maintaining a high degree of co-operation. By contrast, where revenue lagged behind economic growth, the constant need to adjust tax rates would lead to a greater sense of resentment and political difficulties.[22]

The nature of the 'handles' attached to the economy was, in part, dependent on the level of economic development. Presumptive methods of assessment based on external signs of income and wealth were normal in agricultural societies, or where trade and industry were based on small-scale firms with many opportunities for evasion and a dearth of records to establish income or profits. It was difficult to assess the actual income of a farmer or landowner, so that land taxes usually imposed a fixed levy on each field or estate. Presumptive 'assessed' taxes were levied on obvious signs of affluence and conspicuous display, such as the number of windows in a house, the employment of male servants or the possession of a carriage or pleasure horse. The yield of these taxes did not necessarily rise in line with economic prosperity, for they did not directly measure income or wealth; on the other hand, they would not drop in times of depression. The revenue from indirect taxes levied as customs duties on imports and exports, or as excise duties on a range of goods, was inevitably affected by changes in the level of economic activity. However, the impact of economic cycles and growth on yields was influenced by the precise administrative details of the tax. Indirect taxes might fall on a narrow range of goods with a low income elasticity of demand, so that consumption did not rise in proportion to increases in income. For example, the consumption of alcohol in Britain fell at the end of the nineteenth century as income rose and spending shifted to consumer durables with a high income elasticity of demand. If the fiscal system levied duties on

---

[22] See R. A. Musgrave, *Fiscal Systems* (New Haven, 1969), pp. 125–32; R. Rose and T. Karran, *Taxation by Political Inertia: Financing the Growth of Government in Britain* (London, 1986), pp. 53–5, 129–45.

beer and not on bicycles, revenue would lag behind economic growth. Of course, the reverse might equally apply, and a tax might unexpectedly produce a large increase in revenue such as a duty on petrol or motor vehicles. The form of the tax also affected yields. An *ad valorem* tax would produce more revenue in times of inflation and less in times of deflation; a flat-rate duty would not be affected by changes in prices so that the real income of the government would fall in periods of inflation and rise in periods of deflation.[23] The structure of the fiscal system might therefore shift away from indirect towards direct taxes or from direct to indirect taxes, without conscious political decision, simply because of differences in the responsiveness of taxes to economic growth.

Changes in economic organisation allowed the development of new types of 'handles' and administrative procedures. An increase in the proportion of income and output moving through the market meant that the tax base grew and could be more easily tapped, particularly with a shift to larger units of production and distribution. Hawkers and market stalls are more difficult to tax than fixed retail shops, and a large number of shops are more difficult to tax than a smaller number of wholesalers. Similarly, it is easier to tax goods produced in large-scale plant such as breweries or distilleries, where the volume of output may be closely monitored by officials; it is more difficult to tax the production of cloth by scattered domestic workers.[24] However, more routine systems of accounting mean that presumptive methods of taxation can be replaced by direct assessment of income and profits. The movement of people into regular salaried or waged employment allows the tax authorities to obtain information on incomes or even to co-opt employers into deducting tax at source, always provided that their co-operation can be secured. Such an approach is not possible where most people are self-employed or in casual, shifting, employment. The emergence of business corporations creates both opportunities and problems. Should they be viewed merely as collections of individual shareholders who pay taxes on their dividends, or should the corporations themselves be taxed as separate entities in order to provide an additional source of revenue? Should shareholders pay tax on capital gains received from the sale of shares as well as on the dividends? These new 'handles' on the economy may be used or ignored,

---

[23] On the importance of the structure of the tax system in responding to price changes and economic activity in an earlier period, see Gelabert, 'The fiscal burden', pp. 571–6.

[24] For the operation of the Excise, see Brewer, *Sinews of Power*, pp. 101–14. The revenue authorities opposed a sales tax on shops after the First World War because of the difficulties of collection, but accepted a purchase tax levied on wholesalers in the Second World War. See M. J. Daunton, *Just Taxes: The Politics of Taxation in Britain, 1914–1979* (Cambridge, forthcoming).

and are open to contestation. The development of trusts, settlements and corporations also leads to an increasing complexity of legal and institutional forms with opportunities for tax avoidance which requires an increasingly sophisticated legal code. It might be easier to tax industry as it became more bureaucratic and large scale, but at the same time personal consumption might shift to expenditure on services which required new types of 'handles' if revenue were not to lag behind economic growth. Was it feasible to extend indirect taxes from beer and tobacco to expenditure on less tangible consumption on personal services such as restaurants or hair-dressers, holidays or entertainments?[25]

The political and economic dimensions of tax collection could work with each other to create a virtuous circle of trust, or against each other in a downward spiral of tension. The institutional and administrative system might work to create trust in government and amongst taxpayers, which might be reinforced where tax revenues grew in response to economic growth and economic change. On the other hand, trust would be threatened where revenues were inflexible in response to economic change and growth. As a result, tax 'handles' would have to be changed in order to capture revenue from new forms of economic activity or to tap economic growth, which might undermine existing agreements and coalitions, or threaten widely accepted administrative procedures. If these lags and rigidities were allowed to continue, the result might be a crisis of revenue which would destabilise the fiscal system. This directs attention to a third point: the way in which new taxes were developed and the fiscal system reformed.

The introduction of a major new tax is a rarity, and most decisions involve 'fringe tuning' or 'churning', a process by which one tax is slightly increased and another slightly reduced with little immediate impact on the structure of taxation and without affecting the core of the budget. In most cases, 'inertia' of taxation and administration maximises revenues and minimises political costs. However, inertia could also create difficulties. A marked increase in the level of expenditure or a shift in the structure of the economy might create pressure for a change in the tax regime, but the political costs might limit the scope for action and sustain inertia to the detriment of revenues.[26] Equally, political expediency might lead to a change in the tax regime with very little immediate impact on revenues, offering a concession here and imposing a charge there to reflect the government's rhetoric or electoral pressures. This modest 'fringe tuning' of

---

[25] On the discussion of these issues at the end of the First World War, see Daunton, 'How to pay for the war', 910–11.

[26] See Rose and Karran, *Taxation by Political Inertia*, pp. 3–23, 52–3, 68–9, 94–120, 158–66.

taxes might generate political debate out of proportion to the impact on revenue. Such changes could be criticised as inequitable between groups and interests, by reducing taxation on one trade at the expense of another or giving a tax break to one form of income or expenditure and not to others. Where these changes were approved by parliament, resistance could be reduced and legitimacy preserved by participation in a process of negotiation, as in eighteenth-century Britain where trade and regional interests haggled over the customs and excise duties in the Commons.[27] But participation could also cause problems, for tussles over exemptions and tax breaks could bring the fiscal system into disrepute, suggesting that taxes were the result of political favours or advantage, and therefore open to constant challenge and evasion. The problem might be avoided by removing discussion over particular tax rates and exemptions from the chamber, insisting that tax codes concentrate on general principles rather than specific exemptions, and limiting discussion to the level of government expenditure. Such a strategy was adopted in Britain in the nineteenth century, unlike in the United States where the details of taxation of particular trades were fought out in Congress and the fiscal system was riddled with exemptions and concessions. The American tax system was the product of special pleading and favours, with serious consequences for credibility and political legitimacy. The balance between participation and 'log-rolling' was a matter of considerable importance.[28] Marginal adjustments by fringe tuning might also have considerable impact on revenue in the longer term through a cumulative process of compounding, particularly when reinforced by changes in the economic structure. Indeed, modest adjustments and the gradual accretion of taxes with economic change led to an increase in revenue at the least political cost, and politicians had good reasons for avoiding major changes which disrupted existing compromises and balances between interests, as well as leading to collision with entrenched bureaucratic procedures and assumptions.[29]

In contrast to the usual 'churning' of taxes, radical or 'constitutional' reform is extremely rare. Major changes in the tax system create immense political difficulties, and are usually resisted by bureaucrats who are predisposed to collect existing taxes by established procedures and routines. As the Treasury put it, an old tax is no tax for it has entered into calculations of prices and profits; any new tax, however fair and equitable, would

---

[27] For example, P. K. O'Brien, T. Griffiths and P. Hunt, 'Political components of the industrial revolution: parliament and the English cotton textile industry, 1660–1774', *Economic History Review* 2nd ser. 44 (1991), 395–423.

[28] See S. Steinmo, 'Political institutions and tax policy in the United States, Sweden and Britain', *World Politics* 41 (1988–9), 329–72.

[29] Rose and Karran, *Taxation by Political Inertia*, pp. 12–13, 107–9, 172, 218–20.

upset relative prices and economic relations.[30] The detailed technical knowledge of bureaucrats was often used to express extreme scepticism about the feasibility of new taxes and their threat to harmonious relations with taxpayers.[31] The apparent 'obstructionism' of Gladstonian bureaucracy was often in the interests of maintaining public credibility, which had been so hard won. The danger, however, was that officials might also use their expertise to block changes needed to preserve credibility in new electoral or social circumstances. Consequently, a further important variable in the politics of taxation was the ability of permanent officials to shape the tax system by limiting the room for manoeuvre of politicians. In some political systems, officials were permanent with expertise inherited from their predecessors and elaborated into a firmly held set of consistent, long-term, principles. Fiscal policies may then be shaped by a small group of politicians and officials in circumstances of secrecy and with a capacity for continuity. On the other hand, officials might come and go with the party in power, and lack authority.[32] Both approaches could produce a variety of outcomes. Secrecy could protect the tax system from inconsistent, short-term, decisions; it could help to preserve trust in government by protecting the tax system from explicit bargaining by special interests. In Britain, the emphasis on secrecy and the discussion of taxes by a small group of politicians and officials made it possible to limit the influence of interest groups, and so preserve the impression of neutrality, even-handedness and trust. 'Secretive' discussion by a small group might also give considerable influence to officials who had greater continuity and detailed technical knowledge of administration. Their attitude was likely to be cautious, stressing the necessity of preserving existing practices in order to maintain trust and the voluntary compliance of taxpayers. Equally, the system could have serious shortcomings. An unusually determined chancellor or a pressing fiscal need was required to break down the barriers of resistance. As a result, there was a danger that change, when it did come, was driven by an aggressive ideology rather than by concern for administrative or fiscal rationalisation. Changes might not be adequately discussed and assessed before being announced as

---

[30] See below pp. 319–20.

[31] J. A. Kay and M. A. King, *The British Tax System* (Oxford, 1978), pp. 2–3. As they remark, 'The enumeration of endless lists of unimportant objections is a common administrative tactic for resisting change . . . It is extremely unfortunate that the Inland Revenue has cried wolf so often on the impossibility of administering reforms . . . that its views on what is and what is not feasible can no longer be regarded as reliable.' See below pp. 323–7 for the Inland Revenue's objections to graduation of income tax.

[32] See the comparison between Britain and the USA in M. O. Furner and B. Supple, 'Ideas, institutions, and state in the United States and Britain: an introduction', in M. O. Furner and B. Supple (eds.), *The State and Economic Knowledge: The American and British Experiences* (Cambridge, 1990), pp. 35–6.

a *fait accompli*.[33] In Britain, tax proposals emanated from the executive and passed into legislation with the backing of the government's majority in the Commons. Defeat would therefore result in the fall of the government (as in 1852), and it was possible for successive parties to impose mutually inconsistent policies. The permanent officials might therefore have little power beyond a defensive policy of advising against change rather than suggesting reforms to the fiscal system in a positive way. Rigid adherence to established routine could lead to problems by creating lags in the adjustment of the tax system to social and economic change, with lurches in policy rather than coherence. Openness also had its virtues and failings. It could result in a careful assessment of the impact of taxes on the economy and society by discussion between officials, trade associations and unions, and it might result in a stable, coherent, fiscal system. But it could also allow interest groups to secure preferential treatment, and so produce an incoherent tax code which was overwhelmed with exemptions and concessions. Such an outcome was likely where tax laws were negotiated in the chamber rather than imposed by the executive with the support of strong party discipline, so that the tax code was more susceptible to pressure from interests, and permanent officials had less power.[34]

The ability to extract revenue from a more-or-less compliant body of taxpayers, with a greater or lesser degree of mutual trust in each other and in the government, cannot be separated from a fourth point: what was the money spent on, what collective action was undertaken by the state? Whether the tax system was considered to be equitable or inequitable depended on whether the various interests and groups providing revenue felt that the state was spending 'their' money in a reasonable and appropriate way. Clearly, a fiscal system extracting taxes at a higher rate from working-class consumers than from landowners, and using the revenue to support a military establishment or sinecures, was easily criticised as inequitable. Equally, the fiscal system was open to political challenge if it were perceived to be extracting revenue from self-reliant and enterprising middle-class families in order to support passive *rentiers* living on income from government loans, or to provide benefits to an apparently feckless 'underclass'.[35] A high degree of trust in public or collective

---

33 The classic recent case is the poll tax: see D. Butler, A. Adonis and T. Travers, *Failure in British Government: The Politics of the Poll Tax* (Oxford, 1994), p. 303, which points to 'the "elective dictatorship" which gave the government an almost free rein to carry through its poll tax plans'.

34 For a comparison of fiscal policy formation, see Steinmo, 'Political institutions', 329–72, and *Taxation and Democracy: Swedish, British, and American Approaches to Financing the Modern State* (New Haven, 1993).

35 An interesting example is civil war pensions in the USA which took a large part of the revenues of the federal government at the turn of the nineteenth and twentieth centuries.

action therefore depended upon the creation of a widely shared belief
that the tax system was balanced between interests, both in the way revenue was raised and how it was spent. The creation of a sense of balance
involved far more than a simple calculation implied by rational-choice
theory, by which an individual estimated the tax bill for collective action and the benefit received in comparison with private provision. Interests were identified, and notions of 'fairness' were defined, through
a complex process of rhetorical manoeuvres and contestation of meanings. The distinction between 'productive' and 'parasitical' classes, to
take one example, might be drawn in different ways. It might define
active, employed, manual workers in alliance with enterprising industrialists, traders and professionals, in opposition to landowners and *rentiers*. Equally, the line might be drawn between owners of property in
general (landowners, industrialists, professionals with savings for their
old age and dependants, and thrifty workers) on the one hand, against
feckless welfare dependants and selfish organised workers on the other
hand.[36] Politicians did not simply devise fiscal policies to appeal to existing social categories with economically rational, self-interested attitudes to taxation; interests and identities were imagined or constructed
by politicians and the public at least in part through the rhetoric of
taxation.[37]

The measurement of taxable capacity or ability to pay was also contested. Should taxes be 'proportionate', taking the same share of income
from all classes so that the fiscal system did not alter the existing distribution of income and wealth? Should taxes reflect the benefits received
from the state, as a sort of contract with the citizen for the provision of
services? Or should taxpayers pay a variable proportion of their income;
if so, what were the relevant considerations? The definition of income itself was socially constructed. Should payments of interest and charitable
donations be deducted from taxable income? Should savings be encouraged by allowing them to be set against taxable income, or should the
income from savings pay a *higher* rate of tax on the grounds that they
did not rest on current exertion and enterprise? Taxpayers in 'active'

These were seen as partisan and linked to 'patronage democracy'; they contributed to
suspicion towards tax-funded welfare in the early twentieth century. By contrast, as this
study will argue, British spending was seen as fair and non-partisan by the late Victorian
period. See T. Skocpol, *Protecting Mothers and Soldiers: The Political Origins of Social Policy
in the United States* (Cambridge, Mass., 1992).

[36] These contested meanings of parasites and producers were fought in the land campaign:
see A. Offer, *Property and Politics, 1870–1914: Landownership, Law, Ideology and Urban
Development in England* (Cambridge, 1981); and in the discussion over the war debt at
the end of the First World War, see Daunton, 'How to pay for the war', 891.

[37] D. Wahrman, *Imagining the Middle Class: The Political Representation of Class in Britain
c. 1780–1840* (Cambridge, 1995), especially chapter 4.

trades with 'earned' incomes might be privileged over those with 'passive' investments; inherited wealth might be defined as particularly liable to high taxation; or tax breaks might be given to those who were willing to save in order to become self-reliant and provide funds for economic growth. Should occasional windfalls from capital gains be excluded from the income tax, and its coverage limited to regular, recurrent, income? What was the unit of income: should husbands and wives be taxed separately at their individual marginal rate; were they assumed to be in receipt of a single income which was taxed at the highest marginal rate of the husband; or should the combined family income be divided equally between all members, which would reduce the marginal rate of the highest income-earner? Politicians could utilise the rhetoric of taxation in order to define interests by family status, in order to privilege married men with families over bachelors and childless couples, and hence to contain any simple economic divide between rich and poor, capital and labour. The rate of tax might be increased with the level of income, on the grounds that each additional pound of income had a smaller marginal value to the recipient. However, it might also be argued that high marginal rates of taxation undermined incentives and prevented savings from being set aside for new ventures, so harming society as a whole. The answers to these questions implied different visions of society, and were central to political discourse.

Questions of definition applied not only to the income tax but also to indirect taxes and death duties on goods and assets. Discussion of the structure of customs and excise duties entailed economic calculation of their impact on consumption and yields. A high level of duty might result in lower demand and hence less revenue than produced by a modest rate of duty. Politicians and their advisers grappled with these technical considerations of the impact of taxation on consumption and yields.[38] The selection of goods and rates of duty also had moral or normative elements. Even the most ardent supporter of free trade and fiercest critic of indirect taxes accepted taxation of wine, spirits, beer and tobacco, on the grounds that consumption of these goods was 'voluntary' and possibly harmful. Taxes therefore reflected assumptions about useful and harmful, essential and luxury consumption. Commodities might move from one category to another. Tea ceased to be a luxury and became a necessity; the status of sugar was more open to dispute. The existence of endowed charities and trusts created another set of problems of definition and interpretation. Unlike individuals, they did not die and they therefore escaped payment

---

[38] For example, H. Parnell, *On Financial Reform* (3rd edn, London, 1831); see the discussion of the development of these ideas within the Board of Trade by L. Brown, *The Board of Trade and the Free Trade Movement, 1830–42* (Oxford, 1958).

of duties at death. Should they be taxed in some other way? Another complex technical issue, with major consequences for the social structure of Britain, was the taxation of settlements. Most aristocrats did not 'own' their estate, which they held as 'tenant for life' with a reversion to the eldest son. Usually, the settlement was remade on the marriage of the eldest son and the succession was continued to his son as tenant for life. Should this legal device be liable to death duties? In any case, how should death duties be defined? Duties could be imposed on the total value of the estate left at death, at either a flat or a graduated rate. Or the duty might be levied on the amount left to individual beneficiaries, and varied according to the degree of relationship to the deceased. These duties made various assumptions about the entitlement of heirs to their inheritance, and the desirability of conserving or dispersing large fortunes. There was also the issue of what property should be liable. Should 'real' property pay a lower rate than personal property and, if so, where was the line to be drawn? Personal property, such as works of art in a great house, might be 'settled' in order to avoid tax or could be defined as part of the country's 'heritage' with tax privileges. These terms were all open to challenge, and the tax system is therefore a very effective way of articulating assumptions about the market, consumption and social structures.

The process of contestation of language and construction of identities might create an impression that the fiscal system was biassed and inequitable, and so undermine the mutual trust of taxpayers in each other and in the state. Politicians had to draw a fine line so that the legitimacy of the fiscal system was not threatened. On the one hand, they had every incentive to shape the fiscal system by rhetorical devices in order to form identities and create electoral coalitions which were beneficial to them and not to their rivals. On the other hand, they did not wish to undermine the assumption that taxation was equitable, for they could not implement their policies without a secure revenue base. The balance was difficult to maintain, for it was possible that concessions would lead to justified criticisms of self-interest and inequity which would weaken trust and lead to a downward spiral of suspicion about public action. One approach was to stress the fiscal system's role in creating a social contract between classes and interests, claiming that the balance of taxes was adjusted so that it was always seen as 'fair'.[39] This approach would preserve a high degree of trust and political stability, and make the state a neutral adjudicator between interests. But at some point an alternative approach might emerge, and the tax system might become a means of changing

[39] This approach owes much to H. C. G. Matthew, 'Disraeli, Gladstone and the politics of mid-Victorian budgets', *Historical Journal* 22 (1979), 615–43, and R. McKibbin, 'Why was there no Marxism in Great Britain?', *English Historical Review* 99 (1984), 297–331.

the social structure by attacking certain categories of wealth and income. The change might arise from financial pressures on the government to produce more revenue, with the need to justify higher taxes on certain forms of income. It might arise from a shift in definitions of what was 'fair', or from new political calculations with changes in the franchise. The trick was to convince electors and taxpayers – or enough of them – that the new fiscal regime was still within the limits of acceptance and legitimacy.

The history of taxation comprises a combination of these four variables: the institutions of tax assessment and collection; the 'handles' on different forms of income and economic activity; the political processes of tax revision; and the purposes of public action. These factors help to explain the amount of revenue available to the state, the flexibility of its resources, and its ability to adapt patterns of revenue collection. As Theda Skocpol has remarked, 'a state's means of raising and deploying financial resources tell us more than could any other single factor about its existing (and immediately potential) capacities to create or strengthen state organizations, to employ personnel, to co-opt political support, to subsidize economic enterprises and to fund social programs'.[40]

This study applies these variables to Britain over the 'long nineteenth century' from 1799 to 1914. The period begins with the war against revolutionary France which ran, with one short interval, until Britain and its allies emerged victorious in 1815. These wars marked a culmination of the world-wide conflict with the French which started with the accession of William of Orange to the English throne in 1688. The British state was reconfigured as a 'fiscal-military state' based upon the efficient collection of tax revenues to cover the costs of government loans required to support a powerful army and navy. As we have noted, total government expenditure reached 8 to 10 per cent of national income in the eighteenth century; it rose to unprecedented levels during the wars with Napoleon, with a peak of 23 per cent of gross national product (GNP) in 1810. From 1815, expenditure started to drop back to the level of the eighteenth century, at around 8 per cent of GNP. The fiscal-military state was dismantled and new forms of expenditure were held in check. The fall in spending is, at first sight, easily explained. There was a 'peace dividend' with a reduction in military spending and the gradual repayment of the national debt. And the onset of more rapid and sustained economic growth from the second quarter of the nineteenth century meant that existing levels of spending fell as a proportion of the national income. However, there is still

---

[40] Skocpol, 'Bringing the state back in', p. 17.

Table 1.1 *Total government expenditure as a percentage of gross national and domestic product, United Kingdom, 1790–1937*

	GNP		GDP
1790	12	1900	13.3
1800	22	1913	11.9
1810	23	1920	20.5
1820	17	1924	23.6
1830	15	1929	24.5
1840	11	1937	26.0
1850	11		
1860	11		
1870	9		
1880	10		
1890	8		
1900	14		

Source: R. Middleton, *Government versus the Market: The Growth of the Public Sector, Economic Management and British Economic Performance, c. 1890–1979* (Cheltenham, 1996), table 3.1, p. 90, and table 3.2, p. 91.

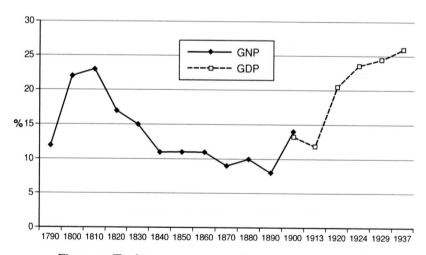

Figure 1.1 Total government expenditure as a percentage of gross national and domestic product, United Kingdom, 1790–1937
Source: R. Middleton, *Government versus the Market: The Growth of the Public Sector, Economic Management and British Economic Performance, c. 1890–1979* (Cheltenham, 1996), pp. 90–1.

something to explain, for peace and economic growth do not automatically lead to retrenchment and falling levels of spending. Indeed, it is often argued that war leads to a displacement of government expenditure to new levels by increasing spending, reforming the fiscal system at a time of emergency and creating legitimacy and capacity for postwar spending. War can therefore lead to the adoption of new programmes without the political costs of raising taxes in peace-time.[41] Both the First and Second World Wars displaced government spending; by contrast, government spending fell back to prewar levels after the wars with revolutionary and Napoleonic France – and stayed there. War-time taxation did not lead to new spending policies at the end of the war; on the contrary, the high costs of postwar debt payments and the incidence of taxation created serious political problems and de-legitimised taxation. The income tax was introduced as a war measure in 1799 and expired in 1816. The subsequent reliance on indirect taxes on trade and consumption threatened trust in the government and in other taxpayers, and the fiscal system was widely regarded as inequitable as a result of the imbalance between the social incidence of taxation and expenditure. The fiscal system also failed to attach adequate 'handles' to the rapidly changing economy.[42] In other words, Britain had created the first successful 'fiscal state' in Europe by 1815 – and now had to redefine it at the end of the war. Politicians were conscious of the need to reshape the 'fiscal constitution', a task undertaken by Peel in his budget of 1842 and confirmed by Gladstone in his budget of 1853. The 'fiscal-military' state of Hanoverian Britain retreated, and the state was reconfigured. The share of GNP taken by public expenditure fell until the end of the nineteenth century, and did not regain its previous peak until the outbreak of the First World War. Between 1850 and 1890, total government expenditure, local and central, grew at a slower rate than GNP, by 0.76 per cent for every 1 per cent rise in GNP. The forms of spending which grew faster than GNP were largely the responsibility of local government: social services (1.48 per cent) and environmental services (1.23 per cent). By contrast, the major forms of central government spending grew less than GNP: debt service

---

[41] W. E. Brownlee, *Federal Taxation in America: A Short History* (Cambridge, 1996), pp. 6–7; A. T. Peacock and J. Wiseman, *The Growth of Public Expenditure in the United Kingdom* (2nd edn, London, 1961), pp. xxxiv–xl, 30, 47–50, 78–80, 108–9.

[42] B. Hilton, *Corn, Cash and Commerce: The Economic Policies of the Tory Government, 1815–30* (Oxford, 1977), provides a detailed account of the complexities of the government's responses to postwar adjustment; G. Stedman Jones, *Languages of Class: Studies in English Working-Class History, 1832–1982* (Cambridge, 1983), chapter on 'Rethinking Chartism' and especially pp. 108–10; P. Harling, *The Waning of 'Old Corruption': The Politics of Economical Reform in Britain, 1779–1846* (Oxford, 1996), pp. 163–78; Wahrman, *Imagining*, pp. 108–44, shows how issues of taxation helped to define middle-class identity and were then subverted to criticise the selfishness of the middle class, pp. 347–8.

(0.38 per cent) and defence (0.92 per cent), with administration more or less in line with economic growth (1.08 per cent).[43] As Michael Mann has pointed out, nineteenth-century states needed less money for war, as a result of a long period of relative peace and a change in military tactics and technology which reduced peace-time defence costs. At the same time, the expansion of a capitalist economy meant that the economies of Britain, Germany, France and the United States grew faster than the state and allowed 'tax relief on a world historical scale'. Although real per capita spending rose, public expenditure fell as a proportion of the national economy from the peak at the turn of the eighteenth and nineteenth centuries. The massive 'militarist state' of the eighteenth century was rolled back and fiscal struggles became less central to politics as 'states eased away from the fiscal crises that had fuelled representative struggle for many generations'. The slack was only partly taken up by civilian spending, which created a new form of state by the end of the nineteenth century, what Mann terms a 'diamorphous civil-military state'.[44] Public expenditure did not regain its previous peak until the outbreak of the First World War, when both civil *and* military spending increased to new levels.

The outcome cannot be simply categorised as '*laissez-faire*', a concept which fails to draw attention to many features of the Victorian state. The Victorian state was concerned to exclude private profit from public action. Private contractors were prevented from running workhouses on behalf of Boards of Guardians; turnpike roads and improvement commissioners, which ran many highways and provided street lighting and watches, were replaced by public bodies. Gas for lights and water for sanitation might be provided by private companies, but they were regulated in order to prevent monopolistic exploitation of the consumer and in many cases were taken into public ownership.[45] At the same time, as many services as possible were left to the market, voluntary associations or local government. Voluntary associations created in the eighteenth and early nineteenth centuries to provide hospitals and schools formed the basis of an active municipal culture from the middle of the nineteenth century. The dismantling of the 'fiscal-military' state made the role of local government more important until the early twentieth century. Between 1850 and 1890, the annual average real rate of growth of central

[43] R. Middleton, *Government versus the Market: The Growth of the Public Sector, Economic Management and British Economic Performance, c. 1890–1979* (Cheltenham, 1996), table 3.1, p. 90.

[44] M. Mann, *The Sources of Social Power*, vol. II: *The Rise of Classes and Nation States, 1750–1914* (Cambridge, 1993), pp. 365–78, 381, 388–9, 504.

[45] See M. J. Daunton, 'The material politics of natural monopoly: gas in Victorian Britain', in M. J. Daunton and M. Hilton (eds.), *The Politics of Consumption: Material Culture and Citizenship in Europe and America* (Oxford, 2001), pp. 75–93.

government expenditure was 1.5 per cent; local government expenditure grew almost twice as fast, at 2.9 per cent.[46] Consequently, the share of local rates in total taxation increased from about 14 per cent in the 1820s to 34 per cent in the 1910s.[47] The central state could concentrate on regulation and administrative oversight of a dynamic commercial economy which could be undertaken by a relatively small administration, in tandem with the law courts and chartered professional bodies such as the Law Society or General Medical Council. A useful shorthand term to describe this reconfigured Victorian state might be a 'delegating-market' state.

The 'fiscal constitution' has been defined as a set of rules to control the desire of politicians and bureaucrats to maximise their revenues. There is, however, another possibility, that the rules were set by politicians and bureaucrats in order to constrain electors and taxpayers, forcing them to *reduce* the level of expenditure from its previous levels. This was the achievement of Robert Peel* and William Gladstone[†] in containing the 'fiscal-military' state. In the mid-nineteenth century, a fiscal constitution was created which re-established a high degree of trust in the government and in fellow taxpayers. The income tax of 1842 created a high level of voluntary compliance to taxation, by relying on a combination

[46] Middleton, *Government versus the Market*, table 3.1, p. 90.
[47] P. K. O'Brien, 'Taxation, 1688–1914', *History Review* Mar. 1997, 6.
* Robert Peel (1788–1850) was the son of a successful industrialist in the cotton industry. He was educated at Harrow and Christ Church, Oxford, and became a Tory MP in 1809. He was under-secretary for war and colonies under Liverpool in 1810–12; chief secretary in Ireland from 1812 to 1818, where he opposed Catholic emancipation and established the police force. He carried through specie resumption in 1819, and was home secretary from 1822 until resigning over Catholic emancipation in 1827. He returned to the Home Office in 1828, and abandoned his hostility to Catholic emancipation. He was prime minister and chancellor of the Exchequer in 1834–5, and formed a new ministry in 1841 which introduced the income tax, reformed banking law and repealed the corn laws. He resigned in 1846 when repeal split the party; he supported free trade and the Whigs. (*DNB*, vol. XLIV, ed. S. Lee (London, 1895), pp. 209–23.)
[†] William Ewart Gladstone (1809–98) came from a Liverpool mercantile family; he was educated at Eton and Christ Church, Oxford, and became a Conservative MP in 1832. He was junior lord of the Treasury in Peel's first administration in 1834, and under-secretary for war and the colonies in 1835. In Peel's second administration, he was vice-president of the Board of Trade in 1841 and president in 1843, resigning in 1845 over the proposal to increase the grant to the Catholic Maynooth college in Ireland. He was secretary for the colonies in 1845–6, and chancellor of the Exchequer in Aberdeen's coalition government, 1852–5. He resigned in 1855 when Palmerston became prime minister, but served as chancellor of the Exchequer in his government of 1859–66. He succeeded Russell as leader of the Liberals in 1867, and formed his first ministry between 1868 and 1874, serving as chancellor of the Exchequer in 1873–4. He resigned as leader of the Liberals in 1875, but returned and formed a second ministry in 1880–5, again serving as chancellor in 1880–2. His third ministry in 1886 fell over home rule for Ireland, and he returned to power for a third and final time between 1892 and 1894. (*DNB, Supplement*, vol. II, ed. S. Lee (London, 1901), pp. 280–329.)

of collection at source and the assessment of tax liability by members of the taxpaying public. At the same time, institutional mechanisms were devised to maintain strict controls on expenditure, and retrenchment created trust in the competence and efficiency of government. The income tax was effective in attaching 'handles' to various sources of income; revenue was buoyant and permitted a gradual reduction of indirect taxes which imposed a burden on international trade and on working-class consumers. The result was to give the government room for manoeuvre in adjusting the fiscal system in order to remove the sense that it was biassed between economic and social interests, and to reshape it in a way which could be portrayed as even-handed. Equity was defined by 'proportionality', a principle which was not seriously challenged during the mid-Victorian debates over the ability of different forms of income to bear taxation. There was also general agreement that the size of the state should be held down as far as possible. Radical and labour politicians feared that a large state would mark a return to parasitical 'old corruption' which had been dismantled with such difficulty. A new equilibrium was created, with a high level of mutual trust and 'voluntary' compliance, and the 'fiscal constitution' was taken out of politics for a generation.

The success of retrenchment and the creation of a sense of equity and even-handedness meant that by the later nineteenth century the state was widely seen as trustworthy and effective in dealing with new social and economic problems. The 'fiscal-military' state haunted radical imaginations; it was exorcised by the success of retrenchment and fears of state spending were removed. In 1836/40, the costs of 'civil government' accounted for only 10 per cent of Britain's gross central government expenditure, when defence accounted for 24.6 per cent and debt charges for a massive 57.7 per cent. Repayment of loans meant that the costs of servicing the national debt fell to 11.7 per cent by 1909/13; the costs of the naval race meant that defence spending rose to 38.0 per cent, but civil government was increased to 31.2 per cent.[48] The 'neutrality' of the state meant that radicals (and especially unskilled unions) were willing to turn to collective action to provide a solution to problems.[49] Historians have pointed to continuities from early nineteenth-century radicalism to Chartism, Liberalism and the emerging Labour party.[50] But there was also a discontinuity: the state became less feared and it was given a more

[48] H. C. G. Matthew, *Gladstone, 1809–1874* (Oxford, 1986), p. 111.
[49] A. E. P. Duffy, 'New unionism in Britain, 1889–90: a reappraisal', *Economic History Review* 2nd ser. 14 (1961–2), 318–19.
[50] See E. F. Biagini and A. J. Reid, 'Currents of radicalism, 1850–1914', in E. F. Biagini and A. J. Reid (eds.), *Currents of Radicalism: Popular Radicalism, 1850–1914* (Cambridge, 1991), pp. 1–19.

positive role. The equilibrium created in the mid-Victorian period was therefore unstable. Successful vindication from fears of an over-mighty state, and the achievement of Gladstone and others in removing taxation from contention and creating a sense of fairness, weakened support for retrenchment which had been integral to the 'Gladstonian fiscal constitution'. This interpretation challenges the orthodoxy that the 'natural' form of the Victorian state was *laissez-faire* and the 'natural' form of the later Victorian period was state growth. Instead, it argues that growth was only feasible as a result of the creation of legitimacy by means of retrenchment and, more importantly, the construction of norms of probity and transparency in the management of state finances.

The process of containing public expenditure may be criticised as socially harmful. The rhetoric of Victorian liberalism stressed the defeat of profligacy and 'old corruption' and the emergence of propriety and fiscal rectitude. But this account could be reversed, by arguing that spending in the eighteenth century maintained security, integrated the kingdom and created a dominant position in world markets for industry and commerce. On this view, the fiscal-military state was a good investment, creating economic hegemony which allowed the Victorians to proclaim the virtues of free trade and a minimal level of spending. The result, so it could be argued, was then too low a level of public expenditure to deal with the social problems of rapid change, an inadequate investment in public health or education. In Patrick O'Brien's view, 'the poor surely suffered most from the Victorian regime's ideology of fiscal parsimony and social neglect'. He criticises Victorian governments for delegating responsibilities for social and environmental services to the local authorities, and for concentrating on defence on the cheap, lapsing into complacency and concentrating on the empire rather than the threat from Germany after 1871. In his view, Victorian politicians were guilty of a massive failure of the liberal imagination.[51]

O'Brien's argument does have its virtues. In the later nineteenth century, liberal free traders ignored the way in which state power was used in the eighteenth century in creating British economic dominance. It is also true that levels of social spending on education and public health were low in the second quarter of the nineteenth century, with harmful results for the well-being of the population.[52] But the case can be pressed too far

---

[51] O'Brien, 'Taxation', 4–6.

[52] S. Szreter and G. Mooney, 'Urbanization, mortality, and the standard of living debate: new estimates for the expectation of life at birth in nineteenth-century British cities', *Economic History Review* 2nd ser. 51 (1998), 84–112, and S. Szreter, 'Economic growth, disruption, deprivation, disease and death: or the importance of the politics of public health for development', *Population and Development Review* 23 (1997), 693–728; N. F. R. Crafts, 'Some dimensions of the "quality of life" during the British industrial revolution', *Economic History Review* 2nd ser. 50 (1997), 633.

with the danger of becoming ahistorical. The costs of the fiscal-military state were high and the burdens of the debt were fiercely contested. The commitment to retrenchment was not an aristocratic policy imposed on the poor, but a deeply held radical belief. A break with the liberal dogma that taxation was a burden on the poor was only possible when trust in the state had been rebuilt, through a long process of debt redemption and fiscal reform. O'Brien argues that the debt could have been reduced by a once-and-for-all tax as David Ricardo* suggested in 1819, but this was not practicable politics – as Ricardo himself admitted. O'Brien's criticism of the central government for relying on local initiatives is based on a normative assumption which runs directly counter to the beliefs of many Victorians who stressed the desirability of creating strong local participatory democracy through public bodies and voluntary associations. And many liberals believed that spending on arms merely created more insecurity and paranoia. We need to understand the views of Victorian politicians towards the state, rather than to castigate them for failing to create a very different state structure based on different normative assumptions. The role of the state was to create the conditions for the emergence of spontaneous, self-governing, associations rather than to encroach on civil society. Victorian Britain did not develop a political theory of a strong state; on the contrary, a strong or bureaucratic state was seen as 'despotic' and mechanical, a sign of the weakness of voluntary associations and localism. By defining the state in this way, it appeared less threatening and there was toleration for its growing collaboration with voluntary bodies.[53] The higher levels of spending on welfare and warfare of the Edwardian period were possible because the serious strains in the fiscal system had been resolved through a process of retrenchment, and tax credibility laid a strong foundation for future

---

[53] On support for retrenchment, see E. F. Biagini, 'Popular Liberals, Gladstonian finance and the debate on taxation, 1860–74', in Biagini and Reid (ed.), *Currents of Radicalism*, pp. 134–62; on the importance of localities and active associational life, see E. F. Biagini, 'Liberalism and direct democracy: John Stuart Mill and the model of ancient Athens', in E. F. Biagini (ed.), *Citizenship and Community: Liberals, Radicals and Collective Identities in the British Isles, 1865–1931* (Cambridge, 1996), pp. 21–44; J. Harris, *Private Lives, Public Spirit: A Social History of Britain, 1870–1914* (Oxford, 1993), pp. 180–3, 196–211, and 'Political thought and the welfare state, 1870–1940: an intellectual framework for British social policy', *Past and Present* 135 (1992), 126, 138–9; on Ricardo, see R. O. Roberts, 'Ricardo's theory of public debts', *Economica* n. s. 9 (1942), 266.

* David Ricardo (1772–1823) was born in London, the son of a Dutch Jew, and was educated partly in Holland. He joined his father's firm of stock brokers, before setting up on his own when he moved away from the Jewish religion. He made a fortune on the Stock Exchange, and turned to economics with the encouragement of James Mill. He retired from business in 1814, and settled on a landed estate in Gloucestershire. His *Principles of Political Economy and Taxation* appeared in 1817, and he sat in parliament between 1819 and 1823, generally supporting the radicals. (*DNB*, vol. XLVIII ed. S. Lee (London, 1896), pp. 93–6.)

government growth. Of course, this Edwardian achievement was not without its problems. At the central level, the fiscal constitution became a matter of dispute between advocates of tariffs and of taxes on socially created wealth or large incomes. At the local level, serious problems started to appear as a result of the limited and regressive fiscal system based on a rate on real property. The success in reforming central taxes, and the failure in extending the local tax base, changed the shape of the British state. The buoyant sources of revenue were all held by the central government, which increased its share of revenue compared with the localities. In Germany, the situation was the reverse: the local states and cities had a wider range of taxes and more buoyant revenues, and the Reich's fiscal resources were limited and contentious.[54] This divergence had significant consequences before, during and after the First World War. Britain was able to secure the resources to fight Germany and to maintain higher levels of postwar spending, without the collapse of public finances which characterised much of continental Europe in the 1920s and 1930s.

The mid-Victorian fiscal system reached its limits by the turn of the nineteenth and twentieth centuries when the costs of naval expansion and the burdens of the Boer war put pressure on national finances, which was compounded by strains in local government and demands for welfare spending. The fiscal system now seemed narrow and unresponsive. The gradual reduction in customs and excise duties meant that their coverage was narrow, and yields did not respond to economic growth. The income tax was more buoyant in response to economic growth, but was limited by the existence of a flat rate. The cost of urban government rose as a result of increased spending on public health, education and the poor law, but the narrow tax base led to greater demands on the central government for assistance. The terms of the 'fiscal constitution' therefore needed to be re-negotiated. One solution was to raise revenue by turning back to customs duties which could be used to reshape the economy through protection and imperial preference. Another solution was to adjust the income tax, with the danger of alienating a large number of electors. The eventual outcome was to reform the income tax by introducing higher rates on large incomes and at the same time reducing the burden on modest middle-class incomes, especially of married men with families. Such a change in the fiscal system had both ideological and administrative implications. First, it meant a change in concepts of 'ability to pay' with a move from simple proportionality to the assumption that large incomes had a greater capacity to pay taxes. It entailed a rejection

[54] See below, p. 376.

of the notion that large incomes were beneficial in providing surpluses for investment, and of the assumption that taxpayers paid the state for the security of their property and lives. These changes were contested, and consent would be threatened unless taxpayers were convinced of the equity of this new definition of ability to pay. Secondly, a progressive tax system required a new method of assessment and collection with the prospect of a more interventionist system of administration, and a potential threat to 'voluntary' compliance. These issues were central to British politics in the interval between the Boer war and the First World War. At the same time as Britain was reforming its income tax, other European countries were struggling to introduce a national or federal income tax. Neither the Reich income tax of 1913, nor the French income tax of 1914, was generally accepted by social interests and classes. On the contrary, they generated serious political tensions with longer-term consequences for war finance and the resolution of postwar difficulties. As we shall see, Britain entered the First World War with a fiscal system better able to secure resources than its allies or enemies.

2   'The great tax eater': the limits of the fiscal-military state, 1799–1842

> ... as to this national *Debt*, as it is called, it is just and proper never to pay another farthing of interest upon it, if the goal of the whole nation, taking one part with the other, require a cessation of such payment. The Fundholder is not to be thought of for a *moment*, if the prosperity and happiness of the nation demand that the interest should no longer be paid. What a monstrous idea, that a *Nation* is to be bound to its ruin by individuals!
>
> William Cobbett, 'Letter II to Mr Peel, 13 Feb. 1831', *Parliamentary Register* 38, reprinted in G. D. H. Cole and M. Cole (eds.), *The Opinions of William Cobbett* (London, 1944), pp. 278–9.

The rise of the fiscal-military state

Between 1688 and 1815, Britain engaged in a long struggle with France for imperial power and trade supremacy. Although there were reverses – most particularly the loss of the Thirteen Colonies in North America – there were compensations in the Indian subcontinent and Australia. By 1815, British economic and imperial power were unrivalled. Success did not rest simply on the exploits of the army and navy, and the heroes commemorated in monuments and myth; it relied just as much on the mundane work of collecting taxes. Britain was a military state in the 'long eighteenth century'; it was also constructing a fiscal state. Effective action by armies and fleets rested on the availability of revenue to maintain naval dockyards and barracks, pay wages and supply food and munitions. As we have seen, a striking feature of the state in eighteenth-century Britain was its ability to appropriate a larger proportion of national income than the French state, with fewer political difficulties.[1] How was this achieved, and what were the consequences for the form of the British state?

Taxes were normally between 8 and 10 per cent throughout the eighteenth century. The 'fiscal-military' state of the eighteenth century came

[1] See Mathias and O'Brien, 'Taxation in Britain and France', 601–50, and Brewer, *Sinews of Power*.

32

under renewed pressure with the unprecedented demands of war with revolutionary and Napoleonic France between 1793 and 1815, when taxation reached 20 per cent of the national income of England.[2] Success did not depend simply on the availability of an increased flow of revenue, for warfare meant that large amounts were spent in a short period of time which far exceeded current income. The fiscal-military state therefore depended upon another crucial feature: the national debt. The steady flow of tax revenues was used to pay interest on loans and to provide a 'sinking fund' for the repayment of the debt; the fiscal system provided lenders with security that the government would not default and that their interest would be paid.[3]

There was a significant change in the capacity of the English and British state to expropriate revenue after 1688. Over the eighteenth century, the fiscal system became more dependent on excise duties, tariffs and stamp duties, with flat-rate direct taxes on incomes and on conspicuous signs of wealth declining in importance. The most important direct tax was the land tax. In theory, this tax was a national rate of 1s, 2s, 3s or 4s in the £ on the income not only of land but also of personal property and office; in principle, it should rise in line with rents, profits and salaries. Reality was different, for the tax was confined to land and its yield did not reflect the actual income from rents: the lowest rate of 1s in £ (5 per cent) was assumed to produce £500,000, rising to a maximum of £2m at 4s (20 per cent). These aggregate sums were divided between counties and boroughs according to their contributions in 1693 rather than by current regional prosperity. Consequently, the tax did not take account of a century of major regional economic adjustments; and neither did it reflect rising rent levels in the later eighteenth century. Indeed, the Financial Reform Association – a radical pressure group – argued in 1860 that the restoration of the land tax to the real level of the 1690s (4s in the £ or 20 per cent on the annual value of all land, buildings, mines and dividends from government loans and public companies) would solve all fiscal problems.[4] The land tax was supplemented by a range of assessed taxes

---

[2] The figures are from O'Brien and Hunt, 'The rise of a fiscal state in England', 129–76; O'Brien and Hunt, 'England, 1485–1815', pp. 53–100.

[3] Dickson, *Financial Revolution*, on the emergence of public debt; Brewer, *Sinews of Power*, chapter 4, on the use of taxes to underpin loans.

[4] On the operation of the land tax, see W. R. Ward, *The English Land Tax in the Eighteenth Century* (Oxford, 1963); on the later complaints, see FRA, *Report on Taxation. Direct and Indirect. Adopted by the Financial Reform Association, Liverpool, and Presented at the Annual Meeting of the National Association for the Promotion of Social Science Held at Bradford, October 1859* (Liverpool, 1859), p. 23, and [C. Tennant], *The People's Blue Book: Taxation As It Is and As It Ought To Be* (London, 1856; 2nd edn 1857; 3rd edn 1862; 4th edn 1872). See also the comments in [W. R. Greg], 'British taxation', *Edinburgh Review* III (1860), 254. Note that the proposal would tax public or joint-stock companies and

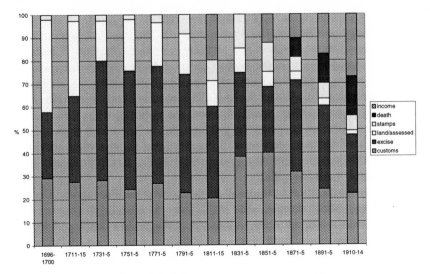

Figure 2.1 Categories of tax revenue as a percentage of all tax revenues, central government of Britain and United Kingdom, 1696–1700 to 1910–14
Source: B. R. Mitchell and P. Deane, *Abstract of British Historical Statistics* (Cambridge, 1962), pp. 386–8, 392–4.

which aimed to tap the income of the rich by taxing signs of conspicuous wealth and display such as male servants, windows, carriages and pleasure horses. However, land and assessed taxes declined from 40.1 per cent of tax revenue of central government in 1696–1700 to 17.4 per cent in 1791–5.[5] The result was an increasing reliance on indirect taxes, in the form of excise duties on a limited range of goods; and duties on exports and imports.

At first sight, customs duties offered a more buoyant tax base and a more effective 'handle' on the economy, for trade was expanding and imports of raw materials such as cotton offered a means of extracting revenue from expanding sectors of the economy. In fact, the share of customs duties fell from 29.2 per cent of central government tax revenue in 1696–1700 to 22.7 per cent in 1791–5, a trend which resulted in part from administrative difficulties and in part from the modification of duties by considerations other than revenue. The customs service was

not private firms, which is an indication of mid-Victorian concerns about the threat of 'impersonal' capital to freedom.
[5] B. R. Mitchell and P. Deane, *Abstract of British Historical Statistics* (Cambridge, 1962), pp. 386–8, 392–3. See also the data of the European State Finance Database at http://www.le.ac.uk/hi/bon/ESFDP/index.html.

Table 2.1 *Structure of tax revenue of the central government, Britain and United Kingdom, 1696–1700 to 1910–14 (percentage)*

	Direct taxes on wealth and income					Indirect taxes on goods		
	Land/assessed	Stamps	Death	Income	Total	Customs	Excise	Total
1696–1700	40.1	1.8	—	—	41.9	29.2	28.9	58.1
1711–15	32.4	2.5	—	—	34.9	27.6	37.5	65.1
1731–5	17.6	2.6	—	—	20.1	28.2	51.7	79.9
1751–5	22.3	1.9	—	—	24.3	24.2	51.5	75.7
1771–5	19.0	3.5	—	—	22.4	26.8	50.7	77.6
1791–5	17.4	8.4	—	—	25.8	22.7	51.5	74.2
1811–15	11.1	8.9	—	19.8	39.8	20.4	39.8	60.2
1831–5	10.5	14.7	—	—	25.2	38.3	36.4	74.8
1851–5	6.5	12.5	—	12.4	31.4	40.1	28.5	68.6
1871–5	3.8	6.3	8.2	10.3	28.6	31.7	39.7	71.4
1891–5	3.0	6.7	12.7	17.2	39.7	24.1	36.2	60.3
1910–14	1.8	6.5	17.0	27.1	52.3	22.3	25.4	47.7

Notes: net income to 1791–5; thereafter gross. The figures exclude income from non-tax revenue such as the Post Office and telegraphs, crown lands. Death duties are included with stamps before 1870. The land and assessed taxes include the land tax, inhabited house duty and taxes on servants, carriages, etc. From 1871, the last category was replaced by excise licences and the revenue was therefore transferred to 'excise'.
Source: B. R. Mitchell and P. Deane, *Abstract of British Historical Statistics* (Cambridge, 1962), pp. 386–8, 392–4.

administratively inefficient. Many officials held their posts through political patronage with a life freehold, which allowed them to draw an income from fees and leave the work to deputies who were paid a modest salary. Merchants might employ these customs officers to assist in the calculation of liability to the complex scale of duties, a procedure which was obviously open to abuse and collusion. In any case, duties on imports and exports were not fixed with revenue considerations alone in mind. There were also issues of national security and imperial preference, which created a desire to protect strategic goods, encourage colonial trade or preserve domestic employment from foreign competition. The complex process of brokerage with trade interests helped to shape political life and to provide links between civil society and the state, but it also limited the government's ability to use customs duties for revenue.[6]

[6] Mitchell and Deane, *Abstract*, pp. 386–8, 392–3; Brewer, *Sinews of Power*, pp. 71, 101, 211–13; on the negotiation of import and export duties, see for example O'Brien, Griffiths and Hunt, 'Political components', 395–423, and N. B. Harte, 'The rise of protection and the English linen trade, 1690–1790', in N. B. Harte and K. B. Ponting (eds.), *Textile History and Economic History* (Manchester, 1973), pp. 74–112.

The greatest increase in revenue over the eighteenth century came from excise duties. There was, again, an administrative rationale, for the excise was collected by efficient bureaucrats rather than by lay commissioners (as with the assessed and land taxes) or sinecurists (as with the customs). Excise officers were paid salaries rather than fees, promoted on merit with a pension on retirement, and controlled and inspected by a hierarchy of gaugers and surveyors under the general supervision of a central Board of Commissioners. Despite the bureaucratic nature of the Excise service, collection of duties did not create serious political tension, for the officers dealt with a relatively small number of producers, usually in large, centralised, plants such as breweries, or dealers in specific commodities. The Excise officers therefore dealt with a small number of large taxpayers rather than with the bulk of the population and compliance could be obtained without too much difficulty. One exception was in Scotland and Ireland, where small-scale illicit distilling was commonplace, and resistance to the payment of excise a point of pride. Compliance here depended on the appearance of large concerns which wished to exploit national markets. In 1824, for example, the first excise licence in Glenlivet was obtained by Smiths, to the chagrin of their neighbours who realised it would bring Excise officers into the glen, and they therefore threatened to burn the distillery. In the late 1820s, troops arrived to prevent illicit distilling and smuggling.[7] On the whole, larger commercial producers had more reason to comply and even to inform on competitors who sought to avoid the duty and steal a commercial advantage; they had an incentive to work with the Excise, negotiating over the precise interpretation of duties to take account of waste or spoiled production.[8]

Potentially, the excise posed a threat to local power structures by creating a source of income independent of parliament and under the control of a powerful central executive. This danger seemed real to country critics of the government who feared that Walpole wished to extend the excise to a wider range of commodities and to create a general excise. The ensuing 'excise crisis' of 1733/4 meant that clear limits were established to the range of excise duties in order to prevent the executive from gaining fiscal

[7] See entry on Smiths of Glenlivet in *New Dictionary of National Biography*, forthcoming.
[8] For example, see the case of the glass industry in T. C. Barker, *The Glassmakers. Pilkington: The Rise of an International Company, 1826–1976* (London, 1977), pp. 34–5, 39, 41–3. The excise duty on glass was extremely high, around twice the prime cost, so there was some incentive to defraud or even bribe the Excise officers. However, the Excise needed to take care that it did not alienate producers. When an attempt was made to tighten up the granting of allowances for waste by taking action against one producer, the courts found in his favour in 1827 and 1828. Despite winning, the costs of the case were high and producers for their part did not wish to alienate the officials. On the whole, it made more sense to ensure that everyone obeyed the rules in order to prevent unfair competition.

independence of parliament. Despite this limitation, excise duties were effective 'handles' on the economy, for consumption of beer, spirits, tea, coffee and industrial goods such as glass rose with prosperity. The share of central government tax revenue supplied by excise duties increased from 28.9 per cent in 1696–1700 to 51.5 per cent in 1791–5.[9] The choice of goods to be taxed rested on moral or cultural assumptions, as well as careful fiscal calculation and political bargaining. In order to secure a steady yield, the government needed to select commodities with a relatively inelastic demand, so that an increase in price did not lead to a collapse in purchases and revenue. These goods might be staple commodities, with the danger of political unrest; or markers of status where the attraction was the exclusivity created by high prices. The fiscal system therefore involved a debate over the nature of commodities as necessities or luxuries, as useful or harmful consumption, as narcotics which threatened control of the self or encouraged health and moral improvement.

The method of assessment and collection of the taxes contributed to the dissipation of tensions. As a general rule, the central government did not rely on government officials in the localities, but worked through justices of the peace drawn from the local gentry and clergy who operated within the limits of statute law. Similarly, collection of the land tax, assessed taxes and later the income tax was delegated to commissioners drawn from the ranks of the local taxpayers which contributed to a high level of consent. Links were created between the state and civil society, so that local structures of power and influence were reinforced rather than subverted by officials from the central government. In the words of Sir Francis Bacon,* the English taxpayer was 'most master of his own valuation' of any nation in Europe.[10] The excise duties *were* collected by an efficient, bureaucratic, central department based at Somerset House in London, but care was taken after 1733/4 that the excise should not threaten existing structures of local power and create hostility to an over-mighty central executive beyond the control of parliament. A crucial element in the success of the British fiscal system was the ability of local representatives meeting in parliament to broker deals between different

[9] On the efficiency of the Excise, Brewer, *Sinews of Power*, pp. 68–9, 101–14, 222; and limits to its extension, Langford, *Excise Crisis*; Mitchell and Deans, *Abstract*, pp. 386–8, 392–3.

[10] Quoted in Braddick, *Nerves of State*, p. 150. As Bacon went on to say, he was also 'the least bitten in the purse'. The achievement of the English state was to increase the 'bite' without threatening the taxpayers' control of valuation: Braddick, *Nerves of State*, pp. 150–1.

* Francis Bacon (1561–1626) was a leading figure in political life under Elizabeth and James I, rising to become lord chancellor in 1618 until he fell from favour in 1621 on charges of corruption and bribery. He was also a philosopher, often seen as the father of empiricism. (*DNB*, vol. II, ed. L. Stephen (London, 1885), pp. 328–60.)

economic interests and regions, bargaining over the imposition of excise or import duties on glass or iron, timber or sugar. The government was anxious to make the duties acceptable in order to ease their enforcement and collection, which created a process of power-broking between the government and groups such as the East India Co. (with its desire to import Indian textiles) and west country clothiers (who were anxious to protect their trade). The complex negotiations in parliament over the structure of duties meant that trade and mercantile interests were incorporated into the state rather than alienated, so legitimising the excise and customs duties. The government's revenue was also closely monitored by the Treasury Commissioners who produced accounts for parliamentary scrutiny, so that there was a reasonable degree of transparency and accountability which increased consent to taxation.[11]

As we have noted, the absence of this process of negotiating and bargaining in France created problems in securing consent to taxation. But the process of negotiation between interest groups and regions within the Commons was also open to criticism of 'log-rolling' or cynical deals between interests (as was to become apparent in the Congress of the United States). This criticism was often made in Britain in the early nineteenth century, and the success of British politicians by the 1840s and 1850s was to 'purge' the fiscal system of special interests and corruption, to make it balanced, equitable and free from any suspicion of deals in the Commons. However, in the eighteenth century a different set of considerations and assumptions existed: it was precisely the ability of trade and regional interests to broker deals which contributed to the success of the fiscal state.

Of course, there were critics of the emergence of the fiscal state and especially of the growth of a 'monied interest' in London based on the sale and transfer of government loans. 'Country' Whigs and Tories were alarmed that the social and political structure was being distorted, undermining the 'republican virtue' of landowners with the time and sense of duty to bear arms to defend the state. David Hume,* for example,

---

[11] Langford, *Excise Crisis*; Brewer, *Sinews of Power*, pp. 131, 147–52; O'Brien, Griffiths and Hunt, 'Political components', 395–423; J. E. D. Binney, *British Public Finances and Administration, 1774–1792* (Oxford, 1958), chapter 5.

* David Hume (1711–76) was born in Edinburgh where he studied law; he lived in France between 1734 and 1737. He failed to obtain chairs in Edinburgh or Glasgow, but did become keeper of the Advocates' Library in Edinburgh in 1752. He resigned in 1757 after he was censured for purchasing French books. He brought Rousseau to Britain and secured a pension, before they quarrelled. He spent periods as a judge-advocate in the army and in diplomatic missions, and was awarded a royal pension to complete his history of England, which appeared between 1754 and 1761. His philosophical works included *Essays Moral and Political* (1741–2), *Philosophical Essays* (1748), *Enquiry Concerning Principles of Morals* (1751) and *Political Discourses* (1752). He was sceptical towards religion,

estimated that there were about 17,000 members of the monied interest in the mid-eighteenth century who posed a serious threat to the traditional authority of parliament and landowners. These *rentiers* might become so powerful that they would be difficult to tax. The monied interest was attacked as 'cosmopolitan' and self-interested; it was able to achieve control over the government and so subvert the constitution. Hume feared the *political* dangers of debt much more than the *economic* burdens on trade and industry. In his view, the debt contained the 'seeds of ruin' through the collapse of free government into 'grievous despotism' as a result of the burden of taxes on the 'independent magistracy', with all property mortgaged to the state and power shared between an absolute monarchy and the holders of government stock. Hume therefore feared that a pluralistic mixing of landed, mercantile and monied interests could not survive, but must result in the dominance of London financiers and *rentiers*. He therefore advocated a voluntary declaration of state bankruptcy or the 'natural death' of the debt.[12]

Such gloomy views of the political consequences of the debt were not shared by everyone, for the ability of the government to raise loans provided the means of protecting English liberties and Protestantism against the menace of French absolutism and Catholicism and, after the revolution, from Jacobinism and Napoleonic ambitions.[13] Indeed, when Edmund Burke* reflected on the revolution in France, he concluded

placing his friend Adam Smith in some difficulties over the posthumous publication of his autobiography and *Dialogues on Natural Religion*. (*DNB*, vol. XXVIII, ed. S. Lee (London, 1891), pp. 215–26; for Hume and Smith, see D. Winch, *Riches and Poverty: An Intellectual History of Political Economy in Britain, 1750–1834* (Cambridge, 1996).)

[12] On Hume, see D. Winch, 'The political economy of public finance in the "long" eighteenth century', in J. Maloney (ed.), *Debts and Deficits: An Historical Perspective* (Cheltenham, 1998), pp. 12–13; J. G. A. Pocock, 'Hume and the American revolution: the dying thoughts of a North Briton', in his *Virtue, Commerce and History: Essays on Political Thought and History, Chiefly in the Eighteenth Century* (Cambridge, 1985), pp. 125–41; I. Hont, 'The rhapsody of public debt: David Hume and voluntary state bankruptcy', in N. Phillipson and Q. Skinner (eds.), *Political Discourse in Early Modern Britain* (Cambridge, 1993), pp. 321–48; D. Hume, 'Of public credit' (pp. 170, 172) and 'Of the independency of parliament' (pp. 14, 26–7, 40–5), in D. Hume, *Political Essays*, ed. K. Haakossen (Cambridge, 1994).

[13] For views on the national debt in the eighteenth century, see J. Hoppit, 'Attitudes to credit in Britain, 1680–1790', *Historical Journal* 33 (1990), 305–22; Pocock, *Virtue, Commerce and History*, pp. 69, 98, 112, 139–40, 196–7, 234–5; Dickson, *Financial Revolution*, especially chapter 2; E. L. Hargreaves, *The National Debt* (London, 1930), chapter 5; and P. Brantlinger, *Fictions of State: Culture and Credit in Britain, 1694–1994* (Ithaca and London, 1996), chapters 2 and 3.

* Edmund Burke (1729–97) was born in Dublin (a Protestant) and educated at Trinity College Dublin; he entered Middle Temple. He started the *Annual Register* in 1759 and became private secretary to W. G. Hamilton (who served as chief secretary in Ireland, 1761–4) between 1759 and 1764; in 1765 he became private secretary to the marquess of Rockingham. He was elected to parliament in 1765, where he supported economical

that the strength of the British system of finance compared with the French was precisely that it allowed a virtuous or 'miscible' collaboration of landed and monied interests in a patriotic alliance.[14] Adam Smith* took a more complicated view of the benefits and shortcomings of the national debt. He accepted that the market for government loans could be beneficial. By creating an asset with some of the character of money, the security of the market in government loans helped to create confidence and stimulated a commercial society. But he also saw problems, for the sums borrowed by the government were deducted from the national stock of capital, so reducing private investment rather than consumption, and shifting workers from productive to non-productive labour. The burden of taxes to service the debt would also restrict private investment in the longer term. Smith drew a distinction between productive and unproductive labour, and between private frugality and public prodigality, yet he was less concerned by the growth of the national debt than Hume, for he accepted that the British system allowed a more harmonious balance of interests than in France. He admitted that the proportion of the national income taken by the state for public purposes would increase with civilisation, and his concern was less to reduce the scale of the state than to ensure that the revenues were raised with least harm to private accumulation, and spent in the most efficient way. Rather than renouncing the debt, he argued that the costs of the empire should be spread to the colonies, in return for political representation in 'the states-general of the British empire'.[15] Representation should therefore be extended as a means of securing taxation – an approach ignored in the case of the American colonies.

The success of the fiscal state in eighteenth-century Britain rested on the system of collection and assessment in the localities, and expression of local and trade interests in parliament. Indeed, the development of a fiscal-military state altered relations between central and local

reform, peace with America, Catholic emancipation, opposed the slave trade and mounted an attack on Warren Hastings and the affairs of the East India Co. He was hostile to the French Revolution, supporting war with France and opposing parliamentary reform at home. (*DNB*, vol. VII, ed. L. Stephen (London, 1886), pp. 345–65.)

[14] E. Burke, *Reflections on the Revolution in France* (London, 1790; Everyman edn, 1910), p. 106.

[15] Smith, *Wealth of Nations*, vol. II, pp. 723, 924–30, 933–4; Winch, *Riches and Poverty*, pp. 115–17, 140.

* Adam Smith (1723–90) was educated at Glasgow University and at Balliol College, Oxford; he was appointed professor of logic at Glasgow in 1751 and professor of moral philosophy in 1752. His *Theory of Moral Sentiments* appeared in 1759, and he became foreign tutor to the duke of Buccleuch, visiting Turgot in Paris and Voltaire in Geneva. He returned to London in 1766 and settled in Scotland in 1767, with a pension from Buccleuch. *The Wealth of Nations* appeared in 1776, and he edited his friend Hume's autobiography in 1777. (*DNB*, vol. LIII, ed. S. Lee (London, 1898), pp. 3–10.)

government. The central government was more concerned with war and imperialism, and securing the necessary resources for the army and navy, than with the intricacies of domestic government which was largely left to local authorities (see chapter 9). These local domestic issues were discussed in parliament, which met for longer periods and devoted much of its time to private, local, bills and the concerns of backbench MPs. It is true that the central government was concerned with the implications of war on the localities, for mobilisation and demobilisation had consequences for crime and poor relief. However, its role was largely to exhort and advise rather than to direct. Many policy initiatives came from the localities, with ministers acquiescing rather than shaping the outcome. This process of central government disengagement from local administration contrasted with the situation in France and Prussia, where central government control *increased* in the eighteenth century in order to mobilise troops and raise revenue. In Britain, the emergence of a powerful central fiscal-military state was complemented by a traditional pattern of local government.[16]

The British state in the 'long eighteenth century' developed a distinctive pattern of taxation. The crown surrendered its ability to live on its own resources, and depended on grants from parliament which was jealous of its power and independence. The selection of taxes rested on a complex process of bargaining, and linked parliament with the concerns of the localities. Unlike in many other European countries, the significant increase in British taxation came in the eighteenth century and some of the problems encountered by continental European states in financing land-wars of the seventeenth century were avoided: the sale of offices, extensive use of tax farmers and the granting of fiscal privileges. The collection of taxes embedded the fiscal system in local sources of power and authority, and created a sense of trust between taxpayers and in the central state. The revenue then supported the use of loans which had a high level of security and marketability. But there were also weaknesses and problems. The process of political bargaining in the Commons was open to the charge of making the fiscal system a means of gaining favours at the expense of other interests. Such a criticism would have special force with demands for parliamentary reform in order to extend the franchise and to redistribute seats to reflect the changing distribution of population and economic activity. The patchwork of local government could also face pressure, as a result of the growth of large new urban communities without formal municipal status, and the closed, self-electing, oligarchies

---

[16] J. Innes, 'The domestic face of the military-fiscal state: government and society in eighteenth-century Britain', in L. Stone (ed.), *An Imperial State at War: Britain from 1689 to 1815* (London, 1994), pp. 96–127.

which dominated many old municipal corporations. The result might be a loss of legitimacy, a failure of the local fiscal state. The unrepresentative nature of municipal corporations created problems in raising taxes and led to a growing reliance on loans – and the mounting debt was increasingly difficult to service. The costs of supporting the poor, and coping with the costs of soldiers' wives and children during war and with the costs of adjustment at peace, fell on the parishes and the poor law. The outcome here was a patchwork of responses from the generous to the miserly, and a growing concern for costs and the reliability of the local agents of government.[17] Although the fiscal system provided the basis for the pursuit of warfare and imperial expansion between the 1690s and 1790s, it was not without shortcomings and limitations. To a large extent, these were masked by external pressures of war, anti-Catholicism and patriotism which created consent to taxation. The fundamental question was: could the British fiscal state survive the still greater demands of the

---

[17] J. Innes, 'Governing diverse societies', in P. Langford (ed.), *The Short Oxford History of Eighteenth-Century Britain* (Oxford, forthcoming); on municipal finance, see E. J. Dawson, 'Finance and the unreformed borough: a critical appraisal of corporate finance, with special reference to the boroughs of Nottingham, York and Boston', PhD thesis, University of Hull (1978). These issues are discussed below in chapter 9, pp. 260–1. On the poor law, see for example P. Mandler, 'The making of the poor law *redivivus*', *Past and Present* 117 (1987), 131–57, on discussions between 'modernising' and traditional approaches; there is a vast literature on the operation of the poor law which ranges from an emphasis on inclusiveness (such as in R. Smith, 'Charity, self-interest and welfare: reflections from demographic and family history', in M. J. Daunton (ed.), *Charity, Self-Interest and Welfare in the English Past* (London, 1996), pp. 23–49) to a stress on exclusion (such as in S. King, 'Reconstructing lives: the poor, the poor law and welfare in Calverley, 1650–1820', *Social History* 22 (1997), 318–38. These issues connect with the debate over the efficiency and modernity of the fiscal-military state, the existence of a 'strong' or 'weak' state in eighteenth-century Britain. The case for a strong and effective state is made in Brewer, *Sinews of Power*, other historians have suggested that the state was 'weak' with a heavy dependence on local initiatives and a diffusion of power, which could have serious flaws or at least required constant negotiation. The difference of interpretation may be overdrawn: the point is how, and to what extent, the central state could rely on local initiatives and create a wide diffusion of initiative in order to mobilise resources, rather than simply creating resistance and a loss of compliance. On this debate, see D. Eastwood, *Governing Rural England: Tradition and Transformation in Local Government, 1780–1840* (Oxford, 1994), who stresses an effective and adaptable local government; J. E. Cookson, *The British Armed Nation, 1793–1815* (Oxford 1997), pp. 1–15, 262–3, who sees a 'thickening' of local government which created patronage and authority out of the reach of the central state, pp. 1–15, 262–3; P. Clark, *British Clubs and Societies, 1580–1800: The Origins of an Associational World* (Oxford, 2000), sees the growth of such a world as an ineffective and unimpressive response to a decline of the central and local state, pp. 175–80, 468, 489; Langford, *Public Life and the Propertied Englishman* on the involvement of a propertied class in local affairs which was carried over into parliament; S. Conway, *The British Isles and the War of American Independence* (Oxford, 2000), pp. 347–53, offers a balanced assessment. These issues are picked up in the conclusion in reference to the 'long nineteenth century'.

Table 2.2 *Taxes collected for central government, 1690–1820*

9 year average centred on	Direct (%)	Indirect (%)	% of indirect taxes	
			Imports	Internal duties
1690	42	58	40	60
1750	28	72	28	72
1800	25	75	50	50
1820	19	81	43	57

Source: P. K. O'Brien and P. Hunt, 'The emergence and consolidation of excises in the English fiscal system before the Glorious Revolution', *British Tax Review* no. 1 (1997), 38–9.

wars with revolutionary and Napoleonic France between 1793 and 1815? And would the tensions and shortcomings be exposed after 1815?

Financing the revolutionary and Napoleonic wars

The French Revolution arose, in part, from a crisis in the fiscal system of the *ancien régime*. The outbreak of war with revolutionary France in 1793 in turn placed strains on the fiscal constitution of Britain. Revenue yields were not expanding in line with the growth of the economy, for the fiscal system did not attach effective 'handles' to economic activity. The failure of the land tax to rise in line with rents was merely one example of the problem, for the eighteenth-century tax system was a patchwork with gaping holes. It was administratively difficult to impose taxes on many forms of income and wealth, and the government instead relied on external signs of prosperity such as keeping a carriage or a male servant, or the number of windows in the house. These assessed taxes did not fall directly on, say, the profits of tenant farmers or urban traders and industrialists. The income from professions and commerce was only taxed through various stamp and registration duties on bills of exchange and legal documents. Despite the attempt to exempt goods purchased by the poor and impose higher duties on luxuries, taxation became more regressive as fiscal burdens mounted.

Reform would create political dangers, and it was only the mounting demands of war finance which eventually forced William Pitt* to alter

---

* William Pitt (1759–1806) was the second son of William Pitt the elder; he was educated at Pembroke Hall, Cambridge, and called to the bar in 1780. He entered parliament in 1781, and was chancellor of the Exchequer 1782–3, prime minister 1783–1801 when he resigned over George III's refusal of Catholic emancipation. He returned to office in 1804. (*DNB*, vol. XLV, ed. S. Lee (London, 1896), pp. 367–86.)

the fiscal system in order to create more effective 'handles'. One possibility was to tax estates at death (see chapter 8); another was to extend the taxation of incomes. In 1798, Pitt converted the assessed taxes into the so-called 'Triple Assessment', a form of graduated income tax based on the payment of assessed taxes in the previous year. Individuals with the largest taxable establishments of carriages and male servants paid five times the previous amount, down to an additional quarter on the smallest establishments. Taxpayers could claim abatements and relief, to ensure that they did not pay more than 10 per cent of their income; the possibilities of evasion and underestimation of income allowed a reduction in liability. Landowners were also given the right to redeem the land tax on any piece of property by paying sufficient government stock into the sinking fund to produce a fifth more interest than the land tax. In order to redeem a land tax of £100 a year, the owner would hand to the government stock producing an annual yield of £120. The terms were simply not attractive to the landowners. The 'Triple Assessment' was therefore disappointing, with a yield of £2m instead of the anticipated £4.5m; the shortfall was made up by £2m from the 'voluntary contribution', a patriotic gesture by taxpayers who felt they were under-taxed.[18]

In 1799, Pitt went a stage further and introduced an income tax at a rate of 2s in the £ on individuals with a total income above £200, with abatements for incomes between £60 and £200.[19] The new income tax offered a much better 'handle' on economic activity, in theory allowing the yield to rise in line with the income of the country. Here was a way of increasing the revenue of the government and reducing Pitt's heavy reliance on loans. The tax was commended by Robert Banks Jenkinson (later Lord Liverpool)* as being 'as near perfection as human wisdom

---

[18] Ward, *Land Tax*, pp. 133–6; J. V. Beckett, 'Land tax or excise: the levying of taxation in seventeenth- and eighteenth-century England', *English Historical Review* 100 (1985), 285–308; J. V. Beckett and M. E. Turner, 'Taxation and economic growth in eighteenth-century England', *Economic History Review* 2nd ser. 43 (1990), 377–403; P. K. O'Brien, 'The political economy of British taxation, 1660–1815', *Economic History Review* 2nd ser. 41 (1988), 20; A. Hope-Jones, *Income Tax in the Napoleonic Wars* (Cambridge, 1939), pp. 14–16; B. E. V. Sabine, *A History of Income Tax* (London, 1966), pp. 23–4. On the land tax, see *Parliamentary History of England from the Earliest Period to 1803*, vol. 23, 2 Apr. 1798, cols. 1360–76, and PP 1870 XX, *Report of the Commissioners of Inland Revenue*, vol. I, pp. 317–18.

[19] Sabine, *Income Tax*, p. 29; Hope-Jones, *Income Tax*, p. 15.

* Robert Banks Jenkinson (1770–1828), second earl of Liverpool, was educated at Charterhouse and Christ Church, Oxford. He visited France in 1789 and witnessed the storming of the Bastille. He became a member of parliament in 1790, and he supported war with France and opposed parliamentary reform. He was foreign secretary 1801–4; home secretary 1804–6 and 1807–9; secretary for war and the colonies, 1809–12; and prime minister, 1812–27. (*DNB*, vol. XXIX, ed. S. Lee (London, 1892), pp. 311–15.)

could devise'.[20] The income tax provided 28 per cent of the additional
tax revenue needed to pay for the war with revolutionary and Napoleonic
France.[21] It was explicitly a war tax, which was temporarily abandoned
in the interlude of peace in 1802/3; when it was restored, the government
held out the prospect that it would be removed with the eventual defeat
of Napoleon. The income tax was therefore a major source of revenue,
but it also threatened a loss of consent. Pitt switched from a voluntary
income tax which appealed to the taxpayer's self-interest to an intrusive,
compulsory, tax which was difficult to enforce. The problem was particularly acute because Pitt's initial form of assessment and collection of
the tax depended on estimating the individual's combined income from
all sources; when the tax was reintroduced in 1803, the tax was instead
divided into various 'schedules' according to different forms of income,
each of which paid separately in the most convenient way (see chapter 7)
and without a need to aggregate income from all sources. This change
meant that the yield of the tax rose and tensions were reduced, yet suspicion still remained which led to the abandonment of the tax after the war.

The external threat from French absolutism and Catholicism, succeeded by the dangers of revolutionary ideology and Napoleonic ambition, justified a fiscal-military state as a means of sustaining the social hierarchy, preserving English liberty, and securing commercial hegemony.
Nevertheless, there were signs that consent and legitimacy were reaching their limits. During the Napoleonic wars, the unprecedented levels
of expenditure were leading to attacks on waste and corruption, with the
belief that parasitical loan contractors and *rentiers* were sucking the blood
of the productive classes. As one disaffected writer complained in 1796,
'The enormous weight of taxes...has reduced the middling classes to
a state of the most pitiable distress.' John Nicholls* feared that the tax
would ruin the middle class, and that it was the unnecessary product
of Burke's persuading the borough mongers that war with revolutionary
France was needed for their security. Few MPs agreed with his suggestion that the great families of Britain should be removed; there was more

---

[20] R. G. Thorne (ed.), *The History of Parliament: The House of Commons, 1790–1820* (5 vols.,
London, 1986), vol. IV, p. 302.

[21] O'Brien and Hunt, 'England, 1485–1815', p. 89.

* John Nicholls (1744–1832) was the son of the physician to George II; he was educated
at Exeter College, Oxford, and became a barrister. He served as an MP in 1783–7 and
1796–1802. He opposed Edmund Burke and the Whig grandees whom he felt were
conspiring against the constitution. He left the Whig Club and became a Friend of
the People and a Friend of Freedom. He became obsessed with the notion that the
Whig aristocracy was subjugating the king and becoming unpopular with the people,
who would overthrow both. Thorne (ed.), *History of Parliament: The House of Commons
1790–1829*, vol. IV, pp. 669–72.

support in the country for his proposition that the middle class was being overburdened. In 1809, an Anglican clergyman remarked that

the middle order must be supported, or the whole fabric will tumble in; if the higher ranks have been oratorically termed 'the corinthian capital of polished society', the middle class is the strong pillar that supports, and lifts it from the dust. It forms that arch in our constitution, which springing from the foundation, supports the superstructure.[22]

Disaffection with the burden of taxation, the notion of the state as a 'tax eater', formed a central tenet in radical rhetoric and in the formation of a middle-class identity.[23] The comments of Francis Burdett* had considerable support. As he put it in 1802,

The income tax has created an inquisitorial power of the most partial, offensive and cruel nature. The whole transactions of a life may be inquired into, family affairs laid open, and an Englishman, like a culprit, summoned to attend commissioners; compelled to wait like a lacquey in their anti-chamber [sic] from day to day until they are ready to institute their inquisition into his property; put to his oath, after all perhaps disbelieved, surcharged and stigmatized as perjured, without any redress from or appeal to a jury of his country... Sir, the repeal of this tax is not a sufficient remedy for its infamy; its principle must be stigmatised and branded.[24]

These fears of an intrusive bureaucracy seemed all the more real at the end of 1814 when the Board of Inland Revenue suspended the lay commissioners who administered the income tax in the City of London and took control into its own hands. This enflamed opinion in the City. As one leading London radical complained, the government officials or surveyors were agents of a 'system of oppression... a tyrannical machine'. Indeed, their duties would 'become so horrible that, like the office of hangman, none but the refuse of society could be induced to take the appointment'. The outcry against the suspensions of the commissioners contributed to the demise of the income tax. In 1816, 22,000 City merchants, bankers

---

[22] Wahrman, *Imagining*, pp. 52, 163; Thorne (ed.), *History of Parliament: The House of Commons, 1790–1820*, vol. IV, pp. 669–71.

[23] Wahrman, *Imagining*, chapter 4.

[24] *Parliamentary History of England from the Earliest Period to 1803*, vol. 36, 12 Apr. 1802, col. 509. Burdett's remarks were quoted in the debates over the reintroduction of the tax in 1842, *Parliamentary Debates*, 3rd ser. 62, 8 Apr. 1842, cols. 146–7.

* Francis Burdett (1770–1844) was educated at Westminster and Oxford. He was in Paris in the early stages of the French Revolution, and returned to England in 1793. He married the daughter of the banker Thomas Coutts, and entered parliament in 1796. He advocated parliamentary reform, attacked the government's policy of war with France and high taxes, and criticised its removal of popular rights and free speech. He stood for Middlesex in 1802, but his election was declared void in 1804 and remained disputed until 1806; he was re-elected for Westminster in 1807 on a platform of reform, and represented the constituency until 1837. He was imprisoned on political charges in 1810 and 1820. Between 1837 and 1844, he was Conservative MP for North Wiltshire. (*DNB*, vol. VII, ed. Stephen, pp. 296–9.)

and traders petitioned against the renewal of the tax.[25] The problem facing the government of Lord Liverpool at the end of the war was how to meet the demands for revenue to fund the national debt, in the absence of the income tax.

Peace and debts

The problems of legitimacy of the tax system grew at the end of the war. The criticism of the tax system and the state it supported was clear in a cartoon of 1829, which portrayed a common view of British society. At the top of the image was a wooden beam, labelled 'manufactures and commerce', which had snapped under the weight of people dependent on it. Desperately clinging to the beam were four tattered workmen; hanging on to their legs were two prosperous businessmen; and clutching at their coat tails was a plump individual, splendidly attired in the robes of a bishop and peer. The caption spelled out the message: 'Manufactures and commerce support the workmen they the merchants and masters who are the chief tax payers and thereby support the great tax eater Church-and-State.'

Peace did not remove the government's need for high levels of revenue, for there were considerable costs of servicing the accumulated national debt. The debt rose from £2m in 1688 or about 5 per cent of GNP to £834m in 1815 or over twice the size of GNP. Although interest rates were halved over the period, payments on the debt rose from under a quarter to over a half of total tax revenues.[26] Indeed, the government was forced to *increase* its debt after the war in order to balance the budget and to maintain the sinking fund intended to pay off the debt. The policy of borrowing made little financial sense, for the new loans paid a higher rate of interest than the old debts they were designed to repay. As Lord Liverpool and William Huskisson* realised, the debt should be reduced

[25] Hope-Jones, *Income Tax*, pp. 2, 28–9, 68–9.

[26] Winch, 'Political economy of public finance', p. 9; P. K. O'Brien, *Power with Profit: The State and the Economy, 1688–1815* (London, 1991), pp. 28–30; O'Brien and Hunt, 'England, 1485–1815', p. 61.

* William Huskisson (1770–1830) was educated in England and then privately at Paris where his uncle was doctor to the embassy; he became private secretary to the ambassador and returned home when the embassy was recalled in 1792. He secured a post to deal with the French *émigrés*, and from 1795 to 1801 was under-secretary for war. He was MP from 1796 to 1802 and 1804 to 1830. He held office as secretary to the Treasury from 1804 to 1806 and 1807 to 1809, resigning as a supporter of Canning. He was colonial agent of Ceylon, with a salary of £4,000, from 1812 to 1823, and minister of woods and forests in 1814. From 1823 to 1827 he was treasurer of the navy and president of the Board of Trade, and from 1827 to 1828 colonial secretary and leader of the Commons. He was killed by a railway engine at the opening of the Manchester–Liverpool railway. He was an expert on issues of finance and trade, and undertook revisions of the tariffs. (*DNB*, vol. XXVIII, ed. Lee, pp. 323–8.)

1   A cartoon from the cover of *State of the Nation*, 1829

Figure 2.2 Debt charges as a percentage of gross expenditure of United Kingdom central government, 1810–1913
Source: calculated from B. R. Mitchell and P. Deane, *Abstract of British Historical Statistics* (Cambridge, 1962), pp. 396–8.

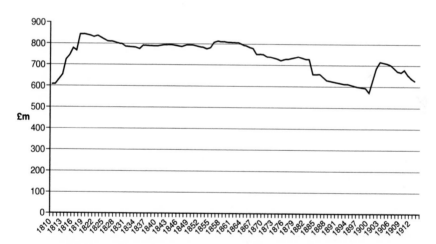

Figure 2.3 Funded and unfunded debt, United Kingdom, £m, 1810–1913
Source: B. R. Mitchell and P. Deane, *Abstract of British Historical Statistics* (Cambridge, 1962), pp. 402–3.

from a budgetary surplus rather than incurring new loans. However, they were constrained by the political difficulties of raising taxes, and by the realisation that payment into the sinking fund was needed to maintain the confidence of the public in government loans.[27] Their problem was how to meet the costs of debt service, given the widespread hostility to 'parasitical' *rentiers* and the absence of any immediate external threat to British security.

Economists were divided over the national debt. On one side, Robert Malthus* argued that the problem at the end of the war was under-consumption, and he argued that *rentiers'* spending on personal services offered a solution. It would 'ensure that consumption which is necessary to give the proper stimulus to production'. In his view, more would be lost 'by the want of consumption than gained by the diminution of taxation'.[28] But such views were denounced by David Ricardo and James Mill[†], as much on political as economic grounds. In order to sustain their anti-militaristic policies, they needed to argue that the national debt was harmful rather than a means of compensating for excessive accumulation of capital and under-consumption. Support of the national debt would be tantamount to arguing for increased expenditure on the army or for salary increases for the civil service; it would justify inefficient spending by a corrupt, aristocratic, government. In Ricardo's view, the debt was 'one of the most terrible scourges ... ever invented to afflict a nation'. His solution was almost as drastic as Hume's and, as he admitted, 'chimerical': to pay off the debt within three to five years by heroic methods of taxation, including a levy on all capital. He was not concerned by the payment of taxes, which were merely a transfer payment from taxpayers to debt holders without any effect on national wealth. His concern was

[27] N. Gash, 'After Waterloo: British society and the legacy of the Napoleonic wars', *Transactions of the Royal Historical Society*, 5th ser. 28 (1978), 155.

[28] T. R. Malthus, *Principles of Political Economy*, vol. I, ed. J. Pullen (Cambridge, 1989), pp. 43, 479–88; also T. Dome, 'Malthus on taxation and national debt', *History of Political Economy* 29 (1997), 275–94.

* Thomas Robert Malthus (1766–1834) was educated at the Warrington Academy (for dissenters) and Jesus College, Cambridge, where he became a fellow in 1793. He became a curate in 1798, the same year as the publication of his *Essay on Population*. In 1805, he was appointed professor of history and political economy at the East India Co.'s Haileybury College. He revised the *Essay* on various occasions, and published *The Nature and Progress of Rent* in 1815. (*DNB*, vol. XXXVI, ed. S. Lee (London, 1893), pp. 1–5.)

† James Mill (1773–1836) was born in Forfarshire, the son of a shoemaker. He was educated in Edinburgh and moved to London in 1802. He wrote for the *Edinburgh Review* 1808–13, and met Jeremy Bentham in 1808, becoming his disciple and advocate. He supported his family by writing; when his *History of India* appeared in 1818 he was appointed to a position in the East India Co.'s administration. He was a member of the Political Economy Club, and encouraged Ricardo. He wrote for the *Westminister Review*, created as a Benthamite journal in 1824. (*DNB*, vol. XXXVII, ed. S. Lee (London, 1894), pp. 382–8.)

much more with the original loan, and its effects on private accumulation. He took a more pessimistic line than Smith who felt that private parsimony could compensate for public prodigality, and that falling profits were a sign of progress and effective competition. Ricardo took a different line, that falling profits would lead to a drop in capital accumulation and that public spending was at the expense of private accumulation. A reduction in state expenditure was central to Ricardo's political economy, in a way it was not to Smith's. It was Ricardo, much more than Smith, who provided the intellectual justification for 'rolling back the state' in the early nineteenth century. His attack on the national debt was part of a wider project of reducing *all* public expenditure as prodigal. In the process, Smith's views on public expenditure were reinterpreted in a Ricardian framework.[29]

If the debt were to be paid off, where could the money be found? One response was to argue, as did the *Courier* in 1816, that 'the income tax is the best means of raising so large a sum with little or no pressure on the poorer classes', and that it was to be preferred to the alternative – to 'grind the rich and poor with enormous increases in Excise and Customs'. Indeed, in 1816 the government of Lord Liverpool attempted to renew the income tax for a further two years. The ambition failed. The return of peace meant that the justification of high expenditure was now removed, and the threat to English liberties was perceived as coming from within the country rather than across the English Channel. 'Can any man pretend', commented the *Edinburgh Review*,

that the people of England would have submitted to the income tax, if they had not been told it was for a season? . . . It is, on every principle, oppressive, contrary to the principles of the constitution, and destructive of individual security. We cannot suppose that a free people will endure it for one instant after the crisis has passed, which alone justified it.[30]

The tax was indeed 'stigmatised and branded' as a threat to English liberty by a tyrannical administration. As one fevered letter to *The Times* put it

---

[29] D. Ricardo, *The Works and Correspondence of David Ricardo*, ed. P. Sraffa with the collaboration of M. H. Dodd (11 vols., Cambridge, 1951–73), vol. I: *On the Principles of Political Economy and Taxation*, pp. 247–8; vol. II: *Notes on Malthus's Principles of Political Economy*, pp. 421, 450; vol. IV: *Pamphlets and Papers, 1815–23*, pp. 149–200; vol. V: *Speeches and Evidence*, pp. 21, 34–5, 38–9; also J. S. Mill, *Collected Works*, vol. IV: *Essays on Economics and Society*, I, ed. J. M. Robson with an introduction by L. Robbins (London, 1967), pp. 1–22; J. S Mill, *Collected Works*, vol. XXII: *Newspaper Writings, I: December 1822–1 July 1831*, ed. A. P. and J. M. Robson (London, 1986), p. 58. Ricardo's views have been discussed in Roberts, 'Ricardo's theory of public debt', 257–66; C. S. Shoup, *Ricardo on Taxation* (New York, 1954); D. P. O'Brien, *The Classical Economists* (Oxford, 1975), pp. 259–65; W. Eltis, *The Classical Theory of Economic Growth* (Oxford, 1984), pp. 219, 221–3; Winch, 'Political economy of public finance', pp. 18–22.
[30] Hope-Jones, *Income Tax*, pp. 116, 119.

in 1816, 'there is the despotic spirit of this inquisitorial impost, its horde of petty tyrants! A government exercising inquisitorial powers may easily extend them...A single root may throw out shoots and suckers on all sides.'[31] The failure to renew the income tax was also influenced, like the excise crisis of 1733/4, by concern that the balance between localism and centralism might be disturbed. A buoyant source of central taxation seemed to threaten the autonomy of the localities, whose own finances were facing difficulties (see chapter 8). The action of the Board of Inland Revenue in suspending the commissioners for the City of London in 1814 formed one part of the wider perception of a threat to the autonomy of justices and local government which created difficulties in the reform of the poor law, introduction of a police force and responses to public health.[32]

The demise of any immediate threat from France after 1815 meant that country gentlemen could now be more critical of the high levels of taxation needed to cover the costs of servicing the debt. They could complain that they were providing money to sustain *rentiers* and financiers who were subverting the social order. They could make common cause with radicals in protesting against the menace of militarism and a luxurious court, the scale of pensions and sinecures, and the depredations of rich financiers and mighty landowners. The issue of the national debt became more pressing and controversial than in the eighteenth century, and the lines of division were redefined. In the eighteenth century, the national debt was attacked by Tories and country Whigs as a threat to social order and the constitution. The wars with revolutionary and Napoleonic France converted many Tories to the approach of Burke, that the debt was a patriotic defence against tyranny. By contrast, opponents of the war and advocates of reform attacked the debt as a burden on the economy and a threat to political liberty through the links with sinecures and 'old corruption'. The government was therefore in considerable difficulty at the end of the war: it was aware of the continued need for revenue and wished to renew the income tax in order to deal with the problem of the debt. But the debt provided a reason for opposing the income tax, as a transfer from producers to parasites, and from those suffering from falling prices (debtors and producers) to those who benefited (creditors and consumers). These identities as producers and parasites, debtors and creditors, were created discursively, through the use of rhetoric rather than a simple expression of existing interests. A distinction was drawn between the 'real' activities of land and production, and artificial monied interests

[31] *Times*, 15 Feb. 1816, quoted in Hope-Jones, *Income Tax*, p. 114.
[32] Hope-Jones, *Income Tax*, pp. 2, 128–9, 133–4.

and speculation which subverted the social order. Investors in war loans, in receipt of high interest rates, gained from the fall in prices; taxpayers complained that the demands on them increased in real terms. Similarly, creditors gained as the real value of their loans rose, and debtors suffered as the burden of repayment and interest increased in relation to their income. Indebted landowners, industrialists and merchants could join in urging the government to reduce salaries, taxes and government expenditure to the prewar level of 1792. Refusal to sanction the continuation of the income tax was one means of forcing retrenchment and, in particular, reducing pensions and sinecures, military spending and half-pay to officers. The attack on 'old corruption' or, in William Cobbett's* phrase, 'the thing', was central to postwar politics. The process of parliamentary negotiation may have helped to create consent and legitimacy in the eighteenth century; now it seemed to many to represent a political system which was biassed and unbalanced, an expression of class power and vested interests.[33]

The government of Liverpool did make considerable efforts to reduce expenditure. In 1822, the Tory government managed to reduce debt charges by converting £150m of the existing 5 per cent stock to a lower rate of 4 per cent; in 1824, a further £70m of 4 per cent stock was converted to 3.5 per cent.[34] In many ways, the achievement of the government of Liverpool in reducing expenditure was impressive. By 1824, Liverpool was willing to admit in private that the country needed *higher* taxes rather than further cuts in expenditure, and that the share of direct taxation was lower than in any other European country.[35] Liverpool did indeed have a point, for the British fiscal system in the 1820s was narrowly based. In Britain, the income tax was introduced in 1799 to extend the land and assessed revenues; these other taxes were not reformed when the income tax was abandoned in 1816 and direct taxes declined in importance. In Britain, the fiscal system became heavily reliant on customs

---

[33] Gash, 'After Waterloo', 152–4; Hilton, *Corn, Cash and Commerce*, Parts I and II.

[34] Gash, 'After Waterloo', 156.

[35] Liverpool to Canning, 19 Oct. 1824, in C. D. Yonge, *The Life and Administration of Robert Banks, Second Earl Liverpool* (3 vols., London, 1868), vol. III, p. 311.

* William Cobbett (1763–1835) was born at Farnham, the son of a labourer. He served in the army between 1783 and 1791, and submitted evidence against officers. He moved to France and then Philadelphia, where he was a bookseller and publisher for loyalists; he shifted to New York in 1797 and to London in 1800, where he became a Tory journalist. From 1804, he was a radical. He farmed in Hampshire from 1804 to 1817, and returned to the United States from 1817 to 1819. He failed to enter parliament in 1821, but eventually become MP for Oldham in 1832. He began *Cobbett's Weekly Register* in 1802, which ran to his death; he supported small farmers and artisans against large landowners, factories and the tax state, combining Tory and radical criticism of social change. (*DNB*, vol. XI, ed. L. Stephen (London, 1887), pp. 142–5.)

and excise duties, with the danger of conflicts between trade interests, between land and commerce, and between rich and poor. The French fiscal system was more flexible and wide-ranging than the British in the early nineteenth century, with a wider range of direct taxes. In France, taxation on external signs of affluence continued with the *contribution personnelle*, above all on residences. The rental value of residences was taken as the most reliable indication of income; the smallest houses were exempt, and a tax was levied on other houses according to a rough estimate of their rental value. Real estate was also taxed by the *contribution foncière*, based on a cadastral survey of the revenue of each parcel of land or building. In addition, the profits of trade and industry were taxed through the *droits de patente*. The *patente* was a form of licence, determined by the presumed profits of an enterprise rather than the actual net income, according to three criteria: the nature of the activity; the scale of the business according to the number of workers, output, raw material consumption and rental value of plant; and the population of the area. Thus a baker with few workers in a small village paid a lower fee than a baker with a large staff in a town. The *patente* applied to entrepreneurial profits, and therefore excluded employees' wages or the salaries of civil servants, the military, clergy and lawyers. As we shall see, these taxes had their problems and the French fiscal system became more rigid as time passed. But what stands out in the second quarter of the nineteenth century is the greater reliance of France on a wider range of taxes than in Britain. In 1840, direct taxes were 37.9 per cent of central government revenues in France, compared with no more than 7.9 per cent in the United Kingdom.[36]

The British government was aware of the dangers of postwar unrest, and conscious that failure to renew the income tax led to a greater dependence on customs and excise duties. Liverpool's administration attempted to reconcile the poor to the 'selfish' removal of income tax by concessions such as abolishing the tax on malt and so reducing the price of beer. But this was also a concession to landowners, who were already facing criticisms of protection of their interests by the corn laws. In 1819, the government again proposed to reintroduce a form of income tax in

---

[36] By 1875, direct taxes were 24.1 per cent of central government revenues in France, still somewhat ahead of the United Kingdom on 20.2 per cent. By 1910, the position was reversed with direct taxes forming 25.7 per cent of central government revenues in France and 31.7 per cent in the United Kingdom. These figures are from P. Flora et al., *State, Economy and Society in Western Europe, 1815–1975. A Data Handbook in Two Volumes. I. The Growth of Mass Democracies and Welfare States* (Frankfurt, London and Chicago, 1983), pp. 301–2, 341–2.

order to produce revenue and to defuse political unrest. The intention was to tax 'realised' capital (that is, spending from assets) rather than earned incomes, and to reduce other taxes which fell on labour. Such a measure would, the secretary to the Treasury argued, 'arrest the progress of those sentiments which if not arrested, must inevitably overturn the constitution and government... Such a measure would be the best practical *Refutation* of the Calumnies of the Demagogues against the Rich.'[37] The attempt failed, for the government had a more immediate need to secure a majority in parliament to pass repressive legislation against the 'demagogues'.

The failure of the government to renew the income tax in 1816 or 1819 meant that the fiscal system was highly dependent on customs and excise duties, hitting trade and industry, and falling more heavily on working-class consumers.[38] The burden of war-time debt and the need to pay interest to *rentiers* from regressive taxes meant that the legitimacy of the fiscal system was called into question on the return to peace to a much greater extent than during the 'long eighteenth century' of warfare. There was a lack of trust that fellow taxpayers were making a reasonable contribution to the expenses of the state, or that the state was spending its revenues in a way that was equitable between classes and interests. In Britain in the 1820s, the state was considered by many to be undemocratic, bloated and inefficient. Politicians came under criticism from a variety of sources, whether from radicals complaining about the subversion of the constitution; from disaffected farmers and gentry concerned about their position relative to the greater landowners and the monied class; or from Evangelical critics of dissipation and luxury. The campaign was self-reinforcing, for the appointment of parliamentary enquiries to rectify one abuse placed more information in the public sphere on related issues, and so led to renewed demands for reform.[39]

Early nineteenth-century radicalism provided the basis of an 'atavistic anti-statism' which formed such an important theme in Victorian liberalism. The radical case was that central government expenditure entailed a transfer payment to aristocrats and financiers, and that reform of the poor law was a blow against the right of the people to tax-funded relief. Such

---

[37] Hilton, *Corn, Cash and Commerce*, pp. 32–3, 82.
[38] O'Brien, 'Political economy of British taxation', 1–32.
[39] Harling, *Waning of 'Old Corruption'*, pp. 137–9, 144–50, 165–78; P. Harling and P. Mandler, 'From "fiscal-military" state to laissez-faire state, 1760–1850', *Journal of British Studies* 32 (1993), 44–70; P. Harling, 'Rethinking "old corruption"', *Past and Present* 147 (1995), 127–58.

anti-statism had a point, for the tax system was regressive after 1816, and expenditure on the army, navy and national debt still accounted for over 70 per cent of central government expenditure between 1861 and 1880. Radicals viewed taxation as a means of sustaining war abroad and exploitation at home, and demanded retrenchment as a means of removing aristocratic hangers-on and ending the depradations of parasitic *rentiers*. What was needed, in their view, was not a mighty state so much as an active civil society based on an associational culture of co-operative societies, trade unions, friendly societies and clubs. Thomas Paine's* 'model of a self-governing, self-helping, libertarian society' and a cheap state had considerable purchase well into the nineteenth century. Only a few radicals such as John Gast† argued that a high income tax could be a means of altering the structure of society by bolstering domestic demand from workers, so removing the need for competition in foreign markets which led to cost-cutting, sweated labour and an attack on artisan republicanism. The radical critique on taxation and the state fed into Chartism, which stressed that the problem of poverty and hardship was political rather than economic in origins, arising from the bias in the tax system against the poor. The solution was therefore political rather than economic, introducing universal manhood suffrage and annual parliaments to secure control over fiscal policy and state expenditure. The aim of Peel and Gladstone was to show that the inequities of taxation *could* be removed through the existing structure of parliament. Their success meant that the radicals and Chartists were largely brought within the realm of the Liberal party which came to represent the continuation of Peelite politics. The achievement of Gladstone was to harness the rhetoric of peace, retrenchment and reform in order to secure the allegiance of

---

* Thomas Paine (1737–1809) was the son of a Quaker stay-maker and small farmer from Thetford. He became an Excise officer in 1761 but was dismissed in 1765 for neglect of duty; he was reappointed in 1768 but left the service in 1774 after leading a campaign for increased pay. He moved to America, and joined the provincial army. His *Common Sense* (1776) set out the steps which led to war, and he held political posts and was given a salary to write. He moved to London, writing *The Rights of Man* in response to Burke's *Reflections*. He fled to France, where he was given the title of citizen in 1792 and elected to the National Convention. He was arrested in 1793, and only escaped with his life as a result of the fall of Robespierre. He published *The Age of Reason* in 1793. He returned to the United States in 1802, where he opposed Washington and the federalists. (*DNB*, vol. XLIII, ed. S. Lee (London, 1895), pp. 69–79.)

† John Gast (1772–1837) grew up in Bristol and was apprenticed to a London shipwright, working at the trade for the rest of his life. He maintained the notion of the 'artisan republic' of self-sufficient men with property rights in their skill, whose position was being undermined by legislation removing their rights and creating an unstable economy based on exports rather than a prosperous home market. See I. Prothero, *Artisans and Politics in Early Nineteenth-Century London: John Gast and his Times* (Folkestone, 1979).

former Chartists and middle-class supporters of Cobdenite free trade.[40] The government of Liverpool had wrestled with the problems of postwar adjustment, starting the process of reform and retrenchment. What he had failed to achieve was a sense of the equity or fairness of the fiscal system which was the task of Peel and Gladstone in their budgets of 1842 and 1853.

[40] Biagini, 'Popular Liberals, Gladstonian finance and the debate on taxation', pp. 137–8; Stedman Jones, *Languages of Class*, chapter on 'Rethinking Chartism', especially pp. 108–10, 176–8; Matthew, *Gladstone 1809–1874*, p. 111; B. Hilton, *The Age of Atonement: The Influence of Evangelicalism on Social and Economic Thought, 1785–1865* (Oxford, 1988); on Gast, see Prothero, *Artisans and Politics*, pp. 220, 226, 256, 335.

3 'Philosophical administration and constitutional control': the emergence of the Gladstonian fiscal constitution

> ... the finance of the country is intimately associated with the liberties of the country. It is a powerful leverage by which liberty has been gradually acquired. Running back into the depths of antiquity for many centuries, it lies at the root of English liberty, and if the House of Commons can by any possibility lose the power of the control of the grants of public money, depend upon it your very liberty will be worth very little in comparison.
>
> W. E. Gladstone, speech at Hastings, *Times*, 18 Mar. 1891

At the end of the Napoleonic wars, the scale of the national debt was at the centre of politics. The transfer of taxes from 'productive' interests to 'parasitical' *rentiers* was a common theme in radical discourse – especially in view of the increase in indirect taxes on trade and consumption, and the protection of landowners through the corn laws. The costs of government seemed excessive, a blatant pursuit of self-interest and sinecures for the hangers-on of the court and government, of militarism and imperialism rather than peace and commerce. The defeat of Napoleon was followed by a new battle against 'waste' and 'corruption', pensions and sinecures, and in favour of peace and retrenchment. The situation was similar at the end of the First World War, when the lower middle class attacked 'waste' by an expanded state bureaucracy; and the Labour party, a new electoral power with the extension of the franchise, demanded a once-and-for-all repayment of the national debt through a 'capital levy' – a proposal suggested by David Ricardo after the Napoleonic wars. Both wars had increased taxation to new (and broadly comparable) levels; both caused immense political difficulties of stabilisation. But there was also a considerable difference. After the First World War, the level of taxation stabilised at a much higher level than in Edwardian Britain: spending was displaced, and the state took a much larger share of national spending in peace-time than it had at any time in the past. After the Napoleonic wars, spending was *not* displaced, and returned to the lower levels of the eighteenth century. The onslaught on the fiscal system was more serious, the loss of legitimacy much deeper.

The task of politicians after the Napoleonic wars was greater than for their counterparts after the First World War: they had to recreate trust in the tax system, which entailed much more than simply reducing 'corruption' and imposing retrenchment. It entailed a long and complex process of reforming administrative and accounting practices, and creating an ethos of 'balance' and fairness through political language and culture. To a considerable extent, the politicians after the First World War were the legatees of this process: the fiscal system after 1918 had not lost its credibility to anything like the same extent as after 1815 or in other countries at the same time. How, then, did politicians after 1815 attempt – and eventually succeed – in reducing the scale of government spending, and in creating trust in the state and in the legitimacy of the tax system? What Gladstone termed the 'principles of philosophical administration and constitutional control' became central to notions of British liberty and identity.[1]

'Old corruption': rhetoric and reality

Historians have devoted much attention to criticisms of the so-called 'old corruption' of Tory governments and the court, which informed radical debate and scabrous cartoons. However, an emphasis on the language deployed by the critics of 'old corruption' may obscure the fact that the actual scale of 'old corruption' was less massive than implied by radical rhetoric.[2] As Harling has remarked, there was a dramatic widening of the gap between radical perception and administrative reality from around 1806, which widened further after the war. 'Economical reform' continued, reducing the scale of venality and cutting levels of expenditure, yet at the same time the attack on 'old corruption' became more intense.[3] Liverpool was remarkably successful in reducing expenditure after the war, but his efforts did very little to blunt the attacks. Of course, criticism of pensions and sinecures was a symbol for the existence of privilege in an unreformed political and fiscal system, which was seen by its critics as skewed against producers to the benefit of 'parasites'. The critics did have a point, for higher landed rents since the late eighteenth century increased the wealth of great aristocratic landowners relative to small owners and

---

[1] For a detailed account of the debates at the end of the First World War, see Daunton, 'How to pay for the war'. The quote from Gladstone (*Parliamentary Debates*, 3rd ser. 170, 4 May 1863, col. 1081) relates to his attempt to impose a tax on charities: see below, pp. 211–13.

[2] W. D. Rubinstein, 'The end of "old corruption" in Britain, 1780–1860', *Past and Present* 101 (1983), 55–86; E. P. Thompson, *The Making of the English Working Class* (London, 1963), p. 676.

[3] Harling, *Waning of 'Old Corruption'*, pp. 137–9, 144–50.

tenant farmers.[4] It would appear, therefore, that the re-establishment of trust in the state and taxation entailed more than a simple reduction in the level of extraction, for criticism mounted even as the 'peace dividend' allowed government expenditure to fall.

One response of politicians to the language of radical critics was to articulate an 'image of probity', stressing office as a public trust and learning a new code of political manners. Between the end of the war and 1830, Tory ministers introduced precisely the measures of economic and administrative reform which radicals believed their greed made impossible. The motivation was to isolate the radicals who demanded sweeping changes in the system of government. By convincing 'respectable' critics – especially independent MPs and disaffected 'country' elements – that a narrow political elite was able to govern efficiently and cheaply, its power could be preserved, the existing political system legitimated, and a widening of the franchise could be avoided. This response of Tory ministers to criticism reduced the threshold for venality, and made the political elite eager to meet public expectations of 'diligent and disinterested service'. Ministers were eager to portray themselves as frugal and honest, basing their claim to authority on their dedication to public duties and their capacity as 'men of business'. However, the shift in the character projected by public men in the early nineteenth century was not entirely successful, for the Tories' attempt to avoid parliamentary reform eventually failed in 1832 in the face of continued demands for constitutional change as a means of removing a parasitical ruling elite. The tax concessions of 1830 left the government open to charges of financial irresponsibility, and failed to contain pressures for parliamentary reform. The symbol of 'old corruption' continued to represent biases in the political system, despite the widening gap between the rhetoric of the radicals and the reality of reduction in expenditure.[5]

The retrenchment of the Tory ministries between 1815 and 1830 did mark a turning point in the fiscal-military state which reduced its claims on the economy below the levels of the eighteenth century.[6] But the shrinking state did not achieve legitimacy and trust as Tory ministers hoped, in part because the strategy was designed to *prevent* a wider definition of citizenship, and in part because the taxes levied to pay for the reduced level of public expenditure were widely (and correctly) perceived to be inequitable. As we have seen, the ministry was forced – against its

---

[4] Harling, *Waning of 'Old Corruption'*, p. 150; I. Dyck, *William Cobbett and Rural Popular Culture* (Cambridge, 1992), p. 135; Daunton, *Progress and Poverty*, pp. 52–6.

[5] Harling, *Waning of 'Old Corruption'*, pp. 138–9, 150–96; S. Collini, *Public Moralists: Political Thought and Intellectual Life in Britain, 1850–1930* (Oxford, 1991), pp. 104–12.

[6] Harling, *Waning of 'Old Corruption'*, pp. 165, 177–8.

better judgement – to abandon the income tax at the end of the war, with the result that it was obliged to rely upon customs and excise duties which fell on working-class consumers and on domestic production.[7] By acceding to pressure for retrenchment through the abolition of the income tax, the ministry was contributing to criticism of the unfair incidence of taxation, to which the radical response was further cuts in expenditure. The attempt to create a sense of trust in a patrician elite and state failed, and the constitutional reform which had been so assiduously opposed by the Tories was introduced by the Whigs in the early 1830s.

In 1832, the parliamentary franchise was re-defined and 'rotten' boroughs removed; in 1835, self-selecting borough councils were replaced by elected councils; the judiciary was reformed; and the privileges of the Church of England reduced. Such institutional reform was portrayed as an onslaught on the structure of 'old corruption' and was linked with a further attack on expenditure. However, the legitimacy of the state was not reasserted, and public agitation mounted in the 1830s with pressure for the removal of agricultural protection and demands for universal manhood suffrage to allow workers to take control of the state. The problem faced by the Whig government was that its policy of retrenchment left it open to charges of financial mismanagement, especially when a serious depression resulted in budget deficits. Although indirect taxes were reduced, the tax system was not reformed by introducing new taxes; the income tax was anathema to radicals as the engine of warfare and a bloated state.[8] Despite the considerable reduction in the scale of the state by 1840, it was still far from achieving legitimacy and trust. Protection of landed interests through the corn laws suggested that policy was still biassed; and the tax system was still heavily dependent on indirect taxes which fell on working-class consumers and middle-class producers.

The creation of a viable rhetoric of legitimacy and trust in the state rested upon the measures of the Conservative ministry of Sir Robert Peel, whose policies were continued within the Liberal party by William Gladstone. They were the heirs to the notion of public duty developed by Tory politicians after the Napoleonic wars, with the difference that it was now integral to their character as public men rather than a (possibly cynical) response to outside pressure. Above all, their devotion to public duty was linked to a claim that they – and the state – were disinterested. Their ambition was conservative, but in a different sense from the postwar Tory ministries which aimed to preserve the rule of a narrow political elite within an unreformed constitution. Rather, Peel concluded that the

[7] O'Brien, 'Political economy of British taxation', 1–32; Hilton, *Corn, Cash and Commerce*, pp. 32–3.

[8] Harling, *Waning of 'Old Corruption'*, pp. 197–227.

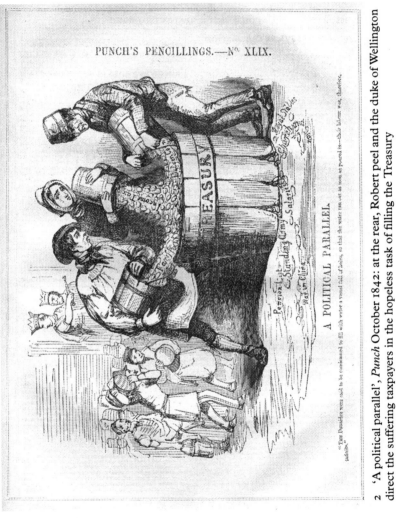

2 'A political parallel', *Punch* October 1842: at the rear, Robert peel and the duke of Wellington direct the suffering taxpayers in the hopeless task of filling the Treasury

best strategy for preserving the rule of the political elite and of protecting property was by adopting policies which were even-handed between all types of property, and between the propertied and the non-propertied. By constraining state expenditure and, as far as possible, excluding the state from involvement with economic interests, it was hoped to protect the political elite from challenge and to define the state as a neutral arbitrator between interests. Politicians should rise above personal greed and self-interest; they should also rise above any temptation to use the state to favour one interest against another, whether a trade group in search of protection or a social group seeking tax breaks. This also meant transforming the role of parliament in the fiscal system, from its eighteenth-century function as a forum to settle competing claims to its Victorian role as the auditor of public expenditure. The Commons was to be purged of fiscal favouritism. How was this project carried out?

'The narrowest limits': constraining the state

In 1828, J. C. Herries* – a member of the Select Committee on Public Income and Expenditure – argued that the first task was 'to ascertain the narrowest limits within which the annual charges for the Public Service could be confined'.[9] The attempt to enforce retrenchment was surprisingly successful, and entailed much more than merely allowing economic growth to reduce government revenue as a proportion of the national income, or cutting the national debt. In addition, restraints were imposed on the level of expenditure which effectively 'chained leviathan'. Many of these devices had existed in Hanoverian Britain, but they were now reasserted and raised to a new level of principle. The result was ambivalent. On one hand, public expenditure was reduced to such an extent that welfare declined: the level of investment in the urban infrastructure was so low that life expectancy in the great cities deteriorated, and there was a failure to invest in education for the masses.[10] The relatively generous

[9] PP 1828 v, *Fourth Report from the Select Committee on Public Income and Expenditure of the United Kingdom. Revenue Expenditure and Debt*, p. 565.
[10] See Szreter and Mooney, 'Urbanization, mortality and the standard of living debate', 84–112; on education, see M. Sanderson, *Education, Economic Change and Society in England* (2nd edn, Cambridge, 1991), and for a discussion of the low level of 'human capital formation' in international terms, see N. F. R. Crafts, *British Economic Growth during the Industrial Revolution* (Oxford, 1985), pp. 63–4, 141, 146, 163–4.
[*] John Charles Herries (1778–1855) was clerk in the Treasury in 1798 and served as secretary to chancellors of the Exchequer; in 1811 he was commissary in chief to the army and in 1814 negotiated financial treaties with the allies. He became auditor of the civil list in 1816, and in 1821 a commissioner to enquire into Irish finances. He entered parliament in 1823, and was appointed financial secretary to the Treasury, where he helped to reform customs duties. He served as chancellor of the Exchequer for a short time in 1827, and became master of the mint in 1828. He was a leading figure on the

levels of English poor relief fell as a proportion of national income. Peter Lindert has estimated that poor relief expenditure in England and Wales fell from 2.7 per cent of gross domestic product (GDP) in 1820/1; it was 1.1 per cent in 1850; and 0.7 per cent in 1880. Levels of public expenditure on education remained low: in 1860, the United Kingdom spent only 0.18 per cent of its GNP on public education, compared with 0.48 per cent in the United States; by 1880, the United Kingdom was spending 0.29 per cent, and the United States had risen to 0.74 per cent.[11] Many historians have therefore argued that there was a failure of collective action in the early Victorian period: spending on poor law fell from its previous high levels, and education did not take up the difference, remaining at lower levels than in the United States, Germany and France. But on the other hand, the 'chaining of leviathan' contributed to the rhetorical task of re-creating confidence in public action and re-establishing trust in the state which had been so seriously eroded after the Napoleonic war. Public action was highly problematic in the second quarter of the nineteenth century as a result of the perceived inequities in the fiscal system and the fear that taxes would be used for militarism and support of unproductive *rentiers*. Constraining the state, creating a sense of credibility in its actions, was a necessary prerequisite for positive action in the future. The emphasis in this chapter is on the means by which the state approached its citizens in the hope of creating consent and trust; it provides a political history of trust. It deals with the rhetoric and administrative processes used by politicians and civil servants in an attempt to elicit a particular response from its citizens. It dissects the creation of a political language and culture, as well as mechanical administrative and accounting procedures. The focus is on how the state viewed its citizens, how it believed its citizens would respond to particular administrative solutions and relationships. Although these approaches were informed by pressure groups and campaigns, they were shaped to a large extent by the cultural assumptions of the political and administrative elite. This elite aimed to present itself and the state as worthy of trust; whether the citizens and taxpayers accepted trust as justified is a separate question. The evidence presented here on the attitude of taxpayers to the state is implicit, emerging from the levels of compliance and yields, and from the policy-makers' own assessment of their success.

Select Committee in 1828, where he 'made the public accounts intelligible which they never were before'. He went on to serve as president of the Board of Trade and secretary of state for war. (*DNB*, vol. XXVI, ed. L. Stephen and S. Lee (London, 1891), pp. 255–8.)

[11] P. H. Lindert, 'Poor relief before the Welfare State: England versus the Continent, 1780–1880', *European Review of Economic History* 2 (1998), 114, and P. H. Lindert, 'Democracy, decentralization, and mass schooling before 1914', Agricultural History Center, University of California, Davis, Working Paper Series no. 104, Feb. 2001, table 3.

This account of taxation is therefore only part of a wider project – a social history of the relationship between the state and its citizens, considering how citizens saw their relationship to each other and to the state.[12]

There was a marked contrast in trends in taxation in the nineteenth century between Britain and other European states. In Britain, the level of taxation fell from 1815 to the end of the century when there was a slight increase; in continental Europe, the reduction in taxes at the end of the Napoleonic wars was modest and soon reversed. In Britain, state expenditure fell as a proportion of GNP between 1820 and 1914, in contrast to France and Germany. In Britain, central government expenditure fell from 12 per cent of GNP in 1830 to 6 per cent in 1880, and stood at 7 per cent in 1910; all spending, including local government, stood at 15 per cent in 1830, 9 per cent in 1880 and 12 per cent in 1910. In Prussia-Germany, central government spending was 17 per cent of national income in 1830, 4 per cent in 1880 and 6 per cent in 1910. In Germany, much spending after unification was at the level of the individual state rather than the Reich: in 1880, at all levels of government, the figure was 13 per cent and in 1910 16 per cent. In France, central government spending was 7 per cent of GNP in 1830, 13 per cent in 1880 and 11 per cent in 1910; at all levels of government, the figure was 18 per cent in 1880 and 15 per cent in 1910.[13] The British state was more effectively constrained than its continental neighbours until the outbreak of the First

[12] One part of this task has been undertaken by D. Vincent, *The Culture of Secrecy: Britain, 1832–1998* (Oxford, 1998), who tries to show both how the state viewed its citizens and vice versa, how the state attempted to keep information from its citizens and how secrecy was challenged. Other areas include the use of medical power over citizens (compulsory vaccination or the notification of diseases); the collection of statistical data both to audit institutions and to measure the economy; the regulation of monopolies to protect consumers; or the creation of coroners' juries to ensure that enquiries into deaths involved citizens as well as doctors. Some of these points are considered in the conclusion.

[13] Mann, *Sources of Social Power*, vol. II, table 11.3, pp. 366–7; D. E. Schremmer, 'Taxation and public finance: Britain, France and Germany', in P. Mathias and S. Pollard (eds.), *Cambridge Economic History of Europe*, vol. VIII: *The Industrial Economies: The Development of Economic and Social Policies* (Cambridge, 1989), p. 362; Harling and Mandler, 'From "fiscal-military" state to laissez-faire state', 59. It may be noted that these figures contradict the contention of L. E. Davis and R. A. Huttenback, *Mammon and the Pursuit of Empire: The Economics of British Imperialism* (Cambridge, 1988), pp. 276–8, that 'England had been and continued to be the most heavily taxed nation in the world' as a result of the costs of defending the empire and its inability to pass the costs to the colonies. Unfortunately, Davis and Huttenback only consider the period between 1865 and 1914, when they claim that taxation as a proportion of net national income rose by a sixth; this ignores the considerable reduction in the proportion between 1815 and 1870, and its stabilisation until the mid-1890s; the increase in Germany and France came earlier, was more rapid and surpassed the British share of GNP from the 1860s. A similar point is made by Michael Mann, who denies that British imperial-military commitments were especially high: he argues that as a proportion of GNP in 1910, military expenditure in Britain was 2.8 per cent, compared with 4.1 per cent in France and 2.9 per cent in Germany: Mann, *Sources of Social Power*, vol. II, p. 377. Similar figures are

World War. This raises the issue posed by Baysinger and Tollison in their study of the fiscal policies of Gladstone: how was leviathan chained and how was the British state able to reduce its claims on GNP to a greater extent than its European counterparts?[14]

The ability to restrict the state and to generate a political culture based on the assumption that it and the political elite were trustworthy did not simply depend upon the assiduous cultivation of a sense of public duty and the notion of a 'neutral' state. Both Gladstone and officials at the Treasury who were reared in the stern tenets of Gladstonian financial orthodoxy were very conscious that new dangers arose from the pursuit of votes by competing politicians as well as from the ambitions of spending departments. The result, they feared, would be a replacement of retrenchment by expenditure unless there were clearly established, rigid, conventions; it was easier to bring down spending from the heights of the Napoleonic wars than to keep it at the new, lower, level. The rhetoric of the neutrality of the state and of public duty, and the appeal to retrenchment and liberty, were sustained by detailed, technical, accounting principles which the Tories started to formulate before 1830, but which became a well-defined system in the middle of the century. These principles formed the links in a chain forged by Gladstone and Treasury officials to constrain the state and its citizens, to make them responsible and prudent.

The first link in the chain was a firm rejection of hypothecation of tax revenue, that is assigning particular revenues to particular purposes. In the eighteenth century, hypothecation was used to create trust in the tax system, by making it clear that certain taxes were earmarked to cover particular loans, and creating confidence that interest would be paid.[15] By the mid-nineteenth century, a different assumption applied, for it was realised that hypothecation would contribute to an increase in the role of the state by treating it as a collection of services and functions, each of which was individually desirable with a protected source of revenue. Revenue should therefore be unified, treated as a single pool of money which was separate from the purposes for which it was raised. This system of 'budgetary unity' was recommended by the Select Committee on Public Monies of 1857 and formalised by the Exchequer and Audit

produced by J. M. Hobson, *The Wealth of States: A Comparative Sociology of International Economic and Political Change* (Cambridge, 1997), table 5.10, p. 171, which puts military spending as a percentage of net national product (NNP) in the period 1870–1913 at 3.1 in Britain, 3.8 in Germany, 4.0 in France and (for 1885–1913) at 5.1 in Russia and 8.2 in Japan.

[14] Baysinger and Tollison, 'Chaining leviathan', 206–13; and see also Leathers, 'Gladstonian finance and the Virginia school of public finance', 515–21.

[15] Brewer, *Sinews of Power*, p. 211.

Departments Act of 1866. This appointed a comptroller and auditor general, who monitored the payment of the gross receipts of the revenue departments into the Bank of England, where they formed a single fund instead of appropriating particular sources of revenue to specific purposes. Money was paid out of a single consolidated fund to cover the expenditure of each department, and any surplus was to be handed over to the National Debt Commission.[16] The entire revenue collected by the state from all sources was paid into the Exchequer rather than diverted into subsidiary funds, and the Commons voted a 'supply' for a particular purpose. Thus the entire revenue of the Post Office was paid into the Exchequer, and the entire costs of operating mail services voted by parliament, rather than the *net* revenue being handed over. The danger of allowing departments to retain revenue, or to be granted certain earmarked taxes, was that they had every incentive to spend and to hand over the minimum net revenue to the Exchequer. The principle was reaffirmed by the Treasury in 1927, as the 'fundamental basis' of British finance and the 'main principle of the Gladstonian reforms'. It gave parliament direct control over expenditure and prevented any head of expenditure becoming stereotyped; it also provided a clear picture of government expenditure as a whole. According to the Treasury, the principle explained the success of Britain in restoring its finances after the First World War compared with France: 'The special accounts, which result from the system of assignment, are the curse of the Continental Budget, as they afford a ready means of cloaking Government liabilities and concealing deficits in a Budget, which balances on paper; but if Parliamentary assent must be obtained for the application of all public resources, it is impossible to disguise the situation.'[17] In the 1920s, the Treasury continued to defend one of the central principles laid down by the mid-Victorian fiscal constitution.

No less important was a second link in the chain: the rejection of *virement* of funds, that is a refusal to move surplus funds from one budgetary

---

[16] PP 1857 (2nd session) IX, *Report from the Select Committee on Public Monies*, pp. 498–9; 29 and 30 Vict. c. 39, 'An act to consolidate the duties of the Exchequer and Audit Departments, to regulate the receipt, custody, and issue of public moneys, and to provide for the audit of the accounts thereof.' The rules were breached at the time of the nationalisation of telegraphs: in 1873, the Post Office was found to have overspent its parliamentary grant. See C. R. Perry, *The Victorian Post Office: The Growth of a Bureaucracy* (Woodbridge, 1992), pp. 126–31. On Treasury controls, see M. Wright, *Treasury Control of the Civil Service, 1854–74* (Oxford, 1969).

[17] PRO, T171/582, Leith-Ross to chancellor, 13 Aug. 1927. Hypothecation has entered political debate in the 1990s and 2000s as a means of justifying socially desirable expenditure by overcoming the resistance to higher taxes in general. The one major exception, bitterly regretted by the Treasury, was the road fund licence which is discussed in detail in Daunton, *Just Taxes*.

head to another. Although revenue was treated as a single sum without any ties to a specific purpose, expenditure was minutely subdivided by annual 'votes' of the Commons for specific functions and tasks. This system contributed to limits on government expenditure. A sum of, say, £1,000 might be voted for the construction of a new vessel for the Royal Navy and £500 for a Post Office in Aberdeen; a surplus of £150 on the first could not be used to cover a deficiency on the second, or diverted to some other purpose such as building a new prison in Manchester or an army barracks in Sydney. Each initiative needed its own 'vote'. The danger of *virement* was that spending would always rise to the available revenue, and would ratchet up expenditure.[18]

The rejection of hypothecation and *virement* depended on the creation of consolidated and simplified accounts. The Select Committee on Public Income and Expenditure in 1828 laid down the general principle 'that no Government is justified in taking even the smallest sum of money from the People, unless a case can be clearly established to show that it will be productive of some essential advantage to them, and of one that cannot be obtained by a smaller sacrifice'. The Select Committee realised that retrenchment was difficult, for each head of expenditure had its own advocates; it was absolutely necessary 'to fix the public expenditure at such an amount that the real wants of the People shall not be made to give way to any imaginary want of the State; the latter arise from so many sources, that it is frequently very difficult to prevent the operation of an undue influence'. The problem, as the Select Committee saw it, was that the Treasury had lost control over spending departments during the Napoleonic war and had not regained authority. The departments laid their annual estimates before the Treasury, but expenditure was not subsequently controlled and it remained under the management of each department. The result was that expenditure was higher than in previous periods of peace: 'Each Department naturally endeavours to exalt its own importance; and wishes to promote its general efficiency, and to have everything in it complete and perfect; hence the desire to secure these objects, rather than the exigency of the Public Service, has had too much influence over a great part of the Public Expenditure.' Crucial to the restoration of Treasury control over expenditure was a clear, uniform, system of accounts so that each sum voted in the annual estimates was applied to the service for which it was intended. Reform of the accounts took a further thirty or so years. The Select Committee of 1828 recommended the introduction of a 'mercantile' system of accounts through the

---

[18] Most academics will recognise the practice of *virement* of money, shifting a balance from the photocopying account to spend more money on seminar expenses: all money is spent, and none is returned to the central university administration.

adoption of double-entry book-keeping.[19] The process was slow, starting with the introduction of commercial accounting methods in the navy in 1831 and army in 1846. In 1857, the Select Committee on Public Monies recommended the extension of the system. The existence of full accounts, the chancellor argued, was essential to provide effective control by the Treasury and parliament; the system of separate votes would only operate if there were an effective check on the issue of money, to ensure that a department did not spend without authority. Although the Exchequer was given powers in 1834 to ensure that separate grants were spent in the way intended by parliament, the check would only be effective if accounts allowed money to be followed from collection to its final appropriation. What was needed, it seemed, was the replacement of the existing 'cumbrous, antiquated, and unmeaning forms' of the Exchequer.[20]

It followed that it was necessary to have annual votes by parliament and that spending plans should not be carried over from year to year. There was a very strong emphasis on the need for constant vigilance by parliament as a protection for the public against the spending ambitions of the executive. Radical reformers argued for an extension of the franchise less for its own sake in creating a more democratic political system than as a means of changing the composition of Members of Parliament, in order to purge the Commons of 'interest' and to make parliamentary control more effective in eliminating militarism and waste. Joseph Hume,* a

---

[19] PP 1828 v, *Second Report from the Select Committee on Public Income and Expenditure of the United Kingdom. Ordnance Estimates*, pp. 6–8; and appendix 53, Treasury minute, 18 Apr. 1828, p. 475.

[20] PP 1857 (2nd session) IX, *Report from the Select Committee on Public Monies*, pp. 498–9 and appendix 1, 'Memorandum on financial control put in by the chancellor of the Exchequer', pp. 519–47. The development of government accounts is part of a wider phenomenon: see M. Poovey, *A History of the Modern Fact: Problems of Knowledge in the Sciences of Wealth and Society* (Chicago, 1998).

* Joseph Hume (1777–1855) was born in Montrose, where his father was a shipmaster; his widowed mother ran a crockery stall. He was apprenticed to a surgeon and then studied medicine in Aberdeen, Edinburgh and London. He became a ship's surgeon in the East India Co. and transferred to the land service as an interpreter and surgeon, as well as holding posts as paymaster. He made a fortune in India and returned to England in 1808. He travelled, and translated Dante, before briefly becoming MP in 1812. He published on savings banks, was active in the Lancastrian school movement and in Indian affairs; he exposed abuses in the East India Co. and favoured free trade to India. He tried, unsuccessfully, to become a director of the company. He re-entered parliament in 1818 and remained, with a short interval in 1841, until his death. He was leader of the radicals, and the main advocate of retrenchment. In 1820, he drew attention to the costs of collecting the revenue, and in 1834 moved the repeal of the corn laws. He maintained a staff of clerks to analyse the returns of public expenditure. He opposed the sinking fund; campaigned against flogging in the army and imprisonment for debt; supported Catholic emancipation; and argued for the repeal of the combination laws. As the *DNB* commented, 'he spoke oftener and probably worse than any other private member'. (*DNB*, vol. XXVIII, ed. S. Lee (London, 1891), pp. 230–1.)

radical MP and himself a beneficiary of 'old corruption' in the East India Co., subjected financial estimates to minute (and tedious) scrutiny, using the material available in the parliamentary library created in 1821. He continued his role as the critic of government waste and the advocate of retrenchment into the debates over the income tax in the 1850s. This role of the Commons in vigilant supervision of spending was important: between 1832 and 1867, parties had limited cohesion and the Commons was seen as an autonomous arena from which the executive could be chosen and prevented from becoming over-mighty. Although the emphasis did shift in the 1870s with a greater stress on the role of strong and stable parties based upon programmes and electoral supremacy, it was still assumed that the Commons would minutely scrutinise spending plans.[21]

The principle was clearly expressed by Gladstone in 1889 when the Conservative chancellor – George Goschen* – broke the rule that the spending plans of the year should be covered by a vote of the revenue of the year. Goschen created a Naval Defence Fund to pay for the construction of battleships, borrowing money which would be repaid out of taxes over the next seven years. The proposal horrified Gladstone as a breach in the constitutional principle that the Commons should not pledge future revenue. Governments would, he feared, soon succumb to the temptation to cast burdens on to the future, so storing up long-term financial difficulties in order to obtain a superficial, short-term, popularity.[22] When Gladstone returned to power, he and his chancellor (William Harcourt)†

---

[21] M. Taylor, *The Decline of British Radicalism, 1847–1860* (Oxford, 1995), pp. 30–2, 45, 135; A. B. Hawkins, '"Parliamentary government" and Victorian political parties, c. 1830–80', *English Historical Review* 104 (1989), 638–69; Harling, *Waning of 'Old Corruption'*, pp. 172–4, 196, on Hume. Interestingly, Hume managed the Working Man's Memorial of Gratitude to Peel, a sign of the radicals' acceptance of the equity of the state: Harling, *Waning of 'Old Corruption'*, p. 255.

[22] PRO, T168/22, E. W. Hamilton Financial Papers 1891–2, quoting Gladstone's speech at Hastings, 17 Mar. 1891, reported in the *Times*, 18 Mar. 1891, p. 11a.

* George Joachim Goschen (1831–1907) was the son of a merchant banker in the City of London, which he joined after education in Germany and at Oxford. He became a director of the Bank of England in 1858 and published *Theory of the Foreign Exchanges* in 1861. He was Liberal MP for the City from 1863 to 1880, serving as vice-president of the Board of Trade in 1865, chancellor of the Duchy of Lancaster in 1866, president of the poor law board from 1868 to 1871 (where he tried to tighten up on the payment of outdoor relief) and first lord of the Admiralty from 1871 to 1874 where he refused to reduce the naval estimates and contributed to the dissolution. He was out of sympathy with Gladstone's foreign policy, and in the home rule crisis of 1886 joined the Liberal Unionists. He was chancellor of the Exchequer in the Conservative government of 1886 to 1892 and first lord of the Admiralty in 1895 to 1900 where he increased the naval estimates. He opposed Joseph Chamberlain's tariff policy and remained a free trader. (*DNB, Second Supplement*, vol. II, ed. S. Lee (London, 1912), pp. 134–40.)

† William Harcourt (1827–1904) was the younger son of an Anglican clergyman and Oxfordshire landowner. He was educated at Trinity, Cambridge, where he was an Apostle.

undid Goschen's 'great constitutional innovation'.[23] The Gladstonian principles were reiterated by Herbert Asquith,* the chancellor in the next Liberal government. Any capital expenditure for army and naval purposes should be provided out of the revenue of the year rather than by borrowing, which confused capital and revenue charges, removed large items of annual expenditure from effective parliamentary supervision and 'inevitably encourages in the spending departments crude, precipitate, and wasteful experiments'. Failure to follow this rule would merely increase the unfunded debt and weaken the state, both because 'it would seriously hamper our borrowing powers if a sudden emergency arose', and because 'the Government is competing for and locking up funds that might otherwise be available for commercial and industrial purposes'.[24]

Although parliament made annual votes on expenditure, its ability to influence the overall structure of expenditure or the shape of revenues was strictly limited. In France and the United States, the chamber and Congress had more direct and detailed control over expenditure. Although there were occasional suggestions that a Select Committee of the Commons should have similar powers,[25] the proposal was always rejected as an encroachment on the right of the executive to propose expenditure. It was for the Commons to approve or reject any particular vote, but not to intervene in making policy. The danger of allowing more power to

He became a successful lawyer, acting for the Metropolitan Board of Works in the scheme to construct the Thames Embankment. He stood as an independent Liberal in 1859 but was defeated. He studied and wrote on international law, especially at the time of the American civil war, and he served on Royal Commissions on naturalisation and extradition. Between 1869 and 1887 he was professor of law at Cambridge, but he was shifting from law to politics. He became a Liberal MP in 1868, and was home secretary in 1880, chancellor of the Exchequer in 1886 and 1892–5; he was also leader of the Liberals in the Commons when Rosebery was prime minister. He resigned as leader of the Liberal party in 1898. He denounced the Boer war and tariff reform. He succeeded to the family estate in 1904, and became liable to the death duties which he had himself reformed. (*DNB, Second Supplement*, vol. II, ed. Lee, pp. 198–212.)

[23] M. J. Daunton, 'The political economy of death duties: Harcourt's budget of 1894', in N. Harte and R. Quinault (eds.), *Land and Society in Britain, 1700–1914* (Manchester, 1996), pp. 149–50.

[24] H. H. Asquith, *Parliamentary Debates, 4th ser. 156*, 30 Apr. 1906, cols. 289–91, 294.

[25] University of Birmingham Library, Austen Chamberlain Papers, AC 17/2/20, deals with the proposal to introduce a Select Committee to examine the details of national expenditure.

* Henry Herbert Asquith (1852–1928) was educated at the City of London School and Balliol College, Oxford; he was called to the bar in 1876 and was made a QC in 1890. He was MP from 1886 to 1918, holding office as home secretary in 1892–5. He was a Liberal imperialist in the Boer war. He became chancellor of the Exchequer in 1905, and held the post until he became prime minister from 1908 to 1916. (*DNB, 1922–30*, ed. Weaver, pp. 29–40.)

the Commons, as James Grigg* pointed out, was deadlock between the executive and Commons, and the possibility that special pleading in the Commons might *increase* spending.[26]

Interest groups were excluded from any bargaining over tax rates or exemptions. Tax legislation was, as far as possible, general rather than particularistic. By contrast, in the United States the tax system was shaped by thousands of exemptions, deductions and credits for various activities in particular locations. Tax laws were written by Congress, which was open to lobbying by interest groups. In Britain, tax measures emanated from the executive, in circumstances of some secrecy: the budget was written by the chancellor, often with minimal discussion with his colleagues in Cabinet, following the advice of a small group of Treasury officials who had a strong commitment to general measures. When Hugh Dalton[†] became chancellor in 1945, he wondered how many members of the Cabinet were normally informed of the budget before it was presented. He felt that practice had varied. As he pointed out, Randolph Churchill[‡] and William Harcourt placed their proposals before the full Cabinet. He might have added that Gladstone's great budget of 1853 was considered by Cabinet on several occasions at length and with considerable divergence of opinion.[27] More recently, chancellors had gone their own way. Dalton himself presented the main lines to the prime

[26] P. J. Grigg, *Prejudice and Judgement* (London, 1948), pp. 66, 68.

[27] M. R. D. Foot and H. C. G. Matthew (eds.), *The Gladstone Diaries*, vol. IV: *1848–1854* (Oxford, 1974), pp. 513–8, and J. Brooke and M. Sorensen (eds.), *The Prime Ministers' Papers Series. W. E. Gladstone*, vol. III: *Autobiographical Memoranda, 1845–66* (London, 1978), pp. 132–45.

* Percy James Grigg (1890–1964) was educated at St John's, Cambridge, and entered the Treasury in 1913. He was secretary to five chancellors of the Exchequer (including Churchill) between 1921 and 1930. He was chairman of the Board of Customs and Excise and of the Inland Revenue; in 1939 he became permanent secretary of the War Office and then joined the government as secretary of state for war from 1942 to 1945. (*DNB, 1961–70*, ed. E. T. Williams and C. S. Nicholls (Oxford, 1981), pp. 460–2.)

† Edward Hugh John Neale Dalton (1887–1962) was the son of the chaplain to Prince George (later George V); educated at Eton and King's College, Cambridge. He was called to the bar in 1914 and served in the war; he joined the economics department of the LSE after the war and was reader between 1920 and 1936. His *Principles of Public Finance* appeared in 1923 and attempted to draw a distinction between academic neutrality and partisan argument; his other main publication was on equality of incomes. He was a Labour MP between 1924 and 1931 and 1935 and 1959. In the war-time coalitions, he was minister of economic warfare, 1940–2 and president of the Board of Trade, 1942–5; in the postwar Labour government, he was chancellor of the Exchequer, 1945–7, chancellor of the Duchy of Lancaster, 1948–50, and minister of town and country planning, 1950–1. (*DNB, 1961–70*, ed. Williams and Nicholls, pp. 266–9.)

‡ Randolph Henry Spencer Churchill (1849–95), younger son of the duke of Marlborough, was educated at Eton and Merton College, Oxford; he was elected a Conservative MP in 1880. He was secretary of state for India 1885–6 and chancellor of the Exchequer and leader of the Commons in 1886, resigning over demands for more finance for the army and navy. He was one of the creators of popular Conservatism. (*DNB, Supplement*, vol. II, ed. Lee, pp. 9–22.)

minister and two senior colleagues, but did not put anything to the full Cabinet until the day before the budget speech, when any major change was impossible.[28] Dalton's experience in 1945 seems to have been the norm by the second half of the nineteenth century, with the chancellor presenting his budget as a *fait accompli* shortly before it was delivered to the Commons. In the late nineteenth century, E. W. Hamilton* of the Treasury presented the chancellor with information on the current state of revenues and expenditure, suggesting the scope for tax concessions or the need for tax increases in the next budget; unless there were major proposals to change the core of the fiscal constitution, the matter did not go any further. The government rarely consulted even its own members, and the passage of the Finance Bill through the Commons was normally guaranteed as a matter of party discipline.[29] This legislation might offer tax breaks to certain activities – for example, the purchase of life insurance – or might grant allowances for children or dependent relatives. However, these measures were of general application, without the exercise of discretion by the tax authorities; there was strong opposition, for example, to anything which would allow firms to apply for tax relief on the application of company reserves to productive investment. The authorities did not wish to become involved in the use of the tax system to encourage particular types of activity, which would simply exacerbate the problems that already existed in defining the general principles in the courts. Their aim was, as far as possible, to write the tax law in such a way that there was no discretion in its implementation; if the government wished to encourage particular activities, it should be in the form of explicit grants which were open to parliamentary scrutiny. As the Inland Revenue argued during the First World War, 'The object of taxation, as known in this country, is solely to provide money; taxes are of general application and, as equality of treatment between taxpayer and taxpayer is a cardinal principle, the scope and conditions of liability are closely defined by statute and discretionary power is taboo.'[30]

[28] BLPES, Dalton Papers, I, diary entry for 7 Dec. 1945.
[29] See Steinmo, 'Political institutions', 329–72.
[30] PRO, T171/168, Reconstruction Committee. Encouragement of industries by means of revision of internal taxation. '1. Memorandum to the chancellor of the Exchequer from the Board of Inland Revenue, E. E. Nott-Bower and N. F. Warren Fisher, 30 Aug. 1916'.
* Edward Walter Hamilton (1847–1908) was born in Salisbury, where his father – a friend of Gladstone – was bishop. He was educated at Eton and Christ Church, Oxford, joining the Treasury in 1870. He was private secretary to Robert Lowe as chancellor of the Exchequer 1872–3 and to Gladstone in 1873–4 and 1880–5. He formed a close relationship with Gladstone. In 1885, he became principal clerk in the finance branch of the Treasury and by 1902 was permanent financial secretary and joint permanent secretary with George Murray. He retired in 1907. His main concern was the financial side of the Treasury, and he mastered the details of the City and banking. He was particularly involved with Goschen's conversion scheme, on which he wrote a book. (*DNB, Second Supplement*, vol. II, ed. Lee, p. 193.)

The ban on hypothecation and *virement*, and the insistence on annual votes, meant that a surplus was possible at the end of the year, either as a result of high tax revenues at a time of prosperity or underspending on any vote. This surplus offered a temptation which self-interested, ambitious, politicians might not resist, and which should be removed from their reach. A chancellor would be able to carry over surpluses in order to make a dramatic reduction in taxation in time for an election, which would turn the tax system into a system of bribery. As Basil Blackett,[*] a Treasury official and writer on taxation, explained in 1910,

there is much objection to using the chance surplus of one year for the ordinary expenditure of the next – such a system would lead to much political jobbery as a strong government would build up a surplus in its early years and use it to remit taxation when its popularity was waning and leave its successors of the opposite party with an empty exchequer.

A further financial convention therefore insisted that any surplus should not be carried forward to the next year. Since 1829, any surplus was transferred to the sinking fund in order to reduce the national debt, so releasing funds which could be more efficiently used elsewhere. Repayment of the national debt would also create confidence amongst lenders that the state was trustworthy, so maintaining British credit and ensuring that the public would lend to the state in times of war when the revenue from annual tax revenues needed to be supplemented.[31] As we shall see, politicians were careful both to limit new loans and to pay off existing debt. In the process, the national debt was transformed from a menace to British liberties to a guardian of British security.

By these means, barriers were constructed to the expansion of the state. These technical accounting procedures and the annual votes of the Commons were erected into matters of high constitutional principle which were integral to English liberty and national identity. In the hands of Gladstone, the annual budget became a matter of high theatricality, or perhaps more accurately of religious ceremony. In Gladstone's view, the

---

[31] PP 1857 (2nd session) IX, *Select Committee on Public Monies*, appendix 1, 'Memorandum on financial control put in by the chancellor of the Exchequer', pp. 519–47; PP 1828 V, *Second Report from the Select Committee on Public Income and Expenditure of the United Kingdom*, pp. 5–7; PRO, T171/9, Basil Blackett, 22 Nov. 1910.

[*] Basil Phillott Blackett (1882–1935) was born in Calcutta where his parents were missionaries. He was educated at Marlborough and University College, Oxford. He entered the Treasury in 1904, serving as secretary to the Royal Commission on Indian Finance, 1913–14, and as Treasury representative in Washington in 1917–19. He was controller of finance at the Treasury from 1919 to 1922 and finance member of the viceroy of India's council from 1922 to 1928; he was a director of the Bank of England from 1929. (*Dictionary of National Biography, 1931–40*, ed. L. G. Wickham Legg, London 1949, pp. 83–4.)

state was more than a collection of individuals. It was an 'organic body' which had 'a national conscience...formed upon a comprehensive idea of right and wrong'. Initially, he believed that the established Church of England provided guidance to the state on what was right and wrong, providing the basis for a moral, organic, state in which all classes could co-operate. In the 1840s, he moved to a new position in which free trade and 'fiscal probity became the new morality'. His budgets forged a connection between economic individualism and probity, self-control and morality, which replaced older notions of obligation and duty in pursuit of a balanced organic society.[32] The budget, and the consolidated fund which brought together all sources of revenue into a single entity, made government finances transparent: it was clear to the public and taxpayers where money came from and where it was going. Above all, spending was open to parliamentary scrutiny on an annual basis. Gladstone's speech of 1891 which denounced Goschen's breach of these principles was, appropriately, delivered at Hastings, a central site in the formation of English national identity which was interpreted by late Victorian historians as a beneficial fusion between the democratic principles of the defeated Saxons and the centralising tendencies of the victorious Normans.[33] The existence of one without the other would lead either to a weak, fragmented, polity or to autocracy; it was necessary to maintain the balance by rigorous financial checks on the ambitions of the executive by local representatives gathered in the Commons. As Gladstone argued in the speech, the finances of the country were 'at the root of English liberty', and rested on parliamentary scrutiny of all public spending.[34] The rhetoric of Gladstonian fiscal orthodoxy was reinforced by administrative checks, parliamentary procedures and a vision of English history which constrained the temptations to spend.

These changes in procedures resulted in a reconfiguration of the central state. As Innes has argued, in the late seventeenth and early eighteenth centuries 'central government became increasingly polyarchic – multi-centred. Power was distributed among a number of institutions, which were co-ordinated by more or less informal co-operation between leading statesmen', and the 'cabinets' of leading ministers mainly dealt with diplomatic and military affairs.[35] The reforms of government accounting procedures and budgetary controls in the second quarter of the

[32] Matthew, *Gladstone, 1809–1874*, pp. 62–3, 76–7.
[33] J. W. Burrow, *A Liberal Descent: Victorian Historians and the English Past* (Cambridge, 1981), p. 143.
[34] PRO, T168/22, Gladstone, speech of 17 Mar. 1891, reported in the *Times*, 18 Mar. 1891, p. 11a. The speech was delivered at the Gaiety theatre, adding a further layer to the construction of national identity in late Victorian Britain.
[35] Innes, 'The domestic face of the military-fiscal state', pp. 98–9.

nineteenth century meant that the business of the central state was much more co-ordinated, through the ability of the Treasury and the chancellor of the Exchequer to control spending plans and of parliament to check the annual votes. The polyarchic structure of the eighteenth-century state gave way to a more unified system at the centre. But the central state also left very large areas of responsibility to local government, especially for investment in the urban infrastructure and welfare spending. Here, as we shall see in chapter 9, a different approach was adopted, with a number of specific taxes for particular functions, often undertaken by specific authorities or after votes by ratepayers. As far as the central state was concerned, leviathan was both chained and worthy of trust from its citizens.

4   'A cheap purchase of future security': establishing the income tax, 1842–1860

I have a strong conviction that the great mass of the lower classes will consider the voluntary determination of Parliament to accept for themselves, and to impose upon the wealth of the country this tax for the purpose of relieving its burdens – I have a strong conviction that it will be generally hailed on the part of the country, as a strong proof of the determination of the upper classes to bear their fair share of taxation.

> Robert Peel on the reintroduction of the income tax in 1842,
> *Parliamentary Debates*, 3rd ser. 61, 18 Mar. 1842, cols. 916–17

... all property ought to contribute to the taxes of the country, which, if they are justly and wisely imposed, ought not to be regarded as a penalty on property, but as the necessary means of rendering property available for the effective use and enjoyment of the owner.

> W. E. Gladstone, *Parliamentary Debates*, 3rd ser. 170, 16 Apr. 1863,
> col. 224g

The creation of strict accounting principles, with transparency and scrutiny, contributed to the establishment of trust in the state. But critics of the fiscal system had another major concern: taxes were inequitable between classes and interests, falling on trade and industry, on producers and poor consumers, to a much lesser extent than on land, on *rentiers*, and the consumers of luxuries. It seems obvious in retrospect that the British tax system from 1816 to 1842 was extremely narrow, and that the abolition of the war-time income tax left the government heavily dependent upon customs duties and a few excise duties, creating a highly regressive fiscal regime which was threatening the legitimacy of the fiscal system and the state. In 1842, Peel reintroduced the income tax in pursuit of the major task of convincing the electors and taxpayers that the allocation of taxation could be fair, marking the voluntary acceptance by property owners and the upper classes of a burden in order to relieve the poor.

In retrospect, viewed from the late Victorian period, the reintroduction of the income tax in 1842 marked the start of a new political economy, providing the basis of economic prosperity and social stability. This was not how it appeared at the time. The strategy was not immediately successful, for the income tax caused dissension rather than acceptance of the equity and balance of the fiscal system, leading to fears that it was a means of providing the state with a new source of revenue for militarism and extravagance. On such a view, the restoration of balance and equity should be secured by cutting spending on the court, debt service and the armed forces. The income tax might simply exacerbate the bias in the fiscal system, falling on active producers of wealth to a greater extent than on passive recipients of income from land or government bonds. Meanwhile, supporters of protection might attack the income tax on different grounds, as a policy designed to provide revenue for the abolition of the corn laws – a self-interested pursuit of the claims of the towns over the country. Although the income tax, like the gold standard, Bank Charter Act and free trade, became central to British identity in the later Victorian period, at the time of its introduction it was highly divisive. The task of Peel was to reintroduce the income tax; the achievement of Gladstone was to make it acceptable, a guarantor of peace and retrenchment, of balance and equity, rather than militarism, extravagance and bias.

Peel's budget of 1842: reintroducing the income tax

Peel was well aware of the tensions over the fiscal system and in 1830, at a time of distress and political unrest, he turned to the possibility of reducing taxes on the 'necessities of the people' as a means of securing stability:

He thought it one of the first duties of the legislature to do all in its power to excite a taste in the humbler classes of society for those comforts and those enjoyments – those luxuries, he might add – of civilised society, the desire for which, and the habitual possession of which, would form the best guarantee that the higher classes could have for the possession of their property and their power, at present enjoyed. It was urged, and with perfect justice, that the remission of taxes was amongst the means by which that most desirable object could be chiefly effected.[1]

Peel's rhetoric is interesting, for he was suggesting that the 'necessities' of the people should now be widened to include comforts and luxuries; the definition of commodities was changing in order to extend participation in the world of goods. Although Peel's tax reductions marked a significant step in retrenchment, they could also be criticised as financially imprudent and a blatant attempt to contain the pressures for parliamentary reform. Would participation in the world of goods be an adequate substitute for exclusion from the world of politics?

[1] *Parliamentary Debates*, new ser. 23, 19 Mar. 1830, col. 658.

In any case, many radicals felt that Peel's concessions were inadequate. Financial reformers such as Charles Poulett Thomson* called for an enquiry into the 'injurious nature' of taxes which fell too heavily on productive industry. In his view, prices were made up of wages and profits, and were set in competition with other countries. Wages had fallen to the minimum, so that taxation must fall on profits and would therefore destroy industry and enterprise. The terrible example of Holland, whose dominance in trade and industry was lost through 'oppressive taxation', provided a warning of what might happen. According to Poulett Thomson, the problem was not so much the *level* as the *incidence* of taxation: taxes fell on raw materials and manufactures at such a high rate that consumption was reduced and revenue fell. A lower rate of duty might lead to higher consumption and revenue.[2] This analysis of higher yields from lower duties was supported by many financial reformers in the 1830s, especially by Henry Parnell's† influential *On Financial Reform*.[3] Customs and excise duties were reduced in the 1830s and 1840s, and contributed to mitigating some of the attacks on the imbalance in the tax system.

Problems still remained and the financial position of the government was weakened as a result of the concessions of the Whigs. In 1842, Peel was faced by a budget deficit and the reintroduction of the income tax offered a more acceptable option than three other possibilities. One was to borrow, which was not desirable in terms of political expediency or the wish to secure financial independence from the City. Peel was left with two different, and contradictory, proposals for changes in indirect taxes. He could reduce duties in the hope that consumption and revenue would rise, a policy which he considered a 'mere delusion'. Indeed, the deficit arose in part from the introduction of the penny post in 1840, which Rowland Hill‡ justified on the grounds that a reduction

---

[2] *Parliamentary Debates*, new ser. 23, 25 Mar. 1830, cols. 857–96.

[3] See Brown, *Board of Trade and the Free Trade Movement*; Parnell, *On Financial Reform*.

* Charles Edward Poulett Thomson (1799–1841) spent time abroad in his father's business before becoming an MP in 1826; he was vice-president of the Board of Trade in 1830 and president in 1834 and became governor-general of Canada in 1839. (*DNB*, vol. LVI, ed. S. Lee (London, 1898), pp. 224–6.)

† Henry Brooke Parnell (1776–1842) came from an Irish landed family; he was an MP in the Irish parliament in 1797 and in Westminster in 1802, where he was a liberal Whig. From 1810, he supported Catholic emancipation. He served as secretary for war in 1831–2, and was both treasurer of the navy and paymaster general of the forces in 1835; he then held the new office of paymaster general from 1836 to 1842. (*DNB*, vol. XLIII, ed. Lee, pp. 342–5.)

‡ Rowland Hill (1795–1879) was born in Kidderminster and was educated at his father's school which he and his brothers subsequently took over; they started an experimental school which was moved to London, and they came into contact with the utilitarians. Hill became secretary to the South Australian Commission from 1835, and proposed a penny post. He held a position in the Post Office from 1840 to 1842, was chairman of

in the postage rate would lead to a massive increase in the business of the Post Office and in its revenue. In fact, revenue fell.[4] The alternative was to raise taxes on working-class consumption which Peel could not contemplate. Despite the concessions during the 1830s, any increase in the taxation of consumption was now politically dangerous at a time of considerable unrest and a well-developed radical critique of the injustices of the tax system. Peel's solution was to introduce an income tax for three years in order to cover the immediate deficiency and to provide sufficient revenue to revise duties, with the hope of stimulating commerce and industry, and reducing the cost of living. The income tax was therefore intended to provide a *temporary* source of income to cover the transition from a regime of high duties and low yields to a dynamic economy based on low duties and high yields.[5] Peel's decision to reintroduce the income tax was less an attempt to increase the revenue of the state at a time of budgetary deficits than a means of removing political tensions and improving governability. His concern was to carry through a process of political and social stabilisation by creating a tax system that was neutral between interests, and offering protection to property in general.

In Peel's view, the income tax was a measure of 'prudential conservatism'[6] which amounted to an insurance policy against more serious attacks on property and political stability. 'My own private opinion', he informed John Wilson Croker* in 1842, 'is that the country is in that state, that the property of the country must submit to taxation, in order to release industry and the millions from it; that the doing so voluntarily and

---

the Brighton railway from 1843, and then returned to the Post Office as secretary to the postmaster general, 1846–54, and secretary to the Post Office, 1854–64. (*DNB*, vol. XXVI, ed. Stephen and Lee, pp. 416–20.)

4 M. J. Daunton, 'Comments', in M. A. Crew and P. R. Kleindorfer (eds.), *Competition and Innovation in Postal Services* (Boston, Dordrecht and London, 1991), pp. 13–16; see also M. J. Daunton, *Royal Mail: The Post Office since 1840* (London, 1985), pp. 19, 22–5.

5 *Parliamentary Debates*, 3rd ser. 61, 11 Mar. 1842, cols. 431, 437–9, 444.

6 The phrase used by H. C. G. Matthew to describe the policy of Peel's political heir, W. E. Gladstone: see H. C. G. Matthew, *The Gladstone Diaries with Cabinet Minutes and Prime-Ministerial Correspondence. Introduction to Volumes XII and XIII, 1887–1896* (Oxford, 1994), p. xxxvi.

* John Wilson Croker (1780–1857) was born in Galway; his father was surveyor-general of the Customs and Excise in Ireland. He was educated at Trinity College, Dublin, and attended Lincoln's Inn. He was a barrister in Ireland, as well as writing poetry and journalism. He became a Tory MP in 1807 and in 1808 was temporary chief secretary in Ireland. He was involved in the founding of the *Quarterly Review* in 1809 and was a leading contributor. He became secretary of the Admiralty in 1809, and held the post until 1830; he reformed the administration. He opposed the reform bill, and left parliament in 1832. Although he was a friend and supporter of Peel, they split over the repeal of the corn laws. (*DNB*, vol. XIII, ed. L. Stephen (London, 1888), pp. 123–32.)

with a good grace, will be a cheap purchase of future security.'[7] Peel justified the tax as a means of integrating classes and defusing social unrest,
which would only be needed for three years as a means of stimulating
economic growth, prosperity and contentment:

Although I admit that the tax may press with additional severity on account of
the uncertain nature of profits on that property which is derived from trade and
professions, yet when I consider that one of the main objects of this measure is to
reduce the duties upon the raw materials of production, and that such a reduction
will give the best chance for a revival of commerce, I cannot but think that the
measures will work for the especial advantage of those who are connected with the
trade of the country. As to those who hold land, or those who derive their incomes
from professions, I have a confident expectation that by reducing the cost of living
I shall compensate them for a great part of their burden, but if I may not offer them
that advantage – yet, if by consenting to such a burden, instead of throwing it upon
the articles of consumption, they diminish the embarrassments of their country,
and take from those who are disposed to agitate the public mind the means of
creating discontent and disunion – if they effect this, surely the compensation
they receive will be ample. I hope that my expectations as to the revival of trade in
three years will not be disappointed – that my anticipations as to the temporary
character of this tax will be realised. Then, when that happy time arrives, when we
shall be enabled to dispense with this tax, then shall we find a revival of commerce
and of industry, and then shall we have the satisfaction of contemplating a people
contented and united, from the proof they will have received that those in the
highest stations, and those who are comparatively affluent, are prepared, in a
crisis of commercial and financial difficulty, to bear their full portion of any charge
which the exigencies of the country may render necessary.[8]

Peel did not expect the income tax to be permanent, and he held out
the prospect that the insurance premium against political disaster could
be allowed to expire once the danger had passed and the economy had
recovered.

By no means everyone was convinced that the income tax was a means
of 'rebalancing' the fiscal constitution, and its periodic renewal remained
the subject of dispute until the 1860s. The rhetoric of both Peel in 1842
and Gladstone in 1853 stressed the role of the income tax in creating balance between classes and interests, in an attempt to counter the claim
that the income tax was simply introducing a further *imbalance* between
classes and interests. Criticism of the income tax came from two different directions that could on occasion make common ground. On the
one side stood the radicals and free traders, and on the other the Tory
protectionists.

---

[7] L. J. Jennings (ed.), *The Croker Papers: The Correspondence and Diaries of the late Rt Hon John Wilson Croker* (2nd edn, 3 vols., London, 1885), vol. II, p. 379.
[8] *Parliamentary Debates*, 3rd ser. 61, 18 Mar. 1842, cols. 916–17.

The reintroduction of the income tax was not received with enthusiasm by many radicals and free traders, who felt that it was being adopted in place of a more desirable policy of retrenchment in government spending, most particularly on war. Despite the fall in the level of government expenditure since 1815, suspicion remained that the income tax would be used to finance militarism and impose burdens on productive, active, enterprise. In the opinion of Henry Brougham,[*] an income tax should only be used in a grave emergency when extraordinary expenditure could not be avoided. It had no place in times of peace, when it 'offers a constant temptation to extravagance', removing the check to 'improvident expenditure, and dispensing with the necessity of seeking a revenue in retrenchment'. The tax was also attacked as a threat to personal liberty, for it would require 'inquisitions scattered throughout the country' to enquire into private affairs. Brougham denied that a tax on income would help the poor, for it would simply diminish the fund for the payment of wages and reduce productive labour; by contrast, taxes on commodities would increase the fund from which productive labour was paid.[9]

Although the introduction of the income tax in retrospect appears to be a precursor to Peel's abolition of the corn laws in 1846, that was not how it appeared at the time. In the 1820s, George Canning[†] – a supporter of free trade – was hostile to the income tax and wished to reduce

9 *Parliamentary Debates*, 3rd ser. 61, 14 Mar. 1842, cols. 508–9; 17 Mar. 1842, cols. 730–49; Hawes, in *Parliamentary Debates*, 3rd ser. 61, 21 Mar. 1842, col. 945; see also Brougham (17 Mar. 1842, cols. 746–7), Howick (18 Mar. 1842, col. 899), Dalmeny (21 Mar. 1842, cols. 979–81), Buller (23 Mar. 1842, cols. 1130, 1134), Russell, 62, 8 Apr. 1842, col. 90. The claim that the income tax was a war tax of last resort was also made by Howick (18 Mar. 1842, cols. 899–900), Labouchere (18 Mar. 1842, cols. 919, 925, 927), Hawes (21 Mar. 1842, cols. 951, 953), Dalmeny (21 Mar. 1842, cols. 979–81); on effect on employment, see also C. Buller 23 Mar. 1842, col. 1128.

* Henry Peter Brougham (1778–1868) was educated at Edinburgh University and became an advocate and barrister. He was a founder of the *Edinburgh Review*, and became an MP in 1810. He supported retrenchment and the reform of charities, law and education; he was active in the Society for the Diffusion of Useful Knowledge and was a founder of the University of London (later University College London). He supported the abolition of slavery but opposed the repeal of the navigation laws. He was lord chancellor from 1830 to 1834. (*DNB*, vol. VI, ed. Stephen, pp. 448–58.)

† George Canning (1770–1827) was brought up by his uncle, a Whig banker, in London; he was educated at Eton and Christ Church, Oxford, and entered Lincoln's Inn. He was hostile to the French Revolution, and was elected to parliament in 1794. He served as under-secretary of state for foreign affairs 1796–9; member of the India board, 1799–1800; paymaster general, 1800–1; treasurer of the navy, 1804–6; foreign secretary 1807–9. He disagreed with Castlereagh at the War Office and fought a duel with him. He was president of the India board, 1816–21 and foreign secretary 1823–7, before briefly holding the posts of prime minister and chancellor of the Exchequer in 1827. (*DNB*, vol. VIII, ed. L. Stephen (London, 1886), pp. 420–31).

direct taxes as a concession to the electorate. Many liberal economists opposed the income tax, preferring to see a reduction in all taxes as a burden on production and criticising the income tax as a discouragement to investment and employment. By contrast, Liverpool – a supporter of protection – wished to raise direct taxes and reduce indirect taxes so that 'we should considerably increase the wealth and resources of the country, by the relief which might be afforded to commerce'.[10] Indeed, the income tax was linked in the eyes of radicals and free traders to *maintenance* of the corn laws and preservation of fiscal inequities. They argued that the people were taxed by the corn laws, paying higher food prices and hence maintaining high rents, which gave money to landowners. The income tax merely took back some of the rent, so that landowners in effect paid nothing to the government; by contrast, other forms of income were hit both by the corn laws *and* by the income tax. Further, rent had escaped any increase in the land tax since 1694, and radicals could argue that the obvious source for any increases in taxation was a reform of the land tax. In the opinion of free traders, maintenance of the corn laws hindered economic growth and reduced tax yields; abolishing the corn laws would allow economic recovery and so make the income tax unnecessary. The income tax was denounced as a means of sustaining agricultural protection, which restricted the market for industry and squeezed the profits of manufacturers:

It is to protect the existence of monopoly, to throw a shield around particular and favoured classes, to sacrifice the prosperity of the many to the interests of the few...It is to uphold the monopolies of the agriculturalist and planter, that [Peel] calls on us to wring the pittance from impoverished industry, and scatters a horde of officials over the land to violate the sanctuaries of private life.[11]

By the late nineteenth century, the income tax and free trade were seen as complementary props of the liberal, free trade, economy; in the early nineteenth century, they were often seen as antithetical.

The income tax was criticised as unfair in its incidence between types of income, imposing an unfair burden on production and enterprise. Critics argued that 'No tax could be devised which would operate more unequally, more unjustly, and more oppressively.' Their case was that the tax fell at the same rate both on 'spontaneous' income from 'permanent property' which could be passed on from father to son, and on transitory

---

[10] Hilton, *Corn, Cash and Commerce*, p. 260.
[11] *Parliamentary Debates*, 3rd ser. 62, 21 Mar. 1842, cols. 979–81 (Dalmeny); see also W. Clay, cols. 963, 971.

or 'precarious' incomes based on personal exertion where money had to be set aside to support dependants.[12] The tax hit

fluctuating income in the same proportion as that which was permanent. The injustice was so flagrant, so outstaring, that it was impossible to exaggerate its deformity...The injustice was to tax men equally whose means were most unequal – rendering a whole life wretched, and preventing the possibility of that caution and providence which might enable an industrious and capable man with a fluctuating income to leave something behind for his family...The reason why the man of fluctuating income was severely taxed was, that the man of landed property might escape taxation. The right hon. Baronet [Peel] did not dare to tax the landowner, and he therefore revenged himself upon the unhappy wretch who owned nothing but the faculty of honestly earning his livelihood.[13]

The solution favoured by Joseph Hume, the leading radical critic of the income tax, was to correct the 'inequity' in two ways. First, expenditure should be reduced so that the revenue from the income tax was not needed. Second, income from the profits of industry should not be taxed, but succession duties should be imposed on inheritance of real property. The benefits of tariff reform and the repeal of the corn laws could then be obtained without the harmful effects of the income tax.[14] On this view, the income tax was simply not needed. Hume later modified his position to accept the income tax, on condition that it was differentiated between forms of income.

The most contentious issue in the ten or twenty years after the reintroduction of the income tax was whether it should be differentiated to take account of the capital lying behind 'spontaneous' income which continued after death, and the need to save from 'precarious' income to provide for old age and dependants. The failure of the income tax to take account of the capital providing a flow of income was denounced for transgressing the 'fundamental principle' that 'all property should pay in proportion to its value'.[15] Precarious incomes were paying a higher effective rate than an income based on absolute possession, for 'industrial earnings are taxed to their full extent, although their dependence on the life and efficiency of those whose labour is indispensable to their production requires that a considerable portion be annually saved'.[16] Consequently, the income tax

---

[12] *Parliamentary Debates*, 3rd ser. 61, 18 Mar. 1842, col. 857 (Baring); 23 Mar. 1842, cols. 1125–6 (C. Buller), 1139–40 (Bowring), 1156 (M. Attwood); 62, col. 89 (Russell) 8 Apr. 1842.

[13] *Parliamentary Debates*, 3rd ser. 61, 23 Mar. 1842, cols. 1167–70 (J. A. Roebuck).

[14] *Parliamentary Debates*, 3rd ser. 62, 25 Apr. 1842, cols. 1079–846.

[15] *Address of the Birmingham Income Tax Reform Association to the Electors of Great Britain and Ireland* (Birmingham, 1857), pp. 5–6.

[16] PP 1861 VII, *Select Committee on Income and Property Tax*, draft report, p. 11. This was written by the chairman, J. G. Hubbard, who failed to secure the agreement of the Committee.

was considered to be inequitable between types of income, creating a bias even as 'it deludes its victims with the belief that they are taxed equally or proportionately with other classes of society'. On this view, Smith's first maxim, that taxation should be in proportion to ability or the revenue enjoyed under the protection of the state, was ignored. The income tax was far from being neutral between interests; it was

> a contrivance of surpassing ingenuity for extracting the largest possible proportion of money from the pockets of the industrious and intelligent *creators* of wealth, in order that a proportionate immunity from taxation may be enjoyed by the *possessors* of wealth; it is a tax upon the working bees of the social hive, for the relief of the drones.[17]

This point dominated discussions on the income tax until 1853 and lingered into the early 1860s, leading to a demand for differentiation between precarious and spontaneous income in order to ensure equity. The advocates of differentiation did not contemplate graduation, which 'arraigns the dispositions of Providence, subverts individual rights, and shows itself to be in principle but a step towards Socialism'.[18] Rather, their concern was to ensure that the tax system was modified in order to ensure intersectoral equity between *sources* of income, and to remove any bias in the social and economic system. Above all, they had no desire to supply the means for an increase in state expenditure which they believed would entail a transfer from productive wealth to aristocratic power and military adventurism. The language of taxation, the definition of different incomes and activities as moral or immoral, socially useful or destructive, precarious or spontaneous, formed a major theme in British politics until about 1860. Of course, the radicals' definition of identities was challenged. A *rentier* receiving 'spontaneous' income from government bonds was an easy target; the widow of an industrialist living off investment income was also in receipt of unearned income and was less easily criticised. The definition of 'spontaneous' income as morally worthless was therefore contested, and the two economic categories were constructed through a highly controversial discursive process.

Free traders and radicals were suspicious of the motives of Peel.[19] His response (and later Gladstone's) was to argue that the income tax was

---

[17] [G. C. Lewis], *The Shade of Cocker and the Chancellor of the Exchequer: A Dialogue on the Income Tax* (London, 1856?), pp. 4–5. This imagined dialogue between a financial reformer and a sceptical chancellor was apparently written by G. C. Lewis. Edward Cocker (1631–75) wrote a text on arithmetic, so that anything 'according to Cocker' was correct.

[18] J. G. Hubbard, *How Should an Income Tax Be Levied? Considered in a Letter to the Rt. Hon. B. D'Israeli* (London, 1852), p. 31, and PP 1861 VII, *Report from the Select Committee on Income and Property Tax*, Q. 1119.

[19] Hilton, *Corn, Cash and Commerce*, pp. 261–5, 267; Taylor, *Decline of British Radicalism*, p. 138.

temporary and would be abolished as soon as retrenchment had done its work: it was simply a socially equitable means of covering expenditure in the interim before economic growth in a free market led to higher tax revenues.[20] Acceptance of the income tax by free traders therefore rested upon acceptance of the argument that it would help to constrain the state, rather than provide it with additional resources. Peel and Gladstone also argued that the tax would create a sense of political responsibility by bringing the public and private choices of electors into line. There was a close correlation between paying income tax and possessing a vote in parliamentary elections under the terms of the Reform Act of 1832. Electors therefore had an incentive to vote for cheap government, for their public choices would have immediate private consequences in their tax bills and the income tax would constrain the fiscal-military state.[21]

This case for the income tax took some time to be accepted. When the income tax was due to be renewed in 1848, Hume again attacked it as a means of paying for militarism and avoiding retrenchment.[22] In Hume's opinion, the income tax was only necessary because of ministerial extravagance; renewal would merely provide ministers with the opportunity to waste money and injure national credit. In his opinion, expenditure on the army was by no means the most sensible way of ensuring the safety of the country:

it was of much greater importance to the peace and security of the State to have a population whose affections should ally them to the crown, and whose minds should be satisfied that justice was done to them by the Government. This would give greater security and stability to the Throne, and tranquillity to the country, than the existence of 100,000 fighting men...The genius of the country was essentially civil, but ministers were making it a military country.[23]

Attitudes to the income tax involved different assumptions about national character and identity, about peace and commerce versus militarism and empire.[24]

The income tax was renewed for a further three years, but a sustained attack was kept up, above all by the Liverpool Financial Reform

---

[20] Peel, *Parliamentary Debates*, 3rd ser. 61, 11 Mar. 1842, cols. 431, 437–9, 444; Biagini, 'Popular Liberals, Gladstonian finance, and the debate on taxation', p. 156.

[21] Matthew, *Gladstone, 1809–1874*, pp. 125–8; Daunton, 'Political economy of death duties', pp. 149–50.

[22] Taylor, *Decline of British Radicalism*, pp. 134, 141.

[23] *Parliamentary Debates*, 3rd ser. 97, 3 Mar. 1848, cols. 197–9.

[24] Taylor, *Decline of British Radicalism*, pp. 134–5, mentions the campaign to reduce spending on imperial defence in PP 1847–8 XXI pt I, *Report from the Select Committee on Navy, Army and Ordnance Estimates*; PP 1849 IX, *First and Second Reports from the Select Committee on Army and Ordnance Expenditure (Ordnance)*; PP 1850, X, *Report from the Select Committee on Army and Ordnance Expenditure (Army)*; PP 1851 VII, *Report from the Select Committee on Army and Ordnance Expenditure*.

Association under the presidency of William Gladstone's brother, Robertson,* and by Richard Cobden in his 'people's budget' of 1849. The FRA and Cobden argued for retrenchment and a massive reduction of customs and excise duties in order to liberate trade. As Hume argued in support of Cobden's demand for a debate on the financial prospects of the country,

No foreign danger, nor necessary cost of the Civil Government, nor indispensable disbursements for the services in our dependencies abroad, warrant the continuation of this increase in expenditure;... the taxes required to meet the present expenditure, impede the operations of agriculture and manufactures, and diminish the funds for the employment of labour in all branches of productive industry, thereby increasing pauperism and crime.[25]

The FRA presented a pitiful spectacle of the fiscal system and financial condition of Britain. The national debt was incurred to protect property, yet the costs were passed with 'reckless disregard' on to the poor and industry, whose pleas for relief were ignored by the government and Commons. The result was a woeful scene, of 'commerce scorned, repulsed, driven away, with fettered industry and despairing industry mourning in her train'. Meanwhile, the income produced by the labour of the poor was transferred to the 'luxurious and idle'. The FRA complained of the widespread and mistaken belief that the 'beautiful superstructure' of lordly England was 'the end of all social good' – to the neglect of the foundations of industry and labour upon which national prosperity were built. What was needed was a reduction in taxes on industry and labour in order to stimulate demand for goods and employment, with the prospect of improvement in social and moral conditions. The outcome would prove to be in the interests of property. 'The time has arrived when, for the sake of its own security, property must bear the burdens of the State and when, to enjoy its rights, it must discharge its duties.'[26]

[25] *Parliamentary Debates*, 3rd ser. 102, 26 Feb. 1849, cols. 123–5.
[26] *FRA, Account of the Formation, Principles and Objects of the Liverpool Financial Reform Association as Embodied in the Speeches Delivered at a Public Meeting Held in Liverpool, Jan. 17, 1849* (London, 1849), p. 5; *Address of the Council of the Liverpool Financial Reform Association to the Tax-payers of the United Kingdom, Showing how the Class for the Protection of Whose Property the National Debt Was Incurred, Changed the System of Taxation, so as to Remove the Burden from their Own Shoulders to Those of the People* (Liverpool, 1849), p. 2. For an account of the movement, see W. N. Calkins, 'A Victorian free trade lobby', *Economic History Revue*, 2nd ser. 13 (1960–1), 90–104.
* Robertson Gladstone (1805–75) was educated at Eton for a time before moving to the College of Glasgow when it was apparent that he would become a merchant; he joined and, subsequently, took over his father's Liverpool merchant house. He declined to enter parliament, and concentrated on Conservative politics on the town council, where he was mayor in 1842. He moved away from Conservatism to Liberalism and radicalism, and from Anglicanism to Unitarianism. (S. G. Checkland, *The Gladstones: A Family Biography, 1764–1851* (Cambridge, 1971).)

The income tax was therefore attacked for unbalancing the fiscal system in favour of property and against the interests of productive industry and labour. The Tory protectionist view was precisely the opposite: the income tax, *in the absence of corn laws to protect agriculture,* created a serious imbalance in the fiscal constitution. In 1842, many landowners were suspicious of Peel's motives in reintroducing the income tax, fearing that it would make the maintenance of import duties - including the corn laws – redundant on revenue grounds. Croker was initially willing to accept Peel's case for the reintroduction of the income tax as a means of integrating classes and defusing social unrest. He certainly did not see it as a means of removing agricultural protection – an issue on which he was later to split with Peel. In his view, the income tax had the 'nature of a *temporary advance* made by wealthy capitalists to relieve and facilitate certain branches of industry which – though now suffering – will by this timely assistance, be enabled to recover themselves, and to repay at no long interval their debt to the general fund'. In Croker's view, the income tax fell on real property and helped to relieve industry of the burden of indirect taxes; there was no basic imbalance in the tax system, and industry should eventually pay back the remissions of taxation designed to get over its immediate difficulties.[27]

Protectionists such as Croker were following in the steps of Malthus, who argued that production and consumption would not automatically reach equilibrium. In order to achieve balanced and sustainable development, the interests of domestic producers should be protected. The solution to economic depression was to boost consumption by creating stable markets at home and in the colonies, and at the same time removing the political threats from Chartism through a socially inclusive economic policy. Their strategy was not based on protection of *agriculture* in particular so much as domestic production in general. As Anna Gambles has remarked,

stable social and economic change should be rooted in secure domestic and colonial markets. Protectionists diagnosed the basic problem of the British manufacturing economy as an unstable balance between its powers of production and the means to consume its product. Thus protecting the incomes of domestic producers was offered as a permanent and inclusive solution to a structural economic problem.

Here they differed from free traders such as Ricardo, who believed that agricultural protection led to an over-extension of agriculture on to

[27] [J. W. Croker], 'Policy of Sir Robert Peel', *Quarterly Review* 120 (Sept. 1842), 485–531, at 492 and see also 512–13.

marginal land, and hence to a reduction in profits throughout the economy with a fall in capital accumulation. At the same time, the corn laws led to high food prices and hence high wages, which contributed to low profits. The protectionists countered that high wages were not caused by the corn laws but by the operation of the labour market; a drop in food prices would not necessarily help industry. Above all, they denied that a reduction in wages and an increase in the share of capital was the key to growth. Rather, the vital point was a balance between production and consumption which would be thrown out of equilibrium by a fall in the share of wages and in consumer demand. Protection would, as G. C. Holland* argued, provide the 'broad basis of home consumption, on which the interests of all classes can alone permanently repose'.[28]

Protectionists could therefore justify their policy as socially inclusive, and castigate free traders for creating economic and political imbalance. The protectionists believed that the power of urban manufacturers led to distorted budgets, so over-turning the balance of interests. In their view, repeal of the corn laws 'symbolised the abandonment, not the embodiment of the British state's impartiality'. It was not simply an appeal to the traditional view that land was the basis of republican virtue, although that was certainly one strand of thought. Above all, the protectionists feared that the Reform Act of 1832 concentrated interests in urban constituencies and so distorted the political process. The result, as Archibald Alison[†] argued in 1839, was that debates over fiscal policy meant 'sacrificing the ultimate interest of the state to the passion for economical reduction on the part of the middle classes of society', which led to a 'progressive unwinding of the springs of the state'. As he complained after the abortive Whig budget of 1831, a balancing of interests was abandoned.[29] The notion of 'balance' in the constitution and between interests was therefore

---

[28] G. C. Holland, *Suggestions towards Improving the Present System of Corn Laws* (London, 1841), p. 31, cited by A. Gambles, *Protection and Politics: Conservative Economic Discourse, 1815–52* (Woodbridge, 1999), pp. 70–1; on the role of protection in preserving consumption, see also Gambles, *Protection and Politics*, pp. 44–5, 54–5, 208–9. The quote from Gambles is in 'Rethinking the politics of protection: Conservatism and the corn laws, 1830–52', *English Historical Review* 113 (1998), 936.

[29] A. Alison, 'Whig and Tory finance', *Blackwood's Edinburgh Magazine* 46 (Oct. 1839), 500, 501, and 'On the financial measures of the reformed parliament. No 1. The Whig budget', *Blackwood's Edinburgh Magazine* 29 (June 1831), 975, quoted in Gambles, 'Rethinking the politics of protection', 946; see also Gambles, *Protection and Politics*, pp. 59–60, 123, 206.

* George Calvert Holland (1801–65) trained as a doctor in Edinburgh and Paris, practising in Manchester and Sheffield. He defended the corn laws. He left medicine to direct bank and railway companies, but failed and turned instead to homoeopathy and mesmerism. (*DNB*, vol. XXII, ed. S. Lee (London, 1891), pp. 139–40.)

† Archibald Alison (1792–1867) was educated in Edinburgh and was a lawyer; he wrote a successful history of Europe, and in 1834 took up the permanent, salaried, post of sheriff

contested, with both sides of the debate claiming that the other was unsettling equity and fairness, and pursuing self-interest at the expense of the public good. Protectionism was justified in the same terms as free trade. It was more than a defensive campaign by particular economic interests eager to preserve their privileges; it was a means of continued renegotiation of the balance of 'reciprocal relations uniting interest to interest, and class to class'.[30]

Many protectionists feared that the repeal of the corn laws in 1846 had upset the balance of interests. They might accept that Peel's budget of 1842 was part of the constant process of preserving balance and offering fair recognition of the needs of the urban consumer. In the words of Croker, it was 'the best combination and adjustment of all interests that our position admits, and the fairest promise of permanent protection to the farmer, and permanent plenty to the people'.[31] But Croker would not accept repeal of the corn laws which he attacked as a partisan policy setting agriculture and industry in opposition, and abandoning a search for balance through reconciliation of economic interests and social classes.[32] The income tax therefore ceased to be part of the negotiation of balance, and became a symbol of imbalance, a fiscal device to provide revenue in place of tariffs.

The income tax was a source of tension, facing attack from two fronts on fundamentally opposed grounds. It was not, at least initially, a means of removing taxation from the political arena; instead, acceptance of the income tax was long-drawn-out and contentious before it was celebrated as a symbol of British superiority over other, lesser, nations with their 'unscientific' fiscal regimes. A central element in this process was Gladstone's budget of 1853, which laid claim to the income tax as a measure of fiscal equity and balance between classes. His success in 1853 stands in marked contrast to the failure of Benjamin Disraeli's* budget of 1852.

of Lanarkshire where he was active in suppressing 'disorder'. He opposed the north in the American civil war, and argued for the necessity both of slavery and protection. He thought Richard Cobden a monomaniac. (*DNB*, vol. I, ed. L. Stephen (London, 1885), pp. 287–90.)

30 Holland, *Suggestions*, p. 22, cited in Gambles, *Protection and Politics*, p. 63.

31 [Croker], 'Policy of Sir Robert Peel', 528, cited in Gambles, *Protection and Politics*, p. 63.

32 Based on Gambles, 'Rethinking the politics of protection', 928–52.

* Benjamin Disraeli (1804–81) was born in London; he was educated privately and entered Lincoln's Inn in 1824, but soon abandoned law and published his first novel in 1826. He was an MP from 1837 to 1876, when he became the earl of Beaconsfield. He opposed Peel and the repeal of the corn laws, and became leader of the Commons in 1848. He was chancellor of the Exchequer in 1852, moving away from protection; and again in 1858–9 and 1866–8. He was prime minister in 1868, and again in 1874–80. (*DNB*, vol. XV, ed. L. Stephen (London, 1888), pp. 101–17.)

Disraeli, Gladstone and fiscal politics

The attitude of Tory protectionists towards fiscal issues started to change after the repeal of the corn laws. Protection was justified, at least in part, as a means of creating a balanced economic, social and political system. The repeal of the corn laws led some protectionists to press for the abandonment of the income tax, in the hope that a return to agricultural protection would be needed on revenue grounds. But others started to take a different attitude, arguing that the role of protection in creating an integrated and balanced society should be transferred to direct taxes. If protection could no longer offer a means of reconciling interests and classes, perhaps a reformed system of direct taxation could fulfil the same integrating function. A good example of the shift in approach is provided by Archibald Alison. He opposed Peel's introduction of the income tax in 1842 but shifted his ground after the repeal of the corn laws. He argued that Peel's reforms led to a dangerous lack of balance between interests and threatened public revenues; his solution was to extend the income tax to smaller incomes in order to give more taxpayers an interest in fiscal conservatism and to create a more equitable taxation of income. As Anna Gambles points out, 'direct taxation was designed to serve the same political and constitutional ends as had protection before 1846'.[33] Hence the campaigns of radicals for reductions in expenditure and a major shift in the tax system were attacked for appealing to the 'passions and selfish interests of the multitudes', so creating 'animosity between class and class, a mistrust of parliament, and ultimately an alienation from the constitution'. Class hostility was harmful, for 'the identity of interest between the poor and the rich is the real irreversible support of the institutions of property'.[34] The issue was how to create a balanced, integrated, society behind constitutional conservatism, and to contain what was seen as selfish interest group politics.

The periodic renewal of the income tax provided the opportunity to press for differentiation. When the initial term expired in 1848, Joseph Hume and other radical MPs were still in favour of abolition; at most, Hume was willing to accept continuation of the income tax for one year as a prelude to its complete abandonment or, at least, reform. When the tax was renewed for three years, he proposed that it be referred to a Select Committee to remove 'gross irregularities'. The motion failed, but Hume and Cobden mounted a campaign to reduce expenditure to the level of 1835, mainly through lower military and naval spending, as a means

---

[33] Gambles, 'Rethinking the politics of protection', 21, citing A. Alison, 'Direct taxation', *Blackwood's Edinburgh Magazine* 61 (Feb. 1847), 243–60.
[34] [T. Spring-Rice], 'Financial prospects, 1849', *Edinburgh Review* 89 (1849), 536.

of reducing customs and excise duties. Such campaigns resulted in the appointment of a number of Select Committees on defence expenditure and official salaries between 1847 and 1851.[35] When the income tax again came before the Commons for renewal in 1851, Hume proposed that it be continued for a year, and that a Select Committee should meanwhile consider ways of removing inequalities between spontaneous and industrious incomes. As Cobden realised, the strategy had its dangers. The proposal to limit renewal to one year would attract support from protectionist MPs who had no intention of reforming the income tax, but every hope that the campaign for differentiation would lead to its collapse and replacement by import duties, a possibility dreaded by free traders such as Cobden. Although Select Committees were appointed under Hume's chairmanship in 1851 and 1852, the involvement of leading protectionists removed any likelihood that taxes on trades and professions would be reduced relative to land and 'spontaneous' incomes. The Select Committee emerged from an alliance of extremes, between free traders who wished to reform the income tax and remove import duties, and protectionists anxious to undermine the income tax as a major source of revenue.[36]

The enquiry soon became lost in the technical details of Hume's own idiosyncratic solution to the inequalities of taxation of 'spontaneous' and 'precarious' incomes. He wished to convert all income into capitalised values, so that taxation could then obey Smith's first maxim of taxation which he defined as in proportion to the *value of property* in the possession of the taxpayer under the protection of the state.[37] The crucial point, as William Farr* argued, was the 'capability to produce value'.[38] A man with an income of, say, £150 a year might receive it from the tail end of a lease or annuity with a few years to run; from a professional or business career subject to the uncertainties of trade and health; or from consols paying

---

[35] Taylor, *Decline of British Radicalism*, pp. 134–5.

[36] *Parliamentary Debates*, 3rd ser. 116, 2 May 1851, cols. 437–8, 442–3, 457–9, 462–3, 477; 5 May 1851, cols. 511–37; 8 May 1851 cols. 726, 727, 732.

[37] PP 1852 IX, *Second Report from the Select Committee on the Income and Property Tax together with the proceedings of the committee, minutes of evidence, appendix and index*, Joseph Hume's draft report, pp. 481–94.

[38] PP 1852 IX, *Second Report from the Select Committee on the Income and Property Tax*, Q. 4913.

* William Farr (1807–83) was born in Shropshire of poor parents; he was adopted by a member of the local gentry whom he assisted in his affairs. Between 1826 and 1828 he studied medicine with a doctor in Shrewsbury and, after receiving bequests from the squire and the doctor, he studied medicine in Paris 1829–31 and University College London in 1832, becoming a licentiate of the Society of Apothecaries. He practised in London, and in 1837 contributed a section on vital statistics to J. R. McCulloch's *Account of the British Empire*. In 1838, he became compiler of abstracts at the Registrar General's Office, and held the post to 1879; he was assistant commissioner for the censuses of 1851 and 1861, and commissioner in 1871. (*DNB*, vol. XVIII, ed. L. Stephen (London, 1889), pp. 226–7.)

interest in perpetuity. Although each person paid the same tax of £10 or 6.7 per cent at a rate of 1s 4d in the £, the capitalised *value* of each income was different: £150 from the tail end of a lease was worth £416, whereas the same income from a trade or profession over fifteen years was worth £1,667, and from consols, £3,750. The tax of £10 therefore ranged from 2.4 per cent to 0.3 per cent on the *value of the income* to its recipient. Farr argued that 'the sublime rule of PROPORTION' meant that income flows should be capitalised in order to take account of their security.[39]

The task was by no means easy, for capitalisation depended on a valuation of all property providing a flow of income, adjusted according to the tenure of property and the age of the recipient in order to produce an actuarial calculation of the expected period of enjoyment of the income. The need to capitalise all incomes would, quite simply, make the income tax impossible to administer. The Inland Revenue feared that capitalising incomes would be 'utterly impracticable', for procedures to obtain returns would be 'inquisitorial' and time-consuming. The attempt would be 'wholly abortive', simply introducing inequalities between taxpayers as a result of anomalies in the highly complex rules applied to different types of property and income.[40] As J. G. Maitland remarked,

the attempt to tax Capital, as such, has always failed in time past, and the increasing complexity of Interest – vested and contingent – present and reversionary –, which increasing civilization naturally brings with it, leads to the conclusion that such an attempt would at the present day, still more signally fail; and further, it would do more injustice in a year than the present tax would do in a century.[41]

Capitalisation of incomes proved a dead-end, and attention turned to a simpler, more approximate, procedure.

The leading, obsessional, campaigner for differentiation was J. G. Hubbard,* whose solution was very similar to the procedure eventually adopted by the Liberal government in 1907 in very different political

---

[39] PP 1852 IX, *Second Report from the Select Committee on the Income and Property Tax*, Hume's draft report, pp. 487, 493; [Lewis], *Shade of Cocker*, pp. 4–7, 12.

[40] PP 1852 IX, *Second Report from the Select Committee on the Income and Property Tax*, spent much time collecting evidence on the capitalisation of incomes; see especially the evidence of William Farr, Qq. 4853–5027, and for a more sceptical view by the Inland Revenue, Qq. 5055–144 and NLW, Harpton Court MS 3421, ff. 1–11 'Memorandum on Mr Muntz's notice of motion for capitalising incomes, with a view to a property tax', Inland Revenue, 12 Nov. 1856. For a critical discussion, see [J. Coode], 'The income tax', *Edinburgh Review* 97 (1853), 530–84.

[41] J. G. Maitland, *Property and Income Tax: The Present State of the Question* (London, 1853), quoted in NLW, Harpton Court MS 3421, ff. 10–11.

* John Gellibrand Hubbard (1805–89) was a merchant in London, with trading and industrial interests in Russia. He was a director of the Bank of England from 1838, and chairman of the Public Works Loan Commission from 1853 to 1889. He was a Conservative MP from 1859 to 1868 and 1874 to 1887. (*DNB*, vol. XXVIII, ed. Lee, pp. 135–6.)

circumstances. He assumed that the recipient of a 'spontaneous' income of £100 in interest from accumulated capital could devote £90 to consumption; by contrast, the recipient of a 'precarious' income of £100 from trade and the professions would set aside £40 as savings and additional capital. Hubbard's proposal was simple: £90 of spontaneous and £60 of precarious income were consumed; earnings from trades and professions should therefore be taxed in the same proportion, at two-thirds of the rate on 'spontaneous' incomes. In his view, the result would be an equitable tax which would not discourage risk-taking and the accumulation of capital, and would establish equity between interests. It would, he believed, follow the principle that 'the imposition of any tax shall leave the power of expenditure exactly as it found it, so that whether an income tax were put on or not, the power of expenditure possessed by those holding different incomes would remain relatively unchanged'.[42] It was designed, therefore, to preserve balance between 'precarious' and 'spontaneous' incomes. It would not change the social structure; rather, the existing tax system distorted society. Of course, Hubbard's scheme rested on the assumption that the recipients of 'precarious' incomes *did* save 40 per cent of their income. The figure had no empirical basis, and there was a tendency to slide into normative statements that recipients of 'precarious' incomes *ought* to save this much. His scheme also assumed that each schedule of the income tax could be assigned to either spontaneous or precarious incomes. As Alfred Milner* pointed out in 1893, schedule

---

[42] Hubbard, *How Should an Income Tax Be Levied?*, pp. 4, 8–15, 47–8; draft report to PP 1861 VII, *Select Committee on Income and Property Tax*, pp. 9–20 and minutes of evidence, Q. 1120.

* Alfred Milner (1854–1925) was born in Germany, where his father was a doctor; he was educated partly in Germany and at King's College London and at Balliol. In 1876, he was fellow of New College, Oxford, before moving to London in 1879, where he was called to the bar in 1881. He turned to journalism, working for the *Pall Mall Gazette* under John Morley and then W. T. Stead. He was active in the university extension movement, and was one of the founders of Toynbee Hall, in memory of his Oxford friend, Arnold Toynbee. He was concerned both with social reform and imperialism. In 1884, he became private secretary to George Goschen, whose views he shared in opposing both Chamberlain's doctrine of 'ransom' and Gladstone's foreign and imperial policy. He was involved with Goschen in setting up the Liberal Unionist Association after the split over home rule, and became his official private secretary in 1886 during Goschen's period as chancellor; in 1889 he went to Egypt as director general of accounts and under-secretary of the finance ministry. On his return in 1892, Goschen appointed him chairman of the Board of Inland Revenue where he was involved in revising the death duties for Harcourt. In 1897, Chamberlain appointed him governor of South Africa, where he remained until 1905. On his return, he worked in the City, in particular for Rio Tinto Co., as well as serving as a member of the Port of London Authority and the Rhodes Trust; he was involved in discussions of national service, imperialism, tariff reform and the promotion of imperial studies in the University of London. He opposed Lloyd George's budget of 1909 and home rule. During the war, he became a member of Lloyd George's war cabinet, and from 1918 to 1921 was secretary of state for the

A on land was clearly spontaneous, and schedules B and E exclusively
precarious income from farming and salaries of office. But he felt that
schedule D confused both types of income. Many professions and trades
were entirely precarious, but profits from large private companies were
in part interest on capital and could be defined as spontaneous. Milner
argued that the difficulty of assigning income of private manufacturers,
bankers and traders was a major obstacle to differentiation; in his view,
the attempt to distinguish between the two forms of income 'would raise
a greater number of intricate points than a whole army of casuists could
determine in a life-time'.[43] This problem might be circumvented by John
Stuart Mill's suggestion of a tax on *expenditure*, with all savings or reten-
tions in the business exempted from tax on grounds both of justice to the
individual and social benefit. He stressed that 'the portion of an income
which was saved and converted into capital should be untaxed', whereas
the existing system taxed savings twice, on the income from which savings were set aside and then again on the income from savings. However,
Mill conceded that his expenditure tax was simply impracticable and he
returned to Hubbard's proposal as the only *practical* solution.

You cannot practically enter into the consideration of what he does save, you must
consider what the class ought to save, and then if you think that, on the whole,
they do save an equivalent amount, you should exempt them...The principle
upon which you are obliged to act, is what he ought to save; the perfect principle
is what he does save.[44]

The approach of Hubbard and Mill was therefore informed by a common
theme: the encouragement of a dynamic economy based on savings, and
a reduction of taxation on 'skill and intelligence'.[45]

Disraeli was a member of the Select Committees of 1851 and 1852,
where he accepted that the income tax was inequitable and should be balanced by differentiation between spontaneous and industrious incomes.[46]
In his abortive budget of 1852, Disraeli aimed to abandon Conservative
support for agricultural protection and to create a new basis for a balanced
integration of interests. Farmers and landowners were offered compensation for the loss of protection by a reduction in the duty on malt, which

colonies. In 1921, he returned to the City and wrote on social and imperial questions.
(*DNB, 1922–30*, ed. J. R. H. Weaver (London, 1937), pp. 589–602.)

[43] Bod. Lib., MS Harcourt dep. 69, ff. 79–93, 'Note on differential income tax', A. Milner,
27 Apr. 1893, and ff. 100–10, A. Milner, 30 Apr. 1893.

[44] PP 1861 VII, *Report from the Select Committee on Income and Property Tax*, Qq. 3543,
3581–4, 3597, 3708–12, 3789.

[45] The phrase is Hubbard's in PP 1861 VII, *Report from the Select Committee on Income and
Property Tax*, draft report, p. 15; see also below, pp. 156–7.

[46] *Parliamentary Debates*, 3rd ser. 96, 2 May 1851, col. 477.

would also benefit working-class beer drinkers. He then proposed a concession to urban, commercial and industrial interests by differentiating the income tax. This was, as Gladstone explained at the end of his life, 'a most daring bid for the support of the liberal majority, for we all knew that the current opinion of the Whigs and Liberals was in favour of this scheme: which on the other hand was disapproved by sound financiers'.[47] The other main element in the budget was an increase in the inhabited house duty to cover defence expenditure, which would fall on urban interests. Of course, the budget proposals could easily be interpreted as an *unbalanced* package, imposing more taxes on urban interests than on agriculture and land. The reduction in the malt tax could be attacked as a means of paying a political debt to agriculture in the unrealistic expectation that 'the occupiers of houses would patriotically submit to increased taxation'.[48] The budget failed, and has been the subject of controversy amongst historians, no less than amongst contemporaries.

One view is that Disraeli was desperately putting together 'a bundle of expedients' in order to create an alliance of two extremes – radical supporters of differentiation and the country party – against the centre. The attempt failed as a result of a revolt of urban interests against higher taxes to relieve land.[49] The alternative view is that Disraeli was making 'a principled and coherent attempt at legislation'. Such an interpretation argues that differentiation was not so much a policy of the radicals who were more concerned with retrenchment, than a Whig policy designed to cover high levels of expenditure. In other words, Disraeli was bidding for the support of the *centre*, attempting to secure a moderate majority and to create a balanced fiscal constitution. This interpretation assumes that Disraeli was attempting to use direct taxes to create a conservative alliance of property, and that his scheme had the support of the majority in the Commons, as offering something to both urban and rural interests. Defeat is then explained by the prime minister's insistence, at the last moment, on adding an increase in the inhabited house duty to cover defence expenditure which alienated urban interests.[50]

Such an interpretation is not entirely convincing. It is a moot point whether differentiation commanded the majority of *moderate* opinion in

---

47 Note written on 14 Sept. 1897, in J. Brooke and M. Sorensen (eds.), *The Prime Ministers' Papers. W. E. Gladstone*, vol. I: *Autobiographica* (London, 1971), p. 77.

48 [G. C. Lewis], 'The fall of the Derby ministry', *Edinburgh Review* 97 (1853), 256–9.

49 R. Blake, *Disraeli* (London, 1966), chapter 15, sees the budget debate of 1852 as one of the crucial points of Victorian history; the quote is from p. 348. See also Matthew, 'Disraeli, Gladstone and the politics of mid-Victorian budgets', 615–43. For an equivocal assessment of the fiscal policies of Disraeli and the Conservative party, see [G. C. Lewis], 'The late elections and free trade', *Edinburgh Review* 96 (1852), 526–66.

50 P. R. Ghosh, 'Disraelian Conservatism: a financial approach', *English Historical Review* 99 (1984), 268–96.

the Commons. Rather, support came from two conflicting groups. The appointment of the Select Committee in 1851 arose from an alliance of extremes between Hume and protectionists who wished to *weaken* the income tax rather than introduce differentiation as a way of making it more equitable and permanent. There were about sixty reforming MPs in the parliament of 1847–52 who allied with the protectionists on taxation. The reformers were ambivalent about taxation. On the one hand, they were suspicious of the 'tax eater' state and wished to cut expenditure as a means of reducing indirect taxes. On the other hand, they realised that revenue from an income tax could allow a reduction in indirect taxes – so long as it did not simply boost public spending.[51] By 1852, radicals such as Hume had dropped their demand for the abolition of the income tax and moved to differentiation as an alternative. Although Disraeli might have been trying to use differentiation as part of a principled policy of integration and fiscal balance, he misjudged the nature and extent of support for differentiation. Many backbench Tories saw support of differentiation simply as a means of disrupting the income tax and forcing a return to protection.[52] His own party had not been converted, and he was going too far, too fast, for his own backbenchers. Certainly, he was not helped by the prime minister's insistence on the inhabited house duty, but Disraeli's scheme was itself flawed. He saw a pragmatic opportunity in the political circumstances of 1852 to create a new, integrated, conservative politics. He failed, because he was seizing the opportunity without a carefully worked out proposal to fulfil his ambition, and because the 'fractured fiscal discourse' in the Conservative party made it impossible to create a consensus behind reform of the income tax *in the absence of protection*. As one cynical commentator remarked, the proposals for fiscal reform lacked 'reality and maturity' and a Professor of Casuistry should be appointed at Westminster to explain the inconsistencies.[53]

The achievement of Gladstone in his budget of 1853 was to make opposition to differentiation into the orthodox position for the next forty years. The defeat of Disraeli's budget, not least as a result of Gladstone's intervention in the debate, and the fall of the Tory government, meant that Gladstone became chancellor of the Exchequer for the first time in December 1852.[54] As he noted in 1854, he faced an alarming prospect:

---

[51] Taylor, *Decline of British Radicalism*, pp. 138–9.
[52] Ghosh, 'Disraelian Conservatism', 276.
[53] Gambles, *Protection and Politics*, pp. 234–8; [Lewis], 'The late elections and free trade', 526–66.
[54] See Blake, *Disraeli*, pp. 345–7. The importance of the budget of 1853 is stressed by Matthew, 'Disraeli, Gladstone and the politics of mid-Victorian budgets'; for a more equivocal assessment, see A. B. Hawkins, 'A forgotten crisis: Gladstone and the politics of finance during the 1850s', *Victorian Studies* 26 (1982–3).

the income tax was about to expire, and 'the wish and intention of a large majority of the House was, that we should not renew the income tax, except on condition of reconstructing it'.[55] Gladstone's strategy in his first budget of 1853 was to balance the fiscal system *without* differentiation, a task which some ministers felt might not be achieved. As Gladstone noted, 'all my proposals had been adjusted with a view of overcoming the great difficulty of differentiation'.[56] In his opinion, differentiation was as much a claim for special treatment by merchants and manufacturers as the demand of landowners for protection by the corn laws, or of shipowners by the navigation laws. Peel saw the dangers in 1842, when he firmly opposed differentiation:

The proposal which I make is a proposal for a tax on the income of this country; and if I once begin to make a distinction with respect to different kinds of income, it will be absolutely necessary that I should abandon the Income-tax . . . If there is to be an Income-tax at all it must be uniformly laid upon all income, and in no case whatever can I allow a distinction to be drawn.[57]

Gladstone had a greater appreciation than Disraeli of Tory suspicions that differentiation would be seen as a further preference to commercial and industrial interests. Although they might support differentiation as a tactic for obstruction, few Tories were convinced that it had positive virtues in creating an integrated society. The ambition of Gladstone, as of Peel before him, was to ensure that the tax system was not disputed between classes, whether between the commercial and industrial middle classes and landowners, or between the rich and poor. Gladstone was more successful than Disraeli in creating consensus in the fractured fiscal discourse of mid-Victorian politics.

An equal rate on *all* forms of income was, in Gladstone's opinion, essential. He feared that differentiation would soon lead to graduation, for the rationale was similar: if taxation were to be proportionate to what the taxpayer could afford, the case applied to the *level* as well as the *type* of income. Graduation was

generally destructive in its operation to the whole principle of property, to the principle of accumulation, and through that principle, to industry itself, and therefore to the interests of both poor and rich . . . it means merely universal war, a universal scramble among all classes, every one endeavouring to relieve himself at the expense of his neighbour, and an end being put to all social peace, and to any common principle on which the burdens of the State can be adjusted.[58]

[55] *Parliamentary Debates*, 3rd ser. 132, 8 May 1854, col. 1469.
[56] Foot and Matthew (eds.), *The Gladstone Diaries*, vol. IV, pp. 513–18.
[57] *Parliamentary Debates*, 3rd ser. 61, 18 Mar. 1842, cols. 914–15.
[58] *Parliamentary Debates* 3rd. ser. 170, 23 Apr. 1863, cols. 617–22.

Above all, Gladstone was concerned that the state should be integrative as well as minimal, and he saw the danger that a breach in the principle of a flat-rate tax would soon make it the subject of demands for concessions from various interests. His strategy was therefore to contain the demands for differentiation, and to make concessions which would not upset the entire basis of the income tax. Indeed, he seemed to be making two contradictory claims at the same time: that the tax was temporary so that there was no point in fine-tuning its incidence between types of property; and that it was a permanent source of revenue for emergencies so that it should not be constantly amended.[59] He opposed differentiation because the income tax was temporary, so that subtle and detailed procedures were unnecessary. The aim was to use taxation to constrain the state, by creating a degree of resistance to tax increases. The income tax would therefore be abolished in return for fiscal responsibility.[60] Yet he also argued that the income tax was suitable for emergencies and would be weakened by constant changes. He advised the Commons never

to nibble at this great question of State policy. Don't let them adopt the plan of reconstructing the Income tax today and saying 'If that does not work, we'll try our hands at it again tomorrow.' That is not the way in which the relations of classes brought into the nicest competition with one another under a scheme of direct competition are to be treated . . . Whatever you do in regard to the income tax, you must be bold, you must be intelligible, you must be decisive. You must not palter with it. If you do, I have striven at least to point out as well as my feeble powers will permit, the almost desecration I would say, certainly the gross breach of duty to your country, of which you will be guilty, in thus putting to hazard one of the most potent and effective among all its material resources . . . I believe it to be of vital importance, whether you keep this tax or whether you part with it, that you should either keep it, or should leave it in a state in which it will be fit for service on an emergency, and that it will be impossible to do if you break up the basis of your income tax.[61]

In 1853, Gladstone offered a concession to the supporters of differentiation without admitting their wider principle, in the hope of containing its appeal. As we have seen, Hubbard and Mill wished to offer tax relief to savings. Hubbard claimed that the only income *enjoyed* by the taxpayer under the protection of the state – Adam Smith's first maxim of taxation – was what he could spend. This interpretation did not commend itself to

[59] Matthew, *Gladstone, 1809–74*, p. 123.
[60] Indeed, Gladstone has been claimed as a precursor of the Virginia school of economics: see Leathers, 'Gladstonian finance and the Virginia school of public finance', 515–21, and Baysinger and Tollison, 'Chaining leviathan', 206–13. However, Biagini feels this strategy applies to 1874 rather than to the 1850s and 1860s: Biagini, 'Popular Liberals, Gladstonian finance and the debate on taxation', p. 156 n. 123.
[61] *Parliamentary Debates*, 3rd ser. 125, 18 Apr. 1853, cols. 1383–4.

Robert Lowe,* who pointed out that income set aside from savings was also under the protection of the state and should therefore contribute to taxation. 'There is a vice of saving as well as spending. Avarice is as odious as prodigality. It is not every man that has an opportunity for saving. Saving implies something to spare after satisfying the wants of the year. To give a remission to savings is, therefore, to give a remission to wealth.'[62] On the other hand, saving was a means towards self-reliance and prudence, and Gladstone offered a concession to a highly specific form of saving which went some way towards meeting the demands for differentiation. He introduced tax relief on premiums for life insurance and annuities designed to provide security in old age and retirement. This was a simpler expedient than the complex and troublesome proposal of Hume to compensate precarious incomes for the savings needed to provide security. Gladstone's concession of 1853 was to outlive its immediate political purpose of preventing a lower rate of tax on earned income, for it continued when differentiation was introduced in 1907, and it was to become a useful means for reducing tax liability as marginal rates rose in the twentieth century.[63] The concession of 1853 was tactical, designed to contain the demands for fiscal reform and to preserve an undifferentiated tax. It was available to *all* taxpayers, and was therefore not divisive between classes. It avoided complicated issues of dividing income into spontaneous and industrious. It appealed to notions of prudence and self-reliance, and was complemented by support for friendly societies and by Gladstone's later creation, the Post Office Savings Bank (1861). Gladstone also used death duties as an alternative means of creating balance in the fiscal system as a whole (see chapter 8). The elaborate

---

[62] Hubbard, *How Should an Income Tax Be Levied?*, p. 15; PP 1861 VII, *Report from the Select Committee on Income and Property Tax*, chairman's draft report, p. 13, and Lowe's draft report, pp. 21–5.

[63] M. Zimmeck, 'Gladstone holds his own: the origins of income tax relief for life insurance purposes', *Bulletin of the Institute of Historical Research* 58 (1985), 167–88. It became an important means of tax avoidance in the twentieth century, and was abolished in 1984 as part of a new policy of encouraging other forms of saving.

* Robert Lowe (1811–92) was the son of an Anglican clergyman, and was educated at Winchester and University College, Oxford. He was called to the bar in 1842 and migrated to Sydney the same year, where he practised law and served on the legislative council as an opponent of the large 'squatters'. He was successful both in the law and in property transactions, and returned to London in 1850, initially as a leader writer on *The Times*. In 1852, he was elected to parliament and served as joint secretary of the Board of Control 1852–5, vice-president of the Board of Trade and paymaster general, 1855–8, vice-president of the Committee of the Council on Education, 1859–64, chancellor of the Exchequer, 1868–73, and Home Secretary, 1873–4. He had a reputation for being brusque, sarcastic and scornful; his proposed match tax of 1871 led to popular protest and was withdrawn. (*DNB*, vol. xxxiv, ed. S. Lee (London, 1893), pp. 197–201.)

attempts of Hume and Hubbard to create equity *within the income tax* gave way to a consensus in favour of an undifferentiated tax. Gladstone argued that a fundamental feature of the fiscal system was the need to strike a balance between different taxes in order to ensure that all forms of income were fairly treated. The key to equitable taxation of spontaneous and precarious income, in the opinion of Gladstone, was the incidence of death duties which could preserve the mid-Victorian fiscal constitution from more fundamental change. Instead of compensating earned incomes by a lower rate of tax to take account of the need to save, why not impose a death duty on the source of spontaneous income? Differentiation in the income tax was both elaborate and unnecessary. Most spontaneous incomes were taxed at source and therefore paid in full; precarious incomes were taxed on the basis of assessment and could be under-reported. In effect, the income tax was differentiated. In any case, there was no reason why a single tax, taken in isolation, should be 'fair'. As Henry Goulburn, the former Chancellor, pointed out,

Human ingenuity had never yet devised a tax that could press with equal severity upon all classes; and the only rational mode of dealing with taxation was to view the whole system together, to correct the inequalities of one tax by the countervailing inequalities of another; so that the balance of the whole system of taxation should press equally and justly upon all classes.[64]

Goulburn's principle was central to the tax system in the second half of the nineteenth century: the important point was whether the tax system *as a whole* maintained an overall balance between classes and interests, rather than whether one tax *in isolation* was equitable.

Although Hubbard was not satisfied and obtained a further Select Committee to consider differentiation,[65] the budget of 1853 marked the end of significant pressure for the next forty or fifty years. The case for differentiation failed in the 1850s and 1860s, in part because of practical administrative considerations which applied most obviously to the capitalisation of income and only to a lesser degree to defining different types of income as spontaneous or industrious. The resolution of the conflict between free trade and protection in the 1850s meant it was more difficult to create an alliance between financial reformers and protectionists. The fractured fiscal discourse gave way to consensus and debates on the 'fiscal constitution' only re-opened when the consensus in favour

---

[64] *Parliamentary Debates*, 3rd ser. 97, 3 Mar. 1848, col. 192; a similar point about the inequality of all taxes was made by Gladstone, *Parliamentary Debates*, 3rd ser. 170, 23 Apr. 1863, col. 617.
[65] This was PP 1861 VII, *Select Committee on Income and Property Tax*.

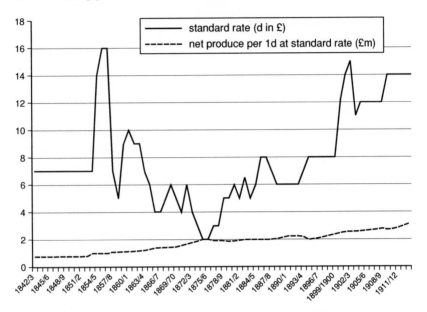

Figure 4.1 Rate and yield of income tax, 1842/3 to 1913/14
Source: PP 1919 XXIII, pt 1, *Report on the Royal Commission on Income Tax*, pp. 131–4.

of free trade was again breached at the turn of the century. The success of Gladstone in removing differentiation from the political agenda did not simply rest on his own political skill in using the budget of 1853 to create a 'social contract' between classes and interests. It also rested on the more general processes which blunted the critical edge of debates on taxation. In large part, the work of 'containing leviathan' had fulfilled its task: attacks on the 'tax eater' state were increasingly strained and pedantic by the 1850s, and the propaganda of the FRA and Financial Reform Union seemed dated and shrill. Could it really be claimed that government departments had an 'uncontrollable thirst for expenditure', and that they were 'masters alike of the Treasury, the House of Commons, and the people'?[66] The voice of Robertson Gladstone as the spokesman of 'financial reform' was obsessive compared with the authority of his brother at the Treasury, and his use of the budget to recreate an organic,

---

[66] On this assessment of the FRA, see Calkins, 'Victorian free trade lobby', 104, and the comments in Taylor, *Decline of British Radicalism*, pp. 93–4; and above, pp. 86–7. The quote is from FRU, *Papers on Taxation and Expenditure Issued by the Financial Reform Union: Number 3, A Budget for 1869 Based Upon Mr Cobden's 'National Budget' Proposed in 1849* (London, 1868), pp. 1–2.

balanced, society. The process was in part based on rhetoric to create a narrative which linked the lower and middle classes as 'the people' in a democratic struggle against the idle and profligate.[67] Peel and Gladstone could portray themselves as men of public duty and trust, who could be relied on to ensure that expenditure was kept to a minimum and to relieve the people from burdens. But this is not to say that the shift was simply in language and rhetoric, for the form of the state itself did change.[68] Rhetorical claims that the state was neutral and balanced between interests, that the parliamentary system could ensure efficiency rather than prodigality, were sustained by the development of more transparent accounting techniques, the long-term fall in expenditure and the reduction in the national debt.

By the last quarter of the nineteenth century the income tax was accepted as a permanent part of the fiscal system, as a valuable tax which had helped to create equity and which sustained British power. The Conservative chancellor, Stafford Northcote, defined the role for the income tax in 1875 which it was to retain for the next twenty years. He pointed out that the income tax in the past had two functions. The first was now complete, as 'an engine for effecting great reforms in our system of taxation'. Indirect taxes had been reduced and the fiscal system was no longer in need of major reform. He held out the prospect that prosperity and an annual growth in revenue would allow the income tax to be held at 2d in the £, which made any complaints about its unfair incidence a matter of insignificance. The income tax could then be used for a second purpose, 'as a war tax, for it raises enormously the power of the country, with reference to any strain upon our military resources'. The income tax would not be kept at a high level designed to maintain an expensive military establishment; it would be 'held in abeyance – ready only for some great emergency, and not to be called upon for trivial occasions'. The fiscal constitution was firmly in place: as Northcote said, it might not be perfect, but it had gone as far as possible in that direction.[69] Of course, the issue would be whether the income tax should become much more than a modest source of revenue in peace, to be held in reserve for emergencies. By the end of the nineteenth century – and especially with the outbreak of the Boer war and the growth of a separate Labour party – the fiscal constitution of mid- and late Victorian Britain was to face new challenges.

[67] E. F. Biagini, *Liberty, Retrenchment and Reform: Popular Liberalism in the Age of Gladstone, 1860–80* (Cambridge, 1992), pp. 11–12.
[68] See the comments of M. Hewitt, *The Emergence of Stability in the Industrial City: Manchester, 1832–67* (Aldershot, 1996), pp. 12–13.
[69] *Parliamentary Debates*, 3rd ser. 223, 15 Apr. 1875, cols. 1034–6.

Accepting the fiscal constitution

The achievement of Peel and Gladstone was apparent in the move of Chartism and radicalism towards 'constitutional radicalism'. The Chartists' attack on a corrupt and repressive state lost force in the 1840s and 1850s as the government showed that it was capable of reform from within.[70] A contrast could be drawn between the British nation and its European counterparts, especially after the revolutions of 1848. Between the revolutions of 1848 and the Paris commune of 1871, the experience of continental Europe differed from that of Britain and helped to transform British liberalism. Former Chartists and middle-class radicals could both express sympathy with nationalist movements in Italy and Poland. Nationalism was contested, speaking both to class and patriotic identities, providing a vehicle for the expression of both shared and antagonistic political beliefs. As Finn argues, neither the ex-Chartists nor the middle-class radicals capitulated, but they both made concessions so that political roles, values and expectations were re-negotiated and liberal culture transformed. Thus nationalist sentiment bridged and expressed class interests. This politics was informed less by issues of 'old corruption' than a new sense of national identity and patriotism based on a contrast between English liberty and continental despotism. Gladstone was a central figure in this change, with his support for nationalism and liberty abroad and at home, and his constant plea for a non-militaristic state based on retrenchment and reform.[71]

Radicalism did not simply disappear with the demise of Chartism, for its decline as an extra-parliamentary movement reflected greater confidence that parliament itself was capable of reforming the state and creating an equitable social order. Radical reformers argued that the Reform Act should be extended in order to eliminate interest from the Commons, which had allowed expenditure to increase in the 1830s and 1840s. Extension of the franchise was less an end in itself than a means of changing the type of MP in order to eliminate militarism through effective parliamentary control over the executive. These radicals obtained support from a variety of MPs with a common interest in controlling expenditure. Independent Liberals also wished to use parliament to control expenditure, but they went on to argue that the wealth of the nation could not increase unless investment was encouraged. Such sentiments led to the

---

[70] Stedman Jones, *Languages of Class*, pp. 177–8.

[71] M. Finn, *After Chartism: Class and Nation in English Radical Politics, 1848–74* (Cambridge, 1993), pp. 6, 10, 59, 188–9, 224–5, 227, 304–5, 307; for a critique, see D. Wahrman, 'The new political history: a review essay', *Social History* 21 (1996), 346–8. On Gladstone, see Biagini, *Liberty, Retrenchment and Reform*, especially chapter 7.

appointment of Select Committees on friendly societies in 1849 and on the savings of the middle and working classes in 1850. As Miles Taylor suggests, these independent Liberals were 'the quiet engineers of mid-Victorian liberalism', and arguably more important than the highly vocal Manchester school of Cobden and Bright. These strands of reform stood at the centre of liberal politics after 1847, both in large urban constituencies and at Westminster, and allowed a *rapprochement* with former Chartists. Rather than simply experiencing defeat, the Chartists were 'reconciled to the mainstream of radical and parliamentary politics'. Members of Parliament were accessible and independent, willing to listen to petitions and representations and to control the executive: this formed part of the liberty of the British subject compared to the continent. Taylor argues that 'Chartism and parliamentary radicalism were interlinked', united in an attempt to create 'accountable popular government' which would monitor the executive through independent MPs representing national, public, interests rather than class, sectional, interests. The Reform Act of 1832 was designed, above all, to increase the effectiveness of the Commons in controlling the executive and expressing public opinion through independent MPs, freed from the constraints of 'influence'. The aim was to increase popular control over the executive, and radical language celebrated the gentlemanly independence and virtue of Members.[72]

This 'radical constitutionalism' flourished to about 1860 and rested on the belief that the Commons would provide the arena for progressive movements to present their case, and for independent MPs to guard the public interest against the executive – not least in protecting the taxpayer from extravagance by ensuring that the executive followed strict rules of economy. The views articulated by MPs such as Joseph Hume therefore had considerable force in the Commons up to 1860, when this brand of constitutional radicalism declined in importance. Independent MPs had less autonomy with the rise of stricter party discipline, when the Commons was expected to provide *support* to the executive. Large urban constituencies were less inclined to delegate and defer to independent MPs, preferring to return local men with a firm grasp of the immediate concerns of the area, its trades and urban government. The rise of nonconformist moralism also contributed to a shift from the independent representative to the 'people'. Meanwhile, the Liberal party was less dependent on urban constituencies, with the recovery of county seats and

---

[72] Taylor, *Decline of British Radicalism*, pp. 30–3, 44–55, 99, 337, 338, 340, 342, 343; PP 1849 XIV, *Report from the Select Committee on the Friendly Societies Bill*, pp. 3–8; PP 1850 XIX, *Report from the Select Committee on Investments for the Middle and Working Classes*, pp. 171–2.

its strength in Ireland, Wales and Scotland. By about 1860, the political context for Hume's campaign for retrenchment and tax reform had passed.[73] The emphasis shifted from the independent MPs' role in controlling expenditure and the legislature's task of imposing checks on the executive, to a greater stress on the control of the taxpayers' demands by the Treasury. The shift had major implications. In the first place, it implied a different attitude towards the franchise. Control over public expenditure no longer depended on the independent Member of Parliament and the reform of the franchise in order to create a responsible Commons. In the debates over the second reform act, the emphasis was on the character of *electors* and the danger that they might vote for expensive policies and redistributive taxation.[74] In the second place, it contributed to a change in the formulation of financial policy. The budget was increasingly shaped by the chancellor with his Treasury officials in conditions of secrecy, and was presented to the Commons for support by a disciplined majority. Although parliament remained important in vetting estimates and making annual votes of expenditure, the task of the independent MP in monitoring the executive was now complemented by the greater power of the chancellor and Treasury in limiting the demands of the spending departments.

In the early 1860s, it was possible to argue that Britain was now a lightly taxed nation. G. W. Norman* suggested that the British fiscal system was 'moderately just and equal, and the government on the whole good'. He pointed with satisfaction to a major fall in British expenditure per capita since 1815, compared with a rise in France where there were additional costs of conscription. Moreover, British national income was twice as high as the French so the real burden of taxation was considerably lower. Norman was confident that the British people 'get a better return for their money paid in taxes than any other European country', with a much smaller army and a civil service between a quarter and a third of the scale of continental Europe. Britain led the way in economy, Norman believed, because the middle class had the greatest influence in the selection of MPs; they were the greatest taxpayers and 'naturally exact stringent attention to economy as one of the first requisites', unlike

---

[73] Taylor, *Decline of British Radicalism*, pp. 340–1.
[74] Taylor, *Decline of British Radicalism*, pp. 333–5.
* George Warde Norman (1793–1882) was a timber merchant trading with Norway until 1830, and a director of the Bank of England from 1821 to 1872. He was an Exchequer bill commissioner from 1831 to 1876, and a founder member of the Political Economy Club. He wrote on currency and taxation. (*DNB*, vol. xli, ed. S. Lee (London, 1895), pp. 112–13).

in other countries where the ruling class might gain from high expenditure. Consequently, the chancellor of the Exchequer was 'one of the strictest economists in the Empire'. Norman's complaint was that Britain was spending too *little* compared with other countries on education and on arts and science.[75]

Norman did have a point, for the project of making the state appear trustworthy by constraining expenditure was not without its dangers. The second quarter of the nineteenth century was marked by a deterioration in the urban environment and in life expectation as a result of low levels of investment in the infrastructure of the great cities.[76] The attack on state expenditure as prodigal and inefficient contributed to a weakening of civic consciousness and of belief in the positive role of public action. Constraining leviathan, in the short and medium term, arose from *distrust* in the state before faith in the positive action of the state was rebuilt. The immediate policy of imposing constraint could therefore produce a different outcome in the longer term, of creating trust in the reliability of state action, of its efficiency rather than prodigality. By placing the fiscal constitution above political debate, public action could be released from its shackles. But in the meantime, much of the positive role of government was delegated to the localities which poses the question of how far local authorities – especially in the great cities – could cope with the pressures placed on them.

The fall in the state's claim on the national economy may be explained by a reduction in the demands of warfare and defence spending compared with the acceleration in growth rates. However, the 'peace dividend' was not experienced immediately, for the massive debts accumulated during the 'long eighteenth century' were only slowly reduced and, in the process, redefined. The national debt moved from a threat to British prosperity, a drain on production and wealth, to a guarantee of national security and strength. Again, this was a triumph of administrative and accounting principles, and of political rhetoric and culture. At the same time, the costs of imperial defence were contested between metropole and periphery. During the 'long eighteenth century', warfare against the French imposed considerable burdens on the domestic economy, and the attempt to shift some of the costs to the empire contributed to the revolt of the Thirteen Colonies in North America. In the aftermath of

---

[75] G. W. Norman, *An Examination of Some Prevailing Opinions as to the Pressure of Taxation in This and Other Countries* (4th edn, London, 1864), pp. 10, 116–21; it is reviewed in [Greg], 'British taxation', 236–46, where other figures are given but the same conclusion drawn, that Britain was not over-taxed.

[76] See p. 257.

the Napoleonic wars, the scale of the debt and the narrow, regressive, fiscal regime created problems of consent within the metropole. Could the reduction of taxation within Britain be achieved at the expense of the colonies and at what cost of compliance? The state was not merely moving responsibilities and burdens to the localities within Britain; it was also engaged in a complex process of allocating fiscal burdens within the empire.

5 'Our real war chest': the national debt, war and empire

...the constitution that admits a debt, carries in its vitals the seeds of its destruction.

> A. Young, *Travels in France during the Years 1787, 1788 and 1789*,
> ed. M. Betham-Edwards (4th edn, London, 1892), p. 337

Ministers are quite aware that they were trenching on the interests both of the capitalist and of the merchant; that they were taxing the colonies, and breaking faith with the public creditor; but they were willing to incur their displeasure to secure the favour of the manufacturers. Such is the consequence of being governed by an administration, who rest on popular favour, and are impelled to sacrifice the best interests of the empire to maintain their interest with the populace in the great cities.

> A. Alison, 'On the financial measures of the reformed parliament.
> No 1. The Whig budget', *Blackwood's Edinburg-Magazine* 29
> (June 1831), 975, cited in A. Gambles, 'Rethinking the politics
> of protection: Conservatism and the corn laws, 1830–52',
> *English Historical Review* 113 (1998), 946

The power of a society to pay debts is proportioned to the progress which that society has made in industry, in commerce, and in all the arts and sciences which flourish under the benign influence of freedom and of equal law. The inclination of a society to pay debts is proportioned to the degree in which that society respects the obligations of plighted faith. Of the strength which consists in extent of territory and in number of fighting men, a rude despot who knows no law but his own childish fancies and headstrong passions, or a convention of socialists which proclaims all property to be robbery, may have more than falls to the lot of the best and wisest government. But the strength which is derived from the confidence of capitalists such a despot, such a convention, never can possess. That strength...flies, by the law of its nature, from barbarism and fraud, from tyranny and anarchy, to follow civilisation and virtue, liberty and order.

> T. B. Macaulay, *The History of England from the Accession of James II*, vol. IV
> (1855; Folio Press edition, London 1986), pp. 249–54

By the end of the Napoleonic wars, the national debt stood at more than twice the gross national product, and interest payments were over half total tax revenues. Not surprisingly, the national debt was viewed with alarm, as a dead weight on the economy, and a burden on productive members of society to sustain parasitical *rentiers* and morally enervating luxury. This debate was intimately connected with other contentious issues of economic policy, for the real burden of the debt would be increased by a policy of price deflation and reduced by a policy of price inflation. Monetary policy was therefore of crucial importance, with the return to gold in 1829, reinforced by the strong link between gold reserves and the amount of money in circulation created by the Bank Charter Act of 1844. Despite the campaigns of the 1880s to loosen the limits on money by adding silver to the monetary base, in the second half of the nineteenth century monetary issues ceased to be so contentious: gold became a guarantee of stability, a natural and providential means of ordering economic affairs which could not be distorted by the meddling of interests. It might almost be said that gold was moral: it created a commercial world in which the amount of money and credit was clearly determined, and anyone who indulged in speculation and an over-expansion of credit would soon be faced with retribution in the form of business failure.[1] Much the same change in cultural meanings may be found in the case of the national debt, which was interpreted by Macaulay in 1855 as a symbol of 'civilisation and virtue, liberty and order'. Individual businessmen were good risks to whom money could be lent in confidence that interest would be paid and the debt honoured, if their reputation was sound. The assessment of their financial probity was in part a matter of their (and their family's) personal comportment, but it was also – and increasingly – a matter of accounting rectitude, a careful keeping of ledgers to allow an assessment of profits, cash flow and assets. Much the same can be said of the state: how could it create a sense of probity and trust, so that it too could borrow large sums of money in an emergency? The general absence of large-scale warfare between 1815 and 1914, and changes in military strategy, meant that the great powers did not need large standing armies as in the eighteenth century. What they *did* need was the ability to produce large sums of money at short notice, in order to build

---

[1] These points are discussed by Hilton, *Corn, Cash and Commerce* and *Age of Atonement*. Although there has been some work on the bimetallic campaign against the gold standard, this was a minority position. The survival of the gold standard is too often seen as simply the product of the self-interest of the City, and there has been surprisingly little work on attitudes towards gold and money, or on the cultural interpretations of gold in the second half of the nineteenth century. On bimetallism, see E. H. H. Green, 'Rentiers versus producers? The political economy of the bimetallic controversy, c. 1880–1898', *English Historical Review* 103 (1988), 588–612, and the response by A. C. Howe, 'Bimetallism, c. 1880–1898: a controversy re-opened?', *English Historical Review* 105 (1990), 377–91. For some comments on the interpretation of gold and money, Brantlinger, *Fictions of State*, chapters 3 and 4.

battleships or to mobilise an army. Confidence in the national debt was therefore crucial, and the willingness of the British public to lend to the state before the First World War stood in stark contrast to the reluctance of the German public.[2]

Another element in the process of constraining the state in reaction to the loss of consent in the second quarter of the nineteenth century was the export of the costs of empire from the metropole to the periphery. The experience of the American war of independence suggested the dangers of this transfer of burdens, but the risk seemed worth taking in the face of political tension at home. Chartist demonstrations on the streets of London and provincial towns were all too visible; the attractions of passing the costs of meeting the urgent domestic demands for retrenchment and free trade to India, the Cape, the Caribbean or Canada were obvious. Discontent there was less immediately threatening – and could be treated with greater force than was prudent at home. The British state might turn a more peaceful, equitable and consensual face to its citizens at home. But could this be at the cost of a more militaristic policy in the colonies, as the level of extraction was increased?[3]

Loans and the national debt

The fiscal-military state of the 'long eighteenth century' rested on the use of tax revenues to provide security for loans. Specific taxes were earmarked for particular loans in order to guarantee an income flow to maintain interest payments, and a sinking fund was introduced by Pitt in 1786 to pay off debt, requiring the government to set aside a fixed amount each year. After 1815, the cost of servicing the debt was the subject of great controversy and Pitt was attacked for relying so heavily on loans in the initial stages of the war. Henry Parnell was typical of many commentators who believed that Pitt had been misled by 'the fraudulence of ingenious reasoning on the part of monied men', and that borrowing would have been unnecessary if he had introduced the income tax at an earlier date.[4]

---

[2] On the failure of the loan in Germany in 1913 and the consequent need to introduce the *Wehrbeitrag* or defence levy, see PRO, T171/167, 'Paper prepared at the request of the chancellor on the German defence levy of 1913'.

[3] On the shift to a more military and repressive policy in the colonies, see for example A. Bank, 'Losing faith in the civilizing mission: the premature decline of humanitarian liberalism at the Cape, 1840–60', in M. J. Daunton and E. Halpern (eds.), *Empire and Others: British Encounters with Indigenous Peoples, 1600–1850* (London, 1999), pp. 364–83, which sees a rise in racist ideology and a more brutal, authoritarian, approach.

[4] Parnell, *On Financial Reform*, pp. 285, 297; see also [J. R. McCulloch], 'Finance accounts of the United Kingdom for the year ended 5 Jan. 1823', *Edinburgh Review* 77 (1823),

Pitt's use of a sinking fund to pay off the debt was criticised. Although Pitt had expected to make payments into the fund from a revenue surplus, the costs of war with France made this impracticable. He was left with a choice of abandoning the sinking fund or preserving it by borrowing money. He took the second course and incurred new, more costly, debt in order to pay off the original, cheaper, loans. At the end of the war, the national debt and the costs of service were high, and some means had to be found to bring them down.[5] This was not an easy task: the recipients of interest on loans were attacked as parasitical *rentiers* battening on productive members of society; and any suggestion that taxes should be increased in order to redeem debt would merely intensify the complaints. The politics of the national debt were of considerable importance until the last quarter of the nineteenth century.

As we have noted, David Hume was fearful of the costs of the national debt and advocated state bankruptcy. Although Adam Smith was more sanguine, he wrote before the huge rise in the debt with the Napoleonic wars, and most classical economists in the early nineteenth century were concerned about the burden. Their fear was that the debt relieved the present and threw a burden on to the future, both by reducing the level of private capital consumption (what later economists term 'crowding out') and by taxation to cover the costs of servicing the debt. Many eighteenth-century commentators believed that tax to cover interest simply transferred income between members of society, without any serious economic consequences. Ricardo continued to accept this position and other classical economists (above all J. R. McCulloch)* admitted that taxation might, up to a certain point, stimulate activity by making producers work harder to maintain their income after tax, as well as encouraging savings. But they also feared that it might rise so high as to destroy initiative and incentive, reducing the funds available for productive investment, and even causing a flight of capital. Stimulation might therefore give way to shock. As John Stuart Mill pointed out, increased government borrowing might not be harmful in a society, like Britain, with abundant capital; it might simply halt capital exports which had not been able to find profitable outlets at home. The test was whether interest rates rose: if they did, Mill felt that the consequences would be serious, indicating that capital was being

---

1–43, for a detailed outline of the attack on the sinking fund as a 'clumsy compound of delusion and quackery' (34).

[5] Hargreaves, *National Debt*, pp. 99–134.

* John Ramsay McCulloch (1789–1864) was educated at Edinburgh University and contributed to the *Edinburgh Review* between 1818 and 1837. His *Principles of Political Economy* appeared in 1825, and he was professor of political economy at the University of London from 1828 to 1837; from 1838 to his death he was comptroller of the Stationery Office. (*DNB*, Vol. XXXV, ed. S. Lee (London, 1893), pp. 19–21.)

withdrawn from the 'wage fund' and so leading to lower wages in addition to the burden of taxes. Most classical economists (with the exception of Ricardo) accepted that governments would need to borrow in war in order to prevent taxes from passing beyond the point of stimulation to create a shock to the economy by exceeding the taxable capacity of the country. But too ready a reliance on loans might simply cast problems into the future. Debt and taxation must therefore be carefully balanced, and the future burden of debt service should be reduced as far as possible. Interest rates might be reduced when peace led to lower costs of borrowing; Ricardo and, at one time, McCulloch argued that the debt might be reduced by a heroic, one-off imposition of a 'capital levy'. But, above all, the repayment of debt should come not from a sinking fund as adopted by Pitt, but from budget surpluses.[6]

Indeed, in 1819 the Commons passed a resolution that a clear budgetary surplus of £5m a year was 'absolutely necessary' in order to reduce the national debt, in place of the existing payments of £15.5m a year into the sinking fund which entailed additional borrowing. However, the available surplus was only £2m, and the chancellor therefore proposed to increase taxes by £3m. The political problem was immediately apparent: the scale of the national debt was resented, yet the only way to reduce the debt was by means of a budgetary surplus which entailed higher taxes and political difficulties. Of course, the radical nostrum was to slash expenditure on 'old corruption' which was difficult to achieve given the high levels of spending on debt service and pensions or half-pay for officers. Despite the tax increases, the government failed to achieve a surplus of £5m, and it also needed to find £10m to pay to the Bank of England as a result of the decision to return to the gold standard. Consequently, the government was forced to borrow. In 1822, a new approach was tried. Payments of pensions and half-pay to army and navy officers amounted to £4.9m in 1822, and would decline over time as they died. The chancellor proposed to replace the high current cost by a lower charge spread over a longer period of time through the so-called 'dead weight annuity'. By selling annuities at a constant charge of £2.8m a year for forty-five years, the government could obtain funds for half-pay and pensions, and make an immediate saving of £2m. However, purchasers were not forthcoming and the scheme was abandoned in 1828.[7]

---

[6] On the classical economists and national debt, see the discussion by O'Brien, *Classical Economists*, pp. 259–65; on J. R. McCulloch, see D. P. O'Brien, *J. R. McCulloch: A Study in Classic Economics* (London, 1970), pp. 237–8, 263–9.

[7] *Parliamentary Debates*, 40, 8 June 1819, cols. 990–7; the resolution was opposed by Hume and Parnell because £3m of the £5m surplus was to be raised by increasing taxes; 3 Geo. IV c. 51, 'An act for apportioning the burthen occasioned by the military and

The Select Committee on Public Income and Expenditure of 1828 was critical of the 'dead-weight annuities', on the grounds that they were an 'intricate contrivance' which merely created new debt rather than a 'real' sinking fund based on a surplus of revenue. The Committee extended its complaints beyond this specific example to a general attack on the government's handling of the national debt and the sinking fund. Its fourth report, under the chairmanship of Henry Parnell, marked the culmination of a campaign against borrowing for sinking funds. In 1822, Joseph Hume proposed thirty-eight resolutions to the Commons in which he attacked the government for borrowing at a higher rate of interest in order to pay off loans at a lower rate of interest. In response, the chancellor reformed the sinking funds in 1823, and held out the prospect of a surplus revenue or 'clear' sinking fund of £5m a year. Once again, the surplus was not available and the government continued to borrow. Hume returned to the attack with a further set of resolutions: the sinking fund was 'founded in fallacy, and has been maintained by delusion'. Although Hume's resolutions were defeated, his opinions were endorsed by the Select Committee of 1828 which was 'impressed with a strong conviction of the sound policy of applying a Surplus Revenue perseveringly in those times during which no extraordinary resources need to be raised, in the reduction of the debts accumulated to defray the expenses of antecedent periods of difficulty and exertion'. Such a course of action was essential for preserving credit and safety in future periods of danger, when it might be necessary to embark on further loans. 'The time cannot be very distant (according to the ordinary vicissitudes of peace and war in the history of human affairs) when the combined weight of the past and present burthens must become too great for the most prosperous people to support, and the fabric of Public credit must crumble under the accumulated pressure.' A reduction in the debt was therefore crucial

naval pensions and civil superannuations by vesting an equal annuity in trustess for payment therefore', 1822; 4 Geo. IV c. 19, 'An act for further regulating the reduction of the national debt', 1823; PP 1828 V, *Fourth Report from the Select Committee on Public Income and Expenditure of the United Kingdom*; PP 1828 V, *Second Report from the Select Committee on Public Income*, pp. 5–7; PP 1857 (2nd session) IX, *Select Committee on Public Monies*, appendix 1, 'Memorandum on financial control put in by the chancellor of the Exchequer, April 1857', pp. 519–47; PP 1890–1 XLVII, *National debt. Report by the secretary and comptroller general of the proceedings of the commissioners for the reduction of the national debt from 1786 to 31 March 1890*, pp. 530–5. For the debate on the national debt and sinking fund, see R. Hamilton, *An Inquiry Concerning the Rise and Progress, the Redemption . . . and Management of the National Debt of Great Britain* (Edinburgh, 1813); W. Grenville, *Essay on the Supposed Advantages of a Sinking Fund* (London, 1827), and the response in W. Cobbett, *Noble Nonsense! Or Cobbett's Exhibition of the Stupid and Insolent Pamphlet of Lord Grenville* (London, 1828), and W. Boyd, *Observations on Lord Grenville's Essay on the Sinking Fund* (London, 1828). For a general account, see Hargreaves, *National Debt*, chapter IX.

for national security in future wars:

The system of borrowing during the war, and gradually redeeming the debt thereby created during peace, is an intermediate course between the resolute exertion of raising at once, by taxes, the whole of the supplies required, and the easier plan of providing for the existing difficulty by the easiest present means, without regard to the interest or safety of future generations.

The Committee would have preferred to apply £5m a year towards debt reduction, on the condition that it could be obtained from surplus revenue. The absence of such a surplus led the Committee to propose the abandonment of a fixed payment and instead to appropriate the 'real surplus' each year. Although the Committee hoped that this might amount to £3m a year, it insisted that it should not be made up from borrowing. These principles were adopted by Henry Goulburn* as a temporary measure in the budget of 1828. In 1829, the existing legislation on the sinking fund was repealed and payment into the sinking fund was set at the surplus of any year. Although Goulburn hoped that the surplus in the budget of 1829 would be £3m, the outcome was only £1.7m and future chancellors were more inclined to give priority to reducing taxes than applying large surpluses to the debt.[8]

The Select Committee of 1828 did not make any explicit recommendations on the desirability of using taxes or loans in order to finance war, but the implication was clear. As Parnell argued in 1831, war finance should rely as far as possible on taxation. The issue appeared as a practical problem during the Crimean war, when more reliance was placed on taxation than in the earlier wars against France. Later commentators came to view it as 'the best financed of our great wars', and it provided a standard of judgement for both the Boer war and the First World War.[9] Reliance upon taxes rather than loans was frequently expressed as an act of justice between the present and future, between a 'manly' acceptance of burdens (which could restrain military adventures) and an irresponsible transfer of costs to posterity (which would remove constraints on

[8] PP 1828 V, *Fourth Report from the Select Committee on Public Income and Expenditure of the United Kingdom*, pp. 561–3; PRO, T171/9, Basil Blackett, 22 Nov. 1910, outlines policy towards the national debt; PP 1890–1 XLVII, *National Debt. Report by the secretary and comptroller general*, pp. 539–42, 552; 10 Geo. IV c. 27, 'An act to amend the several acts for regulating the reduction of the national debt', 1829.

[9] F. W. Hirst, *The Political Economy of War* (London, 1915), p. 143.

* Henry Goulburn (1784–1856) was educated at Trinity College, Cambridge, and became a Tory MP in 1808. In 1810 he was under-secretary in the Home department and in 1813 under-secretary for war and the colonies. As chief secretary in Ireland from 1821 to 1827 he opposed Catholic emancipation and was denounced as an Orangeman. He was chancellor of the Exchequer from 1828 to 1830, home secretary in 1834–5 and chancellor from 1841 to 1846. Peel was responsible for presenting the budgets of 1842 and 1845. (*DNB*, Vol. XXII, ed. L. Stephen and S. Lee (London, 1890), pp. 283–5.)

spending and on militarism). As Gladstone explained, borrowing for war meant

wholesale systematic continued deception upon the people. Under such a system the people do not really know what they are doing. The consequences are adjourned into a far future. What is desirable is that they should know the price they are called upon to pay for the benefits they expect, or the sacrifices they think fit to make in order that that which they do they may do on intelligent and reasonable grounds, not deluding themselves at the cost of bequeathing a charge on posterity.

But it was also realised that there was another, and perhaps more significant, issue, of justice between classes: taxes were paid by workers and industry in order to provide interest to fund-holders. As a result, the rich were 'provided with a savings bank at the expense of the poor'.[10]

Gladstone believed that taxes were less harmful than loans which were drawn from productive capital, so reducing the supply of goods and increasing prices. Loans were therefore paid twice, first in higher prices and secondly in interest. As Gladstone explained,

if you raise war supplies by new taxes, you make each man take his share for himself out of the surplus of his income over his expenditure; but if, on the contrary, you go into the market for a loan, you act directly and to the full extent upon that portion of capital which is immediately available for the promotion of trade. In the one case, you get a large portion of what you want out of a superfluity of capital; in the other case . . . you go directly to that fountainhead where money is supplied, upon which in a great degree the activity of trade and the cheapness of productions must depend.[11]

On this view, taxes were preferable to loans which would waste capital and impose burdens on enterprise. As G. K. Rickards* explained,

The loan system, like an unwholesome stimulant, supplies an artificial energy to the body politic, while it insidiously saps the source of strength, and exhausts the

---

[10] O. Anderson, *A Liberal State at War: English Politics and Economics during the Crimean War* (London, 1967), pp. 206–8, and O. Anderson, 'Loans versus taxes: British financial policy in the Crimean war', *Economic History Review* 2nd ser. 16 (1963–4), 314–27; see also J. E. Cairnes, *On the Best Means of Raising the Supplies of a War Expenditure* (London, 1854), p. 6; G. K. Rickards, *The Financial Policy of War: Two Lectures on the Funding System and on the Different Modes of Raising Supplies* (London, 1855), p. 14; W. E. Gladstone, *Parliamentary Debates*, 3rd ser. 131, 6 Mar. 1854, col. 376.

[11] Gladstone, *Parliamentary Debates*, 3rd ser. 131, 6 Mar. 1854, col. 375. For a brief discussion of Gladstone and loans, see J. Maloney, 'Gladstone and sound Victorian finance', in Maloney (ed.), *Debts and Deficits*, pp. 30–1.

* George Kettelby Rickards (1812–89) was educated at Westminster and Eton, and at Balliol, Trinity, and Queen's Colleges, Oxford. He was a fellow of Queen's between 1836 and 1843, and a barrister from 1837. He was counsel to the speaker of the House of Commons from 1851 to 1882 and Drummond professor of political economy at Oxford between 1851 and 1857. (*DNB*, vol. XLVIII, ed. Lee, p. 261.)

frame. The effect of taxation upon the energies of a nation is widely different. The pressures of taxes, if not excessive in amount or too suddenly imposed, acts as a spur to industry and stimulates individuals to increased exertions in order to discharge the demands of the State without entrenching on their capital. It furnishes new motives, both to exertion and economy. But a loan, imposing on the borrowing generation, as they conceive, only a small fraction of the expense incurred, supplies no such incentive. It rather discourages the endeavour to toil and save...It opens a way to glory or aggrandizement without the struggle and the sacrifice that war involves.[12]

Loans were a temptation to immorality as well as destructive of enterprise and production. Gladstone elevated economic arguments in favour of taxation into a religious and moral principle:

The expenses of a war are the moral check which it has pleased the Almighty to impose upon the ambition and lust of conquest that are inherent in so many nations. There is pomp and circumstance, there is glory and excitement about war...The necessity of meeting from year to year the expenditure which it entails is a salutary and wholesome check, making them feel what they are about, and making them measure the cost of the benefits upon which they may calculate. It is by these means that they may be led and brought to address themselves to a war policy as rational and intelligent beings.[13] Higher taxes were an incentive to conclude peace.

Gladstone therefore doubled the income tax for the duration of the war from 7d to 1s 2d in the £. However, he still had to find additional revenue and his principles collided with political calculation. Gladstone was aware that a further increase in the income tax would lead to agitation for differentiation between types of income. His solution was an increase in consumption taxes, 'in the form which will least interfere with trade, which will least interfere with the innocent enjoyments of the people, and least with consumption ... as compared with the amount of revenue which it is necessary to raise for the purposes of the State'. He therefore increased duties on spirits, sugar and malt, which accounted for about a third of additional war-time taxes. Gladstone was still left with a deficit of about £4m, and he sought power to borrow. He relied on 'evasions and sophistries' to disguise his use of loans, arguing that it was 'a provision for the temporary raising of money' in anticipation of revenue from the new taxes, a desire to provide means in the event of need rather than to meet actual expenditure.[14]

---

[12] Rickards, *Financial Policy of War*, pp. 54–5.
[13] *Parliamentary Debates*, 3rd ser. 131, 6 Mar. 1854, col. 376.
[14] Anderson, *Liberal State at War*, p. 195; *Parliamentary Debates*, 3rd ser. 132, 8 May 1854, cols. 1448, 1452, 1456, 1458–62, 1471.

Gladstone's successor as chancellor, G. C. Lewis,* preferred to avoid moral contortions and he was less dogmatic that taxation was economically preferable to borrowing. In his view, loans might make economic sense for there was a basic difference between the current financial situation and the period of war with revolutionary and Napoleonic France. In the earlier conflicts, government loans traded at a discount and interest rates were high, so that borrowing was very costly and led to rising prices. During the Crimean war, government stock was at a premium, so that it was easy to borrow on decent terms and prices were not affected. Further, the 'Continental system' of Napoleon closed Europe to British goods; during the Crimean war, Europe was open to trade and production was not disrupted.[15] Lewis therefore argued that a high level of taxation might do as much harm as borrowing:

> the encroachment upon the savings of the industrious classes, which would be caused by excessive taxation, would be a greater evil than the abstraction of capital by means of a loan, and its expenditure upon the war ... nothing can be more certain than the effect of excessive taxation in making inroads into the savings of the industrious classes ... Taxes which cripple enterprise and derange industry, or interfere with the ordinary distribution of capital, are more detrimental to the community than loans effected by the Government.[16]

Capital might be sent abroad or wasted, so that government borrowing would not necessarily be at the expense of productive domestic investment.[17] Borrowing could therefore be less harmful, for loans were a voluntary advance by rich capitalists who could afford it, unlike compulsory taxes.[18] There was, therefore, no invariable rule:

> it is quite possible to injure the future and lasting interests of the nation by an overstrained dread of subjecting posterity to obligation. It is better, after all, to succeed to a mortgaged patrimony than to an exhausted estate. To a nation that is advancing in wealth and population, the relative weight of financial burthens is perpetually diminishing. Whether we leave a few millions more or less of debt

[15] G. F. Lewis (ed.), *Letters of the Rt Hon Sir George Cornewall Lewis to Various Friends* (London, 1870), Lewis to Head, 17 Aug. 1855, p. 298.
[16] *Parliamentary Debates*, 3rd ser. 137, 20 Apr. 1855, cols. 1560–1.
[17] Anderson, *Liberal State at War*, pp. 210–11.
[18] Rickards, *Financial Policy of War*, pp. 64–8.
* George Cornewall Lewis (1806–63) was educated at Eton and Christ Church, Oxford. In 1833, he served as an assistant commissioner to enquire into the condition of the poorer classes in Ireland and in 1834 into religious and other instruction. He was a poor law commissioner between 1839 and 1847, when he became a Liberal MP. He was secretary of the Board of Control in 1847, under-secretary for the Home department in 1848 and financial secretary of the Treasury from 1850 to 1852. He edited the *Edinburgh Review* from 1852 to 1855 when he returned to office as chancellor of the Exchequer until 1858. He was home secretary from 1859 to 1861 and secretary of war from 1861 to 1863. (*DNB*, vol. XXXIII, ed. S. Lee (London, 1893), pp. 178–83.)

behind us, may not be a vital consideration; but it is a paramount duty that we owe to our descendants, to adopt no measures that may intrench upon the capital of the country, may undermine its trade, or weighdown those springs of industry which form the perennial sources of national revenue.[19]

A strong case could therefore be made that loans were less harmful to economic prosperity. Indeed, in 1855 even Gladstone accepted that a loan was the only way of dealing with an 'uncontrollable' growth of expenditure:

we cannot possibly expect a free country ...to push the soundest economical doctrines, under all circumstances, to their extremes. You must remember that you have to deal with flesh and blood, and that you cannot ask from flesh and blood more than they can reasonably bear. I go a step further, and I admit that there is a point at which the sudden accumulation of taxation becomes so great an evil, and so great a cause of disturbance to all personal and social relations, that it is better to provide yourself with money up to a certain limit at a pecuniary disadvantage than to carry that disturbance through all ranks of the country.[20]

The national debt was shifting its status, becoming a protector of liberty and prosperity rather than an 'enormous, almost overpowering maw' – provided that it was paid off by budget surpluses after the war. This was the 'intermediate case' between the 'resolute exertion' of higher taxation and the 'easier plan', of borrowing. When the fourth volume of Thomas Babbington Macaulay's* *History of England* appeared in 1855, he mocked those who feared that a heavy debt would lead to ruin by showing how the economy prospered. The debt 'gives to intelligence an advantage over brute force, and to honesty an advantage over dishonesty', so promoting 'happiness and virtue'.[21] Of course, criticisms of the national debt did continue, from Disraeli in *Sybil* to John Ruskin and through to the onslaught on the debt after the First World War which looked back to Ricardo's suggestion of a capital levy. The economist, W. S. Jevons, raised

---

[19] Rickards, *Financial Policy of War*, p. 73.

[20] *Parliamentary Debates*, 3rd ser. 137, 20 Apr. 1855, col. 1594.

[21] Anderson, *Liberal State at War*, pp. 214–16; W. Newmarch, 'On the loans raised by Mr Pitt during the first French War, 1793–1801', *Journal of the London Statistical Society* 18 (1855), 104–40; Brantlinger, *Fictions of State*, pp. 133–4.

* Thomas Babbington Macaulay (1800–59) was educated at Trinity College, Cambridge, and became a fellow in 1824. He was called to the bar in 1826 and wrote extensively for the *Edinburgh Review*. He was appointed a commissioner for bankruptcy in 1828, and was a Liberal MP in 1830 and 1832–4, serving as commissioner of the Board of Control in 1832 and secretary in 1833. Between 1834 and 1838 he was a member of the Supreme Council for India, working on the legal code for India. He returned to London in 1838 and began work on his *History*; the first two volumes appeared in 1848 and the third and fourth in 1855. He returned to parliament between 1839 and 1847 and 1852 and 1856, and served as secretary for war, 1839–41, and paymaster of the forces, 1846–7. (*DNB*, vol. XXXIV, ed. Lee, pp. 410–18.)

a new fear in 1865, when he argued that British coal reserves would be exhausted in a century and that the national debt should therefore be paid off as soon as possible during this 'climax' of British prosperity. He suggested a tax on coal exports to provide the revenue, as well as to cripple competing manufacturers and to conserve British stocks. Such arguments reinforced Gladstone's determination to pay off the national debt; as he informed Jevons, the 'liberation of industry' from taxes had been his priority, and the time had now come to cut the debt. But fears of imminent disaster from the burden of the debt were marginal to British political culture.[22] In the second half of the nineteenth century, Macaulay's position was in the ascendant, and the national debt had become a source of prosperity and security of British liberties, an expression of the moral virtues of a commercial society. In the early nineteenth century, the national debt – like protection – was associated with militarism and warfare. By contrast, free trade would unite nations in peace and prosperity. In the new political and economic circumstances of the second half of the nineteenth century, debt took on a similar role as a mark of commercial probity and capitalist confidence. Macaulay's view was broadly shared by W. E. H. Lecky,* the historian

---

[22] B. Disraeli, *Sibyl, or the Two Nations* (London, 1845; Longman's edn, 1899) pp. 23–5; J. Ruskin, *Fors Clavigera*, vols. XXVII and XXVIII of *Works*, ed. E. T. Cook and E. T. Wedderburn (London, 1903–12): letter 7, 'Charitas' (1870) supported the income tax as 'the only honest and just one', falling on the rich in true proportion to the poor, and argued that no crime was so far beyond pardon as making war machinery; letter 8, 'Not as the world giveth' (1871) expressed hostility to war and war finance; letter 58, 'The Catholic prayer' (1875) argued for a national store to distribute to the poor rather than a national debt which was a 'foul disgrace, at the best. But it is, as now constituted, also a foul crime. National debts paying interest are simply the purchase by the rich, of power to tax the poor'; letter 61, 'The care of Machpelah' (1876) castigated the misery caused by the idle classes. W. S. Jevons, *The Coal Question: An Inquiry Concerning the Progress of the Nation, and the Probable Exhaustion of our Coal-mines* (London, 1865), chapter XVII; J. Morley, *The Life of William Ewart Gladstone* (3 vols., London, 1903), vol. II pp. 57–8; Maloney, 'Gladstone and sound Victorian finance', p. 34. A coal tax was introduced during the Boer war: see below, p. 315, and a revised edition of Jevons's book was issued in 1906, edited by A. W. Flux.

* William Edward Hartpole Lecky (1838–1903) was born in Dublin and educated at Trinity College, Dubin. He published poetry and history and travelled in Spain and Italy; his two-volume account of the decay of superstition and the rise of reason was a great success on its publication in 1865, despite its discursive, even rambling and incoherent, structure. He followed this with his *History of European Morals* in 1869, and his major work, a twelve-volume history of England in the eighteenth century appeared between 1878 and 1892. The final five volumes dealt with Ireland, to correct the attacks on the Irish in J. A. Froude's history. He declined the Regius professorship of history at Oxford. He became a Liberal Unionist in the split over home rule in 1886, and was MP for Dublin University from 1895 to 1902; he supported the creation of a Roman Catholic university in Ireland, and backed Horace Plunkett's schemes for agrarian reform. His *Democracy and Liberty* (1896) was marked by his usual faults of poor structure; as the *DNB* remarked it was a 'storehouse of admirable, if somewhat disjointed, reflections,

of eighteenth-century England. Although he remarked in 1865 that the national debt might be 'the most powerful of all the engines of warfare', he also commented that credit was 'one of the great moralising influences of society, by the immense importance it has bestowed upon character, and one of the great pledges of peace, by the union it has established between different nations'. In Lecky's view, credit would become an agency of peace rather than conflict through the moralising influence of political economy. The ideas of French philosophy were not enough to stop 'colliding passions' and 'it was reserved for political economy to supply a stronger and more permanent principle of unity. This principle is an enlightened self-interest.' Rather than seeing war as a means of securing trade, political economy taught that every nation had an interest in the prosperity of its trading partners, so that 'every fresh commercial enterprise is therefore an additional guarantee of peace'. And the moral truths of political economy would shape policy as industry become the dominant political influence and they were 'realised as axioms by the masses'. In other words, to free traders such as Lecky or Cobden, peace was assured by commerce; and the national debt was not a serious danger, on condition that it was treated like any other commercial credit. Loans should not be used to live beyond the means of the state, as an alternative to taxes; warlike passions could be limited by the immediate impact of military spending on taxation. As Brantlinger remarks, debt became a matter of 'personal culpability', judged by the individual's moral standing or reputation and solvency. In the case of the state, the Bank of England and Treasury were 'economically and morally solvent', handling loans with discretion and probity, under the control of public men of integrity and honesty.[23]

made, on the whole, from a distinctly conservative point of view, and without much hope for the future of democracy. It was largely a doubt, a protest, and a regret.' He was elected a fellow of the British Academy, and appointed to the Order of Merit in 1902. (*DNB, Second Supplement*, vol. II, ed. Lee, pp. 435–40.)

[23] W. E. H. Lecky, *History of the Rise and Influence of the Spirit of Rationalism in Europe* (2 vols., London, 1865), vol. II, pp. 379, 385–95; see Brantlinger, *Fictions of State*, pp. 138–42, which discusses attitudes to debt. The use of taxes to limit militarism was a common theme in Liberal political culture: see below, p. 239–40. On the debates after the First World War, see Daunton, 'How to pay for the war'. Of course, Ruskin had a very different notion of political economy as the creator of 'illth' rather than wealth, and he feared that it did not develop 'manly character' but destroyed it. To Ruskin, 'the real science of political economy . . . is that which teaches nations to desire and labour for the things that lead to life' (J. Ruskin, *Unto This Last: Four Essays on the First Principles of Political Economy* (London, 1862), essay IV, 'Ad valorem'). As we shall see, Edwardian new Liberals (and especially J. A. Hobson) combined Ruskin and Cobden: commerce would only create peace if there were a fair distribution of income and wealth at home; otherwise, the result would be dominance by imperialistic finance in the pursuit of overseas markets. In other words, Lecky's vision of commerce limiting warfare was historically contingent rather than a natural law. See below, pp. 339–49.

Of course, there was always the danger that the absence of a definite commitment to pay a fixed amount would allow chancellors to use surpluses to reduce taxes rather than to redeem debt. In 1875, as Stafford Northcote* pointed out, the system adopted in 1829 had only paid off about £40m of debt. More significantly, the debt was reduced by £120m through the expiry of terminable annuities. These annuities entailed annual payments over a fixed term of years; when they came to an end, the chancellor had a windfall and might be tempted to reduce taxes rather than redeem more debt. Northcote accepted that a reduction of taxes might indeed be desirable when high taxes imposed a burden on the economy. Equally, if taxes were moderate and the economy booming, priority should be given to reducing the debt. He proposed the creation of a fixed debt charge to be paid into a new sinking fund, in order to accelerate the repayment of debt and to impose more discipline on chancellors. The new sinking fund was set as the difference between the 'permanent charge' (set at £28m from 1877/8) and the actual expenditure on debt service. In other words, the chancellor was obliged to budget for £28m but the actual interest payment might be only £20m. Consequently, £8m was paid into the new sinking fund. Any additional surplus was a 'mere windfall resulting from faulty estimating' rather than an integral feature of debt reduction. This new accounting device meant that the chancellor had less power to take any windfall or surplus to reduce taxes. The cost of servicing the debt was reduced in 1889, when Goschen converted existing loans to a lower rate of interest, and as a result the permanent charge was reduced to £25m.[24]

The Liberal chancellor – William Harcourt – expressed the late Victorian consensus to his Conservative successor, Michael Hicks Beach:[†]

---

[24] PP 1890–1 XLVIII, *National debt. Report by the secretary and comptroller general of the proceedings of the commissioners for the reduction of the national debt from 1786 to 31 March 1890*, pp. 558–9; *Parliamentary Debates*, 3rd ser. 223, cols. 1036–43, 15 Apr. 1875; 38 and 39 Vict. c. 45, 'An act to amend the law with respect to the reduction of the national debt and the charge for the national debt in the consolidated fund', 1875; PRO, T171/9, Basil Blackett, 22 Nov. 1910. On Goschen's conversion, see E. W. Hamilton, *Conversion and Redemption: An Account of the Operations under the National Debt Conversion Act, 1888 and the National Debt Redemption Act, 1889* (London, 1889), and Hargreaves, *National Debt*, pp. 194–5.

* Stafford Henry Northcote (1818–87) was educated at Eton and Balliol. He was private secretary to Gladstone in 1842, and became a barrister in 1847. He was elected a Conservative MP in 1855, holding office as president of the Board of Trade in 1866, as secretary for India in 1867, as chancellor of the Exchequer from 1874 to 1880 (and also as leader of the House of Commons in 1876). He was leader of the opposition to Gladstone in the Commons from 1880 to 1885, and became foreign secretary in 1886. (*DNB*, vol. XLI, ed. Lee, pp. 194–9.)

† Michael Edward Hicks Beach (1837–1916) was educated at Eton and Christ Church, Oxford; he became a Conservative MP in 1864. In 1868, he was appointed parliamentary

Table 5.1 *Aggregate net liabilities of the state, 1840–1890*

Close of financial year ending 3 Jan.	£m
1840	837.6
1850	819.8
1860	812.9
1870	783.8
1880	739.5
1890	685.0

Source: PP 1890–1 XLVIII, *Return showing . . .
the aggregate gross liabilities of the state . . . at the
close of each financial year from 1835–6 to
1890–1 . . .*, pp. 328–31.

Of all the articles of prestige that of being the only nation which is really paying off
its debts is in my opinion one of the greatest, and . . . is 'worth many battleships'.
It is a comfortable and reassuring reflection that we could tomorrow from the
Sinking Fund interest borrow 200 millions . . . in case of a great emergency without
additional taxation. This is our real War Chest.[25]

The sinking fund formed the keystone of the arch of late Victorian finance,
reducing the burden of past debt and sustaining the 'extraordinary credit'
of Britain. 'It is in reality the country's reserve fund, or war chest, on which
we can fall back in times of emergency', a proposition soon to be tested
by the Boer war.[26]

Treasury thinking on loans versus taxes was systematised during the
Boer war by E. W. Hamilton. In his view, no politician had adopted an extreme position since Pitt's reliance on loans at the start of the war with revolutionary France. Both Disraeli in 1854 and Gladstone in 1860 admitted
the principle of division between loans and taxes. Above all, the approach
was practical and pragmatic, taking account of the likely cost of the war,
the state of government revenues and the prospect of indemnity from the

---

secretary to the poor law board and then under-secretary of the Home department. He
was chief secretary for Ireland from 1874 to 1878, when he became Colonial Secretary
until 1880. He was chancellor of the Exchequer in 1885 to 1886, when he made way
for Randolph Churchill. He became Irish secretary in 1886–7 and then president of
the Board of Trade from 1888 to 1892; on the return of the Conservative government
in 1895, he became chancellor of the Exchequer and held the office until 1902, facing
the financial difficulties of the Boer war. He opposed tariff reform. (*DNB, 1912–21*,
ed. H. W. C. Davis and J. R. H. Weaver (London, 1927), pp. 253–7.)

[25] Gloucestershire Record Office, 2455 PCC/81, Harcourt to Hicks Beach, 18 Nov. 1895.
[26] PRO, T168/42, memo. by E. W. Hamilton on the sinking fund, 30 Sept. 1897.

enemy. In Hamilton's view, there was no simple, categorical, answer:

You may crush the nation by overloading and breaking down the springs of industry and commerce by an immoderate weight of taxation as much as by charging it with an enormous weight of debt. It may indeed be less injurious to part with capital than with earnings. For, it may well be that a draft on the national capital of the country will by a natural process of adjustment act less injuriously on the labour market than any given scheme of additional taxation.

The experience of previous wars provided some guidance: between 1793 and 1815, Hamilton estimated that taxes covered 47 per cent of the cost of the war and loans 53 per cent; and during the Crimean war, 47.4 per cent and 52.6 per cent. 'Might we not count on ultimately throwing on posterity only as large a proportion (if so large an one) as was thrown thereon by the Crimean war?'[27] In fact, the proportion of loans during the Boer war was considerably higher at 64 per cent. The explanation was, in part, the assumption of Hicks Beach at the start of the war that it would be a 'cheap promenade', costing no more than £10 or £11m which would be paid out of the gold mines of the Transvaal. At the start of the war, taxes were not increased and the ground was not made up as costs escalated to a total of about £250m.[28] The problem was that the Boer War called the fiscal constitution into question, as we shall see in a later chapter. Had the limits of the income tax been reached, and should there be a return to indirect taxes? Or should the income tax be reformed in order to increase the yield still further? The core of the fiscal constitution became a matter of serious contention for the first time in forty or fifty years. The demands for spending by the civilian-military state were increasing from both sides, as a result of the increased costs of defence and the emergence of new electoral imperatives. At the same time, the ability to pass the costs of imperialism to the periphery was coming under strain.

Exporting the fiscal-military state

In 1831, Archibald Alison complained that the Whigs were upsetting the balance of politics and society by reducing taxation on the great cities and manufacturers, and passing the fiscal burdens on to the colonies.[29] At first sight, his argument was a piece of spurious special pleading in favour of West Indian slave owners and sugar planters who were under

[27] PRO, T168/47, vol. IX, misc. memo., 'Taxation versus loans', E. W. Hamilton, 18 Feb. 1900; this memorandum was also in Bradbury's papers, at T170/31.

[28] Hirst, *Political Economy of War*, pp. 146–7.

[29] Gambles, 'Rethinking the politics of protection', 946, quoting Alison, 'On the financial measures of the reformed parliament', 975.

pressure from emancipationists and free traders. But he did have a point, for the fiscal-military state was exported to the colonies as well as reconstituted at home. As we have seen, Adam Smith argued in *The Wealth of Nations* that the North American colonies should contribute to the costs of imperial defence, and he did not accept that Britain should bear the entire cost of maintaining a mercantilist system of trade.[30] Of course, the American colonists rebelled against British attempts to impose more taxes and exposed the limits of shifting taxation from the metropole to the colonies. By contrast, the East India Company was more successful in extracting revenue from India, converting itself from a trading enterprise into a territorial power supported by taxes. Although the Company's attempt to redefine landholding and sovereignty in order to collect taxes more efficiently met resistance in 1781/2, it was overcome more successfully than in North America. As Bayly argues, the fiscal-military state was dismantled (or at least reconfigured) in England and the lowlands of Scotland; the costs were exported to the peripheries of the Scottish highlands, Ireland and, above all, India so that 'the Indian peasant bore a heavy part of the costs of Britain's world role which the British people were not prepared to bear'. This transfer of costs helped the domestic state to 'disarm and civilianise itself'. Britain was able to escape the traumas of 1848 at home, in part, by reducing the fiscal demands for colonial military expenditure and, to a lesser extent, passing costs from the metropole to the periphery in order to secure the loyalty of domestic taxpayers. At the same time, import duties on colonial commodities such as sugar and timber were reduced to benefit domestic consumers at the expense of the West Indies and Canada. Britain escaped riots and revolution at home, at the cost of tensions and fiscal crisis within the empire. The Chartist demonstration in London in 1848 was a tame affair compared with the revolutions in Europe – and in the British empire. In Canada, the parliament was burned down, and there was civil disobedience at the Cape and in New South Wales. In Jamaica, public expenditure was slashed and then suspended as a result of the impact of equalisation of duties on imperial and foreign sugar on its economy, with rioting and the despatch of a warship to impose order. In Ceylon, the attempt to introduce a land tax was successfully opposed by the planters, which meant an increase in indirect taxes at a time of economic crisis. The result was a tax revolt, brutally repressed by imperial authorities. Retrenchment in the colonies avoided the need to increase the income tax in 1848 and so contributed to maintaining peace at home. The outcome in the colonies was very different, for planters and settlers were loathe to impose taxes to meet

[30] See Smith, *Wealth of Nations*, vol. II, pp. 723, 924–30, 933–4.

the costs of government. The parallel with the revolt of the Thirteen
Colonies was obvious to contemporaries, but the outcome was different. As Miles Taylor argues, the empire was preserved by a process of
reform: elected assemblies were created to provide settlers with a sense
of participation; at the same time the payment of a civil list to support
the crown was made permanent rather than a matter for annual vote.
Whether this combination of extending the vote *and* reducing autonomy
could be sustained in the longer term was a different matter; there was a
further rising in Jamaica in 1865. The problems of fiscal compliance in the
colonies therefore remained, and continued to affect policies at home.[31]

Consent to taxation relied, in part, on devolution to local systems of
authority. In the empire, trustworthy and dependable local elites needed
to be created, a task which was by no means easy. Indeed, many of the
themes of the emergence of the tax state in early modern Europe were repeated in new circumstances, with the British state engaged in a complex
process of negotiation with lords and peasants, chieftains and villagers,
over the extraction of any surplus. The outcome was by no means simple or uniform. The issue arose initially in India, where the ability of
the East India Co. to extract revenues depended on a changed notion of
sovereignty. In Indian theory and practice, sovereignty and the right to
land rested on a complex and shifting hierarchy of rights, rather than on
absolute dominion or ownership. The right to collect land revenue was
separate from the right to collect 'rents', and both proprietorship and
revenue extraction were overlapping and multiple. The East India Co.
took a simpler view, and replaced multiple claims on the land by single
proprietorship. This meant shifting from an unstable hierarchy of king-
ship and rights, and converting the *zamindars* into proprietors of the land
akin to an English territorial aristocracy. Their proprietorship of the land
was confirmed or created, and linked with the collection of revenue on
behalf of the government. A failure to hand over revenue to the East
India Co. could then lead to a loss of proprietary rights. This pattern
was systematised in Bengal in 1793 in the so-called 'permanent settlement' which gave a definite proprietorship to the land, often to people
who previously had only a share in the estate, and fixed the government's

---

[31] C. A. Bayly, 'Returning the British to south Asian history: the limits of colonial hegemony', *South Asia* n.s. 17 (1994), 16, 18–19, and 'The British military-fiscal state and indigenous resistance: India, 1750–1820', in Stone (ed.), *Imperial State at War*, pp. 322–54;
M. Taylor, 'The 1848 revolutions and the British empire', *Past and Present* 166 (2000),
146–80. For one view on the use of fiscal policies to consolidate the British state by
addressing regional imbalances in Ireland and Scotland, see A. Gambles, 'Fishing for
free trade? The political economy of fisheries policy in Britain and the UK, 1780–1850',
Journal of British Studies 39 (2000), 288–316, who argues that fiscal inducements were
given to the Celtic fringe.

claim on revenue.[32] Although it was some time before an efficient system of collection and administration emerged, the permanent settlement transformed the revenue base of the Raj. Payments were defined and no longer open to bargain, and the liabilities fell on the land and its owners whose identities were carefully recorded. The East India Co. had therefore aligned itself with the large proprietors at the expense of the peasantry.[33]

The permanent settlement gave the East India Co. more revenue which helped to pay for an army and hence for the extension of its rule. The Company's collection of revenue was stricter than other rulers in India, with fewer opportunities for money to escape in costs of collection or aid to farmers and landlords. Although the new system alienated many groups who lost their previous position in the hierarchy of rights, the crisis passed and stability was created by turning the Indian landlords into something akin to the territorial aristocrats of England – or, perhaps a better analogy, of Scotland where the clan chieftains were converted into proprietors of landed estates rather than guardians of the clans' lands.[34] The permanent settlement contained the revolt against taxation by 'establishing a countervailing interest in property', creating intermediaries who reduced the need for direct contact between the Company and the mass of the population.[35] However, the paramount need for support from the territorial aristocracy also limited the ability of the Company to extract revenue from the land.

Similar problems arose with the permanent settlement as with the land tax in England: the government did not obtain any share of increased profits with the extension of cultivation or improvement in productivity, and could not respond to changes in the relative prosperity of different regions and crops. W. Muir,* senior member of the Sudder Board of Revenue in the North-Western Provinces, explained that the government lost compared with the proprietors it had created by granting them

---

[32] Bayly, 'British military-fiscal state', pp. 322–54.

[33] P. G. Robb, *Ancient Rights and Future Comfort: Bihar, the Bengal Tenancy Act of 1885, and British Rule in India* (Richmond, 1997), pp. 40, 45, 66–7.

[34] Bayly, 'British military-fiscal state'; on Scotland, see A. McInnes, *Clanship, Commerce and the House of Stuart*, 1603–1788 (East Linton, 1996).

[35] Robb, *Ancient Rights and Future Comfort*, pp. 67, 216.

* William Muir (1819–1905) was born in Glasgow, the son of a merchant; he was educated at the Universities of Glasgow and Edinburgh, and joined the East India Co. in 1837. He was closely involved with the assessment of land revenues, and in establishing the permanent settlement in the North-West Provinces after the 'mutiny'. He rose to be lieutenant-governor of the North-West Provinces from 1868 to 1874, financial member of the council 1874–6 and a member of the Council of India in London from 1876 to 1885. He was principal of Edinburgh University from 1885 to 1905, and he wrote extensively on the history of India and Islam. (*DNB, Second Supplement*, vol. II, ed. Lee, pp. 659–61.)

absolute rights over the land. The result was 'simply to enhance the value of their property by alienating a profitable right of Government, without any equivalent, and at the expense of the other portions of the community, on whom will fall the burden of making good the prospective loss thus created'. One solution was the *temporary* settlement that was adopted in the North-Western Provinces in 1833. A proprietary right to land was granted after careful enquiry and registration; the government's claim to revenue was periodically reassessed so that it could share in the increased value of land. This was linked with a greater concern for the tenant right of the *raiyatwari* or cultivator of the soil, and with a system of direct rule through a local official of the Company who worked with the customs of the mass of the population and the village headman. It meant close personal administration and greater power of fiscal extraction. Both the permanent and temporary, the *zamindar* and *raiyatwari,* systems were based on working with the agrarian structure of India, by different routes. The balance of argument ebbed and flowed over the nineteenth century. The rebellion of 1857 arose, in part, from a more interventionist and anti-landlord policy by Company officials.[36] As a result, Muir and the lieutenant-governor of the North-Western Provinces felt that the temporary settlement, despite its fiscal benefits, should be replaced by a permanent settlement which removed the dangers of political tensions at each revaluation. Above all, they believed that a permanent settlement offered an incentive to proprietors to improve their estates, in the knowledge that they would obtain the entire profit. The lieutenant-governor of the provinces explained that

the limitation of the Government demand in perpetuity, will, in much larger degree, lead to the investment of capital in the land. The wealth of the agricultural classes will be increased. The prosperity of the country and the strength of the community will be augmented. Land will command a much higher price. The prospective loss, which the Government will incur by relinquishing its share of the profits arising from extended cultivation and improved productiveness, will be partly, if not wholly, compensated by the indirect returns which would be derived from the increased wealth and prosperity of the country at large.

The permanent settlement was a strategy to encourage investment and productivity by the proprietors, with the political benefits of securing their loyalty to the Raj. As the lieutenant-governor remarked, 'the absolute limitation of demand upon their land will be received by an agricultural people with the highest satisfaction, and will produce, if anything can, feelings of attachment to the Government, and of confidence in its desire

---

[36] Robb, *Ancient Rights and Future Comfort,* pp. 216–17; E. Stokes, *The Peasant and the Raj* (Cambridge, 1978), chapter 2.

to promote the best interests of the country'.[37] The argument continued, for in the 1870s opinion was swinging back in favour of temporary settlement and reliance on personal administration.[38]

In 1858, the crown assumed direct rule of India from the East India Co. The finances were in a poor state, for debt had been mounting for twenty or so years, and had soared as a result of military expenditure in suppressing the 'mutiny' of 1857. The government of India had a large deficit and turned to Britain for assistance. The British government was alarmed, for this pressure from India threatened the process of retrenchment at home. The secretary of state for India (a member of the British Cabinet and conscious of domestic political pressures) insisted that the revenue of India should be increased in order to reduce the debt, create a balanced budget and maintain payments of the so-called 'home charges'. India should be making a contribution to Britain for the costs of government and defence rather than seeking assistance from the Treasury. But from where could the revenue be raised?[39] The problem with extending the permanent settlement was that revenue from the land tax was static. Muir assumed that encouragement of investment by proprietors would lead to economic growth and hence to increased revenues from other duties. In fact, the government of India was obliged to raise existing taxes and to impose new ones. Tariffs, stamp duties and salt duty were increased, and an income tax was introduced in 1860; at the same time, expenditure was cut. The finances of India were brought into balance, the debt reduced and the British Treasury freed of demands for assistance. By the 1870s, the taxes imposed in order to restore financial equilibrium could be reduced. The income tax was abolished in 1873, and import duties were reduced and finally removed in 1882.[40] Meanwhile, a new provincial

[37] PP 1867 L, *Copy of correspondence between the secretary of state for India in council and the government of India in 1865, 1866 and 1867 on the subject of the permanent settlement of the land revenue in India*, 'Minute of W. Muir, esq., senior member of the Sudder Board of Revenue, on the expediency of forming a permanent settlement of the North-Western Provinces, dated 5th December 1861', pp. 286–91; 'Minute by R. Money, esq., junior member of the Sudder Board of Revenue, North-Western Provinces, dated 21st December 1861', p. 299; 'Minute by the Honourable the Lieutenant Governor of the North Western Provinces, in the Revenue Department, under date the 27th May 1862', pp. 300–1.

[38] Robb, *Ancient Rights and Future Comfort*, p. 221; but see his general comments on the alliance with *zamindars* in Bengal, pp. 235–8, 282–6.

[39] PP 1859 session 1 XIX, *Copy of financial despatch to the government of India, 19 January 1859. Review of the finances of India as shown in the actual accounts of 1856–7 and as estimated for 1857–8 and 1858–9*, pp. 17, 30–1; PP 1859 session 1 XIX, *A copy of financial dispatches between the government of India and the secretary of state for India respecting new loans required for India and of all notifications of the government of India concerning the public debt*, pp. 35–6, 38–9.

[40] PP 1900 XXIX, *Final Report of the Royal Commission on the Administration of the Expenditure of India*, pp. 589–600, 678–85.

rate on land was introduced by Lord Mayo,* the governor-general. His aim was to impose controls on spending by making local government responsible for finding revenue from their own resources, so creating an incentive for economy and permitting a reduction in taxation.[41] In the 1860s, 1870s and early 1880s, Indian finances therefore gave an impression of financial prudence and good management: the debt was reduced, the budget was in balance, the home charges were met and taxes were reduced. Financial relations between Britain and India were put on a new footing by the Select Committee of 1874 which established the basis for apportioning charges between the two countries. Although India was not expected to relieve British expenditure, it should share in the costs of the empire of which it was part; these charges should be carefully calculated and fixed over a period of years.[42] Here was a period of financial harmony, when the costs of rule in India did not greatly affect the British Treasury.

The sense of fiscal well-being did not continue into the later nineteenth century. As early as 1874, Sir John Strachey[†] was concerned that taxes were leading to feelings of 'suspicion and dissatisfaction'. Strachey was optimistic that revenues would increase with economic prosperity, and that surpluses would allow a remission of taxes – as they did for the next decade.[43] By contrast with the permanent settlement, taxation of the land for local purposes was resented and threatened the alliance between the

---

[41] PP 1874 XLVII, *Copy of a paper entitled 'Observations on some questions of Indian finance, by Sir John Strachey'*, 6 Feb. 1874, pp. 249–50, 256; see also PP 1878–9 LV, *Copy of a circular to all local governments and administrations in India, dated Simla, 16 June 1879, in explanation of the present financial position of the government of India, and of the recent orders issued regarding the reduction of expenditure and the revision of provincial assignments*, pp. 569–73. On the system of devolution and its limits within India, see D. Kumar, 'The fiscal system', in D. Kumar (ed.), *The Cambridge Economic History of India*, vol. II: *c. 1757–c. 1970* (Cambridge, 1983), pp. 905–10.

[42] PP 1874 VIII, *Report from the Select Committee on East India Finance*, pp. 4–5.

[43] PP 1874 XLVII, *Copy of a paper entitled 'Observations on some questions of Indian finance, by Sir John Strachey'*, 6 Feb. 1874, pp. 245–82.

* Richard Southwell Bourke, 6th earl of Mayo (1822–72) came from an Irish landed family, and was educated at Trinity College, Dublin. He was an MP from 1847 to 1869 and served as chief secretary of Ireland in 1852, 1858 and 1866; he was appointed viceroy of India in 1869 and held the post until his assassination. (*DNB*, vol. VI, ed. L. Stephen (London, 1886), pp. 21–4.)

† John Strachey (1823–1907) was educated at Haileybury and entered the Bengal civil service in 1842, rising to become lieutenant-governor of the North–Western Provinces between 1874 and 1876. He was appointed finance member of the governor-general's council in 1876, resigning in 1880 as a result of seriously underestimating the cost of war in Afghanistan. He was a member of the Council of India between 1885 and 1895. With his brother Richard (1817–1908) he played a major role in decentralising provincial finances, abolishing internal customs and extending free trade. He helped to consolidate British government in India after 1857, and was associated with philosophical radicalism. (*DNB, Second Supplement*, vol. III, ed. Lee, pp. 437–9.)

Raj and the *zamindars*.[44] From the mid-1880s, the situation started to change and the fiscal situation become much more difficult. A decline in the value of silver against gold meant that the rupee depreciated against sterling, so increasing the burden of the 'home charges'. At the same time, military expenditure rose. The permanent settlement meant that other taxes had to be raised: the land tax declined from 52 per cent of government revenue in 1861–5 to 49 per cent in 1891–5 and 28 per cent in 1921–5.[45] The income tax was reintroduced in 1886, salt duties were increased in 1888 and import duties imposed in 1894.[46] These taxes laid the basis for an expansion in the Indian state, but also caused problems. The imposition of the income tax, without offering political representation, would cause problems: it contradicted the thrust of Gladstonian rhetoric that payment of the tax was linked to political responsibility. The salt duties were unpopular, a tax on a necessity which could be exploited by nationalists. The solution preferred by the government in India was to impose import duties, which could be justified as protecting Indian businesses against British competition, and would limit the need for other, less popular, internal taxes. But the government in Britain had other considerations in mind. Import duties – especially on cotton goods – would hit British exporters, and above all Lancashire. The cotton interest was well organised and vocal, and the parliamentary constituencies in Lancashire were crucial in winning elections in the late nineteenth and early twentieth centuries. The secretary of state for India needed to strike a balance between electoral considerations at home and the desire of the government in India to impose import duties.[47] The government in India appealed for 'liberal treatment' of the 'home charges', arguing that India was bearing an undue share of the costs of the army for the empire as a whole. Although the Royal Commission on the Administration of the Expenditure of India was not convinced by these pleas, there were clear signs that a limit to fiscal extraction was reached.[48] After about 1880, the situation

---

[44] Robb, *Ancient Rights and Future Comfort*, p. 68.

[45] Calculated from B. B. Misra, *The Administrative History of India, 1834–1947: General Administration* (Bombay, 1970), pp. 364–5 quoted in Robb, *Ancient Right and Future Comfort*, p. 68 n. 89.

[46] PP 1900 XXIX, *Final Report of the Royal Commission on the Administration of the Expenditure of India*, pp. 594–7.

[47] On import duties and cotton, see I. Klein, 'English free traders and Indian tariffs, 1874–96', *Modern Asian Studies* 5 (1971), 251–71; and for the postwar outcome when the balance shifted from Lancashire to India, C. Dewey, 'The end of the imperialism of free trade: the eclipse of the Lancashire lobby and the concession of fiscal autonomy to India', in C. Dewey and A. G. Hopkins (eds.), *The Imperial Impact: Studies in the Economic History of Africa and India* (London, 1978), pp. 35–67.

[48] PP 1900 XXIX, *Final Report of the Royal Commission on the Administration of the Expenditure of India*, pp. 589–600, 678–85, 691.

of the early and mid-Victorian period was reversed. Compliance and trust in the fiscal constitution was strengthened at home and it was easier to extract revenues within Britain; at the same time, resistance increased in the colonies and the power to tax in India declined. As Peter Robb has remarked, 'resistance to British rule was fueled by attempts to extend the amounts and scope of taxation'. The incidence of taxation rose, less for military purposes and more for active intervention in social change and economic development. In redefining the boundaries of state action, the British government in India was also encouraging nationalist demands for participation.[49]

India was the most significant part of the empire, both in terms of potential revenue and costs. In other colonies, taxation resembled the fiscal system of eighteenth-century Britain in raising revenues from readily identifiable goods and commodities. In Jamaica, for example, customs duties accounted for 55.5 per cent of revenue in 1869. The internal revenues consisted of an excise duty on rum (16.6 per cent) and spirit licences (2.3 per cent); the other major sources of revenue were a tax on horses, asses, wheels and livestock (6.1 per cent), a duty on houses (4.0 per cent), trade licences (1.6 per cent) and quit rents or land tax for (1.9 per cent).[50] The limits of taxation were clear in Jamaica, with the revolt of 1865 and its brutal suppression by Governor Eyre.[51] Taxation in Britain could be portrayed as equitable and balanced; in Jamaica, it still had more in common with the fiscal regime challenged within Britain by the radicals and Chartists.

In the later nineteenth century, the British empire expanded in Africa, with a new set of fiscal concerns. In Jamaica, the government could tax export commodities such as sugar and rum; in many African countries, external trade was minimal and confined to certain districts so that there was less scope for taxation of imports and exports. The difficulties are apparent from the 'hut tax' revolt in Sierra Leone in 1898 which again turned on the creation of local allies and devolved systems of authority. Taxation was not unknown, for chiefs imposed levies. The problem was that the hut tax was an additional imposition rather than a substitute, and it did not incorporate the existing authority of the chiefs who felt their power was threatened. The governor defended the tax on the

[49] Robb, *Ancient Rights and Future Comfort*, p. 70.
[50] PP 1871 XLVIII, *Return of all taxes and imposts from which the revenues of the several colonies of the British empire are raised, together with the gross amount yielded by each tax or impost*, pp. 716–20, for Jamaica.
[51] B. A. Knox, 'The British government and the Governor Eyre controversy, 1865–75', *Historical Journal* 19 (1976), 877–900, and C. Hall, 'Competing masculinities: Thomas Carlyle, John Stuart Mill and the case of Governor Eyre', in her *White, Male and Middle Class: Explorations in Feminism and History* (Cambridge, 1992), pp. 255–95.

general principle of 'the right of the Government to compel the governed to contribute towards the support of the Government which ensures them the security of life and prosperity, just laws and all the other benefits of the most advanced civilisation'.[52] Similarly, the introduction of a poll tax in Natal in 1905 contributed to the revolt of the Zulus in 1906. As the criminal magistrate in Durban realised, the Zulu opposed the tax because it was 'calculated to disturb their social system'.[53] The outcome in South Africa was the imposition of white dominance by military power; in west Africa, without a settler population, a different solution was needed.

The answer, it seemed, was to incorporate the chiefs into the system of British rule rather than to undermine their authority. The approach was most clearly stated by Frederick Lugard* who argued that direct taxation made more sense in west Africa, not least for the moral effects on the population: the need to pay taxes would encourage economic development rather than warfare, and it would also permit the abolition of slavery and forced labour. Direct taxation was therefore an agency of civilisation. However, the situation differed between areas of west Africa. In some districts, mainly Islamic areas, there were already native rulers or emirs who could collect the taxes in accordance with previous custom, and the revenues would then be shared with them as rulers and judges. Such a strategy meant that a considerable part of the taxes remained in the hands of the local elites to provide the revenue for 'native administration', a form of delegated authority or indirect rule. In other cases, native rulers were absent or weak and taxes had not previously existed. Here, Lugard proposed to create a new form of authority based on village heads or chiefs paid salaries out of the revenue they collected. In these cases, the revenue would be paid over to the government rather than to 'native treasuries' as was the practice in the more highly organised native administrations. By these means, it was hoped to replace forced labour and slavery as the way of supporting rulers who would now earn their incomes by an active role in administration; the former slaves would pay taxes to the

[52] PRO, CO/267/438, governor's confidential despatch of 28 May 1898, governor's secret despatch to the secretary of state, 28 May 1898, cited in L. Denzer and M. Crowder, 'Bai Bureh and the Sierra Leone hut tax war of 1898', in R. I. Rotberg and A. A. Mazrui (eds.), *Protest and Power in Black Africa* ((New York, 1970), p. 177.

[53] S. Marks, 'The Zulu disturbances in Natal', in Rotberg and Mazrui (eds.), *Protest and Power*, p. 224.

* Frederick John Dealtry Lugard (1858–1945) pursued an army career in India and Africa, before moving into colonial administration as high commissioner of north Nigeria from 1900 to 1906 and governor of Hong Kong from 1907 to 1912. He returned to Nigeria, as governor of both north and south, from 1914 to 1919, where he developed indirect rule based on native institutions. (*DNB, 1941–50*, ed. L. G. Wickham Legge and E. T. Williams (London, 1959), pp. 532–7.)

state in return for their freedom. As Lugard put it,

> The object in view is to retain as far as possible the ancient tribute as sanctioned by Native law and customs, and to preserve the individuality of the institutions of the country; to utilise the Native machinery for the purpose; and to introduce some uniformity and equality in the incidence of taxation in the different provinces. The result it aims at is to emancipate the people from indolence on the one hand and forced service on the other, and to raise them to a plane of greater communal and individual responsibility.

Taxation was therefore part of a strategy to recreate indigenous social systems and political authority through a system of assessing, collecting and spending taxes. It would link the local elites with British rule, and replace the existing system of slave raiding, forced labour and impositions.[54]

The result was a contest over the allocation of revenue. The 'native treasuries' retained half of the proceeds of direct taxes and handed the remainder to the British administration, so creating an impression that the revenue belonged to the emirs who were simply paying a tribute to the government for protection. Not all British administrators accepted this proposition. Local officials and provincial lieutenant-governors usually supported strong native administration, but the governor and the Colonial Office in London were more eager to secure greater control over the amount allocated to the localities. This contest ebbed and flowed in the early twentieth century, and was linked with another debate over the form of tax in previously untaxed districts. Should it be a tax on income with an individual assessment and collection in the hands of local chiefs? This so-called emir's tax would entrench indirect rule and weaken the centre. Or should it be a simple poll tax, collected by the government – a so-called king's tax which gave more power to the central administration? The emir's tax had the virtue of creating native administrations as a means of authority, but reduced the ability of the British authorities to secure revenue. The king's tax might provide the British government with more control over revenues, at the expense of anti-tax revolts.[55] In west Africa, as in India, the British authorities were caught in a difficult balancing

54 F. J. D. Lugard, *Political Memoranda: Revision of Instructions to Political Officers on Subjects Chiefly Political and Administrative*, 1913–18 (3rd edn, reprinted London, 1970), 'Memorandum No. 5: Taxation', pp. 163–215. This memorandum was originally issued in 1905, and revised in 1917. In Nyasaland, taxation of Africans fluctuated between a poll tax, hut tax and combination of the two. Taxation was seen as a way of creating a workforce: in 1901, the rate was increased with the proviso that it would be halved on proof of a month's paid employment with a European: see S. Roberts, 'The direct taxation of Africans in the Nyasaland protectorate, 1892–1939: some determinants of revenue policy', *British Tax Review* (1967).

55 J. White, *Central Administration in Nigeria, 1914–1948: The Problem of Polarity* (Dublin and London, 1981).

act between a desire to create local systems of authority which implied handling control of revenues to local elites, and a wish to secure revenue to meet the costs of imperial rule from London. Despite the concerns of the government in London to ensure that the colonies paid for defence, the imperatives of securing local support for imperial rule imposed strict limits. After all, there was little to be gained by extracting more taxes at the expense of unrest and hence increased costs of military intervention.

The development of taxation for the central state in Britain was part of a triangular relationship. The decline of the fiscal-military state in the early and mid-Victorian periods was achieved, in part, by passing costs both to local government within Britain *and* to the colonies. In a sense, the policy adopted by Mayo within India was at one with the policies within Britain. By ensuring that the costs of government fell on the localities, on Birmingham or Bihar, financial rectitude could be established by making sure that the beneficiaries of expenditure also paid the costs. By the end of the nineteenth century, the process of delegation both to the localities within Britain and to the colonies was starting to falter. As we shall see in chapter 8, the mounting costs of local government in Britain led to a demand for more assistance from the centre. Similarly, concerns for political stability and peace in the colonies created limits to the transfer of tax revenues to the metropole; there was a greater incentive to use taxation to encourage economic development within the colonies and to give more power to local elites. The constraints on the British fiscal state would therefore be challenged, and the limits of the civilian-military state created in the nineteenth century were being reached.

6 'The sublime rule of proportion': ability to pay and the social structure, 1842–1906

> ... the ideal of an equitable tax has as many shapes as Proteus.
>
> G. W. Hemming, *A Just Income Tax How Possible*
> (London, 1852), p. 4

> The subjects of every state ought to contribute towards the support of the government, as nearly as possible, in proportion to their respective abilities; that is, in proportion to the revenue which they respectively enjoy under the protection of the state. The expence of government to the individuals of a great nation, is like the expence of management to the joint tenants of a great estate, who are all obliged to contribute in proportion to their respective interests in the estate.
>
> Adam Smith's first maxim of taxation,
> *An Inquiry into the Nature and Causes of the Wealth of Nations*,
> ed. R. H. Campbell, A. S. Skinner and W. B. Todd
> (2 vols., Oxford, 1976), vol. II, viib, p. 825

> The income of every man employed in industry, and in the accumulation of property, ought to be untaxed; but on the other hand ... all property such as land, houses, or property fixed, capital, testable, or moveable, formed a fit subject for taxation. The injury to the community would be less, by confining the tax to the product of capital, and not to the profits of industry.
>
> Joseph Hume, opposing the reintroduction of the income tax,
> *Parliamentary Debates*, 3rd ser., vol. 62,
> 25 Apr. 1842, cols. 1082–3

> ... it is desirable in a high degree, when it can be effected, to connect the possession of the franchise with the payment in taxes.
>
> W. E. Gladstone, 1859, quoted in H. C. G. Matthew,
> *Gladstone, 1809–1898* (Oxford, 1997), p. 127

> ... taxation ought to involve equality of sacrifice, and I do not see how this result is to be obtained except by some form of graduated taxation – that is, taxation which is proportionate to the superfluities of the taxpayer.
>
> C. W. Boyd (ed.), *Mr Chamberlain's Speeches*,
> vol. I (London, 1914), 'The radical programme',
> speech delivered at Warrington, 8 Sept. 1885, p. 193

At the basis of all tax systems are assumptions about how best to measure the capacity of the taxpayer to bear the demands of the state for
revenue. Obviously, revenue can only be extracted where there is a surplus above mere subsistence; and the rate of extraction should not be
increased to such an extent that the yield starts to decline. As we noted
earlier in the discussion of the national debt, classical economists accepted
that taxation might create a stimulus to additional effort up to a certain
point when it gave way to 'shock'. However, any assessment of what
'capacity' might entail, and at what point stimulus might become shock,
involved a wide range of social and political calculations and assumptions which would be influenced by shifts in the nature of the economy,
in social structure, in political ideology and in the franchise. Fiscal history, as Joseph Schumpeter remarked in the difficult circumstances at the
end of the First World War, provides an insight into 'the laws of social
being and becoming and into the driving forces of the fate of nations',
both as an agent of change and, even more, for its 'symptomatic significance (in so far as everything that happens has its fiscal reflection)'. As he
remarked,

That men should contribute to the expenses of the State according to their 'ability'
is accepted by every one as the essence of fairness, and 'ability to pay' has long
been the first principle, indeed the very catch-word, of its subject ... But what
that phrase shall be taken to mean at the practical stage where the relative tax
burdens of two individuals must be settled, seems even further from common
acceptance to-day than it has been during the past twenty years.[1]

Taxation entailed conflicting claims on the surplus of society. As
Schumpeter pointed out, 'The kind and level of taxes are determined by
the social structure, but once taxes exist they become a handle, as it
were, which social powers can grip in order to change this structure.'[2]
Debates over tax policy therefore expose tensions and debates over the
form that society should take. Should taxes on 'active' entrepreneurs be
reduced and taxes on income from accumulated wealth or land be increased? Should savings for retirement and support of dependants, or
gifts to charity, be encouraged? Should individuals be taxed or did ability
depend on family responsibilities and incomes? Political parties did not
simply represent the fiscal priorities of various pre-existing social groups,
for these interests and identities were constructed through a rhetorical
process and shaped by the language of politics. Fiscal policy defined as

---

[1] Schumpeter, 'The crisis of the tax state', p. 7.
[2] Schumpeter, 'The crisis of the tax state', p. 17; see also R. Goldschied, 'Sociological
approach to the problems of public finance', in R. A. Musgrave and A. T. Peacock
(eds.), *Classics in the Theory of Public Finance* (London, 1967), pp. 202–13.

well as expressed identities. Further, the conflicting rhetorical construction of identities was linked with a debate over the extent to which the existing social structure was 'natural' or pathological and in need of correction. Should taxation remove money for the government and leave the social structure unchanged; or should it remove money in order to alter the social structure, for reasons of social equity or economic efficiency? Of course, there was also a fear that an attempt to alter the social structure might actually harm the economy, by removing incentives and depressing savings by the rich. Such issues were obviously central to political debate, and also to economic theory.

Economists and taxation

Economists played a leading role in debates over the incidence of taxation, grappling with the question of the claims of the government on income. The relationship between developments in economic theory and in policy are complex, and it is by no means the case that changes in economic thought had a simple expression in the fiscal system. However, leading civil servants did read economics, and there was a constant interchange of ideas and expertise. The emergence of statistics and their utilisation by economists depended on the collection of data by the government, not least from the tax system. The growth of economic knowledge was closely associated with the state, and the line between the emerging profession of economics and public service was more permeable than some historians have assumed. At the very least, economics could provide a justification for policies adopted for other reasons. The state might need to collect more revenue to fund war or social reform; or politicians might wish to alter the tax system for cynical electoral advantage, in response to pressure from particular groups in society, or to resolve social and economic problems. The language of economics could provide *post hoc* justification and authority. Above all, the debates over taxation referred to economists, using their language and concepts while often failing to grasp the logic of their argument, and frequently reworking the terms. The issue, therefore, is how the ideas of political economy enter into a more general political culture.[3]

A leading concept in the mid-nineteenth century was 'proportionality', the notion that each taxpayer paid the same proportion of income

---

[3] The current work of Adam Tooze will provide a detailed account of these issues; I am grateful to him for conversations on these points. Frank Trentmann's analysis of free trade provides a model of the way economic ideas penetrate political discourse and culture. On the relation between the state and economic knowledge, see the comments in Furner and Supple, 'Ideas, institutions, and state', pp. 3–39.

to the state in return for protection and security. This was Adam Smith's first maxim of taxation, but it was open to a number of different interpretations. The most obvious meaning was that all taxpayers should pay the same *share* of their income to the state. The analogy was with the tenants of an agricultural estate. A tenant with a quarter interest in an estate, worth say £2,000, should pay a quarter of the costs of management, say £200. A tenant with a half share worth £4,000 would pay half the costs of management, say £400. Both were paying 10 per cent of their income. Similarly, an artisan with an income of £100 and a wealthy industrialist with an income of £1,000 should both pay the same proportion of their incomes to the state for the costs of government. This 'proportionality' might be achieved by a mixture of taxes with different incidences, so that the artisan would be taxed through his beer and tea; these commodities would form a much smaller proportion of the income of a wealthy industrialist who would also pay income tax and death duties. The important point was to ensure that the tax system *as a whole* fell proportionately on all levels and forms of income so that it was neutral and left the social structure as it was found. This may be termed the 'benefit approach' or *quid pro quo* principle, based on the notion of a social contract: the taxpayer pays for the benefit received from the state and the distribution of income and wealth is taken as given.[4]

Smith's maxim could also be read as supporting a second approach, of 'ability to pay' which could be measured in a number of ways with different assumptions and implications.[5] It could be simply a refinement of proportionality. Thus income from accumulated capital could have a greater ability to pay, on the grounds that it offered a steady income regardless of the risks of trade or personal circumstances, and the underlying asset survived for dependants and heirs. By contrast, income from trade and professions was disrupted by ill-health or economic depression, and it disappeared at death. It was therefore necessary to save in order to provide for dependants. On this view, proportionality was not defined by identical *gross* incomes, and a more sophisticated measure of

---

[4] O'Brien, *Classical Economists*, p. 241. For fuller discussions of benefit approach, see examples of this approach in E. R. A. Seligman, *Progressive Taxation in Theory and Practice* (2nd edn, Princeton, 1908), chapter 2, and historical appendices I and II on how the benefit approach could lead to both proportional and non-proportional taxation; and R. A. Musgrave, *The Theory of Public Finance* (New York, 1959), chapter 4.

[5] O'Brien, *Classical Economists*, p. 241. O'Brien places Bentham and David Hume in the 'benefit' school and Mill and McCulloch into the ability school. See also Seligman, *Progressive Taxation*, chapter 3, on the 'faculty theory' and historical appendices III, IV and V on how it might lead to proportional, degressive or progressive taxation; and Musgrave, *Theory of Public Finance*, chapter 5, on the 'ability to pay' approach.

proportionality should differentiate between 'spontaneous' income and 'industrious' or 'precarious' income. Such an approach did not necessarily attempt to use taxation to change the social structure, but simply sought to take account of differences between sources of income in order to ensure that the real burden of taxation was proportionate on precarious and spontaneous incomes. The issue of differentiation of tax on *forms* of income was the most contentious area of fiscal debate in the mid-nineteenth century, and Gladstone feared that it would set class against class – industrialists versus landowners or producers versus *rentiers*. Taxation could therefore become a source of tension rather than a social contract and a source of stability. As we have seen, one of Gladstone's achievements was to marginalise the demand for differentiation in the 1860s for a generation, until it reappeared as an important theme in the policy of the Liberal government of 1906.

Differentiation could also be justified as a means of encouraging growth by removing any penalty against 'active' capital and enterprise. This point could be generalised, to argue that 'ability' to bear taxation should reflect, above all, the impact on growth. J. R. McCulloch stressed the need to adjust taxes between sectors of the economy in order to encourage growth. Indeed, debates over taxation until the end of the nineteenth century were more concerned with the intersectoral incidence of taxation between industry and agriculture or producers and *rentiers* than with interpersonal incidence of taxation for individual welfare. Although high indirect taxes in the second quarter of the nineteenth century were regressive, much of the debate was expressed in sectoral terms, of the protection of agriculture or monopolists at the expense of productive workers and industry. In the mid-Victorian period, the concern for balancing the tax system between sectors, and the marked reduction in indirect taxes, meant that interest in the interpersonal incidence of taxation was marginalised. In the early nineteenth century, the high level of indirect taxes could be criticised for skewing the incidence of taxes between sectors of the economy; at the same time, as a secondary issue, it could express a lack of balance between rich and poor. By the late nineteenth century, indirect taxes were much lower and could be interpreted as a reasonable payment for the benefits offered by the state. Indeed, the reformed system of indirect taxes meant that they were often seen as 'voluntary'. McCulloch argued that the individual taxpayer could make a personal decision to purchase taxed commodities, in effect assessing his own ability to pay by reduced consumption. Many Liberals accepted the same point, on the grounds that taxed commodities such as beer and tobacco were not necessities and might even be harmful narcotics. Of course, such a view did not take account of the preferences of consumers and whether they wished to reduce their consumption of taxed commodities and purchase a different selection of goods.[6]

The approach of McCulloch did not consider whether the rich had a greater ability to pay than the poor, and concern for the interpersonal incidence of taxation only emerged as a major issue at the end of the nineteenth century. The limits of the mid-Victorian position were drawn by John Stuart Mill. He rejected the notion of 'benefit' on the grounds that the poor actually needed *more* protection – an argument justifying regressive taxation which Mill felt was unacceptable on other grounds. In his view, government was a concern for all, and it was simply not possible to ask who received more or less benefit. Everyone should pay compulsory taxes for benefits received by all members of society, in the same way that voluntary subscriptions were paid to an association in which all the members had an interest. In a voluntary body, 'all are thought to have done their part fairly when each has contributed according to his means, that is has made an equal sacrifice for the common object; in like manner should this be the principle of compulsory contributions'. Benefit was therefore irrelevant and Mill defined Smith's first maxim as 'equality of sacrifice'. Taxation 'should be made to bear as nearly as possible with the same pressure upon all'. However, Mill did not accept that equality of sacrifice implied a graduated income tax. He was only willing to admit that taxes should not affect the income needed for the 'necessaries of life'. Thus a tax of £5 from an income of £50 would affect the ability to buy necessities, whereas a tax of £1,000 on an income of £10,000 might not. This tax of 10 per cent was not equal in its sacrifice, and the solution was to remove taxes from the basic income 'needful for life, health, and immunity from bodily pain'. In order to fulfil this principle he was willing to make a modest change to the operation of the income tax. As it stood, the *entire* income was liable to tax once the exemption limit of £150 was passed. Thus an income of £149 paid no tax, but £150 paid tax on the entire amount (£4 7s 6d). Mill argued that an income of £151 should pay tax on £1. As a general principle, equality of taxation in proportion to means implied that tax should only be levied on the excess above expenditure on 'necessities' or subsistence income, with allowances for both small and precarious incomes:

The rule of equality and of fair proportion seems to me to be that people should be taxed in an equal ratio on their superfluities; necessaries being untaxed, and

---

[6] O'Brien, *Classical Economists*, p. 241 and O'Brien, *McCulloch*, pp. 233–5. On the Liberal argument that indirect taxes were 'voluntary' by the last quarter of the nineteenth century, see below p. 222.

surplus paying in all cases an equal percentage. This satisfies entirely the small amount of justice that there is in the theory of a graduated income tax, which appears to me to be otherwise an entirely unjust mode of taxation, and in fact, a graduated robbery. What gives it plausibility is the fact, that at present the lowest incomes which are taxed at all are overtaxed.[7]

Mill was not prepared to go further towards a graduated income tax. He did not accept that the income of £10,000 should bear a higher rate than 10 per cent, for this 'is to lay a tax on industry and economy; to impose a penalty on people for having worked harder and saved more than their neighbours'. A graduated taxation of *income* would therefore harm growth and enterprise; taxation of *inherited wealth* was a different matter. As he put it, 'impartiality between competitors would consist in endeavouring that they should all start fair, and not in hanging a weight upon the swift to diminish the distance between them and the slow'. Further, he argued that the luxuries consumed by the poor should pay indirect taxes. Exemption from taxes only covered necessaries, and any money diverted to 'indulgences' should pay to the expenses of the state.[8] Mill was therefore taking a restricted view of the welfare implications of taxation, relying on a simple distinction between necessaries and indulgences.

The position adopted by McCulloch and Mill was overturned by the marginal revolution in economics at the end of the nineteenth century. Alfred Marshall's *Principles* stressed the marginal costs of producing another unit of output, and the marginal satisfaction to be derived from consuming it. In this approach, an additional pound did not produce the same satisfaction for someone in receipt of an income of £1,000 as for someone in receipt of an income of £100. The meaning of equality of sacrifice was more complicated than in the past, as writers at the end of the nineteenth century entered into confused discussion of what their predecessors meant by the words equal or proportionate, and how this should be rephrased in the new vocabulary of marginalism. Did equal sacrifice mean each taxpayer should surrender the same proportion of their total utility? That is, the aim should not be to take 10 per cent from all income levels (£5 from an income of £500 and £10 from an income of £1,000), but

---

[7] See Mill's evidence to PP 1852 IX, *Second Report from the Select Committee on the Income and Property Tax*, Qq. 5222–69, 5277–447, and PP 1861 VII, *Report from the Select Committee on Income and Property Tax*, Qq. 3539–44, 3567, 3578–97; J. S. Mill, *Principles of Political Economy*, ed, W. J. Ashley (London, 1909), pp. 804–9. The imposition of income tax on the entire income once it passed the threshold was a source of irritation; employers might opt to pay their staff just below the threshold, which the Inland Revenue (unsuccessfully) tried to define as evasion. See PP 1852 IX, *First Report from the Select Committee on the Income and Property Tax*, Qq. 3019, 3020, 3235.

[8] Mill, *Principles*, ed. Ashley, pp. 804–9; PP 1861 VII, *Report from the Select Committee on Income and Property Tax*, Qq. 3581–97; O'Brien, *Classical Economists*, pp. 241–2, 252.

rather to extract the same proportion of happiness or satisfaction, which varied according to income. Or did it mean an equal *marginal* sacrifice in order to produce minimum disutility? By this definition, the aim was to calculate the additional satisfaction produced by the final increment of income, and to ensure that the rate of taxation on that income imposed the same loss of utility or satisfaction. Thus the final £10 of income for someone earning £500 might produce three times as much satisfaction as the final £10 for someone earning £1,000, so that the tax rate could be three times as high on the larger income with the same marginal disutility. Of course, the maxims of Smith could be reinterpreted to justify new definitions of equity, providing intellectual authority and status, and an impression of continuity with cherished principles deeply rooted in British political culture.[9]

F. Y. Edgeworth,[*] the professor of political economy at Oxford, embarked on a complex and even convoluted and elusive project of using marginal theory to create a 'pure theory of taxation'. He started from a 'hedonistic' principle of taxation, that is the sacrifice of happiness by the taxpayer, and he assumed that the test of government action in taxation was the 'greatest-happiness principle'. This approach derived from the utilitarian philosopher Jeremy Bentham[†] and, in a sense, the marginal revolution in economics involved a reworking of Bentham's concern with the means of creating the greatest sum-total of happiness in society. The pursuit of his principle led Bentham to argue for equality; Edgeworth would not go so far. He followed Henry Sidgwick[‡] in his

---

[9] See the discussion in F. Y. Edgeworth, 'Minimum sacrifice versus equal sacrifice', in his *Papers Relating to Political Economy*, vol. II (London, 1925), pp. 234–42 (reprinted from 'The subjective element in the first principles of taxation', *Quarterly Journal of Economics* 24 (1910), 459–70), and 'The pure theory of taxation', pp. 107, 115–16 (reprinted from *Economic Journal* 7 (1897), 46–70, 226–38, 550–71); and Seligman, *Progressive Taxation*, pp. 213–5.

[*] Francis Ysidro Edgeworth (1845–1926) was the step-nephew of Maria Edgeworth, the novelist. He was educated at Oxford, and became professor of political economy at King's College, London, in 1888 and then Drummond professor of political economy at Oxford from 1891 to 1922. He was editor, chairman of the editorial board and joint editor of the *Economic Journal* from 1891 to 1926. He was mathematical in his approach, publishing *Mathematical Physics* in 1881. (*DNB, 1922–30*, ed. Weaver, pp. 284–5.)

[†] Jeremy Bentham (1748–1832) was educated at Westminster School and Queen's College, Oxford; he was called to the bar but devoted most of his time to writing on politics and jurisprudence. *Fragments on Government* appeared in 1776 and *Introduction to Principles of Morals and Legislation* in 1780, and he wrote extensively on poor laws, prison reform, education and parliamentary reform. He was involved in establishing the *Westminster Review* in 1823. He was best known for his principle of the 'greatest happiness of the greatest number' or utilitarianism. (*DNB*, vol. IV, ed. L. Stephen (London, 1885), pp. 268–80.)

[‡] Henry Sidgwick (1838–1900) was educated at Rugby and Trinity, Cambridge, where he became a fellow in 1859. He was appointed to a lectureship in philosophy in 1869

concern (similar to Malthus's criticism of the old poor law) that those who gained from redistribution of income might simply take more leisure or have more children, so that there was less to distribute and the average income would support a larger population. He also accepted Mill's fear that equality was a threat to liberty and might not be

> consistent with that multiform development of human nature, those manifold unlikenesses, that diversity of tastes and talents, and variety of intellectual points of view, which not only form a great part of the interest of human life, but by bringing intellects into stimulating collision, and by presenting to each innumerable notions that he would not have conceived of himself, are the mainspring of mental and moral progression.

Edgeworth agreed with Mill and Sidgwick that 'dull equality' would threaten liberty and knowledge, which were maintained by the rich and leisured. And people had different natures and different capacities, so that equality of incomes would lead to an *unequal* distribution of happiness. The pursuit of equality by means of taxation might remove incentives to saving and enterprise above a certain level of income, so limiting the growth of the community's wealth. This might be offset by an increase in the savings of the poor, by 'investment of capital in persons by way of education', and an increase in the efficiency of the poor. As a result, Edgeworth claimed to have returned to the position of Mill, that equality had to be tempered by common sense – an argument for 'the limitation of inheritances and the taxation of unearned increments'. In reality, Edgeworth went beyond Mill to accept a progressive income tax. He did not accept equal marginal sacrifice was practicable, for it was impossible to know the exact relationship between an increase in income and a decrease in satisfaction, or the speed with which gratifications were satiated. Further, the benefits of general public expenditure could not be allocated to individuals in order to measure the satisfaction derived from their payment of taxes. The principle of 'minimum sacrifice' avoided the problem of incomplete information. Edgeworth suggested collecting all taxes from the small number of incomes with the lowest final utility. This did not require a precise measure of the relationship between resources and satisfaction, beyond the general proposition that utility did not increase proportionately to means. In other words, there would be less loss of satisfaction to society as a whole by taking all taxes from millionaires with very low marginal utility from their final *tranche* of income than by taking money from a larger number of smaller incomes which would

and to the chair in 1883 which he held to 1900. He supported women's education at Cambridge, and his wife became president of Newnham College. (*DNB, Supplement,* vol. III, ed. Lee, pp. 342–5.)

impose taxes on people with a higher marginal utility from their final *tranche* of income. The result would not be complete equality, but a *levelling* of the higher incomes which would lead to the minimum aggregate sacrifice. As he explained to the Royal Commission on Local Taxation in 1899, in allocating taxation 'the *prima facie* best distribution is that the whole amount should be paid by the wealthiest citizens. The incomes above a certain level should all be reduced to that level; the incomes below that level should be untaxed, the level being determined by the amount which it is required to raise.' This levelling principle should be moderated by prudence, to avoid driving capital out of the country, or 'awakening the predatory instincts of the poor'.[10]

The appearance of Edgeworth's 'pure theory' in 1897 came after the introduction of graduated death duties in 1894, and the conversion of Harcourt to a progressive income tax which was blocked at that time by administrative obstacles. The importance of Edgeworth (and other economists) was less in initiating change in fiscal policy than in removing the intellectual authority of the opponents of progression. The process continued with the appearance of A. C. Pigou's* *Wealth and Welfare* in 1912, the first attempt to apply Marshall's marginalism to welfare economics. Pigou defined economic welfare as the satisfaction connected

---

[10] Edgeworth, 'The pure theory of taxation', in *Papers Relating to Political Economy*, vol. II, pp. 100–18; he cited Mill, *Principles*, Book II, chapter 1, section 3 (at p. 211 of the Ashley edition), and H. Sidgwick, *Principles of Political Economy* (2nd edn., London, 1887), chapter 7, on 'economic distribution'. Sidgwick argued that a more equal distribution of wealth would *prima facie* increase happiness, but that it was necessary to allow for loss through increased idleness, decreased saving, lessened efficiency of capital, pressure of population and checks to the growth of culture. It was impossible to dispense, as Communists proposed, with individualistic stimulus, but socialism was not open to the same objection, and some progress in that direction by a gradual and judicious extension of government was compatible with sound economic theory. Bentham's case for equality is in his *Constitutional Code for the Use of All Nations and All Governments Professing Liberal Opinions* (London, 1830), Book I, chapter iii, sec. v. For Edgeworth's comments to the Royal Commission on Local Taxation, see 'Answers to questions put by the local taxation committee', in *Papers Relating to Political Economy*, vol. II, pp. 130–1. These reflections of Edgeworth are significant for the development of utilitarian thinking from Bentham to Sidgwick. As Robert Skidelsky argues, Sidgwick attempted to create a secular philosophy in place of theology, keeping economics as part of ethics; he was a Benthamite, arguing that the crucial problem was the relationship between rational egoism (pursuit of individual happiness) and rational benevolence (pursuit of universal happiness). The problem was how to get people to pursue the second. He failed in his attempt to find an answer, but he 'made Cambridge Benthamite in its social reasoning'. Marshall detached economics from ethics, but still followed the 'hedonistic calculus'. See R. Skidelsky, *John Maynard Keynes*, vol. I, *Hopes Betrayed, 1883–1920* (London, 1983), chapter 2.

* Arthur Cecil Pigou (1877–59) was educated at Harrow and King's College, Cambridge, where he read history and moral sciences. He became a fellow of King's in 1902 and succeeded Marshall as professor of economics in 1908, holding the post to 1943. (*DNB*, *1951–1960* ed. E. T. Wilson and H. M. Palmer (London, 1971), pp. 814–17).

with earning and spending the national dividend. His concern was with
the creation of the largest possible national dividend, which would be
reduced if the marginal net product of resources was unequal between
different uses. The question was: how could resources be allocated to ensure the desirable outcome of an equal marginal net product in all uses?
The solution was, in part, to control monopolies and to remove impediments to mobility of labour and capital. But another possibility was to
transfer resources from the rich to the poor. The result would be an increase in the commodities consumed by the poor, at the expense of those
consumed by the rich and by machines. Pigou felt that a loss of income
by the rich would leave their efficiency virtually unchanged, whereas an
increase in consumption by the poor would produce a higher rate of return – and the same would apply compared with the use of marginal
resources in machinery, so long as the poor invested in themselves in a
competent manner. Here was the problem: Pigou felt that they could not
be trusted, and should therefore be under control and direction. Further, resources would not produce a higher rate of return if transferred
to 'defective' or elderly members of society, and should be concentrated
on two categories: normal men in middle life to cover sickness and unemployment; and above all, the minds and bodies of 'sound' children.[11]
Such an approach did not consider the marginal satisfaction of individuals and instead concentrated on their efficiency – a line of argument which
connected with the concerns for Britain's competitiveness and with the
debates over 'eugenics' and the character of the British race.

These economists were not arguing for equality of income and wished
to contain 'predatory instincts' and socialist ambitions. Their definition
of fiscal justice might still assume that the existing distribution of property
and income only needed to be changed to a modest extent rather than to
alter the structure of society in any fundamental way. Edgeworth's starting point was the amount of revenue needed by the government, which
was still around 10 per cent: he simply wished to allocate this amount
with the minimum sacrifice, and did not assume a marked increase in
spending and taxation. Indeed, it could be argued that higher marginal
tax rates simply removed the distortions created by a single flat rate of
tax which imposed an unequal sacrifice on different sources and levels
of income. Nevertheless, the shift in economic theory did alter the terms
of debate over taxation, providing intellectual authority for progressive
taxation as a prudent measure to increase the sum total of happiness and
the size of the 'national dividend'. Economic ideas provided a large part
of the meanings and vocabulary of political debate, and limited possible

[11] A. C. Pigou, *Wealth and Welfare* (London, 1912), especially chapter 9.

alternatives.[12] The point is apparent in 1909, when opponents of Lloyd George's 'people's budget' turned to Alfred Marshall to supply them with intellectual authority – which was not forthcoming. He refused to denounce the budget as socialist, as a device to remove responsibility from individuals and pass it to the state. Instead, Marshall believed that cautious redistribution from poor to rich would be beneficial. 'For poverty crushes character: and though the earning of great wealth generally strengthens character, the spending of it by those who have not earned it, whether men or women, is not nearly an unmixed good.' Spending by the rich tended to lower their character; and he felt that a small check to the growth of their capital would merely lessen the trend to export capital to other countries. Indeed, state spending might be beneficial, so long as it was not used for 'foolish ostentatious expenditure' as by private persons. 'The notion that the investment of funds in the education of the workers, in sanitation, in providing open air play for all children etc tends to diminish "capital" is abhorrent to me.' As Marshall pointed out to Helen Bosanquet in 1902, a leading figure in the Charity Organisation Society and a member of the Royal Commission on the Poor Laws,

the high consumption of the rich seems to me excessive and to necessitate in effect a meagre life on the part of others... Is the share of the total price of products which goes to manual labour as large as is compatible with a wholesome and 'free' state of society? Could we by taking thought get the work of our great captains of industry and financiers done with rather less of their present huge gains?

The way Marshall posed these questions indicated that the 'context for refutation' had changed, so that the onus rested on opponents of redistribution to indicate that it would harm freedom and efficiency.[13]

Of course, debates over the 'fair' incidence of taxation extended beyond formal economics to moral definitions of luxuries or necessaries, of deserved and undeserved incomes or wealth, of producers and parasites. The terms and arguments of economists were diffused and popularised in a much less systematic way, entering into political culture through specific debates and locales which affected the rhetoric adopted by the participants. The rest of the chapter considers some of the contexts for discussion of the burden of taxation – and one place to start is the connection with the franchise and parliamentary reform.

[12] See Furner and Supple, 'Ideas, institutions, and state', p. 15.
[13] Marshall's views are in J. K. Whitaker (ed.), *The Correspondence of Alfred Marshall, Economist*, vol. III: *Towards the Close, 1903–1924* (Cambridge, 1996), pp. 231–4, and A. C. Pigou (ed.), *Memorials of Alfred Marshall* (London, 1925), pp. 443–4. I would like to thank Tamotsu Nishizawa for these references. The notion of the 'context for refutation' is from S. Collini, *Liberalism and Sociology: L. T. Hobhouse and Political Argument in England, 1880–1914* (Cambridge, 1979), p. 9.

The franchise and taxation

The different interpretations of benefit and ability were not simply abstract ideas, for they were intimately connected with the changing electoral system and social structure. Peter Lindert, for example, has pointed to the importance of demography and income distribution. He suggests that the larger the proportion of elderly in any society, the greater the likelihood of support for social spending, not simply for pensions but for the poor, unemployed and ill. In his view, the ageing of the population in the later nineteenth and early twentieth centuries helps to explain the increase in social spending. A second factor is income distribution or what he calls 'social affinity'. In some societies, the distribution of income is skewed so that the median voter is poor relative to average income. In this case, the majority of the electorate would have low incomes and would vote for taxation of the rich and redistribution to the poor. In other societies, the income of the median voter was closer to the income of the rich, so there was less likelihood of progressive, redistributive, taxation. The issue was: to whom did the bulk of the electorate have the greatest affinity? Crudely, Britain would fit the first and the United States the second situation.[14] Equally, it would be possible to think of other structural features which influenced attitudes to taxation: the scale of business enterprises and threat of monopoly profit; the extent of ownership of real property and the chance of capital gains; the nature and extent of charitable activity; or marital and family status.

These structural features did have a role to play in shaping attitudes to taxation, but we should be wary of determinism. Affinity, after all, is not a simple reflection of distribution of income – and the construction of statistics on income distribution is itself a social phenomenon which needs to be understood. The tax system did not simply emerge from the existing distribution of income; rather, at some point the distribution of income became a significant ideological issue and social 'fact'. Indeed, data on the distribution of incomes and wealth were largely products of fiscal information, as in the work of Leo Chiozza Money* and Josiah

---

[14] P. H. Lindert, 'The rise of social spending, 1880–1930', *Explorations in Economic History* 31 (1994), 1–37, and P. H. Lindert, 'What limits social spending?', *Explorations in Economic History* 33 (1996), 1–34.

* Leo George Chiozza Money (1870–1944) was born in Genoa. He was managing editor of Commercial Intelligence 1898–1903, and revised the Board of Trade Returns in 1903; he was a witness to the Select Committee on Income Tax in 1906, and a member of the Select Committee on Home Work, 1907–8. He was elected a Liberal MP in 1906, and was parliamentary secretary to the ministry of shipping, 1916–18. He resigned this post and joined the Labour party, failing to win a seat in 1918. He served on the Royal Commission on the Coal Industry in 1919, but his career was then blighted by sexual scandal. (*Who Was Who, vol. IV: 1941–50* (London, 1952), p. 806.)

Stamp.[15]* The emergence of income distribution (and redistribution) as a political issue was mediated by political culture through changing definitions of 'social affinity'. This was not simply a matter of income levels, for workers might have affinity with employers as active, productive, members of society against parasitical *rentiers* and the feckless poor. Further, artisans might consider state spending as a means of sustaining warfare and officialdom rather than as a means of improving their own welfare. The issue, therefore, is not simply the impact of the social structure on political attitudes; it is how the social structure was perceived. This point may be extended to demographic structures. The important consideration might not be the ageing of the population, for concern about a fall in the birth rate might lead to tax breaks for family men with children at the expense of elderly childless couples or the unmarried. The definition of the tax code by demographic categories was a complex cultural process which is entirely absent from Lindert's analysis.

Much the same point of cultural construction applies to the franchise and taxation. Victorian politicians were well aware of the connection between the franchise and the tax system, and there was a widely shared assumption that the franchise and taxation should be connected in some way. The basis of the fiscal constitution of Peel and Gladstone was that a 'self-taxing class of income-tax paying electors' were trustees who paid direct taxes in order to relieve non-electors who were liable to indirect

---

[15] L. G. Chiozza Money, *Riches and Poverty* (London, 1905). See also the work carried out by Josiah Stamp within the Inland Revenue: *British Incomes and Property: The Application of Official Statistics to Economic Problems* (London, 1916), who discusses the use of tax data by earlier writers, and points to many of the difficulties and failings in their estimates. See chapter 13 on 'The distribution of income and the number of taxpayers', and the attempt of Dudley Baxter to make estimates for 1865/6, with assistance from the Inland Revenue; and of Leone Levi for 1850/1, 1879/80 and 1882/3.

* Josiah Charles Stamp (1880–1941) was born in London, the son of a shopkeeper. He entered the Inland Revenue as a boy clerk in 1896, and took an external degree in economics from the LSE in 1911, followed by a DSc in 1916 for *British Incomes and Property*. He was assistant secretary of the Inland Revenue between 1916 and 1919, when he became secretary and director of Nobel Industries and in 1926 president of the London, Midland and Scottish Railway until his death. He was a member of the Royal Commission on Income Tax of 1919/20 and the Committee on National Debt and Taxation of 1924–7, and he served on the Economic Advisory Council from 1930 to 1941, as well as becoming a director of the Bank of England in 1928. He was British representative on the Dawes (1924) and Young (1929) committees on German reparations. In addition, he was an active member of the Methodist church, president of the Abbey Road Building Society, governor and then chairman of the LSE and president of the Royal Statistical Society. His publications included *British Incomes and Property* (1916), *Fundamental Principles of Taxation in the Light of Modern Developments* (1921), *Wealth and Taxable Capacity* (1922) and *Taxation during the War* (1932). He was killed, with his wife and eldest son, in an air raid. (*DNB, 1941–50*, ed. Legg and Williams, pp. 817–20).

taxes.[16] But it was not entirely clear that the relationship between taxation and the franchise of 1832 was soundly based. We have noted that Joseph Hume feared that parliament was dominated by the possessors of real property who were loathe to pay their 'fair' share of taxes, passing taxes on to the enterprising members of society. But a greater concern arose from the fact that the threshold for the payment of income tax was fixed at £150 in 1842, a relatively high figure which meant that many voters did not contribute to the income tax. Electors would therefore not necessarily be led towards fiscal responsibility through self-interested opposition to higher taxes, for any voter with an income below £150 might vote for expensive programmes without bearing the cost.

In 1852, Charles Babbage* calculated that 850,000 out of a million voters were below the income tax threshold, which gave them an incentive to impose a higher rate of tax on the minority. He was alarmed at the political dangers. 'Amidst the political errors of the present century, I know none possessing so revolutionary a character – none so calculated to accelerate its destructive course by its own accumulated momentum – none which, although seemingly fatal only to the rich, is in reality fatal to all industry.'[17] Babbage was not alone in this view that it would be 'unsafe and unjust' to introduce universal suffrage which would allow the working classes to dominate the electorate. After all, they contributed only 31 per cent of taxes and could opt to pay nothing by reducing their consumption of dutiable goods. An extension of the franchise to the lower orders at the same time as they were relieved from indirect taxation was, so the Edinburgh Review complained, 'of questionable policy and uncertain issue' in creating a financially irresponsible electorate with the power to increase expenditure, without themselves bearing the cost.[18] Babbage's solution was to reduce the exemption level and disenfranchise anyone who claimed it. His approach was based upon a 'bargain and sale' (or benefit) theory of the state, by which taxes were paid for the protection of property and the person, and for permission to use the institutions

---

[16] Matthew, Gladstone, 1809–1874, p. 127.

[17] C. Babbage, Thoughts on the Principles of Taxation with Reference to a Property Tax and its Exceptions (London, 1852), reprinted in M. Campbell-Kelly (ed.), The Works of Charles Babbage, vol. v: Scientific and Miscellaneous Papers, II (London, 1981), pp. 52–3.

[18] [W. R. Greg], 'The expected reform bill', Edinburgh Review 95 (1852), 262.

* Charles Babbage (1791–1871) was educated at Peterhouse, Cambridge; he was a founder member of the Astronomical Society in 1820, and its secretary until 1824. In 1823, he received a grant from the government to make a 'difference engine' to carry out mathematical calculations; a grant for a new design was withdrawn in 1842. The attempt to construct the engine was an obsession. He was Lucassian professor at Cambridge between 1828 and 1839 (without giving any lectures), and a founder of the Statistical Society in 1834. He published The Economy of Manufactures in 1832 and Table of Logarithms in 1827. (DNB, vol. II, ed. Stephen, pp. 304–6.)

provided by the state. He argued that it cost *more* to protect small than large capitalists, for a vendor of apples on the street corner needed the police to prevent theft of the stock, whereas a great merchant house such as Barings was able to shift its capital around the globe and so avoid risk.[19] Few commentators went so far as Babbage, and we noted earlier that his regressive interpretation of benefit was rejected by Mill. However, support for the 'bargain and sale' or benefit approach was widespread. The FRA treated taxation as payment for services rendered in proportion to those services; the revenue was a National Insurance Fund from which the state provided personal security, enjoyment of property and 'full liberty for the exercise of his industry and skill in every honest and lawful vocation'. The FRA argued that taxation was a modest payment for the protection of the person, and an additional payment for the protection of property according to its value. Such an approach led one reformer to propose a capitation tax on everyone over the age of fourteen. The FRA was more cautious, for a 'poll tax' would be a greater burden on an unskilled labourer than on an artisan – and life was simply more valuable to a rich man. The tax on property already fell on workers through higher rents, so that any new tax on wages could be seen as double taxation. In the view of the FRA, any tax on wages should take the form of a small poundage collected by the employer. As the FRA pointed out, 'it might be of great advantage that every citizen should feel such individual interest in good and economical Government as a direct and known payment towards its expenses would, undoubtedly, be calculated to excite in him'. Such logic led Joseph Hume to suggest a reduction in the threshold of income tax to £60 during the Crimean war, in order to impose fiscal responsibility on lower-middle-class and working-class advocates of militarism.[20]

Gladstone took a similar, if less extreme, line, hoping that electors who paid income tax would be fiscally prudent, both for their own sake and as trustees of non-electors who paid indirect taxes. In his budget of 1853, he was concerned to adjust the tax threshold so as to create fiscal responsibility amongst electors, with a close connection between voting and payment. In 1853, he reduced the threshold for the payment of income tax

---

[19] Babbage, *Thoughts on the Principle of Taxation*, p. 49; a similar point was made in [Coode], 'The income tax', 544–8. See also the comments on his scheme by G. W. Hemming, *A Just Income Tax How Possible* (London, 1852), pp. 5–7, as 'dangerous, if not unsound' on the grounds that the state did more than protect natural rights existing before civil society; in fact, much property was created by the state, such as the right to pass property to heirs and copyright.

[20] [Tennant], *The People's Blue Book*, p. 236, and the criticism of the capitation tax in [Greg], 'British taxation', 253–6; FRA, *Report on Taxation*, pp. 7, 21. The debate over income tax and the working class is covered by O. Anderson, 'Wage-earners and income tax: a mid-nineteenth century discussion', *Public Administration* 41 (1963), 189–92.

from £150 to £100, with a lower rate for the incomes between £100 and £150. An income of £100 was, he remarked, 'the dividing line . . . between the educated and the labouring part of the community', and between the voter and the non-voter. He was restoring the link between voting and the income tax: the franchise was based on a £10 household qualification, and he estimated that an income of £96 was needed to qualify. As he remarked, 'I do not think that a £10 franchise can in the fair meaning of the word be said to be within the reach of the working man.'[21] He pointed out in 1863 that incomes of £100 to £150 had benefited from the prosperity of trade and the fall in indirect taxes, and it was an act of justice to those with incomes above £150 that small incomes should 'make some contribution to the fund by means of which such great benefit, common to all classes, had been realized'.[22]

The extension of the franchise in 1867 changed the situation and threatened to break the link between the vote and income tax. In 1866, Gladstone's plans for reform of the franchise were cautious. He proposed to reduce the qualification in boroughs from an annual rental of £10 to £7, a figure chosen with care (and with a similar logic to Lindert). As Gladstone pointed out, a rental of £6 would give the working class a clear majority in urban constituencies – in other words, the median voter would be poor and would not pay direct taxes. Gladstone was not in favour of delivering 'the majority of town constituencies into the hands of the working class'. Instead, he wished to give the vote to skilled workers who could show 'self-command, self-control, respect for order, patience under suffering, confidence in the law, regard for superiors'. These were the men who belonged to friendly societies and to trade unions with welfare schemes, whose rights of association would be accepted by the state. And these skilled workers might well be eager to support a policy of retrenchment, content to provide their own welfare through subscriptions to their own organisations rather than through redistributive taxation and demeaning dependence on the state. However, the failure of Gladstone's modest proposal and the introduction of a much wider household franchise by Disraeli *did* give the working class a majority of the urban electorate. Gladstone accepted the *fait accompli*, and even made himself appear as its main architect. But he was also anxious to ensure that extension of the franchise did not produce class warfare and higher expenditure. In Gladstone's view, there was no reason to expect that these workers, if given the vote, 'would act together as a class' – and his

---

[21] H. C. G. Matthew, *Gladstone, 1809–1898* (Oxford, 1997), p. 127; his calculations on the effect of the £10 household qualification are in W. E. Gladstone, *Speeches on Parliamentary Reform* (London, 1866), p. 53.

[22] *Parliamentary Debates*, 3rd series 170, 16 Apr. 1863, cols. 224j–k.

political rhetoric and programme were designed to fulfil that expectation by stressing issues of civil and national rights, peace and reform, and encouragement of self-help organisations.[23]

The reduction in the threshold of the income tax and a rise in incomes with economic growth meant that the number of people charged to the income tax at the lowest level under schedule D rose from 75,577 in 1868/9 to 195,296 in 1869/70 and to 273,554 in 1873/4, bringing more electors within the tax to create a more disciplined, fiscally responsible, electorate, highly sensitive to the rate of income tax. Even so, the bulk of the electorate did not pay income tax: in 1881, there were 1.2m county and 1.9m borough electors in the United Kingdom.[24] This circumstance gave new force to Gladstone's ambition of abolishing the income tax which might become a powerful engine for expenditure rather than a means of 'constraining leviathan'. During his chancellorship of 1860 to 1866, he considered means of abolishing the income tax on several occasions, but these became more realistic in 1873/4 when there was a prospect of a budgetary surplus. The plan did not succeed – and had less support than Gladstone might have hoped. Abolition might have thrown the government back on to indirect taxes which would divide the Liberal party. Indeed, the income tax found defenders both amongst the radicals and free traders who had earlier feared it as an agent for militarism. Joseph Chamberlain, who had so successfully created an urban alliance of skilled workers, nonconformists and industrialists in the Liberal caucus of Birmingham, was fierce in his condemnation of Gladstone's plan as 'simply an appeal to the selfishness of the middle classes'. The danger, it seemed both to Chamberlain and to Conservative politicians, was less from the class interests of workers than from the middle class. In fact, the government fell and the Liberals lost the election so that Gladstone did not have a chance to carry out his plans.[25]

[23] Matthew, *Gladstone, 1809–1898*, pp. 139–42.

[24] Biagini, 'Popular Liberals, Gladstonian finance and the debate on taxation', p. 150, citing PP 1873 XXXIX, *Return showing the number of persons charged to the income tax . . .*, p. 297, and PP 1878–9 XLII, *Return of the number of persons charged to the income tax for the year ended . . . 5 April 1873 to 1878*, p. 234; H. J. Hanham, *Elections and Party Management: Politics in the Time of Disraeli and Gladstone* (London, 1959), pp. 403–4.

[25] The plans for 1860 to 1866 are mentioned by E. W. Hamilton in BL Add. Mss 48,654, Hamilton Diary, vol. XXV, f. 56, 25 Nov. 1890. On Gladstone's views of the franchise and his plans to abolish the income tax, see Matthew, *Gladstone 1809–1898*, pp. 123, 127, 139–42, 222–5; the quote from Chamberlain is on p. 225, from *Fortnightly Review* 22 (Oct. 1874), 412. The Board of Inland Revenue thought that there was a high likelihood that the tax would be repealed and issued circulars urging the speedy completion of the assessment: see B. E. V. Sabine, 'The abolition of income tax: a dream of 1873/4', *British Tax Review* (1973). Biagini, *Liberty, Retrenchment and Reform*, on support for retrenchment; on Chamberlain's attempts to create an alliance of industry and labour (with varying success) in Birmingham, Sheffield and nationally, see

The immediate impact of 1867 was less of a threat to the minimal state than Gladstone feared. The median elector might be relatively poor, with an income below the average – but the fiscal threat was not apparent and the Liberal party was able to continue as a cross-class alliance. By the 1890s, strains were becoming more obvious. The explanation was, in part, the mounting costs of imperial defence and naval expenditure which were already apparent in the early 1890s, before the costs of the Boer war led to renewed debate on the fiscal constitution. Further, pressure for social spending was also emerging. Although old age pensions were one element in this shift to tax-funded welfare, the explanation was not simply the emergence of an older population and electorate. In the 1890s, the growth of unskilled trade unions was challenging the Lib–Lab alliance and reliance on self-help welfare. Skilled men might be able to pay for welfare benefits through their unions and friendly societies; unskilled workers could not afford the subscriptions and started to press for a more active state intervention. The question was: who should pay?[26] As we shall see in the discussion of death duties in chapter 8, the budget of 1894 marked the start of a change in attitudes within the Liberal party which were realised when the Liberals returned to power in 1906.

Differentiation and graduation

As a result of changed electoral circumstances at the end of the nineteenth century, differentiation returned to the political agenda with a more radical edge than in the 1840s and 1850s. Differentiation could simply be a means of adjusting the incidence of taxation between types of income, without any wider implication. It could imply a moral view of society, based on the assumption that some forms of property and income were more deserving and socially beneficial than others. On this view, taxation should become an instrument to break the dead-hand of passive, accumulated, *rentier* wealth in order to benefit active producers and risk-takers, and to promote a dynamic economy. Such an approach could appeal to industrial capitalists, defining themselves against landowners and *rentiers*. By the early twentieth century, it could also lead to a far wider challenge to capitalism in general. 'Spontaneous' income could be redefined as 'unearned', received from wealth created by the enterprise of society as a whole and misappropriated by private individuals. What society had created could be legitimately reclaimed by society, an argument that implied a radical redefinition of property rights. This approach to

P. Marsh, *Joseph Chamberlain: Entrepreneur in Politics* (New Haven and London, 1994), chapters 3, 4, 5.

[26] On these debates within the trade unions, see Duffy, 'New unionism in Britain'.

unearned, socially created, wealth was initially limited to land whose value was seen as rising through the dynamism of house-builders or factory-owners rather than any enterprise of the landowners who monopolised a scarce resource. Labour and industrial capital were thus united against landowners; coal miners and their employers could make common cause against the owners of minerals who charged high royalties. Here was the basis of Chamberlain's doctrine of ransom, a dangerous word implying coercion or brigandry. In Chamberlain's rhetoric, the landowners had destroyed the common property and natural rights of the people, and he claimed that property must now pay a 'ransom' for its security, a substitute for the natural rights which had been lost.[27] This proposal might appeal to the urban working class of Birmingham, creating a link with industrialists against a common foe. However, the definition of socially created wealth could be extended to include industrial wealth, produced at the expense of workers and consumers. The case for differentiation could therefore shift from a moderate claim for equity between spontaneous and precarious incomes to an attack on land, or a more general socialist attack on wealth as part of a policy designed to create equality and fundamentally change the distribution of income and wealth.

When differentiation was finally introduced in 1907, it was followed in 1909 by a progressive, graduated, income tax. As we have seen, Gladstone marginalised demands for differentiation, which he feared as a means of setting class against class and as a step in the direction of graduation. But in the 1840s and 1850s, even the fiercest supporters of differentiation were strongly opposed to graduation. John Stuart Mill is a case in point: he accepted differentiation and rejected graduation of the income tax, despite his realisation that it was easier for a rich person to pay a tax of 10 per cent than a poor person:

I do not see how you can, either with justice or policy, tax a person more heavily because he earns more, or because, after having earned more, he saves more. I do not think you can lay a tax upon energy, or industry, or prudence. It seems to me that even upon the question of justice, apart from policy, there is no stronger or more valid principle than that of not giving any advantage to self-indulgence, even though the effect may be to give some advantage, or rather, not to interfere with the natural advantage of the rich over the poor.

What Mill *did* accept was graduation of the succession duty at death, on the grounds that inherited wealth was received without exertion, as 'a privilege which he owes to the existence of law and society, to which the

---

[27] Marsh, *Joseph Chamberlain*, pp. 186–7, 202; see C. W. Boyd (ed.), *Mr Chamberlain's Speeches*, vol. I (London, 1914), p. 137, speech on 'The doctrine of ransom' at Birmingham, 5 Jan. 1885.

State is entitled to annex conditions'. His policy was 'to allow people to retain the full advantage for their lives of what they have acquired; but the State may deal with it on the occasion of succession' so allowing the pursuit of active industry and enterprise and diffusing inherited wealth.[28]

The approach of Mill and Hubbard to taxation was therefore informed by a common theme: the encouragement of a dynamic economy based on savings, and a reduction of taxation on 'skill and intelligence'. They supported differentiation and opposed graduation from a common concern to encourage savings. Differentiation would lessen the burden on risk-taking. By contrast, graduation punished the 'prudence and virtue' of those who added to the wealth of the country, penalising the accumulation of capital and discouraging enterprise.[29] However, the policy of differentiation advocated by Hubbard and Mill appears, at first sight, to have an ambivalent or even contradictory attitude towards savings. A lower level of taxation of earned incomes was designed to stimulate savings and accumulation. However, future flows of income from savings out of earned income would then pay a *higher* rate of taxation. Advocates of differentiation simultaneously argued for tax policies designed to *encourage* saving and capital accumulation over consumption, and for higher taxes on income from savings which would *discourage* accumulation. As a result, Mill has been accused by at least one commentator of confusion in failing to appreciate the relationship between capital and growth, and of being more concerned with issues of equity than efficiency.[30] The point was not lost on contemporary critics of differentiation, who could not see why a widow receiving interest from savings from her husband's earnings should be penalised by a higher rate of tax. Why should the widow of a small manufacturer with children to educate pay a higher rate of tax than a prosperous barrister with fewer family responsibilities? Was it justice, Gladstone wondered, to put a higher tax on widows and orphans supported by annuities in order to 'put a lower tax upon your bankers and brewers and upon your physicians and lawyers'? Should life annuitants, comprising desolate widows, orphaned daughters and defenceless women, pay a higher rate of tax than prosperous bankers and brewers, physicians and lawyers? Here was Gladstone's objection: whatever the inequalities in the incidence of income tax between spontaneous and precarious incomes, there were other inequalities and anomalies *within* each

---

[28] PP 1861 VII, *Report from the Select Committee on Income and Property Tax*, Qq. 3578–97, 3708–12, 3757, 3770.

[29] PP 1861 VII, *Report from the Select Committee on Income and Property Tax*, draft report, p. 15, Qq. 747–50, 1119.

[30] M. Veseth, *Mountains of Debt: Crisis and Change in Renaissance Florence, Victorian Britain and Postwar America* (New York and Oxford, 1990), pp. 115–16.

category so that some 'spontaneous' incomes were more deserving than others. How could any fiscal policy choose between them with fairness?[31]

Nevertheless, criticism of Mill and Hubbard for failing to understand the connection between savings, capital accumulation and growth is not entirely reasonable. After all, much saving escaped a higher rate of tax on 'unearned' income. Most industry and trade was in the hands of family firms and partnerships, so that profits retained in the business to create capital would provide precarious or *earned* income since it was still actively engaged in trade. The scope of differentiation would therefore be confined to *passive* savings outside the firm, and did not affect active accumulation. Both Mill in his writings on political economy, and Hubbard in his own business life in the City of London, opposed joint-stock companies as inefficient and a threat to competition; their vision rested on family firms with active owners. The entire thrust of liberal, free trade, economics was in favour of active participation in small firms and associations, rather than passive investment.[32] The definition of income from dividends from public companies was significant. Should it be counted as 'earned' income, since it involved ownership and risk in the same way as private partnerships; or as passive, spontaneous, income akin to government bonds or debentures? Hubbard's answer was that it was 'spontaneous' income derived from invested property so that it should be liable to a higher rate of tax. The important point was that it did not entail *personal* involvement, and the underlying asset survived illness or retirement. Although partnerships and companies in the same line of business might seem indistinguishable, Hubbard argued that there were real differences which affected their tax position:

In a trading company the labour of the clerks, managers, and directors is all paid for; reserves are made for depreciation, casualties, or exhaustion, and the dividends represent the net return for the capital invested by the shareholder.

In a private partnership the management and supervision are carried on by the partners in the firm; some may provide the capital, some the supervision, but the profits combine the reward for the management and the returns for the capital; they are industrial profits divisible amongst the partners. The partners contributing capital only, are called sleeping partners and there may be no important difference, so far as their personal fortunes are concerned, between them

---

[31] Gladstone's views were explained to Asquith when he was considering the introduction of differentiation in 1907: see PRO, T172/22, 'Memorandum to the chancellor of the Exchequer', 26 Mar. 1907. See *Parliamentary Debates*, 3rd ser. 125, 18 Apr. 1853, cols. 1368–83.

[32] See F. Trentmann, 'Political culture and political economy: interest, ideology and free trade', *Review of International Political Economy* 5 (1998), 232, and also T. Alborn, *Conceiving Companies: Joint-Stock Politics in Victorian England* (London, 1998).

and the shareholders of a public company; but the shareholders of a company can always secure a limited liability, which partners in a private firm cannot. Practically, the tax collector knows nothing of sleeping partners; it is the entirety of the partnership, the firm, which he assesses; and whatever the proportions in which capital and labour are contributed, the partnership is entitled to the character and privileges of an industrial pursuit.[33]

Hubbard would therefore give a private partnership (such as his own firm in the City) the benefit of a lower rate of tax; as soon as the concern was transformed into a public company, dividends would pay a higher rate. Of course, some money would be diverted from the private partnership into secure assets such as land or government bonds in order to provide for widows and dependent children, free of the risks of the family firm and the perils of unlimited liability. Hubbard was himself a major purchaser of land, and most reasonably prosperous families created trusts and settlements to provide for family members outside the firm.[34] But the search for family security was at the expense of funds for the active, dynamic, sector of the economy. It was one thing to support risk-taking businessmen by reducing their tax liability so that they could save to support their dependants; it was quite another thing to allow these passive dependants to have tax breaks. In other words, Mill's and Hubbard's fiscal policy was entirely consistent with a particular social vision and a distinctive understanding of the sources of growth in a dynamic, risk-taking, economy. The eventual adoption of differentiation in 1907 arose from a different set of political calculations and ideological assumptions, which created a strong link with graduation.

Gladstone was hostile to 'progression' as 'generally destructive' of the principle of property, accumulation and industry, and hence against the interests of rich and poor. It would be the cause of 'universal war, a universal scramble among all classes, every one endeavouring to relieve himself at the expense of his neighbour, and an end being put to all social peace, and to any common principle on which the burdens of the State can be adjusted'. However, he did accept an element of graduation within 'moderate bounds'. In 1864, he contemplated graduation of the inhabited house duty, so that it would rise from 8d in the £ on houses rented at £10 or less a year to 3s 4d on houses rented at more than £500. As he remarked, such a scheme was innocent of the confiscatory principles implied by a

---

33 PP 1861 VII, *Report from the Select Committee on Income and Property Tax*, draft report, p. 14.
34 Hubbard's own sons overlooked this need to establish a divide between the family assets and the firm, and kept the inheritance of other members of the family in the business, with disastrous results: see M. J. Daunton, 'Inheritance and succession in the City of London in the nineteenth century', *Business History* 30 (1988), 272–6.

graduated income tax. Indeed, Gladstone felt that the inhabited house duty was preferable to the income tax and might form a replacement – an ambition he never achieved. In addition, he accepted a modest degree of 'degression' or abatement in the income tax in order to adjust the incidence of taxation to the 'relative poverty among men'. Gladstone accepted that there was a 'sore place' for incomes between £100 and £200, where the tax was more accurately levied than on many trades and professions:

As a general rule, the concerns of those who possess only these smaller incomes are more transparent, so to speak, than the private affairs of their richer fellow-countrymen. Every neighbour can see through them; they may be said to live in glass houses; deception, if they are disposed to deceive, would be for them almost wholly impossible. They pay the tax fully and readily, and they see or they surmise that many persons above them in the world, are not and cannot be always brought to account with equal strictness.[35]

His solution was to replace the lower rate of tax on incomes from £100 to £150. Instead, there would be a single rate of tax, moderated by a new 'abatement' or tax-free allowance on incomes from £100 to £200.

The change had an important psychological advantage of making everyone sensitive to the same rate of tax. The difference between degression and progression was important. Progression imposed a *higher* rate of tax on the rich and would therefore be resented as an act of confiscation. Degression was a *reduction* in the liability of smaller incomes, a concession to respectable affluence rather than an imposition on the rich. The graduation of tax was therefore kept within 'moderate bounds'. Such an approach also had administrative advantages. Collection of tax at source required the deduction of tax at a standard rate from each category of income or schedule – rent, dividends, salary – without the need to estimate an individual's aggregate income from all sources. But degression and progression applied to *total* income which created administrative difficulties. Degression had an important advantage over progression: tax was initially deducted at the standard rate so that taxpayers had an incentive to make a voluntary return of their total income which would lead to a *refund* of tax. A progressive system would *increase* liability to tax, and compulsory returns would be needed with greater resistance to divulging total income. Degression could be portrayed as another means of legitimating the income tax by reducing the burdens on those with least capacity to pay, so containing any pressure to redistribute income or to

[35] *Parliamentary Debates*, 3rd ser. 170 16 Apr. 1863 col. 224l–m, and 23 Apr. 1863, col. 622; BL, Add. MSS 48, 654, Hamilton Diary, vol. xxv, ff. 56–7, 25 Nov. 1890; BL, Add. MSS 44,789, f. 1, 'Two schemes of graduated house duty', 10 Feb. 1864.

Table 6.1 *Number of persons charged to schedule D of the income tax, United Kingdom, 1854 and 1868*

	1854		1868	
	Number	%	Number	%
Under £100	23,692	8.4	76,888	19.2
£100 and under £200	174,741	61.9	191,342	47.9
£200 and under £300	35,063	12.4	56,933	14.2
£300 and under £1,000	39,070	13.8	58,834	14.7
£1,000 and under £5,000	8,655	3.1	13,434	3.4
Above £5,000	1,261	0.4	2,166	0.5
Total	282,482	100.0	399,597	100.0

Source: PP 1870 XX, *Report of the Commissioners of Inland Revenue on the duties under their management for the years 1856 to 1869 inclusive,* vol. II, pp. 580–4.

Table 6.2 *Changes in the structure of income tax, 1842–1905*

1842/3 to 1852/3	7d in £ on incomes above £150
	Effective rate of tax on all incomes above £150: 2.9 per cent
1853/4	Incomes of £100 to £150: 5d in £, effective rate of 2.1 per cent
	Incomes above £150: 7d in £, effective rate of 2.9 per cent
1863/4	Single rate of 7d in £ for incomes above £100
	Abatement of £60 on incomes under £200
	I.e. an income of £150 paid on £90
1872/3	Abatement increased to £80 on incomes over £200
1876/7	Abatement of £120 on incomes under £400
	Incomes under £150 exempted from tax
1890/1	One rate for incomes above £150
	Abatement of £120 on incomes £150 to £400
1894/5	One rate on incomes exceeding £160
	Abatement of £160 on incomes above £160 but not exceeding £400
	Abatement of £100 on incomes above £400 but not exceeding £500
1898/9	One rate on incomes above £160
	Abatement of £160 on incomes exceeding £160 but not £400
	Abatement of £150 on incomes exceeding £400 but not £500
	Abatement of £120 on incomes exceeding £500 but not £600
	Abatement of £70 on incomes exceeding £600 but not £700
	Income of £200 paid on £40: effective rate 0.67 per cent

Source: PP 1870 XX, *Report of the Commissioners of Inland Revenue on the duties under their management for the years 1856 to 1869 inclusive,* vol. II, p. 568; PP 1881 XXIX, *Supplement to the 24th Report of the Commissioners of Inland Revenue on the Inland Revenue for the year ended 31 March 1881, being a continuation of the tables of accounts contained in volume II of the report of 1870,* p. 510; PP 1900 XVIII, *43rd Report of the Commissioners of Her Majesty's Inland Revenue for the year ended 31 March 1900,* pp. 473, 478.

set one class against another. It was one strand in the creation of cohesion and stability by portraying the tax system as balanced, sustaining a state which was neutral and above the selfish tussle of interests. This neutral state would also be constrained, for a standard rate with concessions to lower incomes imposed limits on the yield of the income tax. Any increase in government revenue would require a higher standard rate and lead to resistance; in a progressive system, the majority of taxpayers might be tempted to pass higher costs to a minority of taxpayers with high incomes. Until the end of the nineteenth century, Gladstone's project of a minimal state with low, constrained, taxation was widely shared by the organised working class and radicals who feared that taxation would be used to finance war rather than provide welfare for the poor, and there was little support for the use of taxation to redistribute income and change the social structure.[36] However, abatements could also be used by creative chancellors as a means of manipulating the electorate by reducing the level of taxation of significant categories of voters in a bid for support (see chapter 8 on Harcourt's budget of 1894).

Balancing the fiscal system: direct versus indirect taxation

In 1842, the British fiscal system was marked by a greater reliance on indirect taxes than many other European countries which had a wider range of taxes on specific forms of income and wealth. In the 1820s and 1830s, discussion of indirect taxes concentrated on the need for rationalisation, and reformers such as Parnell argued that a reduction from the existing high rates of duty would lead to increased consumption of imported goods and hence to improved yields. He was not necessarily arguing that the contribution of indirect taxes to government revenue should be reduced, but rather that the yield should be produced with least distortion to trade and burdens on the taxpayer. Adam Smith's second, third and fourth maxims stressed that the amount, time and manner of payment should be clear, for the convenience of the taxpayer and to limit the power of the tax gatherer. In Smith's opinion, a considerable degree of inequality in the incidence of taxation was less of an evil than a small uncertainty. Taxes should be collected at a time and manner convenient to the taxpayer, and in his opinion the payment of small amounts through purchases of goods had the advantage that it gave freedom over payment. Further, 'every tax ought to be so contrived as both to take out

---

[36] Biagini, 'Popular Liberals, Gladstonian finance and the debate on taxation', pp. 134–62. Gladstone's proposal on the inhabited house duty are in BL Add. Mss 44,798, f. 1, 'Two schemes of graduated house duty', 10 Feb. 1864.

Nº XLI.—INDIRECT TAXATION.
MULTUM IN PARVO

3 'Indirect taxation', *Punch* May 1842: the taxpayer is terrorised by goblins of indirect taxation

and to keep out of the pockets of the people as little as possible, over and above what it brings into the publick treasury of the state'. In other words, the costs of collection should be modest; the tax should not obstruct industry; it should not tempt taxpayers to evade and then to face ruinous fines; and it should not cause vexation through 'odious examinations'. Failure to observe these principles would make the tax more of a burden to the people than it was a benefit to the state.[37] Indeed, free traders were not entirely hostile to indirect taxes. The Whig *Edinburgh Review* argued that taxation on consumption 'operates with perfect fairness between individuals', for it was paid by taxpayers 'according to their means, defined and limited by their expenditure' which could be adjusted by their own free will. Indeed, it could even be argued that 'taxation of the poor man is *entirely voluntary*. He assesses himself and he need not contribute one farthing to the revenue unless he pleases. No actual *necessary* of life is taxed.' The claim also raises an interesting question of the definition of

[37] Smith, *Wealth of Nations*, vol. II, VIIb, pp. 825–6; Parnell, *On Financial Reform*, pp. 1–17, argued for tax reform on the principle of 'levying the revenue which is wanted for the public service in such a manner as to occasion the smallest possible loss of money and enjoyment to the contributors, and the least possible impediment to the progress of national industry and national wealth' (p. 17).

necessities. The *Edinburgh Review* pointed out that, with the exception of beer, most taxed commodities were relatively new to Britain. Hence tea, coffee, sugar, tobacco

are in no fair and intelligent sense *necessaries*... They are all luxuries and super-fluities: – it is very right that the working man should have them, if he chooses; but why, any more than the rich man, he should have them without paying for them, it is impossible to see. If he can purchase them, it is because he has money to spend on superfluities, and the portion of his income that he can set aside for superfluities is surely a fair subject for taxation. If he pays any tax at all, it is because he has stepped voluntarily into the taxpaying class.[38]

It might be doubted that working-class consumers would so readily accept this argument, which was directed against the more doctrinaire free traders and especially the FRA. Their response was simple, to argue that consumption of these new commodities was beneficial, a sign of progress. As John Noble explained, the 'whole framework of our civilisation... is based upon the fact that the luxuries of the past are the necessaries of the present; if this principle were carried out to its legitimate conclusion we should relapse into barbarism'.[39] Issues of indirect taxation therefore raised important issues of the morality of consumption, of the line between necessities and luxuries or indulgence.

Some commentators felt that the distinction between direct and indirect taxes had little significance, for the important issue was their ultimate incidence. J. R. McCulloch pointed out that both direct and indirect taxes hit the 'labouring classes'. He assumed that indirect taxes could not be shifted to other classes, and therefore fell on the working-class consumer. Equally, the income tax reduced the fund for the payment of wages and hit workers.[40] Consequently, there was no benefit for workers in a shift from indirect to direct taxes, for both were paid by the workers. Other commentators feared that the hostility of the poor might lead to their exemption from taxation; at the same time, the upper classes could use their control of the legislature to reduce their own burdens. On this argument, the incidence of taxation fell heaviest on the 'intermediate order' of the middle class. 'It is simply an abuse of power – the violation by the strong of the rights of the weak; for there cannot be a clearer right in civil society than that of bearing no more than an equal share of the public burdens.'[41]

---

[38] [Greg], 'British taxation', 262–3.
[39] FRU, *Papers on Taxation and Expenditure Issued by the Financial Reform Union. Number 2. J. Noble, Suggestions for a Revision of Taxation* (London, 1868), p. 2.
[40] J. R. McCulloch, *A Treatise on the Principles and Practical Influence of Taxation and the Funding System* (London, 1845), pp. 157–8, 377.
[41] [H. Merivale], 'M'Culloch on taxation and funding', *Edinburgh Review* 82 (1845), 367–80.

Such an approach gave more emphasis to the adjustment of the income tax to relieve professional incomes and, to a lesser extent, trade and industry which had derived some benefit from a reduction in duties.

In the 1840s and 1850s, Cobden and the FRA took a more dogmatic and assertive view of the need to cut or even abolish indirect taxes. They argued for an abolition of duties on trade on the grounds that reliance on consumption or 'stomach' taxes 'makes the poor man pay much more than the rich man, in proportion to their respective means'.[42]

To what, under such a crushing load of taxation, has the poor man to look for comfort and happiness? Shelter, food, fuel, *all* taxed, *all* put beyond his reach, except the almost spontaneous productions of the earth – potatoes, water, and mud. On the first two he may, perhaps, hold together in physical existence his body and soul, and with the last build himself a miserable cabin; but what the ultimate result of such a state of millions will be, let the present and recently past condition of Ireland answer. And yet to this state is the present system of taxation hurrying us.

Such a system of taxation would call the legitimacy of government into question, and 'true conservative policy points out the necessity of removing such sources of discontent'.[43] The dangers were obvious: 'Indirect Taxation *is* essentially and unavoidably a conflict of class interests, – a direct provocative to class hatreds.'[44] Further, indirect taxes might undermine prudence, for they were paid 'unconsciously'. The outcome might therefore be extravagant expenditure. After all, voters would be able to shift costs, surreptitiously, on to the mass of consumers.

It is because the public money has been easily, and furtively got, that it has been badly spent. It is because the Taxes are no longer direct and open, but hidden in duties on commodities, and paid mainly by the masses, that a scandalous indolence and laxity in all that regards the expenditure of the public money, and slavish submission to the invasion of a privilege for which its predecessors fought and bled, have become the distinguishing characteristics of the modern House of Commons.[45]

Above all, indirect taxes might lead to expenditure on war. Direct taxes were now reinterpreted, not as a means of funding war but of ensuring peace through fiscal discipline. 'Happy would it have been for England, if there had been such a check on unjust, unnecessary, and aggressive wars as Direct Taxation would have afforded.'[46] The extreme financial reformers did admit one major problem with the abolition of indirect

[42] FRA, *Report on Taxation*, p. 18.
[43] FRA, *Financial Reform Tracts, 3, Taxation Part I* (London, 1848), pp. 6–7.
[44] FRA, *Report on Taxation*, p. 17.
[45] FRA, *Report on Taxation*, p. 11; also FRU, *Papers on Taxation and Expenditure . . . Number 2*, p. 3.
[46] FRA, *Report on Taxation*, p. 12.

taxes: the poor would not contribute to the costs of government and would have no motivation to be responsible political citizens, and we have noted the proposal of a capitation tax or poundage on wages in order to create a recognition of the need for economy and fiscal discipline.[47]

Free traders and financial reformers also attacked indirect taxes for obstructing industry and enterprise, and preventing the 'free exercise of capital'. Abolition of indirect taxes and substitution of direct taxes would lead to untrammelled commerce and make Britain the emporium of world trade. It would lead to peace, for the whole of mankind would become customers and 'the bare idea of war would soon be scouted by the common sense and common interests of the whole family of man'.[48] It would create 'profitable employment and a self-supporting people, with all the energy and independence which such a population gives to a nation'. This would secure peace at home as well as abroad, for the alternative would be 'idleness and want, trenching upon and ultimately absorbing the property of others, till the end be anarchy, if not violent and bloody revolution'. Indirect taxes led to a shortage of profitable employment for capital at home, and hence to foreign speculation and 'artificially fiscally-created pauperism' with crowded gaols and workhouses.[49] The abolition of these duties would create a prosperous home market and provide work for the unskilled, so emptying gaols and workhouses. Direct taxation would also benefit landowners, both morally and economically. Indirect taxes gave a 'premium . . . to the privileged classes to withdraw their capital and themselves from the offices of production to live partially or entirely in idleness'.[50] Direct taxes would lead to an expansion of consumption and production, and therefore raise land values. 'There is no conflict of class interests involved in the substitution of Direct for Indirect Taxation.'[51] As one member of the FRA, explained in 1848:

their quarrel was this: it was industry against idleness – it was the working bees against the drones – and they claimed that every man who was able and willing to work should have the free unlimited market of the world to work in, as God gave it to him, and by the blessing of Providence they would win it for him yet . . . They had been ruled over by the idle men of the community, by men whose boast it had been that neither they nor their fathers ever earned an honest penny by their industry – and they had taxed them at their pleasure, for their own benefit. Now, that must no longer be the case. Let them lay the taxes so that they should bear their fair share of the burden; and depend upon it, they would look after the expenditure in a very different fashion . . . In this great work . . . he

---

[47] See above p. 151.
[48] *Times*, 16 Jan. 1857.
[49] FRA, *Financial Reform Tracts, 3, Taxation Part I*, p. 7; FRA, *Report on Taxation*, pp. 28–9.
[50] FRA, *Financial Reform Tracts, 15: Direct Taxation* (London, 1850?), p. 1.
[51] FRA, *Report on Taxation*, p. 17.

trusted they should have the assistance of all the industrious classes of the empire, from the highest to the lowest. It was every working-man's question; it was every tradesman's question; it was every merchant's and banker's question; and every shopkeeper's question.[52]

The fiscal rhetoric united industrious producers against idle parasites. It should also be read as part of the debate with protectionists who had their own vision of a balanced community based on a strong domestic market. To them, repeal of protective duties led to a dangerous reliance on foreign markets at the expense of home markets, and industrialists were behaving in a selfish manner at the expense of the rest of society. To the financial reformers, domestic consumption could be boosted by abolishing indirect taxes; the landowners were behaving selfishly and needed to be brought into the industrious community. A similar argument was resurrected and extended by J. A. Hobson and the new Liberals before the First World War.

The rhetoric of parasites versus producers and of hostility to indirect taxes, became rigid dogma in the early twentieth century as part of the Liberal defence of free trade. In the 1840s, 1850s and 1860s, most politicians – both Liberal and Conservative – were more cautious and realistic than the FRA and FRU. The issue was where to set the balance between direct and indirect, between 'sensible' or vexatious and 'insensible' or hidden taxes. One leading Whig politician, G. C. Lewis, took a sensibly pragmatic line in the face of demand for major cuts in indirect taxes at a time of trade depression. Taxation, he felt, was being wrongly

Table 6.3 *Direct and indirect taxes, collected by central government, United Kingdom, 1841/2 to 1901/2 (percentage)*

	Indirect	Direct
1841/2	73.0	27.0
1861/2	62.2	37.8
1881/2	59.5	40.5
1901/2	47.5	52.6

Source: PRO, T168/58, E.W. Hamilton, Financial Papers 1902/3.

[52] FRA, *Financial Reform Tracts, Number 6, The National Budget for 1849 by Richard Cobden MP in a Letter to Robertson Gladstone, President of the Financial Reform Association of Liverpool, with a Report of the Public Meeting Held at the Concert Hall, Liverpool, December 20, 1848, at which the Budget was Announced to the Nation* (London, 1848?), pp. 13–14.

blamed for difficult economic conditions.[53] The danger of repealing indirect taxes and relying too heavily on income tax was that it 'cripples our power of increasing taxation for an extraordinary or temporary purpose, and renders it necessary on any such occasion to have recourse at once to borrowing'.[54] In Lewis's view, Gladstone's strategy in his budget of 1860, of increasing the income tax in order to make significant cuts in indirect taxes, was

> founded upon liberal and philanthropic views, which proceed upon the assumption that everything is to march uninterruptedly to its pre-appointed end. If these anticipations are all verified, there will be an increase in our foreign trade, an extension of our manufactures, an improvement in our working classes, and a consequent increase in the productiveness of the remaining taxes. There will likewise be more pacific and settled relations between England and France, and a consequent reduction of armaments on both sides of the Channel.[55]

Lewis rejected such hopes as unrealistic, and instead favoured Arthur Young's* proposition that a tax system should have a great variety of incidence as a means of assisting equality, by 'bearing lightly on an infinite number of points, heavily on none'. Lewis added a further requirement: 'moderation of the rate'. No tax was defensible if it was excessive, whatever its incidence or method of collection; by contrast, 'a moderate tax can often be paid without serious inconvenience', whatever its other shortcomings.[56] In Lewis's opinion, taxes should not be expected to meet unrealistic standards of equity.

It could also be argued that indirect taxes were less troublesome to collect. As the *Edinburgh Review* remarked, reliance on direct taxes entailed 'the fixed, definite, and unrelenting demand of the collector'; by contrast, indirect taxes of commodities meant that 'the price of the article and the tax are so blended as to be indistinguishable'. The *Edinburgh Review* doubted the wisdom of making taxes as visible and onerous as possible as a means of imposing fiscal discipline on the voter, and instead

---

[53] Lewis (ed.), *Letters of George Cornewall Lewis*, Lewis to Head, 24 Nov. 1848, pp. 188–9; Lewis to Head, 4 Sept. 1849, p. 210.

[54] Lewis (ed.), *Letters of George Cornewall Lewis*, Lewis to Head, 12 Mar. 1860, pp. 376–7.

[55] Lewis (ed.), *Letters of George Cornewall Lewis*, Lewis to W. R. Greg, 24 Mar. 1860, p. 378.

[56] NLW, Harpton Court MS 3605, undated notes on taxation, NLW, Harpton Court MS 3463, citing A. Young, *Travels in France during the Years 1787, 1788 and 1789 Undertaken More Particularly with a View to Ascertaining the Cultivation, Wealth, Resources and National Prosperity of the Kingdom of France* (Bury St Edmunds, 1792), p. 531.

* Arthur Young (1741–1820) was born in London; his father, the rector of Bardfield in Suffolk, was chaplain to the speaker of the Commons. He was apprenticed to a merchant in Lynn, and spent periods as a farmer, journalist and agent to an Irish landlord. He wrote extensively on agriculture in England, Ireland and France, and was appointed secretary to the Board of Agriculture in 1793. (*DNB*, vol. LXIII, ed. S. Lee (London, 1900), pp. 357–63.)

stressed the virtues of ease of collection. 'What, if he naturally prefers insensible perspiration to forcible extraction? . . . Taxation must of necessity be a painful operation; it is simple cruelty and folly not to perform it under the influence of chloroform.' The best mode of imposing taxes was therefore the least unpleasant and the least felt, and the *Edinburgh Review* argued that was indirect taxation. Of course, it was the 'unconsciousness' of indirect taxes which alarmed financial reformers, who 'would have taxation made as ostensible and vexatious as possible, in order that, being annoying to the people to pay and difficult for the Government to collect, there should be a constant and combined pressure towards its reduction to the smallest practicable amount'.[57] By the end of the nineteenth century, the Treasury took a different view, that the need of foreign (and especially Latin) countries to 'hide' taxes in the price of goods was a sign of a lack of consent to direct taxation. Far from indirect taxes being easier to collect, the Treasury argued that a need to check the accounts of thousands of shopkeepers would cause tension and resistance.[58]

Until 1860, the government increased both direct *and* indirect taxes when it needed more revenue. This was most obvious in the Crimean war. In 1854, Gladstone doubled the income tax to 1s 2d in the £, and Lewis added a further 2d in 1855; at the same time, indirect taxes were increased. At the outbreak of the Crimean war, Gladstone initially announced that 'we cannot add and do not advise you to add one farthing to the indirect taxation of the country', but later in 1854 he increased duties on spirits, malt and sugar. Gladstone was forced into the change by necessity, and was careful to limit himself to duties 'which will least interfere with trade, which will least interfere with the innocent enjoyments of the people, and least with consumption – which will, in fact, cause the smallest deduction from the comforts, the advantages, and the enjoyments of the people, as compared with the amount of revenue which it is necessary to raise for the purposes of the State'. His successor, G. C. Lewis, was more favourably disposed to a wide range of taxes and he made further additions to spirits, sugar, coffee and tea.[59] Even so, the revenue from the additional war taxes was about £24m from income tax and £13.5m from indirect taxes.[60]

Gladstone was not dogmatically committed to the abolition of indirect taxes, for his constant theme was balance between different forms

---

57 [Spring-Rice], 'Financial prospects, 1849', 519–20, 530–7; [Greg], 'British taxation', 259–60.
58 Hence its opposition to a sales tax after the First World War: see Daunton, 'How to pay for the war', 911–12.
59 Anderson, *Liberal State at War*, pp. 201–6; *Parliamentary Debates*, 3rd ser. 132, 6 Mar. 1854, cols. 371–2; 132, 8 May 1854, col. 1452.
60 The estimate of S. C. Buxton, *Mr Gladstone as Chancellor of the Exchequer* (London, 1901), p. 144.

of taxation. He wished to remove differential duties between colonial and foreign goods, and protective duties of domestic producers, for these merely distorted trade. These duties meant that consumers paid more for their goods, but much of the money went to the producers rather than to the state. Generally, Gladstone wished to reduce indirect taxes in order to benefit consumers through lower prices, stimulate trade and remove burdens on the poor – but he felt that revenue duties were acceptable within reason. Certainly, they should not be reduced or removed at the expense of imposing burdens on income tax which he wished to abolish. Gladstone's definition of the limit of indirect taxes was most clearly expressed in his budget of 1860 which stands alongside his first budget of 1853 in defining the Gladstonian fiscal constitution.

When Gladstone presented his budget in 1860, he faced a prospective deficit of £9.4m. The income tax had been renewed for seven years in 1853 and the war duties on tea and sugar were also due to expire. Clearly, he had some difficult choices to make in covering the deficit. Should he introduce a 'niggardly budget' (retaining war-time duties on tea and sugar and raising income tax to 9d) or a 'more generous budget' (income tax at 1s and the removal of war-time duties on tea and sugar)? Although Gladstone claimed that, in principle, he was in favour of reducing duties on these items of 'universal consumption', he opted to retain them. People were prosperous and able to pay, and they were entirely revenue duties without any protection of domestic production or differential between foreign and colonial goods. He argued that 'it is a mistake to suppose that the best mode of giving benefit to the labouring classes is simply to operate on the articles consumed by them. If you want to do them the *maximum* of good, you should rather operate on the articles which give them the *maximum* of employment.' This entailed setting trade free to create more employment at higher wages. Hence his support for the Cobden–Chevalier treaty of 1860 which reduced tariffs on goods between Britain and France, and his wider strategy of removing almost all the surviving differential or protective duties. The repeal of the corn laws in 1846 did not mark the immediate adoption of free trade; it was only the mid-point of a long period of decline in the average tariff. The budget of 1860 virtually completed the process. As Gladstone pointed out twenty years later, two principles should be followed: there should be no protective duties on raw materials, food or manufactures; and the revenue from duties should come from the smallest number of goods. In pursuit of these principles, he abolished duties on almost 400 goods, leaving nominal 'registration' duties on a number of imports and exports, and significant non-protective revenue duties on about fifteen commodities. Amongst other changes, he aimed to abolish the duty on paper, a proposal of great symbolic value in removing the tax on information and knowledge which would appeal to the radicals with their demand for a cheap press. As he pointed out, his proposals amounted to an abandonment of the principle of protection, 'so that the consumer will know that every shilling he pays will go to the revenue, and not to the domestic as against the foreign producer'. He was confident that the loss of revenue from indirect taxes of about £4m would result in an increase in trade and prosperity. The question then was: how to make good the loss of revenue and cover the deficit? He decided against the 'more generous' option of abandoning the war-time duties on sugar and tea and imposing an income tax of 1s in the £. Instead, he retained these duties and opted for an income tax of 10d on incomes above and 7d on incomes below £150. In other words, he covered his massive concessions by means of duties on items of 'universal consumption' and maintaining some of the increase in the income tax.

Gladstone was lyrical on the benefits of the budget, which continued his project of 1853 of integrating society and creating stability, contentment and self-reliance. It would

scatter blessings among the people ... You are not forging mechanical helps for men, nor endeavouring to do that for them which they ought to do for themselves; but you are enlarging their means without narrowing their freedom, you are giving value to their labour, you are appealing to their sense of responsibility, and you are not impairing their sense of honourable self-dependence.

He drew a fanciful analogy between monarchs in the past who scattered coin amongst the crowds on their progress around the country. Now, the queen was scattering blessings in a different way, by

wise and prudent laws ... which do not sap in any respect the foundations of duty or of manhood, but which strike away the shackles from the arm of industry, which give new incentive and new reward to toil, and which win more and more for the Throne and for the institutions of the country the gratitude, the confidence, and the love of an united people ... that which stirs the flame of patriotism in men, that which binds them in one heart and soul, that which gives them increased confidence in their rulers, that which makes them feel and know that they are treated with justice, and that we who represent them are labouring incessantly and earnestly for their good – is in itself no small, no feeble, and no transitory part of national defence.

There was, therefore, no need to spend large sums on defence and warfare, for a policy of free trade and prosperity created international harmony which removed the need to construct expensive fortifications against the French. It would also create a loyal, dependable, population which could be called on to protect the country from its enemies. The abolition of protective duties would also, as he pointed out in 1880, purge politics of corruption for they simply bolstered 'the most selfish instincts of class against the just demands of the public welfare', giving producers 'power and influence largely gotten at the expense of the community, to do battle, with a perverted prowess, against nature, liberty and justice'.[61]

Gladstone's proposals were highly contentious, for his policy was in clear opposition to many (even most) members of the Cabinet, and the repeal of the paper duties brought him into collision with the Lords, leading to the first major constitutional battle between the two Houses since 1832. The repeal of the paper duties was attacked on the grounds that it added 1d to the income tax, and it only passed the Commons on a narrow majority. When the proposal went to the Lords as a separate measure apart from the budget, it was rejected and so opened a constitutional controversy. The Lords had no power to impose taxation or amend a money bill. The argument in favour of their action turned on the claim that refusal to *repeal* a tax was not the same as refusal to *impose* a tax. The prime minister, Lord Palmerston,* was not convinced of the need to repeal the duty, and he acquiesced in the decision of the Lords. Gladstone did not, and denounced the 'gigantic and dangerous innovation' of the Lords. The Commons agreed with Gladstone, stressing their control over issues of taxation and their power to impose and remit taxes. In 1861, the paper duties were included in the same bill as the rest of the budget, and placed beyond the power of the Lords.[62]

---

[61] *Parliamentary Debates*, 3rd ser. 156, 10 Feb. 1860, cols. 818–19, 826, 830–8, 850, 867–72; details are in S. C. Buxton, *Finance and Politics: An Historical Study, 1789–1885* (2 vols., London, 1888), vol. I, chapters 10, 11, 12; Buxton, *Mr Gladstone as Chancellor*, chapters 3 and 4 on the budget of 1860, chapter 8 on purging the tariff; Matthew, *Gladstone, 1809–1898*, pp. 113–14, 124–5; W. E. Gladstone, 'Free trade, railways and the growth of commerce', *Nineteenth Century* 7 (1880), 374, 377. For a brief discussion of Gladstone on indirect taxes, see Maloney, 'Gladstone and sound Victorian finance', pp. 41–4. According to Nye, net customs revenue as a percentage of net export values stood at 53.1 per cent in Britain and 20.3 per cent in France in 1821–5; the figures were 11.5 and 5.9 per cent in 1861–5. By 1881–5, the relative position was reversed, with Britain at 5.9 per cent and France at 7.5 per cent: J. N. Nye, 'The myth of free trade Britain and fortress France: tariffs and trade in the nineteenth century', *Journal of Economic History* 51 (1991), 26.

[62] Matthew, *Gladstone, 1809–1898*, pp. 113–14; Buxton, *Mr Gladstone as Chancellor*, chapter 9; and Buxton, *Finance and Politics*, vol. I, pp. 211–14 and chapter 13 on the paper duty.

* Henry John Temple, 3rd viscount Palmerston (1784–1865) was born in London and educated at Harrow, Edinburgh and St John's College, Cambridge; he was an Irish peer, and could therefore sit in the Commons and he was an MP from 1807 to his death. He was lord of the Admiralty in 1808, secretary at war (with responsibility for finance) from 1809 to 1828, and foreign secretary in 1830, a post he held with only a short gap to 1841, and again from 1846 to 1851. He was home secretary (with intervals) between 1852 and 1855, and prime minister in 1855–8 and 1859–65. Like Gladstone, he started out as a Tory; he moved towards the Whigs, and unlike Gladstone pursued imperialistic and expansive foreign policies. (*DNB*, vol. LVI, ed. Lee, pp. 16–33.)

In his budget of 1861, Gladstone argued the case for both direct *and* indirect taxes in a passage often cited in later discussions:

> I never can think of direct or indirect taxation except as I should think of two attractive sisters who have been introduced into the gay world of London, each with an ample fortune, both having the same parentage – for the parents of both I believe to be Necessity and Invention – differing only as sisters may differ...I cannot conceive any reason why there should be unfriendly rivalry between the admirers of these two damsels; and I frankly own, whether it be due to a lax sense of moral obligation or not, that as a Chancellor of the Exchequer...I have always thought it not only allowable but even an act of duty to pay my addresses to them both. I am, therefore, as between direct and indirect taxation, perfectly impartial.

Reduction of indirect taxes was justified on political, social and moral grounds, for it 'knit together the interests and feelings of all classes of the community'. At the same time, it led to material prosperity. But the task was not to destroy indirect taxes: it was to prune the tree and make it more vigorous. 'Its condition recalls to my mind the tree of golden leaves which has been described by Virgil, from which his hero was ordered to pluck a branch, and on whose trunk, the moment one branch had been plucked, another took its place.' Indirect taxes therefore had a major role in Gladstone's fiscal constitution: protective and differential duties were anathema; revenue duties were acceptable on condition they did not distort the economy or threaten social harmony. He did not believe that indirect taxes should be reduced at the expense of direct taxes – and he argued for the abandonment of the income tax. However, he pointed out in 1861 that 'I really cannot conceive that my responsibility to abolish the tax is that absolute and unconditional responsibility wholly apart from any question of the amount of expenditure for which provision is to be made.' In 1861, he made only a small surplus: he repealed the paper duties, kept the tea and sugar duties for a further year, and reduced the income tax to 9d for the last three-quarters of the year. He wooed both sisters – but his flirtations were emotionally fraught.[63]

In 1861, Gladstone remarked that taxation was higher than it had ever been at a time of peace in Europe.[64] For the next generation, chancellors experienced much more favourable circumstances. The rate of economic growth rose in the middle of the nineteenth century and the yield of taxes increased. In 1842–3, each 1d of income tax produced £772,000 revenue; in 1860–1, this had risen to £1,122,000; the growth continued, to £1,588,000 in 1870–1, £1,867,000 in 1880–1 and £2,214,000 in 1890–1.[65] At the same time, costs of defence and warfare were modest,

---

[63] *Parliamentary Debates*, 3rd ser. 162, 15 Apr. 1861, cols. 584–6, 592–3.
[64] *Parliamentary Debates*, 3rd ser. 162, 15 Apr. 1861, col. 594.
[65] Stamp, *British Incomes and Property*, table G4, pp. 318–19.

for Britain was not involved in European warfare, most imperial wars were small scale, and military technology and strategy did not require large standing armies or huge fleets. Most of the cost of social welfare was incurred at the local level. There was therefore some room for manoeuvre in reducing taxes, and chancellors had to decide which sister should be courted most assiduously. Gladstone did contemplate abolishing the income tax in the 1860s and in 1873/4, possibly at the expense of an increase in the inhabited house duty or in death duties.[66] Although he did not achieve his ambition, the rate of income tax was reduced from its peak of 1s 4d in the Crimean war; it was cut after the war to 5d, but subsequently raised to a peace-time peak of 10d in 1860. By 1863, it was down to 7d, in 1864 to 6d, in 1865 to 4d. Despite these considerable concessions to income tax, duties were also cut. The duty on tea rose from 1s 6d to 1s 9d in the war; by 1865 it stood at 6d. Similar cuts were made to the sugar duty, and the concessions to the two sisters were about equal.[67] Would chancellors be able to continue their delicate task of flirting with both sisters?

In 1870, Robert Lowe reiterated Gladstone's policy. He anticipated a surplus of £4.5m, and had to decide on the concessions to direct and indirect taxes. He took a different, and equally fanciful, analogy: that taxpayers were like animals living at great distances below the water, surviving because of 'equalisation of pressure'. It followed that the pressure of taxation would be felt most lightly if spread over a number of sources, rather than placing some taxpayers under intolerable pressure and giving 'undeserved ease' to others.

I am not willing...to let go any great branch of Revenue that is levied with tolerable ease and without any grievous pressure...while reducing the burdens of the people to the very lowest possible amount, I shall not willingly let go altogether any branch of Revenue which I think can be collected without imposing any great suffering upon the community.

In pursuit of this policy, he reduced the income tax to 4d (a concession of £1,250,000) and cut the sugar duty by half (a concession of £2,350,000).[68]

The chief difficulty experienced by Lowe, so it seemed, was 'to know how to get rid of all the money which persisted in pouring in upon him. The general impression at the time was that the country need never fear either a deficiency of receipts or a shrinking of revenue.' Economic growth and prosperity meant that yields rose, and chancellors had considerable

[66] See p. 153.
[67] Buxton, *Mr Gladstone as Chancellor*, pp. 144–6.
[68] *Parliamentary Debates*, 3rd ser 200, 11 Apr. 1870, cols. 1626, 1638–42.

room for concessions. At the same time, the reduction in the cost of servicing the national debt, the absence of large-scale military commitments and the low level of social spending meant that central government expenditure grew less rapidly than the economy. In 1871, Lowe made a serious miscalculation when he announced in the budget his intention of introducing a new duty on matches in conjunction with an adjustment to the succession duties – a proposal which caused outcry and deputations of poor matchmakers from the East End. The budget was withdrawn, and Lowe returned to a safer policy of making more concessions. He reduced the duty on sugar to such a low rate in 1873 that his Conservative successor, Stafford Northcote, abolished it in 1874. Lowe also abolished the remaining registration duty on corn in 1873. In the opinion of Sydney Buxton, the budget of 1873 departed from Lowe's own principle of 'equalisation of pressure' and embarked on a new policy. As Buxton commented, duties previously abolished had been protective or unremunerative. The budget of 1873 marked a new approach, of abolishing 'simple duties on articles of general consumption' which were inexpensive to collect and not harmful to trade. The result was that the range of indirect taxes was reduced to a few commodities, and purely revenue duties had been abandoned.[69]

The major question for the future was: what would happen when taxes needed to be increased rather than reduced? The marked reduction in indirect taxes changed the position, for free trade was defined according to the standards of 1873 rather than 1860. Gladstone removed protective duties and retained a small number of revenue duties which were compatible with free trade. The reliance on a few duties had significant political consequences by the end of the nineteenth century, for these

---

[69] Buxton, *Finance and Politics*, vol. II, especially chapters 23 and 25 on Lowe and 27 on Northcote. The comments of Buxton on Lowe are on pp. 157–9. On the match tax debacle, see Morley, *Life of Gladstone*, vol. II, pp. 373–4. His proposed Latin pun to be printed on the match stamp – *Ex luce lucellum* – might, remarked Morley, 'divert a college common room' but seemed flippant. The tax was discussed by W. S. Jevons, *The Match Tax: A Problem in Finance* (London, 1871) who accepted its unpopularity. However, he defended the tax on general grounds, arguing that 'all classes of persons above the rank of actual paupers should contribute to the state in the proportion of their revenues'. Relief to the poor might seem desirable, but Jevons warned against 'ill-considered humanity': the result might be to harm the poor by imposing taxes on capital which would leave for foreign countries and colonies and reduce employment of the poor. He doubted the wisdom of relying so heavily on a narrow basis of indirect taxes, and argued that taxes on necessities were acceptable to secure some contribution from the mass of the population. Such a tax was preferable to excessive taxation of profits, provided that industrial materials were not taxed, and there was no protection. Jevons was continuing some of the themes of writers such as Babbage (above, pp. 150–1) and was looking forward to Robert Giffen (below, pp. 311–13).

remaining articles tended to form a declining share of total consumption. Any additional revenue was likely to require a reimposition of the sugar duty or an increase in the range of duties – proposals now interpreted as an onslaught on free trade. It proved difficult to draw a distinction between revenue duties and protective duties, and the reductions in the budgets of 1873 and 1874 became sacrosanct to most Liberals and more generally embedded in British political culture.

The marked divergence between Britain and other European countries dates from the end of the nineteenth century, when British duties failed to rise as other countries started to move to protection (see chapter 10). The emphasis in the historical literature on the repeal of the corn laws in 1846, and its connection with the income tax in 1842, obscures an important point: excise duties formed the basis of free trade finance up to the 1860s. By the end of the century, the situation was different, for the share of indirect taxes in many other European countries rose, whereas in Britain it fell. Part of the explanation was the structure of the direct tax system, which was able to tap the benefits of economic growth in Britain compared with the more stereotyped direct taxes in much of continental Europe where revision was more problematic.

British politicians and civil servants constantly stressed the modern, scientific, nature of the British tax system after 1842 in comparison with the archaic and 'unscientific' nature of European taxation. In fact, the reintroduction of the income tax marked a convergence with France by extracting revenue from a similar range of incomes. Between 1816 and 1842, Britain lacked the range of taxes on different forms of income found in France and other European countries. After 1842, the British income tax had certain similarities with the direct taxes in France, for the use of different schedules with different methods of assessment and collection meant that the effective rate of income tax varied between types of income, in much the same way as the specific taxes levied on particular forms of income in other European countries. Thus schedule A covered income from real estate and was equivalent to the *contribution foncière* levied in France on the income from buildings and land. Schedule D taxed the profits of trade, industry and the professions, and was equivalent to the *droits de patente*, a form of licence on industry, trade and the professions. The *patentes* were introduced in 1791, replacing the guilds when they were swept away and business was opened to anyone who paid the *patente*. In Britain, guild powers withered away and did not provide the basis for an alternative system of state taxation. The income tax was therefore akin to the French system in certain respects, marking an extension of the fiscal system to similar elements of the economy.

Nevertheless, the British tax system diverged from the French in the way 'handles' were attached to different forms of income. The method of assessment and collection in Britain contributed to the high degree of consent to taxation and tax yields were more responsive to economic growth. The main difference between direct taxation in the two countries was that the British system offered greater flexibility and freedom from political tensions in tapping the tax base. A comparison between the *droits de patente* and schedule D on profits makes the point. The *patentes* were a fixed charge determined by the type of business and the population of the area, plus a proportional charge according to the rent of business premises assessed by the local mayor and the agent of the finance ministry. Such an approach was not necessarily less effective than the British system of self-assessment of income; in both cases, the issue was how best to attach a 'handle' to an elusive form of income, where the taxpayers had many opportunities for concealment and under-assessment. However, the *patentes* were less responsive to changes in the structure of the economy or levels of activity: they were essentially licence fees for particular trades, and did not rise in step with economic growth or changes in the structure of the economy. Further, the *droits* created a plethora of separate tax categories according to region and trade so that any adjustment of the tax was exceedingly difficult, involving detailed bargaining over the precise rate for this trade or that region. By contrast, schedule D – whatever the dangers of under-assessment – did not create serious tensions between classes and interests. The chancellor of the Exchequer could alter the rate of taxation from *all* schedules by a single adjustment of the rate of income tax in the £, which was not possible for French finance ministers who needed to adjust a range of separate taxes, a process which was complicated and politically sensitive. Similarly, revenue from taxes on land, dividends or employment was less likely to rise in line with the increase of the tax base in France. In Britain, schedule A reflected the actual level of rents paid by tenants, whereas in France it rested on a lagged bureaucratic reassessment of estimated rents. Similarly, schedules C and E were effective in extracting income from government stocks and employment. In France, door and window taxes and the *contribution personnelle mobilière* did not rise in line with total national income. The two tax systems therefore differed in their effectiveness in attaching handles to the tax base. The scope for adjustment of existing direct taxes was limited in France, and their replacement by a new income tax posed still greater problems. Consequently, the French government became more dependent on general indirect taxes which rose in line with economic activity. In Britain, the shift to direct taxes was facilitated by the attachment of effective handles to the economy, quite apart from any ideological commitment.[70]

The outcome was a marked change in the structure of taxation in Britain and France. Between 1816 and 1842, Britain was more dependent on consumption taxes than France; between 1842 and the First World War, the share of direct taxes rose in Britain and fell in France. The French tax system started to produce social and political tension, in contrast with the widely shared sentiment that the British fiscal system was even-handed between interests and classes. Of course, there was also a political case in support of a conscious, graduated, shift in the fiscal structure in favour of direct taxes which was central to the conception of the British state. By the end of the nineteenth century, the FRA's rigid opposition to indirect taxes was central to Liberal rhetoric in the form of support of the 'free breakfast table'. The shift away from indirect taxes had gone so far that problems were starting to arise. The fiscal system was reaching its limits, forcing a reconsideration either of the flat-rate income tax or the extension of indirect taxes to a wider range of goods.

Conclusion

When Peel reintroduced the income tax in 1842, he aimed to balance the budget in two senses: first, by removing the deficit left by the Whigs and restoring order to government finances; and secondly, by establishing a sense of equity between different types of wealth and income. In 1846, he took a further step by abolishing agricultural protection. His policy was continued by Gladstone, most notably in his budget of 1853. Peel and Gladstone established the principle that the state should not appear to favour any particular economic interest, and that taxes should be a carefully devised system of checks and balances. Any bias in the income tax against 'industrial' or earned income (which was liable to loss during ill-health or trade depression) compared with 'spontaneous' or unearned income (which was supported by capital assets producing income regardless of health or economic depression) should be balanced by taxation of property at death, rather than by turning the income tax into an arena for conflict between interests. Gladstone appealed to radical assumptions, arguing that a minimal state and retrenchment would remove the source

---

[70] R. L. Koepke, 'The *Loi des patentes* of 1844', *French Historical Studies* 11 (1979–80), 398–430. Of course, in France the income tax and graduation were tainted by Jacobinism or extreme socialism; they only slowly came to be seen as equitable and fair. See J.-P. Gross, 'Progressive taxation and social justice in eighteenth-century France', *Past and Present* 140 (1993), 121, 123–5.

of revenue which sustained parasitical hangers-on and fuelled warfare: retrenchment offered peace and liberty. Peel and Gladstone articulated a language of public trust.[71]

The creation of at least an *appearance* of neutrality was achieved more successfully in Britain than in other European countries.[72] The willingness of the elite to shoulder the burdens of the income tax and to abandon the corn laws marked a triumph of 'disinterestedness'. The success of the policy was clear in 1848, when revolutions in the rest of Europe contrasted with the demise of Chartism. The radicals of mid-Victorian Britain were willing to trust elite politicians such as Peel and Gladstone, and to accept the legitimacy and 'neutrality' of the state, rather than to castigate politicians as selfish and corrupt, and the state as a special interest. Radicalism became constitutional, working through parliament in order to control expenditure and to monitor the executive, and this continued into the Labour party's adoption of a similar strategy of parliamentarism.[73] However, Labour did not simply succumb to the hegemony of Gladstonian finance. The creation of a high degree of trust in the state and in public action permitted a shift in attitudes, away from criticism of the state as prodigal to acceptance of the state as efficient. The success of the Gladstonian project could lead to its subversion: if the fiscal system was fair and balanced, why not use it to pay for tax-funded welfare and other collective action?

These debates over the technicalities of ability or capacity to pay taxes raise fundamental issues about the nature of the state and its relationship with its citizens. Was the citizen entering into a contract with the state, paying for the protection of property? But it was realised by Hemming in 1852 that property might itself be created by the state, so that there was not a simple contract between two parties: one had called the other into existence. The point was accepted by J. S. Mill, who assumed that inherited property depended on 'artificial' legal institutions and could therefore be heavily taxed by the state – not least because it was passive.

---

[71] Harling, *Waning of 'Old Corruption'*, pp. 228–54; Harling and Mandler, 'From "fiscal-military" state to laissez-faire state', 70; Hilton, *Corn, Cash and Commerce*; Matthew, 'Disraeli, Gladstone and the politics of mid-Victorian budgets'; Matthew, *Gladstone, 1809–1874*; Biagini, 'Popular Liberals, Gladstonian finance and the debate on taxation', pp. 134–62; Biagini, *Liberty, Retrenchment and Reform*; McKibbin, 'Why was there no Marxism in Great Britain?'; on the emergence of free trade as an orthodoxy, see A. C. Howe, *Free Trade and Liberal England, 1846–1946* (Oxford, 1997), chapter 4.

[72] G. Eley and D. Blackbourn, *The Peculiarities of German History: Bourgeois Society and Politics in Nineteenth-Century Germany* (Oxford, 1984), pp. 105, 122, 125, 256–85.

[73] D. Read, *Peel and the Victorians* (Oxford, 1987), pp. 288–9, 319; Biagini, *Liberty, Retrenchment and Reform*, pp. 6–8 and *passim*; on Labour and parliamentarism, see P. Ward, *Red Flag and Union Jack: Englishness, Patriotism and the British Left, 1881–1924* (Woodbridge, 1998).

These issues were often debated by laying claim to a particular definition of Adam Smith's first maxim, contesting the meaning of the enjoyment of property. In the mid-Victorian period, the radical implications of these debates were contained; at the close of the century, they reappeared with new force. Socially created or unearned wealth did not 'belong' to the owner but to the community which had called it into being. The definition of 'enjoyment' was transformed by the influence of the marginal revolution in economics, with its realisation that the satisfaction derived from an additional pound was much less for someone earning £10,000 a year than someone subsisting on £75 a year. Of course, politicians were also acutely aware of the electoral implications of the extension of the franchise. But until 1894, the potentially explosive forces were contained: they were to be released at the end of the century by the costs of warfare, and changes in attitudes to social spending.

7 'The minimum of irritation': fiscal administration and civil society, 1842–1914

The tax which each individual is bound to pay ought to be certain, and not arbitrary. The time of payment, the manner of payment, the quantity to be paid, ought all to be clear and plain to the contributor, and to every other person. Where it is otherwise, every person subject to the tax is put more or less in the power of the tax-gatherer, who can either aggravate the tax upon any obnoxious contributor, or extort, by the terror of such aggravation, some present or perquisite to himself. The uncertainty of taxation encourages the insolence and favours the corruption of an order of men who are naturally unpopular, even when they are neither insolent nor corrupt. The certainty of what each individual ought to pay is, in taxation, a matter of so great importance, that a very considerable degree of inequality, it appears, I believe, from the experience of all nations, is not near so great an evil as a very small degree of uncertainty.

> Adam Smith's second maxim of taxation, *An Inquiry into the Nature and Causes of the Wealth of Nations*, ed. R. H. Campbell, A. S. Skinner and W. B. Todd (2 vols., Oxford, 1976), vol. II, viib, pp. 825–6

...the policy of the law hitherto has been...not to make the collection depend upon the will of the Government, because it was thought more consistent with constitutional law, to entrust the amount to local parties, and that those who may have the confidence of their neighbours shall be employed for this purpose.

> Sir Robert Peel, *Parliamentary Debates*, 3rd ser. 61, 18 Mar. 1842, col. 912

The primary object of good administration is to promote efficiency, which in Income Tax matters results in the smooth working of the machine in such a way as to produce the full measure of revenue with the minimum of irritation to the taxpayer and with the least possible inequity between one taxpayer and another...an administration that is sympathetic and scrupulously fair, while adopting proper safeguards against evasion, can do much to reconcile the taxpayer to his lot, and convince him that within the limits of the Statutes the tax has been laid upon him with due care and justice.

> PP 1920 XVIII, *Report of the Royal Commission on the Income Tax*, p. 177

The Englishman has a genius for co-operating with the tax-collector.

> J. M. Keynes, 'Notes for the budget statement, 1941', in J. M. Keynes, *The Collected Writings of John Maynard Keynes, XXII Activities, 1939–45. Internal War Finance*, ed. D. Moggridge (London, 1978), p. 302

'To tax and to please', Edmund Burke remarked in 1774, 'no more than to love and to be wise, is not given to men.'[1] Pleasure in the payment of taxes is scarcely possible, yet collection could entail less animosity and discontent by creating 'voluntary' compliance and mutual trust. The 'relations of extraction' between taxpayers and the state could be formulated so as to foster a widely shared belief that the bargain between the state and the citizen was 'fair', both in the way revenue was extracted and the way it was spent. Consent was contingent on the belief that no group was unduly penalised or favoured in the collection or expenditure of taxes, and on the assumption that politicians and civil servants could be trusted to spend the money as promised. Of course, 'fairness' was an ideological construct or rhetorical device which rested upon a particular definition of equity, and was open to contestation, as indicated in the previous chapter. But, so long as the definition was widely accepted, and the tax system was considered fair and legitimate, the collection of taxes was possible with a minimum of tension.

The collection of customs and excise duties became highly routine in the second half of the nineteenth century. Excise duties were limited to a small range of goods, and collection was relatively simple: a small, efficient, bureaucracy dealt with large producers such as brewers or tobacco merchants. There was minimal interference with retailers or customers – a consideration which explained resistance to a wider sales tax at the end of the First World War.[2] Similarly, the simplification of import and export duties meant that administration became more routine: few goods were involved, and duties were levied by weight and measure rather than the complex scales of the early nineteenth century. As the Customs Board explained, Gladstone's budget of 1860 'carried the process of simplification of the tariff almost to the extremest limit of which it was susceptible'. At the start of the nineteenth century, there were 1,500 different rates in duty in Britain; in 1860, there were twenty-six broad categories, of which ten were 'countervailing' duties on imported duties, designed to balance excise duties levied on domestic production. Two other duties were set to expire, leaving only fourteen duties for revenue purposes. The process continued: the small surviving duties on timber and corn were abolished in 1866 and 1869; and the duty on sugar was halved in 1873 and removed in 1874. Only nine principal duties remained, and in 1896/7 only four commodities supplied 96.1 per cent of the revenue – foreign spirits,

---

[1] E. Burke, 'Speech on American taxation', in E. Burke, *The Writings and Speeches of Edmund Burke*, vol. II: *Party, Parliament and the American Crisis*, ed. P. Langford (Oxford, 1981), p. 454.
[2] See Daunton, 'How to pay for the war', 911–2.

tobacco, tea and wine.[3] In 1863 and again in 1886, a merger was considered between the Inland Revenue and Customs, completing the process of consolidation started in 1848 when the Board of Excise was incorporated into the Board of Inland Revenue. The proposed merger did not come about; instead, the Excise was removed from the Inland Revenue and united with Customs in the budget of 1908, so creating a clear administrative divide between direct and indirect taxes. As a result, there were two distinct Boards for direct and indirect taxes, and two bodies of advice and expertise, which helped to shape the tax system in the later nineteenth and twentieth centuries.[4] Above all, the Inland Revenue felt that its methods of collection were less intrusive and contentious than indirect taxes, with their need to pry into the books and personal affairs of a large number of traders and businesses.

It is extremely difficult to measure the attitudes of taxpayers to the system of fiscal administration, and much of this chapter deals with the government's view of civil society and its perception of how consent should be achieved. The concern is largely with the reaction of politicians and civil servants to how they thought taxpayers did, or might, react to patterns of administration. There was a considerable degree of self-awareness and critical assessment of how the collection of taxes might be viewed, and a realisation that compliance would be secured through a careful presentation of the state to its citizens, and that bounds could not be safely transgressed.[5] As we have argued, a major achievement of the British state after 1842 was to remove the sentiment that the fiscal system was 'unfair', and that the state was prodigal and inefficient. This rhetoric of 'fairness' influenced fiscal policy, for it could not be exposed as an empty sham without serious political costs; the state was constrained from raising revenue in a way which was openly inequitable between classes or interests.[6] But consent did not depend only on the creation of a sense of

---

[3] PP 1898 LXXXV, *Customs tariff of the United Kingdom from 1800 to 1897, with some notes upon the history of the more important branches of receipt from the year 1660*, pp. 39–41.

[4] PP 1863 VI, *Report from the Select Committee on Inland Revenue and Customs Establishments*, p. 311; PRO, IR74/181, 'Memorandum for Sir M. Hicks Beach on the proposed amalgamation of the Board of Customs with the Board of Inland Revenue', Sir A. West, 7 Jan. 1886; B. Mallet, *British Budgets, 1887–88 to 1912–13* (London, 1913), p. 290.

[5] A similar point can be made from the reform of the inquest: should this be passed over to experts, or should it involve general practitioners, with a greater understanding of the context of a death, and a jury meeting in public? As Ian Burney says, the association of the inquest with 'English liberties' was a constitutive feature of debates about its future, creating a 'framing discourse': much the same could be said of debates over the involvement of lay commissioners and assessors in the tax system. See I. A. Burney, *Bodies of Evidence: Medicine and the Politics of the English Inquest, 1830–1926* (Baltimore, 2000). I would like to thank Peter Mandler for drawing my attention to this parallel.

[6] McKibbin, 'Why was there no Marxism in Great Britain?'

balance and equity: it also rested on the precise methods of administration which allowed the revenue to be extracted from the taxpayer with 'the minimum of irritation'. The procedures adopted in 1842 became central to the income tax, a crucial feature of the Victorian fiscal constitution to which officials at the Inland Revenue and Treasury appealed whenever chancellors proposed a reform. The administrative procedures started to harden into dogma, providing officials with a means of blocking change through their immense technical knowledge of the machinery of assessment and collection. There was a danger that, at some point, official resistance would call consent into question and make the tax system rigid in the face of social change. New political circumstances could mean that consent would come to depend on graduation of tax rates, but the Inland Revenue might insist that a single standard rate of tax was essential for ease of administration. Similarly, a change in economic structures might mean that incomes from employment became more numerous with a need to change the methods of collection of taxation in order to minimise friction.

The income tax was a source of pride and celebration at least by the end of the nineteenth century. Indeed, the apparent ease of operation of the income tax and its wide acceptance by the taxpaying public contributed to the decline in indirect taxes and the rise of direct taxes up to and beyond the First World War. For all the earlier tensions, the income tax became a significant feature in British national identity, a mark of the secure relationship between subject and state in contrast with what were perceived to be more despotic or bureaucratic nations of Europe. On this view, other nations were forced to rely on indirect taxes as a result of their failure to negotiate a harmonious and co-operative relationship with civil society; in Britain, such a relationship had been established and should not, on any account, be threatened by 'inquisitorial' state action. Of course, much of this case was rhetorical rather than an accurate description of administration in different countries. Nevertheless, it was of considerable importance in creating consent to income tax and erecting formidable barriers against reform of the fiscal constitution. The Treasury and Inland Revenue appealed to this rhetoric in a long, and eventually unsuccessful, rearguard action against graduation. It was also used, with greater success, at the end of the First World War to block the adoption of indirect taxes. The decision of other countries to adopt sales taxes was taken as proof that the relationship between the taxpayer and the state was less satisfactory than in Britain, where the income tax was widely accepted as legitimate. The aim of this chapter is to assess the ways in which the state negotiated its relations with its citizens in the collection and administration of taxes and, above all, the income tax where the potential for tension was greatest.

Assessment and collection of the income tax

The income tax introduced by Pitt in 1799 required taxpayers to divulge their entire income, which was then taxed as a whole. When Henry Addington* reintroduced the tax in 1803, after the short-lived peace of 1802–3, he abandoned the attempt to assess total income and the tax was divided into separate schedules or types of income (see table 7.1). The benefits of schedular taxation were obvious in the great improvement in yields: a tax rate of 2s in the £ produced £5,628,813 in 1801; a rate of 1s in the £ produced £5,341,907 in 1803.[7] In 1842, Peel re-enacted Addington's approach as codified in the Income Tax Act, 1806. Collection at source on particular types of income was preferred to direct assessment of total income which was 'much more inquisitorial, more vexatious, and more difficult'.[8] Taxes from different categories of income could be levied in different ways. Tax was collected at source from rents and dividends in schedules A and C, and from official salaries in schedule E. This procedure was seen by many as the key to the success of the British tax system after the reintroduction of the income tax in 1842, allowing it to be 'levied with a minimum of friction and a maximum of result', and allowing collection 'to the utmost farthing which is due' from dividends, salaries and rent, without any disclosure to the tax authorities.[9] Of course, there were attempts at evasion. In 1843, a Welsh landowner was found to have asked his tenants to under-report their rent so reducing his tax liability under schedule A and their own under schedule B. Indeed, one culprit was himself an assessor, who returned his rent as £60 rather than £64. But such cases of collusion did not cause much concern to the Inland Revenue which stressed the virtues of ease of collection at source.

---

[7] Hope-Jones, *Income Tax*, pp. 22–3.
[8] PP 1852 IX, *First Report from the Select Committee on the Income and Property Tax*, C. Pressly of Inland Revenue, Q. 367.
[9] PP 1852 IX, *First Report from the Select Committee on Income and Property Tax*, Q. 373.
* Henry Addington (1757–1844) was the son of a physician; he was educated at Winchester and Brasenose College, Oxford. He entered parliament in 1783 and was speaker from 1789 to 1801, when he became chancellor and prime minister. He quarrelled with Pitt, a childhood friend, in 1803 and resigned in 1804. He served as president of the council for a short time in 1805 and again in 1812; he was home secretary in Liverpool's government from 1812 to 1821, with a reputation for repression. He remained in the Cabinet until 1824, and opposed both Catholic emancipation and the reform bill. (*DNB*, vol. I, ed. Stephen, pp. 117–21.)

Table 7.1 *Income tax schedules*

Schedule A: rents of real estate and houses
Tax was paid at source by deduction from the rent, so that the owner of property received the income net of tax. The tax was on the gross rent, without an allowance for repairs or improvements. In 1894, when the death duties were reformed, a concession was granted to schedule A: a deduction of 10 per cent was allowed from the income of land and 15 per cent from the income of houses. The income tax rate was effectively reduced as a compensation for the graduated taxation of real property at death.

Schedule B: profits from the occupation of land i.e. farming
The tax could not be paid at source, for the profits depended upon a large number of transactions as crops were sold and seeds, implements and animals purchased. In order to remove the need for farmers to produce complicated returns, it was assumed that profits amounted to three-quarters of rent in England and a half in Scotland. In 1842, the proportions were reduced to half and a third; and in 1851, farmers were permitted to pay tax on their actual profits when these were lower.

Schedule C: profits from government stock and dividends
The tax was deducted at source when the Bank of England paid the interest on stock.

Schedule D: profits from trade, commerce and the professions
It was not possible to collect the tax at source, for the profits rested upon a large number of transactions; neither was it possible to take rent (or any other simple measure) as an indicator of profits. The assessment of the tax therefore rested upon an assessment of the profits of the individual trader or professional. Tax was paid on the basis of average income of the previous three years in order to smooth out fluctuations of trade, unlike other schedules which paid on the basis of the preceding year. The procedure adopted for government stock was extended to companies which were treated as withholding agents in the payment of dividends. Income tax was paid at the standard rate on profits, and when dividends on shares and interest on stock were distributed, they were paid net of tax. Anyone who was exempt from tax, or paid a lower rate, claimed repayment of the tax from the authorities.

Schedule E: salaries and pensions from office
In the case of employment from office, income tax was deducted from the salary or pension at source, which was paid net of tax. When the income tax was introduced, payment of a regular annual salary was not common outside the government service. Employers made a return of their staff to the tax officials, who claimed payment of tax from the employees, but with the growth of larger, bureaucratic, organisations such as railway companies or joint-stock banks, the payment of salaries net of tax was extended to them.

Source: A. Hope-Jones, *Income Tax in the Napoleonic Wars* (Cambridge,1939), pp. 20–1; PP 1870 XX, *Report of the Commissioners of Inland Revenue on the duties under their management for the years 1856 to 1869 inclusive*, vol. I, pp. 326, 328.

E. W. Hamilton expressed a common view that the ease of collection of the income tax 'is one of the wonders of the world. It is the envy of other nations.'[10] An American commentator in 1910 agreed, arguing that 'it obviat[es] the necessity for inquisitorial proceedings upon the one hand, while removing the opportunity for fraud and evasion upon the other'.[11] The schedular system meant that it was no longer necessary to establish the entire income of an individual taxpayer, so reducing the scope for clashes between taxpayers and officials of the Inland Revenue; and collection at source limited the opportunity for under-assessment and evasion. It was repeatedly argued that such a system meant that the relations between taxpayer and tax collector were trouble free, and collection at source was considered to be 'at the very root of the British income tax system...Without deduction of tax at source the revenue is wholly dependent upon the care and accuracy with which the taxpayer makes up his Income Tax Return; evasion is simple.'[12] The entire tax receipt under schedules A, C and E was collected at source, and formed 63.5 per cent of the net revenue from the income tax in 1855/6. The proportion fell to 36.0 per cent in 1910/11, but an increasing proportion of income under schedule D from dividends on shares in public companies was deducted at source, as well as regular salaries under schedule E (see table 7.2). In 1905, 70 to 80 per cent of tax was collected either at source, or on income which could be verified in some way.[13]

Collection at source was not possible for incomes from unincorporated businesses in schedule D, that is the profits of professions or family firms and partnerships. Here, tax liability was determined by lay commissioners and assessors so that the income tax was less intrusive and the relationship between the state and civil society was not threatened. It was argued that taxpayers were protected against an over-powerful bureaucracy and a grasping state by relying on members of the taxpaying class to assess and collect taxes, and to arbitrate in disputes. Of course, an administrative system operated by taxpayers was susceptible to under-assessment of incomes, and a fine line needed to be drawn between the benefits of consent and the dangers of evasion. Permanent officials had powers to

[10] PP 1905 XLIV, *Report of the Departmental Committee on Income Tax*, p. 221; PRO, T168/68, miscellaneous memorandum by E. W. Hamilton, volume XIII, 'Graduation of income tax', Hamilton to chancellor of the Exchequer, 6 June 1906; administration is outlined in PP 1870 XX, *Report of the Commissioners of Inland Revenue*, vol. I, pp. 307–13. PRO, IR40/308, Thomas Kite, assistant inspector, Hereford, 11 Feb. 1843, and J. Timm, solicitor to Inland Revenue, 17 Feb. 1843.

[11] K. K. Kennan, *Income Taxation: Methods and Results in Various Countries* (Milwaukee, 1910), pp. 58, 73–4.

[12] PRO, T176/18, undated and unsigned paper, ff. 17–18.

[13] PRO, T176/18; PP 1905 XLIV, *Report of the Departmental Committee on Income Tax*, p. 223.

Table 7.2 *Net receipt from income tax by schedule, United Kingdom, 1855/6 and 1910/11 (per cent)*

	1855/6	1910/11
Schedule A (rent)	47.2	25.3
Schedule B (farming)	5.6	0.5
Schedule C (dividends)	10.4	4.0
Schedule D (trade and professions)		
Public companies and foreign dividends		38.7
Trades and professions		20.1
Total	30.9	58.8
Schedule E (employment)	5.9	6.7
Supertax		4.6

Source: PP 1857 (1st session) IV, *First Report of the Commissioners of the Inland Revenue*, pp. 251–2; PP 1911 XLV, *Return showing for the year ended 31 March 1911 (1) the amount contributed by England, Scotland and Ireland respectively to the revenue collected by imperial officers (2) the expenditure of English, Scottish and Irish services met out of such revenue; and (3) the balances of revenue contributed by England, Scotland and Ireland respectively, which are available for imperial expenditure . . .*, p. 415.

monitor the system and prevent obvious cases of fraud and evasion, which would threaten mutual trust between taxpayers. Compliance would break down if one taxpayer thought that another was evading proper payment; commitment to taxation rested upon the belief that fellow taxpayers were at least as reliable and trustworthy as oneself. But care had to be taken that bureaucratic powers were not increased too far, for this would be interpreted as an act of 'despotism' by the government which would undermine the relationship between the taxpayer and the state, and threaten consent to taxation. A careful balance needed to be struck between incorporating taxpayers into the administrative system in order to secure a high level of acceptance of taxation at the cost of a certain degree of avoidance; and the creation of a more bureaucratic system which would remove anomalies and abuses at the expense of tension or unrest. Of course, this line shifted as the structure of the taxpaying class altered: when miners came within the reach of the income tax in the First World War, they were suspicious of a tax system which incorporated mineowners into assessment and collection. There was always a danger that the Inland Revenue would become more concerned to maintain tried and tested administrative procedures than to respond to the changing social relations of extraction.

The administration of the income tax depended on a hybrid system of lay and professional administrators which was crucial to achieving consent and minimising resistance. Collection and assessment of the income tax were based on the existing machinery of the land and assessed taxes, which passed responsibility to the taxpaying class. In each county division in England, the grand juries selected commissioners of land tax from those liable to the tax, who met a property qualification of real estate worth £100 a year; they appointed commissioners of general purposes with a qualifying income from all sources of £200 a year who had responsibility for the income tax. These general commissioners had considerable discretion and ought to be, remarked Pitt, 'persons of a respectable situation in life; as far as possible removed from any suspicion of partiality, or any kind of undue influence: men of integrity and independence'. They in turn appointed assessors who chose the collectors, with the same person often holding both appointments. The assessors and collectors were usually tradesmen in town and small farmers in the country, and held office on the same principle as parish officers such as the overseers of the poor; they were drawn from the residents of the parish and held office for a year with the threat of a fine if they refused. In 1860/1, there were about 54,000 assessors in the United Kingdom. The collector and assessor were each recompensed by a commission of 1.5d on every pound of tax collected. Finally, additional commissioners were selected by the general commissioners from residents with an annual income of £100. These officials were all drawn from the taxpaying public, and were not members of the state bureaucracy. The general commissioners appointed a clerk to provide administrative support, who was paid by them from a commission on the tax collected. Most clerks had another occupation such as a solicitor, and they were independent of the government. The additional commissioners were also assisted by clerks who were paid directly by the central government, but they were employed part-time rather than permanent officials. Administration of the income tax therefore rested upon the local community, utilising the same type of people who served as justices of the peace, and was characterised by Gladstone as the collection of taxes 'through the medium of a voluntary agency'.[14]

[14] *Parliamentary History of England from the Earliest Period to 1803*, vol. 34, 3 Dec. 1798, col. 6; on administration, see PP 1870 XX, *Report of the Commissioners of Inland Revenue*, vol. I, pp. 308–10; PP 1862 XII, *Select Committee on Inland Revenue and Customs Establishments*, evidence of C. Pressly, chairman of Inland Revenue, Qq. 163, 167–8; PP 1863 VI *Select Committee on Inland Revenue and Customs Establishments*; *Parliamentary Debates*, 3rd ser. 173, 8 Feb. 1864, col. 234; C. Stebbings, 'The clerk to the general commissioners of income tax', *British Tax Review* (1994): B. E. V. Sabine, 'The general commissioners', *British Tax Review* (1968).

Local, lay, administration was co-ordinated by a central body in London, the commissioners for the affairs of the taxes who were appointed in 1785 to provide some general oversight of the land, house and assessed taxes. In 1799, the commissioners took responsibility for the income tax, and in 1805 three commissioners for special purposes were appointed to deal with the income tax. The special commissioners had oversight of the largest returns in schedules A and C. The Board of Inland Revenue, as the central office at Somerset House eventually became known, was responsible for ensuring that the tax was administered uniformly throughout the country by informing general commissioners of changes in the law and supplying them with standard forms. Nevertheless, considerable discretion was left to the localities, in part as a self-protective measure to distance the central administration from the pressures of interest groups.[15] The Board did have permanent officials throughout the country in the form of surveyors who administered the house tax. They were given responsibility for monitoring the new income tax, working through the general commissioners and seeking advice from the special commissioners at Somerset House. The operation of the income tax was therefore based on a compromise between two styles of fiscal administration, of the land and assessed taxes which relied on the local taxpayers, and the excise duties operated entirely by permanent officials of the central government.[16] Care was needed to preserve the compromise, for an attempt to shift the balance between local delegated powers and central supervision threatened consent, and contributed to defeat of the income tax after the Napoleonic war. The general commissioners were widely seen as the protectors of citizens against oppression.[17]

Every three years, the assessors left a form for the assessment of schedules A and B at each house worth more than £10 a year. They also issued returns under schedules D and E by drawing up lists of everyone likely to be liable under schedule D, requesting employers to produce names of staff, and fixing a general notice to the doors of churches and chapels. The returns of schedules A, B and E were checked by the assessors, who estimated the value of any property which was not returned or where information was incomplete.[18] There was little room for evasion in these

---

[15] The use of the word commissioner for a variety of categories led to confusion, and the Taxes Management Act, 1880, referred to the commissioners at Somerset House as the Board of Inland Revenue; PP 1920 XVIII, *Report of the Royal Commission on the Income Tax*, recommended that this terminology be used for future legislation. See below pp. 207–10 on depreciation allowances.

[16] Hope-Jones, *Income Tax*, pp. 18–19, 24–5, 28–32; PP 1920 XVIII, *Report of the Royal Commission on the Income Tax*, p. 178.

[17] Kennan, *Income Taxation*, pp. 55, 68–9, 114.

[18] PP 1920 XVIII, *Report of the Royal Commission on the Income Tax*, pp. 186–7.

cases: the valuation of land could be estimated without too much difficulty, and there was little doubt about interest from government stocks in schedule C, or about public incomes and pensions in schedule E. The surveyors reviewed the forms, and acted as assessors in the second and third years. The general commissioners approved the assessments, and their clerks issued notices to taxpayers with a right of appeal to the general commissioners; the collector then requested payment. Tax was deducted from rent by tenants, who paid it with their own tax, and by the Bank of England and government from schedules C and E. The greatest problem arose in the case of schedule D, where the profits of trade and professions were less clear and more difficult to check. Here was the role of the additional commissioners with personal knowledge of local trades. They had a clear sense of what was reasonable; more to the point, they established the consent of taxpayers. Returns of income under schedule D were sent to the assessor who estimated the amount due from anyone who neglected to make a return; the clerk to the general commissioners produced a list which was sent to the surveyor to check on doubtful cases and to enter the assessable profit from the accounts of public companies. The additional commissioners then made an assessment of income on the basis of information in the returns, the estimates of assessors and surveyors, and company accounts. The general commissioners issued notices for the payment of tax and announced the date for appeals. If the surveyor was not satisfied, he had the right to object to any assessment and to propose a surcharge, with a right of appeal by the taxpayer. Most cases were settled as a result of the surveyor's examination of the evidence, but the final decision rested with the general commissioners who could, if they wished, turn to three referees, one nominated by the taxpayer, a second by the general commissioners and the third neutral. There was no appeal against the general commissioners on a point of fact; a dispute on a point of law could go to the High Court. The general commissioners signed the assessments, which often became a formality; more significantly, they had a quasi-judicial function of adjudicating on claims for exemptions or abatement, hearing appeals and imposing penalties.[19] The ultimate determination of tax liability therefore rested in the hands of members of the taxpaying public rather than state officials, and the whole process was remarkably free of executive power and court decisions.

Since the income tax was intended as a temporary measure for three years, Peel turned to the legislation of 1806 rather than proposing any major changes which would suggest permanence. Above all, Peel was concerned to secure consent, and the continued involvement of lay

[19] PP 1920 XVIII, *Report of the Royal Commission on the Income Tax*, pp. 199–200.

commissioners and assessors was crucial to a high degree of voluntary compliance. Experience showed that the procedures of 1806 were more likely to create consent and trust, particularly at a time of suspicion about the government's intentions. One result of Peel's commitment to the administrative procedures of 1806 was that the income tax did not immediately apply to Ireland. There was no land tax in Ireland and hence no commissioners; the tax could therefore not be collected through the use of lay auxiliaries, and the use of government officials would create resentment and tensions.[20] Where Peel *did* make changes, they were designed to reinforce consent. Peel realised that the 'chief force of the objection as to the inquisitorial nature of the assessment' was in schedule D. In London, Bristol, Hull and other provincial towns, commissioners were appointed by 'special direction', which gave a formal role to various influential institutions and so helped to secure acceptance of the fiscal system. In the City of London, for example, commissioners were nominated by the Corporation, Bank of England and several leading dock, insurance and chartered companies. Such a procedure gave at least symbolic independence from the executive. Peel also realised that taxpayers might prefer not to divulge their affairs to neighbours who were serving as lay assessors, with the possible threat to their credit. He therefore offered taxpayers the option of dealing with distant, impersonal, special commissioners drawn from permanent officials at Somerset House and Treasury nominees. In fact, the power was little used: the special commissioners assessed only 2,388 of 380,000 individuals liable to schedule D in 1867/9.[21] The major role of the special commissioners was, in fact, to assess dividends and salaries paid by railway companies. In 1853, the special commissioners were also used by Gladstone in order to extend the income tax to Ireland – a centrally controlled, bureaucratic, form of collection which departed from the established pattern in Britain.[22]

---

[20] *Parliamentary Debates*, 3rd ser. 61, 11 Mar. 1842, col. 445.

[21] PP 1852 IX, *Second Report from the Select Committee on the Income and Property Tax*, appendix pp. 912–13; *Parliamentary Debates*, 3rd ser. 61, 18 Mar. 1842, cols. 910–12; 5 & 6 Vict. c. 35, 'An act for granting to Her Majesty duties on profits arising from property, professions, trades and offices until 6 April 1845'; PP 1920 XVIII, *Report of the Royal Commission on the Income Tax*, pp. 179–80, 186; Hope-Jones, *Income Tax*, pp. 15–16; PP 1870 XX, *Report of the Commissioners of Inland Revenue*, vol. I, pp. 308–10, 327–8; PP 1905 XLIV, *Report of the Departmental Committee on Income Tax*, pp. 222–3.

[22] *Parliamentary Debates* 3rd ser. 125, 18 Apr. 1853, cols. 1392–3, 1402–3; PP 1870 XX, *Report of the Commissioners of Inland Revenue*, vol. I, p. 310; 16 & 17 Vict. c. 34, 'An act for granting to Her Majesty duties on profits arising from property, professions, trades, and offices', 1853. The extension of the income tax to Ireland raised major questions of the costs of famine relief which were met in part from loans and in part from a rate paid in Ireland. Russell failed to extend the income tax to Ireland in 1848/9 as a better way of covering these costs. In Britain, radicals complained that Irish landowners were escaping their obligations and therefore imposing higher taxes on British taxpayers. In Ireland, the

What stands out in the mid-nineteenth century is the small scale of the bureaucracy required by the income tax. In 1870, there were only 361 surveyors, assistant surveyors and inspectors in Britain.[23] What remained to be seen was whether the administration of the income tax could continue to rely on the procedures of 1806, or whether there would be a shift in the boundary between lay and official, local and central control. A related issue was the ability of a schedular income tax to meet demands for revenue or to preserve a balanced fiscal system. Fiscal necessity or arguments of social justice might make it desirable to impose a higher, graduated, tax on large incomes, which would require a return to the taxation of global incomes adopted in 1799.

The British tax authorities were inclined to exaggerate the harmony of this system of administration, as we shall see in the next section. They also drew a strong – and exaggerated – contrast between their approach and continental Europe. Although local Assessment Commissions did exist elsewhere, they were criticised as the creatures of state officials, so that 'in Continental States the Government is in the long run supreme in matters of assessment'. In Prussia, for example, the head of the local community sat as the president of the Preliminary Commission which produced lists and returns. These were sent to the Assessment Commission headed by a state official, with a majority of members elected by councils and the remainder appointed by the government of the department. In addition, there was a Special Commission of Appeal for each department, in part appointed by the departmental government and in part elected by the provincial committee, with the president appointed by the minister of finance who had responsibility for the entire process of assessment.[24] The contrast with Britain was less stark than the Inland Revenue and Treasury wished to suggest, for there was a clear desire to involve local *elected* representatives in comparison with self-selected commissioners in Britain. The main difference in the process of administration was that in Prussia the elected members of the committees were part of the same machinery as the state officials; in Britain, there was a clear demarcation with a greater sense of lay control. But the main difference between Prussia and Britain arose from the different structure of the Reich and United Kingdom.

burden of the debt (£4.4m) and anticipated interest charges (£3m) was insupportable. In 1853, the debt was written off in return for the extension of the income tax to Ireland. See Morley, *Life of Gladstone* vol. I, pp. 465–7, 646–7; P. Gray, *Famine, Land and Politics: British Government and Irish Society, 1843–50* (Dublin, 1999), pp. 248, 275, 301–3, 313, 317, 324, 333.

[23] PP 1870 XX, *Report of the commissioners of Inland Revenue*, vol. I, p. 307.

[24] PRO, T168/96, 'Differentiation and graduation in the income tax and estate duty and some comparisons with foreign and colonial systems', B. Mallett, Dec. 1905; see also PP 1905 LXXXV, *Reports from His Majesty's representatives abroad respecting graduated income taxes in foreign states*, pp. 49–51, 67–9.

The income tax was introduced in Prussia in 1894, and the individual states resisted proposals by the Reich to introduce its own income tax which would threaten their revenues and change the balance of power between states and Reich. The eventual adoption of an income tax by the Reich in 1913 was associated with a serious fiscal and political crisis. The Reich's income tax lacked legitimacy and consent, less because of the method of collection and assessment than as a result of tensions within a federal system and the perception that the Reich was biassed between classes.[25] Here was the main divergence – yet the system of administration adopted in Britain did mitigate some of the problems of compliance which are a natural feature of any tax system. It was at least a comforting myth of political culture that the Englishman, unlike his less fortunate fellow Europeans, did have a genius for co-operating with the tax collector – and one which was constructed through a language of constitutional liberties.

Compliance, avoidance and evasion

How was the Board of Inland Revenue to respond to problems of compliance, avoidance and evasion? A balance had to be struck between intrusive measures with the danger of alienating taxpayers and acceptance of a degree of evasion in order to secure compliance. If evasion and avoidance were allowed to go too far, the fairness of taxation would be called into question and taxpayers would justify evasion on the grounds that others were doing the same or worse. Compliance depended on a degree of trust between taxpayers, an acceptance that most people adhered to basic honesty. Once this assumption was threatened and compliance was eroded, the tax authorities would need to impose stronger measures which would undermine the willingness of taxpayers to co-operate and drive up the costs of collection.

The Inland Revenue and Treasury defended the general commissioners 'as a buffer between the Taxpayer and the Crown' and an 'ancient bulwark of safety' for the public, and argued that the hybrid form of administration helped to secure consent.[26] Nevertheless, officials at Somerset House and the Treasury were aware of the shortcomings of delegating powers to the taxpaying class, and (in the opinion of one critic) 'has fretted and

---

[25] J. M. Hobson, 'The tax-seeking state: protectionism, taxation and state structures in Germany, Russia, Britain and America, 1870–1914', PhD thesis, University of London (1991), p. 106; Hobson, *Wealth of States*, chapter 2; N. Ferguson, 'Public finance and national security: the domestic origins of the First World War revisited', *Past and Present* 142 (1994), 155–64; J. von Kruedener, 'The Franckenstein paradox in the intergovernmental fiscal relations of imperial Germany', in Witt (ed.), *Wealth and Taxation*, pp. 111–23.

[26] PRO, T171/120, '1915', unsigned and undated.

strained at the gentle check and restraint imposed by the wisdom of those who devised the system'. Reforms were indeed proposed on a number of occasions but were restricted by opposition in parliament and the country so that the authorities were making a rhetorical case of the virtues of delegation, despite their awareness of the practical shortcomings.[27] The limits of local autonomy and delegation and central oversight, of a degree of evasion in return for consent, had to be carefully negotiated through a discourse of English 'liberties' and constitutional proprieties. This was a common theme in mid-Victorian Britain, with the desire of government officials to inspect and control, and of 'experts' to apply their authority, colliding with pressure to preserve the autonomy of local action and the participation of citizens. The central state embarked on the creation of systems of information gathering and inspection, with more than twenty central inspectorates established between 1832 and 1875 to monitor and enforce local administration of laws and standards. The Inland Revenue was part of this bureaucratic machinery of information gathering and surveillance. As Miles Ogborn has remarked, each arena of policy created different regimes of power and knowledge, whether it be the administration of the poor law, the establishment of police forces or monitoring of public health. What was involved was not a simple shift of a fixed amount of power between locality and centre: the nature of power emerged in different forms for different purposes, and varied between locations, through a process of contestation and negotiation. Localities might sidestep attempts to control the poor law guardians by developing new initiatives through the town council or charities. Government officials might sidestep elected local authorities to work with bodies of experts, or might create their own inspectors throughout the country. Administration of taxation was one element in this wider (and open-ended) process.[28]

The assessors and collectors might be in a difficult position. Small traders, appointed by their parish, were often 'placed between two conflicting interests, that of the Crown and of their customers in trade'. Some did refuse to undertake the task, such as William Comerford Casey, a soap manufacturer of Wavertree in Lancashire who was fined £10 in 1850 – one of seven declining to serve in the Prescot division of Lancashire between 1850 and 1856. Critics of the system pointed out that these parish officers

---

[27] For a critical outline of these proposals, see PRO, T171/120, 'Administration of income tax'.

[28] This approach owes much to the work of historical geographers who are concerned with the spatial restructuring of the state: see especially M. Ogborn, 'Local power and state regulation in nineteenth-century Britain', *Transactions of the Institute of British Geographers* n.s. 17 (1992), 215–26; F. Driver, *Power and Pauperism: The Workhouse System 1834–1884* (Cambridge, 1993).

could not be punished or dismissed for failing to make an assessment or setting it too low. In 1862, Charles Pressly, the chairman of the Inland Revenue, felt that the long survival of the income tax meant that it was time to replace the existing 'vicious organisation' by a 'proper machinery' of permanent officials. Indeed, he argued that most taxpayers would prefer to be assessed by a government official in preference to giving information of their income to a local parish officer.[29] Gladstone agreed that the Board of Inland Revenue did not have sufficient control over the entire process of assessment and collection. In 1864, he proposed that the Board should have power to appoint its own officials as collectors. His case rested on the need to protect the parishes from responsibility for default by collectors. Although they were parish officers, the parish had no control over their appointment and efficiency: they were nominated by assessors, who were in turn nominated by the commissioners. Gladstone proposed that the Board should have power to give notice of its intention to take over the collection of income tax in any area outside London; it would not proceed if a third of the general commissioners objected. The change was therefore permissive, and would simply place collectors in England on the same basis as Scotland, where the collection of land and assessed taxes was made by officials since 1833, and Ireland. Nevertheless, the proposal had to be withdrawn. After all, the income tax was meant to be temporary, so why was change necessary? Might it not give the government more patronage, in order to deal with a minuscule loss of revenue from defaulting collectors? And was it a 'breach of parliamentary faith', given that Peel introduced the tax on the express condition that it should be locally assessed? This apparently trivial issue raised important matters of principle over the accountability of delegated powers.[30]

Robert Lowe returned to the issue again in 1870, when he announced, somewhat cautiously, that he intended to seek the opinion of the Commons 'whether the time has not arrived when we might put an end to the system of collecting taxes through parochial officers'. He reported the

[29] PP 1863 VI, *Report from the Select Committee on Inland Revenue and Customs Establishments*, draft report by T. B. Horsfall, p. 313; PP 1856 L, *Collectors' fines (Prescot division): return of all persons with their names and occupations in full, on whom fines have been levied from 1 Jan. 1850 to 23 June 1856 in the Prescot division in the county Palatine of Lancaster, for refusing to act as collectors and assessors of government taxes* ..., p. 25; PP 1862 XII, *Select Committee on Inland Revenue and Customs Establishments*, evidence of C. Pressly, Qq. 163, 470–3. Whether taxpayers agreed with Pressly is a different matter; see the correspondence in *The Times* in 1896 complaining of the peremptory nature of communications from the Inland Revenue: C. Stebbings, 'One hundred years ago: "official insolence"', *British Tax Review* (1996).

[30] *Parliamentary Debates*, 3rd ser. 173, 8 Feb. 1864, cols. 234–42; 175, 9 June 1864, cols. 1463–85; PP 1871 XXXVII, *Return of the amount of income tax collected in Great Britain together with the percentage of loss upon such amount*, p. 227.

Inland Revenue's opinion that many collectors were illiterate, corrupt and 'utterly indifferent to the interests of the Exchequer'. Gladstone's attack on the collectors rested on his claim to protect the parishes; Lowe tried a different line, suggesting that they thwarted the wishes of the Commons. By appealing to the well-developed *amour propre* of MPs, he was attempting to turn the charge of unconstitutional behaviour against the collectors rather than the supposedly despotic executive.[31] In 1871, the Inland Revenue proposed a more sweeping change. The general commissioners would be retained, for the Inland Revenue felt

it would be difficult to devise a better mode of ensuring fairness and impartiality, and (what is perhaps of equal moment) the conviction in the mind of the taxpayer that they are ensured, than by the establishment of such a tribunal of appeal as that of the District Commissioners, composed as it is of independent gentlemen, conversant, from their residence in the neighbourhood, with all the circumstances necessary to enable them to form a correct judgment, and elevated by their position above all suspicion of undue bias to one side or the other.

But the Board felt that the security provided by the commissioners was largely as an appeal body. By retaining its appellate function and transferring assessment and collection to the surveyors, administration would be simplified and the interests of the taxpayer protected. The proposals failed. The Board felt that reform was only possible with the approval of the general commissioners, and their opinions were accordingly canvassed. When 270 opposed the change against 261 in favour (with 66 neutral), the Inland Revenue advised the Treasury not to proceed from fear of 'vehement opposition' in parliament. [32] A measure of reform *was* achieved in 1879, when the general commissioners were permitted to hand responsibility for collection to the Board of Inland Revenue. Unlike in 1864, the initiative rested with the commissioners and many large towns in England devolved collection of schedules D and E to the Board in order to relieve the parishes from liability for default.[33]

In 1887, the position of assessor was again challenged, when the government proposed granting power to the Board to transfer assessment to the surveyor when a vacancy occurred, and to abolish the position of collector for schedules D and E. The result was outrage, especially in the City of London. J. G. Hubbard, the veteran income tax reformer, denounced the proposal as a threat to liberty and justice. The government

[31] *Parliamentary Debates*, 3rd ser. 200, 11 Apr. 1870, cols. 1611–12.

[32] PP 1871 XXXVII, *Copies of the circular letter addressed by the Board of Inland Revenue to the District Commissioners of Taxes in England and Wales, 16 May 1860*, pp. 235–7.

[33] PP 1900 XVIII, *43rd Report of the Commissioners of Her Majesty's Inland Revenue for the year ended 31 March. 1900*, pp. 473–4; PRO, IR74/94, 'Poundage to assessors and collectors of income tax'; see also T171/120, 'Administration of income tax'.

might just as well, he argued, pass authority to the police. Any change would be

> extremely detrimental to the interests of the taxpayers and unfair towards those who had so long been labouring under the oppressive weight of a most tyrannical measure... The present Assessors whom they had selected with very great care were gentlemen known in their neighbourhood, who had a general view, not only of what business was, but of the way in which business should be conducted and accounts kept, but the official Surveyor or assessors would really know nothing about it, and would go upon one principle which was engraved upon the portal of the Inland Revenue Office, if it could be seen – 'g-r-a-b'.[34]

After this rebuff, only minor changes were introduced in 1891 and 1892 when the payment of assessors, collectors and clerks by poundage was replaced by fixed payments.[35] The system was not fundamentally changed until the 1920s, when the commissioners were largely confined to an appellate function, and assessment and collection transferred to officials. In many ways, the change merely reflected reality, for the commissioners usually confirmed assessments rather than taking an active role.[36]

The biggest problem of compliance and avoidance arose in income from unincorporated businesses in schedule D, where there was 'a substantial amount of fraud and evasion'.[37] In 1870, the Board of Inland Revenue claimed that 40 per cent of assessments were under-stated, and in 1893 the chairman – Alfred Milner – assumed that there was, in effect a 20 per cent reduction in the income tax from trade and professions.[38] Indeed, taxpayers could easily justify evasion as a means of securing

---

[34] *Times*, 19 Aug. 1887.

[35] PP 1900 XVIII, *43rd Report of the Commissioners of Her Majesty's Inland Revenue for the year ended 31 March. 1900*, pp. 472, 474; PRO, IR 74/94, 'Poundage to assessors and collectors of income tax'.

[36] See *Just Taxes* for the political controversy over the proposal of PP 1920 XVIII, *Royal Commission on the Income Tax*, at a time of considerable criticism of state powers at the end of the war. The administrative and judicial functions of the commissioners are discussed in C. Stebbings, ' "A natural safeguard": the general commissioners of income tax', *British Tax Review* (1992), 398–406, and C. Stebbings, 'The general commissioners of income tax: assessors or adjudicators?', *British Tax Review* (1993). In their appeal role, the commissioners moved from investigating and collecting evidence, to deciding on the evidence placed before them by the parties concerned. Stebbings argues that the commissioners, despite their claims to neutrality, are in reality often seen as lacking independence from the Inland Revenue as a result of their origins in the collection and assessment of the tax. She feels that their independence and impartiality now need to be strengthened. The point has wider implications for the rights of citizens against the state: reliance on co-operation with local elites might have provided some protection in the past, but the institutional patterns which emerged now fail to provide an adequate defence.

[37] PP 1905 XLIV, *Report of the Departmental Committee on Income Tax*, p. 223.

[38] PP 1870 XX, *Report of the Commissioners of Inland Revenue*, vol. I, pp. 336–7; Bod. Lib., MS Harcourt dep. 69, ff. 100–10, A. Milner, 30 Apr. 1893; see also G. H. Blunden, 'The future of the income tax', *Economic Journal* 2 (1901), 166, and the critical comments of J. Ingenbleek, *Impôts directs et indirects sur le revenue: la contribution personelle en Belgique,*

'fairness'. Arthur Chamberlain,* giving evidence on behalf of the Birmingham Chamber of Commerce excused a high level of evasion on the grounds that the method of ascertaining business income was unfair with respect to depreciation and obsolescence. 'A sense of unfairness combined with powerlessness to obtain justice, or what is believed to be justice, leads to the belief that you may meet fraud with fraud – hence evasion.'[39] Under-assessment of income was accepted by the perpetrators as an act of justice rather than simple self-interest, an attitude which posed a serious threat to the revenue.

Surveyors had similar concerns about the difficulties in obtaining information from employers. The act of 1842 only required private employers to provide a list of the names and residences of their employees, without indicating incomes and hence liability to tax. In order to get around this shortcoming, surveyors requested (without any powers of compulsion) lists of anyone earning more than £100, to catch those who might pass the tax threshold when other income was taken into account. In 1860, James Akroyd, a leading textile manufacturer in Halifax, complained of those 'oppressive and unconstitutional powers which *compel* us to turn *Informers* against persons in our employment'. Although Akroyd reluctantly provided lists of their workers, non-compliance was difficult to handle. There were no powers against those who declined to provide information on *incomes* and local commissioners were reluctant to impose penalties for failing to supply lists of names and addresses. Consequently, there were problems in assessing taxes from employment. Charles Senior, the surveyor in the Black Country, reported in 1860 that major industrial concerns were not making returns of their employees. In the case of Chance Brothers, a major glass manufacturer, only 26 of 128 employees earning between £100 and £300 a year paid tax. Senior felt an example should be made of the worst cases. However, care had to be

---

l'Einkommensteurer en Prusse, l'income tax en Angleterre (Brussels and Leipzig, 1908), pp. 312–14. Evasion is also considered by Stamp, *British Incomes and Property*, pp. 315–29, who argued that it was a modest figure around 1913: of a gross assessment of about £1,167m, he put evasion at about £17m (compared with Chiozza Money's estimate of £70m).

[39] PP 1905 XLV, *Report of the Departmental Committee on Income Tax*, Qq. 1888, 1890, 1905.

* Arthur Chamberlain (d. 1813) was the younger brother of Joseph, and a partner in Smith and Chamberlain, a firm of brassfounders, from 1863. He was a Birmingham city councillor like his brother, whose political career he assisted. He had an ability to rescue companies; his greatest success was Kynochs, a manufacturer of ammunition and cordite. Joseph helped to bring down Rosebery in 1895 over the low stocks of cordite held by the army; and the firm had a close relationship with the War Office in contracts for supplies. Lloyd George mounted a vicious attack on Joseph's links with Birmingham businesses which had made the city the arsenal of empire, attacking his family as profiteers. Arthur remained committed to free trade and, unlike his brother, was hostile to trade unions. (Marsh, *Joseph Chamberlain*, pp. 18, 85, 321, 364, 494, 502–4, 569, 663.)

taken not to trespass on local autonomy, and much depended on securing the voluntary co-operation of employers, which would be threatened by too draconian a use of legal sanctions beyond a few exemplary cases. Attempts to increase the powers of the Inland Revenue met resistance. In 1861, the chancellor of the Exchequer sought powers to compel joint-stock companies to return the names and addresses of all employees liable to income tax. He withdrew the proposal after it was attacked as 'coercion and inquisitorial interference'. In 1871, power was sought to require all employers to return the income of their workers, as well as their names and addresses. The proposal was strongly criticised in parliament as 'unnecessary and unjust'. It turned employers into informers, and implied that clerks were less honest than traders in making an accurate return of their own income. In any case, the information might be misleading: many workers paid their own subordinates out of the sum received from the employer; and the family income was often supplemented by other sources. Although the chancellor felt that it was in everybody's interest to make collection of taxes simple and cheap, he felt it prudent to drop the proposal.[40]

The powers of the Inland Revenue to deal with false – or non-existent – returns were limited. A third of tax forms were not returned, and failure to submit a form was only subject to a penalty if it could be proved that there was in fact a liability for tax. The Inland Revenue feared that taxpayers calculated that the risk was worth taking, for the penalties for failing to make a return or for submitting a false return were small and did not involve publicity. Of course, the additional commissioners and surveyors were not obliged to accept the income given in the return so that one way of proceeding with cases of suspected evasion was to assess tax on a higher income or to impose a surcharge. The taxpayer had a right to appeal, which gave the commissioners power to call for accounts and to charge triple duty where the appeal failed. Obviously, the taxpayer would not appeal where the tax was still under-assessed, and the power of the Inland Revenue was reduced by strict time limits. A surcharge could only

---

[40] PRO IR40/904, Charles Senior, report to the Board of Inland Revenue, 19 Apr. 1860; IR40/1090B, Thomas Irving to secretary of Inland Revenue, 12 Nov. 1860; J. Ackroyd to J. Timm, solicitor of the Inland Revenue, 23 Nov. 1860; Inland Revenue to Messrs Ackroyd and Son, 3 Dec. 1860; J. Ackroyd and Son to Inland Revenue, 28 Dec. 1860; IR40/904, C. Senior to J. Timm, 19 Apr. 1860; Income Tax. Schedule D. Evasion of Duty, J. Timm, 25 Apr. 1860; see also IR40/799, on cases of tax evasion in Birmingham, 1858–60. On the attempt to impose an obligation on employers, see *Parliamentary Debates*, 3rd ser. 164, 19 July 1861, cols. 1166–9 and 201, 9 June 1870, cols. 1810–13. Forms with the column for incomes were in fact printed and issued in the City and, as the Inland Revenue remarked, no one objected: PP 1871 XXXVII, *Copy of a letter from the clerk to the commissioners of income tax for the City of London as to returns required from private employers of the salaries which they give to their clerks; also, of a memorandum from the Board of Inland Revenue thereupon*, pp. 231–2.

be made within one year and a supplementary assessment within four months, so that there was a strong possibility of escaping liability. Between April 1842 and April 1851, there were only 239 prosecutions of income taxpayers for failing to make a return or making a false return, and not one actually went to trial. As the solicitor of the Inland Revenue pointed out, it was virtually impossible to get evidence against a taxpayer for a false return of income under schedule D, for 'the amount of his profits is known only to himself'. In his view, the existing system resulted in a lack of official oversight, with the prospect of evasion. Consequently, 'the powers of the Department are inadequate to cope with causes of persistent and deliberate evasions of duty, continued it may be, over a long series of years, without detection, seeing that, if finally detected, only a small portion of the evaded duty can be legally recovered, and only very insignificant penalties can be inflicted'.[41] The Inland Revenue favoured an extension of the period for surcharges and supplementary assessment to six years, and the solicitor to the Inland Revenue argued that the only remedy was to make under-assessment a police court offence punishable by a fine, with the threat of 'disagreeable notoriety'. However, there was also a danger that these proposals would be counter-productive. The authorities needed to prove that the return was knowingly false, and the complexities of tax law meant that the defendant would have the benefit of the doubt in most cases, at the expense of ill-feeling between taxpayers and tax officials.[42] Nevertheless, attitudes did change. As the Select Committee of 1905 pointed out, the main concern of the public was no longer a feeling that the income tax was inquisitorial and oppressive. Rather, consent was more likely to be called into question by the ability of some taxpayers to evade payment and hence to impose a greater burden on those less able to evade tax. The Select Committee therefore proposed stricter administration of the tax, by making returns compulsory, increasing penalties and extending the period of surcharge.[43] But reform was delayed until after the First World War which imposed immense strains on the existing system of administration, and led to the appointment of a Royal Commission on the Income Tax.[44]

The smooth operation of an increasingly complex tax system came to rely less on the existence of lay assessors and commissioners than on the

[41] PP 1905 XLIV, *Report of the Departmental Committee on Income Tax*, pp. 223–5, and appendix I (a) the prevention of fraud and evasion, pp. 251–4.

[42] PP 1905 XLIV, *Report of the Departmental Committee on Income Tax*, appendix I (a), the prevention of fraud and evasion, p. 252, and evidence of F. C. Gore, Qq. 783–6, and W. Gyles, Qq. 902–3; PP 1852 IX, *First Report from the Select Committee on the Income and Property Tax*, evidence of J. Timm, Qq. 394–403, 414–15, 454–5.

[43] PP 1905 XLIV, *Report of the Departmental Committee on Income Tax*, pp. 224–5.

[44] This is discussed in more detail in Daunton, *Just Taxes*.

relationship between the Inland Revenue and the taxpayers' professional advisers. These professional advisers and the revenue authorities had a relationship of mutual support: the advisers needed a degree of confidence in the competence of the authorities in interpreting rules; and the authorities needed a degree of confidence in the integrity of the professionals. The crucial bodies in the provision of tax advice were the Law Society and the Institute of Chartered Accountants, whose role may be understood in the context of two features dating from the seventeenth century. The first feature was the notion that the ideal form of law was precedent and immemorial custom, which guaranteed freedom and liberty. David Sugarman suggests that the definition of freedom under the law linked 'Englishness' with law and liberty, and legitimated the state. The second feature was the emergence of a public sphere in the eighteenth century, in the form of clubs or voluntary hospitals or paving commissioners which constituted civil society and often utilised private legislation to provide services. The combination of these two elements meant that the state was careful not to interfere with the professions, which gave them a high degree of autonomy at a time when self-governing professions in France and Germany were being subjected to state control.[45] The result was important not only for the professions, but for constituting the British state.

The treatment of company accounts provides one example of the divergence between Britain and continental Europe. In Britain, company legislation imposed a minimal need for financial reporting to a public body, and the role of accountants in auditing companies was not strictly monitored by the state. This professional autonomy connects with the operation of the tax system, for legislation gave little or no guidance on what was meant by the crucial phrase 'an act done to further the purposes of trade'. The interpretation of these words affected tax liability. Until 1874, disputes over definitions were left to the local commissioners, who were not necessarily legally trained; there was a lack of clear case law and the possibility of wide variation between districts. In 1874, both the crown and taxpayers were given the right to request the commissioners to 'state a case' before the High Court on the grounds that their decision was erroneous in law; the issue could then be argued by barristers before a judge. Legal and economic considerations became intermeshed, for decisions had considerable implications for industrialists

---

[45] D. Sugarman, 'Bourgeois collectivism, professional power, and the boundaries of the state: the private and public life of the Law Society, 1825–1914', *International Journal of the Legal Profession* 3 (1996), 257–301; on the distinctiveness of English law and the importance of judges compared with the greater role of academic law and codification in Germany, see R. C. van Caenegem, *Judges, Legislators and Professors: Chapters in European Legal History* (Cambridge, 1987). I would like to thank Alistair Reid for this reference.

who wished to argue that profits should be net of running costs and depreciation, or of mineowners who wished to set the exhaustion of coal
against profits. Further, the proper role of the courts became a matter
of considerable concern. Should they be used to regulate government
functions, or become an intrinsic part of the administrative machinery of
a complex society? Most lawyers were doubtful. The barrister employed
to advise the tax authorities was A. V. Dicey,* the leading opponent of
'collectivism'. Dicey and the Law Society were hostile to 'officialism', arguing that lawyers should not become means to an administrative end of
applying complicated statutes. Lawyers had a strong professional ideology as the defenders of individual rights, linked with an *ad hoc* approach
and resistance to general principles, which gave considerable significance
to informal understandings between the revenue authorities, accountants
and lawyers. In reaching their decisions, the courts therefore tended to
use a traditional, *ad hoc*, common law approach. The result, it has been
suggested by Raymond Cocks, was 'massive problems':

Just because the interpretation of revenue statutes is a craft with its own, almost
intuitive qualities, the drafting of revenue statutes is a nightmare. The possible
responses of civil servants, accountants, tax advisers, solicitors, barristers and
judges are so numerous that, with a view to eliminating uncertainty, the draftsman
has to produce very detailed legislation indeed. And the result of course is the
all but overwhelming weight and complexity of modern tax statutes. The strange
legacy of the mid-Victorian determination to deal with revenue cases in what was
seen as being a 'common sense' manner is the creation of a body of law that
is frequently far beyond the grasp of the most intelligent and 'common sense'
citizen.[46]

The involvement of the lay commissioners and lawyers in the definition
of tax law led to a confused, diffuse, *ad hoc* body of case law, which
parliamentary draftsmen sought to control through ever more complex
and technical acts. Particularly with the increase in taxes and death duties

[46] R. Cocks, 'Victorian barristers, judges and taxation: a study in the expansion of legal
work', in G. R. Rubin and D. Sugarman (eds.), *Law, Economy and Society, 1750–1914:
Essays in the History of English Law* (Abingdon, 1984), pp. 445–69; see also Sabine, *A
History of Income Tax*, p. 106. Two examples of the legal interpretation of taxation are
considered below: charities and depreciation. As we shall see, the application of 'common
sense' was not agreed by all judges: some took a liberal and 'sensible' view of the meaning
of statutes, but most judges were literalist in their construction of statutes. Cock's point
remains, that the tax code was highly complex and confusing.
* Albert Venn Dicey (1835–1922) was educated at Balliol, and was fellow of Trinity
College, Oxford, from 1860 to 1872. He was called to the bar in 1860 and was junior counsel to the Inland Revenue, 1876–90; he became a QC in 1890. From 1882 to
1909 he was Vinerian professor of English law and fellow of All Souls College, Oxford.
Dicey was a convinced unionist and opponent of 'collectivism'. He published *Introduction
to the Study of the Law of the Constitution* (1885), *Digest of the Law of England* (1896) and
Law and Public Opinion in England (1905). (*DNB, 1922–30*, ed. Weaver, pp. 259–61.)

during the First World War, solicitors became tax advisers, explaining the implications of the annual budget and devising means to reduce liability. As the Inland Revenue closed one door, lawyers found a new loophole and the tax code became ever more complex.[47]

The combination of centralised bureaucratic and local lay control was important in gaining acceptance of the income tax during the nineteenth century. It helped to establish the legitimacy of the tax and to remove the sense of intrusion by an over-mighty executive. It was also a characteristic feature of the British state which was heavily reliant on the delegation of powers.[48] The registration and control of the medical and legal professions, for example, were in the hands of the General Medical Council and the Law Society rather than government agencies; and the auditing of company accounts was passed to members of the Institute of Chartered Accountants with relatively weak requirements of disclosure of financial information in published accounts. There was always the danger that delegated powers could be used in the self-interest of the professions rather than to protect the public, or that auditors might be captured by the companies on whom they were reporting. The same dangers might apply to co-option of taxpayers as a guarantee of fairness and equity. The result might be to obscure other deep inequities and create barriers to the reform of the tax system in a manner which many felt would be more just and fair. However, delegation might assist the legitimation of taxation, reducing the problems of compliance so that the state was 'stronger' and more effective. The state might therefore be able to take over functions at the expense of other areas of civil society, so permitting more generous welfare expenditure and weakening the voluntarism which characterised the British state in the nineteenth century. The legitimacy of the tax system and a high degree of consent were major factors in determining the boundaries of the state. A constant stress on the administrative efficiency of the income tax and on high levels of compliance could be used to limit changes within the income tax, and in particular to block progression. However, at the end of the First World War, the Inland Revenue's emphasis on the virtues of direct taxes in securing consent and the dangers of indirect taxes in alienating shopkeepers and other small businesses, contributed to maintaining a redistributive system of income tax.[49] The legitimacy of central government taxes compared with local taxes

---

[47] D. Sugarman, 'Simple images and complex realities: English lawyers and their relationship to business and politics, 1750–1950', *Law and History Review* 11 (1993), 277.

[48] This struck the Belgian commentator J. Ingenbleek when he concluded that British fiscal administration based on self-government could not apply to continental Europe where other habits and contingencies applied: *Impôts directs et indirects*, pp. 307, 309–10.

[49] Daunton, 'How to pay for the war', 910–13.

also contributed to a shift from a regressive local property tax to tax-funded welfare.[50] The creation of widespread acceptance of the fiscal system in mid- and late Victorian Britain had long-term consequences for the structure of the British state.

Defining income

As we have seen, the income tax imposed different effective rates on different types of income as a result of the method of assessment and collection. Of course, some reformers wished to go a step further by differentiating the tax rate between 'precarious' and 'spontaneous' incomes. Such a distinction entailed difficult issues of definition, of a moral as much as an economic nature. There was also a wider semantic point: what *was* an income? In schedule A, income was taken to be the gross rent received by the owner of land and houses without any allowance for repairs, depreciation or improvements until the concession of 1894 (see below). Presumably, a landlord was expected to obtain a higher income from improvements which were therefore not set against tax. But should an increase in the value of property be taxed as income when it was realised? A ground landlord paid tax on the annual ground rent received during the term of a lease, but would he also pay tax on the capital value of the buildings taken into his possession when the lease expired? Similarly, tax was deducted at source from dividends; would gains on the capital value of shares be taken as income when they were realised? The answer left a degree of discretion to the Board: any transaction in the nature of trade was taxable, but a capital gain apart from normal trade was not taxable. In schedule D, legislation referred to taxation of 'the annual profits or gains' from trade, commerce and professions which was interpreted as meaning annually recurring and reasonably secure income, rather than all sources of income during the year. Thus 'casual profits' or one-off sums were not taxed.[51]

---

[50] M. J. Daunton, 'Payment and participation: welfare and state formation in Britain, 1900–51', *Past and Present* 150 (1996), 169–216.

[51] L. H. Seltzer, *The Nature and Tax Treatment of Capital Gains and Losses* (National Bureau of Economic Research, New York, 1951), pp. 1–16, 256–62; P. H. Wueller, 'Concepts of taxable income I. The German contribution', *Political Science Quarterly* 53 (1938), 85, notes that there was no systematic concept of income in Britain, and that economists accepted the Inland Revenue's approach, for example A. Marshall, *Official Papers*, ed. J. M. Keynes (London, 1926), p. 338; and A. C. Pigou, *A Study in Public Finance* (London, 1928), p. 98. PP 1920 XVIII, *Report of the Royal Commission on the Income Tax*, p. 108, did not attempt a definition and instead relied on a tautology: 'If there is any class of income that does not fall within the words that impose the charge in any one of the Schedules, that class of income is not within the scope of the Income Tax.' Of course,

The British income tax therefore drew a distinction between annual income (which was liable to taxation) and capital gains (which were not). By contrast, the tax systems of many other countries took account of capital as well as income in assessing ability to pay tax and adopted a fundamentally different conception of income. In the German states, for example, the income tax was complemented by the *Erganzungssteuern* or supplementary taxes and the *Vermogenssteueren* or net fortune tax, a form of tax on wealth regardless of realisation.[52] In the federal income tax in the United States, realised capital was taxed – the sale of an investment for more than its initial cost was taken as income during the year. In Britain, capital gains were excluded from income on the grounds that they were irregular, lacking a continuing source such as employment or a business. Further, a tax on both the capital and the income it produced was taken to mean double taxation: it was assumed that realisations were reinvested so that the annual yield would be taxed in future years. Of course, there was no guarantee that realised capital gains *would* be reinvested, for they could be used to increase consumption without paying tax. This possibility became reality after the Second World War when high levels of income tax on dividends increased the attractions of non-taxed capital gains. However, capital appreciation was not a major issue in the nineteenth century, and assets were in any case taxed at death.[53] It did become an issue in a rather different way, through debates on socially created wealth or rent from about 1900. Many Liberals argued that land was in fixed supply, and any rise in its value was the result of the enterprise of the community; it was therefore socially created and should be appropriated by the community. The argument could be extended to apply to other forms of socially created wealth in industrial capital; as we shall see, this issue was central to debates on taxation within the Labour party in the early twentieth century.[54]

The difference in the conception of income in Britain and the United States rested in part on the economic and social structures of the two countries. More people lived on relatively fixed and secure incomes in Britain than in the United States, where there was a greater expectation of making profit from swift changes in the value of land or securities.[55] Capital gains were a major source of large fortunes in the United States,

there *was* debate over the nature of earned and unearned, industrious and spontaneous income.

[52] Wueller, 'Concepts of taxable income, I', 88–9.

[53] H. B. Spaulding, *The Income Tax in Great Britain and the United States* (London, 1927), pp. 18–19, 34–6, 120–1; Seltzer, *Nature and Tax Treatment of Capital Gains*, p. 38. On the debates after the Second World War, see Daunton, *Just Taxes*.

[54] See below, pp. 349–60.

[55] Spaulding, *Income Tax in Great Britain and the United States*. pp. 133–5.

such as the appreciation in the value of land in New York which produced the immense fortune of the Astors, or the increased value of oil fields which aggrandised the Rockefellers.[56] However, the difference was not simply between a more stable pattern of wealth in Britain and a more speculative economy in the United States. The definition of income in Britain owed much to the legal traditions of settled estates in an agrarian economy. The crucial point was the different notion of the principal or asset to be conserved. In Britain, the emphasis was on the actual physical piece of land or *res* rather than its value.

In an agrarian economy, income arose after a lapse of time from a continuing, fixed, source such as a farm or, to use the analogy of William Pitt, the fruit from a tree. The income could be used independently of the source from which it came, provided that the physical asset of the farm or tree survived. In the case of settled aristocratic estates, a distinction was drawn between the income of the estate (which was available to the life tenant or beneficiary to spend) and the principal or capital of the land from which the income was derived (which was not available for disposal). Increases in the capital value of the estate were not available as income to the life tenant, except through a larger flow of income in the future. The same applied to trusts such as marriage settlements which held securities to provide an income for women. The courts held that profits from realisation were part of the trust fund, and were not available to the trustees to disburse as income to the beneficiary. The duty of the trustees, in other words, was to maintain the *res* which formed the basis of the trust rather than a stable capital value. Suppose that a trust held £1,000 in stocks which rose in value to £1,200: it was the *res* of the stock itself which comprised the capital and not the £1,000 initially invested, so that the £200 gain was not available as income. Suppose the value of the stock fell to £800: again, the concern was the particular stock and not the sum of £1,000, so that the entire interest could be used as income without requiring the trustees to divert it to preserve the value of the fund. Essentially, a physical definition of capital as *res* was extended from land to securities, and was incorporated into the income tax. 'Income tax, if I may be pardoned for saying so', commented Lord Macnaghten* in

---

[56] Seltzer, *Nature and Tax Treatment of Capital Gains*, pp. 5–6.

* Edward Macnaghten (1830–1913) was the son of an Irish baronet and MP, the former receiver of the court of chancery in Calcutta. He was born in London and educated at Trinity College, Dublin, and Trinity, Cambridge, where he became a fellow in 1853. He was called to the bar in 1857, practising as an equity junior and becoming a QC in 1880. He was elected to parliament for Co. Antrim in 1880, and declined appointment as home secretary in 1886. He became lord of appeal in ordinary in 1887 – an unprecedented appointment straight from the bar without holding a lower judicial post. He was active in the Lords on Irish and legal bills, and signed the Ulster covenant in 1912. He was

1901, 'is a tax on income. It is not meant to be a tax on anything else.'
The lord chancellor was of a similar mind in 1903:

Was it the intention of the Income Tax Acts ever to tax capital as if it was income?
I think it cannot be doubted, upon the language and the whole purport and
meaning of the Income Tax Acts, that it never was intended to tax capital – as
income at all events... I do not think it is a matter on which one can dogmatize
very clearly. Where you are dealing with income tax upon a rent derived from
coal, you are in truth taxing that which is capital in this sense, that it is a purchase
of the coal and not a mere rent. The income tax is not and cannot be, I suppose
from the nature of things, cast upon absolutely logical lines, and to justify the
exaction of the tax the things taxed must have been specifically made the subject
of taxation.

Since there was no definition of either 'income' or 'capital' in the income
tax acts, the issue was therefore thrown back to the courts for interpretation, suggesting the complexities and confusions of tax law. The American law started from the same assumptions as English law, but in 1913 the
Supreme Court modified the *res* concept of capital and ruled in favour
of taxing corporations' realised capital gains under the Corporation Tax
of 1909. The principal was defined as the quantity of money or value of
the asset; any realised appreciation in its value was a taxable gain.[57]

The British approach had implications for the treatment of investment
in industry. In Britain, capital losses and depreciation could not be deducted from liability for tax. Tax was deducted from the profits of a
company at the standard rate. Dividends were paid to shareholders net
of income tax; anyone who was below the tax threshold or paid at a reduced rate would then make a claim for repayment. Profits retained in
the firm as a reserve for depreciation or new plant and machinery were
taxed at the full standard rate. No allowance was available for depreciation and obsolescence of the physical plant or machinery of the factory or
mine, so inflating taxable profits and creating a bias against capital inten-
sive investments. However, the three-year average of actual expenditure

chairman of the Council of Legal Education between 1895 and 1913, helping to create a
new system of professional training. (*DNB, 1912–21*, ed. Davis and Weaver, pp. 361–2.)
[57] Seltzer, *Nature and Tax Treatment of Capital Gains*, pp. 25–46, 257; N. Isaacs, 'Principal:
quantum or res', *Harvard Law Review* 46 (1932–3), 776–81; R. Lachs, 'Income tax on
capital profits', *Modern Law Review* 6 (1942–3), 148–56; *The Law Reports 1901. House
of Lords, Judicial Committee of the Privy Council* (London, 1901), HL (E) 1900, London
County Council and Attorney-General, pp. 35–6; *The Law Reports 1903. House of Lords,
Judicial Committee of the Privy Council* (London, 1903), HL (E) 1903, Secretary of State
in Council of India and Sir Andrew Scobie, pp. 302–3; Wueller, 'Concept of taxable
income, I', 85, notes that early nineteenth-century English economists were preoccupied
with 'factorial' distribution rather than personal distribution which had more impact on
the concept of income; and P. H. Wueller, 'Concepts of taxable income, III: the American
contribution', *Political Science Quarterly* 53 (1938), 557–8; R. F. Magill, *Taxable Income*
(New York, 1945).

on repairs of premises or the supply and repair of implements could be set against tax, so encouraging repairs of existing plant rather than its replacement.[58] The cost of mending a broken cog-wheel could be set against tax, but not the cost of scrapping an entire machine which was worn out or superseded by a more efficient model. The flaws were admitted by the chairman of the Inland Revenue in 1905. As he remarked, the income tax was defined in 1842 and 1853 as a duty on profits. In his view, it was 'incontrovertible' that the profits of a coal mine which cost £100,000 to open and equip, and produced a profit of £10,000 a year for forty years, was £400,000 less £100,000. But the acts were based on the assumption that the income tax was temporary, so that profits were assessed over the short rather than long term. As he admitted, it was curious that it took so long to accept that profits were what remained after deducting the outgoings needed to produce the earnings.[59]

In practice, local commissioners and surveyors adopted a more liberal approach. 'Supply and repairs' came to be interpreted as renewals – a definition without legal authority and not applied consistently to all districts. In 1878, depreciation was explicitly recognised for the first time. The local commissioners were given legal authority to 'allow such deduction as they may think just and reasonable as representing the diminished value by reason of wear and tear during the year of any machinery or plant used for the purposes of the concern'. Even so, the extent of the concession was imprecise, and was fairly narrowly interpreted. In the case of the *Caledonian Railway Co.* v. *Banks* (1880), the commissioners and courts ruled that allowances could only be granted for actual expenditure on repairs rather than a decline in the value of rolling stock which did not need repair. Clearly, rolling stock and engines were less valuable as a commodity for sale after five years than when new, but the commissioners refused to make any allowance on the grounds that they had not been repaired. The court upheld this view, arguing that the crucial point in determining value was the ability to produce the same amount of profit with the same outlay rather than 'the value of the plant as merchantable or marketable articles'. In other words, there was no concession for replacing old but serviceable plant.[60] Similarly, iron and coal companies were not allowed to make a deduction for the exhaustion of minerals and the costs of sinking new pits to replace those which were exhausted. In the view of the

---

[58] Veseth, *Mountains of Debt*, p. 118.

[59] PP 1905 XLIV, *Departmental Committee on Income Tax*, appendix III, 'Memorandum submitted by Sir H. Primrose: c. depreciation of assets charged to capital account', pp. 258–63.

[60] *Reports of Tax Cases under the Act 37 Vict cap 16 and under the Taxes Management Act*, vol. I: *1875–1883* (London, 1884), Court of Exchequer, Scotland, Second Division, 1880: *Caledonian Railway Co.* v. *Banks* (surveyor of taxes), pp. 487–501.

courts, 'capital expended in the sinking of pits must necessarily become exhausted and lost sooner or later, that is foreseen when the expenditure is made'. The investment might produce an overall profit at the end of the period or a loss; but as far as the court was concerned, the only concern was the amount of income produced year by year. In the case of *Coltness Iron Co. v. Black*, the court ruled that no account could be taken of how the income was earned, whether from invested capital or skill, whether it was temporary or permanent, steady or fluctuating. The court was adamant that the act of 1842 took the 'full amount of the balance of profits' without considering any capital employed in the concern; this definition of profit was a different matter from the ordinary commercial accounts of the company, which took note of the working expenses, interest payments on capital and the state of the capital account. None of this was of any consideration for assessing the income tax:

> If any part of the capital is lost, or if, from the nature of the business, the capital employed can never be recovered or restored, that is an element of primary importance in fixing the financial condition of the Company and the true amount of its net earnings. But the statute refuses to take an ordinary balance sheet, or the net profits thereby ascertained, as the measure of the assessment, and requires the full balance of profits, without allowing any deduction except for working expenses, and without regard to the state of the capital account or to the amount of capital employed in the concern, or sunk and exhausted, or withdrawn.[61]

Although the courts were correct in their interpretation of the act of 1842, there was a clear tension between the understanding of profit in commercial accounts and in tax law. The income tax simply did not take account of the employment of capital in the estimation of profit, and did not allow for investment in newer, more expensive and productive plant.

In practice, the Inland Revenue did not object to local commissioners granting allowances for substituting new equipment by writing down obsolete equipment by an annual allowance for depreciation. But the practice was not uniform, with the exception of an explicit provision of an annual allowance of 4 per cent of the prime cost of ships. Allowances varied with the discretion of local commissioners, and the Inland Revenue did not publicise its willingness to condone depreciation. In 1897, the Association of Chambers of Commerce complained that no allowances were made for replacing obsolete equipment. The Treasury responded by informing local surveyors that an allowance could be granted when new machinery was introduced, up to the value of the *existing* rather than the new machine. However, these allowances were only offered in response to

---

[61] See *Reports of Tax Cases*, vol. I, in *re Adie and Sons*, in the Exchequer, Scotland, 1875, pp. 1–4; *Forder v. Handyside*, in the Exchequer, England, 1876, pp. 65–70; and *Coltness Iron Co. v. Black*, in the Court of Exchequer, Scotland, 1879/80, pp. 287–324.

specific requests, without explaining the policy to manufacturers. There was considerable local variation between trades and districts, for the Inland Revenue felt that the initiative should come from trade associations which could make agreements on behalf of organised traders. The outcome was a lack of consistency. In Huddersfield, for example, 7.5 per cent was allowed on spinning, dyeing, carding and finishing machines, but in Bradford 5 per cent on looms. The allowances were fixed as a proportion of the value of machines, regardless of actual investment or the accounting practices of a particular firm. Arthur Chamberlain argued that firms should only be taxed on the income available for distribution, so that *any* amount of depreciation should be accepted and all retained profits should be free of tax. The tax system was therefore biassed against capital-intensive industry and favoured the continued use of existing capital.[62] Certainly, the issue could cause tension between taxpayers and the Inland Revenue and call consent into question. It became particularly significant after the First World War, with the need to invest in new plant at a time of high levels of taxation which made industry sensitive to the treatment of depreciation allowances. In 1918 allowances were finally offered for obsolescence, on condition that a replacement was made. Even so, relief was on historic rather than replacement costs of plant which was open to criticism at a time of rapid inflation.[63] The politics of company taxation could become a major point of contention between the government and industrial organisations.

Companies, charities and co-operatives

The definition of capital and income, and their liability to taxation, raises another issue: were corporations themselves taxable entities apart from the individual shareholders? In the case of the United States, a corporation was an entity separate from its shareholders and was liable to taxation in its own right. Indeed, taxation of corporations dated from 1909, prior to the reintroduction of a federal income tax in 1913. This reflected the

[62] Seltzer, *Nature and Tax Treatment of Capital Gains*, pp. 256–7; *Parliamentary Debates*, 2nd ser. 239, 4 Apr. 1878, col. 552; PP 1905 XLIV, *Departmental Committee on Income Tax*, evidence of A. Chamberlain, Qq. 1905, 1908–9, 1911–12, 1929 and *Report*, pp. 231–3; appendix III, 'Memorandum submitted by H. Primrose: c. depreciation of assets charged to capital account', pp. 258–63; appendix IV, 'Statement showing the special rates of allowance for the wear and tear of machinery and plant', p. 264; appendix V, 'Copy of letter from the chancellor of the Exchequer dated 28 May 1897 to the secretary of the Association of Chambers of Commerce on wear and tear of machinery', p. 265. PRO, T171/38, Finance Bill, 1913, Income Tax 12, schedule D, allowance for depreciation of machinery and plant; Veseth, *Mountains of Debt*, p. 119.
[63] Daunton, 'How to pay for the war', 898–9; the issue of inflation was raised more urgently after the Second World War, see Daunton, *Just Taxes*.

concern in the United States about the monopoly power of large business corporations, their impact on small farmers and urban consumers, and their threat to civic republicanism. In the 1890s, the Populists and Democrats wished to use the income tax to break down bastions of economic power; the adoption of the corporate income tax or 'special excise tax' in 1909 was in many ways a defensive move to prevent a more radical onslaught. In the United States, business corporations were at the centre of political debate before the First World War, and they were treated as separate entities. Corporations were taxed on their own earnings, and any distributions were taxed again as the income of the shareholders. By contrast, the British income tax treated companies merely as withholding agents who forwarded tax to the Inland Revenue, rather than taxable entities in their own right.

The underlying theory is that the income tax is to be imposed only on individuals and in accordance with their taxable capacity... A corporation is regarded merely as a device by means of which a number of individuals can conveniently do business, and it is not looked upon as a separate object of taxation. It is not in itself a potentially taxable person, but is an aggregation of persons who may or may not be taxable.[64]

The first challenge to this position came in the First World War, when companies paid a tax on any increase in their profits above a prewar standard. But this excess profits duty was abandoned as profits returned to prewar levels, with the danger that a fall in profit rates *below* prewar levels would oblige the government to repay duty. Although the government did introduce a corporation tax after the war, which was consciously modelled on the American system, it was seen as an emergency measure and was abandoned in 1924.[65]

There was one partial and temporary exception to the exemption of corporate bodies from taxation. In 1799, Pitt exempted the income of any 'Corporation, Fraternity, or Society of persons established for charitable purposes only' from income tax, and the exemption survived in 1842. However, Peel felt that they should contribute to public revenues and in 1845 he suggested a separate tax of 6d in the £ on charities. The proposal was not adopted, which raised an issue of equity: many endowed charities were criticised as corrupt and inefficient, serving the needs of a small group rather than society as a whole. The issue reappeared in Gladstone's 'deadly encounter with the so-called charities' in 1863. As we shall see in chapter 8, Gladstone extended the succession duty to real property and

[64] J. D. Buenker, *The Income Tax and the Progressive Era* (New York and London, 1985); Brownlee, *Federal Taxation in America*: pp. 36–43, 46; Spaulding, *Income Tax in Great Britain and United States*, pp. 35, 86–93; Kennan, *Income Taxation*, pp. 280–2.

[65] Daunton, 'How to pay for the war', 896–901, 914.

settled personalty, and he felt that endowed charities which did not die should not escape this tax as well as income tax. The result was that individual taxpayers, 'the fathers of families, men labouring to support their wives and children', paid more to provide exemptions to charitable bequests which were often merely designed to gain 'credit and notoriety' for the donor.[66] Gladstone argued that the situation had changed since charities were first granted exemption: at one time they were crucial to the provision of education and the relief of the poor, but now the state was making grants and tax exemptions were unnecessary. Many endowed charities were also seen as inefficient survivors of the world of unaccountable, unreformed corporations. Their exemption offended against 'the sound general principle that all property ought to contribute to the taxes of the country, which, if they are justly and wisely imposed, ought not to be regarded as a penalty on property, but as the necessary means of rendering property available for the effective use and enjoyment of the owner'. He therefore proposed to balance the death duty falling on other property by an annual corporation tax on the income of endowed charities such as Oxford and Cambridge colleges, public schools and the livery companies of the City which were frequently attacked by radicals for misusing funds for the personal benefit of members. As Gladstone pointed out, the state was handing a subsidy of £216,000 to charities, in breach of the rules of careful parliamentary scrutiny applied to other expenditure. Indeed, the charities might be useless or even harmful. In Gladstone's opinion,

If this money is to be laid out upon what are called charities, why is that portion of the State expenditure to be altogether withdrawn from view... and to be so contrived that we shall know nothing of it and have no control over it; so that, while to every other object recognised by the State as fit to be provided for out of the public funds, we apply every year a vigilant eye with a view to modification

[66] Exemption was given by 39 Geo. III c. 13 s. 5, and 5 & 6 Vict. c. 35 s. 105. Gladstone referred to Peel's proposed tax in 1845 in *Parliamentary Debates*, 3rd ser. 170, 4 May 1863, col. 1075. On the attack on endowed charities, see D. Owen, *English Philanthropy, 1660–1960* (London, 1964), chapter VII on Brougham's attack on the charities and the establishment of the Charity Commission by the Charitable Trusts Acts, 1853 and 1860, and pp. 318–21; the reference to 'deadly encounter' is on p. 331. There was a long-standing concern with the ability of charities to accumulate large amounts of land, which would disinherit heirs, limit the land market and create inefficient institutional management of estates. They were covered by the law of mortmain which banned the gift of land (which was extended by the courts to cover shares in canals and railways) to corporate bodies. This limitation was relaxed in some cases, such as colleges in Oxford and Cambridge, and the Ecclesiastical Commissioners. But the law was confused or contradictory. Not only was the acquisition of land controlled; so was the alienation of land. Charities might use bequests to buy property; parliament was then concerned that it should not be sold, in order to ensure that the assets were properly used. Alienation was controlled by the Charity Commission. On the complex and confused legal position of charities, see C. Stebbings, 'Charity land: a mortmain confusion', *Journal of Legal History* 12 (1991), 7–19.

or retrenchment, here we continue an exemption, and, pluming ourselves upon our liberality, we leave this great expenditure entirely in the dark, and waive in favour of these institutions, not only the receipt of a certain sum of money, but the application of all those principles of philosophical administration and constitutional control which we consider necessary for the general government of the country and the management of our finances?

Gladstone felt that 'voluntary' charities were preferable to endowed charities, for they involved the donors in running the societies, creating an active citizenship and accountability, a process of careful 'philosophical administration' rather than a desire for posthumous fame. Since donations to these societies came from taxed income, they were penalised in competition with endowed charities which did not pay tax on the income from their estates and investments. The proposed corporation tax met strong resistance, and Gladstone was astonished 'by the skilful manner in which the charitable army, so to call it, has been marshalled'. He withdrew the measure in the face of this opposition inside and outside the Commons.[67] The corporation tax was eventually introduced in 1885, placing a tax of 5 per cent on endowed charities. However, exceptions were made for religious and charitable purposes, education and anything to the benefit of the public at large or ratepayers in any location. Consequently, about 90 per cent of endowments escaped the tax, which fell mainly on the City livery companies, Inns of Court and City of London corporation. The yield in 1912/13 was a mere £49,441.[68]

Charities were therefore exempt from income tax on their receipts of rents and dividends, which raised the question of how to define a charity. There was a danger that the charities could be used as a means of tax avoidance, using the legal form as a mask for self-interest. Could private schools or sporting clubs claim charitable status and so escape any tax? In 1842, the right of any charity to exemption from income tax was decided by an official answerable to the special commissioners who initially applied the wide, all-encompassing Elizabethan definition of charity as relief of poverty, advancement of religion and education, and a highly

[67] *Parliamentary Debates*, 3rd ser. 170, 16 Apr. 1863, cols. 224d–g, and 4 May 1863 on the Customs and Inland Revenue Bill, cols. 1072–102 for Gladstone and cols. 1102–35 for the debate. The speeches are also in W. E. Gladstone, *The Financial Statements of 1853, 1860–63* (London, 1863), pp. 365–71, 435, 438, 458. See also H. C. G. Matthew (ed.), *The Gladstone Diaries*, vol. VI: *1861–68* (Oxford, 1978), 'Memorandum on charities, 24 April 1863', p. 197, and on the withdrawal, 4 May 1863, p. 199. For an account of the issue, see Owen, *English Philanthropy*, pp. 330–3; see also Matthew, *Gladstone, 1809–1898*, p. 139.

[68] See H. C. G. Matthews (ed.), *Gladstone Diaries*, vol. X, 1881–3 (Oxford, 1990), p. 29, for Gladstone's request to C. Herries of the Inland Revenue, 5 Mar. 1881, to consider an annual tax in lieu of death duties on charities; PRO, IR 74/241, 'Memorandum on the scope and yield of corporation duty, 1915'.

general category of 'public purposes'. In 1856, he took a more restrictive definition but on his retirement in 1863, the solicitor of the Inland
Revenue still felt that exemptions were too generous and the Board of
Inland Revenue sought advice from the Treasury. Although the Treasury
did rule in favour of the wider, Elizabethan, definition of charity, it also
suggested that the Charity Commission should carry out an enquiry into
the largest tax-exempt charities in London. The Charity Commission
report was favourably disposed to the charities, although it did expose
shortcomings in the operation of Christ's Hospital, a school in the City
of London, which was taken up by the Endowed Schools Commission's
reform of charitable or 'public' schools. The outcome, therefore, was
scrutiny and reform rather than revolutionary change.[69]

The Inland Revenue remained concerned about the loss of revenue.
The Treasury felt that the present administration of charitable exemptions was unsatisfactory, and urged the Inland Revenue to apply the existing rules and prevent 'any further extension of the inconvenient latitude
which already exists' until the matter was settled by parliament. The danger was that the Inland Revenue might seem to change the rules without
parliamentary sanction. In 1887, the Inland Revenue again tried to limit
exemption to charities for the relief of poverty, when they denied the
status of a charity to a trust established by the Moravian church to support missions and to provide a school for the children of missionaries.
J. G. Hubbard was provoked into action on behalf of the Church Building Society which was also denied exemption. He secured figures from
the Inland Revenue on the scale of tax relief: in all, £2,050,962 was re-
funded to charities, of which £778,528 went to education, £534,701 to
hospitals, £236,523 to pensions funds, £193,834 to doles, £157,101 to
almshouses and £102,232 to religion.[70] Clearly, considerable sums were
at stake, and the issue was eventually resolved by the Law Lords in 1891
in *Special Commissioners of Inland Revenue* v. *Pemsel*, a test case arising
from the status of the Moravian missions.

The Law Lords resolved the dispute over the status of the Moravian
church in its favour, accepting the wider Elizabethan definition of charity.
Judges were not entirely agreed on the correct approach to interpreting
statutes, whether by a 'sensible' or a 'literal' reading. As Macnaghten

[69] PP 1865 XLI, *Copies of correspondence between the Treasury and the Board of Inland Revenue
in August and September 1863 respecting the exemption from income tax of rents and dividends
applied to charitable purposes and of correspondence between the Treasury, the Home Office
and Charity Commissioners, respecting an inquiry into the management of certain charitable institutions, together with the reports of the Charity inspectors by whom such inquiry was conducted,*
pp. 7–13, 36–109; Owen, *English Philanthropy*, pp. 324–9, 333–4.
[70] PP 1865 XLI, *Copies of correspondence*, Treasury minute, 30 Sept. 1863, p. 11; Owen,
English Philanthropy, pp. 334–5.

pointed out, the Inland Revenue – with the support of some senior judges – argued that the intentions of the legislature were to be found in the popular and ordinary use of the word 'charity'. The Scottish courts followed this line of argument, pointing out that the word could not be read in the technical sense of English law in a measure designed to cover all three kingdoms; it must follow the ordinary sense of the relief of poverty. On this definition, charity would not cover conversion of the heathen. But Macnaghten insisted that meaning was to be found in the technical legal definition of the words in the statutes, which were the four categories defined by Elizabethan statutes. Macnaghten was also critical of the Inland Revenue for setting aside established practice on its own decision, without the involvement of parliament. This judgement involved an important point in legal philosophy: everything depended on the will of parliament, which could only be understood through the technical, legal, meanings of words rather than their everyday sense. The 'rule of exclusion' adopted by most judges rested on interpreting statutes by a literal interpretation, without any consideration of the debates within parliament or public statements of the legislators. After all, there might be many expressions of views and it would be difficult to discover the real intention; it was better to rely on the text of the act. This was, of course, precisely the issue involved in the courts' refusal to permit businesses to set depreciation of capital against tax.[71] As a result of the Pemsel decision, any receipts from dividends or earnings by a charity were exempt from income tax.

In effect, the Inland Revenue had to decide in each case whether a society was charitable or not according to the Elizabethan definition of charity. A review in the 1920s found a mass of contradictions and anomalies, and proposed some rules to introduce clarity. Although the Young Men's Christian Association was a religious organisation, it was not granted exemption for it provided subscribers with social and recreational activities. A community of contemplative monks would pay tax, for their prayers were not in the public interest; if they also undertook social work, they would be exempt. The Cobden Club was denied charitable status, for it was in pursuit of a particular political programme; the League of Nations Association was given charitable status. Professional education was exempt; professional associations designed to protect their members were not. So the list continued, as the Inland Revenue tried to classify a huge

---

[71] *Reports of Tax Cases*, vol. III: *1890-1898* (London, 1899), *Special Commissioners of Income Tax v. Pemsel*, House of Lords 1890 and 1891, pp. 53–103, 333–5; van Caenegem, *Judges, Legislators and Professors*, pp. 17–18. I am grateful to Louise Tee for her comments on the interpretation of tax legislation.

range of activities and prevent charitable status becoming a means of tax avoidance.[72]

Of course, voluntary charities received most of their income from donations from previously taxed earnings rather than interest and rents on endowments which secured tax exemption. Should donors to voluntary societies be allowed to set their gifts against tax? If voluntarism was morally desirable, as Gladstone argued, should subscriptions have tax relief in order to encourage an active civil society and prevent further expansion of the boundaries of the state? In fact, Gladstone assumed that equity should be established by taxing endowed charities rather than by extending relief to voluntary charities.[73] The voluntary hospitals raised the issue of tax relief on donations in 1914 and again after the war when they were joined by the universities. The Inland Revenue and Treasury resolutely opposed any concession. As the Treasury remarked, the state would 'become a compulsory subscriber to all charities, whatever their objects'. The Inland Revenue was concerned that donations would be used to reduce personal tax liability, allowing individuals to avoid their contribution to public spending in favour of their own preferences. As a result, the government would be making concealed subsidies to a variety of purposes, which might be contradictory – both for the conversion of Catholics to Protestantism and of Protestants to Catholicism. The Inland Revenue was also concerned that it would be granting tax relief to a rich man in order to support schools and hospitals for others, and at the same time denying tax relief to a poorer man struggling to pay for his own son's education or his wife's medical treatment. The Inland Revenue adopted a common civil service ploy: one concession would be the thin end of the wedge, for accepting the claim of charities would soon create an unanswerable case for making *all* payments on health and education free of tax. The Inland Revenue was therefore hostile to tax breaks on donations to voluntary societies and argued that any public support for social purposes should be explicit:

If it is accepted that it is desirable to encourage philanthropic gifts on public goals, the State should make direct and open grants towards the charitable object which it is in the public interest to foster rather than that the burden should be distributed unequally through the community through the medium of taxation reliefs, unequal and unaccompanied by even the smallest measure of public control.

When a concession *was* granted, it was unintentional and unwelcome to the Treasury. High tax rates after the First World War led to tax avoidance by means of a specified annual gift by deed of covenant to members of

---

[72] PRO, IR75/70, Report of the Charity Committee, 1926.
[73] *Parliamentary Debates*, 3rd ser. 170, 16 Apr. 1863, col. 224g.

the family who paid no tax or a lower rate. In order to control avoidance, the Finance Act of 1922 ruled that covenants of less than six years should pay tax. This attempt to close one loop-hole created an opportunity for charities: the implication was that any covenant of seven years *was* tax exempt. Charities therefore offered tax-free covenanted subscriptions. The result was an indiscriminate state subsidy to all bodies regarded as charities, with a considerable loss of tax revenue. The Inland Revenue put the loss of revenue at about £100,000 in 1927 and £1m by 1934.[74] Despite the Gladstonian belief in the benefits of active participation in voluntary associations, the Treasury was alarmed that it was subsidising activities over which it had no oversight and preferred state-funded collective action as more economical and accountable.

The Inland Revenue was faced with a number of other definitional problems in dealing with mutuals and co-operatives owned by their members, who took profits in a number of ways. In the case of a mutual insurer, such as the Norwich Union or Equitable Life, members benefited (in theory, at any rate) from lower premiums than charged by their commercial rivals and there was no income to be taxed. But what about co-operative societies which paid a 'dividend' to its members at the end of the year, allocating any trading surplus to shareholders in proportion to their purchases from the store? Private traders argued that the co-operative movement was given preferential treatment: the dividend and any surplus retained within the organisation was not taxed. The Inland Revenue insisted that there was no cause for complaint, and that the position of the societies arose from administrative pragmatism rather than principle. Most members of co-operative societies were workers who fell below the threshold for payment of income tax, and the Inland Revenue argued that deduction of tax at source would simply result in the trouble and expense of repayment, with resentment and tension. Further, it could be argued that the societies did not make a profit: they charged their members a margin above the cost price of goods so that the dividend 'is clearly not profit, but merely a return to members of sums which they have paid for their own goods in excess of the cost price'. The societies

---

[74] PRO, IR 63/103, 'Finance bill, 1923: exemption of donations to universities from taxation', Board of Inland Revenue, undated; T172/1400, Royal Commission on the Income Tax: memorandum by the Board of Inland Revenue on the subject of the exemptions from income tax enjoyed by charities, Nov. 1919; T171/60, Budget 1914. Income Tax (1). 'Inland Revenue note on proposal for the allowance of income tax on the amount of a taxpayer's subscription to charities, 7 May 1914'; T171/176, 'Contributions to hospitals, universities, etc: note by the Board of Inland Revenue', 15 May 1920; T171/318, Forber to chancellor of Exchequer, 5 July 1934. See also Daunton, 'Payment and participation', 192–3; Owen, *English Philanthropy*, pp. 336–8. On the change in 1922, see D. Shopforth, 'Charitable covenants by individuals: a history of their tax treatment and their cost to the Exchequer', *British Tax Review* (1986).

were seen as valuable means of encouraging thrift. Of course, the societies might decide to use some of this margin to build new stores, which did give them an advantage over their competitors. In effect, the societies had cheaper untaxed sources of internal funds than their commercial rivals, who had some reason to be aggrieved.[75] Clearly, such discussions raise a major issue of the nature of ownership and property rights which also appeared in the tax treatment of partnerships versus companies in the debate over differentiation, in the definition of charity and in the interpretation of mutuals. The theme reappears in chapter 9, in the debate over the 'taxing' powers of public utilities.

Taxation and the family

The definitions of income and taxable entities were connected with a further major issue: the nature of the family. The argument in favour of differentiation was based on the need for men in receipt of precarious or industrious income to set aside savings to support themselves in retirement and their widows and dependants after their death. This point could easily be extended to argue that the tax system should recognise the costs of supporting children, at least until the age of sixteen or the end of secondary education. Although children's allowances were part of the original income tax in 1799, they were not part of the tax code in 1842 and were only reintroduced in 1909 (see chapter 11). Until then, no allowance was permitted for family responsibilities and a bachelor paid the same rate as a married man with dependent children. But what would happen when a man married a woman with her own source of income? Before the Married Women's Property Act of 1870, the legal position was clear: the property of a woman passed to her husband on marriage, and any income of a married woman living with her husband was treated as belonging to him. Consequently, any exemption or abatement enjoyed by a woman before marriage was lost. Thus a small investment income of £50 received by a woman would be added to her husband's income of, say, £140. Neither would be liable to tax as single people; as a married couple, they could exceed the threshold and pay tax on £190.

The Married Women's Property Act of 1870, and the further measure in 1882, allowed women to hold property in their own right, and it might be assumed that their income would now be separately assessed for tax. In fact, the tax position of married women did not change, for

---

[75] PRO, IR 74/69, 'Income tax: exemption in favour of co-operative societies'; IR74/21, 'Income tax in relation to co-operative societies', Jan. 1903; PP 1905 XLIV, *Report of the Departmental Committee on Income Tax*, pp. 241–3.

the Inland Revenue continued to insist that a husband and wife received a *single* income, regardless of the ownership of property or the source of earnings. Harcourt's budget of 1894 granted a concession to married women, allowing separate assessment where they had an independent *earned* income and the joint income did not exceed £500. However, the Inland Revenue interpretation was highly restrictive, limited to earnings from employment such as teaching where the woman's income was clearly distinct. The Inland Revenue feared that a wider definition would be exploited as a means of tax avoidance. In family enterprises such as shops or small workshops, revenue would be lost by 'splitting' income between husband and wife to reduce liability on what was, in effect, a single enterprise. Income from trade was therefore excluded until 1897, when separate assessment was allowed if the wife's trade were entirely independent of her husband, and carried on in separate premises. The Revenue's desire to limit the scope of separate assessment was not simply the result of patriarchal assumptions, for there were good reasons to be concerned about tax avoidance by traders assessed under schedule D. 'There is no class of people who are more generally under-assessed than shop-keepers in a moderate way of business', Milner pointed out, and

the moment it is conceded that a married woman may claim separate exemption or abatement in respect of her earnings *from trade generally*, the revenue authorities will be exposed to claims on the part of the wives of all traders who can by any possibility be alleged to take any share in conducting their husband's businesses... Such a danger must at all hazards be avoided.

Neither did the concession extend to separate assessment of income from investments, for a married couple might easily allocate their investments between themselves in order to reduce liability. Issues of the right of married women to be treated as autonomous individuals came into conflict with the Inland Revenue's justifiable fear that married couples would exploit separate assessment in order to avoid tax.[76]

Even when husbands and wives were permitted to opt for separate assessments, their joint incomes were still aggregated to decide the marginal rate and the husband was responsible for payment. In other words, income could not be allocated between a couple to keep both below the threshold for payment of the standard rate or super tax. As the Inland Revenue pointed out, this would be a concession to the rich at the

---

[76] PRO, IR63/5, 'Income tax on married women's property: claim to exemption or abatement', A. Milner, May 1895.

expense of other taxpayers who would have to pay a higher rate to cover the loss of revenue.[77] Concern for equity between income levels was more significant than concern for the rights of women. In the view of the Inland Revenue, a married couple pooled their incomes and should therefore be assessed on the joint total; they had more ability to pay than a bachelor and a spinster living separately on the same income. 'The incomes of both are applied to satisfying the needs of the same circle, viz: the household, and are rightly chargeable as one income.'[78]

The Inland Revenue's approach was tested in 1912. Mr Wilks, a school teacher with a salary of £171 15s, refused to pay income tax on his wife's earnings as a surgeon of about £700. The Inland Revenue soon found itself in a difficult legal position in taking action against Mr Wilks. He claimed that he did not have enough money to pay his wife's tax bill and that the household goods could not be distrained since they belonged to his wife. He was therefore sent to prison. The case exposed the Inland Revenue to criticism for maintaining the assumption of 1842 that the wife's income belonged to her husband. It was attacked not only by supporters of women's rights such as Bertrand Russell, but also by right-wing critics of the state who argued that Wilks's imprisonment typified the insatiable demands of the state for revenue, and the 'far too great eagerness to press certain parts of our fiscal system with undue vigour'.[79] The Inland Revenue's point about the loss of revenue was a serious one and not simply an expression of its undoubtedly patriarchal assumptions about household structure. Most of the benefit would go to relatively affluent families with unearned incomes, by splitting investments in order to remain below the threshold for super-tax. The government preferred to proceed by making concessions to married couples in a different way. Husbands were awarded allowances against tax for wives and children, to be set against their income. This approach reflected patriarchal assumptions that male heads of household should support their wives and families; it appealed to concerns about sustaining a strong imperial race; and it could be justified as a means of encouraging responsible parenthood by the middle class rather than feckless behaviour by the poor. It also made good political sense by reducing the tax liability of an

77 PRO, T171/166, N. F. W. Fisher to A. Chamberlain, 31 Mar. 1919; 'Husband and wife: separate treatment for income tax and super tax purposes. Note by the Board of Inland Revenue', 28 Apr. 1919; 'Note on Mr Locker-Lampson's proposed motion on the adjournment on 19 March 1919', Board of Inland Revenue, 19 Mar. 1919.

78 PRO, T171/37, 'Income tax: proposals for separate assessments of the incomes of husband and wife'.

79 PRO, IR74/43, 'Memorandum by P. Williamson, 9 Oct 1912'; undated and unsigned typescript; Niemeyer to Bradford, 1 Oct. 1912; J. E. Piper, 2 Oct. 1912; Times, 4 Oct. 1912.

important group of modest middle-class incomes.[80] The government was able to divide the electorate by marital status and family responsibilities, so containing opposition to higher levels of income tax and supertax. Bachelors or affluent childless couples would pay in full; married men with families received allowances which reduced their tax liability (see chapter 11).

The British approach to family income differed from other countries in assuming that all income should be aggregated in the hands of the male head of household. When the income tax was introduced in France, the entire income of the family was divided between its members so that the tax liability of larger families was reduced. This reflected the strongly pro-natalist and maternalist assumptions of French policy, and complemented the payment of family allowances to women. In Britain, trade unions were opposed to family allowances paid to women, which would weaken their claim to a 'male breadwinner' wage; by contrast, French unions were weaker and employers' associations supported family allowances as a way of reducing wage demands. In Britain, the demand for separate taxation of women and for family allowances were linked to feminism, and seemed to destabilise family structures as in the case of the Wilks. By contrast, in France, support for allowances and tax splitting came from social Catholics as a way of supporting larger families.[81]

In the United States, 'tax splitting' was introduced in 1948, allowing married couples to split their income equally regardless of who earned it, and so reduce their marginal rate. This measure arose from complications over the different property systems of individual states and their connection with taxation. A number of states had 'community-property laws' which assumed that husband and wife had an equal interest in income earned by a spouse and in property acquired during the marriage. In 1930, the Treasury argued that the husband controlled the 'community' and that the wife could not have income for tax purposes. However, the Supreme Court ruled against the Treasury and argued that the husband was simply the *agent* of the community, so that each spouse should pay tax on half the community property. Since the federal income tax followed state property law, the tax position of families in community-property states was more favourable. Not surprisingly, some states adopted community-property regimes from 1939 to 1947; more

---

[80] PRO, T171/166, 'Note by the Board of Inland Revenue on the cost of certain possible reliefs from income tax in favour of small taxpayers', 24 May 1919.
[81] On the difference between French and British attitudes to family allowances, see S. Pedersen, *Family, Dependence, and the Origins of the Welfare State: Britain and France*, 1914–45 (Cambridge, 1993).

surprisingly in view of the fiscal advantages not all states followed their example. Opposition to adoption of community-property systems arose from hostility to the notion that a wife had an interest in the earnings and property of the community, as well as from legal difficulties in inserting a new definition of property into common law regimes. In common law states, income splitting could be achieved by creating a husband–wife partnership; in these cases, the federal tax authorities determined as a matter of fact whether the wife was active or contributed her capital. Their decisions reflected notions of gender roles, assuming that the wife owed her husband unpaid services so that the partnership was invalid; the British case is very similar. The introduction of income splitting in the United States in 1948 resolved problems with both ploys for reducing tax liability. It simply affected the federal tax code and not property rights or gender roles. It did not involve the issue of control over community property; and did not entail the wife's taking an active role in the partership. Debates over income tax codes therefore reflect different assumptions about family structures and gender. In the case of Britain, the absence of tension between two different property regimes allowed the Inland Revenue to hold to its position for much longer.[82]

The income tax raised a number of major problems in defining both income and the entity which was liable – capital gain or income, corporations or shareholders, families or individual members. The decisions reflected legal traditions, the balance of economic and political interests, concern for revenue and patriarchal assumptions. Similarly, indirect taxes were permeated with moral and social assumptions about consumption, and played a major role in shaping the market through the definition of what constituted a necessity and a luxury. The 'cheap loaf' is only the most obvious case. When Lowe reduced the sugar duties, he pointed out that it 'is not a stimulant, but it is, in the highest degree, a nutritive'.[83] The repeal of the paper duty was linked with the spread of knowledge and intellectual endeavour. In the late Victorian and Edwardian period, Liberals and Labour demanded the 'free breakfast table', arguing that taxes on necessities – tea, coffee, sugar – should be repealed. Most indirect taxes fell on tobacco, beer and spirits, which were not covered by the general opposition to indirect taxes. As Philip Snowden pointed out, these taxes were evidence of ill-spent means which should be spent on 'necessary and beneficial consumption'.[84] Attitudes to indirect taxation were permeated with moral assumptions about consumption, in the same

[82] C. C. Jones, 'Split income and separate spheres: tax law and gender roles in the 1940s', *Law and History Review* 6 (1988), 259–310.

[83] *Parliamentary Debates*, 3rd ser. 200, 11 Apr. 1870, col. 1641.

[84] P. Snowden, *Labour and National Finance* (London, 1920), p. 20.

way as discussions of direct tax were couched in terms of unproductive and productive wealth, precarious and spontaneous earnings.

Conclusion

One point which runs through this discussion of the administration of the fiscal system is the constant reiteration of the need to maintain consent by the taxpayer. Officials at the Inland Revenue and Customs and Excise returned again and again to this issue, in part as a device to limit the independence of politicians. Their immense technical knowledge could block action by politicians, preventing what they saw as dangerous innovation. Repeatedly, the official line was to find reasons why change was impossible or undesirable – whether it be graduation or differentiation, or the introduction of new indirect taxes. On the whole, officials in the nineteenth and early twentieth centuries were reactive and negative; it took a strong-willed and informed chancellor to force through any change. But it would be wrong to suggest that officials were simply a force for inertia. They did have a serious point: their priority was the need to protect the revenue and the consent of taxpayers, against the desire of politicians to use the fiscal system for social or electoral purposes. By the end of the nineteenth century, the leading officials at the Inland Revenue and Treasury were the custodians of the Gladstonian fiscal constitution as politicians started to move in new directions, reflecting different electoral considerations and ideological influences. Between Harcourt's budget of 1894 and Lloyd George's budget of 1914, the fiscal constitution was re-shaped. The politics of taxation became a matter of high political drama and contention, after forty years of general acceptance.

8 'The right of a dead hand': death and taxation

If it be said, as it may with truth, that those who have inherited the savings of others have an advantage which they may have in no way deserved, over the industrious whose predecessors have not left them anything; I not only admit, but strenuously contend, that this unearned advantage should be curtailed, as much as is consistent with justice to those who thought fit to dispose of their savings by giving them to their descendants...

The inequalities of property which arise from unequal industry, frugality, perseverance, talents, and to a certain extent even opportunities, are inseparable from the principle of private property, and if we accept the principle, we must bear with these consequences of it: but I see nothing objectionable in fixing a limit to what any one may acquire by the mere favour of others, without any exercise of his faculties, and in requiring that if he desires any further accession of fortune he shall work for it...

With regard to the large fortunes acquired by gift or inheritance, the power of bequeathing is one of those privileges of property which are fit subjects for regulation on grounds of general expediency...I conceive that inheritance and legacies, exceeding a certain amount, are highly proper subjects for taxation.

> J. S. Mill, *Principles of Political Economy*, ed. W. J. Ashley
> (London, 1909), pp. 219, 228, 809

Nature gives a man no power over his earthly goods beyond the term of his life. What power he possesses to prolong his will after his death – the right of a dead hand to dispose of property – is a pure creation of the law, and the State has the right to prescribe the conditions and limitations under which that power shall be exercised. The right to make wills or settlements or successions is the creation of positive law.

> W. Harcourt, *Parliamentary Debates*, 4th ser. 33,
> 16 Apr. 1894, cols. 489–90

The fiscal history of Victorian Britain may too easily be written in terms of the emergence of the income tax, from its reintroduction by Sir Robert Peel in 1842 through to the creation of a more sophisticated system of graduation by *levels* of income and differentiation by *forms* of income in the early years of the twentieth century. The income tax, so it would appear from this narrative, provided a secure, flexible and widely accepted source of revenue for the British state in contrast to many other European countries, where the introduction of the income tax remained contentious up to the First World War. Certainly, the proportion of revenue from direct taxes rose between 1842 and 1914. According to Colin Matthew, the proportion of the United Kingdom's central government revenue from indirect taxes fell from 78.7 per cent at the start of Victoria's long reign (1836/40) to 48.8 per cent at the end (1901/5).[1]

What is often missed is the importance of death duties in the general shift of the British fiscal system from indirect taxes on consumption to direct taxes on income and wealth. In 1871, death duties were 7.6 per cent of the tax revenue of the central government, rising to 9 per cent in 1881, 11.8 per cent in 1891 and 14.0 per cent in 1901 (see also Table 2.1).[2] The significance of death duties to the British fiscal system was not simply their own yield, but also their contribution to the success of the income tax. The death duties operated as a 'balance' in order to create a sense of equity and fairness in the income tax, and helped to defuse other political tensions. Indeed, it could be argued that the imposition of death duties *solved* political difficulties by defusing tensions over the income tax in the mid-Victorian period, through removing the criticism that it was inequitable between precarious income from trade and industry, and spontaneous income from investments. And in 1894, the chancellor of the Exchequer – William Harcourt – made reform of the death duties central to a shift in the fiscal constitution. Graduated taxation of estates at death was more easily accepted than graduation of income tax, and prepared the way for the later reforms of Asquith and Lloyd George.

Forms of death duty

There were four separate death duties in Britain until Sir William Harcourt simplified them in his budget of 1894: probate, legacy, succession and estate (see table 8.1). As he pointed out, there were two forms of death duty: the first (class A) simply considered the *size* of the estate, without regard to the ultimate destination; the other (class B) took

[1] Matthew, *Gladstone, 1809–1874*, p. 126 and see above, pp. 161–77.
[2] Mitchell and Deane, *Abstract*, pp. 393–4. For a general account of inheritance taxes, see L. Dunn, 'A history of inheritance taxes in England', PhD thesis, University of London (1956).

account of the *recipient* of the estate.[3] The oldest duty fell into the first category: the probate duty dating from William of Orange's reform of the finances of the English state to wage war against the French. As first introduced in 1694, it was a simple flat-rate stamp duty but pressure of war finances meant it was transformed in the late eighteenth century into a sliding scale according to the total value of personal property left by the deceased. The legacy duty followed the second principle. It was introduced by Lord North on a modest scale in 1780, as a stamp duty on any bequest of personal property. North was not able to adopt a full-scale tax on collateral successions such as existed in Holland and explained by Adam Smith in *The Wealth of Nations*. The stamp duty was only expected to produce £21,000 a year, and even this modest sum turned out to be optimistic. The stamp was paid on receipts, and executors and beneficiaries could simply dispense with them in order to evade the tax.[4] In 1796, William Pitt proposed a full-scale tax on collateral successions to produce £250,000 a year. The duty fell on the sum received by *individual* beneficiaries and varied according to their relationship with the deceased.

These two duties favoured real property, which was not liable to tax. The exclusion of real property from the probate duty is understandable, for the annual land tax was imposed on real property and a complementary duty on *personal* property made political and fiscal sense. However, the level of land tax was fixed, despite the marked increase in rent levels in the later eighteenth century, and Pitt was aware that land was relatively lightly taxed.[5] His intention in 1796 was therefore to impose the legacy duty on 'collateral successions' on landed as well as personal property. The legacy duty was fiercely criticised by Charles James Fox, the great opponent of Pitt and the French wars. Fox feared the 'novelty of the principle of a tax on capital' which would 'enable the state to seize upon the whole property of the country'. Above all, any tax on land fuelled 'country' fears of the intentions of the government. A legacy duty on land, claimed one alarmed Member of Parliament, was 'a political measure immoderately increasing the influence of the Crown, and full of danger in its obvious consequences to the constitution and freedom of the country'.[6] The taxation of real property passed the Commons by the very narrowest of margins, on the casting vote of the speaker of the House. Pitt felt that the political dangers were too great and withdrew the measure, with a loss

[3] *Parliamentary Debates*, 4th ser. 33, 16 Apr. 1894, cols. 485–6.
[4] S. Dowell, *A History of Taxation and Taxes in England from the Earliest Times to the Present Day*, vol. II: *Taxation from the Civil War to the Present Day* (London, 1884), pp. 173–4, 213–14; Smith, *Wealth of Nations*, vol. II, viih, p. 859, of 5 to 30 per cent.
[5] For the incidence of taxes, see O'Brien, 'Political economy of British taxation'.
[6] Quoted in Buxton, *Finance and Politics*, vol. I, pp. 117–18.

of about £140,000 of revenue.[7] The legacy duty on personal property was also attacked on the grounds that it applied to *all* successions, whatever the degree of relation. As one MP complained in 1805:

It was peculiarly directed against the ill-favoured and against the ancient maiden, against the diseased, the lame and the blind. They were more objects of pity than of taxation. If the tax were to be imposed, the first two years of income of it ought to be laid out in hospitals and nunneries, that the objects of it might be permitted to starve decently.[8]

In 1815, widows were exempted from the duty (see table 8.1). The choice of rates for different degrees of relation clearly indicated assumptions about moral entitlement to inheritance.

The introduction of the income tax in 1799 offered another way of reaching income from real property. Its abandonment in 1816 meant that land was taxed at a very low level and a larger proportion of government revenues came from indirect taxes on customs and excise which hit the working class, industry and commerce. As the Anti-Corn Law League argued, landowners' rents were supported by protective duties, yet their incomes were escaping taxation. The probate and legacy duties were part of this inequitable fiscal system, for they fell on *personal* property and hence on accumulations from the earnings of merchants, manufacturers and the professions, and exempted landed property. Indeed, landed aristocrats and gentry might be able to avoid taxation even on their personal property. The exclusion of real estate from the duties extended to freehold houses, including fixtures such as mantelpieces, immovable statues, frescoes and panelling. Paintings and tapestries incorporated into the structure of the house were therefore exempted from tax.[9] Further, personal property could escape tax if defined as 'heirlooms' forming part of the settled estate. Heirlooms were initially confined to monuments, weapons, armour and pennons which expressed the status of the family. This definition was widened in the eighteenth century to cover new symbols of aristocratic status such as plate, jewellery and works of art acquired by connoisseurs on the Grand Tour. As one judge remarked in 1740 in justifying the new definition of heirlooms in a settlement, 'Clauses of this Nature are intended as Monuments of Great Families to

---

[7] Dowell, *Taxation and Taxes*, vol. II, pp. 214–15.

[8] Quoted in Thorne (ed.), *The History of Parliament: The House of Commons, 1790–1820*, vol. V, pp. 245–6.

[9] The cases (*Scarsdale* v. *Curzon*, 1 J and H 40, 1859–60, and *D'Eyncourt* v. *Gregory*, 3Eq 382, 1866) are in P. Mandler, 'Art, death and taxes: the taxation of works of art in Britain, 1796–1914', *Historical Research*, 74 (2001), 272–3, which provides an excellent account of this topic and the cultural assumptions in the death duties in relation to the possessions of the landed elite.

Table 8.1 *Death duties prior to the reforms of 1894*

Probate duty

Levied on: personal property
to include everything which the deceased possessed of value, paid out of the estate before division

Rate: ad valorem, by the amount left
1881 tariff: £1 per £50 up to £500 net
£1 5s per £50 up to £1,000 net
3% of value above £1,000 net

In 1888, half of the proceeds was paid to local authorities in aid of local taxation.

Legacy duty

Levied on: personal property
paid by the individual on the property to which he/she succeeds, at the time of succession

Rate: varied according to the relationship of the legatee to the deceased
levied on the saleable value on receipt of the legacy

1815 tariff:		
widows	exempt
lineal descendants	1%
brothers, sisters and their descendants	3%
uncles, aunts and their descendants	5%
great-uncles, aunts and their descendants	6%
any other person	10%

In 1881, personal estates up to £300 were exempted; and lineals were relieved from the payment of legacy duty where probate duty had been paid (the level of probate duty was increased to protect revenue).

Succession duty: 1853

Levied on: real property and settled personal property
applied the legacy duty to bequests payable out of or charged on real estate, i.e. it taxed what was left untouched by the legacy duty.

Rate: The rate of legacy duty was levied on the capitalised value of the 'years of enjoyment' or life interest. Assume a man aged thirty-five succeeded to 100 acres worth £5,000, with a net income of £150; the value of an annuity of £150 for a man aged thirty-five would be calculated from life tables, which gave £2,362. The tax on this sum could be paid in eight half yearly instalments, with the balance being remitted in the case of death. In 1888, the existing rate remained in force for property which was liable to probate duty as well as succession duty (for example, leaseholds). For other property, the rate was increased by 0.5 per cent where it passed to lineals and 1.5 per cent where it passed to non-lineals.

1888 tariff:		
lineal descendants	1.5%
brothers, sisters and their descendants	4.5%
uncles, aunts and their descendants	6.5%
great-uncles, aunts and their descendants	7.5%
any other person	11.5%

Table 8.1 *(cont.)*

Estate duty: 1889
Levied on: real property and personal property
Rate: 1 per cent duty on all personal estates of £10,000 and above, however divided;
                in the case of landed property and settled personalty, it was levied where
                the value received by a *single* heir amounted to £10,000, which was
                calculated on assumptions which placed it below the capital value

---

Note: Leaseholds were defined as personal property for the probate duty, and as real property for the legacy and succession duties.
Source: S. C. Buxton, *Finance and Politics: An Historical Study, 1783–1885* (2 vols., London, 1888), vol. I, pp. 117–18, and vol. II, pp. 292–8, 384–5; S. C. Buxton and G. S. Barnes, *A Handbook to the Death Duties* (London, 1890), pp. 1–65.

support the Honour and Dignity of them.'[10] Pitt's legacy duty of 1796 explicitly exempted 'every article of plate, furniture, or other things not yielding any income', provided they were inherited by persons without the power to sell. In other words, personal property inherited as an heirloom through a settlement could not be taxed unless the settlement came to an end at some point in the future, giving the heir an absolute right in the property.[11]

These biases in death duties were open to challenge. As Joseph Hume remarked in 1842, the exclusion of real property from duties in 1796 was 'class legislation' which could only be explained by the failure to represent the people in parliament: 'it must be evident to every person, that to refer such a question as this to the House of Commons as at present constituted, was to refer it to a jury of landowners, whose interests were opposed to those of the country at large'. The government stood accused of failing to balance the fiscal constitution and treating all interests with 'equal justice'. Instead, it was 'maintaining the interests of the landed proprietors in opposition to those of the country in general'.[12] The issue continued to rankle. 'Let us not boast of English freedom or of equality before the law, while this injustice remains', complained Richard Cobden. 'In what form could aristocratic privilege assume a more offensive and costly aspect than in that of a bold and palpable exemption from taxation.'[13] Indeed, in 1842 Lord John Russell* argued that reform of

[10] See the discussion in Mandler, 'Art, death and taxes', 273–4; the judge's comment is cited by Mandler from *Gower v. Grosvenor*, Barn C 56–7, 1740.
[11] The complications are covered by Mandler, 'Art, death and taxes', 274–7, discussing 36 Geo. III c. 52 s.14. Of course, it was difficult for the revenue authorities to keep track on when duties did become liable; see the attempt to tighten procedures (283).
[12] *Parliamentary Debates*, 3rd ser. 62; 26 Apr. 1842, col. 1153.
[13] FRA, *Financial Reform Tracts, Number 6, The National Budget for 1849*, pp. 8–12.
* Lord John Russell (1792–1878) was the third son of the 6th duke of Bedford, educated at Westminster and Edinburgh. He became a Whig MP in 1813, supporting parliamentary

death duties was 'fairer, better and more just' than the 'unavoidable and unnecessary' income tax which would hit active, earned, incomes.[14]

In 1853, Gladstone turned to the taxation of estates at death as part of his strategy of creating a fiscal system which could be portrayed as fair between classes and interests. Gladstone's budget involved, amongst other changes, the creation of a third death duty to balance the fiscal system: the succession duty. As we have seen, the income tax was subject to severe criticism from many radicals and supporters of the Anti-Corn Law League. In their view, the answer was not the introduction of a new tax but the imposition of strict economy and retrenchment, which would allow the *repeal* of taxes. Government spending was seen as leading to waste and extravagance, creating a class of parasitical office-holders and sustaining militarism. The income tax was also, in the view of many merchants and manufacturers, unfair in its incidence between different forms of income. As Gladstone remarked, there was a widely expressed feeling that 'the operation of the income tax is severe upon intelligence and skill as compared with property'.[15] The Financial Reform Association, and many Liberal MPs, argued that the income tax should be differentiated by the source of income, in order to fall more heavily on 'realised' or 'spontaneous' unearned incomes derived from investments and assets, than on 'precarious' earned incomes which involved the risks of trade or personal exertion. But Gladstone opposed differentiation of the income tax, for he had grave doubts about the possibility of distinguishing between individuals and groups on such a basis. Above all, such a strategy would destroy the income tax and the fiscal constitution by setting one class against another. Gladstone argued that the correct way of proceeding was by considering the tax system as a *whole* and seeking a remedy for the unequal incidence of the income tax elsewhere.[16] He seized upon reform of the death duties as a means of preserving the balance of the fiscal system and as a safer alternative to differentiation.[17]

Gladstone argued that the grievance that 'intelligence and skill under our system of taxation pay too much, and property too little' could be

reform. He held office as paymaster general 1831, home secretary 1835 and colonial secretary 1839. He supported repeal of the corn laws, and became prime minister on Peel's resignation, from 1846 to 1852. He was foreign secretary in 1852–3 and remained in the Cabinet without office; in 1854–5 he was president of the council and secretary of the colonies for a short period. He returned to office as foreign secretary between 1859 and 1865 and prime minister 1865–6. (*DNB*, vol. XLIX, ed. S. Lee (London, 1897), pp. 454–64.)

14 *Parliamentary Debates*, 3rd ser. 62, 8 Apr. 1842, cols. 96–7, and 26 Apr. 1842, cols. 1139–167.
15 *Parliamentary Debates*, 3rd ser. 125, 18 Apr. 1853, cols. 1386–7.
16 *Parliamentary Debates*, 3rd ser. 125, 18 Apr. 1853, cols. 1386–7.
17 *Parliamentary Debates*, 3rd ser. 132, 8 May 1854, cols. 1468–9.

met through a 'safe, honourable and efficacious' mechanism: the adjustment of death duties by a new succession duty which extended the legacy
duty to *all* successions to real property and settled personalty as well as
personal property.[18] Here was a second tax of Harcourt's class B. This
legacy duty offered, in Gladstone's view, the safest way of ensuring that
real property did not escape its fair share of national taxation and that
intelligence and skill were not over-taxed. Generally, the taxation of property – for example, by differentiating the income tax between spontaneous
and precarious incomes – posed dangers which were avoided by the use
of death duties:

The greatest mischief of taxes upon property is the liability of a constant recur-
rence of those struggles of classes which are often associated with them. But in
carrying into effect this increase in the legacy duty, you have this great advantage,
that the liability to pay occurs only within the limitation which the laws of a higher
power have ordained, that it only occurs once, on the death of a man ... this is a
most weighty consideration for those whose duty it is to inquire how they can best
neutralise the social dangers incident to all questions connected with the taxation
of property.[19]

Real property should therefore pay death duties, but Gladstone did not
accept that the rate should be the *same* as on personal property.

The justification for charging different duties was that land and houses
suffered from the additional burden of local taxation or rates, as well as
paying the land tax and the income tax on the flow of rents. Rateable
property was, remarked Gladstone, 'now struck in both ways' through
the legacy and probate duties as well as local rates on real property. It
was only fair, therefore, that death duties should take less from 'rateable
property' than from personal property which did not pay these additional burdens, and Gladstone concluded that the fairest method was
to charge the successor to real property on the *life interest* rather than
the capital value.[20] Personal property therefore paid legacy duty on the
full capital value of the bequest, whereas real property received 'more ten-
der consideration' and paid succession duty on the value of the life interest, with the right to pay over four years and a refund in the event of death
(see table 8.1).[21] The inequality of death duties on real and personal property was deliberate. Gladstone carefully shaped the system in order to
compensate for the burden of income tax on 'precarious' earned incomes
which did not arise from possession of personal or real property, and to
adjust the impact on real and personal property to take account of the

[18] *Parliamentary Debates*, 3rd ser. 125, 18 Apr. 1853, col. 1394.
[19] *Parliamentary Debates*, 3rd ser. 125, 18 Apr. 1853, col. 1395.
[20] *Parliamentary Debates*, 3rd ser. 125, 18 Apr. 1853, col. 1397.
[21] Buxton, *Finance and Politics*, vol. I, p. 118.

burden of local taxation.[22] Gladstone also retained the heirloom clause of the legacy duty. Although the new duty was to apply to the life interest in real property and settled property, heirlooms were still exempt. The result was a bias in the tax system, for the heirloom clause exempted old master paintings collected by aristocrats on the Grand Tour and was less likely to apply to modern British paintings collected by the *nouveaux riches* who did not adopt the same legal forms for inheritance as the landed elite.[23]

Gladstone promised in 1853 that the income tax would ultimately be abolished and he hoped that the yield from the succession duty would contribute to this ambition. In his view, death duties were more acceptable than income taxes. However, the revenue from the new duty did not fulfil his expectation of producing £2m a year; as late as 1885, the yield was only £935,000.[24] The opportunity to redeem his pledge did seem to have arisen in 1873/4, when a budget surplus of £6m was anticipated. The loss of revenue from the income tax would be met, he intended, by 'a proposal to reconstruct and enlarge the death duties. Direct taxation of a kind most vexatious to trade and industry was to be removed; direct taxes, the least of all unfavourable to trade and industry, and going, as a direct tax should wherever possible go, straight to property, was to be imposed.'[25] He lost the election of 1874 and the opportunity passed, but it is clear that Gladstone viewed death duties as preferable to income tax in its incidence on different types of income, and its minimisation of social conflict.

Just why were death duties more acceptable to Russell and to Gladstone? It was not simply that death duties were a means of avoiding the greater dangers of differentiation. There was also a sense that inherited wealth was the product of social and legal structures, and had not been earned by the efforts of the recipient. The active pursuit of wealth was desirable; the passive enjoyment of wealth might entail a loss of dynamism. As we have seen, this attitude was reflected in Gladstone's attitude to the income of endowed charities from investments in comparison with associations deriving their income from annual donations. The first led to trustees and boards to manage the assets, without personal

---

[22] Gladstone's strategy in 1853 is explained in Buxton, *Mr Gladstone as Chancellor*, pp. 13–16, 122–3, 135–7.

[23] Mandler, 'Art, death and taxes', 276–7.

[24] S. C. Buxton and G. S. Barnes, *A Handbook to the Death Duties* (London, 1890), pp. 22, 25–6.

[25] W. E. Gladstone, 'Lecky's History of England in the eighteenth century', *Nineteenth Century* 21 (1887), 934–5; see the exchange between Gladstone and Lecky which indicates that Gladstone did not make this intention public and merely referred at the time to 'judicious adjustments' of taxes and the need to make them more equitable: W. E. H. Lecky, 'Mr Gladstone and the income tax', *Nineteenth Century* 22 (1887), 54, and W. E. Gladstone, 'Mr Lecky and political morality', *Nineteenth Century* 22 (1887), 281. See also Buxton, *Finance and Politics*, vol. II, pp. 166–7.

involvement; the second entailed the active participation of donors. Endowed charities did not die and therefore escaped payment of death duties; in his view they should therefore be liable to an annual tax.[26] In other words, Gladstone wished to encourage active accumulation of wealth and active involvement in the management of associations rather than passive enjoyment. There was a general acceptance that estates at death had a higher capacity to bear taxation than other forms of income and wealth. Indeed, acceptance of this proposition was to prove a point of entry for more radical approaches to taxation.

Death duties and local taxation

The issue of death duties connected with the vexed topic of local taxation which raised larger revenues than the central government and paid for massive programmes of investment in the urban infrastructure. The only form of local taxation was the rate on real property, and Gladstone accepted that it should therefore pay less to central taxation in order to ensure equity. This became a matter of controversy in 1885, when he proposed changes to the death duties in order to increase revenues and prevent a large deficit. Gladstone suggested an increase in the succession duty on real property, and to impose a 5 per cent income tax on corporations and endowed charities in lieu of death duties. The budget was rejected, the Commons passing a motion that it 'declines to impose fresh taxation on real property' until ratepayers were offered relief 'in respect of local charges imposed on them for national services'.[27] In other words, property was burdened with local taxation in order to provide services such as education which did not simply benefit local property values. It was left to the Conservative chancellor, George Goschen, to put central government support for local finance on a new basis in 1888. He handed local authorities the revenue from certain licence duties and half the proceeds of the probate duty. The aim was to reduce the burden of local rates on real property by transferring specific sources of central government revenue. This would also protect the government from an open-ended commitment to provide grants for specific purposes, for the revenue from the licences and probate duty would be clearly defined. Local authorities would therefore need to show care and economy, rather than turning to the central government to provide them with grants. In future, local authorities would receive half the proceeds of the probate duty – a tax on *personal* property – which would reduce pressure on local rates on *real*

---

[26] Matthew, *Gladstone, 1809–1874*, p. 139, on the abortive scheme of 1863; and see above pp. 211–13.

[27] Buxton, *Finance and Politics*, vol. II, pp. 297, 314–16.

property. In order to preserve the balance in the fiscal system as a whole, Goschen then increased the succession duty which fell on *real* property (see table 8.1). By these means, he claimed that he was preserving the balance in the fiscal system as a whole by a compensating adjustment of the death duties and local rates.[28] These complex and confusing changes had little impact on the revenue of the government, but they did have significance in defining electoral identities.

Liberal politicians were alarmed that Goschen's proposal would be seen as a means of relieving the burdens of urban ratepayers and so undermining their support in the towns. The rates did not fall only on landowners, but also on factories, mines, ironworks, railways and so on – what was termed 'visible personalty'. The Conservatives could therefore claim to be helping urban ratepayers in general rather than landowners in particular. The Liberals counter-attacked, arguing that Goschen had destroyed rather than preserved the balance of the fiscal system: by relieving real property from local taxation, there was no longer any justification for its more favourable treatment in national taxation. Henry Fowler,* a leading Liberal politician, pointed to two inequalities in the tax system: in local taxation, real property paid more than its fair share; and in national taxation, real property paid less than its fair share. In Fowler's opinion, Goschen relieved real property of too much of its liability to local taxation; over-payment had given way to under-payment. Consequently, the only justification for the favourable treatment of real property in central taxation had been removed and Liberals should now press for absolute equality. Fowler assumed that real property accounted for 45 per cent of all property and personal property for 55 per cent, yet their respective contributions to the death duties were £1,420,000 and £6,970,000. 'We *must* raise and fight this issue *now*', he insisted. Goschen's scheme was, in his opinion, a measure of self-interest designed to help landowners.[29] It provided the Liberals with the opportunity for political advantage.

---

[28] The best account of local taxation and debates over the land is Offer, *Property and Politics*.
[29] Bod. Lib., MS Harcourt dep. 23, ff. 203–9, Fowler to Harcourt, 4 Apr. 1888.
* Henry Hartley Fowler (1830–1911) was born in Sunderland, the son of a Wesleyan minister. He moved to Wolverhampton in 1855, to practise as a solicitor. He entered municipal politics, serving as mayor in 1863 and as MP from 1880 to 1908. He held office as under-secretary for home affairs in 1884 and financial secretary to the Treasury in 1886. He was a leading critic of Conservative finances in opposition from 1886 to 1892, and resumed office as president of the Local Government Board in 1892 until 1894, when he became secretary of state for India. He was a director of the National Telephone Co. from 1897 and president from 1901. He supported the Boer war and opposed tariff reform. In 1905, he became chancellor of the Duchy of Lancaster, and from 1908 to 1910 lord president of the council. (*DNB, Second Supplement*, vol. II, ed. Lee, pp. 49–52.)

Fowler was simply arguing for the restoration of equity of treatment between types of property, by rebalancing the fiscal constitution. Gladstone accepted his logic and moved an amendment to Goschen's measure, that 'the Duties accruing upon deaths should be so fixed as to equalize the charges upon real and personal property respectively'.[30] After all, Gladstone had deliberately designed the succession duty to be more lenient on real property than the probate duty on personal property, precisely to take account of the burden of the rates; the reduction in the incidence of rates meant that the duties should now be equalised.[31] His ambition was 'that the Death Duties ought to be equal upon realty and personalty',[32] which would increase government revenue with less harm to trade and industry than other taxes proposed by the government. 'The present enormous disparity under the Death Duties', he remarked, 'between the charge upon realty and the charge upon personalty has only been tolerated because of the advantage enjoyed by personalty in respect of the limited contribution to the rates, and, in regard to a great portion of personalty, its not being liable to any contribution at all to the rates.'[33] The advantage to personalty in local taxation should, he felt, be cancelled by grants from national taxation which fell more heavily on personal property.[34] The favourable treatment to realty under the death duties should then be removed by equalising the rates on personal and real property.[35] Goschen did the opposite: he transferred revenue levied on *personalty* by the probate duty in order to reduce the burden of rates on *real* property. The inequality of the death duties in favour of real property had 'lost its whole and only justification'.[36] Although the enormous increase in the level of rates meant that all ratepayers had a strong claim to assistance, Gladstone felt that landowners had the weakest case. Indeed, he accused them of hypocrisy and deceit in pleading the cause of *all* forms of real property and appealing to urban MPs for support, without drawing attention to the incidence of taxation. 'The landed proprietors, in fact, posed as the sympathising friends of the urban communities', claiming a common grievance when they were in fact deriving large profits from the expenditure of the rates, which increased the value of their property

---

[30] *Parliamentary Debates*, 3rd ser. 325, 23 Apr. 1888, col. 190.

[31] For Gladstone's reaction, see *Parliamentary Debates*, 3rd ser. 325, 23 Apr. 1888, cols. 190–214.

[32] *Parliamentary Debates*, 3rd ser. 325, 23 Apr. 1888, col. 192.

[33] *Parliamentary Debates*, 3rd ser. 325, 23 Apr. 1888, col. 192.

[34] *Parliamentary Debates*, 3rd ser. 325, 23 Apr. 1888, col.192.

[35] *Parliamentary Debates*, 3rd ser. 325, 23 Apr. 1888, col.197; Buxton, *Finance and Politics*, vol. II, appendix M, pp. 384–5.

[36] *Parliamentary Debates*, 3rd ser. 325, 23 Apr. 1888, col. 199. In 1885, Gladstone had of course proposed to increase the death duty on real property *without* a compensating concession to the rates. See Buxton and Barnes, *Death Duties*, pp. 27–8.

and were in any case often paid by their tenants through increased rents. The claim of owners of 'visible personalty' for relief was greater than the owners of real property, for nearly all the increase of rates fell on them and they were also hit by death duties. As Gladstone argued, the owners of visible personalty were contributing through the probate duty to the fund from which they were compensated for the heavy burden of rates; landowners received compensation from the fund without making a contribution.[37] The case for equalising the death duties was therefore accepted by Gladstone in 1888 as a necessary step to restore balance to the tax system.

Goschen made a further attempt at reform in 1889, when he introduced a completely new 'estate duty'. As far as the Liberals were concerned, he simply made a bad situation worse. Goschen argued that the existing death duties *were* balanced between real and personal property, and instead he pointed to another discrepancy: small properties paid relatively more than large properties. He proposed an additional tax on estates of £10,000 and above, in the form of a charge of 1 per cent on the capital value of both realty and personalty. Here was a further duty of class A. He argued that the inequalities of the existing death duties between personalty and realty were justified; his aim was to add a new tax which was *equal* between personalty and realty. In fact, he treated realty more favourably than personalty, reflecting political pressure from the landed interest for assistance in the face of the agricultural depression. The duty was charged on the full value of personalty whether it was left to one person or divided between several. On realty, it was charged only where an *individual* succession exceeded £10,000. Further, the duty on personalty was paid at once; on realty, it could be spread over four years. The duty was levied on the full capital value of personalty but on a restricted value of land.[38] Despite Goschen's initial intention, in practice the new estate duty introduced a higher rate of tax on personal than on real property, and exacerbated Liberal criticism that the death duties were too favourable to realty now that the incidence of local taxation had been reduced.[39]

Liberal critics of the death duties found a mass of inequalities and anomalies in the death duties as left by Goschen in 1889. 'The history of Death Duties', remarked Sydney Buxton* and George

---

[37] *Parliamentary Debates*, 3rd ser. 325, 23 Apr. 1888, cols. 206, 209–11.
[38] This was a highly technical point: see Buxton and Barnes, *Death Duties*, pp. 31–3, 50.
[39] Buxton and Barnes, *Death Duties*, pp. 29–33.
* Sydney Charles Buxton (1853–1934) was educated at Clifton and Trinity College, Cambridge. He served on the London School Board from 1876 to 1880, and was elected a Liberal MP in 1883. He served as under-secretary of the colonies from 1892 to 1895, postmaster general from 1905 to 1910 and president of the Board of Trade from 1910 to 1914. He was governor-general of South Africa from 1914 to 1920. (*DNB, 1931–40*, ed. Legg, pp. 131–2.)

Barnes,* 'has been one long tale of tinkering and tacking.' Instead of dealing with the duties as a whole, chancellors had modified the existing duties or created a new duty in order to meet the demands for revenue, with the result that there were 'subdivisions, eccentricities, and anomalies without end, and which together form a maze which no one who has not devoted much time and patient study to the subject can hope to unravel'.[40] The attempt of Buxton and Barnes to unravel the maze in their *Handbook to the Death Duties* merely set out what had been explained by Gladstone in the Commons, that the greater part of the contribution to local taxation was paid by real property which did not make an adequate contribution to national taxation. But it was one thing to suggest that anomalies existed; it was another to propose a practical scheme for reform. Should the entire system of death duties be swept away and a new consolidated duty put in its place or should there be a further adjustment to equalise the incidence of the duties? But, even more important, what was the intention: to restore balance within the tax system as a whole, or to use the death duties as a means of *increasing* the incidence on certain types of income and property? Here was the radical claim, that landed property was peculiarly liable to taxation. In this view, the value of land was socially created and should therefore be taken by the community. Far from land being over-taxed by the local rates, it was grossly under-taxed. The crucial issue shifted from the impact of indirect taxes on the necessities of the poor, to the burden of local taxation and income tax on the working class and lower middle class.[41] Central to the debate was the emergence of the 'land question' which marked a major turning point in late Victorian politics.

The land question and the reform of death duties

Gladstone's strategy in 1853 was to adjust death duties to the precise level which compensated real property for its higher burden of local taxation, while at the same time ensuring that it paid sufficient to offset the differential impact of income tax on precarious and realised income. It

---

[40] Buxton and Barnes, *Death Duties*, pp. 33–4.
[41] Biagini, 'Popular Liberals, Gladstonian finance and the debate on taxation', p. 150.
* George Stapylton Barnes (1858–1946) was born in India, the son of the foreign secretary in India; he married Buxton's sister. He was educated at Eton and University College, Oxford, and was called to the bar in 1883. In 1886, he acted as counsel to the Board of Trade in bankruptcy cases; he was an official receiver in 1893 and senior receiver in 1896. He joined the Board of Trade as comptroller of the companies' department, 1904–11 and labour department, 1911–13. In 1913, he was second secretary and in 1915 joint permanent secretary of the Board of Trade. He served as a member of committees to amend company laws (1906), to remodel the statutory forms of railway accounts and statistics (1909) and for new capital issues in the war (1915). From 1916 to 1921 he was a member of the council of the viceroy of India. (*Who Was Who*, vol. IV, p. 62.)

was a clever and careful balancing act which used the death duties to create a sense of equity and fairness in the tax system as a whole. The death duties were part of a system of *proportionate* taxation, by which each social group or type of income should pay the same rate when all claims were taken together. By the 1880s, this approach was under threat. The level of local taxation was increasing as a result of expenditure on education, public health measures, slum clearance, and the costs of poor relief and public order. Local sources of revenue were under strain, and the correct response became a matter of deep political division, within as well as between parties. The Conservatives argued that real property was bearing an increasing burden of rates and that it should be *relieved*, as in Goschen's scheme of 1888. The reaction of Gladstone and Fowler in 1888 was to argue that too much relief had been offered to land. However, they continued to view the death duties as a device to balance the fiscal system as a whole, by ensuring that land paid its fair share of the total tax bill from local rates, income tax and death duties. Their criticisms of the reforms of 1888 and 1889 continued to be based upon the assumptions of *proportionate* taxation.

A new view was emerging in the Liberal party around 1890, associated with Henry George's* *Progress and Poverty*: far from being over-burdened by local taxes, land was escaping its proper contribution. In part, the argument rested on the belief that owners of property shifted the incidence of rates to tenants and occupiers through increased rent, but the case went much further. The increase in land values – so it was argued – was entirely a result of the enterprise of the community, through the individual initiatives of traders, industrialists and house owners, and collective investment in the infrastructure. It was socially created and should therefore be taken by the community as its own. The burden of taxes on land should be far higher, and Goschen's scheme of relieving the rates on real property at the expense of national taxes was a retrograde

---

* Henry George (1839–97) was born in Philadelphia where his father was a clerk in the customs house and a publisher of religious tracts. He worked as a clerk, went to sea and trained as a printer, moving to the west coast where he spent a long period drifting and in poverty. He worked as a journalist, and in 1871 published *Our Land and Land Policy* which noted the increase in land values alongside growing poverty, arguing that private ownership and rent were robbery of labour. He elaborated the case, after reading Ricardo and other economists, in *Progress and Poverty* which appeared in a private edition in 1879 and a regular edition in 1880. He moved to New York and visited Ireland and England, writing *Irish Land Question* in 1881 and coming into contact with the Irish Land League. In 1883, he returned to England and lectured to the Land Reform Union, returning again in 1884/5 and making seventy-five speeches in thirty-five cities. He stood as mayor of New York in 1886, and returned to England again in 1888 and 1889. (*Dictionary of American Biography*, vol. IV, ed. A. Johnson and D. Malone (New York, 1931), pp. 211–15.)

step.[42] What was needed was an *increase* in the incidence of taxes on real property and on unearned incomes.

When the Liberals returned to power in 1892 in Gladstone's last government, it fell to William Harcourt to find an answer. Should he follow Gladstone's approach of 1888 that relief to the rates and real property should be complemented by a full equalisation of death duties, and adjust death duties to balance the fiscal system and preserve proportionality? A balanced tax system in the 1850s required variation in the incidence of death duties; in the 1890s, shifts in other taxes meant that balance required equalisation. On such an account, the aim remained constant: to keep the fiscal ship on an even keel by adjusting the ballast. Or should Harcourt go a stage further, using the death duties to increase the tax burden on land, on the grounds that it had a greater capacity to pay? Or should he follow a different strategy, moving away from Gladstonian fiscal orthodoxy while still pursuing Gladstone's aim of using the tax system to build from the centre to the extremes, to maintain an integrated, legitimate, social and political system without setting groups against each other? In the new circumstances of the 1890s, with the emergence of a powerful radical group and the development of a working-class political presence, a strategy for integration would need to move beyond 1853. Harcourt's ambition was, indeed, to attempt the third option, which seemed the best electoral strategy to avoid alienating middle-class voters and at the same time to retain the allegiance of radicals.

Harcourt had a difficult task when he took up the office of chancellor of the Exchequer in 1892, for he faced the prospect of a budget deficit as a result of the large naval building programme of the previous Conservative administration. Already in 1888/9, Goschen experienced pressures on government revenue which were to force a reassessment of the structure of taxation during the Boer war with the mounting burdens of military expenditure. In order to finance the naval programme, Goschen drew on the savings produced by conversion of the national debt to a lower rate of interest in 1888, but he also needed to increase revenue from taxes on beer and the new estate duty. These taxes were disliked by brewing and landed interests within the Conservative party, and were welcomed by many Liberals dedicated to temperance and hostile to accumulated wealth. What the Liberals could *not* condone was Goschen's 'great constitutional innovation' of a separate Naval Defence Fund of £10m to be paid out of taxes over the next seven years. The proposal horrified Gladstone, who held that it was crucial for the Commons to fix expenditure from year to year (see chapter 3). His concerns were shared by E. W. Hamilton

[42] This change in perceptions is analysed by Offer, *Property and Politics*.

at the Treasury, who feared 'it is mortgaging a part of the taxes too far ahead for expenditure of a kind over which Parliament likes to have annual control'.[43] Gladstone and Harcourt attempted to contain naval expenditure, a frustrating experience which finally prompted Gladstone's resignation in 1894. Naval expansion was, he felt, 'the greatest and richest sacrifice ever made on the altar of militarism. It is absolute insanity ... I dread the effect which the proposals may have on Europe. The peace of Europe is my primary consideration. Financial considerations such as the sounding of the death-knell to the Sinking Fund are merely secondary.'[44] For his part, Harcourt feared that 'we have come to the end of our taxation tether in times of peace', and he attempted to ensure that naval spending should 'be cut according to the financial cloth'.[45] Death duties could be justified as a means of shackling the state and so reducing the desire for military adventures, in much the same way that the income tax would make an expensive foreign policy unpopular. As T. H. Farrer* remarked, the naval programme 'was due, not to the demands of those who consume the bulk of dutiable articles, but of naval men, of amateurs, of those who pay direct taxes'. The fiscal system must therefore be amended to ensure that 'those who call the tune must pay the piper':

It is often said that direct taxation, and especially graduated direct taxation, is dangerous with a democracy, because the masses will, under such a system of taxation, have the excitement of spending the money without the burden of paying it. But in the case of naval and military expenditure it is not the masses, but the classes, who call for it; and, therefore, if we wish to keep it within limits it is upon the classes and not upon the masses, that the burden should fall.[46]

Death duties could be justified on the grounds of Gladstonian retrenchment – as a means of establishing electoral responsibility and constraining militarism – rather than as a radical onslaught against property.

---

[43] BL, Add. MSS 48,650, Hamilton Diary, f. 69, 5 Feb. 1889; ff. 61–2, 24 Feb. 1889; f. 72, 9 Mar. 1889.

[44] As reported by Hamilton in D. Brooks (ed.), *The Destruction of Lord Rosebery: From the Diary of Sir Edward Hamilton, 1894–5* (London, 1986), entry for 22 Mar. 1894, p. 126.

[45] Brooks (ed.), *Destruction*, p. 16, and entries for 13 Nov. 1894, p. 189; 28 Nov. 1894, p. 193; 14 Dec. 1894, p. 197; 11 Jan. 1895, pp. 204–5; 16 Jan. 1895, p. 208.

[46] T. H. Farrer, 'Sir William Harcourt's budget', *Contemporary Review* 66 (1894), 153, 164, and T. H. Farrer, 'The imperial finance of the last four years, III', *Contemporary Review* 58 (1890), 497.

* Thomas Henry Farrer (1819–99) was educated at Eton (where he was a friend of Stafford Northcote) and at Balliol. He was called to the bar in 1844 and left practice in 1848 to draft bills at the Board of Trade. He became assistant secretary to the marine department of the Board of Trade in 1850, assistant secretary in 1854 and permanent secretary 1865–86. He attacked Goschen's finance, and was a member of the London County Council 1889–98. He took a leading part in the Gold Standard Defence Association and was president of the Cobden Club in 1899. (*DNB, Supplement*, vol. II, ed. Lee, pp. 201–2.)

A second source of financial pressure came from local government –
and above all, from that other creation of the Conservative government,
the London County Council (LCC). The politics of London were crucial
to the Liberal government, for metropolitan constituencies could win or
lose a general election.[47] The London Liberal and Radical Union argued
that the gain of twelve London seats in the election of 1892 was largely due
to the expectation that a Liberal government would relieve the pressure
on ratepayers in poorer areas of London; it was feared that the gains
of 1892 would be jeopardised if the next election took place before some
measure of financial relief.[48] 'The feeling about taxing Owners is intense',
commented Farrer, 'and it is formidable because there the Labour party
and the Ratepayers pull together. It would take very little to make an Irish
land question in London.'[49] There was a growing demand for a radical
policy directed against Rent, the value of land arising from its scarcity
rather than the energies of the owner. The Progressives and Liberals
who controlled the LCC were divided between more conservative figures
such as Farrer and Lord Rosebery,* and radicals such as J. W. Benn[†]
and Sidney Webb[‡] who gained the upper hand in 1892. Their differences

---

[47] P. Thompson, *Socialists, Liberals and Labour: The Struggle for London, 1885–1914* (London,
1967), p. 90; K. Young, *Local Politics and the Rise of Party* (Leicester, 1975), pp. 42, 223.

[48] Bod. Lib., MS Harcourt dep. 187, f. 126, memo by the executive committee of the
London Liberal and Radical Union, 9 Jan. 1893; and ff. 134–5, resolutions passed at a
meeting of the Council of the London Liberal and Radical Union, 8 May 1893.

[49] Bod. Lib., MS Harcourt dep. 119, ff. 111–5, Farrer to Harcourt, 23 Nov. 1892.

* Archibald Philip Primrose, 5th earl of Rosebery (1847–1929), was educated at Eton and
Christ Church, Oxford, succeeding to the earldom in 1868 and announcing his support
of the Liberal party in 1869. He was active in support of Scottish claims, serving as
under-secretary of the Home Office with special charge for Scottish business in the
Lords in 1881. He travelled to Australia and New Zealand 1883–4 and developed his
ideas of the empire as a commonwealth of nations. He was lord privy seal in 1885 and
foreign secretary in 1886. He helped to reconcile Liberals to imperialism, and proposed
reform of the Lords to make it an effective second chamber. He was chairman of the
LCC in 1889–90. As foreign secretary from 1892 he clashed with Harcourt over imperial
policies in Uganda and Egypt; he became prime minister on Gladstone's resignation in
1894, in preference to Harcourt who led the party in the Commons. He resigned as
leader of the party in 1896, became president of the Liberal League in 1902 which
marked a split in the party over empire, and severed his links with the party in 1905. He
opposed home rule and denounced the budget of 1909. (*DNB, 1922–60*, ed. Weaver,
pp. 687–96.)

[†] John Williams Benn (1850–1922) was born in Cheshire, the son of a clergyman. He
moved to London where he became a publisher, and served as a Liberal MP 1892–5
and 1904–10; he was elected to the LCC in 1889 and was chairman 1904–5. (*Who Was
Who*, vol. II: *1916–28* (London, 1929), p. 62.)

[‡] Sidney James Webb (1859–1947) was born in London; his father was a public accoun-
tant and his mother a hairdresser. He was educated at the Birkbeck Institute and City
of London College, working as a clerk in the City in 1875–8 and then in the civil service
1878–91. He was called to the bar in 1885, when he joined the Fabian Society, and
was a member of the LCC from 1892 to 1910. In 1892 he married Martha Beatrice
Potter (1858–1943), the daughter of a wealthy industrialist. They wrote *History of Trade*

were clear in the debate over the land question. 'A course of lessons in the "law of rent"', remarked Webb, 'will usually convert a mere Radical into something very like a Socialist', which was precisely what Farrer and Rosebery feared.[50] In January 1893, thirty-five Liberal MPs, forty members of the LCC, and representatives of various Liberal and radical clubs, urged Harcourt to introduce the taxation of land values. This was, they argued, preferable to the reform of the death duties:

> It is said that in place of this cardinal reform, other measures are to be substituted, such as the increase of the probate duty and its application to land; this, however, excellent in itself, would fail to meet the necessity of the case, as no sufficient amount can be raised by a death duty, which is operative on an average once only in twenty years, and which can easily be evaded . . . These proposals, therefor [sic], are manifestly an inadequate alternative for the direct Taxation of Ground Values; this impost alone can extract from land owners a sufficient contribution to meet the expenditure by which land values are created.[51]

Harcourt was under considerable pressure from some groups within the party to launch an explicit attack on landowners and Rent, rather than to restore proportionality. There were serious political dangers: failure to obtain such a measure would alienate radicals from the Liberal government, while success would alienate moderate sentiment. An explicit attack on the land threatened to use the tax system as part of the conflict between classes so firmly rejected by Gladstone. The solution, as Farrer realised, was 'a large reform of Imperial Taxation – which will itself be one of the best cards you can play in the political game of the future'.[52]

Harcourt had, therefore, to meet the pressures of the navy for money as well as containing the grievances of occupying ratepayers, and controlling the London radicals with their sweeping schemes for local taxation. He needed to find a policy to contain the demands of the radicals, without alienating middle-class voters and driving them into the embrace of the Conservatives. To Farrer and Harcourt, death duties were the best solution to both problems. They offered a means of raising money for the navy

Unionism (1894), *Industrial Democracy* (1897) and the history of English local government in nine volumes between 1906 and 1929. They founded the London School of Economics in 1895 and drafted the minority report of the Royal Commission on the Poor Laws, 1909. Sidney was on the executive of the Labour party from 1915 to 1925 and drafted *Labour and the New Social Order* (1918). He became a Labour MP 1922–9, president of the Board of Trade in 1924, and secretary for the dominions and colonies in 1930–1. (*DNB, 1941–50*, ed. Legg and Williams, pp. 935–40.)

[50] Young, *Local Politics and the Rise of Party*, pp. 42, 223; Thompson, *Socialists, Liberals and Labour*, pp. 90–9; J. Davis, *Reforming London: The London Government Problem, 1855–1900* (Oxford, 1988), pp. 119–22, 149–52.
[51] Bod. Lib., MS Harcourt dep. 187, ff. 127–31, memorial to Harcourt, 23 Jan. 1893.
[52] Bod. Lib., MS Harcourt dep. 119, Harcourt to Farrer, ff. 116–7, 24 Nov. 1892; ff. 198–202, 25 Dec. 1892.

and for local services, which could be justified on Gladstonian grounds as an attempt to limit militarism while also going some way towards meeting the radicals' attack on the unearned increment. Indeed, by limiting the force of the radical attack on land, reform of death duties might make the position of land more stable. Of course, it was a commonplace of liberal economics, most clearly stated by J. S. Mill, that property left at death was peculiarly liable to taxation: it would not affect *active* capital, and inheritance depended upon social institutions. Reform of the death duties could therefore be seen as a measure of prudential conservatism in favour of enterprise. The issue was how far to go.

Gladstone was wary about any proposal for graduation, denouncing even Goschen's modest scheme of 1889 on the grounds that it might eventually 'amount to confiscation'.[53] He merely wished to restore proportionality and to balance the tax system between precarious and spontaneous incomes, rather than to favour one against the other. Gladstone informed Harcourt in July 1892 that something should be done to *equalise* the death duties. This could easily be justified on the grounds of proportionality, adjusting the incidence on different types of property to balance the tax system. A similar position was adopted by Rosebery, Richard Haldane* and the Liberal imperialists who sought to make a new appeal to the middle and upper classes alienated from the party by Gladstone's sectional or 'faddist' Liberalism – his alliance with the Irish and lack of support for imperialism. The 'Limps' were concerned at the extent to which the party had become one of protest, and they aimed to attract 'the centre, the great mass of voters' by appealing to the 'old Liberal spirit which existed before the split of 1886' and reconstructing the link between the party and 'the great mass of British public opinion'.[54] The strategy, as Haldane saw it in 1888, was 'to get back the support of that minority of the upper and middle classes, which does naturally, but at present does not, vote with them'.[55] As Beatrice Webb remarked, the strategy of the Limps defined the centre as 'the capitalist or professional

[53] BL Add MS 48,650, Hamilton Diary, f. 114, 2 May 1889.

[54] H. C. G. Matthew, *The Liberal Imperialists: The Ideas and Politics of a Post-Gladstonian Elite* (Oxford, 1973), quoting Haldane (p. 130), Rosebery (p. 130) and Ferguson (p. 131); also pp. 132–3. On the loss of wealth in 1886, see the comments of P. W. Clayden, *England under the Coalition* (London, 1892), p. 150.

[55] R. B. Haldane, 'The Liberal party and its prospects', *Contemporary Review* 53 (1888), 160, quoted in Matthew, *Liberal Imperialists*, p. 130.

* Richard Burdon Haldane (1856–1928) was educated in Edinburgh and Göttingen, and was called to the bar in 1879, becoming a QC in 1890. He was a Liberal MP from 1885 to 1911, serving as secretary of state for war, 1905–12, and lord chancellor, 1912–15. He was active, with the Webbs, in university reform in London and in financial issues. He was lord chancellor in the first Labour government in 1924. (*DNB, 1922–60*, ed. Weaver, pp. 380–6.)

man who desires little social change and the Empire maintained'. In her opinion, a preferable electoral strategy was to appeal to 'the great lower middle and working class'.[56] These debates over the tax structure connected with the fundamental dilemma of the Liberal party from the late 1880s, the concern that it might lose moderate, middle-class, support.

Harcourt's ambition in 1894 was to appeal to the members of the middle class at the lower levels of liability to income tax who dominated the electorate. Reform of the death duties was a key element in his strategy. Although Harcourt was sceptical of Gladstone's Irish policy, in other respects he was a representative of the problem as defined by the Liberal imperialists. He was a 'faddist', whose support for temperance alienated support; and he was a staunch opponent of expenditure on the navy and imperial adventures. It would be easy to conclude that his budget of 1894, which reformed death duties and introduced a new principle of graduation by the size of the total estate, was a further attack on property owners, alienating them from the party and driving them into the arms of the Conservatives. This was certainly what Rosebery feared, and Harcourt's son Lewis (Loulou)* reported that he was 'fighting like a demon' against the steepness of the graduation of death duties. 'R. said "We shall lose all the monied mercantile classes and what shall we do then at the Election? and how can we find money to fight it? The split in the Liberal Party will become horizontal and not vertical".'[57] Harcourt's strategy was different from the Liberal imperialists, yet he did not have much sympathy with the radicals. He was building support from the centre, defined as the lower levels of income taxpayers. He was not appealing to them on the basis of imperialism, but through an astute strategy of tax concessions, with reform of the death duties as one part of a wider fiscal strategy to secure allegiance from a crucial electoral interest. Harcourt was attempting three things: the provision of funding for the navy, while controlling the more extravagant demands of the Admiralty; the containment of the radicals in London, while convincing them that action was being taken; and an attempt to shape the tax system in the interests of the lower levels of income taxpayers.

---

[56] Matthew, *Liberal Imperialists*, pp. 130–3; B. Webb, *Our Partnership*, ed. B. Drake and M. I. Cole (London, 1948), p. 225.

[57] Bod Lib., MS Harcourt dep. 406, ff. 88–90, 2 Apr. 1894.

* Lewis Harcourt (1863–1922) was private secretary to his father 1881–6, 1892–5 and 1895–1904, and a Liberal MP 1904–16. He helped form the Free Trade Union. He held office as first commissioner of works 1905–10, secretary of state for the colonies 1910–15, and returned to the office of works 1915–16. He committed suicide to prevent being exposed as a paedophile.(*DNB, 1922–60*, ed. Weaver, pp. 390–2; M. Parris, *Great Parliamentary Scandals: Four Centuries of Calumny, Smear and Innuendo* (London, 1995), pp. 84–6.)

The budget of 1894: progression and the estate duties

Action on the death duties was clearly necessary when the Liberals came to power, if only to reduce the existing confusion to order. Gladstone instructed Harcourt to equalise death duties and restore proportionality. It was, however, possible to go a step further, graduating the death duties and using them as the main source of additional revenue on the ground that accumulations of wealth were better able to bear taxation and that death duties were more suited to both graduation and differentiation than the income tax. This was the position of Sydney Buxton. He argued in favour of the death duties as a means of raising additional revenue, on psychological grounds: death duties, he claimed, were less unpopular than other forms of taxation for liability for payment arose with accession of wealth, and heavier rates charged to non-lineals were more readily accepted because the bequest was more unexpected.[58] Death duties also had an economic advantage over other taxes, for 'their levy or increase does not in any way fetter or disturb trade or industry, or affect the spending power of existing incomes. In their effect they are neutral, and in this neutrality lies their greatest merit.'[59] He rejected the view that death duties were a tax on capital, which would reduce the yield from other taxes by destroying capital. Capital was not 'destroyed' so much as redistributed, and the revenue derived from death duties enabled the reduction of other taxes which were more disruptive of trade.[60] Buxton argued that graduation could more easily be applied to death duties than to the income tax on purely administrative grounds. The income tax was collected on different forms of income according to 'schedules' so that there was no need to calculate the aggregate income of each taxpayer, which would become necessary with the imposition of a graduated income tax. Buxton feared that the need to declare the total income of each taxpayer would lead to tensions, and would make for difficulties in graduating the income tax. 'In the case of Death Duties, however, the introduction of even an elaborate scheme of graduation would involve no change in the system of levy; for already the value of the property to be taxed has to be declared. Thus it would be as simple to raise the necessary taxation on a graduated as on a uniform scale.'[61] Buxton also felt that the death duties could be used to equalise the taxation of permanent and precarious incomes. The income tax pressed on precarious incomes derived from intelligence and skill; by taxing the capital from

[58] Buxton and Barnes, *Death Duties*, p. 67.
[59] Buxton and Barnes, *Death Duties*, p. 68.
[60] Buxton and Barnes, *Death Duties*, pp. 69–70.
[61] Buxton and Barnes, *Death Duties*, pp. 72–4.

which permanent incomes were derived, the tax system would be more balanced.[62]

Harcourt was willing to go further than either Gladstone or Buxton, for he requested officials at the Treasury to prepare for the equalisation of death duties, and for the graduation of both death duties *and* income tax. In 1863, Gladstone warned against the dangers of graduating the income tax beyond exemption for small incomes, expressing alarm that if 'you adopt it as a general rule of your legislation it merely means universal war – a universal scramble amongst all classes, every one endeavouring to relieve himself at the expense of his neighbour – and an end being put to all social peace and to any common principle on which the burdens of the state can be adjusted'.[63] By the early 1890s, many Liberals *were* prepared to graduate the income tax, feeling that Gladstone was concentrating too much on Irish home rule and neglecting attractive domestic policies. A deputation of MPs urged Harcourt that 'man cannot live by Home Rule alone' and pressed for a 'good English programme', including a radical budget. Lewis Harcourt agreed, and pitied Gladstone for his naive belief that equalisation of the death duties was sufficient: 'Poor man! We should want a great deal more than that . . . we must have a revolutionary Budget next year.'[64] Harcourt was under considerable pressure to overhaul the income tax as well as the death duties, and in January 1894 he received a memorial from ninety-four Liberal MPs who complained that

the principle of adjusting the burden of taxation according to the ability to bear it is flagrantly violated in our present fiscal arrangements . . . the weight of taxation, which is really felt as a severe burden, by persons of small means, ought to be diminished by a much heavier assessment upon persons of fortune who do not at present feel the burden at all, and whose share of taxation might be greatly increased without even then imposing upon them any substantial sacrifice.

This was a clear rejection of the principle of proportionate taxation and a new definition of 'capacity'. They urged consolidation of death duties on realty and personalty, and the introduction of a graduated scale, complemented by graduation and differentiation of the income tax. By raising additional revenue, it would then be possible to reduce taxes on tea, coffee and cocoa and introduce a 'free breakfast table'. As Lewis Harcourt remarked, 'For many years the budgets have been more or less rich men's budgets – it is time we should have a poor man's budget.'[65] As it turned out, these ambitions were not fully realised. Despite the sympathy of

---

[62] Buxton, *Finance and Politics*, vol. II, p. 173; Buxton and Barnes, *Death Duties*, p. 74.

[63] *Parliamentary Debates*, 5th series 170, 26 Apr. 1863, col. 622.

[64] Bod Lib., MS Harcourt dep. 383, ff. 2–3, Lewis Harcourt journals, 19 July 1892, and ff. 20–2, 21 July 1892.

[65] Bod. Lib., MS Harcourt dep. 122, ff. 21–7, memorial to Sir William Harcourt, 12 Jan. 1894.

PUNCH, OR THE LONDON CHARIVARI.—May 12, 1894.

HAMLET AND THE SKULL.

HAMLET (Sir W. H—RC—RT). "THIS FELLOW MIGHT BE IN'S TIME A GREAT BUYER OF LAND, WITH HIS STATUTES, HIS RECOGNISANCES, HIS FINES, HIS DOUBLE VOUCHERS, HIS RECOVERIES," &c., &c.

4 'Hamlet and the skull', *Punch* 12 May 1894: William Harcourt revises the estate duties

Harcourt for a graduated income tax, graduation was confined to the death duties.

Harcourt could easily justify the reform of the death duties by a need to sweep away existing complications, and to tackle the inequalities in the treatment of different types of property. As he explained, policy in the past had been to deal with inequalities by piecemeal changes, which 'only left confusion worse confounded' and resulted in what he called 'tessellated legislation'. The time had come to reform the whole edifice, and to stop using the death duties as compensation for other fiscal inequalities. The answer was to have one death duty of class A and one of class B. The probate and estate duties were merged as a new estate duty on the value of all property, real or personal, left at death. The rate was graduated, rising from 1 per cent on estates of £100 to £500 to a maximum of 8 per cent on estates of £1m and above. Similarly, the succession and legacy duties under category B, falling on beneficiaries, were placed on the same basis so that they were equal in their incidence. Smaller properties were relieved of the duty, so that the overall result was to reduce the level of taxation on small estates and to increase it on the larger estates at death. Overall, Harcourt expected an increase in the yield of death duties of £3.5m to £4m a year, to about £14m.[66] The ultimate yield was to prove disappointing.

The apparent rigour of the death duties was moderated by generous terms for valuation of land, and by Harcourt's sensitivity to the problems of settled estates. Settled land could not easily be sold to cover the duty and was therefore only liable once in the course of a settlement rather than on each succession. In return for this concession, Harcourt imposed an additional settlement estate duty of 1 per cent. In fact, liability was easily covered by taking out a life insurance policy. However, the new duties did also produce one unexpectedly large source of income. Heirlooms and settled personalty were liable to pay duty at the *next* succession which produced £20m, or twice the expected yield.[67] Landowners soon demanded that heirlooms be exempted, and Hicks Beach somewhat reluctantly made a concession in 1896. He exempted settled personalty in the form of paintings, books, works of art, scientific collections, 'or other things not yielding income as appear to the Treasury to be of national, scientific or historic interest'. These items would be exempted so long as they were settled, so escaping the provision of 1894 that duty should be paid once within each settlement. Hicks Beach had opened a large loophole in the death duties. At most, Harcourt was willing to accept exemption for works of art of 'national and historic interest' which were left to a public collection.[68] By contrast, Hicks Beach had

---

[66] The duties were outlined in *Parliamentary Debates*, 4th ser. 33, 16 Apr. 1894, cols. 484–98.

[67] Mandler, 'Art, death and taxes', 289, citing PRO, IR74/2, 'Finance Act, 1894. Experience of the first year of the new Estate Duty', A. Milner to M. Hicks Beach, 12 Aug. 1895, and T168/33, 'Death duties, 1895–6'. A. Milner, 10 Apr. 1896.

[68] Mandler, 'Art, death and taxes', 289, citing Finance Act, 1896, section 20, on Hicks Beach's concession, and, for Harcourt's views at the time of his budget, *Parliamentary Debates*, 4th ser. 26, 2 July 1894, cols. 726–36, 10 July 1894, cols. 1344–57, 1361–72,

made a large concession to the landed class, without any recompense to the public. As Harcourt remarked, it was 'an enormous present to the richest millionaires in the country'. One young Liberal MP – David Lloyd George* – gave notice of his hostility to the landed aristocracy by moving an amendment to allow public access to any work of art exempted from tax.[69] He did not succeed, and landowners were very generously treated by the Treasury's interpretation of the concession. The state was involved in the art market, defining national or historic interest as, in effect, the entire contents of country houses, even to the extent of furniture, china, tapestries and minor paintings. As one judge remarked, such things were 'the legitimate appurtenances of a ducal residence'. Hicks Beach's concession was extended far beyond his initial intentions, and claims for exemption were particularly pressing after 1906 as death duties rose to new levels. Lloyd George was now in a position to take action. Rather than removing the exemption from aristocratic collections, he extended exemption to *unsettled* personalty much to the chagrin of the Inland Revenue's art adviser who now needed to inspect the collections of the *bourgeoisie*.[70]

Despite its shortcomings, reform of the death duties in 1894 gave Harcourt a degree of credibility in the eyes of radicals. Although the death duties gave Harcourt part of the revenue he needed, it was by no means sufficient. His initial intention was to produce additional revenue by a further increase in the income tax, and higher duties on beer and spirits.[71] There were obvious political dangers in this package, and Harcourt therefore hoped to adjust the burden of taxation in order to minimise opposition. He was clearly convinced that increased levels of government spending had changed the politics of taxation. It was not expedient to impose more burdens on the poor through duties on beer; it was necessary to moderate the pressure of income tax on small incomes;

1381–2; and 27, 16 July 1894, cols. 38–46. See also C. Stebbings, 'One hundred years ago: works of art', *British Tax Review* (1996).

[69] Harcourt's comment is from *Parliamentary Debates*, 4th ser. 42, 7 July 1896, cols. 993–4, and Lloyd George's intervention is in *Parliamentary Debates*, 4th ser. 42, 14 July 1896, cols. 1497–9, both from Mandler, 'Art, death and taxes', 289–90.

[70] Mandler, 'Art, death and taxes', 295.

[71] Bod. Lib., MS Harcourt dep. 398, f. 8, 27 Dec. 1893, f. 17, 1 Jan. 1894; 399, ff. 27–8, 12 Jan. 1894.

* David Lloyd George (1863–1945) was born in Manchester, the son of a teacher who died in 1864; he was brought up by his mother and uncle, a shoemaker, in Caernarfonshire. He became a solicitor in 1884 and was a Liberal MP from 1890 to 1945. He opposed the Boer war and aristocratic privilege, and resisted the payment of rate revenue to support Church of England and Roman Catholic schools. He became president of the Board of Trade 1905–8, chancellor of the Exchequer 1908–15, minister of munitions 1915–16 and prime minister from 1916 to 1922. (*DNB, 1941–50*, ed. Legg and Williams, pp. 515–29.)

and the only way in which this could be achieved was by imposing a sur-tax on large incomes. 'I *must* deal with the Income Tax as it would be impossible in the present state of opinion to raise the larger amount from indirect taxation, and if the Income Tax is to be continued as it clearly must at a high level it will be indispensable to reform it at both ends.'[72] But this ambition of creating a progressive, graduated, income tax was ruled out before he presented his budget to the Commons. His plan was to impose a surtax of 0.5d in the £ on incomes above £5,000, rising by 0.5d for each additional £5,000 up to £100,000. Lewis Harcourt reported that his father was 'getting enthusiastic over it and says that some powder is wanted to charge the gun if so heavy a projectile as our deficit is to be fired'.[73] The attraction of the scheme was clear:

It is plain that with the increased and increasing expenditure Income Tax must be treated as a permanent tax. It is essential therefore to redress its admitted inequalities. It is generally felt that it presses too heavily on the lower and too lightly on the higher rates of income. You must therefore have what may be called a normal Income Tax with (1) alleviation at the lower end (This is effected by the allowances under £500) (2) You must also have enhancement at the upper end.

In other words, incomes below £500 would get allowances to reduce their liability; between £500 and £5,000 they would pay the full normal rate; and above £5,000 they would also pay a graduated surtax.[74] Such was Harcourt's plan, which was only partly implemented as a result of the obstruction, ostensibly on administrative grounds, from leading officials (see chapter 10).

In 1894, Harcourt's plans of reforms of the income tax were therefore restricted. Instead, he abandoned graduation at the top end by adding a surtax on large incomes. Instead, he raised the rate by 1d in the £ and re-turned some of the proceeds to limit opposition. He granted a concession to property owners under schedule A, by allowing them a 15 per cent re-duction on gross income to cover outgoings on repairs and maintenance. The concession cost about £610,000 and sacrificed a large part of the income from the new death duties. More importantly, Harcourt made a further concession to small income taxpayers. His Conservative counter-part, Michael Hicks Beach, realised that reform of the death duties was not justified simply on grounds of raising revenue.[75] Rather, it was part of a new fiscal and electoral strategy. Harcourt revised the income tax at the bottom end, so that small incomes paid *less* despite the increase in the standard rate. The existing threshold for payment of income tax was

---

[72] Bod. Lib., MS Harcourt dep. 70, ff. 56–7, Harcourt to Milner, 19 Feb. 1894.

[73] Bod. Lib., MS Harcourt dep. 399, ff. 45–6, 7 Feb. 1894.

[74] Bod. Lib., MS Harcourt dep. 70, ff. 40–3, notes on surtax, undated, [1 Feb. 1894?].

[75] See comments of Hicks Beach, Gloucestershire Record Office, 2455, PCC/12, Hicks Beach to Balfour, 8 May 1894.

£150 a year; incomes between £150 and £400 a year had an abatement of £120. In Harcourt's opinion, incomes of £400 to £500 were most in need of relief: 'They are a large and most deserving class, mostly emerging into the independence they have earned for themselves, and rising by their own industry from the stratum of exemption to that of Income-Tax paying means.' Accordingly, Harcourt increased the threshold for payment of tax to £160, and offered an abatement of £160 on incomes up to £400. He then introduced a new abatement of £100 for incomes from £400 to £500.[76] The increase in the standard rate of tax therefore did not affect incomes below £500. These concessions benefited a large number of people, on modest middle-class incomes, who were precisely the electoral group to which the Liberal party needed to appeal.

Harcourt could interpret the estate duty as a form of graduation and differentiation which would help 'precarious' incomes from trade and employment. In other words, he could link the estate duty to a rhetoric of support for enterprise and risk-taking against unearned incomes from accumulated wealth. Graduation of estate duty could be presented as equivalent to a graduated income tax, without its shortcomings. Indeed, E. W. Hamilton, a leading representative of Gladstonian fiscal orthodoxy, was willing to support a graduated estate duty. It was easier to collect because it did not involve inquisition. It affected only incomes derived from capital, and exempted incomes from salaries which were dependent on the life of the individual who earned the income. It did not affect anyone with an income of less than £1,000 a year, and would not operate in the life of present owners.[77] Hamilton was clearly willing to support the estate duty as preferable to differentiation and graduation of the income tax. Harcourt assured the Commons that by means of the estate duty 'you do arrive at the result which is aimed at in the demand for a graduated Income Tax falling upon what are called "spontaneous", as distinguished from "industrial" incomes'.[78] By making some simple actuarial calculations, the periodic impact of the duty could be expressed as an annual income tax. Assuming a return of 4 per cent, a personal estate of £37,500 would produce an income of £1,440; the additional estate duty was equivalent to an annual income tax of 1.25d. On a personal estate of £200,000 producing an income of £7,680, the additional duty was equivalent to 6.25d annual income tax; and on a personal estate of £1,200,000 producing an income of £45,080 to 10d.[79]

[76] *Parliamentary Debates*, 4th ser. 33, 16 Apr. 1894, cols. 499–501.

[77] Bod. Lib., MS Harcourt dep. 65, ff. 1–4, 7 Apr. 1894.

[78] *Parliamentary Debates*, 4th ser. 33, 23 Apr. 1894, cols. 502–3.

[79] Bod. Lib., MS Harcourt dep. 65, ff. 1–4, E. Hamilton, 7 Apr. 1894; he also made some 'rather fanciful' calculations for income from real property in MS Harcourt dep. 65, ff. 78–82, 13 Apr. 1894. In 1906, the same point was still being made by H. W. Primrose

Harcourt was only able to introduce his budget against the strong opposition of Rosebery, who succeeded Gladstone as prime minister in 1894. Rosebery feared that it might be interpreted as an attack on landowners, so alienating the 'last relics' of property owners in the party who would become 'an active and alarmed adversary'. In Rosebery's opinion, it was desirable to preserve the aristocracy, for 'a plutocracy of the American type would be a bad substitute for the landed class in Great Britain'. Rosebery feared that the Liberals would lose support from the prosperous, without securing the allegiance of the less well-off. Men earning £500 were, he felt, neither sufficiently numerous nor given to gratitude. Above all, he was alarmed by 'a horizontal division of classes in this country in which the Liberal party would rest on nothing but a working class support without the variety and richness and intellectual forces which used to make up that Party'.[80] Harcourt was not impressed, and announced that 'there is nothing to do with such rubbish as this sort except to treat it with the contempt it deserves'. He informed Rosebery that he cheerfully accepted the animosity of the landowners, who were simply losing privileges they should never have possessed. In reality, his concessions on schedule A returned much of the taxation, and in many ways he was *containing* more radical attacks. He was convinced that his strategy made electoral sense, for incomes under £500 accounted for 90 per cent of the electorate. As he tactlessly informed Rosebery, the best way to get their gratitude was to earn it; the fault lay with leaders of the party who alienated support 'by appearing as the defenders of fiscal privileges and exemptions of the wealthy which are universally condemned'.[81]

The Liberal party was able to portray Harcourt's measure as 'a great Democratic Budget'. The reform and simplification of the death duties would mean that 'land which has hitherto paid far too little, now has to pay as much as (though not more than) any other kind of property'. Graduation of death duties meant that the millionaire would pay proportionately more than a man worth £1,000. It reduced the impact of income tax on everyone under £500. 'The BUDGET is a FAIR BUDGET. It is an HONEST Budget – it pays its way. It lays down the important and far-reaching principle that extra taxation ought to fall on THOSE WHO CAN BEST AFFORD TO PAY. It removes some of the unjust PRIVILEGES which the landlords have possessed in the past.'[82] The thrust of the budget

of the Inland Revenue: PRO, IR74/11, 'Note as to methods of estimating the annual tax on property which would be equivalent to the present occasional taxes on transmission of property at death', 3 July 1906.

[80] Bod. Lib., MS Harcourt dep. 57, ff. 77–89, Rosebery, 3 Apr. 1894.

[81] Bod. Lib., MS Harcourt dep. 57, fos. 93–109, 4 Apr. 1894.

[82] Liberal Publication Department, leaflet 1653, 'The budget: what it is and how it was carried', in Bod. Lib., MS Harcourt, dep. 125.

was to assist 'higher-paid workmen, clerks, struggling professional men, the smaller shopkeepers, manufacturers and agriculturalists'.[83] He could point to the graduated death duties as an act of social justice between 'precarious' or industrious and 'spontaneous' or passive incomes, and he could suggest to the radicals that he was taking action against socially created rents. Harcourt was pursuing the same end as Gladstone: to use the tax system to unite rather than divide classes. He was building from the middle out, offering concessions to the lower level of income taxpayers. The increase in death duties helped to contain pressure from radicals for an attack upon land, without mounting an onslaught on land as a separate fraction of capital. It appealed to the radicals, and contained their pressure for wider – and possibly wilder – schemes. As Farrer remarked, the budget would 'rank with the great efforts of Sir R. Peel and Mr Gladstone', and would 'properly take its place amongst the great measures which have helped to reconcile capital and labour; have adapted the demands of government to the altered circumstances of society; and have advanced the welfare of the people'.[84] Of course, whether landowners and the Conservatives agreed was a different matter. Harcourt's conception of 'balance' was a construction which appeared distinctly unbalanced and redistributive to the Conservatives – not to say Rosebery. But in the changed political circumstances of the 1890s, this was no bad thing in Harcourt's view: landowners had already abandoned the Liberal party and the greater need was to secure support from radicals, nationalists, the lower middle class and working class.

Death duties were therefore central to debates over the fiscal constitution of Britain in the nineteenth century. Taxation of estates at death seemed more acceptable to many politicians than taxation of current incomes, on the grounds that it did not harm active enterprise, and that the right to inherit was something secured by the state and its laws. Although the ambition of Gladstone to replace the income tax by death duties was not realised, death duties did remain central to his vision of the equity of the tax system. Above all, he was anxious that the income tax should not be used to set one class or interest against another, and he used death duties in order to convince the supporters of differentiation of the income tax between spontaneous and precarious incomes that balance was restored by taxation of estates at death. To Gladstone, the death duties were a means of ensuring that no form of income paid a greater or lesser proportion in tax. This allowed him to defuse the campaign for differentiation in the mid-Victorian period. By 1894, the approach of Harcourt was different. The extension of the franchise, the rise of the

[83] *Birmingham Daily Post*, 23 Apr. 1894, quoted in Brooks (ed.), *Destruction*, p. 24.
[84] Farrer, 'Sir William Harcourt's budget', 153, 164.

303   PUNCH, OR THE LONDON CHARIVARI.   [June 30, 1894

DEPRESSED DUKES.

Duke of D-v-nsh-re. "If this Budget passes, I don't know *how* I'm going to keep up Chatsworth!"

Duke of W-stm-nst-r. "If you come to that, we may consider ourselves lucky if we can keep a Tomb over our Heads!"

5   'Depressed dukes', *Punch* 30 June 1894, contemplate the loss of their estates

land question, and concerns about local taxation, meant that pressure for differentiation and graduation was more intense and had more radical implications than in the mid-Victorian period. Death duties were part of Harcourt's strategy of containment, showing the radicals that he was taking action without accepting their wilder claims. Above all, he wished to reduce the burden of taxation on small middle-class incomes, whose votes were so important. By offering them abatements to their income tax, and using the death duties as a means of hitting large unearned incomes, he could pose as the friend of hard-working, risk-taking, independent and self-sufficient families.

Harcourt was therefore moving towards the fiscal and electoral strategy which was adopted and extended by Asquith and Lloyd George between 1907 and 1914, *ahead* of the Conservatives' search for a strategy based on tariff reform. However, there were important differences between Harcourt and his successors. Unlike Asquith, he was not proposing differentiation between industrious and spontaneous income – or what was now termed with a more obvious moral connotation, earned and unearned income. Unlike Lloyd George, he was not attacking land outright. What Harcourt aimed to achieve was equality between duties on real and personal property which would remove a potential grievance against landowners and contain the radical critique. Indeed, Milner assured Hicks Beach that equalisation of the death duties was in the best interests of landowners. The 'indefensible' preferential treatment of real property by the death duties meant that landowners lost more through their inability to secure redress of their 'just claims' for relief from local taxation. Milner estimated that the net additional cost of Harcourt's death duties on land would be £600,000 a year, and 'If that sacrifice, by putting land for the first time on a footing of equality with other property with respect of burdens common to all enables it to make out a case for relief from burdens peculiar to itself the sacrifice may after all turn out a blessing in disguise.'[85] The equalised death duty was an insurance premium rather than extortion. By 1907, the situation had changed, with a greater need of the Liberal party to face the challenge of tariff reform on one side and the growth of a separate Labour party on the other. In these new electoral circumstances, death duties had an even greater appeal as an attack on 'unproductive' wealth. In 1907, Asquith increased the estate duty to a maximum rate of 11 per cent, and Lloyd George took it up to 15 per cent, with a settlement estate duty of 2 per cent.[86] Perhaps the dukes did, after all, have reason to be depressed.

[85] PRO, IR74/2, 'Finance Act 1894. Experience of the first year of the new Estate Duty', A. Milner to M. Hicks Beach, 12 Aug. 1895.
[86] Mallet, *British Budgets*, p. 490.

[Tocqueville's analysis of America and France] led him to attach the utmost importance to the performance of as much of the collective business of society, as can safely be so performed, by the people themselves, without any intervention of the executive government ... He viewed this practical political activity of the individual citizen, not only as one of the most effectual means of training the social feelings and practical intelligence of the people ... but also as the specific counteractive to some of the characteristic infirmities of Democracy, and a necessary protection against degenerating into the only despotism of which in the modern world there is real danger – the absolute rule of the head of the executive over a congregation of isolated individuals, all equal but all slaves. There was, indeed, no immediate peril from this source on the British side of the channel, where nine-tenths of the internal business which elsewhere devolves on the government, was transacted by agencies independent of it; where Centralisation was, and is, the subject not only of rational disapprobation, but of unreasoning prejudice; where jealousy of Government interference was a blind feeling preventing or resisting even the most beneficial exertion of legislative authority to correct the abuses of what pretends to be local self-government, but is, too often, selfish mismanagement of local interests, by a jobbing or *borne* local oligarchy ... I have steered carefully between the two errors, and ... have ... insisted with equal emphasis upon the evils of both sides, and have made the means of reconciling the advantages of both, a subject of serious study.

J. S. Mill, *Collected Works*, vol I: *Autobiography and Literary Essays*, ed. J. M. Robson and J. Stillinger (London and Toronto, 1981), pp. 201–3

The radical demand for a minimal state and free trade in mid-Victorian Britain did not entail a simple pursuit of individual economic self-interest. Rather, the aim was to break down the privileges of chartered monopolies and create an active associational life based on the participation of citizens.[1] In the words of Eugenio Biagini, Gladstonian liberalism rested on 'the identification of liberty with self-government, high esteem for a life of public service and the related civic virtues, the idealisation of

---

[1] On the culture of free trade, see Trentmann, 'Political culture and political economy'.

"independence", and an emphasis on self-help and education as moral imperatives'.[2] Above all, John Stuart Mill stressed the need for active participation in the local community, based on the positive liberty of 'Athenian democracy' in order to limit the potentially harmful moral consequences of an increase in the size of towns and the complexities of economic life. In small communities with face-to-face relations, a shop-keeper could only deceive his customers once without a loss of reputation; in a large town, a shopkeeper was driven to obtain customers by grandiose and misleading claims about the qualities of his goods. In other words, 'public opinion degenerated from rational check to an irrational phe-nomenon easy to manipulate'. What applied to retailers might equally apply to politicians, resulting in the decline of a cultivated elite of 'public moralists' who relied on logical argument, and a rise in a more populist approach in a commercial society of individuals pursuing private inter-ests. These dangers could only be avoided by cultivating direct, popular, participation and civic virtue – and preventing it from degenerating into selfish mismanagement.[3]

Mill believed that local government was a protection against the po-tentially despotic power of the executive over isolated individuals. But it could be interpreted in a less positive way, as a sign of meanness rather than participation, a danger of which Mill was aware. One modern his-torian, Patrick O'Brien, criticises Victorian politicians for their strategy of devolving administrative and fiscal responsibilities to the localities as part of 'the Victorian regime's ideology of fiscal parsimony and social neglect'. In his view, the central government was able to avoid the 'dif-ficult and unpopular tasks' of raising taxes for public services, and in-stead concentrated on foreign and strategic policies.[4] His criticism of the parsimony of early Victorian governments is supported by the dete-rioration in life expectancy and infant mortality in British cities in the second quarter of the nineteenth century. The expectation of life at birth in cities in England and Wales with a population of more than 100,000 fell from thirty-five in the 1820s to twenty-nine in the 1830s, before a significant improvement raised life expectancy to thirty-eight in the 1870s and forty in the 1880s.[5] Under-investment in the infrastructure of public health in the late eighteenth and early nineteenth centuries had

[2] Biagini, 'Liberalism and direct democracy', pp. 22–3.
[3] Biagini, 'Liberalism and direct democracy', pp. 29, 30–1, 36. On the notion of 'public moralists', including Mill, see Collini, *Public Moralists*.
[4] O'Brien, 'Taxation', 7.
[5] Szreter and Mooney, 'Urbanization, mortality and the standard of living debate', table 6, 104.

serious consequences for welfare. Failure to invest sufficient sums in the urban environment in the early nineteenth century was, in the words of N. F. R. Crafts, 'one of classic market failure – suboptimal expenditure on public goods in the context of free rider problems, unequal incidence of benefits, and a narrow tax base'.[6] Investment in the urban environment could have raised the efficiency of the economy and produced a decent rate of return, but it was not in the interests of any single industrialist to stop polluting the air or rivers, and to pay for new sewers or paving. The starting point for the analysis of local government finance must be to consider the political circumstances which led to such an outcome. Why was there a failure of investment in the second quarter of the nineteenth century that led to urban squalor and declining life expectancy?

The problem was eased, in an admittedly partial and regionally varied way, in the second half of the nineteenth century by re-establishing the conditions for collective action. The gain in life expectancy in the last quarter of the century was largely the result of improvements in the urban environment brought about by capital investment in sewers, water supply and paving; by improved standards of cleansing and regulating the city; and by the provision of isolation hospitals and maternity clinics. Local authorities were responsible for an increasing share of total government expenditure. In the 1820s, local taxes accounted for about 14 per cent of total taxation; by the First World War, the proportion had increased to 34 per cent.[7] As Charles Feinstein has shown, capital formation by local authorities accounted for 95 per cent of all public investment between 1870 and 1914, and for a sizeable share – 11 per cent in the 1870s and 15 per cent in the 1890s – of gross domestic fixed capital formation.[8] By 1914, local authority debt had risen to £656.2m, not far short of the national debt which stood at £706m.[9] Despite the continued influence of penny-pinching ratepayers, investment in the urban infrastructure did

---

[6] Crafts, 'Some dimensions of the "quality of life" during the British industrial revolution', 633–4; see also J. G. Williamson, *Coping with City Growth during the Industrial Revolution* (Cambridge, 1990), and J. C. Brown, 'The condition of England and the standard of living: cotton textiles in the north-west, 1806–50', *Journal of Economic History* 50 (1990), 591–614; on the gains as a result of intervention in public health, see S. Szreter, 'The importance of social intervention in Britain's mortality decline c. 1850–1914: a reinterpretation of the role of public health', *Social History of Medicine* 1 (1988), 1–37, and A. Hardy, *The Epidemic Streets: Infectious Disease and the Rise of Preventive Medicine, 1856–1900* (Oxford, 1993).

[7] O'Brien, 'Taxation', 6.

[8] C. H. Feinstein, *National Income, Expenditure and Output of the United Kingdom, 1855–1965* (Cambridge, 1972), table 39, T85–6.

[9] J. F. Wilson, 'The finance of municipal capital expenditure in England and Wales, 1870–1914', *Financial History Review*, 4 (1997), 31.

rise in the later Victorian period until it hit the limits of the local tax base around 1900, at the same time as a rise in the cost of borrowing money.

Why was there an increase in investment in the second half of the nineteenth century that led to considerable improvements in urban mortality and life expectancy? In part, the answer was through considerable private investment by large-scale gas, water and transport companies, as well as by the myriad small builders and house owners. Both forms of private investment posed political difficulties. The companies usually held local monopolies, with what amounted to 'taxing' powers over consumers. Consequently, there was concern to limit their ability to charge high prices or extract excessive profits, resulting in controls which might act to limit future investment or lead to public ownership. By contrast, investment in the housing stock was highly fragmented between landowners, builders, house owners and the providers of mortgages. Housing formed the major source of local government revenue through its liability to rates – and entailed complex political negotiations. The house owners might collect the rates on behalf of the local authority, in return for a commission – but might not be able to pass them on to the tenants. Local finance might therefore erode profits in housing and hamper future investment.[10] The focus in this chapter is on public investment, asking how the circumstances were created for a greater level of collective action. The task was by no means simple and unproblematic. Additional spending might be desirable to resolve the problems of urban health, public order and economic efficiency, and many government departments were eager to encourage local authorities to invest in drains, reservoirs, schools and hospitals. But who should pay, in what way, for large-scale, capital-intensive, investments in huge engineering works, and for the increased costs of providing an expanding range of municipal services? Were local taxes fairly distributed between different interests and incomes, and was it fair to impose charges on the localities rather than central government? Might increased spending by the localities force the government to make grants or offer loans, so undermining attempts by the Treasury to hold down taxes and redeem the national debt? How should the Treasury deal with the potential threat to its control over public spending and debt? The spurt in investment by local authorities raised issues of mind-numbing technical complexity and political difficulties.

[10] I have dealt with both of these aspects elsewhere: see 'The material politics of natural monopoly', and *House and Home in the Victorian City: Working-Class Housing, 1850–1914* (London, 1983).

The failure of urban expenditure

During the eighteenth century, the rise of a powerful fiscal-military state to wage war against the French was linked with the disengagement of the central state from social policy and public order, which were left to the localities. The outcome was different in France and Prussia, where the attempt of the central state to mobilise resources led to the creation of new central agencies in the localities. In the case of Britain, as Joanna Innes has remarked, 'both initiative and practical administrative responsibility may be said to have devolved on to local authorities, who – with much experience behind them and with a well-developed and increasingly ambitious and reflective culture of public service to sustain them – were at least reasonably well equipped to respond to this challenge'.[11] But there were also problems, for the population of Britain was rising to unprecedented levels and moving into towns. There was no systematic connection between the size of towns and the structure of government, for some of the largest towns of the early nineteenth century – such as Manchester and Birmingham – did not have municipal corporations, and relied as best they could on a variety of powers and institutions – on manorial courts, county justices, market charters, parish vestries or improvement commissions. As Innes remarks, traditional urban forms had fossilised in apparently irrational patterns.[12]

Corporations might represent an active civic culture, and could respond to the needs of the town through ownership of property, markets and harbours, and by sponsoring improvements. Nevertheless, corporations were increasingly open to criticism by the end of the eighteenth and beginning of the nineteenth century. One of their major concerns was to regulate trade and apprenticeship, protecting freemen of the town from competition. Increasingly, this role was open to legal challenge and ideological attack as irrelevant to a competitive, commercial, economy. Similarly, the representative function of corporations was open to doubt. Many corporations fell into the hands of one political or religious group, undermining the corporation's claim to defend the economic interests of the town as a whole. The use of revenues from corporate property, tolls and dues became a subject for contention, for corporation finances lacked transparency and were attacked for misallocating the community's resources for partisan ends. As a result, a 'closed', self-electing, body had problems in levying rates on the town as a whole, with the result that

---

[11] Innes, 'Domestic face of the military-fiscal state', pp. 96, 102; see also D. Eastwood, *Governing Rural England: Tradition and Transformation in Rural England, 1780–1840* (Oxford, 1994), pp. 1–4.
[12] Innes, 'Governing diverse societies'.

most urban improvements were financed from borrowing, with a mounting burden of debt.[13]

Nevertheless, the absence, or ineffectiveness, of a corporation did not necessarily prevent towns from responding to problems of governance. Existing powers could be turned to new uses, to rival or replace the corporation: manorial courts, market charters, courts leet, parish vestries or county JPs. New bodies were also created. Voluntary associations proliferated to provide schools, hospitals, libraries, literary and philosophical societies, mechanics institutes, botanic gardens.[14] Unlike the closed and secretive corporations, membership was open to anyone paying a subscription, and actions were recorded in published accounts and reports which were debated at public meetings. Commissions were established by local, private, acts to pave, light and watch areas of the town, with their own independent rating powers. The commissioners were usually appointed *ex officio* or co-opted. Despite the 'irrationality' of the structure of urban government, it was sufficiently flexible to deal with urban growth in the eighteenth century, so that life expectancy rose and infant mortality fell. Problems were to arise in the second quarter of the nineteenth century, when public health deteriorated and the failure of collective action was more apparent.

In the late eighteenth and early nineteenth centuries, the institutions of the state, local corporations, the Church of England and charitable foundations of all kinds from universities to almshouses were attacked on the grounds that they were not accountable to the public in the exercise of their rights and the performance of their duties. The conservative defence was that institutions were accountable to the *law* which imposed specific obligations, as well as to the crown and to God. Any reform should come from *within* the institutions which were aware of the complications of the situation, rather than from ignorant outsiders; at most, parliament should enable rather than compel reform; the bodies were assumed to be behaving in a conscientious manner and only needed to be shown how to undertake voluntary reform. Such an approach has been defined by Geoffrey Best as 'trustworthy unaccountability'.[15] The conservative defence of charitable foundations and corporations rested on the belief that those running them had the desire to behave in a conscientious manner in order to fulfil their obligations, which should be sustained through public

[13] Innes, 'Governing diverse societies'; Dawson, 'Finance and the unreformed borough'.
[14] On the creation of these associations, see Clark, *British Clubs and Societies*, who suggests that they were an ineffective response to the weaknesses of formal government; and Langford, *Public Life and the Propertied Englishman*, for a more positive view. See also above, p. 42 n. 17.
[15] G. F. A. Best, *Temporal Pillars: Queen Anne's Bounty, the Ecclesiastical Commissioners and the Church of England* (Cambridge, 1964), pp. 178–83.

trust and encouragement. The Whigs were more inclined to suspect that the institutions were sources of privilege without responsibility, which were in need of regulation and accountability to an outside body. In the second quarter of the nineteenth century, livery companies in the City, almshouses and Oxford and Cambridge colleges were criticised for misusing funds for the benefit of their members and 'taxing' other members of society by avoiding their fiscal responsibilities.[16] Major enquiries were launched into the estates of the Church of England, endowed charities, municipal corporations and schools in order to create a greater degree of public accountability through elective processes and active parliamentary reforms. Similar issues arose with respect to companies – often monopolies – supplying gas or water. The shareholders and directors of these utility companies had similar powers to the old chartered monopolies such as the East India Co. in fixing prices and 'taxing' consumers. They therefore needed to be regulated to prevent their charging high prices. Public bodies, charities and companies were part of a single discourse on accountability and taxation.[17]

One response to the pressures on urban governance was to create cheap and simple procedures to establish *ad hoc* bodies to undertake paving, lighting and watching. The Lighting and Watching Act of 1830 removed the need for an expensive private act to establish each new improvement commission; in future, any three rated inhabitants in a community in England and Wales could request a meeting and a commission would then be created so long as it was approved by a three-quarters majority. Rather than being co-opted or appointed *ex officio*, the commissioners were now elected on a franchise giving more weight to large property owners: a householder with property assessed for the poor rate at up to £50 had one vote, with an additional vote for each £25 up to a maximum of six. This graduated franchise followed the precedent of the Sturges Bourne Act of 1818, a permissive measure allowing parishes to replace 'open' vestries by 'close' or elected vestries under the guidance of larger ratepayers which would bring the poor law under the control of larger ratepayers rather than potential beneficiaries. The principles of 1818 and 1830 were opposed by the alternative approach of J. C. Hobhouse's* permissive act

---

[16] On charities, see above pp. 211–17 and for an account of the debate over the public responsibilities of charities, see Owen, *English Philanthropy*, chapter 7.

[17] This issue is explored in more depth in Daunton, 'Material politics of natural monopoly'.

* John Cam Hobhouse (1786–1869) was educated at Westminster and Trinity College, Cambridge, where he founded the Cambridge Whig Club. He travelled with Byron, and was his executor. He contested Westminster as a radical in 1819, and was imprisoned for breach of privilege; he was elected in 1820. He was active in support of Greek independence. He held office as secretary at war 1832–3 and Ireland 1833, when he resigned over the house and window tax. He was defeated at Westminster, and elected

of 1831, which allowed parishes to establish select vestries on the basis of one ratepayer, one vote. In 1833, the Whig government went some way towards Hobhouse's position. The act of 1830 was amended so that five ratepayers could call a meeting, at which a smaller majority of two-thirds was needed to establish a commission, which would then be elected on the basis of one ratepayer, one vote.

These divergent approaches to the franchise had major consequences for collective action and public expenditure. On the one hand, wide participation in 'open' vestries meant that those who paid little or nothing in rates could take control of spending and of taxation, a prospect which caused considerable alarm at a time of high poor law expenditure. On the other hand, the unrepresentative nature of 'closed' corporations and charities with their self-selecting and self-interested governing bodies, as well as co-opted or *ex officio* improvement commissions, created problems of legitimacy and consent to taxation. When these bodies were reformed, the choice of franchise had major consequences for spending on social capital. Hobhouse's principle of one ratepayer one vote potentially gave power to small ratepayers to incur expenditure which fell most heavily on large property owners. The prospect alarmed the duke of Wellington,* who condemned Hobhouse's Act 'for leaving the property of every man at the disposition of the rabble of his parish, particularly in the towns'. But the result might well be parsimony rather than extravagance, for most votes were held by small property owners – investors in small houses to rent, or shopkeepers and traders – who feared that public spending would hit their profits. A franchise based on one vote per ratepayer might entrench lower-middle-class ratepayers, with a concern for parsimony and a lack of interest in collective spending. By contrast, a graduated franchise gave more power to large property owners and ratepayers who

---

for Nottingham 1834–47, and for Harwich from 1848. He was commissioner for woods and forests in 1834, president of the Board of Control 1835–41 and 1846–52. (*DNB*, vol. XXVII, ed. Lee, pp. 47–50.)

* Arthur Wellesey, first duke of Wellington (1769–1852) was educated at Eton, Brussels and Angers military academy; he entered the army in 1786, and was MP from 1790 to 1795. He served in India from 1797 to 1805, in both military and civil administration, and returned as an MP from 1806 to 1809 serving as chief secretary in Ireland 1807–9. He then commanded the army in Portugal, Spain and France; he was ambassador in Paris in 1814 and at the Congress of Vienna in 1815. In 1815, he commanded the army at Waterloo at the final defeat of Napoleon. He was in the Cabinet as master-general of ordnance from 1818 to 1827, opposing Catholic emancipation and recognition of the independence both of the Spanish colonies in Latin America and of Greece. In 1828, he became prime minister and carried Catholic emancipation against his own opinions. He resigned in 1830 rather than accept parliamentary reform, returning to office as prime minister and home secretary in 1834, and as foreign secretary in Peel's first administration in 1834. He was a Cabinet minister without office from 1841 to 1846. (*DNB*, vol. LX, ed. S. Lee (London, 1899), pp. 170–223.)

might have an interest in imposing strict economy in poor relief. However, they might take a different line on spending on the urban infrastructure (whether from self-interest in improving the efficiency of their business, or a wider sense of public trust) so that plural voting might break the hold of lower-middle-class retrenchment.[18]

The different approaches to the franchise in the Lighting and Watching Acts of 1830 and 1833 re-emerged in two major reforms: the Poor Law Amendment Act of 1834 and the Municipal Corporations Act of 1835. The poor law adopted a graduated franchise as a means of imposing strict control on spending which many reformers felt was excessive and counter-productive in encouraging feckless behaviour by the poor. In the opinion of reformers, control of the old poor law in England was not in safe hands, unlike in Scotland where the larger landowners secured control from the middle of the eighteenth century. In England, the granting of relief was in the hands of the overseers of the poor, who were answerable to the residents of the parish. Although they might take a harsh line towards claimants in order to hold down taxes, they might also incur heavy expenditure out of a self-interested calculation that they might themselves be applicants in the future, or in order to pass the costs of maintaining seasonal labour on to the public purse. Further, the poor law was part of a system of social order based on deference and discretion. An unsuccessful applicant for relief could appeal against the decision of the overseers to any justice in the county, who could order that relief be granted. In theory, the discretionary power of the justices created a sense of deference within a paternalistic or hierarchical social order. However, the experience of agrarian unrest in the early 1830s suggested that deference was no longer effective, and a different form of authority was emerging, based on the certainty of punishment and the use of a professional police force. Reform of the poor law was designed to remove entitlements to welfare by breaking the power of beneficiaries and ensuring that local power was in 'reliable' hands. Parishes were grouped together into Unions, with elected Boards of Guardians. The power of beneficiaries was reduced by a system of plural voting for larger taxpayers: owners of property assessed at up to £50 had one vote, with a further vote for each £25 of rateable value up to a maximum of six; ratepayers had one vote for assessments up to £200, rising to a maximum of three votes for property rated at £400 and above.

[18] For an outline of the different franchises, see J. Prest, *Liberty and Locality: Parliament, Permissive Legislation and Ratepayers' Democracies in the Nineteenth Century* (Oxford, 1990), pp. 8–9, 12–13. He does not consider the implications of the different franchises, either for accountability or responses to the urban problem. See also P. M. Ashbridge, 'The power and the purse: aspects of the genesis and implementation of the Metropolitan Poor Act, 1867', PhD thesis, University of London (1998), chapter 2.

These scales were revised in 1844, and were later adopted by the Public Health Act of 1848 and the Local Government Act of 1858: owners or occupiers of property assessed below £50 had one vote, rising in steps for each additional £50 to a maximum of six votes as an owner or occupier. Further, election to the Board was confined to larger owners and occupiers of property, and JPs were *ex officio* members.[19] The poor law was therefore made 'safe' and expenditure was brought under control.

Unlike the poor law, reform of the municipal corporations in 1835 adopted one vote for each ratepayer. The Municipal Corporations Act did little to create fiscal capacity to respond to the problems of public health, and Simon Szreter has gone so far as to argue that reform *weakened* the responsiveness of towns and resulted in political and administrative paralysis. At first sight, the franchise appears more democratic than in the case of the poor law, but there was little danger of Wellington's fears being realised. The municipal franchise was dependent on the prompt payment of rates, so that securing the vote was a financial transaction which potential voters might decide to forgo. A large number of ratepayers were excused payment, or the rates were simply not collected because of administrative difficulties and the poverty of the occupiers. The size of the electorate was also influenced by how the rates were fixed by the local council and their officials, for they could control whether any particular property exceeded the threshold for the vote. The franchise was therefore actively constituted rather than passively granted. Control over local government fell into the hands of small shopkeepers, house landlords and small manufacturers who did not wish to pay for the costs of pollution or poor sanitation; they were anxious to hold down rates which would fall on their assets and profits. The narrowness of the tax base and the limited franchise therefore led to a constant danger that a policy of expenditure would produce political nemesis. Although the Municipal Corporation Act broke the hold of self-electing oligarchies and created the *potentiality* for levying a rate on the entire town by linking taxation with representation, in the short term the structure of the franchise gave power to supporters of retrenchment. In many cases it also replaced a patrician oligarchy of local gentry and urban merchants who were willing to embark on collective spending on urban improvements. Before 1835, their problem had been that unreformed corporations lacked legitimacy: it was difficult to impose taxation with the result that many fell into debt. But the reformed corporation did not solve the problem, for it might undermine an older civic or corporate culture without creating a new commitment to collective action and municipal dignity. Co-operation

---

[19] Prest, *Liberty and Locality*, pp. 15–16; Mandler, 'The making of the new poor law *redivivus*'; Ashbridge, 'The power and the purse', chapter 2.

gave way to mutual suspicions. As Szreter puts it, 'It was much easier to agree to disagree, and for each to get on with minding his own business, in accordance with the liberal and libertarian precepts of the age.' The emphasis was on retrenchment, with less ability to negotiate a political bargain to promote expensive investment.[20]

Of course, investment in the urban infrastructure could be left to private enterprise, but problems arose here as well as with public spending. Until the 1850s, joint-stock companies were established either by charters granting monopoly rights or by act of parliament. Monopolistic trading companies such as the Hudson Bay Co. or the East India Co. were denounced by radicals as part of the system of 'old corruption', and the same critique applied to the West India Dock Co. in London which was granted power to force traders to use its facilities. Here was another form of taxation without representation, the imposition of a charge without accountability to the consumer or 'tax' payer.[21] There were similar concerns that railways were exploiting traders and 'corrupting' parliament through vested interests. In 1844, the Railway Act laid down a number of provisions to protect the consumer, including the right of the government to nationalise the railways after twenty-one years. The act was devised by Gladstone as president of the Board of Trade, and in 1865 he was willing to implement nationalisation by purchasing the lines and then leasing them back to commercial firms under the supervision of a government board.[22] As William Farr argued in 1873, 'The East India Co. and the Railway Companies fell into many errors, and even crimes,

[20] Szreter, 'Economic growth', 705–6; Prest, *Liberty and Locality*, p. 17; G. B. A. M. Finlayson, 'The politics of municipal reform, 1835', *English Historical Review* 81 (1966), 673–92; G. B. A. M. Finlayson, 'The Municipal Corporation Commission and Report, 1833–35', *Bulletin of the Institute of Historical Research* 36 (1963), 36–52; P. Salmon, 'Electoral reform at work: local politics and national politics, 1832–41', DPhil thesis, University of Oxford (1997). The classic account of ratepayers' reaction is E. P. Hennock, *Fit and Proper Persons: Ideal and Reality in Nineteenth-Century Urban Government* (London, 1973); E. P. Hennock, 'Finance and politics in urban local government in England, 1835–1900', *Historical Journal* 6 (1963), 212–25. The problems of local government finance are also dealt with by Offer, *Property and Politics* . See also Williamson, *Coping*, pp. 294–8, and A. S. Wohl, *Endangered Lives: Public Health in Victorian Britain* (Cambridge, Mass., 1983); D. Fraser, *Urban Politics in Victorian England: The Structure of Politics in Victorian Cities* (Leicester, 1976); on the local response to the Municipal Corporation Act, and the nature of pre-reform government, see Dawson, 'Finance and the unreformed borough'. On the difficulties of rating small property, see PP 1837–8 XXI, *First Report from Select Committee on Rating of Tenements*, Qq. 108–10, 375–9, 1010–1, 1512–17, 2641–7, 2795, 3357–63.
[21] Daunton, *Progress and Poverty*, p. 294 . For a recent account, which links debates over the East India Company to debates on domestic companies, see Alborn, *Conceiving Companies*, chapter 2.
[22] F. Dobbin, *Forging Industrial Policy: The US, Britain and France in the Railway Age* (Cambridge, 1994); Matthew, *Gladstone, 1809–1874*, pp. 119–20.

at their origin, but they have rendered imperishable services to mankind; and they have alike earned, and are destined to receive the same apotheosis – Absorption into the Sovereign Power.' Both could be criticised on the same grounds as the 'fiscal-military state' and 'old corruption', that they benefited a small group at the expense of the bulk of the population, and could only be purged by nationalisation or by regulations imposed by disinterested public servants. The East India Co. was absorbed into the 'sovereign power' in 1858; the railway companies escaped nationalisation until 1947. However, the companies *were* forced to accept state arbitration of disputes with traders over their rates in the Regulation of Railways Act of 1868 and the Railway and Canal Traffic Act of 1873. In the case of railways, as with other elements in the infrastructure, the issue was where to fix the boundary between the private sphere of large-scale business and the public sphere of government. As Timothy Alborn argues, the outcome depended on the politics of joint-stock companies, on the relationship between customers (with their concern for charges), shareholders (with their concern for profits), employees (with their concern for wages) and management (with their concern for long-run stability).[23]

What was the result in the case of urban utilities such as gas and water, and later tramways and electricity, or docks and harbours? These concerns required large amounts of capital, and they did not fit into the norm of control and ownership by a family or partnership. They might therefore be perceived as 'corrupt' in using their power against consumers without the discipline of competition or political control, as examples of what may be termed 'untrustworthy unaccountability'. To an extent, utility companies could be seen as mimicking the form of voluntary associations: the right to participate rested on the ownership of a share with a small denomination in the same way that a voluntary hospital was managed by its subscribers. As a result, serious political conflicts might be avoided, at least for a time. The problem was that the utility companies soon diverged from this model, and were open to the same criticism as the East India Co. and the railway companies, as self-interested monopolists with the power of taxation of consumers through high charges or poor quality gas and water, without the chance of representation. The utility companies were not able to escape from political difficulties by moving away from a local customer base, and they were always liable to pressure from the consumers of gas and water who had political power through their vote in borough elections.

[23] Alborn, *Conceiving Companies*, Part III, deals with railways; the quote from Farr is on pp. 51–2. See also Dobbin, *Forging Industrial Policy*.

One response to the monopolistic hold of gas companies was to set up rival 'consumer' companies in which customers and shareholders controlled the concern in the same way as subscribers to voluntary associations. Another response was to limit the power of the companies by pitting one against the other. Both approaches failed, for understandable economic reasons: entry costs were high, and companies preferred to form monopolies to supply a town or (in the case of London) a distinct territory.[24] John Stuart Mill expressed deep unease about the outcome, arguing that monopolistic companies were not accountable. In theory, shareholders had power over the directors of companies; in practice, he feared that their input was minimal. By contrast, government agencies were more accountable to electors. As Mill saw it, any 'delegated management' was likely to be 'jobbing, careless and ineffective' compared with personal management by the owner, but these faults were even more likely in the case of large companies than the state. Despite the dangers that a powerful state bureaucracy would keep citizens in a child-like condition, Mill felt that the threat posed by company control of gas and water was even greater: the companies were more irresponsible and unapproachable than the government, and had the power to levy what was, in effect, a compulsory tax. Mill felt that the utility companies were comparable with the dangers of the fiscal-military state and protection: 'a government which concedes such monopoly unreservedly to a private company does much the same thing as if it allowed an individual or an association to levy any tax they chose, for their own benefit, on all the malt produced in the country, or on all the cotton imported into it'. What was needed, therefore, was strict regulation over private companies to control their prices and profits or to give the right of public purchase at fixed intervals. On such a view, the companies were a threat to a freely competitive market, and control over their power was needed to complement the removal of customs duties or chartered monopolies.[25] Protection of consumers against exploitation by 'natural monopolies' might therefore require a more active local state, the creation of an 'Athenian democracy' in which all citizens could participate and which might well take the utilities into public ownership.

In the early and mid-nineteenth century, the increasing size and complexity of cities, with their massive problems of pollution and sanitation, required an unprecedented scale of investment in the urban infrastructure. However, the institutional structure did not provide the necessary

[24] D. A. Chatterton, 'State control of public utilities in the nineteenth century: the London gas industry', *Business History* 14 (1972), 166–78; the issue is considered at more length in Daunton, 'Material politics of natural monopoly'.

[25] Mill, *Principles*, chapter XI of Book IV.

framework for investment. Both the municipal system and private concerns were highly contested, and taxpayers and consumers lacked a sense of trust in them. What was needed was a resolution of these tensions and a removal of suspicion, in order to break constraints on investment. Until investment could be increased, the urban environment would continue to deteriorate with alarming consequences for life expectancy and the efficiency of the urban economy.

The creation of collective spending

The problem of investment in the urban infrastructure could only be resolved – or at least lessened – by establishing a framework for both public and private action. Obviously, the deterioration in the urban environment, with the dangers of a sudden and squalid death from cholera or typhoid, provided an incentive, but that is not the whole answer. Conditions do not lead to action in any direct way, for as Christopher Hamlin points out, the 'intolerability thesis . . . neglects to explore how the verdict of intolerability was arrived at and by whom, and why the mountains of filth were tolerated one day and declared intolerable the next'. Sanitary reform was more complicated than a simple story of supporters of dirt and cheap government battling with the proponents of rationality and progress. Rather, the circumstances in which local councils and officials took decisions should be seen as one of 'bewilderment and frustration with technical and legal complexities and fear of taking the wrong step'. In his case studies of the introduction of sewage works in the industrial town of Merthyr Tydfil and the resort of Leamington Spa, Hamlin finds that the trigger in both cases was legal: an injunction from a private party to stop pollution of the river, using common law procedures. Of course, the injunction did not provide an answer to the fundamental question of where the money should come from in order to solve the problem; and the decision over the best form of sewage disposal also had financial implications. Similarly, municipal purchase and improvement of the water supply in the spa and residential town of Cheltenham and the industrial town of Wakefield arose from the same concern that the water company's proposed change in the existing supply would threaten the prosperity of the town. In Cheltenham, the company wished to supplement water pumped from wells with water from the Severn, which would destroy the town's reputation as a spa. In Wakefield, the company proposed to replace polluted water from the river with pure, hard, water from wells so creating problems for large woollen manufacturers who wanted soft water for cleaning and dyeing. The appeal to sanitary issues was only part of a wider set of concerns, and can only be understood within a more

complex interplay of interests. Certainly, Hamlin's emphasis on the difficulties in deciding between competing technical options has its validity.[26]
However, such an approach may all too easily lead to a detailed account
of battles over which source of water or what form of sewage treatment
should be adopted in one town after another. It is also possible to suggest
a number of more general changes which increased the effectiveness of
local institutions in responding to the enormity of investment in the infrastructure and in the provision of a wider range of services. At least two
issues needed to be resolved: the creation of political support for taxation;
and the ability to borrow large sums of money to purchase private utilities and invest in a wide range of expensive facilities from new drainage
systems to schools, roads, public parks and art galleries.

Extension of the franchise in the Second Reform Act of 1867 and
the Municipal Franchise and Assessed Rates Acts of 1869 weakened
the power of ratepayers' retrenchment. The local electorate quadrupled
to 60 per cent of working-class men, most of whom did not pay their
rates in person but 'compounded' it as part of the rent handed to their
landlord. As a result, the electorate was less sensitive to costs than the
narrow, property-based electorate after 1835 – a point realised by supporters of the short-lived amendment to the Second Reform Act which
disenfranchised 'compounders' and required direct payment as a condition of the vote. Wellington's fear was now more realistic. At least in
some towns and in some circumstances, new forms of cross-class alliance
could be forged, creating what Szreter has called a 'neo-patrician political leadership'.[27] More prosperous businessmen started to seek public
office as a mark of honour and dignity, and the culture of voluntary asso-
ciationalism moved into the municipality. The municipal arena became
the space within which a wider range of interests in the town could seek
influence, and the municipalities entered a new phase in providing parks,

[26] C. Hamlin, 'Muddling in Bumbledom: on the enormity of large sanitary improvements in
four British towns, 1855–1885', *Victorian Studies* 32 (1988–9), 55–83; on the differences
over water purity, see C. Hamlin, *A Science of Impurity: Water Analysis in Nineteenth-
Century Britain* (Bristol, 1990).

[27] Hennock, *Fit and Proper Persons*, p. 12, shows that the municipal electorate as a percentage
of the population was 3 per cent in Birmingham in 1841 and 1861, rising to 18 per cent
in 1871 and 19 per cent in 1911; in Leeds, the proportion was 10 per cent in 1841, 13
per cent in 1861, 19 per cent in 1871 and 20 per cent in 1911. J. Davis and D. Tanner,
'The borough franchise after 1867', *Historical Research* 69 (1996), 306–27, discusses
the parliamentary franchise; for the impact of granting the vote to compounders, see
313; Szreter, 'Economic growth', 717. On the short period of disenfranchisement of
compounders and the problems this caused, see *Parliamentary Debates*, 3rd ser. 190, 19
Mar. 1868, cols. 1893–921, and 197, 21 June 1869, cols. 360–80; PP 1867–8 XIII, *Report
from the Select Committee on Poor Rates Assessment together with proceedings of the Committee,
Minutes of Evidence and Appendix*; D. Englander, *Landlord and Tenant in Urban Britain,
1838–1918* (Oxford, 1983), pp. 85–100.

libraries, art galleries, town halls or water works. As Morris remarks, 'the word "municipal" was closely associated with notions of local pride, of improvement and of achievement'.[28] The corporate or civic culture of the eighteenth century could now re-emerge at least in some boroughs in the new guise of an active municipal culture. Of course, considerable variations still existed, depending on the local political and social circumstances, with some towns lagging far behind their neighbours in their willingness to invest in the urban infrastructure. Nevertheless, in aggregate investment did increase in the last quarter of the nineteenth century, and Joseph Chamblerlain's activities in Birmingham were not, as some historians have suggested, merely a sign of what might have been.[29]

The change was the result of a combination of forces. In part, dissenters and evangelicals transferred their energies from voluntary societies to the municipality, as in the case of Joseph Chamberlain* who was elected to the Birmingham council in 1870 as a result of his interest in education.[30] In part, it was the result of economic self-interest, for investment in the infrastructure often made good business sense in securing supplies of cheap water for industrial processes or, more generally, increasing the efficiency of the urban economy at a time when many firms relied on 'externalities'. Small, competitive, family firms had weak internal managerial hierarchies and relied on external bodies to provide training or marketing, to deal with labour relations and to cope with social welfare. Chambers

[28] R. J. Morris, 'Structure, culture and society in British towns', in M. J. Daunton (ed.), *Cambridge Urban History of Britain*, vol. III: *1840–1950* (Cambridge, 2000), p. 412.

[29] The classic account of differences in local political circumstances and the power of ratepayers is Hennock, *Fit and Proper Persons*; for a good example of the differences between neighbouring towns in investment in public health, see K. S. M. Göschl, 'A comparative study of public health in Wakefield, Halifax and Doncaster, 1865–1914', PhD thesis, University of Cambridge (2000). F. M. L. Thompson, 'Town and city', in F. M. L. Thompson (ed.), *The Cambridge Social History of Britain 1750–1950*, vol. I, *Regions and Communities* (Cambridge, 1990), places more emphasis on the failure of investment and sees Chamberlain as merely a symbol of what might have been; this is to miss the considerable increase in aggregate spending on public investment up to the early twentieth century when higher interest rates, overseas investment and the limits of local taxation imposed constraints on spending.

[30] Hennock, *Fit and Proper Persons*, pp. 83, 93.

* Joseph Chamberlain (1836–1914) was educated at University College School; he joined a firm of screw manufacturers in Birmingham 1854–74; he was chairman of the National Education League of Birmingham in 1868 and the National Education League in 1870. He served as mayor of Birmingham 1873–5, and became Liberal MP for the city in 1876. He took office as president of the Board of Trade in 1880, but was out of sympathy with his colleagues, adopting imperialistic policies in foreign affairs and radical policies at home which he advocated in his unofficial Liberal programme. He was president of the Local Government Board in 1886, but resigned over home rule and established the Liberal Unionists. He was secretary of state for the colonies in the Conservative administration from 1895 to 1903, resigning in order to mount his campaign for tariff reform. (*DNB, 1912–21*, ed. Davis and Weaver, pp. 102–18.)

of Commerce could handle complex legal issues and establish a framework within which individual concerns could operate, by creating agreed contracts and codes of arbitration, as well as bargaining with the central state over issues such as cotton duties in India. In the mid-nineteenth century, formal internal managerial hierarchies were weak and there was considerable delegation of authority over recruitment or work discipline to workers on the shop-floor. Associations were created at the level of the town in order to negotiate with workers and establish a degree of order in a highly competitive market. Although the individual firm could not determine the selling price of its output and could not individually control wage costs, it *was* possible to limit the degree of competition and uncertainty by ensuring that firms agreed on wage rates and were tied to a set timetable for re-negotiation. The individual firm therefore 'externalised' industrial relations by delegating negotiation with unions to an association operating outside the firm at the level of the town or industrial region.[31] Much the same 'externalisation' applied to the development of new techniques and industrial training, where firms were slow to develop their own internal research and development or training. In many cases, information and techniques were shared between inter-related firms specialising in parts of a process within the craft community of a town such as Sheffield or a district such as Clerkenwell. When this approach started to falter at the end of the nineteenth century, industrialists turned to public provision through schools of art and design or technical colleges, relying on public institutions to provide training outside the firm.[32] Similarly, family firms relied on local social networks which created trust and reputation, and allowed entrepreneurs to insert themselves into circuits of credit and subcontracting.[33] These networks were external to the individual firm, based on the local community through the chapel, Chamber of

---

[31] For example, W. Lazonick, *Competitive Advantage on the Shop Floor* (Cambridge, Mass., 1990); H. F. Gospel, *Firms and the Management of Labour in Modern Britain* (Cambridge, 1992); R. Price, *Masters, Unions and Men: Work Control in Building and the Rise of Labour, 1830–1914* (Cambridge, 1980); J. Zeitlin and C. Sabel, 'Historical alternatives to mass production: politics, markets and technology in nineteenth-century industrialisation', *Past and Present* 108 (1985), 133–76; D. Reeder and R. Rodger, 'Industrialisation and the city economy', in Daunton (ed.), *Cambridge Urban History*, vol. III, pp. 554–7.

[32] P. Johnson, 'Economic development and industrial dynamism in Victorian London', *London Journal* 21 (1996), 27–37; H. F. Gospel (ed.), *Industrial Training and Technological Innovation: A Comparative and Historical Study* (London, 1991).

[33] For example, S. Nenadic, 'The small family firm in Victorian Britain', *Business History* 35 (1993), 86–114; J. Brown and M. B. Rose, 'Introduction', in J. Brown and M. B. Rose (eds.), *Entrepreneurship, Networks and Modern Business* (Manchester, 1993), p. 3; M. B. Rose, 'Beyond Buddenbrooks: the family firm and the management of succession in nineteenth-century Britain', in Brown and Rose (eds.), *Entrepreneurship*, pp. 127–8; on credit matrices, see P. Hudson, *The Genesis of Industrial Capital: A Study of the West Riding Wool Textile Industry, c. 1750–1850* (Cambridge, 1986), pp. 105–207, 262–5.

Commerce, charities or town council. The economy of expanding towns in the nineteenth century did not depend simply on investment in factories and machines, in urban infrastructure and services, but also on the accumulation of trust. The ability to insert a firm into a fragile network of credit was critical to success, and was carefully cultivated and monitored through religious bodies, participation in commercial associations and involvement in philanthropic bodies. Participation in the civil society of the town had a clear economic rationale in creating reputation which could then be generalised to the municipal authority as a body of trustworthy members. In the words of Simon and Nardinelli, 'the talk of the bourgeoisie, not the smoke of the factory, was the defining characteristic of the modern city economy' – information on who was a safe risk, the latest market trends, the newest technical development could determine success or failure. This myriad activity also provided the basis for a strong municipal culture, and led to a greater sense of trust between taxpayers and of consent to public action.[34]

The development of a municipal culture would have little practical importance without the availability of funds. The provision of expensive sewage treatment plants or water works was not only controversial as a result of conflict over the best engineering solution; the choice of techniques was influenced by their cost and by the fundamental issue of who should pay. The willingness of councils to spend on expensive solutions involving large-scale capital expenditure depended on the availability of cheap loans and conflict arose over the terms for local authority borrowing. Central government departments with an interest in encouraging investment in public health or education would prefer fairly generous terms, allowing authorities to borrow over long periods at low interest rates, either from the government or from private investors. But the Treasury had different considerations in mind. Might cheap loans encourage wasteful and ineffective spending, and were the authorities able to control their budgets and keep up repayments? Might the localities compete with the government in loan markets, or push up the public debt which the Treasury was so anxious to reduce?

A balance had to be drawn between strict controls which frustrated activity, and a set of accounting rules sufficiently strong to establish the legitimacy of public action by creating transparency, accountability and trust. During the second and third quarters of the nineteenth century, we have seen how the *central* state created a much greater sense of trust in taxation through a clear set of accounting rules which ensured that

---

[34] C. J. Simon and C. Nardinelli, 'The talk of the town: human capital, information and the growth of English cities, 1861–1961', *Explorations in Economic History* 33 (1996), 384–413; Morris, 'Structure, culture and society in British towns', pp. 410–14.

every item of expenditure was voted annually by parliament, with complete transparency. The aim was to prevent expenditure from running out of control, and to establish trust in the integrity and honesty of government. The same project of creating trust and accountability had to be carried out in local government so that economy could be defined not simply as low expenditure, but as efficient, remunerative and controlled spending. Once the central state had confidence in the efficiency and reliability of local government, devolution of spending had a number of virtues. As Sir Charles Wood* remarked to Lord John Russell in 1850, 'it is evidently wise to put as little on the Government whose overthrow causes a revolution as you can and to have as much as you can on the local bodies which may be overthrown a dozen times and nobody be the worse'.[35] The strategy is apparent in the controversial area of education, where government funding collided with religious susceptibilities. When School Boards were created in 1870 to fill gaps in voluntary provision of education, the Education Department in London was eager to displace conflict from Whitehall to the localities, and in 1887 it called for further devolution as part of this strategy.[36] As the Sanitary Commission explained in 1871, the aim should be 'not to centralise administration, but on the contrary to set local life in motion'.[37] In 1889, John Morley[†] argued that 'decentralisation' had the advantage of delegating to local bodies any 'affairs dangerous in the hands of government'. He was thinking of highly controversial and divisive issues such as compulsory land purchase or control of the drink trade which might threaten the legitimacy of the central state,[38] but his sentiment might be extended to cover other

---

[35] Quoted by P. J. Waller, *Town, City and Nation: England, 1850–1914* (Oxford, 1983), pp. 244–5.

[36] G. Sutherland, *Policy Making in Elementary Education, 1870–95* (Oxford, 1973), pp. 92, 94–5.

[37] Quoted in J. Davis, 'Central government and the towns, 1840–1950', in Daunton (ed.), *Cambridge Urban History*, vol. III, p. 268.

[38] BL, Add. MS 48, 651, Hamilton Diaries, vol. XXII, f. 132, 20 Nov. 1889.

* Charles Wood (1800–85) was educated at Eton and Oriel College, Oxford. He was a Liberal MP from 1826 to 1866, holding office as joint secretary to the Treasury in 1832, secretary to the Admiralty in 1835, chancellor of the Exchequer in 1846, president of the Board of Control in 1852, first lord of the Admiralty in 1855 and secretary of state for India, 1859–66. (*DNB*, vol. LXII, ed. S. Lee (London, 1900), pp. 353–4.)

† John Morley (1838–1923) was educated at Cheltenham College and Lincoln College, Oxford. From 1860 he worked as a journalist in London, editing the *Fortnightly Review* between 1867 and 1882. He came into contact with J. S. Mill and Joseph Chamberlain, and supported disestablishment, secular education, land reform, progressive taxation and a pacific foreign and imperial policy. He published a *Life of Cobden* in 1881, and was elected to parliament in 1883. He broke with Chamberlain over Ireland, and was chief secretary in Ireland from 1892 to 1895. He opposed the Boer war, in alliance with Harcourt. He wrote the life of Gladstone (3 vols., 1903). He returned to office as secretary of state for India, 1905–10. (*DNB, 1922–30*, ed. Weaver, pp. 616–24.)

issues with the potential for disruption. The process has been termed 'peripheralisation': politicians at the centre aimed to create autonomy for 'high' politics through delegation to reliable and dependable 'local elite collaborators' in the localities.[39] It was by no means a simple and straightforward task.

London offers a good example of the processes by which large-scale spending became possible. The issue of finance was crucial to the construction of the new system of main or 'intercepting' sewers designed to prevent the discharge of effluent into the Thames. The existing sewers were simply intended to cope with rainwater, and householders were forbidden from discharging into the sewers until 1815. The change in policy created a disjuncture between the interests of the private water companies (which increased their profits by a greater use of water closets) and the commissioners of sewers (who did not have the financial resources to increase the capacity of the system). The profit of the companies was also earned at the cost of a serious threat to public health, for the Thames provided the water supply for many Londoners. Although the eight district commissions of sewers were merged into a single metropolitan commission in 1847, their revenue from the sewer rate remained limited. The commissioners resigned in protest in 1852, and their successors failed to raise a loan on the security of the rate in 1853. The crisis in the provision of an adequate system of sewers for London is a clear example of the problems of collective action in the second quarter of the nineteenth century.[40]

The institutional structure changed with the creation of the Metropolitan Board of Works (MBW) in 1855, whose members were drawn from the parish vestries and city corporation. However, the financial problems were not resolved. The cost of new sewers was formidable, rising from an initial estimate of £2.8m to an eventual expenditure of £4.1m. How could this large sum be obtained? The original intention of the government was to grant powers to the MBW to borrow from the Treasury on the security of the rates, but this was dropped from the act and very strict controls were imposed. The funding of the scheme was seriously hampered by a limited definition of liability to tax. Ratepayers would only pay when they derived direct advantage from the new sewers, and could appeal to the Quarter Sessions if they received less benefit than others from the scheme. In other words, the taxpayer was defined as an individual consumer who paid a charge for a particular service rather than for collective investment

[39] J. Bulpitt, *Territory and Power in the United Kingdom: An Interpretation* (Manchester, 1983), pp. 3, 60–6, 143–61.
[40] S. Halliday, 'Sir Joseph Bazalgette and the main drainage of London', PhD thesis, London Guildhall University (1998), pp. 22, 36–7, 41–2, 50, 56–7.

in the health of the metropolis. The ability of the MBW to incur expenditure was also controlled, for any sum in excess of £50,000 had to be approved by the Commissioners of Public Buildings and Works, and any sum above £100,000 by parliament. These constraints were removed in 1858, much to the alarm of Gladstone. He argued that London – the richest city in the world – should bear the cost of cleaning its own river; in his view, costs and benefits should be symmetrical both for individuals and for cities. Despite Gladstone's opposition, the MBW obtained power to raise £3m by bonds and debentures, underwritten by the Treasury so that money could be obtained at low interest rates. The loan would then be repaid over forty years from a main drainage rate of 3d in the £ from all parts of London without any right of repeal by individual taxpayers; the power of blocking expenditure above £50,000 was also removed. In 1863, Gladstone – despite his earlier reservations – approved a further loan of £1.2m. In the 1850s and 1860s, strict rules were devised for the provision of loans with clearly defined sources of revenue to provide security, so establishing confidence in lending to the MBW and creating a sense of trust in the efficiency of public investment.[41]

The debate over the taxing and borrowing powers of the MBW was played out for the nation as a whole, continuing the discussions of 1830 and 1833 over the most appropriate franchise. The power of small ratepayers might create parsimony and poor sanitation; how much power should be given to supporters of sanitary reform, who formed a minority of the electorate, in order to force collective expenditure against a cautious majority? The acts of 1830 and 1833 required a *majority* of three-quarters or two-thirds of ratepayers before the structure of the vestries could be altered. By contrast, the Public Health Act of 1848 permitted a *minority* of ratepayers – 10 per cent – to petition the General Board to implement the act. Alternatively, the General Board could itself intervene if the death rate was high. The town council could, if it wished, implement the act or a separate Local Board of Health might be established with a graduated franchise as in the case of the poor law. The council (or local board) then had unprecedented powers to borrow, with the consent of the General Board, up to a year's assessable value and to mortgage the rates for 30 years. The act of 1848 therefore gave considerable power to an active minority to force change, and small penny-pinching ratepayers were at a disadvantage in gaining control of the local board. Not surprisingly, there was outrage at the centralising tendencies of the General Board and the marginalisation of the small property owner. In 1858, the Public Health Act returned to the earlier principles of 1830 and 1833. The role of the

---

[41] Halliday, 'Sir Joseph Bazalgette', pp. 82–3, 106–10, 201, appendix 3.

General Board in implementing the act was removed. Instead, a meeting of ratepayers could be called, by twenty ratepayers for a motion to adopt powers or by one ratepayer to block adoption; in either case, a majority of two-thirds was needed to enforce or suspend the act. The terms of 1848 were therefore unusual, and the normal method of establishing consent to taxation was through a ratepayers' plebiscite. Such an approach applied, for example, to the Museums Act of 1845, the Bath-houses and Wash-houses Act of 1846 and the Libraries Acts of 1850 and 1855. Similarly, the Borough Funds Act of 1872 insisted that a municipality must secure the approval of a public meeting of owners and ratepayers before promoting a private bill to take on some new power. In effect, referenda were used to prevent extravagance and to establish consent. As a result, ratepayers could oppose schemes which they felt inappropriately expensive, such as in Islington where they voted against the use of rates to support a public library in 1855, 1870, 1887 and 1897. Not everywhere was so penny-pinching as Islington, which was declining into a poor inner city borough in the late nineteenth century. In many provincial towns, it was easier for industrialists and merchants to mobilise resources for collective action, perhaps by offering philanthropic donations to start the process.[42] On the one hand, the system permitted 'economists' to block spending on new services; on the other hand, the use of plebiscites established a framework for the creation of consent to specific forms of collective spending.

Power to tax was not enough, for many of the new functions required large capital expenditure which could not be provided by an annual flow of revenue. Local authorities needed to borrow, and the weakness of the capital market in the early nineteenth century needed to be tackled. Loans sanctioned by the Public Health Act of 1848 amounted to £2.96m by 1871, and under the act of 1858 to £7.36m; further loans were obtained under private acts. The problem, as the Local Government Board (LGB) saw it, was that investment in social capital was still hindered by the difficulties of securing flexible, convenient and cheap loans. The Public Works Loan Commission (PWLC) was set up in 1817 to make loans to projects of 'public interest', but the terms laid down in the Public Works Loans Act of 1853 were stringent. Money could only be borrowed for twenty years, and the terms were not easy; in 1859, the rate was set at 5 per cent. At the time of the Lancashire cotton famine, loans were offered at 3.5 per cent to provide work relief and this concession was extended to sanitary authorities by the Public Health Act, 1872. The approach of the LGB was to urge favourable terms for public loans in

[42] Prest, *Liberty and Locality*, pp. 30, 35, 42–5; A. Clinton and P. Murray, 'Reassessing the vestries: London local government, 1855–1900', in A. O'Day (ed.), *Government and Institutions in the Post-1832 United Kingdom* (Lampeter, 1995), pp. 70–1.

order to encourage spending – a policy which brought the Board into conflict with the Treasury. Gladstone and his chancellor, Robert Lowe, opposed low interest rates on the grounds that they were hidden grants. The chairman of the loan commissioners – J. G. Hubbard in a new guise – strongly supported stringent terms, arguing that 'the State has no business to be a money lender at all. It is only from exceptional necessity that the existence of such a Board as that over which I preside can be tolerated'. The LGB (and other spending departments) therefore collided with the Treasury over the terms of public loans. The Board aimed for lower interest rates and longer periods for repayment, while the Treasury held out for a higher rate and shorter periods, arguing that public loans should only be available as a last resort. In 1873, the Board won a partial victory over the Treasury, with a rate of 3.5 per cent on loans of thirty years. In 1875, the Treasury succeeded in restoring a fixed rate of 5 per cent; in a short-lived experiment, each department was required to produce an annual statement of all public loan requirements for inclusion in a Public Works Loan Bill, to be voted by parliament. In 1879, each local authority was limited to £100,000 a year from the PWLC, and in 1900 large authorities were debarred. Although parliament did make loans available for specific purposes, such as housing at $3\frac{1}{8}$ per cent, on the whole government loans became the preserve of small authorities which were not able to turn to the capital market.[43]

The concern of the Treasury should be understood in the context of problems with the national debt in the mid-1870s, for loans to local authorities from the PWLC were recorded as additions to the national debt – a simple accounting procedure which led to considerable concern, especially since the National Debt Commission (NDC) seemed to be heading for insolvency. The trustee savings banks handed their deposits to the NDC which used the money to buy government stock for redemption; the banks were guaranteed a fixed rate of interest which was above market rates so that the NDC was making a loss on the transaction.[44] When Stafford Northcote created a new sinking fund to pay off the national debt in 1875, he barred loans to local authorities from the funded debt of long-term consols. Consequently, local loans fell on the unfunded debt which consisted of more costly short-dated Exchequer bills and bonds. As far as Joseph Chamberlain was concerned, there was no problem about increased local authority debt which created an asset. But the Treasury

[43] C. Bellamy, *Administering Central–Local Relations, 1871–1919: The Local Government Board in its Fiscal and Cultural Context* (Manchester, 1988), chapter 3; Wilson, 'Finance of municipal capital expenditure', 34–6.

[44] H. O. Horne, *A History of Savings Banks* (London, 1947); Daunton, *Royal Mail*, pp. 92–106.

saw matters differently, fearing the impact of large local loans on money markets. In 1880, pressure on the unfunded debt was somewhat reduced by allowing the NDC to use deposits of the Post Office Savings Bank (POSB) for local loans. Further, Goschen decided to create a distinct local loan fund at the NDC in 1887, on the grounds that local loans inflated the apparent level of national indebtedness and harmed the credit of the nation. Goschen and the Treasury aimed to create transparency and greater accountability, for any deficiency in the local loan fund would now be obvious and would be made up by a specific parliamentary vote, so removing any danger of a hidden subsidy to local loans.[45]

In fact, larger authorities obtained most of their loans through the money market rather than from the government. These loans needed to be sanctioned by a private act or by the LGB, and local authorities had problems in issuing loans in an effective manner until the 1870s. In most cases, authorities raised loans for specific purposes, and borrowed at fixed interest rates for fixed periods on the security of property or the rates. With the partial exception of bonds used for the largest projects of the MBW and the Mersey Dock and Harbour Board, the loans were not transferable or tradeable. The aim of the LGB and the local authorities was to reform this system in order to create an active market, by consolidating separate debts and making loans easily transferable. Councils would then be able to exploit movements in the money market, paying off loans incurred at times of high interest rates and taking out new loans at lower rates. But the LGB's desire to allow easier access to the money market collided with the Treasury's concern for financial discipline. In 1875, Northcote's Local Loans Act took a more restrictive view than the Public Health Act of the same year. The first measure insisted on loans of thirty years, confined to permanent works approved by the LGB for the proper execution of statutory powers, and secured by a mortgage on revenues. The second measure proposed a term of sixty years, for any capital expenditure approved by any department. The Treasury also tried to impose stricter accountability. Loan accounts were to be audited, to ensure that debts were being repaid. Pressure from the Association of Municipal Corporations and Joseph Chamberlain meant that the audit was dropped, but professional treasurers did improve financial controls within local authorities in the later nineteenth century. The Local Loans Act is striking as much for what it failed to do as for what it achieved. It did not extend the sources of local government loans; it did not allow consolidation of loans or re-borrowing to exploit movements in interest rates. The solu-

[45] Bellamy, *Administering Central–Local Relations*, pp. 86–92; Wilson, 'Finance of municipal capital expenditure', 34, 39.

tion came through the initiative of large authorities which issued stock on the London and provincial stock exchanges. The approach was pioneered by the MBW in 1869, when it obtained permission to issue 3.5 per cent loan stock, which could be traded and used to pay off earlier loans obtained at higher interest rates. Other large authorities followed in the 1870s, and in 1888 general power to issue stock was granted to the new county councils. In 1889, model clauses were agreed for private acts, and in 1890 the LGB obtained power to sanction stock issues by urban local authorities. The large authorities increasingly issued local stock, leaving smaller authorities to rely on mortgages approved by the LGB, and the smallest to depend on public loans.[46]

The ability of local authorities to borrow on a large scale was also affected by general movements in financial markets. In the 1890s, capital exports fell and interest rates were low. Local authorities were therefore able to secure loans on favourable terms, incurring new expenditure and replacing old loans on better terms. Money flowed into the PWLC as authorities paid off their loans and savers placed money in the POSB where the fixed interest rate of 2.5 per cent was now very generous. As a result, local authorities could borrow more easily and on more favourable terms, which allowed a higher level of investment in the cities of Britain. In 1889/90, loans accounted for 10.9 per cent of the total income of local authorities in England and Wales; the proportion rose to 23.3 per cent by 1904/5.[47] The money market became much tighter with the boom in foreign investment from 1905. Interest rates rose, so placing greater restraints on local authorities and making the Treasury concerned that it would be competing with local authorities for limited funds in the money market. By 1912/13, loans were down to 11.1 per cent of the total income of local authorities in England and Wales.[48] The LGB had to counter the alarm of the Treasury and ensure that local authorities were financially stable and able to secure funds to carry out the duties placed on them by the government. These difficulties help to explain the fall in local government's share of investment in social overheads and infrastructure before the war, and the general fall in investment in this sector. Nevertheless, capital formation in social overheads and infrastructure was the most rapidly growing sector of the British economy between 1850 and 1910.[49]

---

[46] Bellamy, *Administering Central–Local Relations*, chapter 3; Wilson, 'Finance of municipal capital expenditure', 35–8.

[47] G. C. Baugh, 'Government grants in aid of the rates in England and Wales, 1889–1900', *Historical Research* 65 (1992), 235–7.

[48] Baugh, 'Government grants in aid', 235–7.

[49] R. Millward and S. Sheard, 'The urban fiscal problem 1870–1914: government expenditure and finances in England and Wales', *Economic History Review* 2nd ser. 48 (1995), 5, 22; Bellamy, *Administering Central–Local Relations*, pp. 94, 99; C. H. Feinstein and

The finance of the poor law was also reformed in the 1860s, allowing the construction of a wider range of institutions – asylums, hospitals, orphanages – which involved considerable capital expenditure and running costs. The intention was, in part, to tighten the granting of outdoor relief which reached new levels in the 1860s. The construction of institutions required a 'radical restructuring' of the financial system of the poor law. Although the act of 1834 created unions, individual parishes within the union still contributed in proportion to the number of paupers relieved, so that wealthy parishes with few paupers did not contribute in proportion to their rateable value. The financial resources of the union were therefore limited, and capital expenditure was difficult. The poorest parishes paid the bulk of the cost of relief, while suburban and rural parishes escaped. Not surprisingly, ratepayers in the poorer parishes were obsessed with economy which could mean a disinclination to build expensive specialist institutions. The system was partially reformed in 1861, when the cost of the 'irremovable poor' (residents of three years with a right to relief) was placed on the union as a whole. The process was completed by the Union Chargeability Act of 1865, when the union was treated as a single fiscal unit and parishes contributed in proportion to their rateable value; the period of irremovability was also reduced to one year.[50]

The shift from parishes to unions did not solve the problem in London, where whole unions in the East End were dominated by the poor, and rich unions in the West End did not contribute. In 1867, the Metropolitan Poor Act established a Common Poor Fund for London, in order to redistribute fiscal resources from west to east. This measure, like the act of 1865, was inspired by two connected policies. The first was construction of institutions to provide specialist 'curative' treatment, such as the hospitals of the new Metropolitan Asylums Board (MAB) established in 1867. The second was the provision of deterrent workhouses as part of the campaign against outdoor relief. Treatment of the sick poor in separate institutions made it possible to treat the remainder in a harsh manner. As a result, the level of outdoor relief in England and Wales declined from around 45 per 1,000 population in the 1850s and 1860s

S. Pollard (eds.), *Studies in Capital Formation in the United Kingdom, 1750–1920* (Oxford, 1988), tables 13.1, 13.2 and 13.3 on fixed assets in gas, water and electricity; tables 16.2, 16.3, and 16.5 on education, medical and poor law services and other public services; compare with table 11.2 on mining and quarrying and table 12.4 on manufacturing. A. Offer, 'Empire and social reform: British overseas investment and domestic politics, 1908–14', *Historical Journal* 26 (1983), 119–38.

[50] M. E. Rose, 'The crisis of poor relief in England, 1850–90', in W. J. Mommsen (ed.), *The Emergence of the Welfare State in Britain and Germany, 1850–1950* (London, 1981), pp. 52–3; F. Driver, *Power and Pauperism: The Workhouse System, 1834–1884* (Cambridge, 1993).

to 22.1 per 1,000 in 1908. Meanwhile, the level of indoor pauperism rose modestly from 6.5 per 1,000 in 1850 to 6.8 in 1908, with a more marked increase in costs. Between 1871/2 and 1905/6, the number of indoor paupers rose by 76 per cent and the cost by 113 per cent. The full implementation of the principles of 1834 depended on heavy capital expenditure, as did the attempt to deal with the curse of infectious diseases by erecting isolation hospitals. But it was crucial that spending remained in dependable hands, which explains the structure of the new MAB. The MAB could call on the fiscal resources of London as a whole, but the elected members were supplemented by government nominees who diluted the representative basis of local government at the same time as the parliamentary franchise was extended. This provided a safeguard against radicals who had campaigned for equalisation of the rates and might increase spending in the poor districts at the expense of the rich. At the same time, these nominees were a counter-weight to penny-pinching attitudes by small property owners so that more could be spent on metropolitan health. Care had to be taken that the local auxiliaries were both dependable and willing to undertake necessary expenditure in an efficient and cost-effective manner. Trustworthy accountability was created: the narrative of reform of the parliamentary franchise needs to be supplemented by a greater appreciation of the complexities of the franchise for local government.[51]

Not only was collective public action made more responsive; investment by privately owned utility companies was also controlled in order to protect the consumer from the 'taxing' powers of natural monopolies. The control and ownership of large business enterprises was fought out in similar terms to debates over the franchise, often with the same vocabulary and with similar concerns about the precise relationship between owners and consumers as between taxpayers and beneficiaries of public spending. The Gas Works and Water Works Clauses Acts of 1847 limited the dividend paid to shareholders to 10 per cent; when this level was reached, any two gas consumers could apply to the Quarter Sessions for a reduction in price. In the 1860s, it was usual to add a maximum price and to give power to arbitrators appointed by the Board of Trade. In the case of gas, from the mid-1870s the 'maximum dividend' system was increasingly replaced by sliding scales by which gas prices and dividends were automatically adjusted: a fall in the price of gas by 1d would permit

[51] Rose, 'Crisis'; M. E. Rose (ed.), *The Poor and the City: The English Poor Law in its Urban Context, 1834–1914* (Leicester, 1985), for the application of the poor law in various towns; on the MAB, see the contribution by P. Ryan, 'Politics and relief: East London unions in the late nineteenth and early twentieth centuries', pp. 140–1. Driver, *Power and Pauperism*, especially chapters 4 and 5; Ashbridge, 'The power and the purse'.

an increase in the dividend of 0.25 per cent, and vice versa. The aim was to create a common interest of shareholders and consumers in efficiency and improvements in productivity, which might have deleterious effects on wages and workers. The development of tramways and electricity relied on the alternative method of control suggested by J. S. Mill: establishing the public's right to a 'reversionary profit'. The Tramways Act of 1870 gave the local authority power to grant a licence for a fixed interval of twenty-one years, with the right to purchase at 'then value' when the term expired; the same power was granted in 1882 for electricity. There was, therefore, a deep-seated concern about the powers of these 'natural' monopolies, and the need to create methods of democratic accountability in cases of 'delegated management'.[52] Indeed, the outcome was often a shift to public, municipal, ownership from the middle of the nineteenth century.

The utilities were less successful than the railways in preserving private ownership and preventing absorption into the 'sovereign power' of the state. The explanation was, in part, that regulations limited the ability of companies to pursue efficient economic strategies, by reducing their profitability and removing the security for long-term investment. Above all, utilities had a political problem: consumers were largely coterminous with the voters within a municipality. In the case of the railways, it was difficult for local traders to overcome the national power of directors and shareholders drawn from all parts of the country, particularly when dividends were preserved at a high level.[53] It was a different matter in the case of the utilities, for consumers were local electors and it proved difficult for the managers and directors to pose as their representatives. Indeed, many consumers felt that the best way of creating participation and democratic accountability was through municipalisation, so making

---

[52] There is an extensive literature: see, as examples, J. A. Hasson, 'The growth and impact of the British water industry in the nineteenth century', *Economic History Review* 2nd ser 38 (1985), 531–47; D. Matthews, 'Laissez-faire and the London gas industry in the nineteenth century: another look', *Economic History Review* 2nd ser 39 (1986), 244–63; Chatterton, 'State control of public utilities'; PP 1918 III, *Select Committee on Gas Undertakings (Statutory Prices)*; R. Millward, 'The emergence of gas and water monopolies in nineteenth-century Britain: contested markets and public control', in J. Foreman-Peck (ed.), *New Perspectives on the Late Victorian Economy: Essays in Quantitative Economic History* (Cambridge, 1991), pp. 96–124; J. P. McKay, *Tramways and Trolleys: The Rise of Urban Mass Transport in Europe* (Princeton, 1976); J. Foreman-Peck and R. Millward, *Public and Private Ownership of British Industry, 1820–1990* (Oxford, 1994); J. Kellett, 'Municipal socialism, enterprise and trading in the Victorian city', *Urban History Yearbook* (1978), 36–45; M. Falkus, 'The development of municipal trading in the nineteenth century', *Business History* 19 (1977), 134–61; on telegraphs and telephones, Perry, *Victorian Post Office*. I have considered the issues in 'Material politics of natural monopoly'.

[53] Alborn, *Conceiving Companies*, Part III.

the consumer coterminous with the owner and offering an opportunity, through council elections and meetings, to participate in management.

Ownership of utilities also appealed for a further, related, reason: it offered a solution to the limited tax base of local government by making profits available for public purposes. The income might be used in order to reduce rate demands and so circumvent the threat of a ratepayers' revolt; or it might be devoted to other purposes, such as in Birmingham where the profits from the gas undertaking were channelled into the provision of an art gallery. Indeed, Joseph Chamberlain was able to portray municipal ownership as a form of accountable and efficient joint-stock company or voluntary association, where the interests of all were in harmony, and the opportunity of 'corruption' removed:

The leading idea of the English system of municipal government is that of a joint-stock or co-operative enterprise in which the dividends are received in the improved health and the increase in the comfort and happiness of the community. The members of the Council are the directors of this great business, and their fees consist in the confidence, the consideration, and the gratitude of those amongst whom they live. In no other undertaking, whether philanthropic or commercial, are the returns more speedy, more manifest or more beneficial.[54]

Where utilities did survive in private hands, the explanation was partly political: a lack of identity between the area served by the company and the limits of the local authority. The lack of administrative symmetry between companies and local authorities was most obviously apparent in London, where the companies covered a larger area than any single vestry or metropolitan borough, and there was considerable concern about granting more power to the LCC. In other cases, the utility covered adjacent authorities which would need to combine to negotiate terms and administer the service – an outcome usually defeated by jealously independent municipalities. Private concerns were also likely to survive where local authorities had alternative sources of revenue, or low levels of population growth meant there was little pressure on resources.[55]

The development of joint-stock companies and public utilities is all-too-often relegated to a marginal, technical, position in the literature on

---

54 Quoted in L. Jones, 'Public pursuit of private profit? Liberal businessmen and municipal politics in Birmingham, 1865–1900', *Business History* 25 (1983), 240–59.
55 On the fiscal incentives for municipalisation, and the political problems which could arise, see Foreman-Peck and Millward, *Public and Private Ownership*, chapter 4, on profit levels in public ownership and pp. 176–81 on revenue as a reason for municipalisation; R. Millward and R. Ward, 'The costs of public and private gas enterprises in late nineteenth-century Britain', *Oxford Economic Papers* 39 (1987), 719–37; R. Millward, 'From private to public ownership of gas undertakings in England and Wales, 1851–1947: chronology, incidence and causes', *Business History* 35 (1993), 1–21; Millward and Sheard, 'The urban fiscal problem'.

the nineteenth century. In fact, the scale of investment was remarkable and of great importance for the performance of the economy. The capacity to invest such large sums was political as much as economic, and should be cast in the same mould as debates over the nature of the state. The language used, and the themes debated, were part of a discourse on the nature of taxation in its broadest sense: attacks on the corn law could be set in the same framework as attacks on the natural monopolies of gas and water. Reforming the state of 'corruption' and establishing standards of accountability and public trust entailed reform of the utilities which were supplying the services of the expanding towns and cities of Victorian Britain. Similarly, the municipal corporations and poor law unions were able to move away from a narrow concern for economy to a greater capacity to incur new capital expenditure and to develop a wide range of services, with a greater degree of trust between taxpayers and local institutions, and between the central state and dependable 'auxiliaries'. What remained to be seen was how far the process could go before serious strains emerged.

The fiscal crisis of the local state

Strains did start to appear from the 1890s, when the mounting costs of local government placed considerable pressure on a local tax base narrowly confined to a property tax – the rates. In theory, the rates were levied on moveable (personal) as well as immoveable (real) property, but in practice became limited to the annual value of real property on the grounds of administrative convenience – a pattern formally approved by the Poor Rate Exemption Act of 1840.[56] In England and Wales, the gross rateable value of each property was estimated and adjusted to take account of the cost of repairs and other charges; the authority then set a rate in the £ which was separately collected for the poor law, education, public health and the municipality. By the late nineteenth century, the rateable value of most towns was rising less than the costs of local government, not only because of the addition of new functions but also because many prosperous suburban areas were outside the municipal boundaries and so escaped contribution. The impact of local taxes on the housing market caused concern, especially from about 1900. In England, occupiers were liable for rates, which created administrative problems. Working-class tenants with weekly lets moved frequently, and even where tenants did stay, few poor families on minimal resources were able to set aside money from their weekly wage to meet the annual rate demand. As a

---

[56] E. Cannan, *The History of Local Rates in England* (London, 1896), pp. 85–101.

result, much working-class housing was effectively exempted from rates in the early nineteenth century. The solution was 'compounding': councils paid a commission to owners of working-class houses to pay the rates direct to the council; the owners hoped to collect the rates by an addition to the weekly rent charged to the tenant. A change in tenants was therefore immaterial, the budgetary problems of poor families were eased, and the yield of the rates improved. However, by the end of the century councils wished to reduce the 'compounding' allowance in order to improve the yield of the rates. At the same time, owners of working-class property were alarmed at the decline in their profits. The building boom of the late 1890s led to a glut of houses, coinciding with stagnation in working-class incomes. Owners faced difficulties in passing higher rates to their tenants, with the result that profits and property values fell in the Edwardian period. Although the system was rather different in Scotland, the outcome for profitability was similar. In Scotland, most property was held on long lets, so that collection of the rates was less problematical; the rates were also levied as separate charges on owners and tenants. Compounding was therefore unusual. However, complaints about the inflexibility of long lets resulted in legislation in 1911 to change the tenure of Scottish housing. Short lets were introduced, with a consequent need to adopt compounding. The owners' allowance was set at a low level, less than the commission they paid to their own agents for collection of rent. Profit margins were therefore squeezed, and Scottish owners had the same problems as their English counterparts in passing on higher rates to their tenants.[57]

Not surprisingly, many owners of house property complained about the 'unfair' incidence of the rates. Why should the owners of houses pay rates on their entire income, unlike a lawyer or merchant who only paid on a modest office rather than their fees and commissions? Why should house owners pay rates in order to provide poor relief to dockers thrown out of work as a result of seasonal trade in the port, whereas merchants and shipowners largely escaped local taxation? Social commentators also realised that rates were regressive, for housing formed a higher proportion of expenditure by families on low incomes. And the complaint of local authorities, expressed through the County Councils Association, the Urban and Rural District Association and Association of Municipal Associations was that national services were falling on the rates and should be transferred to national taxation.[58] The solution to these problems became a

---

[57] Daunton, *House and Home*, chapter 9, on rates and compounding, pp. 132–9 on Scottish tenure; Englander, *Landlord and Tenant*, chapter 6, on compounding and chapter 8 on Scotland; Offer, *Property and Politics*, Part IV.

[58] Daunton, *House and Home*, pp. 218–19, 231; PRO, T172/30, local taxation and imperial contributions, 1908.

pressing issue at the end of the nineteenth century and early twentieth century.

There were a number of possible solutions. One was to widen the local tax base by introducing new taxes under the control of the local authorities. At the end of the nineteenth century and early years of the twentieth century, the main suggestion from radical Liberals and Labour was a tax on land values which led to a highly charged debate and minimal yield. In any case, the revenue was to go to central government.[59] Other possibilities were floated, such as a local death duty or a local income tax. The problem was how exactly to localise the income tax. Should it depend on the place of origin of the income, which would benefit the major business centres from which dividends and interest were paid? Or should it be the place of receipt of income? The problem was that tax was deducted at source at the place of *origin*, so that localisation by place of *residence* would entail compiling a return of income from all sources, which the Inland Revenue opposed. Not only would it undermine the confidentiality of tax returns; it would also provide an incentive to false declarations and so threaten good will in the tax system. In any case, it would mainly benefit prosperous residential areas and would not help poorer towns.[60] Consequently, local authorities did not obtain any significant new tax, unlike the central government which secured revenue from a wider range of taxes with a buoyant revenue. Local authorities remained dependent on a narrow property rate which explains the attraction of supplementing the rates through municipal trading.

The contrast with other European countries was striking, where most local authorities had a range of taxes in addition to property taxes. In Germany, for example, the income tax was levied by state and local governments; the local authority could either determine its own rate to add to the state tax or could levy it separately. The problem in Germany was that the federal Reich had difficulties in introducing its own income tax.[61] In the case of Britain, the central government was very jealous of its own taxing powers and at most ceded the revenue of certain taxes (such as the licence duties in 1888) to the localities. However, this policy was intended to *limit* local demands on the central government, by replacing grants for specific purposes by defined and limited income streams. The payment of grants from central taxes to the local state immediately raised serious

[59] This was considered in more detail in connection with death duties in chapter 8.

[60] PRO, IR74/118, 'Proposals to localise the income tax', W. J. Braithwaite, 27 June 1910.

[61] Hobson, *Wealth of States*, pp. 62–6; M. Newcomer, *Central and Local Finance in Germany and England* (New York, 1937), pp. 3, 11–13. The contrast with Germany was considered in PRO, T171/47, which contains two Inland Revenue notes on taxation of the working class in Germany and abroad; and T171/74, 'State grant to local government authorities in Prussia', W. H. Dawson, 8 Apr. 1904, and 'German national and local taxation'.

issues of accountability. In the nineteenth century, the central government could rely on the localities to take responsibility for major areas of spending on public health, poor relief and education. Local politicians were considered to be dependable and fiscally responsible; the central government would ensure that spending plans and loans were realistic, but its direct financial contribution to local government was minimal. In the twentieth century, local politicians might be seen as unreliable and fiscally irresponsible, with serious consequences for the central state whose financial contribution would increase and threaten control over the budget. 'Athenian democracy' could become a source of danger which national politicians and the Treasury wished to bring under control.

Grants-in-aid of local rates started in 1835, with modest payments towards the costs of criminal prosecutions and transferring prisoners to the ports for transportation. Additional grants were added as time passed. In 1849, the poor law guardians were given the salaries of teachers in workhouse schools and the auditors of union accounts, as well as half the salaries of poor law medical officers. In 1857, the central government paid a quarter of the salaries and clothing of provincial police; in 1865, grants were made to the London fire brigade, in 1874 to maintenance of the lunatic poor in asylums and in 1887 a quarter of the cost of maintaining main roads.[62] The approach was piecemeal and small scale, designed to secure a particular administrative result. Despite their modest scale, the Treasury was already concerned at the implication of these grants for control over national finances. Treasury orthodoxy stressed that local authorities would be encouraged in the ways of financial rectitude by ensuring that increased spending had an immediate effect on local taxpayers. There was a danger that central government subventions would weaken the need for prudence. As Charles Wood pointed out, overly generous grants from the centre might threaten the 'economy and efficiency' of local administration.

If the local administrator knows that he and his neighbours have to pay nothing, the greatest motive for economy is taken away in those matters where the expense may be kept down by his care and attention. For this reason I should be most unwilling to take the *whole* of any charge altogether on the public funds.

On the other hand local administration often degenerates, and mistaken views of various questions are taken, so that it needs a certain amount of check and control from a more enlightened central body, removed from local influence and prejudice... With a contribution from the public comes without any possible objection the power and right of central inspection and control, and it is to this central body that we must look to check local abuses.

---

[62] PRO, T168/82, 'Grants in aid of local rates', Vincent Griffiths, 12 May 1876.

In Wood's view, the virtues of local autonomy must therefore be combined with central control.[63]

This was not as easy as it might appear, for a commitment by the central government to pay a proportion of local expenditure created two problems. An increase in local expenditure would oblige the central government to increase its own expenditure, regardless of the state of national finances, and the Treasury would demand strict monitoring of local government to ensure that the grants were spent effectively, so creating a costly and time-consuming process of approval and audit.[64] The Treasury much preferred an alternative approach: to fix the amount of central government subvention, so removing the danger of an upward drift of grants in line with local spending, and ensuring that additional costs fell on ratepayers who would have a strong incentive to vote for 'responsible' government. The position was most clearly stated in 1881 by a committee chaired by J. G. Dodson,* the president of the Local Government Board, which concluded that subventions should no longer be led by the demands of local authority expenditure, but should be 'stereotyped' to create an incentive for economy. In Dodson's view, this could be achieved by assigning the proceeds of specific taxes to local authorities.[65]

Such an approach had already been proposed by George Goschen during his period as Liberal president of the Local Government Board. In 1871, he suggested assigning the inhabited house duty to the local authorities, and he returned to the issue in 1888 as chancellor in a Conservative government. His predecessor as chancellor, Michael Hicks Beach, had put forward a different solution, of widening the basis of local taxation to 'the profits derived from capital invested in personal property as well as in real property'. In effect, this would amount to a local income tax and the Inland Revenue argued that it would be very difficult to 'localise' incomes in a particular local authority area.[66] Instead, the Inland Revenue suggested an easier method: to hand over easily localised taxes such as excise licences and inhabited house duty on the lines proposed by Goschen in 1871 and Dodson in 1881.[67] These proposals formed the basis of

[63] PRO, T168/82, memorandum, Lord Halifax, 4 Dec. 1872, and also see 'Local taxation', R. Lowe, 8 Nov. 1872.

[64] Bellamy, *Administering Central–Local Relations*, pp. 24–6.

[65] Bellamy, *Administering Central–Local Relations*, pp. 37–8.

[66] PRO, T168/82, 'Local taxation: 1, Copy of reference by the Chancellor of the Exchequer, 21 Dec. 1885'.

[67] PRO, T168/82, 'Local taxation: 2, Report dated 6 Jan. 1886 on foregoing reference'; see also 'Local taxation: further report, 1 March 1886'.

* John George Dodson (1825–1897) was educated at Eton and Christ Church; he was called to the bar in 1853 and was a Liberal MP from 1857 to 1884. He was deputy speaker from 1865 to 1872, president of the local government board 1880–2 and chancellor of the Duchy of Lancaster 1882–4. (*DNB, Supplement*, vol. II, ed. Lee, pp. 144–5.)

Goschen's assigned revenues of 1888. Instead of making grants in proportion to specific forms of expenditure, Goschen gave local authorities the income from licences collected in their area, plus a proportion of the revenue from probate duty allocated according to their share of the previous grants. The revenue would increase modestly over time as the yield of licences and probate rose, but it was hoped that pressure for further subventions would be contained and the local authorities could be left to get on with their business. The system had the great virtue in the eyes of the Treasury that the revenue was strictly defined, and unlike grants-in-aid did not give a sense of inexhaustible relief. There was less need for strict central government control over the localities. Goschen's system attempted to limit the grants paid to local government to precisely defined sources of revenue. In this case, 'hypothecation' made sense for it set definite limits to grants from the central government, containing expenditure more rigorously than proportionate grants. In 1889/90, government grants amounted to 11.4 per cent of the total income of local authorities in England and Wales, compared with 48.3 per cent from rates and, as we have noted, 10.9 per cent from loans; by 1904/5, grants were 13.6 per cent of income, and most of the increased expenditure of local authorities came from loans.[68] What remained to be seen was how long the line could be held.[69]

Goschen's attempt to define the relation between local and central taxation was soon embroiled in a controversy over the incidence of local and central taxes on different forms of income and property. In the third quarter of the nineteenth century, the concern of Gladstone was simply to ensure that different forms of national and local taxes were 'balanced' so that each form of income and property paid no more or less than its due proportion. Gladstone argued that rates fell on real property and so 'balanced' the lower burden of income tax on 'spontaneous' compared with 'industrious' incomes, and of death duties on real compared with personal property. The debate was soon to move beyond a concern for balance to a much more radical position that land had a particular ability to bear taxation. Liberal views started to shift from the 1870s, and attitudes to the incidence of local taxation on different forms of income and property formed an ideological fault-line between parties.

The Local Taxation Committee was formed in 1869, a pressure group of landed and agricultural interests which argued that land was *over-*taxed. It made common cause with urban interests in urging that the cost of 'national' or 'imperial' services should be transferred to the central government. Indeed, the government was defeated in 1872 on a motion

---

[68] Baugh, 'Government grants in aid', 235-7.
[69] Offer, *Property and Politics*, chapter 13; Daunton, *House and Home*, pp. 217-18.

that parliament would only accept legislation placing additional burdens on the rates on condition that the central government made a contribution. One possible Liberal response was to divide rural and urban interests against each other, by claiming that landowners were *under*-taxed and that the occupiers of urban buildings were paying too much for local government. But this was not yet a clear ideological divide, for senior Liberal politicians could still argue that land was *over*-burdened by local taxation.[70] In the 1870s, Liberal interest in the 'land question' focussed on the power of great estates to control the land market and on the injustices of the leasehold system. According to this view, landowners held land off the market to charge excessive prices, and the leasehold system created slums by removing any incentive for house owners to maintain the houses in the final years before the leases expired and the property reverted to ground landlords, without compensation. In the 1870s, the main demand of radicals within the Liberal party was to create a more active land market by removing the legal impediments which allowed great owners to manipulate the market. Liberals started to demand a right for occupiers to renew leases or to purchase the freehold.[71]

Goschen's scheme of 1888 was still challenged by Gladstone on the grounds that he upset the balance of the tax system by relieving real property from too much of the burden of local taxes (see chapter 8). In the next few years, the terms of the debate shifted, as a result of the changed composition of the Liberal party after the split over Ireland in 1886, and the impact of Henry George's *Progress and Poverty*. George's extreme 'single tax' position held that all taxes could – and should – be replaced by a tax on land values which were an unearned increment created by the enterprise of other members of society. His analysis brought earlier radical, Chartist and Ricardian ideology back to the centre of Liberal politics, with its assumption that landowners gained at the expense of small-holders and common rights, increasing rents and battening on the wealth of productive classes. In the 1880s and 1890s, the debate was pushed beyond the demand for a free market in land to a larger claim that landowners were passive and parasitical, gaining an unearned, socially created, increment at the expense of active productive interests.[72]

[70] See PRO, T168/82, 'Memorandum by Lord Halifax, 4 Dec. 1872' and 'Local taxation', R. Lowe, 8 Nov. 1872; Bellamy, *Administering Central–Local Relations*, pp. 24, 28–9, 33–4.

[71] D. A. Reeder, 'The politics of urban leaseholds in Late Victorian England', *International Review of Social History* 6 (1961), 413–30; Bellamy, *Administering Central–Local Relations*, pp. 28–34; Offer, *Property and Politics*, chapter 11; Daunton, *House and Home*, pp. 227–30; PP 1886 XII, 1887 XIII, 1888 XXII, 1889 XV, 1890 XVIII, 1890–1 XVIII, 1892 XVIII, *Report and Proceedings, Select Committee on Town Holdings*.

[72] Offer, *Property and Politics*, chapter 12.

The changing emphasis within the Liberal party is apparent in the struggle for power within the new London County Council which was created at the same time as Goschen's reform of local taxation. As we noted in chapter 8, there was a split within the Liberal members between radicals and progressives such as Benn and Webb, and more conservative figures such as Rosebery and Farrer. The LCC's Local Government and Taxation Committee was asked to consider whether the costs of permanent improvements should be borne by the owners of property. Under the chairmanship of Farrer, the Committee came to a temporising recommendation that acts allowing the LCC to raise loans should contain a provision that interest charges and repayment should fall on the various classes of persons interested in London property, in such a manner as parliament directs; and that no contract should allow owners of property to shift the burden on to other people. In other words, if rates rose, owners of property should not increase the rent paid by the occupiers. The question of *how* charges should be allocated between different classes was not resolved, and a divide started to open within the ranks of the Liberals.[73]

The radicals defeated Farrer and Rosebery, taking control of key positions on the LCC in 1892. Farrer feared that tension over local taxation might produce a common front of ratepayers and the left against landowners. His solution was two-fold: to divide the rates between owners and occupiers in order to create a sense of fairness in the allocation of burdens; and to impose a municipal death duty to assist the 'groaning occupier'. Farrer strongly resisted any taxation of the unearned increment; his aim was to remove a grievance and 'render the title to land more stable' rather than to attack the landed interest. By contrast, radicals saw a municipal death duty as merely a short-term measure before taxation of ground values was adopted. Rosebery was defeated within the LCC in 1892; as Liberal prime minister in 1894–95, he faced pressure to adopt a more radical attack on landowners. When the Liberals returned to power in 1906, taxation of land values was supported by a large number of MPs, and became a major theme in Lloyd George's budgets.[74]

---

[73] Thompson, *Socialists, Liberals and Labour*, pp. 91–9; Davis, *Reforming London*, pp. 119–22, 149–52; LCC Minutes of Proceedings January–December 1889, minutes of 21 May 1889, Report of the Local Government and Taxation Committee, 15 May 1889, pp. 352–3.

[74] Bod. Lib., MS Harcourt dep. 119, ff. 111–15, Farrer to Harcourt, 23 Nov. 1892 and 11 Nov. 1892, ff. 83–4; MS Harcourt dep. 187, B. F. C. Costelloe, 'Memorandum as to the finance of the London County Council', Oct. 1892, ff. 86–93, and memorial to Harcourt, 23 Jan. 1893, ff. 127–31; Farrer, 'The imperial finance of the last four years, III', *Contemporary Review* 58 (1890); LCC Minutes of Proceedings July–December 1892, adjourned report of the Local Government and Taxation Committee, 16 Nov. 1892, 29 Nov. 1892, pp. 1122–5, and 1 Dec. 1892, pp. 1142–4.

The assigned revenues did not provide a permanent solution to the problem of local government finance. The attempt to control local claims on the central government was soon subverted by the renewed growth of proportionate grants linked to local expenditure for particular purposes. The spending departments were generally in favour of proportionate grants, which encouraged local action and initiative. The Treasury was less impressed, arguing that open-ended proportionate grants exposed national finances to constantly mounting demands. In order to protect itself, the Treasury therefore insisted on cumbersome administrative controls over local authority schemes. The Treasury preferred strict financial limits on the subventions, so protecting the central government from demands for money and permitting a relaxation of administrative controls, for any increase in expenditure would have an immediate impact on local ratepayers and make them more cautious in supporting expensive policies. But the approach of 1888 came under severe pressure. The revenue from excise licences on dogs or carriages rose only by a small amount, at a time when the costs of local government were increasing by a much greater amount. Further, the distribution of the probate duty reflected the payment of grants in the past rather than the current expenditure of councils and changes in the distribution of population. Goschen's system was inflexible and unresponsive, and the assigned revenues were soon supplemented by further grants for particular purposes, such as education, roads, small-holdings, housing, maternity and child welfare, treatment of venereal diseases and tuberculosis. In 1895, a further transfer of the revenue from the land tax and inhabited house duty was considered to relieve local taxation; in the event, the Conservative government offered an alternative (and partisan) relief to local taxation in the form of a partial derating of agricultural land.[75] As the assigned revenues declined in importance and 'percentage' grants increased, so the issue of the fiscal responsibility of local government and electors returned to haunt supporters of economic and prudent local government. Farrer feared that subsidies to the rates from non-local sources would reduce the motives for economy.

What I dread above all things is that any class of persons – whether Tradesmen, Landowners, Parsons or Local Authorities should get the power of dipping their hands into the common purse, for the due filling of which they are not responsible. To place in their hands special taxes is one thing: to give them fixed sums is another

---

[75] Bellamy, *Administering Central–Local Relations*, pp. 51–2; PP 1901 XXIV, *Final Report of Royal Commission on Local Taxation (England and Wales)*, pp. 426–9, 431–9; Daunton, *House and Home*, pp. 218, 223; PRO, T168/78, 'Memorandum by F. L. Robinson', 30 Jan. 1895, and 'Relief to agricultural land', M. E. Hicks Beach, 9 Mar. 1896; T168/35, Hamilton to Hicks Beach, 19 Oct. 1895; Offer, *Property and Politics*, chapter 14.

and a less good thing. But to give them indefinite and constantly increasing claims is the worst of all.

The problem, then, was how to provide subventions to localities without creating the capacity for expenditure out of general taxes.[76]

The solution favoured by the Treasury was to draw a clearer line between local and imperial services and taxes. When Reginald Welby,* the former head of the Treasury, advised the LCC in 1898 that it did not get its proper share of revenue from Goschen's scheme, he proposed a transfer of 'national' services to central taxation and management. As a Treasury man, the attraction was clear: central management and funding established firm control over spending, and prevented local authorities from ratcheting up the contribution from the Exchequer. Welby's position was developed and amended by the Treasury representatives on the Royal Commission on Local Taxation in 1901. E. W. Hamilton and George Murray† proposed that expenditure should be divided into two categories. The first should consist of 'onerous' services required by the state, such as relief of the poor, care for lunatics or provision of schools. Although the central government should provide a large part of the funding, it did not necessarily follow that it should take over administration which would over-burden government departments and lose the benefits of local knowledge. The second should consist of purely local services which were beneficial to the ratepayer and should therefore be financed from local taxation in proportion to the benefit received. By dividing the services in this way, Hamilton and Murray hoped to resolve the vexed issue of the amount of government assistance to the localities: the government would determine the amount of contribution as a

---

[76] PRO, T168/82, Farrer to Hamilton, 4 Apr. 1897.

* Reginald Earle Welby (1832–1915) was the son of a clergyman, educated at Trinity College, Cambridge. He entered the Treasury in 1856 and became an 'enthusiastic disciple' of Gladstonian and Cobdenite finance; he succeeded Farrer as president of the Cobden Club. He was assistant financial secretary in 1880, and was promoted to permanent secretary between 1885 and 1894. He was elected an alderman of the LCC and served as chairman in 1900. He was a free trader and an exponent of rigid economy. The *DNB* commented that he was slow in coming to a decision and loved to potter over details, but that he was hard-working, with proficiency in the minutiae of public finance. He believed in a strong Treasury to check public expenditure. He was also, in the words of the *DNB*, 'a bachelor of bachelors', well known in London Society, a gourmet and stickler on the details of civility. (*DNB, 1912–21*, ed. Davis and Weaver, p. 563.)

† George Herbert Murray (1849–1936) was the son of a clergyman and fellow of All Souls; he was educated at Harrow and Christ Church, Oxford. He entered the Foreign Office in 1873 and transferred to the Treasury in 1880, serving as private secretary to Gladstone from 1892 to 1894, and then to Rosebery. He was chairman of the Board of Inland Revenue 1897–9 and secretary of the Post Office 1899–1903, returning to the Treasury as permanent secretary in 1903, jointly with Hamilton until 1907 and then alone until 1911. On retirement, he was a director of the Westminster Bank and the Southern Railway. (*DNB, 1931–40*, ed. Legg, pp. 637–8.)

block grant established by various statistical criteria of need and local fiscal capacity, fixed for a period of time. Local authorities would not have an open-ended commitment to spend as much as they wished on 'onerous' services, with the central government footing a proportion of the bill. The Treasury strongly supported 'stereotyping' in place of assigned revenues, which were now criticised for introducing the heresy of hypothecation, breaking the doctrine that 'all revenue raised by the State should be paid into the Exchequer, and that all expenditure for which the State was responsible should be issued out of the Exchequer'. Revenues should be firmly distinguished as local and part of the budget of local authorities, or central and covered by parliamentary votes.[77]

The division of services into 'onerous' and 'beneficial' merely raised a new set of questions which were difficult to resolve at a time when the structure of *national* taxation was also in contention, and the incidence of local taxes on different forms of property was a matter of controversy. If 'onerous' burdens were to be covered by central taxes, should these take the form of indirect taxes or a more progressive income tax? Should 'beneficial' services be paid by landowners who received an 'unearned' increment from higher land prices? Difficulties of localising income meant that most local revenue would be raised from immobile property, but who should pay and how should 'benefit' be defined? Even the Conservative chairman of the Royal Commission, Lord Balfour of Burleigh,* admitted that 'there is a considerable amount of agreement that the Urban Land Holder has got a very good bargain and that it is quite fair to squeeze him a bit if it can be done without the introduction of obnoxious principles, and without the risk of unfairness to him'. His modest proposal of a stamp duty on contracts for letting building land was taken much further in association with Hamilton and

---

[77] Bellamy, *Administering Central–Local Relations*, pp. 52–4; PRO, T168/82, 'Memorandum on questions to be dealt with in the final report', E. W. Hamilton and G. H. Murray, 15 Oct. 1898, and 'Memorandum on imperial relief, on local burdens and on the system of imperial and local taxation', E. W. Hamilton, Mar. 1897; PP 1901 XXIV, *Final Report of the Royal Commission on Local Taxation (England and Wales)*, Minority Report by Sir Edward Hamilton and Sir George Murray, pp. 563–4.

* Alexander Hugh Bruce, 6th baron Balfour of Burleigh (1849–1921) was born in Alloa, and educated at Eton and Oriel College, Oxford. He was a member of the Factory Commission, 1874–5; chairman of the Educational Endowments Commission, 1882–9; of the Welsh Sunday Closing Commission, 1889; of the Metropolitan Water Supply Commission, 1893–4; of the Rating Commission, 1896; of the Royal Commission on Food Supply in Time of War, 1903; of the Royal Commission on Closer Trade Relations between Canada and the West Indies, 1909; and of the Committee on Commercial and Industrial Policy after the War, 1916–17. He was private secretary to the Board of Trade, 1889–92. (*Who Was Who*, vol. II), p. 35.

Murray.[78] They suggested dividing the rateable value of a property between permanent and 'wasting' assets. This entailed placing more taxes
on the site value, which increased as a result of public expenditure on improvements. Consequently, 'urban site value is a form of property which
from its nature is peculiarly fit to bear a direct and special burden in
connexion with "beneficial" local expenditure'. The proceeds of the tax
should be passed to the local authorities, for their efforts produced the
higher site values in the first place. By contrast, the structure erected
on the land was 'wasting and perishable', requiring constant repair and
renewal.[79]

The proposals of Hamilton and Murray were taken still further by
radical Liberals, who wished to appropriate the 'unearned increment'
created by the community, so reducing the taxation of active, enterprising,
industrialists or builders.[80] It became a central plank in Lloyd George's
rhetoric of an attack on landowners in the budget of 1909, when he
suggested a tax of 1d in the £ on the capital value of land, and a tax of
20 per cent on any increment in land value at the time of sale (in effect
a capital gains tax on one form of property).[81] In 1913, he proposed a
further tax on land by means of a separate rating of sites.[82] Quite apart
from any revenue, the principle of site valuation was seen as a means of
creating a more dynamic economy:

Under the present rating system the better the use to which property is put the
heavier becomes the burden the ratepayer has to bear. If it is put to an inferior
use, the ratepayer's burden is lightened; while if left unused, no rate whatever is
levied. In other words, local taxation is now levied in such a way as to hinder
and penalise enterprise, industry and progress, and to encourage the withholding of land from its best use... From these evil results all ratepayers suffer, and
the growth and progress of the whole town is shackled and retarded... The substitution of Site Value for Rateable Value is not so much a means of adjusting

[78] PRO, T168/56, Balfour of Burleigh to Llewellyn-Davis, 15 Dec. 1900.
[79] PP 1914 XXIV, *Final Report of the Royal Commission on Local Taxation (England and Wales)*,
'Report on urban rating and site values, by Lord Balfour of Burleigh, Lord Blair Balfour,
Sir Edward Hamilton, Sir George Murray and Mr James Stuart', pp. 585, 587.
[80] See for example, PRO, CAB37/117/92, 'Land taxation: the rating of site values; a national
site tax', D. Lloyd George, 13 Dec. 1913.
[81] PRO, CAB37/98/44, 'The taxation of land values', D. Lloyd George, 13 Mar. 1909: for
the best account of the development of his policy, see Offer, *Property and Politics*, chapters
19 and 22, and B. B. Gilbert, 'David Lloyd George: land, the budget and social reform',
American Historical Review 81 (1976), 1058–66; B. B. Gilbert, 'David Lloyd George: the
reform of British land-holding and the budget of 1914', *Historical Journal* 21 (1978),
117–41.
[82] PRO, CAB37/117/92, 13 Dec. 1913, 'Land taxation: the rating of site values; a national
site tax', pp. 8–9; the scheme was elaborated in CAB37/117/96, 'Taxation and rating of
land values', 24 Dec. 1913. See also T171/73, 'Budget 1914. Land taxation. Rating of
site value. Cabinet memorandum etc.'

inequalities of burden between individuals or classes or ratepayers as a means of removing the existing shackles and penalties by which industry is impeded and enterprise discouraged.[83]

The Liberal land campaign was designed to release the shackles on enterprise, to create an alliance of productive workers and industrialists against parasitic landowners which would marginalise Labour and retain support from the middle class.[84] Others were less convinced, pointing to a variety of inconsistent motives and fearing that 'It is this confusion of thought which makes what is reasonable and by itself doubtless not unpopular, detestable and a source of dread to the loyal voter of all classes.'[85] The rhetoric might fail in its purpose, by alienating property in general. Conservative politicians could easily produce a different rhetoric based on the identity of landowners and industrialists as different forms of property against threats from the property-less. As we shall see, the concept of Rent was taken in new – and threatening – directions as a means of attacking the unearned wealth of industrialists, so weakening the Liberal rhetoric and confirming the Conservative case (see below, pp. 349–60). The land campaign failed to resolve the Liberal's political problem; and it did not produce any significant revenue before it was abandoned after the war.[86]

By the First World War, the structure of local government finance had not been satisfactorily reformed by either the Conservative or Liberal governments. By 1912/13, government grants had only risen to 13.9 per cent of the total income of local authorities in England and Wales, and the share of loans had dropped as a result of competition with overseas investment; as a result, there was greater pressure on the rates at a time of severe depression in the housing market.[87] The final report of the Royal Commission on Local Taxation in 1901 did not provide any easy answer, and the Conservative government simply continued with the existing system by adding more assigned revenues and further grants for particular services.[88] The Liberal policy of land taxation proved to be a chimera, and did nothing to solve the pressing problem of grants to local authorities. Indeed, Lloyd George alienated the local authorities when he proposed that the land taxes should go to *national* revenue. He also proposed to

---

[83] PRO, T168/95, E. W. Hamilton to chancellor, 25 May 1906; T171/69, 'IIA, Probable effects of the transfer of a portion of the rates from the basis of rateable value to that of site value, E. J. Harper, 15 December 1913'.

[84] Bod. Lib., MS Asquith 25, Lloyd George to Asquith, 5 Dec. 1913, ff. 63–6.

[85] Bod. Lib., MS Asquith 22, ff. 98–9, letter circulated by Asquith from a writer who represented a Midlands constituency.

[86] See Offer, *Property and Politics*, pp. 399–400, 403.

[87] Baugh, 'Government grants in aid', 235–6.

[88] Bellamy, *Administering Central–Local Relations*, p. 53.

'stereotype' the revenue from the tax on motor vehicles and public house licences. The Association of Municipal Corporations (AMC) mounted a campaign against Lloyd George's failure to meet their grievances, and he did concede half the revenue from the land taxes – a concession with no practical consequence in view of their failure to produce revenue.[89] The immensely detailed technical task of reforming financial relations between central and local government was passed to a departmental committee in 1911, under the chairmanship of the government's leading account-ing officer, the comptroller and auditor general, Sir John Kempe.* His report in 1914 rejected the attempt to draw a clear line between onerous and beneficial services as pointless and meaningless. He proposed the replacement of assigned revenues by block grants for specific purposes according to formulae which would take account of the local need for each service and the fiscal capacity of the authority.[90]

The AMC was wary of Kempe's plan, fearing that the result would be 'a sweeping change of the whole principles of local government'. The AMC accepted the need for control where grants were *proportionate* to expenditure, for local extravagance would lead to higher national taxes. The use of capitation grants according to population and other statis-tical measures would reduce the need for tight central controls, which the AMC welcomed. But it remained sceptical of the government's in-tention, fearing that the result might not be greater autonomy for local government. Might the government simply lay down service levels and standards which all authorities were expected to meet? The Association feared that the central government might insist that grants should be used to provide additional services rather than to reduce the rates, so that 'the Government Department would become the real rating authority and the Local Authorities would to a most serious extent lose their local control of the amount of annual expenditure.' The outcome would be 'the estab-lishment of bureaucratic government in lieu of local self government'. In the opinion of the AMC,

the presumption ought to be that the Corporations who are answerable to their electors are the best judges of the requirements of their districts ... We are doing

---

[89] Bellamy, *Administering Central–Local Relations*, p. 57.

[90] Bellamy, *Administering Central–Local Relations*, pp. 58–60; PP 1914 XL, *Final Report of the Departmental Committee on Local Taxation in England and Wales*, pp. 543–647.

* John Arrow Kempe (1846–1928) was the son of a clergyman, and was educated at St Pauls School and Trinity College, Cambridge. He joined the Treasury in 1867 and was private secretary to Northcote as chancellor between 1874 and 1880. He left the Treasury in 1894 to become deputy chairman of Customs until 1904, when he became comptroller and auditor general to 1911. He was chairman of the local taxation committee in 1911–14 and a member of the Royal Commission on the civil service in 1915. (*Who Was Who*, vol. II, 29 p. 445.)

this work and spending our time very willingly indeed in the public service, and we do hope that a very large discretion will be left to the Authorities of this country generally who have done their work so well.

This argument could be used by penny-pinching authorities who wished to use grants to keep down the rates. But block grants might also be used to penalise progressive councils who would not be able to secure additional funding for new initiatives. The use of block grants would limit the freedom of councils to provide poor services; it would also prevent progressive councils from raising standards and adding new functions. Lloyd George's response to the AMC stressed that grants would ensure that all authorities undertook particular tasks.

It has been put as if it were purely a question of the municipalities and the ratepayers. But what it means is, that the taxpayer for the first time is entering into a sort of partnership even as far as bringing in a very substantial amount of cash, and I think he is entitled to have a voice in the management at any rate which is proportionate to the contribution which he makes.[91]

Although Lloyd George accepted the case for reform in 1914, nothing was done before the war and block grants were only finally introduced in 1929 by Winston Churchill and Neville Chamberlain.[92] The tangled structure of local government finance had not been resolved by the First World War. One response was to side-step the issue by moving the finance of services to the central government. Old age pensions in 1908 reduced the pressures on the poor law and transferred part of the support of the elderly to the general taxpayer. In 1911, unemployment and health insurance took a different approach in order to avoid placing more pressure on the income tax with the danger of alienating middle-class voters. Instead, the cost fell on contributions from employees and employers, with a small additional payment from the central state. This shift in the provision of welfare from local to central taxation or contributory insurance could be interpreted as the point at which the role of local government and the active municipal culture started to decline. As Melling has remarked, 'the political settlement of the mid-Victorian period enabled industrialists to concentrate their energies on local government and district trade associations'; the emergence of insurance schemes meant that centralised federations of employers needed to negotiate with the government.[93] The pressures of the war, with the need to negotiate with the government over

---

[91] PRO, T172/126, Finance Bill, 1914: deputation from the Association of Municipal Corporations to the chancellor of the Exchequer, 3 July 1914.

[92] See Daunton, *Just Taxes*, for a full discussion.

[93] J. Melling, 'Welfare capitalism and the origins of welfare states: British industry, workplace welfare and social reform, c. 1870–1914', *Social History* 17 (1992), 471, 477.

supplies of raw materials, and over prices and profits, took the trend still further. Moreover, the structure of industry started to shift from small-scale family concerns relying on the external economies of the city, to larger concerns with stronger internal managerial hierarchies and a division between ownership and control. Local reputation and the municipal culture of the mid-Victorian period were less significant, and active participation of the urban elite in city government started to decline. On such an interpretation, local government declined in importance, to be fought over by the lower middle class and Labour.[94] Local government might simply be less dependable than in the mid-Victorian period. The abolition of plural voting for the poor law in 1894 meant that the potential beneficiaries of welfare might once more take control, especially with the extension of the franchise in 1884 and 1918. In the depression of the 1920s, Conservative politicians and civil servants were uneasily aware of the possibility that Labour might utilise the local poor law to drive up the costs of welfare, so that control shifted to larger – and more dependable – units of local government or to the central government.[95]

Certainly, the failure to reform local taxation was to pose a serious threat to local autonomy over the course of the twentieth century. But the extent of decline at the outbreak of the First World War should not be exaggerated. The central government took over some functions, but this might release local authorities to develop new services. The most obvious was public housing after the First World War, and many local authorities developed a wide range of maternal and infant welfare services. Local authority spending on welfare was still 40 per cent of the total expenditure on welfare between the wars, and the allocation of resources made a real difference to patterns of mortality.[96] In some towns, such as Nottingham and Leicester, small firms and local initiatives remained important, with a concern for externalities and an active municipal culture. In other cases, the urban elite retreated, and local initiatives could scarcely cope with the decline of the economic base of towns dependent on ship-building or cotton. But this is not to say that local government in cities such as Glasgow or Manchester simply collapsed. The retreat of the middle class gave an opportunity to Labour to increase the social functions of urban government between the wars. The Labour party

94 For example, R. Trainor, 'The middle class', in Daunton (ed.), *Cambridge Urban History*, vol. III, pp. 699–712; B. M. Doyle, 'The changing functions of urban government: councillors, officials and pressure groups', in Daunton (ed.), *Cambridge Urban History*, vol. III, pp. 298–301; and Morris, 'Structure, culture and society in British towns', pp. 418–19.
95 A. Crowther, *British Social Policy, 1914–39* (Basingstoke, 1988).
96 M. Dupree, 'The provision of social services', in Daunton (ed.), *Cambridge Urban History*, vol. III, pp. 388, 391.

built up support in working-class neighbourhoods, developing a ward organisation with female membership, so compensating for the difficulties experienced by trade unions during the depression. Labour could represent itself as the party of effective urban government, rather than trade union self-interest. The ward structure and female participation turned attention to the provision of municipal services, especially for women and children. The retreat of the urban elite from urban government meant that Labour became the main supporters of an active municipal culture against 'ratepayers' concerned to hold down local spending.[97]

In 1914, municipal government was still important and expanding, and it could be argued that it remained dynamic into the 1920s and 1930s. But the failure to reform urban finance did impose a serious constraint. By contrast, the buoyancy of the yield of central government taxation, and above all the increasing importance of a progressive income tax, meant that there was a marked divergence between the fiscal capacity of the local and central state. The cross-class alliance over municipal government of the mid-Victorian period was fragile. The spending power of large urban authorities alarmed local ratepayers as well as the Treasury which feared a loss of control of national budgets; and Labour politicians realised that the progressive income tax offered a way of funding social services by redistribution between rich and poor, depressed and prosperous areas. The failure to reform the rates in the late nineteenth and early twentieth centuries, and the creation of a 'modern' income tax with wide legitimacy, led to a long-term shift in the relative importance of local and central government.

[97] Reeder and Rodger, 'Industrialisation and the city economy', pp. 572–92; M. Savage, 'Urban politics and the rise of the Labour party, 1919–39', in L. Jamieson and H. Corr (eds.), *State, Private Life and Political Change* (Basingstoke, 1990), pp. 204–23; M. Savage and A. Miles, *The Remaking of the British Working Class, 1840–1940* (London, 1994), pp. 68–9, 82–5.

10   'The end of our taxation tether': the limits
of the Gladstonian fiscal constitution,
1894–1906

It is when the financial situation presents difficulties that a statesman
of genius and originality – a PITT, a PEEL, or a GLADSTONE – finds his
opportunity. There is now as good reason as there was in 1841 or 1853
for reconsidering and revising our financial system as a whole, and in a
bold and comprehensive way.

Times, 27 Feb. 1899

... the proportion of public burdens borne by the working classes has
been decreasing during the last thirty years ... The question for Chancellors of the Exchequer of the near future will be, – 'Is it fair to continue to
make alterations of the fiscal system in this sense?' The answer ... would
seem to be that, if we accept the principle of equal sacrifice ... the process of decreasing the burdens of the working classes should now cease.
But if, on the other hand, we believe in proportional sacrifice it is reasonable to continue this process still further.

C. P. Sanger, 'Is the English system of taxation fair?',
Economic Journal 9 (1899), 16–17

By the early 1890s, strains were appearing in the Gladstonian fiscal constitution as a result of tensions over the Conservative naval building programme and the mounting costs of urban government. Consequently,
definitions of 'balance' were called into question. Goschen faced these
issues in his attempt to impose a limit on the demands of local government
in 1888, but the costs of urban government continued to rise in the 1890s
(see chapter 9). His breach of Gladstonian principles of finance with the
Naval Defence Fund outraged Gladstone (see chapter 8), but continuing pressures for military and naval spending proved too strong to resist
and led to his resignation in 1894. Goschen's successor as chancellor,
William Harcourt, was concerned by 1894 that 'we have come to the end
of our taxation tether in times of peace'.[1] The sentiment was shared by
E. W. Hamilton at the Treasury, who pointed to 'the formidable fact that
unless this country is prepared to take a new fiscal departure we shall

---

[1] Brooks (ed.), Destruction, p. 189, 13 Nov. 1894.

soon be unable to cope with our huge and increasing expenditure. I am certain that finance is going to be the crux ahead for the Government of the day in the near future.'[2]

It was widely believed that a fiscal era was drawing to a close. Robert Giffen[*] pointed out that retrenchment in government expenditure in mid-Victorian Britain had gone further than elsewhere in Europe. Taxation was low and higher expenditure on some services was compensated by a reduction in the debt charge. Indeed, the level of debt per capita fell from £33 9s 3d in 1836/7 to £16 6s 6d in 1896/7.[3] But circumstances were changing at the end of the century, with greater expenditure on defence and mounting pressure for spending on welfare in what Michael Mann has called the 'diamorphous half-military, half-civil state'. For most of the nineteenth century, the state had shrunk in relation to the growth of the economy and civil society. At the end of the century, another change was becoming apparent: an increase in the power of the military as a po-litical force and changes in military technology; and an increase in the scope of the civilian state.[4] Retrenchment created consent to taxation, legitimising the state and collective action, and hence allowing a reac-tion against cheap government. Consequently, the future seemed to hold out the prospect of 'a gradual and insidious growth of public charges outstripping the natural increase of revenue'.[5] Ministers and officials re-alised that pressure for higher expenditure was mounting: existing services

[2] Brooks (ed.), *Destruction*, p. 246, 2 May 1895.

[3] PRO, T168/34, 'Memorandum written in preparation of the budget of 1897/8', E. W. Hamilton, 17 Apr. 1897.

[4] The point was noted by Robert Giffen in his series of (anonymous) articles in *The Times* in 1899, which were extracted and dissected by the Treasury: PRO, T168/43, R. Giffen's article in *The Times*, 13 Feb 1899. The point is made by Mann, *Sources of Social Power*, vol. II, pp. 394–5. This change in the nature of the state is a major topic: on the power of the military, and the alliance formed with science in pursuit of power rather than peace at the end of the century, see F. Turner, *Contesting Cultural Authority: Essays in Victorian Intellectual Life* (Cambridge, 1993), chapter 8, 'Public science in Britain, 1880–1919', and D. Edgerton, *England and the Aeroplane: An Essay on a Militant and Technological Nation* (Basingstoke, 1991). The ability of the military to secure popular support, par-ticipating in the political process and constraining politicians, appears in K. T. Surridge, *Managing the South African War, 1899–1902: Politicians v Generals* (Woodbridge, 1998). The literature on welfare is massive: for one useful account of the emergence of welfare as a central feature of high policy around 1900, see J. Harris, 'The transition to high pol-itics in English social policy, 1880–1914', in M. Bentley and J. Stevenson (eds.), *High and Low Politics in Modern Britain* (Oxford, 1983), pp. 58–79.

[5] PRO, T168/5, 'Some remarks on public finance', E. W. Hamilton, 24 July 1895.

[*] Robert Giffen (1837–1910) was assistant editor of *The Economist* 1868–76 and chief of the statistical department of the Board of Trade 1876–97; he edited the *Journal of the Statistical Society* 1876–91 and wrote extensively on economic issues, including *Essays in Finance* (London, 1880–6) and *Economic Enquiries and Studies* (London, 1904). He became a Liberal Unionist in 1886 and subsequently a unionist free trader. (*DNB, Second Supplement*, vol. II, ed. Lee, pp. 103–5.)

such as education were growing; new demands were appearing for old age pensions with the possibility of 'a boundless subsidy from the State'; agriculture was appealing for relief; India was demanding a reduction in its military charges; and the armed forces had ambitious spending plans. As E. W. Hamilton pointed out in 1895, times had changed since Robert Lowe remarked that his chief difficulty was knowing how to get rid of the money which 'persisted in pouring in upon him'. The days of 'leaps and bounds' in revenue had ended: 'We are now in days of "leaps and bounds" of expenditure, when the chief difficulty of the Finance Minister of this country is, or soon will be, how to raise money sufficient to cover the demands which "persist in pouring in upon him".' The danger noted by Hamilton soon appeared: as a Cabinet paper pointed out in 1901, the normal expenditure of the central government (excluding the costs of war in South Africa) increased from £105.1m in 1895/6 to £147.6m in 1901/2. A rise in expenditure of more than 40 per cent in six years made the financial resources of the government a matter of some urgency.[6]

It was not clear that the existing structure of taxation could meet the demands for revenue, for 'the basis of taxation has been perilously narrowed'.[7] It was precisely the question of how best to widen the tax base which formed the central issue of British politics at the turn of the century. The core of the fiscal constitution was contested and the outcome was by no means certain. What caused Harcourt particular concern and despondency was the likelihood that fiscal pressures might breach the policy of free trade. He saw as early as 1893 that

The only question is what are to be the new taxes and what shall be their amount. It may be that our vast and growing expenditure and the urgent requirements on every side for increased estimates have made our present system of taxation altogether inadequate. A McKinley tariff which raises an immense revenue upon every article of consumption may have become inevitable, but I am afraid I am too old to adopt new ideas and I hardly think that I shall be the Finance Minister to make such a proposal. I have been brought up in the old fashioned principles of public economy and I shall not regret it if my last political efforts are made in its defence.[8]

His own approach to this process of reassessing the fiscal constitution was to introduce graduated death duties and to increase the yield of the income tax by adjusting the incidence in a way which would retain

---

[6] PRO, T168/5, 'Some remarks on public finance', E. W. Hamilton, 24 July 1895; CAB 37/58/85, 'Growth of expenditure', Sept. 1901.

[7] Times, 27 Feb. 1899, commenting on Giffen's articles: extracted in T168/43, Financial Papers, 1898–9.

[8] Bod. Lib., MS Harcourt dep. 222, ff. 7–11, W. Harcourt to Acland, 9 Jan. 1893. The McKinley tariff of 1890 increased American import duties.

electoral support. Others were less convinced, and felt that the limits of direct taxation had been reached. In their view, the time had come for a return to the proportions of direct and indirect taxation of the 1860s. These debates over the tax system ran alongside discussion of free trade, for a return to the share of revenue from indirect taxes of the 1860s might be linked with the use of import duties in retaliation against other countries. In 1903 these discussions were brought to a new intensity by Joseph Chamberlain's campaign for tariff reform. His programme polarised debates, pushing the Liberals into a more dogmatic defence of free trade and rejection of indirect taxes. The opportunity for a pragmatic adjustment of customs duties was lost in the debate over his more ambitious programme, with a consequent need to find alternative sources of revenue. The fiscal constitution established by Peel in 1842 and confirmed by Gladstone's budget of 1853 was re-opened: it remained to be seen which statesman of 'genius and originality' would draft the new fiscal constitution.

Indirect taxes and tariff reform

The steady movement away from customs and excise duties towards direct taxes led many politicians and economists to argue that the fiscal system had become too narrow and inflexible. Should the British fiscal system return to the relative proportions of direct and indirect taxation during the 'golden age' of Gladstone's term as chancellor between 1859 and 1866, when indirect taxes still provided about 60 per cent of the revenue of the central government? After all, indirect taxes are not in themselves intrinsically unfair or 'unscientific', for everything depended on the choice of goods and the rates of duty, and Gladstone had courted the two sisters of direct and indirect taxes. It might even be argued that the limitation of customs and excise duties to a few items (especially beer and tobacco) at high rates made a narrow range of indirect taxes *more* regressive than a wider selection of goods or the imposition of duties on luxury consumer goods purchased by the well-off.

The only increase in indirect taxes since 1878/9 was in duties on beer and spirits which could be justified by the Liberals as a measure of moral reform. Apart from alcohol, the only other duties producing significant revenue were on tobacco and tea. As the Treasury pointed out, the yield from existing duties was not likely to rise, for consumption of 'harmful and dispensable luxuries' was falling. In a telling remark, the Treasury commented that these were the most suitable objects of taxation, so excluding taxes on goods and services with a rising demand (see figure 10.1 for structure of indirect taxes in 1890–1).[9] The Treasury calculated that

[9] Bod. Lib., MS Harcourt dep. 118, ff. 1123–6, [E. W. Hamilton?], undated.

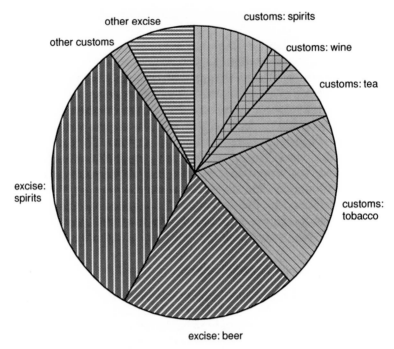

other excise

customs: spirits

other customs

customs: wine

customs: tea

excise:
spirits

customs:
tobacco

excise: beer

Figure 10.1 Major categories of customs and excise duties, United Kingdom, 1890/1
Source: PP 1890–1 XLVIII, *Finance accounts of the United Kingdom, years ended 31 March*, pp. 18, 20.

indirect taxes rose from £1 7s 3d per indirect taxpayer in 1861/2 to £1 9s 11d in 1901/2, or by 10 per cent; meanwhile, real wages had risen substantially so that taxation of indirect taxpayers fell by 17.5 per cent compared with their means. By contrast, direct taxes rose from 16s 11d per direct taxpayer in 1861/2 to £1 12s 11d in 1901/2 or by 94.5 per cent, which amounted to an increase of 21 per cent in relation to means.[10] These figures could be interpreted in two ways, as an entirely appropriate measure of equity between classes, or as a serious deterioration in the position of direct taxpayers which should be rectified.

In the opinion of Hamilton, the shift from indirect to direct taxes was reasonable and even desirable:

The burden of taxation...has been largely transferred from the community at large to the shoulders of those who are, *prima facie*, best able to bear it...This

[10] PRO, T168/62, 'Comparative burthen of taxation in 1861/2 and at the present day'.

diminution of indirect taxation, or of taxation on commodities, which must press most severely on the poorest classes relatively to their means, has undoubtedly done much to remove inequalities of taxation.[11]

Where, then, should the new sources of revenue be found? Hamilton had posed a puzzle to which he had no answer.[12] More than anyone except Gladstone, he was the voice of fiscal orthodoxy and the personal embodiment of the mid-Victorian fiscal constitution. Hamilton's despondency about any major change in the fiscal system indicates the limits reached by the Gladstonian constitution by the end of the nineteenth century which was placed under immense strain by the Boer war. His policy rested upon a defence of the *status quo*, in a vain attempt to prevent the introduction of either graduation of the income tax or tariff reform. Indeed, it may be argued that his refusal to contemplate a wider system of indirect taxation before the issue hardened into dogma with Chamberlain's tariff campaign made the adoption of a graduated income tax more likely as the only possible alternative.

Hamilton's advice to Michael Hicks Beach, the chancellor between 1895 and 1902, repeatedly stressed the limits of action. Hamilton had few expectations that existing taxes, whether indirect or direct, could be raised. Indirect taxes fell on goods such as spirits whose consumption was already declining or which were politically sensitive, such as beer and tobacco. Tea was the only 'necessity' which was taxed and with some prospect of bearing a higher duty; Hamilton believed it should be held in reserve for use in a war emergency. He was no more hopeful about direct taxes. He believed that death duties had reached the highest level which would be tolerated, and income tax was already too high for a time of peace. It was, he argued, 'the one direct tax of all others to which resort is had most easily, and thus most fittingly, if we are involved in war'. In his view, the level of income tax in peace-time 'ought to be low enough to admit of its being easily and immediately raised to meet a crisis. In fact, a moderately low Income Tax constitutes one of the principal reserves of this country; indeed, there will not be a sound state of finance until the Income Tax is materially reduced.'[13]

Hamilton was therefore left with a choice between broadening the basis of the fiscal system either by imposing a completely new tax or by reintroducing an old tax. His process of reasoning indicates the limits to the fiscal constitution at the end of the century. He felt that a new direct tax was not practical politics, and the last attempt at a new indirect

[11] PRO, T168/34, E. W. Hamilton, 17 Apr. 1897; he calculated that indirect taxes fell by 4s 5d and direct taxes rose by 13s per capita between 1836/7 and 1896/7.
[12] PRO, T168/5, 'Some remarks on public finance', E. W. Hamilton, 24 July 1895.
[13] PRO, T168/69, 'Mr Speyer on national finance', E. W. Hamilton, 25 June 1905.

tax – Lowe's proposed match tax of 1871 – had ended in disaster. He therefore came by a process of elimination to his one possibility – the reimposition of an old indirect tax, and preferably a customs duty which was easier to collect than an excise duty. The process of elimination was then transferred to the list of goods formerly liable to customs duties. Hamilton insisted that the customs duty must be compatible with the free trade policy of the previous sixty years. Free trade was, he argued, concerned with consumers who formed the majority of the population whereas protection was more concerned with the interests of the seller, and this distinction was 'specially necessary in a country like ours which cannot feed itself and which is an essentially manufacturing country'. Hamilton viewed manufacturers as consumers of imported raw materials with interests in common with working-class consumers of food. He also insisted that duties should only be used to obtain revenue, preferably at a modest rate and without increasing the price of a commodity more than the amount paid to the Exchequer. They should on no account be protective, and the best way of guarding against this possibility was by selecting a commodity which was not produced at home. Once again, he proceeded by a process of exclusion which left him with a highly restricted choice. He dismissed the small registration duty on corn introduced by Peel when he repealed the protective corn laws in 1846. This duty was removed by Lowe in 1869, and Hamilton feared that its reintroduction would be denounced as a first step back to protection. Thus at the end of an exhaustive process Hamilton came to a less than startling solution to the fiscal problems of Britain in the late nineteenth century: restoration of the import duty on sugar which had been reduced to a very low rate by Robert Lowe and then repealed by Stafford Northcote in 1874. This was the only commodity produced overseas and not at home which would produce a large revenue at a moderate rate, without threatening free trade. Hamilton had laboured and produced the least evil tax which scarcely offered the opportunity for a marked expansion in the limits of the state.[14] After all, the point was to stress the revenue limits to spending rather than to find new, buoyant, sources of revenue to fuel the growth of the state.

Essentially, Hamilton was defending the relationship between direct and indirect taxes admitted by Gladstone in the third quarter of the nineteenth century, and he had no desire to overturn the fiscal constitution. He opposed both protection and Liberal advocates of the 'free breakfast table' who wished to repeal duties on tea and coffee, which would

---

[14] PRO, T168/5, 'Some remarks on public finance', E. W. Hamilton, 24 July 1895; he repeated the exercise in 1901, T168/52, 'The financial problem', E. W. Hamilton, 31 Jan. 1901.

lead to a still narrower fiscal base with alarming political repercussions for 'the more democratic we become, the less can we afford to let the masses go "scot free" of taxation'.[15] His concern arose in part from the old Gladstonian dread of warfare and the belief that payment of taxes was a necessary constraint on militarism. He stressed that 'the soundest of doctrines is that taxation should involve representation: not much less sound appears to me to be the inverse doctrine, representation should involve taxation (of some kind, however light)'.[16] The force of this argument increased with the fear that an untaxed electorate would be able to secure social reform and pass the costs on to others. What was needed was balance, with the reimposition of indirect taxation complemented by a 'counter-balancing turn of the screw' of direct taxation:

Ever since Mr Gladstone likened direct and indirect taxation to 'two attractive sisters' to both of whom addresses ought to be paid at the same time, it has generally been held that when additional revenue is required it shall be raised partly by one and partly by the other; but in the absence of there being any real test of the equity of our taxation system, no principle is involved by the double 'addresses', and, as a matter of fact, addresses have been paid in a much more marked fashion during the last 30 years to direct than to indirect taxation. Owing to this tendency, the two sisters hold the balance about evenly at the present moment; and it is probable that financiers will for some time to come lay themselves out to maintain the evenness of the balance, though, even in this too, no principle is involved. That is to say, their aim will be to avoid upsetting seriously the present balance.[17]

It was a cautious policy, designed to preserve the *status quo*. Hamilton was avoiding the issue which came to dominate Edwardian politics: should one of the sisters be wooed and the other spurned?

Indeed, it was easy to draw a different conclusion from the figures on the rise of direct and decline of indirect taxation. An alternative view held that the 'classes' (that is, the aristocracy and wealthy middle class) were over-taxed and the 'masses' under-taxed, so that indirect taxation should be increased in order to restore balance and justice to the fiscal constitution. As *The Times* remarked, the political attraction of direct taxes was that they fell on a limited number of people and 'the victims are comparatively powerless and have been compelled to pay what they look upon, not unreasonably, as a form of blackmail'.[18] Such a position was strongly argued by Milner in 1895, who felt that there was 'fiscal danger . . . in stringing the bow of direct taxation much more tightly'. In

[15] BL Add. MS 48,651, Hamilton Diary, vol. XXII, f. 132, 20 Nov. 1889.

[16] BL Add. MS 48,652, Hamilton Diary, vol. XXIII, f. 23, 4 Jan. 1890.

[17] PRO, T168/52, 'The question of new taxation discussed', E. W. Hamilton, 13 Dec. 1901.

[18] *Times*, 27 Feb. 1899, extracted in PRO, T168/43.

his view, it was 'Free Trade...gone mad' to reject increases in indirect taxes and in particular to oppose a 'light all-round import duty'. He denied that such a policy was protectionist:

I consider myself as fond a Free Trader as John Wesley was a good Christian. But I know I do not belong to the orthodox and Infallible sect, any more than Wesley belonged to the Church of Rome (the *only* Church in its own opinion)...What I object to is the Athanasian Creed system in economics. I think it between ourselves, just childish. Yet that is what the orthodox Free Traders have come to. They no longer argue. It is enough for them to say 'Oh! that is against Free Trade' (as defined *nota bene* by themselves).

In his view, free trade had hardened into dogma and so limited the government's freedom of manoeuvre on revenue grounds. He argued that a change of emphasis was needed, away from a desire to hold down prices to benefit the consumer to a new concern for the producer:

The producer would gain, and he too is a British citizen. The nation, as a whole, would not be a penny the poorer, though *the mere consumer*, the man, who neither as a workman nor as a shareholder in any industrial enterprise, has any interest in the price of articles produced in Great Britain, might be at a little disadvantage. But this is a small class, which has been uniformly and enormously benefited by the course of economic development for many years. The very slight disadvantage which that class ought not, *by itself alone*, to stand as an absolute bar to any fiscal measures, assuming that on general grounds they would be desirable.[19]

In the opinion of Frank Trentmann, such a change in discourse from the consumer to the producer was at the heart of British politics at the turn of the century. In fact, what was involved was more than a simple change from one to the other, for the terms were defined against each other in a continuing dialogue. How would a particular form of consumption shape the productive system, and vice versa?[20] Milner was not alone in his views. In 1895, H. W. Primrose* of the Customs and Excise commented

---

[19] PRO, T168/34, 'Note on the concluding portion of Sir E. Hamilton's memorandum', A. Milner, 31 July 1895; A. Milner to E. W. Hamilton, 15 Aug. 1895.

[20] For his approach, see Trentmann, 'Political culture and political economy'; F. Trentmann, 'The strange death of free trade: the erosion of "liberal consensus" in Great Britain, c. 1903–1932', in Biagini (ed.), *Citizenship and Community*, pp. 219–50; F. Trentmann, 'Wealth versus welfare: the British left between free trade and national political economy before the First World War', *Historical Research* 70 (1997), 70–98; F. Trentmann, 'Civil society, commerce and the "citizen-consumer": popular meanings of free trade in late nineteenth- and early twentieth-century Britain', *Center for European Studies Working Paper* 66.

* Henry William Primrose (1846–1923) was educated at Balliol College, Oxford; he was a cousin of Rosebery. He joined the Treasury in 1869, served as private secretary to the viceroy of India from 1880 to 1884 and to Gladstone in 1886. He was secretary of the Office of Works from 1887 to 1895. He became chairman of the Board of Inland

that 'responsible politicians on the Liberal side would be glad to see the area of indirect taxation widened, and would not undo what had been done in that way'.[21] He was able to appeal to another of Gladstone's *obiter dicta*, that

on occasions of great emergency, when large demands are to be made on the people, I think you must have a partial resort to indirect taxation; and on occasions when demands less large are to be made on the people, if those demands have a character of apparent permanence, then also, I think, you ought to call in the aid of indirect taxation.[22]

Perhaps it was unsurprising that the 'great emergency' of the Boer war led the chairman of the Customs to remark in 1901 that 'we have reached a crisis in our financial history which offers us an unique opportunity of adding to the number of the sources of our public revenue with the least amount of opposition'.[23]

The strongest, and most public, case was made by Robert Giffen, who wrote a series of articles in *The Times* based on his knowledge and expertise as the former chief of the statistical department of the Board of Trade. Giffen complained that the reduction of customs duties had gone further than anticipated even by Cobden and Bright, and that the need for additional revenue should be met by restoring the proportions between direct and indirect taxes of the 1860s. In Giffen's view, the fiscal system was too narrow and overly reliant on the income tax; indirect taxes were far too limited, reduced to a few duties at too high a level, with an over-dependence on alcohol and tobacco. Such a pattern 'has neither the merit of striking the community in a great variety of ways nor the merit of rapid expansion on an emergency'. Consequently, each supposedly temporary increase in expenditure was met from the income tax. The result was a gradual, and largely inadvertent, shift in the proportions of direct and indirect taxes which was accepted by chancellors who realised its popularity. In *The Times*'s view, the high level of income tax survived only because it fell on a class which was 'numerically insignificant at the polls'. Giffen felt that the income tax was initially imposed as a temporary measure to reform indirect taxes; when it became permanent it was on the basis of a modest rate in normal times to be increased in periods

Revenue 1899–1907, and was a member of the Royal Commission on the Civil Service (1912) and Railways (1913). He shot himself in Kensington Gardens. (*DNB, 1922–30*, ed. Weaver, pp, 696–7.)

[21] PRO, T168/35, H. W. Primrose to E. W. Hamilton, 22 Oct. 1895.

[22] *Parliamentary Debates*, 3rd ser. 205, 1 May 1871, cols. 2014–15; this was cited in PRO, T168/52, 'The financial problem', E. W. Hamilton, 31 Jan. 1901.

[23] PRO, CAB37/58/93, 'Extension of the basis of indirect taxation', 7 Oct. 1901.

of emergency. In his view, the equity of this arrangement had been destroyed by making the high rate of income tax permanent. Further, this posed problems in raising taxes to cope with emergencies which would weaken the credit of the government and lead to borrowing. Giffen therefore argued for a *reduction* in the normal rate of income tax in order to provide a reserve for emergencies. Meanwhile, reinstating taxes on corn and sugar would not take the proportion of indirect taxes back to the 1860s. After all, these duties were accepted by Cobden, and Gladstone had planned to abolish the income tax. 'To oppose such taxes on free trade grounds is simply free trade run mad, or political free trade, and not the free trade of economists and students of finance, or commonsense men of business.'

Giffen's case rested on a particular view of equity. He gave more weight to pragmatism, convenience and the needs of the state than to the pursuit of theoretical justice. He also rejected the assumption that a reduction in income tax relieved the rich at the expense of the poor, for 'there is no room for considering nicely in a homogeneous State how much falls, in the first instance, on the rich and how much on the poor, since the burden in the end is equally adjusted'. A reduction in direct taxes on the rich would benefit the poor, for the result would be an increased accumulation of capital and hence higher wages. As *The Times* put it, 'The rich man's one luxury from an economic point of view is employment of labour.' It followed that Giffen was opposed to 'rubbishy ideas' of graduation of the income tax and to measures of taxable capacity which he saw as fatal to the 'sober ideals' of English finance and the welfare of the state:

no class of people in any community is in a position to say that one kind or amount of income can bear a higher proportion of taxation than another kind or amount. All are citizens owing an equal duty to the State, and there is really no common measure of their ability except the income they receive under the protection of the State. Taxable capacity is a something supposed to remain over after certain wants have been provided for, as it is supposed that as incomes rise the taxpayer can pay more in proportion to the State with less privation than if he had a small income. But all this is mere imagination...As far as one can know, wants are in all cases curiously proportioned to the income, and the privation caused by any proportionate burden must also be proportional.

Here was a defence of the *status quo* far removed from the marginal revolution in economics: the richer the individual, the greater his or her wants, so that the loss of an additional pound of income was just as painful as to the poor. Further, justice could not exist in a fiscal system based on few indirect taxes which allowed many to escape. The main principle of Giffen's fiscal policy was simple: 'the practical golden rule surely is to have a sufficient number of sources of revenue, with the rates of all the taxes as moderate as possible to make it tolerably certain that no class is excessively pressed in the first instance and that the burden in all probability is equally diffused'.[24] His position was, therefore, close to Lowe's 'equalisation of pressure'.

There was strong official and orthodox support for a modest reversal of the trend from indirect to direct taxes, and such a change was justified as compatible with 'sound' rather than dogmatic free trade. Indeed, this reading of the historical record could be justified. The free traders at the Board of Trade in the 1830s and 1840s did not see anything wrong in principle with obtaining revenue from import duties on tea, coffee and sugar. These commodities were not necessities; they did not enter into the costs of production of industry; and they did not lead to higher wages and hence to higher costs for export industries. As Lucy Brown remarked, 'there was nothing in the Board of Trade in 1840 comparable to the late Victorian propaganda for the "free breakfast table".[25] Indeed, we have seen that the dominant attitude in the Liberal party did not change until the 1860s. These views on the desirability of a modest extension of revenue duties were complemented by a growing feeling amongst industrialists that dogmatic free trade failed to take account of the inequalities of competition with other countries. The erection of tariff barriers by other countries, and the negotiation of most-favoured nation agreements after the American tariff of 1890 and the German tariff of 1902, meant that the world of Cobden was in retreat. Subsidised competition through bounties on sugar beet or shipping led to a questioning of free trade which now allowed British consumers to purchase foreign goods at artificially reduced prices. Adherence to a rigid policy of free trade could be criticised for distorting the market and playing into the hands of monopolists. On such an interpretation, unilateral free trade was no longer working and the best way of preserving an open world economy was through retaliation and the negotiation of reciprocal deals. The aim was not 'insular protectionism' which would create an isolated autarkic economy, but an aggressive policy to reverse the slide into world-wide protectionism. As Frank Trentmann remarks, there was a 'widening, if sometimes grudging acknowledgement among liberal opinion that Cobdenism had become an anachronism in the age of new mercantilism'. Reciprocity and retaliation

---

[24] This material comes from the series of articles in *The Times* from 'A correspondent', Robert Giffen, on 'Twenty years finance': they appeared on 13, 16, 21, 27 Feb. 1899 with a leading article on 27 Feb. 1899; there were further articles on 'The reform of taxation', 5 Mar. 1901, on 'The present financial position', 27 Mar. 1899 and 11 Apr. 1899, with a leading article on 10 Apr. 1899. These were all extracted and commented on in PRO T168/43 and T168/53. See also R. Giffen, 'Some economic aspects of the war', *Economic Journal* 10 (1906), 205–6.

[25] Brown, *Board of Trade and the Free Trade Movement*, p. 157.

might be needed in order to equalise conditions. At the same time, the case for a revenue tariff was obvious to free traders who were concerned by the burden of the income tax. Thus Bernard Samuelson, an industrialist and Liberal free trader, was able to propose a 10 per cent tariff in 1901 in order to raise revenue and to provide a bargaining counter in negotiations with other countries. However, Chamberlain's advocacy of tariff reform soon polarised the debate into two extreme positions of absolute free trade and imperial preference, so excluding the less doctrinaire middle ground of retaliation and a revenue tariff. Although the case for both retaliation and widening the tax base had considerable support, polarisation between unadulterated or dogmatic free trade and the root-and-branch reforms of Chamberlain pushed these possibilities off the political agenda.[26]

The issue of how to increase the government's revenue became critical in the Boer war, the most expensive military engagement since the Crimean war. Initially, the chancellor was sanguine about the costs of the war. In October 1899, he argued that the financial estimates of the war had been calculated with care and accuracy, and that brilliant successes by the army would mean a speedy end to conflict, when the costs could be passed to the taxpayers of the Transvaal. He argued that an increase in indirect taxes would harm commerce; and an increase in the income tax from a high level of 8d in the £ would create resentment. He therefore merely asked for power to raise a loan.[27] The optimism was misplaced, as brilliant success turned to disaster, and the careful estimates of cost proved to be far too low. In his budget of March 1900, Hicks Beach faced the need to raise taxes. Hamilton's advice was to follow the precedent of the Crimean war by raising about 47.4 per cent of the costs of the war from taxes, and to balance direct and indirect taxation in 1900/1.[28] Hicks Beach accepted that the proportion of direct and indirect taxation was fair and he did not propose any material change in the balance of the tax system: he courted the two sisters, raising the income tax, and also the duties on beer and spirits, tobacco and tea.[29] His budget of 1901 aimed to raise 50.3 per cent of revenue from direct taxes, marking the first time that direct taxes were over half the total. He followed Hamilton's advice and reinstated the sugar duty which could be justified as consistent

[26] F. Trentmann, 'The transformation of fiscal reform: reciprocity, modernization, and the fiscal debate within the business community in early twentieth-century Britain', *Historical Journal* 39 (1996), 1005–48.

[27] *Parliamentary Debates*, 4th ser. 77, 23 Oct. 1899, cols. 509–17.

[28] PRO, T168/47, miscellaneous memoranda, 'Taxation versus loans', E. W. Hamilton, 18 Feb. 1900, and E. W. Hamilton to the chancellor, 24 Feb. 1900.

[29] *Parliamentary Debates*, 4th ser. 80, 5 Mar. 1900, cols. 53–78.

with free trade: sugar was not produced at home, so protection was not involved. The precedent of Gladstone could be called into service, for he had raised the duty during the Crimean war, and he argued in 1860 that the labouring classes should bear part of the cost of war in the interests of peace and economy.[30] Further, the duty was justified on grounds of equity between different classes. Figures were produced to show that a labourer with an income of 24s a week paid 9.4 per cent of his income in taxes if he drank spirits, but only 0.9 per cent if he was a teetotaller and non-smoker. By contrast, a clerk on £700 paid 6.4 per cent. The sugar duty would raise the tax paid by the labourer to between 9.9 per cent and 1.4 per cent; the clerk would pay 6.5 per cent. In other words, the labourer could opt to avoid taxation by giving up his spirits, beer and tobacco, whereas the clerk had no choice about paying his income tax.[31]

The pressure of war finance also led to consideration of reintroducing a general registration duty of 1d a hundredweight on all imports. Despite his earlier reservations, Hamilton was now willing to accept the duty on the grounds that it was so low as to be imperceptible and without any protective element. However, political sensitivity over the effect on raw materials and competitiveness meant that the duty was only applied to corn – a commodity with a large political resonance. The government also introduced an export duty of 1s a ton on coal in 1901. Peel had introduced a duty of 4s a ton on coal exports in 1842, but had abandoned it in 1845 in the face of opposition from coal owners. Nevertheless, the duty had some advocates at the time of the Cobden–Chevalier treaty with France in 1860, on the grounds that Britain was living off its capital by exporting a natural resource. The duty would – so it was hoped – be paid by the foreigner. Hamilton argued that Britain had a monopoly at least in steam coal so that this branch of the export trade would not suffer and the duty would largely fall on consumers outside Britain – a proposition which was rejected by south Wales coal owners who were well aware of their high costs and the demands from workers for higher wages. Despite his assumption that the industry would not suffer, Hamilton doubted that such a duty was desirable either on principle, as a return to 'a somewhat antiquated fiscal system', or on practical grounds. After all, the only way to conserve resources would be through a prohibitive duty – and that would hit a major export trade, with serious consequences for shipowners. Although Hamilton preferred to restrict himself to a duty on sugar, the export duty on coal was introduced and (as in 1842) soon led to strong opposition from coal owners. The fiscal innovations of the Boer war were few and modest, and did little to increase the government's sources of revenue.[32]

Hicks Beach was not confident that Hamilton's fiscal strategy could survive, but did not have any major proposals of his own. He was alarmed by an underlying growth in 'normal' expenditure of 40 per cent between 1895 and 1901 which had only been met because tax yields were high as a result of a strong economy and the war-time emergency taxes. What would happen with an economic down-turn and pressure to remove war taxes on the return to peace? 'I can conceive no financial methods which could long provide for such a rate of increase in time of peace', he warned Salisbury in 1901. Although he was willing to contemplate a small duty on corn, meat or petrol, he was opposed to any measures which marked a return to protection – despite the recommendation from some officials that he introduce import duties on grain and meat. The alternative was to slash expenditure, which would be difficult given the demands for public spending on health, education and the navy. Hicks Beach had reached the limits of the Gladstonian fiscal state.[33]

The return of peace raised the question whether the duties introduced to meet the war emergency should be repealed, or extended to place the fiscal system on a new basis. The answer offered by C. T. Ritchie,* who became chancellor in 1902, failed to convince his Cabinet colleagues. He realised that increases in 'normal' expenditure meant that only a quarter of 'war taxes' could be removed. Although he wished to give priority to cuts in income tax, he saw the need to reduce indirect taxes as well in order to avoid the politically damaging argument that the rich were benefiting at

---

[32] On the registration duty, PRO, T168/45, 'The proposed duty of 1d per cwt on imports', T. W. Pittar, 13 Sept. 1899; on the coal tax, T168/47, 'Export duty on coal', E. W. Hamilton, 23 Feb. 1900, and E. W. Hamilton to chancellor, 24 Feb. 1900; for general discussion, T168/52, 'The financial problem', E. W. Hamilton, 31 Jan. 1901, and 'The question of new taxation discussed', E. W. Hamilton, 13 Dec. 1901. For the comments of the leading coal owner and Liberal MP, D. A. Thomas, on the coal tax, see *Parliamentary Debates*, 4th ser. 152, 18 Apr. 1901, cols. 715–18.

[33] PRO, CAB37/58/109, M. E. Hicks Beach, Oct. 1901; Gloucestershire Record Office 2455, Hicks Beach to Salisbury, 13 Sept. 1901; see also Hamilton's warnings about peace-time expenditure and the need to retain the sugar duty, T168/49, 'The financial outlook', E. W. Hamilton, 27[?] Mar. 1901. The proposal for import duties on grain and meat came in CAB37/58/93, 'Extension of the basis of indirect taxation', 7 Oct. 1901.

* Charles Thomson Ritchie (1838–1906) was educated at the City of London School, and joined his father's firm of East Indian merchants and jute spinners of London and Dundee. He was a Conservative MP from 1874 to 1905. In 1879 he was chairman of the Select Committee to consider measures to protect West Indian cane sugar from European subsidies to sugar beet; he took office as financial secretary to the Admiralty 1885–6, and as president of the Local Government Board 1886–92 where he was responsible for setting up county councils. He was president of the Board of Trade 1895–1900, home secretary 1900–2 and chancellor of the Exchequer 1902–3; he opposed Chamberlain and tariff reform. (*DNB, Second Supplement*, vol. III, ed. Lee, pp. 202–8.)

the expense of the poor. Indeed, the Conservative party's agent feared that the corn duty gave an immense political advantage to the Liberals who would be able to blame it for rising prices and falling employment. The outlook was gloomy for the Conservatives, who feared that 'we may...at any moment have the little loaf *versus* the big loaf brought permanently against us'. Ritchie was concerned that the high level of income tax and rising prices might well produce 'a violent reaction, resulting in sweeping and ill-considered reductions in our defensive expenditure'. He could not borrow without damaging credit, and he insisted that it was essential to preserve a substantial sinking fund. The only solution, it seemed, was a reduction in army expenditure in order to cut the income tax and repeal the corn duty.[34] This package of measures exposed a deep division over the future direction of fiscal policy.

Ritchie was attacked in some quarters for reducing direct taxes much more than indirect taxes: he took 4d off the income tax, a concession about four times the cuts in indirect taxes. The justification for his decision was that the balance had still moved towards direct taxation and away from indirect taxation since the outbreak of the war: indirect taxes were estimated to yield 50.9 per cent of total tax revenues in 1903/4 compared with 52.1 per cent in 1899/1900. Further, a temporary increase in income tax was 'a special implement of war', suitable to meet a temporary need, and a war-time increase should therefore not become permanent in peace. A reduction in indirect taxes was politically dangerous, for the working-class contribution to taxes had fallen as their political power had increased. The process should be halted, argued one Treasury official,

unless we are to arrive at a state of things in which preponderant power will be in the hands of those who can, if they so chose, exempt themselves from any share in the expenses of Government. The working classes as a whole are quite as largely and directly concerned in the maintenance of the services for which our increased expenditure has to provide as the rest of the community. And there are some of the existing items of expenditure, and many among those which from time to time are pressed on Parliament, which are directly and specially for the benefit of the working classes. The free grants for elementary education involve an annual expenditure of close upon 3 millions, which is practically put straight into the pockets of the parents of children in elementary schools.[35]

---

[34] PRO, T168/57, 'A provisional forecast, 1903/4', E. W. Hamilton, 11 Nov. 1902, and 'Exchequer revenue and expenditure, 1903/4', W. Blain, 24 Jan. 1903; CAB37/63/148, 'Preferential treatment', 31 Oct. 1902; CAB37/63/155, 'Colonial preference', C. T. Ritchie, 15 Nov. 1902; CAB37/63/170, 'Public finance', C. T. Ritchie, 23 Dec. 1902; CAB37/64/15, 'Our financial position', C. T. Ritchie, 21 Feb. 1903.

[35] PRO, T168/52, 'The financial outlook of 1904/5', E. W. Hamilton, 11 Feb. 1904; CAB37/66/61, 'Direct and indirect taxation: memorandum by Mr Blain', May 1903.

Here, it seemed, was precisely what Gladstone had feared: the ability of electors to use taxes for personal gain by passing the costs of social policies on to others. The constraints on leviathan seemed, to this civil servant, to be in danger of snapping. On this view, Ritchie should have gone further in shifting the balance of the tax system from direct to indirect taxes, retaining the corn duty as the foundation for a new policy of tariff reform and imperial preference. Above all, Joseph Chamberlain had the courage – or foolhardiness – to challenge the basis of the Victorian commercial policy and fiscal constitution by proposing a tariff to produce revenue and provide protection. He was returning to the ideas of the Tory protectionists of fifty or sixty years earlier, arguing for a new fiscal balance to protect producers.

The result of Joseph Chamberlain's campaign was to remove the possibility of pragmatic, technical, revision of indirect taxes designed to counter other countries' protectionist duties or to produce additional revenue for the government. Instead, debate was dominated by a much more divisive and controversial ideology of tariff reform and imperial preference, linked with a highly contested vision of Britain's future. The result was to constrain both the Liberals and Conservatives. The Liberals' commitment to free trade made it difficult for them to argue for an increase in indirect taxation on *revenue* grounds. Meanwhile, the ability of the Conservatives to argue a pragmatic, limited, case for tariffs as a means of offering protection and revenue was overwhelmed by Chamberlain's grand schemes. As a result, the fiscal constitution was contested in a way it had not been during the previous forty or fifty years, a period marked by general agreement on the parameters of the state when politicians fought over details and skirmished at the margin. Chamberlain's dramatic gesture transformed the debate on the structure of taxation, but not in the way he intended. The outcome was to *confirm* the shift away from indirect taxes. The solution to the narrow fiscal base was not a revenue tariff; it was a restructuring of the income tax through a surtax on large incomes, an adjustment of its incidence on smaller incomes and the adoption of differentiation. The Gladstonian fiscal constitution was modified in a fundamental way.

In September 1903, Ritchie resigned as chancellor and was succeeded by Joseph Chamberlain's son, Austen.* He inherited a deteriorating

* Austen Chamberlain (1863–1937) was the son of Joseph; he was educated at Rugby and Trinity College, Cambridge. He was a Liberal Unionist MP from 1892 to 1937: he was lord of the Admiralty 1895–1900, financial secretary to the Treasury 1900–2, postmaster general 1902–3, chancellor of the Exchequer 1903–5. He returned to office in the war as secretary of state for India 1915–17, a member of the War Cabinet in 1918, chancellor of the Exchequer 1919–21, and leader of the Conservatives in 1921–2. He was foreign

financial situation, with no prospect of tax cuts and an imperative need to increase taxes in order to avoid a serious budget deficit in 1903/4 and 1904/5. One possibility was to cut naval and army expenditure, which he argued would actually improve Britain's ability to wage war: 'Our defensive strength rests upon our financial not less than upon our military and naval resources and I am bound to say that in the present condition of our finances it would, in my opinion, be impossible to finance a great war, except at an absolutely ruinous cost.' But there was no escape from the need to find additional tax revenue. Hamilton pursued his usual cautious approach of excluding possibilities: all that remained after his ruthless pruning was (once again) the duty on sugar, which could if doubled raise the entire £6m needed by the chancellor. However, Hamilton was reluctant to recommend that the whole increase should come from indirect taxation, especially compared with concessions to income taxpayers in 1902, for 'an increase of the duty, without any concurrent addition to direct taxation, involves so radical a change in our long-accepted financial system'.[36]

The policies of Joseph Chamberlain were anathema to Hamilton and the Treasury who opposed any reversal of the trend in the fiscal constitution towards equal shares of direct and indirect taxes. Their opposition rested less on grounds of principle than a desire to preserve the existing relations of extraction which ensured wide acceptance of the tax system. The problem with tariff reform was that

great changes in taxation are involved, and this of itself is a very serious matter; for, with a case of so difficult and abstruse a problem as the incidence of taxation, it is certain there is much truth in the old maxim that 'an old tax is no tax', and in the saying that 'sooner or later, taxation, if undisturbed, finds its own level'.[37]

Existing taxes allowed taxpayers to adjust their prices and expectations. By contrast, 'a new tax is the tax that is most felt', for 'the principal hardship, if not injustice, of taxation is *change* in it, which involves great friction in passing on the charge', upsetting the calculations made by members of society in their relations with each other and with the state.[38] New taxes would also disrupt the economy and 'anything that tends to divert trade from its natural channel and to disturb its settled course is "a leap in the

---

secretary 1924–9 and first lord of the Admiralty in 1931. (*DNB, 1931–40*, ed. Legg, pp. 163–8.)

[36] University of Birmingham Library, AC 17/2/17, 'The financial situation', Austen Chamberlain, 7 Dec. 1903 (also in CAB37/67/84); AC 17/2/29, 'The financial outlook of 1904/5', E. W. Hamilton, 11 Feb. 1904 (also in PRO, T168/52).

[37] University of Birmingham Library, AC 17/2/5, 'The fiscal problem', paper to Cabinet by Treasury, 25 Aug. 1903.

[38] PRO, T168/64, miscellaneous memo vol. XII, 'The incidence of taxation', E. W. Hamilton, 12 May 1904.

dark", and consequently, attended with danger; for trade, like credit, is a very sensitive plant, of slow growth. It is easy to disorganize and lose trade; it is most difficult to organise and make it.'[39] Hamilton therefore preferred an increase in the rate of income tax. Although he stressed 'the enormous importance of keeping the income tax at a comparatively low rate in times of peace, in order that it may constitute a ready reserve in times of emergency', he felt that the 'normal' rate of income tax should in future be 11d or 1s rather than 7d or 8d, and the 'war reserve' should be 2s rather than 1s 4d.[40] Hamilton was mounting a holding operation to preserve the existing balance of direct and indirect taxation, without a marked shift to tariffs or a radical revision of the income tax.

It was clear to Austen Chamberlain that the budget of 1904 'will mark a critical moment in the fortunes of the Government and the Party'. A more heroic solution was required to deal with the 'extremely gloomy' financial outlook, and the answer was obvious to him: a policy of tariff reform and imperial preference as proposed by his father, based on a strategy of attack rather than a timid, vacillating and defensive stance. Although the Chamberlains' case for tariff reform was defeated in the general election of 1906, it had a major influence on the subsequent development of trade and fiscal policies by *excluding* a revenue tariff. After all, it was possible to argue for protection of industry and an increase in indirect taxation *without* supporting the full programme of tariff reform and imperial preference. Joseph Chamberlain made it extremely difficult to separate them, and as a result he fundamentally narrowed the range of policy options available to Edwardian governments. The problem was apparent to George Goschen who accepted the case for broadening the basis of taxation yet refused to support Chamberlain on the grounds that his policy was inspired by protection.[41] Austen Chamberlain denied the charge:

an old Chancellor of the Exchequer like yourself must feel that the base of our fiscal pyramid is dangerously narrow. Of Beach's 'broadening' taxes, corn has gone, coal is going . . . , sugar is threatened. Every existing tax is as high or higher than it ought to be; and the only alternative offered to a general tariff for revenue is to pile on the weight on the apex of the pyramid by further graduation of the death duties, by graduation of the income tax, and by raiding land and capital wherever found – ground rents, royalties and so forth. Can you contemplate such a programme with equanimity? Yet how can you fight it without a practical alternative?[42]

Chamberlain's assessment of the situation had a ring of truth. Even when the financial situation was less strained, Harcourt had graduated death

[39] University of Birmingham Library, AC 17/2/5, 'The fiscal problem'.
[40] PRO, T168/52, 'The financial outlook of 1904/5', E. W. Hamilton, 11 Feb. 1904.
[41] University of Birmingham Library, AC 17/3/52, letter from G. J. Goschen, Nov. 1905.
[42] University of Birmingham Library, AC 17/3/53, Austen Chamberlain to Goschen, 14 Nov. 1905.

duties and threatened to graduate the income tax. Goschen was equally correct that the driving force of Chamberlain's policy *was* protection of industry; as he pointed out, less than a tenth of the argument for tariff reform referred to broadening the basis of taxation.[43] It was precisely the connection between protection and indirect taxes, the attack on the shibboleth of free trade, which marginalised Liberal opponents of higher, graduated, income taxation. The containment of Harcourt's proposals for graduation in the budget of 1894 was not to survive when the Liberals next came to power.

Containing graduation

The initial, hesitant, step towards progressive taxation came with Harcourt's budget of 1894. As we have seen in chapter 8, Harcourt turned to the death duties as a means of raising money for the navy, which could be justified on Gladstonian grounds of limiting militarism by making the advocates of imperial expansion pay. The extension of death duties also went some way towards meeting the radicals' attack on the unearned increment. Of course, it was a commonplace of liberal economics, most clearly stated by John Stuart Mill, that property left at death was more liable to taxation than *active* capital. Reform of the death duties could therefore be seen as a measure of prudential conservatism in favour of enterprise.

The issue was how far to go. Gladstone did contemplate graduation of the inhabited house duty and Hamilton accepted in 1894 that this offered 'the best guage of the spending power of the people'.[44] A modest degression of income tax on small incomes was compatible with the Gladstonian fiscal constitution, as part of an attempt to bring as many people as possible within the tax system, taking the tax threshold lower down the income scale without imposing undue hardship and resistance. Both Hamilton and Gladstone were loathe to go beyond the existing income tax exemptions and abatements for small incomes. Degression had, it seemed, already gone too far, and Gladstone criticised any extension of total exemption which would remove the sensitivity of voters to the consequences of voting for expensive policies. He was therefore opposed to the extension of relief to small taxpayers proposed by Northcote in 1876 and by Harcourt in 1894. Although taxation of estates at death was justified in terms of the attack on 'dead' capital, Gladstone was wary

---

[43] University of Birmingham Library, AC 17/3/54, Goschen to Austen Chamberlain, 20 Nov. 1905.

[44] BL Add. MS 48,654, Hamilton Diary, vol. XXV, f. 57, 25 Nov. 1890; BL Add. MS 48, 652, vol. XXIII, ff. 98–9, 27 Mar. 1890; Brooks (ed.), *Destruction*, 15 Mar. 1894, pp. 124–5.

about graduation of the duty. He denounced even Goschen's modest scheme of 1889, of a duty of 1 per cent on estates above £10,000. As Hamilton explained, this was 'the thin end of the wedge to a graduated system of taxation, which is pretty certain to be expanded in the future'. Gladstone shared his concerns, fearing that the graduation of estate duty and more generous income tax exemptions were already subverting the fiscal constitution. He 'was prepared to accept, in the abstract, graduated taxation, but it was attended with dangers; for where was it to stop? If pressed, it might amount to confiscation.' Gladstone merely wished to restore proportionality and to balance the tax system between precarious and spontaneous incomes, rather than to favour one against the other. Gladstone defined graduation as an 'equitable distribution of taxation', a careful assessment of the tax system to ensure that each form of income and property paid its fair burden which should be achieved by 'compensatory taxes' rather than graduation of any particular tax. Gladstone's response to the introduction of graduated death duties in 1894 was unenthusiastic resignation. He accepted that 'graduated taxation in principle was not unjust', and that 'so long as this "iniquitous abominable and accursed" military expenditure had to be incurred, it was permissible and even necessary'. However, he was reluctant to accept a progressive income tax.[45]

Gladstone was therefore wary about any extension of graduation, and we have seen that his sentiment was shared by Rosebery, Haldane and the Liberal imperialists who sought to make a new appeal to the middle and upper classes who had, in their opinion, been alienated from the party by 'faddist' Liberalism, the alliance with the Irish, and lack of support for imperialism. Acceptance of graduation would merely provide new evidence that the party was in the grip of radicals. Although Harcourt had little sympathy with the radicals, he was equally hostile to the Liberal imperialists. He preferred to build support outwards from the centre which he defined as the lower level of income taxpayers. Reform of the death duties was only one part of a wider fiscal strategy to secure the allegiance of this crucial electoral interest. Graduation would allow an adjustment of the income tax on smaller incomes, a strategy crucial to the fiscal politics of Harcourt and, later, of Lloyd George and Winston Churchill.* The package of measures in Harcourt's budget of

---

[45] BL Add. MS 48,652, vol. XXIII, f. 118, 18 Apr. 1890; Brooks (ed.), *Destruction*, p. 129, 3 Apr. 1894; MS 48,650, Hamilton Diary, vol. XXI, f. 90, 2 Apr. 1889; f. 95, 11 Apr. 1889, ff. 101–2, 16 Apr. 1889, f. 114, 2 May 1889; MS 48,653, vol. XXIV, f. 86, 25 July 1890; Brooks (ed.), *Destruction*, p. 159, 31 July 1894.

* Winston Leonard Spencer Churchill (1874–1965) was the son of Randolph Churchill; he was educated at Harrow and Sandhurst, joining the army and also working as a war correspondent. He became a Unionist MP in 1900, moving to the Liberals in 1904 in opposition to tariff reform. He became parliamentary under-secretary of the colonies

1894 prefigured the approach of the Liberal government from 1906 and laid the basis for a 'modern' progressive tax system.[46] As his Conservative counterpart – Michael Hicks Beach – realised, reform of the death duties was not justified simply on grounds of raising revenue.[47] Rather, it was part of a new fiscal and electoral strategy. Harcourt was convinced that the politics of taxation had changed, and that a return to indirect taxation was politically impossible. Reliance on higher rates of income tax therefore meant that it was 'indispensable to reform it at both ends'. As we have seen in chapter 8, he made two complementary proposals, to add a surtax at the top end and to increase abatements on smaller incomes.[48]

In 1894, Harcourt fought a losing battle for graduation against the forces of fiscal orthodoxy within the Treasury and Inland Revenue. 'It is a great disadvantage in these Radical days', Lewis Harcourt confided to his journal, that the leading officials at the Treasury and Inland Revenue were old colleagues of Gladstone and Liberal imperialists, and that they 'should regard themselves as the sentinels of the Landlord and Capitalist class'.[49] The old guard at the Treasury and Inland Revenue were clearly formidable opponents of change, basing their opposition to graduation of the income tax on a highly developed and articulate set of assumptions about the nature of the British fiscal system and the relationship between the state and taxpayers. Their case rested on the collection of income tax at source so that it was not necessary for the Inland Revenue to be aware of the total income received by any individual under each head. The taxpayer need only divulge his total income voluntarily, in order to get the return of tax deducted at source from incomes which fell *below* the threshold. Graduation would entail a major adjustment in the tax system, by compelling taxpayers to divulge their total earnings in order to

---

in 1906; he was president of the Board of Trade 1908–10, home secretary 1910–11, and first lord of the Admiralty 1911–5. In 1915 he became chancellor of the Duchy of Lancaster, but resigned to join the army. He returned to office as minister of munitions in 1917–18, secretary of war and air in 1918–21 and colonial secretary in 1921–2. He was out of the Commons from 1922 until 1924, when he returned as a Conservative until 1964. He was chancellor of the Exchequer 1924–9, and split from the party over the India bill in 1931. He was prime minister 1940–5 and 1951–5. (*DNB, 1961–70,* ed. Williams and Nicholls, pp. 193–216.)

[46] B. K. Murray, *The People's Budget, 1909/10: Lloyd George and Liberal Politics* (Oxford, 1980), p. 16.

[47] See comment of Hicks Beach, Gloucestershire Record Office, 2455 PCC/12, Hicks Beach to Balfour, 8 May 1894.

[48] Bod. Lib., MS Harcourt dep. 398, f. 8, 27 Dec. 1893, f. 17, 1 Jan. 1894; dep. 399, ff. 27–8, 12 Jan. 1894, ff. 43–4, 14 Jan. 1894, f. 24, 30 Jan. 1894, ff. 45–6, 7 Feb. 1894; dep. 57, ff. 55–9, Harcourt to Rosebery; dep. 70, ff. 40–3, notes on surtax, 1 Feb. 1894[?], ff. 56–7, Harcourt to Milner, 19 Feb. 1894; PRO, CAB37/98, no. 45, Income Supertax, L. Harcourt, 25 Mar. 1901.

[49] Bod. Lib., MS Harcourt dep. 406, f. 21, 16 Mar. 1894.

pay *more* tax. Milner explained the Inland Revenue's case. 'The Income Tax . . . *lends itself ill to graduation*, because the material facts, on which such graduation is based, can only be supplied by the individual taxpayer, who has the strongest motive for, and infinite means of, concealment.' The clauses in the budget bill providing powers to collect the necessary information 'must be stringent, and their inquisitorial character is certain to provoke discussion'. The opponents of graduation argued that it was not simply a matter of troubling 10,000 people who would ultimately pay the surtax. Rather, it was necessary to send forms to 100,000 people in order to discover who was liable. Milner assumed that 80 per cent would not reply, and it would not be possible to know whether their silence arose because they did not have an income of £5,000 or because they were concealing their income. It would therefore be necessary to have powers of compulsion, despite the fact that in four cases out of five there would be nothing to tax:

Experience shows, that the irritation caused by the inquiries of the tax gatherer is universal: it is not confined to the persons whom he is ultimately seeking to charge. We should be making a hundred incidental enemies for every recalcitrant, or mendacious, plutocrat whom we were trying to run in . . . is the game worth the candle? Would this extra million a year not be dearly bought if it involved setting up a feud, so long happily avoided, between the public generally and the vast body of persons, often not very well-mannered or very literate, who are concerned in the collection of the taxes.[50]

The danger, as Milner saw it, was that the change to the tax system would cause 'indirect injury to the Revenue' through a loss of compliance which would 'outweigh the meagre pecuniary result'.[51] Accordingly, Harcourt abandoned the surtax in 1894 in the face of opposition from Hamilton and Milner. As Harcourt explained, the Inland Revenue 'are strongly of opinion that the measures of penal discovery and irritating inquisition which would be involved . . . would render the collection of the Income Tax so odious as to imperil its existence, and in all probability make it impossible to maintain the tax'.[52]

Much the same case was argued by the older generation of officials in 1906. Primrose doubted that 'some 15,000 of the most powerful of the community would tolerate tamely such an inquisition into their private

[50] Bod. Lib., MS Harcourt dep. 70, ff. 160–6, 'Memorandum on various proposed changes in the income tax', A. Milner, 9 Mar. 1894.

[51] Brooks (ed.), *Destruction*, pp. 124–5, 15 Mar. 1894, and p. 129, 3 Apr. 1894; PRO, T168/96, Milner's memo on income tax graduation, 1894.

[52] Bod. Lib., MS Harcourt dep. 405, ff. 57–8, 10 Mar. 1894; *Parliamentary Debates*, 4th ser. 33, 16 Apr. 1894, col. 502.

affairs as would be inevitable with a system of Progressive Income Tax? Or would any reasonable person wish to subject them to such an inquisition, if he realised that little or no profit to the community would result from it?' The result would be tension in assessment and collection of taxes, which would alienate the lay commissioners.[53] Graduation, therefore, would imperil the high level of consent to the income tax:

> The collection is one of the wonders of the world. It is the envy of other nations. We must do nothing to imperil this productivity...When it is said that other countries graduate the tax with success, can we say for certain that it is with success when the amounts which the tax produces are mere fleabites as compared with the huge sums raised in this country? If therefore the best authorities cannot promise you an increase of revenue by resort to graduation which at the same time is not confiscation, are you not perilously near incurring a loss? And would it not be better to look elsewhere for introducing the system of graduation?[54]

The Select Committee of 1906 reported on the 'practicability' of graduating and differentiating the income tax. Although it concluded that graduation could be extended by the use of degression and abatements, a limit would be reached when the level of abatements required a large increase in the 'normal or foundation' rate of tax so that the total amount collected was considerably above the amount retained by the government, with inconvenience to taxpayers and to trade and commerce. The committee felt that the existing system would remain practicable if abatements were extended from the existing figure of £700 to incomes of up to £1,000. The committee also felt that graduation by means of a super-tax levied by means of personal declaration of income was practicable, if it were decided to impose a much higher rate of tax on large incomes, above say £5,000. The Committee wished to retain collection at source, but also felt that a compulsory declaration of the total income of all taxpayers was desirable in order to prevent even the existing evasion and avoidance of tax. The Select Committee was, therefore, not convinced by the claims of the Inland Revenue that collection at source was incompatible with graduation.[55]

The Inland Revenue concentrated on the administrative difficulties of graduation, but Primrose also expressed concern about the economic impact of higher levels of tax. Although his concern for administration and compliance might have been genuine, it was certainly allied to a predilection in favour of the existing distribution of income and wealth. Might a

---

[53] PRO, T168/96, memorandum by H. W. Primrose, 22 June 1903, 'Graduation of income tax, practicability thereof'.
[54] PRO, T168/68, 'Graduation of income tax', E. W. Hamilton to chancellor, 6 June 1906.
[55] PP 1906 IX, *Report from the Select Committee on Income Tax*, pp. 661–7.

graduated income tax remove income which would otherwise be saved, so reducing the amount of capital and increasing its price? Primrose argued that capital would be scarcer and more expensive, so that the distribution of income would shift in favour of capital and against labour, with a reduction in employment and wages. In other words, the existing distribution of income was in the interests of workers as well as capitalists. Primrose rejected the notion that graduation meant taxation by ability to pay, for the amount of income did not take account of the obligations of landowners compared with *rentiers*, of assured compared with precarious incomes or of family men compared with bachelors. Primrose took the line that equality of treatment would require *all* of these factors to be considered in order to avoid still greater inequalities and anomalies – and that any such attempt to establish the surplus income of each taxpayer would be impossible and would merely create 'irritation and controversy to an extent that would quickly render the special tax odious'. This criticism was extended to differentiation as well as graduation. Supporters of differentiation argued that a higher rate of tax on unearned incomes would encourage active, precarious, income. Opponents objected that a heavier tax on unearned income from capital would simply discourage capital accumulation, so leading to higher interest rates and hindering industrial growth.[56]

Graduation of death duties was more readily acceptable to officials because it avoided the practical difficulties of imposing a varying rate of income tax, and did not entail inquisition into the affairs of the living.[57] As we have seen, taxation of estates at death was justified because the power

---

[56] PRO, T168/96, W. Blain, 5 June 1906; PP 1905 LXXXV, *Reports from His Majesty's representatives abroad respecting graduated income taxes in foreign states*, 'Introductory report', B. Mallet, July 1905, pp. 37–51; PRO, T168/96, 'Differentiation and graduation in the income tax and estate duty, and some comparisons with foreign and colonial systems', also in PP 1906 IX, *Report from the Select Committee on Income Tax*, appendix 1, 'Paper handed in by Mr Mallet. Differentiation in the United Kingdom and foreign countries, etc. compared', pp. 917–25; Bod. Lib., MS Harcourt dep. 69, ff. 79–93, note on differential income tax, A. Milner, 27 Apr. 1893; PRO, T168/96, 'Graduation of income tax, practicability thereof', H. W. Primrose, 22 June 1903; T171/1, 'Finance Bill, 1901. Mr Herbert Lewis's amendment as to rate of income tax', H. W. Primrose, 6 June 1901 (also in T168/96); T168/69, 'Mr Speyer on national finance', E. W. Hamilton, 25 June 1905; T168/68, E. W. Hamilton to Henry, 18 Sept. 1905; T168/68, Hamilton to chancellor, 11 Jan. 1906; PRO, T168/68, miscellaneous memoranda by E. W. Hamilton, vol. XIII, 'Graduation of income tax', Hamilton to chancellor, 6 June 1906, and Hamilton to chancellor, 11 Jan. 1906; T168/96, 'Income tax committee: memorandum of evidence to be given by Sir H. W. Primrose' (also at PP 1906 IX, *Report from the Select Committee on Income Tax*, appendix 13, 'Paper handed in by Sir H. W. Primrose, 25 July 1906. Memorandum of evidence to be given by Sir H.W. Primrose, chairman of the Board of Inland revenue', pp. 960–4.

[57] BL Add. MS 48,652, Hamilton Diary, vol. XXIII, ff. 78–9, 8 Mar. 1890.

to dispose of property after death was 'a privilege so highly artificial that
there may be less scruple in attaching to it somewhat onerous conditions',
and it affected only incomes derived from capital rather than incomes
from trade and professions.[58] Officials also argued that the death duties
made differentiation of the income tax redundant. Attempts were made
to estimate the combined impact of the income tax and death duties on
'spontaneous' compared with 'precarious' incomes by adding the annual
cost of insurance policies to cover the death duty. An unearned income of
£200 would pay 2.6 per cent tax and insurance, compared with 1 per cent
on an earned income of £200; these figures rose to 5.9 per cent and 3.8 per
cent on £500 and 7.4 per cent and 5 per cent on £1,000. The effective level
of differentiation was greater, for earned incomes were under-assessed by
about 20 per cent, whereas investment incomes were assessed at source at
the full amount. Consequently, unearned incomes were probably taxed
at double the rate of earned incomes. The 'inevitable conclusion' drawn
from these figures by Bernard Mallet* was that the British tax system was
already equitable between earned and unearned income, exceeding the
level of differentiation in Prussia. 'The demand for the "differentiation"
of the English Income Tax', he concluded, 'could hardly be maintained
if the action of the Death Duties in burdening capital, and the income
from capital, were generally realised.'[59] The answer, it seemed to him,
was to adjust the relative weights of income tax and death duties rather
than to change the nature of the income tax. In any case, the distinction
between spontaneous and precarious incomes was not clear-cut and did
not measure the capacity to pay tax. As Milner pointed out, the result
might be to place a heavier burden on weaker shoulders so that a widow
with £500 a year from investments to support herself and her children
might pay more than a barrister with earnings of £5,000 a year.[60]

In 1894, Harcourt admitted defeat of graduation of the income tax
on administrative grounds. However, he made clear his commitment to
the principle of graduation and was confident that means could be found

---

[58] See above, chapter 8; the quote is from PRO, T168/96, memorandum by H. W.
Primrose, 6 June 1901, on income tax graduation, also in PP 1906 IX, *Report from the
Select Committee on Income Tax*, appendix 13.

[59] PRO, T168/96, 'Differentiation and graduation in the income tax and estate duty, and
some comparisons with foreign and colonial systems', B. Mallet, Dec. 1905, also in
PP 1906 IX, *Report from the Select Committee on Income Tax*, appendix 1.

[60] Bod. Lib., MS Harcourt dep. 69, ff. 79–93, 'Note on differential income tax', A. Milner,
27 Apr. 1893.

* Bernard Mallet (1859–1932) was educated at Clifton College and Balliol College,
Oxford; he joined the Foreign Office in 1882 and moved to the Treasury in 1885. He
was commissioner of the Inland Revenue 1897–1909 and registrar-general of England,
1909–20. He served as president of the Royal Statistical Society 1916–18 and of the
Eugenics Society in 1929. (*Who Was Who*, vol. III (London, 1941), p. 894.)

for implementing the proposal. Indeed, Reginald Welby at the Treasury felt it was possible to make a start with a surtax on very large incomes which 'would be found in the long-run conservative'.[61] Graduation was therefore postponed rather than abandoned. He did reform the lower end of the income tax. As we have noted in chapter 8, in this respect he was moving towards the fiscal and electoral strategy adopted by Asquith and Lloyd George between 1907 and 1914, before the Conservative campaign for tariff reform. Nevertheless, there were important differences between Harcourt and his successors. Unlike Asquith, he was not proposing differentiation between earned and unearned income within the income tax. The demand for differentiation was to emerge more strongly after 1900 with the development of a radical critique of socially created wealth and Rent which grew out of the attack on landowners – a different argument from Hubbard's concern in the mid-nineteenth century to balance the taxation of spontaneous and precarious incomes rather than to define land as peculiarly liable to taxation.[62]

At the end of the nineteenth century, senior civil servants of the Treasury and the Inland Revenue formed a massive dead-weight against change, using their immense authority to preserve the *status quo* against Liberal advocates of graduation. As we have noted, Hamilton was also opposed to any significant increase in indirect taxes which would threaten a reversal of the long trend towards direct taxes. By the end of the century, the advice of Hamilton created rigidities and inflexibilities, imposing strict limits to the revenues of the government – precisely the outcome he preferred. But the official position was by no means uniform. Some officials argued that the balance between direct and indirect taxes could be adjusted by returning to the proportions of the 1860s, which was compatible with free trade. This position was compromised by Chamberlain's campaign for tariff reform. Other officials, mainly of a younger generation, accepted that the fiscal system would become more dependent on the income tax, which should be reformed. In their opinion, the imperatives of compliance had changed: the existing system would soon meet resistance, and the incidence of the tax needed to be adjusted to ensure continued acceptance of fairness and equity. Hamilton's commitment to earlier norms of balance and equity would now *threaten* rather than preserve the legitimacy of the fiscal system. A new generation of officials at the Treasury and Inland Revenue accepted the need for reform of the income tax in order to solve pragmatic issues of revenue and

[61] Bod. Lib., MS Harcourt dep. 70, Harcourt to Milner, 10 Mar. 1894, ff. 172–9, Milner to Harcourt, 12 Mar. 1894, ff. 142–3, Welby to Harcourt, 11 Mar. 1894.

[62] See above, p. 255.

compliance. The Liberal government had a similar concern with the need to secure revenue, but also had a pressing need to develop a clear electoral strategy to ensure that it retained the support of working-class electors without alienating middle-class income taxpayers. How were they to resolve the problem, and how successful were they in redefining the fiscal constitution?

[The reports of the Select Committees of 1905 and 1906] were followed, in 1907 and subsequent years, by a series of legislative changes that have profoundly modified the old and simple outlines of the tax. It is from 1907 that the modern Income Tax counts the years of its life.

PP 1920 XVIII, *Report of the Royal Commission on the Income Tax*, p. 106

Formerly the only question of the tax-gatherer was 'How much have you got?'... But now a new question has arisen. We do not only ask today, 'How much have you got?' we also ask, 'How did you get it?' Did you earn it by yourself, or has it just been left you by others? Was it gained by processes which have done no good to anyone, but only harm?

W. S. Churchill, *Liberalism and the Social Problem* (London, 1909), pp. 377–8

The amount of socially-created wealth increases annually. The share of the workers remains stationary or declines. Social reform should aim at securing for the common good the use and benefit of all socially-created wealth. In the hands of a democratic Government, Finance can be a very potent instrument to that end.

The Labour Party. Ninth Annual Conference, 1909 (London, 1909), appendix II, 'The incidence of taxation', memorandum by the Executive Committee, p. 102

The defeat of the Conservatives in the general elections of 1906 and 1910 removed the possibility of a shift to indirect taxation by the introduction of tariff reform. Instead, the Liberal government transformed the income tax by adopting both differentiation and graduation, as well as introducing new taxes on land and increasing death duties (see table 11.1). In the 1840s and 1850s, Hume and Hubbard argued for differentiation as an act of justice between spontaneous and industrious incomes, a demand Gladstone resisted from a fear that it might set class against class. Certainly, Hume and Hubbard never contemplated graduation, for they wished to create an active, dynamic, economy of risk-takers in search of profit, based on private rather than corporate capitalism. Gladstone was concerned that differentiation might nevertheless lead to graduation and his alarm appears justified, for graduation soon followed the introduction of differentiation in 1907. When differentiation returned to the political agenda, it had very different connotations from the case made by Hume and Hubbard. It was now part of a wider attack on the landed interest and 'socially created wealth', in which differentiation and graduation were two means in pursuit of the same end. The electoral context had changed, with an extension of the franchise and the emergence of a separate Labour party. Differentiation now offered a way of appealing to radical attacks on 'unearned' or 'socially created wealth' as well as favouring active enterprise over passive accumulation. Graduation was the other element in the strategy, adjusting the tax rate to ability and producing more revenue to meet the needs of the government to finance social reform and military expenditure, and to provide a free trade alternative to tariff reform. A further change went back to the income tax of Pitt and Addington: tax allowances for family responsibilities which could be used to justify higher rates on taxpayers who did not have family responsibilities, and to secure the support of crucial groups of the electorate who were relieved of taxation. The income tax code became more complicated, with a plethora of allowances for small incomes and earned incomes, for wives, children and dependent relatives. The definition of 'capacity to pay' became more sophisticated, with a much greater concern for how much was earned, by what means, and to maintain what responsibilities. The language of taxation articulated the normative assumptions of politicians about the social structure, and helped them to define identities and interests to shape the electorate.

Although the transformation of the income tax by the Liberal government of 1906 to 1914 marked a departure from the Gladstonian fiscal constitution, it could still be interpreted as an act of justice between taxpayers designed to ensure that taxes had the same impact *at the margin* for everyone. A new sense of balance and equity could be achieved. A graduated and differentiated tax was justified as a means of ensuring that the marginal impact on the final pound of an income of, say, £10,000 from investments was the same as on the final pound of an income of, say, £500 from earned, precarious, income. Such an approach could appeal to modest middle-class incomes (and especially to married men with families) as a means of establishing an equitable, balanced, fiscal system. The strategy of politicians in both the Liberal and later the Conservative party was to produce a 'dip' in the incidence of taxation on married men with families at the lower levels of liability to income tax in order to preserve the loyalty of a significant electoral constituency, and to secure political support for higher general levels of taxation. The fiscal system could also be used in a more radical manner, in order to *alter* the balance of society in pursuit of a particular vision of equity. In other words, politicians might no longer seek to present the tax system as neutral, maintaining the existing social structure and ensuring that the marginal incidence of taxation was the same for all. Their rhetoric might now rest on an active use of the tax system to reshape society according to (highly contested) normative assumptions of equity and social justice. Many progressives in the Liberal and Labour parties argued that large incomes were socially created and led to a skewed and deformed social structure; the role of the tax system should be to capture this unearned increment and make it available for social purposes. The income tax could become precisely what Peel and Gladstone always feared – the locus of deep political and social tension which would threaten its status as a widely accepted means of raising revenue for the state.

These debates entailed a battle over the 'core' of the fiscal constitution rather than skirmishes at the margin, and they were part of a wider debate about Britain's future identity. The Peelite and Gladstonian fiscal constitution was threatened by a combination of the financial pressures of the Boer war, the demands for social reform and the costs of local government. As we have seen, the mounting costs of urban government collided with an inflexible and regressive system of local taxation, so that the boundaries between local and national finance had to be redefined, either by shifting responsibilities from the localities to the centre or by channelling new sources of funds from the centre to the localities. This concern for local taxation connected with major issues of social policy, for it involved the future of the locally funded poor law, and the extent to which social services should be financed through central taxes or self-financing insurance schemes. The solution favoured by Chamberlain was imperial preference: import duties would provide revenue for social reform, and at the same time foster a strong market for British goods at home and in the empire, so creating higher wages and steadier employment which would solve the problems of poverty and unemployment. The Liberal response rested on a continued commitment to free trade, and the belief that an 'open' economy offered prosperity. This could be linked with the radical attack on the unearned increment in land as a means of increasing revenue and of reducing the burden on 'active' property. Such an approach could be presented as a means of uniting the enterprising, active and productive members of society of all classes against passive parasites; it could also be extended from a critique of land to a wider attack on all forms of socially created Rent. Proponents of this view argued that a redistribution of wealth and income would solve the problems of poverty and unemployment, by creating a more dynamic economy based on a stronger domestic market. Such an approach might move away from a simple Cobdenite belief in the virtues of free trade to a more active role for the state in ensuring that socially created wealth was not misappropriated by private individuals. Rejection of protection and support of free trade might therefore rest on reshaping the domestic market to create a stronger demand for goods and for labour. This might entail a transfer of resources from rich to poor which could command considerable support as a measure of social justice and national efficiency. It might go further to a demand for social ownership and the replacement of private property which would alienate many middle-class voters who might well define themselves as property owners in alliance with landowners and investors in government bonds or shares in public companies. But in addition to these ideological assumptions and political calculations, opinion shifted within the Treasury and Inland Revenue as officials came to accept the need for change. In part, this was an adjustment to their new political masters. However, officials also had their own, more pragmatic, reasons for accepting the need for change in the fiscal constitution.

Accepting change: the official view

The adoption of graduation and differentiation reflected a change in the balance of power at the Treasury and Inland Revenue as well as shifts in political rhetoric and electoral calculation. A younger generation of officials at the Treasury and Inland Revenue felt that reform would not be so harmful and might well be essential in order to secure revenue. Indeed, they realised that, given the shift in electoral realities and social assumptions, resistance to change was more likely to jeopardise consent than a desperate attempt to preserve the *status quo*. Hamilton retired in 1907, and Lloyd George marginalised other officials in favour of John Bradbury*

---

* John Swanwick Bradbury (1872–1950) was born in Cheshire, the son of an oil merchant. He was educated at Manchester Grammar School and Brasenose College, Oxford, joining the Colonial Office in 1896 and then the Treasury. He became private secretary to Asquith in 1905, and in 1908 head of one of the divisions of the Treasury. He worked on the 1909 budget, planned the finances of the health insurance scheme, and served as insurance commissioner from 1911 to 1913. He was joint permanent secretary of the Treasury from 1913 to 1919, with responsibility for finance. He left the Treasury to serve as delegate to the Reparation Committee 1919–25; he was chairman of the Food Council 1925–9 and also a director (for the government) of the Anglo-Persian Oil Co. He was a member of the Macmillan Committee on Finance and Industry 1929–31: he supported the gold standard and felt that problems arose from the high standard of living; his dissenting memorandum argued for strict economy in public expenditure. (*DNB*, *1941–50*, ed. Legg and Williams, pp. 98–9.)

at the Treasury and Robert Chalmers,* a 'partisan Liberal', at the Inland Revenue.[1] The younger men in the Treasury and Inland Revenue moved beyond Hamilton's restrictive notion of possible tax changes which offered a limited range of options to politicians. Primrose was horrified, commenting to Hamilton in 1907 that he was 'startled' that proposals for graduation emanating from the Treasury went further than the most 'predatory' members of the Select Committee of 1906. As he pointed out, the Select Committee had merely said that a super-tax was practicable, not that it was desirable, and 'it would be very unfortunate if ideas more revolutionary than any that the Committee ventured to hold, should take their rise from the Treasury itself'.[2]

The Treasury and Inland Revenue officials shifted from finding reasons to block change desired by politicians, to showing how change was feasible without a loss of compliance. Instead of finding administrative reasons for rejecting change, they now sought to show that change was compatible with existing administrative procedures. They were more concerned about the 'elasticity' of the revenue which they believed would be improved by graduation. Clearly, the existing system of abatements imposed limits, for a sizeable increase in the normal or standard rate would entail the collection of large sums of money to be returned to those entitled to abatements. Degression and abatements therefore only made sense so long as the income tax remained at a modest rate.[3] The existing system of abatements imposed serious limits on the revenue of the government: a high standard rate of tax could be borne by large incomes but would cause hardship on small incomes. The consequent need to increase abatements led to a complete loss of revenue from small incomes. It made more sense to have a progressive scale so that *some* revenue could be raised from smaller incomes. In other words, graduation was as much about the need to extract some revenue from smaller incomes as it was about extracting more taxation from large incomes.[4]

The standard rate of tax with abatements and degression was already more progressive than the Prussian income tax. In Prussia, the income

---

[1] Murray, *People's Budget*, pp. 77, 80.
[2] PRO, T168/96, H. W. Primrose to E. W. Hamilton, 3 Feb. 1907.
[3] PP 1906 IX, *Report from the Select Committee on Income Tax*, pp. 661–7.
[4] PP 1920 XVIII, *Report of the Royal Commission on the Income Tax*, p. 132.
* Robert Chalmers (1858–1938) was educated at the City of London School and Oriel College, Oxford. He joined the Treasury in 1882 and was chairman of the Board of Inland Revenue 1907–11 before returning to the Treasury as permanent secretary 1911–13. He was governor of Ceylon 1913–16 and temporary under-secretary of Ireland in 1916, before becoming joint permanent secretary of the Treasury 1916–19. He was a member of the Royal Commission on Oxford and Cambridge Universities in 1920–2, and Master of Peterhouse, Cambridge, from 1924 to 1931. His pomposity and cynicism are said to have concealed his sensitivity. (*DNB, 1931–40*, ed. Legg, pp. 154–5.)

exemption was set at a lower level (£45), so that the income tax fell more heavily on small incomes than in Britain, and affected more people. In Britain, only about 2.3 per cent of the population was assessed, compared with 11.1 per cent in Prussia. In Britain, no tax was paid until an income of £150 was reached, whereas in Prussia taxation started at 0.67 per cent on an income of £45 and reached 1.7 per cent at £150. The British rate then rose to a maximum of 5 per cent at an income of £750 and above, whereas in Prussia it gradually rose to a peak of 4 per cent on extremely large incomes above £100,000.[5] This comparison suggested that the British income tax was modest at the lower level of liability: the problem was that it peaked too soon. The heaviest burden, proportionately, was on incomes between £700 and £2,000 to £3,000, so that a reasonably affluent member of the middle class such as a successful lawyer or doctor paid at the same rate as a 'mendacious plutocrat'. As Reginald McKenna* pointed out,

it is the resistance of these persons to the tax which stands most in the way of raising it...The class of persons earning incomes between £700 and £2,000 or £3,000 a year are formidable as a body by their influence on public opinion...By giving them the relief to which they have a claim the tax is rendered far more elastic.[6]

Of course, this class was also likely to abandon the Liberals for the Conservatives and tariff reform if they felt that their interests were ignored in favour of a search for working-class votes and expensive schemes of tax-funded welfare.

There were electoral and fiscal reasons for relieving certain middle-class taxpayers in order to secure their adherence to a higher general level of extraction. It was also clear from evidence produced in the debate over Irish home rule and the financial contribution of Ireland to the union

[5] PRO, T168/96, 'Differentiation and graduation in the income tax and estate duty, and some comparisons with foreign and colonial systems', B. Mallet, Dec. 1905; PP 1905 LIII, *Return showing which of the colonies have established systems of graduated income tax levied at different rates on earned and unearned incomes, or both, with particulars in each case of the rate of tax and the system of assessment and collection*, pp. 185–281, and *Further return*, pp. 283–353; PP 1905 LXXXV, *Reports from His Majesty's representatives abroad respecting graduated income taxes in foreign states*, 'Introductory report', B. Mallet, July 1905, p. 40.
[6] PRO, T172/22, R. McKenna to chancellor, 'Income tax committee', 17 Dec. 1907.
* Reginald McKenna (1863–1943) was born in London, the son of a civil servant. He was educated at Trinity Hall, Cambridge, and was called to the bar in 1887. He was a Liberal MP from 1895 to 1918, serving as financial secretary to the Treasury 1905–7, president of the Board of Education 1907–8, first lord of the Admiralty 1908–11, home secretary 1911–15 and chancellor of the Exchequer 1915–16. He refused the chancellorship in 1922, but was later willing to accept if he could be found a seat in the City of London. From 1917 he was a director, and from 1919 to 1943, chairman of the Midland Bank. (*DNB, 1941–50*, ed. Legg and Williams, pp. 551–5.)

that the poor were taxed heavily in relation to their income. Leo Chiozza Money estimated that in 1904, 800,000 taxpayers had incomes of £160 to £700; a further 235,000 had incomes of £700 to £5,000, and only 15,000 above £5,000. However, these largest incomes amounted to £240m, compared with £250m and £340m. According to Chiozza Money, the burden of all taxes (direct and indirect) was equivalent to 18.5d in the £ (7.7 per cent) on incomes of £160 to £700, and reached a peak of 21.4d (8.9 per cent) on incomes of £700 to £5,000 before falling back to 18.9d (7.9 per cent) on incomes above £5,000. The rate for those *below* the income tax threshold was 14.9d in the £ (6.2 per cent). In his view, 'the question of ability to pay is practically disregarded by our present taxation', with the great mass of the people paying almost the same rate as the very rich. The solution was to raise additional revenue from the income tax without affecting the most numerous class of taxpayers, by imposing a super-tax on incomes above £5,000.[7] As one official remarked, with touching faith in the willingness of the rich to pay rather than to evade tax:

It is the existence of so much income in the shape of incomes far above the average level that makes the incidence of a uniform rate of tax inequitable, and calls for redress by means of a supertax... The objections to supertax are mainly based upon the assumption that the people subject to the tax will regard it as unjust, and will do all in their power to evade it. This idea does not appear to take sufficiently into account the disposition of an Englishman to respect the law because it is the law. It also ignores the fact that the supertax is imposed as a measure of justice. The persons subject to it would be all people of educated intelligence, fully qualified to appreciate the reasons which make it equitable that they shall contribute to the Income Tax in a higher proportion than those who are less fortunate... There seems little reason to suppose that people of position and reputation will incur the risks of evasion in order to escape a burden which they cannot deny to be justly their due.[8]

The existing income tax therefore lacked flexibility as a means of raising revenue, which would be improved by graduation.

The argument of Primrose that graduation would hit savings and accumulation, making capital dearer and so shifting the distribution of income against labour, was also dismissed by a new generation at the Treasury. People with moderate incomes in the middle class, who did not pay supertax, could be relieved of taxation and would therefore be able to save more than previously. Their savings would compensate for any reduction of

7 PRO, CAB37/87/28, 'Notes on the incidence of taxation in the UK', L. G. Chiozza Money, Mar. 1907; see also Chiozza Money, *Riches and Poverty*. Figures provided by the Inland Revenue are in PRO, CAB37/87/24, 'Income tax', H. W. Primrose, 1 Mar. 1907.
8 PRO, CAB37/87/22, 'Supertax', 26 Feb. 1907.

accumulation by the wealthy. A more radical argument was put forward by Chiozza Money, that the state could use tax revenue to raise capital for productive industry which was otherwise 'wasted' in 'luxurious and harmful expenditure' or sent overseas.[9]

The administration difficulties were minimised by the new generation of officials. Instead of stressing to the problems of getting tax returns from the rich, they pointed out that most people affected by a surtax already made a return under schedule D – and indeed that returns should become compulsory for *all* taxpayers to reduce evasion and avoidance. The practical difficulties stressed by Milner and Primose were now rejected as 'trivial'. Collection at source already existed alongside individual assessments of all incomes up to £700 for abatements. As a result, perhaps 750,000 taxpayers out of a million already declared their total income. It was simple to check returns, for example by comparing dividend income and lists of shareholders in public companies. The argument was turned around, from opposing a return of total income on the grounds that taxpayers would be reluctant to provide information to increase their liability, to a realisation that most of the necessary information was already supplied by taxpayers.[10] A cynical interpretation would be that Milner and Primrose had simply used administrative pettifogging to block changes they found ideologically repellant. But this would be to miss two other explanations. First, there was a genuine concern for compliance amongst revenue officials, which was used after the First World War against higher *indirect* taxes. Second, the long experience and continuity of officials in the British civil service (by comparison with the short-term political appointments found in the United States) created a massive dead-weight of authority and tradition which was difficult to shift. The corollary was that once it *did* shift, the new system was readily incorporated into the traditions of the civil service.

Above all, evidence on the experience in foreign countries and the empire indicated that graduation and differentiation were feasible. Graduation took three forms: in many German states, bands of income paid the same fixed sum of tax; in Switzerland, bands of income paid a percentage rate; and in Scandinavia and the Netherlands, it was linked with abatements. Only Britain relied entirely on abatements and exemptions. Differentiation was also found in most tax systems, by one of four methods.

---

[9] For Primrose, see above, pp. 325–6; the criticism of his approach is in PRO, T168/96, comment on H. W. Primrose, 'Graduation of income tax, practicability thereof', 22 June 1903; and on Chiozza Money, PP 1906 IX, *Report from the Select Committee on Income Tax*, appendix 14, 'Paper handed in by L. G. Chiozza Money', p. 965.

[10] PRO, T168/96, 'Note on income tax reform', 5 June 1906; PP 1906 IX, *Report from the Select Committee on Income Tax*, p. 662 and appendix 14, 'Paper handed in by L. G. Chiozza Money', pp. 966–7.

One was a combination of an income tax and a tax on capital or property, such as the supplementary *Erganzungssteuer* in Prussia. The second was distinct taxes on earned and unearned income, as in Bavaria and the Netherlands. The third, adopted in Italy and Spain, was to vary the rate on income from different sources, within a single income tax. The fourth system was separate, compensatory, taxes, either instead of differentiation in the income tax (as the death duties in Britain), or in addition to it, as in Italy, Spain and the Netherlands. Comparison with other countries led to a more pragmatic attitude by a new generation of officials. As they realised, graduation and differentiation were already accepted in the British fiscal system to a greater extent than in other countries; it was simply that they were more disguised in the form of death duties and abatements.[11] Previously, officials and politicians had drawn the conclusion that differentiation was redundant; now, the argument was turned around, to claim that the principle had been accepted so that differentiation of the income tax was a sign of continuity rather than rupture.

Acceptance of graduation and differentiation could be portrayed as an innocuous attempt to correct extreme disparities and an uneven distribution of taxation on rich and poor rather than as a major breach of principle. Such an approach could be presented as a measure of social justice without destroying private capital, and even preserving it against radical challenge. Graduation could be portrayed as a prudent measure, and fears that progression would lead to confiscation or appropriation were taken much less seriously than in France, where progressive taxation was synonymous with extreme socialism.[12] In Britain, the situation was somewhat different. The income tax was initially associated with militarism rather than with socialism, until Gladstone successfully transformed it into the prop of free trade and retrenchment. It was relatively easy to introduce an element of graduation into the income tax without causing a political crisis, by justifying it as a measure of social justice and prudence rather than an attack on property. After all, Adam Smith's first maxim of taxation laid down that people should contribute to government 'as nearly as possible in proportion to their respective abilities' and 'the revenue they enjoy'. It was relatively easy to justify graduation by the huge intellectual authority of Smith, through a shift in the reading of his maxim to suggest that ability increased with the size of income,

[11] PRO, T168/96, 'Differentiation and graduation in the income tax and estate duty, and some comparisons with foreign and colonial systems' (also in PP 1906 IX, *Report from the Select Committee on Income Tax*, appendix 1, pp. 917–25; PP 1905 LXXXV, *Reports from His Majesty's representatives abroad respecting graduated income taxes in foreign states*, 'Introductory report', B. Mallet, July 1905, pp. 37–51.
[12] Gross, 'Progressive taxation and social justice', 80–1, 121–3.

and that enjoyment was determined by the marginal value of each additional £ of income. This new reading of Smith was in accord with the writing of leading economists such as Marshall, Edgeworth and Pigou. Although few people read (or understood) this more recondite, technical, economics, the professional interpretation of the welfare implications of taxation was part of the wider shift in political culture. The work of economists provided intellectual sanction, putting older interpretations of equity and ability on the defensive, reflecting the more general shift in political discourse towards the necessity of creating an efficient and competitive economy, and a more integrated society, whether to sustain a strong imperial race or to improve the welfare of the poor.

Liberal imperialists and new Liberals

The change in fiscal policy made electoral sense for the Liberal party. The existing scale of degression meant that the income tax fell most heavily on modest middle-class incomes who were likely to defect from the Liberal party to the Conservatives. What was needed was a fiscal system which could relieve them of taxation, and appeal to a rhetoric of active enterprise against parasitical plutocrats – particularly if a connection could also be made to working-class concerns. Here was an explanation of the attack upon land as a parasitical fraction of capital which appealed to the radical wing of the Liberal party. This was electorally attractive to many in the Edwardian Liberal party at a time when landowners had already shifted to the Conservatives. It offered a means of uniting rural attacks upon alien landowners in Ireland, Wales and Scotland with urban concerns for the reform of local taxation and a resolution to the housing problem. The blame for urban problems could be laid at the door of rapacious landowners charging a high price for sites, without contributing to the costs of government whose spending had increased land values.[13] Secondly, it offered an alternative to the Conservative electoral strategy of tariff reform. The intention of Chamberlain was that duties on imports and imperial preference would create a stable domestic and imperial market for British goods, which would lead to steady employment and higher wages, so solving the problems of poverty. At the same time, import duties would produce revenue for social reform (especially old age pensions), without raising the price of food which would still be available from the empire on preferential terms. It was a policy designed to improve national production by appealing to urban producers drawn

---

[13] For the land question, see Offer, *Property and Politics*; for a comment on Lloyd George and land, see Gilbert, 'David Lloyd George: land, the budget and social reform'.

6 'Tax land *not* food': poster reprinted from the *Morning Star* news-paper: the Liberal government wished to tax land rather than food; the House of Lords attempted to block the 'people's budget' of 1909

from both the working class and industrialists.[14] Of course, the Liberals could mount an attack on Chamberlain for breaching the policies of free trade which had secured British prosperity for the previous half century, and interpret his policy as an onslaught on the 'free breakfast table' designed, whatever he claimed, to benefit the landed class. But it was also necessary to develop a positive policy. One solution was Liberal imperialism, which was associated with Rosebery and Haldane.[15] Another was new Liberalism, whose main proponents were L. T. Hobhouse,[*] J. A. Hobson[†] and L. G. Chiozza Money.[16]

Both groups were in agreement over the need to maintain free trade and to introduce social reform, for reasons which were to an extent contradictory. The aim of the 'Limps' was to maintain a strong empire based upon an efficient domestic economy and fit imperial race, which required a free trade solution to the problems of unemployment and poverty. From 1898, they were increasingly concerned about government finance with

---

[14] For one, controversial, view of the politics of Chamberlain's proposal, see E. H. H. Green, *The Crisis of Conservatism: The Politics, Economics and Ideology of the British Conservative Party, 1880–1914* (London, 1995), and E. H. H. Green, 'Radical conservatism: the electoral genesis of tariff reform', *Historical Journal* 28 (1985), 667–92.

[15] The classic account of Liberal imperialism is Matthew, *Liberal Imperialists*; see also B. Semmel, *Imperialism and Social Reform: English Social-Imperial Thought, 1895–1914* (London, 1960).

[16] On new Liberalism see P. F. Clarke, *Liberals and Social Democrats* (Cambridge, 1978), and M. Freeden, *The New Liberalism: An Ideology of Social Reform* (Oxford, 1978).

[*] Leonard Trelawny Hobhouse (1864–1929) was a descendant of John Cam Hobhouse; he was educated at Corpus Christi College, Oxford, where he was tutor in 1890 and fellow in 1894. He was on the staff of the *Manchester Guardian* from 1897 to 1902, and was appointed professor of sociology at the LSE in 1907. His main publications were *The Labour Movement* (1893), *The Theory of Knowledge* (1896), *The Mind in Evolution* (1901), *Morals in Evolution* (1906) and *The Metaphysical Theory of the State* (1918). (*DNB, 1922–30*, ed. Weaver, pp. 420–1.)

[†] John Atkinson Hobson (1858–1940) was born in Derby, the son of a newspaper proprietor. He was educated at Derby School and Lincoln College, Oxford; on graduating, he taught classics until 1887 and then worked as a university extension lecturer until 1897. He developed his idea of under-consumption (with A. F. Mummery) in *The Physiology of Industry* (1889), arguing for graduated taxation. He was influenced by Ruskin, and wrote a study of him in 1898, as well as a biography of Cobden. He wished to nationalise monopolies and standardised industries, and retain individual enterprise where taste and skill were important to expressing the personality of the consumer and the producer. He believed that under-consumption led to over-saving and hence a flight of capital in search of imperialism; free trade would only lead to peace on condition that income was redistributed at home. He set these views out in *The Evolution of Modern Capitalism: A Study of Machine Production* (1894), *Imperialism: A Study* (1902), *The Economics of Distribution* (1900) and *The Industrial System: An Inquiry into Earned and Unearned Income* (1909). He was involved with L. T. Hobhouse and other 'new Liberals' in *The Nation*; he opposed the Boer war; and helped form the Union of Democratic Control in the First World War. During and after the war, he published *Democracy after the War* (1917), *Taxation in the New State* (1919) and *The Economics of Unemployment* (1922). (*DNB, 1931–40*, ed. Legg, pp. 435–6.)

the rise in government expenditure under the Tories. But they did not think that retrenchment was the answer, for the increase in expenditure was the result of the development of an 'organic state'. As Haldane put it, 'we are spending more because we have a larger house, a larger family, a higher way of living, new necessities which have come from an improved condition of things'.[17] Although the 'Limps' hoped to hold down expenditure on old age pensions which did nothing to help 'efficiency', they accepted that social spending would increase and that existing sources of revenue were inadequate. They came to the view that Gladstonian finance was designed for a different conception of government – and having rejected tariffs as a source of revenue, direct taxes were the only solution. Haldane argued at the time of the 1902 budget that Britain had not 'exhausted the resources of civilisation in respect of income tax...I do not think we have got to the limit of direct taxation even yet.' The Limps therefore moved towards differentiation and graduation in the income tax, less as a device for redistribution and social reform than as a means of securing revenue for expenditure on efficiency.[18]

The new Liberals supported graduation of the income tax on somewhat different grounds. In their view, imperialism was the problem and social reform the cure.[19] Hobson and Chiozza Money argued that investment in imperialism was wasteful and sustained militarism in the interests of a small class of financiers and aristocrats. Free trade in itself did not lead to peace as Cobden believed, for the trade system might arise from a maldistribution of income which removed the incentive for domestic investment, and created low-waged employment in services and basic export commodities. The high levels of income of the rich meant that they 'wasted' their money on luxury imports and on the employment of servants, creating a dependent, deferential, class and turning the south of England into a playground for a leisured elite. Even so, they could not spend all of their income, and the consequent 'over-saving' could not find an outlet at home, given the 'under-consumption' of the poor. The result was a flood of capital into foreign investments, so provoking imperial warfare. In other words, Cobden's dream of peace and retrenchment could only be fulfilled by redistributing income at home in order to prevent a pathological trade system. The financiers who inspired the Boer war were similar to the corrupt aristocratic elite denounced by Cobden; it was not enough to sweep away the power of the aristocrats and to leave individuals to pursue profit in a capitalist economy, in order to create

---

[17] Quoted in Matthew, *Liberal Imperialists*, p. 252, from *Parliamentary Debates*, 4th ser. 105, 21 Apr. 1902, cols. 828–9.

[18] Quoted in Matthew, *Liberal Imperialists*, p. 255, *Parliamentary Debates*, 4th ser. 106, 21 Apr. 1902, cols. 827ff; generally, see Matthew, *Liberal Imperialists*, pp. 250–7.

[19] Clarke, *Liberals and Social Democrats*, chapter 3.

harmony and prosperity. The result might simply be the emergence of a new form of corruption. Although Hobson remained a committed free trader, he did not accept that the existing trade system was natural. He wrote a biography of Cobden – and also of Ruskin, with his rejection of the simple pursuit of profit and the dangers of creating 'illth' rather than wealth. In Ruskin's view, the pursuit of profit at the expense of quality of work or enjoyment of the worker was degrading, removing a sense of pride and fulfilment. A redistribution of income would address this problem, for increased incomes for the poor would create discriminating consumers who could purchase the products of craftsmen rather than workers treated as mere cogs in the economic machine. Ruskin wished to end the separation of work and enjoyment, the processes of production and consumption, in order to create work for all valued for its own sake. He wished to combine 'honest production, just distribution, wise consumption'. Hobson accepted the force of this argument, and tried to find an answer to the social question posed by Ruskin: 'How can society consciously order the lives of its members so as to maintain the largest number of noble and happy human beings?' Where Hobson differed was in his solution, for he did not follow Ruskin's own distinctive solutions of creating guilds to replace capitalist employers. Rather, he stressed the use of the tax system to redistribute income and wealth, in order to create a buoyant domestic economy and to cut the tap-root of imperialism. He was uniting Cobden and Ruskin, arguing for a free trade economy and the pursuit of profit whilst ensuring that the result was not imperialistic adventures and the material and spiritual immiseration of the poor.[20]

Ruskin was contemptuous of political economy. By comparison, Hobson wished to revise Ricardo's economics in pursuit of his social vision, by redefining and extending the concept of Rent which came to provide the intellectual basis of new Liberal policies. The everyday meaning of the word 'rent' is the sum paid by a tenant for the use of a house or farm. It was given a more technical meaning by Ricardo. A farmer on fertile soil paid rent to his landlord, and received a profit from the sale of grain. When the population increased and demand for food rose, less fertile land was taken into cultivation until the point at which no profit

[20] On the need to redistribute income and wealth at home to create a strong domestic market, see J. A. Hobson, *Imperialism: A Study* (London, 1902; 2nd edn 1905); and Chiozza Money, *Riches and Poverty*. For Hobson's biographies, see *John Ruskin: Social Reformer* (London, 1898), quotations from pp. 155, 310, and *Richard Cobden: International Man* (London, 1918), and an interesting discussion by H. C. G. Matthew, 'Hobson, Ruskin and Cobden', in M. Freeden (ed.), *Reappraising J. A. Hobson: Humanism and Welfare* (London, 1990), pp. 11–30. After the war, Hobson worked out these ideas in the ILP's programme, *The Living Wage*: see N. Thompson, 'Hobson and the Fabians: two roads to socialism in the 1920s', *History of Political Economy* 26 (1994), 203–20.

was possible. As prices rose, the farmer on the fertile soil was able to make a higher profit – in other words, his profit was higher than normal and he received a Rent. Ricardo argued that the landowner would be able to increase the charge for the use of the land, so that the Rent would be expropriated by the landlord rather than the tenant; over time, the share of income taken by land would rise at the expense of other forms of profit, and the economy would reach a 'stationary state'. Ricardian Rent initially applied to land and it formed the basis of the continued radical attack on aristocratic landowners up to the First World War, especially as popularised by Henry George. On this view, landowners had a monopoly and were able to charge higher prices as a result of the enterprise and initiative of other members of society who wished to build houses or factories. However, the notion of Rent could be extended to other situations. As a result of superior business skills, access to a patent or high-grade mineral resources, or a monopoly in the provision of gas to a town, a business might secure a profit or Rent greater than the normal run of firms. In Ricardian economics, Rent was ethically neutral. It would usually be short term, until other firms entered the market, or the Rent-seeking behaviour of monopolies could be controlled by government regulation or public ownership. Hobson gave the notion of Rent a more critical edge, with a moral dimension; he took the radical attack on land and extended it to Rent in general as 'unearned' and available to the community.

Hobson took a different approach from Marx, who assumed that value was created by labour and that capitalists expropriated the surplus value in excess of the cost of subsistence. In Marxist economics, the distribution of surplus value formed the basis of conflict between classes which would be resolved by revolutionary destruction of the capitalist order. By contrast, Hobson assumed that capitalism could be reformed by political action: he was, to use Peter Clarke's terminology, a 'moral reformer' who believed that peaceful change was possible through the moral initiative of individuals. At the basis of Hobson's theory of Rent was the concept of under-consumption and his theory of surplus value. Hobson divided the value of land, capital and labour into 'subsistence payments' – the return needed to bring them into use – and the 'gratuitous surplus' of socially created earnings which was 'not necessary to maintain or promote socially serviceable processes of production or consumption'. Hobson argued that industrial reality differed from economists' assumptions of free competition, for in every process one or other of the factors of production was scarce as a result of natural limits or social constraints; it could therefore extort a surplus in excess of the normal price at which land, labour or capital would otherwise be available. Hobson denied that the high return was beneficial in attracting resources to achieve the highest return and hence to stimulate growth. Rather, he believed that any surplus was 'waste' which led to inefficiency. A monopoly of education, for example, led to scarcity payments for certain forms of mental labour, resulting in a flooding of other labour markets and a fall in wages which removed any stimulus for improved efficiency. Thus lawyers controlled access to training and obtained high incomes; other people were forced into clerical work where salaries were consequently depressed. Similarly, an industrial monopoly meant that capital invested there achieved a higher return than the normal level needed to secure funds. The high return was not 'socially serviceable in the sense of stimulating increased production'. In other words, much of the surplus above the necessary current costs of production 'goes in overpayments which check, instead of stimulating, efficiency and progress, while other parties of the system, especially the lower grades of labour, are deprived of the share needed to evoke, educate and support the growing efficiency requisite for participation in the more rapid march of modern industry'. These Rents, 'forced gains' or 'excessive payments' were unearned and the whole of the surplus was a legitimate source of public revenue, to be removed by public ownership of industry or by taxation. Accordingly, 'subsistence payments' should be tax free, and all taxation should fall on the 'gratuitous' or 'unproductive' surplus.[21]

How could the unproductive surplus be reached? Hobson admitted the difficulties of devising a tax system to measure the surplus and he simplified by assuming that the unproductive surplus varied with the *size* of income, and could therefore be reached by graduated income and inheritance taxes:

No one will dispute the fact that an increasing proportion of high incomes can be taken by taxation, without impairing the incentives of the owners of the land, capital or ability, from which these incomes are derived, from applying them now to production. When it is clearly and generally recognised that this is equivalent to an admission that these elements of income, thus taken in taxation, are not earned by their recipients, but are attributable to social causes of scarcity value, it will be understood that no injurious burden or sacrifice is imposed, no confiscatory policy pursued, but that the state is simply seeking to collect a portion of the social income.

[21] For Hobson's economics, see Clarke, *Liberals and Social Democrats*, especially pp. 47–53, 125–7, his views are set out in J. A. Hobson, *The Industrial System: An Inquiry into Earned and Unearned Income* (London, 1909), especially chapters 4 and 14; J. A. Hobson, *The Science of Wealth* (London, 1911), especially chapters 5 and 6; and J. A. Hobson, *Taxation in the New State* (London, 1919), pp. 10, 103; see also J. A. Hobson, *The Evolution of Modern Capitalism: A Study of Machine Production* (London, 1894); J. A. Hobson, *The Problem of the Unemployed: An Enquiry and An Economic Policy* (London, 1896); J. A. Hobson, *The Economics of Distribution* (London, 1900).

However, the element of surplus varied between incomes of the same size – for example, depending on the size of the family – and Hobson suggested that the unproductive surplus might also be reached by taxing expenditure on luxuries such as motor cars or jewellery. By contrast, protective duties reduced the aggregate wealth of the world and the share taken in wages, and so enhanced the surplus. Progressive taxation of savings and unearned income by death duties, a graduated income tax and taxation of land values would reduce savings, increase incomes and consumption and create a prosperous domestic economy, purged of poverty and the drive for imperial adventures. By this means, Hobson was combining Cobden's belief in free trade and international peace with Ruskin's attack on political economy for worshipping wealth at the cost of life. Trade would lead to peace – on condition it emerged from a strong domestic economy. The distribution of income and wealth at home should allow discerning consumers to purchase goods produced by workers able to express their identity and creativity.[22]

The economics of Hobson remained contentious, and he was dismissed by professional economists as an 'economic heretic' until J. M. Keynes paid him a tribute in the *General Theory*.[23] However, the underlying assumptions of Hobson were readily incorporated into Liberalism by another route, the Idealist philosophy of Hobhouse.[24] In Hobhouse's words, 'the central point of Liberal economics ... is the question of social service and reward'. As he put it,

the general problem in economics is not to destroy property, but to restore the social conception of property to its right place under conditions suitable to modern needs ... It is to be done by distinguishing the social from the individual factors in wealth, by bringing the elements of social wealth into the public coffers, and by holding it at the disposal of society to administer to the prime needs of its members.

Such an approach rested on the assumption that all property was social, and that ownership was conferred and protected by the 'organized force' of society. Value and production contained a large social element, for

---

[22] Hobson, *Industrial System*, pp. 131, 134, 136, 232, 235.

[23] Hobson called his autobiography *Confessions of an Economic Heretic* (London, 1938); on Hobson and Keynes, see Clarke, *Liberals and Social Democrats*, pp. 226–34, 271–3. Their approaches were in reality different: Hobson stressed the dangers of over-saving and the economic benefits of spending'; Keynes gave more weight to investment.

[24] On the importance of Idealism, and the differences between the approaches of the Bosanquets and Hobhouse, see Harris, 'Political thought and the welfare state', and S. Collini, 'Hobhouse, Bosanquet and the state: philosophical Idealism and political argument in England, 1880–1918', *Past and Present* 72 (1976), 86–111.

an individual could do very little by his unaided efforts in a modern industrial economy. Hobhouse wished to stimulate individual efforts, to extend their scope by removing impediments to self-help and initiative. The role of the state was to 'secure the conditions upon which mind and character may develop themselves', allowing 'its citizens to win by their own efforts all that is necessary to a full civic efficiency. It is not for the State to feed, house, or clothe them. It is for the State to take care that the economic conditions are such that the normal man . . . can by useful labour feed, house and clothe himself and his family.' In other words, self-sufficiency and responsibility were impossible unless individuals had a living wage; the answer to poverty was not to create dependence on the state, with a loss of autonomy, but to build character through personal responsibility.

The solution was to transfer resources from the rich who were appropriating income and wealth created by society:

an individualism which ignores the social factor in wealth will deplete the natural resources, deprive the community of its joint share in the fruits of industry and so result in a one-sided and inequitable distribution of wealth. Economic justice is to render what is due not only to each individual but to each function, social or personal, that is engaged in the performance of useful service, and this due is measured by the amount necessary to stimulate and maintain the efficient exercise of that useful function. This equation between function and sustenance is the true meaning of economic equality.

Hobhouse was here expressing the same sentiment as Hobson, in a different ethical language. His problem was how to identify and extract social value or surplus for the public use, how to ensure that everyone received the remuneration needed to supply their best efforts and to maintain efficiency. Hobhouse was anxious not to take violent action which would threaten initiative and originality, or diminish capital; he advocated a 'gentle and slow-moving policy of economic reorganization' informed by experience, in pursuit of 'economic justice as the maintenance of social function':

The true function of taxation is to secure to society the element in wealth that is of social origin, or, more broadly, all that does not owe its origin to the efforts of living individuals. When taxation, based on these principles, is utilized to secure healthy conditions of existence to the mass of the people it is clear that this is no case of robbing Peter to pay Paul. Peter is not robbed. Apart from the tax it is he who would be robbing the State. A tax which enables the State to secure a certain share of social value is not something deducted from that which the taxpayer has an unlimited right to call his own, but rather a repayment of something which was all along due to society.

This revenue could then be used for the common good, such as investment in public health, and in ensuring that everyone received sufficient income to stimulate their effort and preserve their efficiency – and no more. Hobhouse was far from advocating socialism; he wished to preserve and extend personal initiative, and to combine social and individual factors by defining the rights of individuals in terms of the common good. By these means, Hobhouse legitimated the place of the state in arranging distributive justice in a way far removed from Gladstone's definition of neutrality and balance. The role of the state was ethical, to establish the ideal world of positive liberty and freedom for all its members.[25]

'Limps' and new Liberals took somewhat different approaches to imperialism, but they were agreed on the need to defend free trade from Chamberlain's protectionism and to invest in the British people. It was therefore possible for them to work together in many cases. An ardent free trader and imperialist such as Winston Churchill could seize upon many of the terms and concepts of the new Liberals. It meant that Asquith, who was closely linked with the 'Limps', introduced differentiation as chancellor in 1907, and then as prime minister accepted graduation. Of course, Liberal politicians were also concerned with electoral realities: how to prevent the defection of working-class voters to Labour, how to meet the demands of Labour for expensive schemes of social reform without alienating middle-class voters? Chamberlain's campaign for tariff reform aimed to appeal to working-class interests by offering employment in a stable, protected, market with welfare benefits to be paid from tariff revenues. The Liberals needed to counter his proposals, with the danger that increasing the rate of income tax to finance reform would alienate middle-class votes – and also to contain Labour demands for a right to work and tax-funded welfare. One solution was to opt instead for contributory insurance schemes which placed the cost upon employees and employers rather than the taxpayer, which meant that workers were paying for their own social welfare rather than receiving a transfer payment from the rich and from socially created wealth.[26] Liberal fiscal policy therefore had to

[25] The quotations are from L. T. Hobhouse, *Liberalism* (London, 1911), pp. 158–9, 188–212; for a discussion of Hobhouse's thought, see Collini, *Liberalism and Sociology* especially pp. 115–20, 123–37; and for his particular view of Idealism, Collini, 'Hobhouse, Bosanquet and the state'.

[26] On the Liberal need to find an alternative to Labour's redistributive policies and a claim for a right to work, see E. P. Hennock, *British Social Reform and German Precedents: The Case of Social Insurance, 1880–1914* (Oxford, 1987), pp. 206–9; for Treasury hostility to non-contributory pensions, see J. Macnicol, *The Politics of Retirement in Britain, 1878–1948* (Cambridge, 1998), p. 163.

find an alternative to the programme of tariff reform which would also satisfy the demands of Labour, without causing such alarm to middle-class voters that they would seek refuge with Chamberlain as the lesser of two evils. The pressures on the Liberal government cannot be fully appreciated without considering the development of the Labour party's fiscal ideology.

Rent and socially created wealth: Labour's fiscal policy

Labour thinking had many similarities with new Liberalism and its concern for socially created wealth. Indeed, many of the advocates of new Liberalism joined the Labour party after the war. However, there were tensions – never entirely resolved – over the use of taxation as a means of liberating character and individualism (as in Hobson and Hobhouse) and the desire to replace private property. Above all, Sidney Webb produced his own version of the theory of Rent at about the same time as Hobson, with different implications for policy and the nature of society.

Webb agreed with Hobson in rejecting the Marxist theory of labour value; unlike Hobson, he accepted that value was determined by neo-classical marginal utility theory through the interplay of demand and supply curves. The demand schedule was the utility to the consumer of the final, marginal, purchase; the supply schedule was the cost to the producer of the final, marginal, item; price was created by the operation of the market in allocating resources to maximise everyone's utility or satisfaction. Such an approach assumed a basic harmony of interests, rather than the inherent conflicts of Marxism. Where Webb and the Fabians departed from neo-classical economists was in arguing for the existence of a large element of socially created value which had nothing to do with merit or ability. Webb extended Ricardo's definition of Rent to cover interest, wages, salaries and profits as well as land, arguing that all were determined in the same way, and that all who drew such incomes were *rentiers*. The normal economic wage was derived by the most unskilled worker at the margin of cultivation with minimal capital; anything above this was Rent. Although the higher incomes of some workers might be explained in part by ability, any variation in the rate of return to *capital* was the result of 'opportunity' or chance, and was therefore an 'unearned' income received without commensurate work. In capitalist societies, many incomes were unethical and allowed consumption of goods and services without producing an equivalent amount for the community. Scarce ability was also socially created, so that solicitors received a higher income because of restrictions in the number of places for the children of the

PUNCH, OR THE LONDON CHARIVARI.—October 27, 1909.

SOCIALISM

OLD LIBERALISM

Bernard Partridge

FORCED FELLOWSHIP.

Suspicious-Looking Party. "ANY OBJECTION TO MY COMPANY, GUV'NOR? I'M AGOIN' YOUR
WAY"—(aside) "AND FURTHER."

7 'Forced fellowship', *Punch* 27 October 1909: old Liberalism forms
an uneasy relationship with socialism

poor at grammar schools or university.[27] The Webbs' definition of Rent provided 'an ethical touchstone for evaluating the wealth and income of every man'. It was based upon 'a substitution of the motive of public service for the motive of self-enrichment...which will make "living by owning" as shameful as the pauperism of the wastrel'. On the one side, there was the socially undesirable, parasitic, class made up of the 'functionless rich – of persons who deliberately live by owning instead of by working, and whose futile occupations, often licentious pleasures and inherently insolent manners, undermine the intellectual and moral standards of the community'. These people had accepted the immoral and 'morbid obsession' which had dominated western Europe for the past 300 years, that 'man in society is and should be inspired, in the exercise of his function, by the passion for riches'.[28] On the other side were people who made a contribution to society, to whom Rents should be reallocated. Ethically unearned income and wealth should be taken by the government, as the collective property of the English nation rather than individuals.

The Webbs' approach had clear similarities with Hobson's in its definition of socially created wealth. The greater difference was in the means by which the unearned increment or unethical Rent should be captured by the community, and the nature of society and individual responsibility.

---

[27] S. Webb, 'The rate of interest and the laws of distribution', *Quarterly Journal of Economics* 2 (1887–8), 200, 208, and S. Webb, 'The rate of interest', *Quarterly Journal of Economics* 2 (1887–8), 472. Webb was responding to F. A. Walker, 'The source of business profits', *Quarterly Journal of Economics* 1 (1886–7), 265–88, who argued that the surplus of the higher grade of employer, after paying wages, materials and machinery, was what he produced over and above the lowest grade of employer with equal amounts of labour and capital. In other words, it was his own creation, produced by his business ability which raised him above the employer of the no-profit class. Profits fell into two elements: the normal interest on capital and rent of ability to produce more from a fixed amount of capital. Rent was an ethically neutral term for a justified surplus. It was in the interests of the community and wage-earners that industry should be restricted to these men, who would run firms for profits which would benefit rather than harm the workers. Walker was seeking to explain why profits, *pace* Ricardo and Mill, did not decline. See also Thompson, 'Hobson and the Fabians', 203–20. For the development of Fabian notions of Rent, see for example Fabian Society, *Capital and Land* (Fabian Tract 7, London, 1888); Fabian Society, *English Progress towards Social Democracy* (Fabian Tract 15, London, 1890); Fabian Society, *The Unearned Increment* (Fabian Tract 30, London, 1891); Fabian Society, *The Difficulties of Individualism* (Fabian Tract 69, London, 1896); Fabian Society, *Socialism and Superior Brains* (Fabian Tract 146, London, 1909); and S. and B. Webb, *Problems of Modern Industry* (London, 1898), p. 472.

[28] D. M. Ricci, 'Fabian socialism: a theory of rent as exploitation', *Journal of British Studies* 9 (1969–70), 105–21; also W. Wolfe, *From Radicalism to Socialism: Men and Ideas in the Formation of Fabian Socialist Doctrine, 1881–89* (New Haven, 1975); S. and B. Webb, *A Constitution for the Socialist Commonwealth of Great Britain* (London, 1920), pp. XII, 80, 350–1.

Both Hobson and the Webbs were reformers rather than revolutionaries, accepting that the state could acquire socially created value through a gradual and peaceable process on behalf of the community which had created it and to whom it properly belonged. But Hobson and Hobhouse diverged from the Webbs, for they were 'moral reformers', stressing the role of the state in removing impediments to individual character. By contrast, the Webbs and the Fabians were 'mechanical reformers': change came from experts who reformed the machinery of society, rather than from the spontaneous actions of the people. Their approach differed from the new Liberals who accepted much of the critique of socially created wealth, but also stressed the need for a transformation of *character*. By contrast, the Webbs argued that the citizen owed a duty to the state to remain fit and healthy, and could be trained and directed by the state. The contrast is most explicit in the case of labour exchanges. To William Beveridge and Churchill, the exchanges were simply means of providing information, to assist workers in finding a position; to the Webbs, they should be compulsory, forming part of an organised labour market. The Webbs stressed the role of the state and collective action above individual moral responsibility. In their view, Rent had nothing to do with personal morality or responsibility, and arose from the economic structure; character merely responded to changes in the social structure created by the state. Neither did the Webbs seek the creation of enjoyable and creative production, to cater for discriminating consumers. Unlike Hobson (and Ruskin), they stressed the efficiency of large-scale production, and the need to replace the waste of consumer choice. The growth of large units of production in private hands was simply a step towards large-scale production in the hands of the state.[29]

[29] The terminology is that of Clarke, *Liberals and Social Democrats*, p. 5: 'mechanical reform' is what Hobhouse called 'official socialism', based on a contempt for liberty arising from a confusion of liberty and competition, and with a measure of contempt for humanity 'as in the mass a helpless and feeble race, which it is its duty to treat kindly. True kindness, of course, must be combined with firmness, and the life of the average man must be organized for his own good . . . It is a scheme of the organization of life by the superior person, who will decide for each man how he should work, how he should live, and indeed, with the aid of the Eugenist, whether he should live at all or whether he has any business to be born' (Hobhouse, *Liberalism*, pp. 169–71). See also for a study of the main protagonists in the Royal Commission on the poor laws with their different assumptions about the ability of character to rise above circumstances, A. M. McBriar, *An Edwardian Mixed Doubles: The Bosanquets versus the Webbs: A Study in British Social Policy, 1890–1929* (Oxford, 1987); for differences over labour exchanges, see B. B. Gilbert, 'Winston Churchill versus the Webbs: the origins of British unemployment insurance', *American Historical Review* 71 (1966), 846–62; and for the difference between the Webbs and Hobson over the ILP's *Living Wage* in the 1920s, see Thompson, 'Hobson and the Fabians'. On the need for government action to force men to be moral, see Ricci, 'Fabian socialism', 119.

Many members of the Labour party did not go so far as the Webbs, and attached importance to character, individual fulfilment and participation. There was common ground between 'mechanical' and 'moral' reformers over the need to acquire unearned or socially created wealth for the community, and to bring remuneration into line with service. Where they differed was in the extent to which reform was compatible with private ownership: should the taxes be used to create distributive justice within a free market; or were they to be used to *replace* the free market and capitalism by a new social order? The result was an unresolved ambiguity within the Labour party. These issues were debated within the Labour Representation Committee (LRC) and Labour party from 1900, which brought together a mixture of trade unionists in pursuit of their legal rights and free bargaining, with members of the Independent Labour Party (ILP) and Social Democratic Federation (SDF). The more abstract ideas of Hobson and Webb entered political culture through these debates, forming a strong set of moral assumptions which were to inform Labour thinking to the Second World War and beyond.

At the LRC's first annual conference in 1901, an ILP motion was accepted as a test for all candidates: privately owned capital had an inevitable tendency to monopoly, and private control was 'disastrous to the welfare of the consuming public, inimical to the social and political freedom of the people, and especially injurious to the industrial liberty and economic condition of the workers'. The solution proposed by the ILP was to transfer private monopolies to public control in 'an Industrial Commonwealth founded upon the common ownership and control of land and capital and the substitution of co-operative production for use in place of the present method of competitive production for profit'. The Marxist SDF added a further condition, that candidates should recognise 'class war as the basis of working-class political action'. Although these resolutions were passed by conference, trade union representatives were not entirely convinced and were more inclined to see the LRC and Labour party as a means of defending their bargaining position.[30] The rhetoric was dangerous, for it threatened to marginalise Labour as a special interest against the public and property; the success of the party was more likely to rest on its ability to portray itself as the guardian of the national interest against waste and exploitation.

Where trade unionists and socialists could agree was in rejecting Chamberlain's policy of tariff reform, despite his attempts to argue that workers would benefit from full employment and high wages in a

---

[30] *Report of the First Annual Conference of the Labour Representation Committee, 1901* (London, 1901), pp. 20–1.

protected market. As a motion introduced by Philip Snowden* asserted, protection would do nothing to help the unemployed or to improve wages; it would merely foster socially created wealth and 'enable the landlord classes to exact a heavier toll than ever from the labour of the nation, and encourage the growth of trusts and other forms of monopoly in private hands'.[31] As Ramsay MacDonald[†] remarked, tariff reform promised to broaden the base of taxation, but simply meant 'increasing the number of victims of unjust taxation' so that the rich could escape:

> Protection meant that the costs of industry should go up, that the cost of production should be increased, that the facilities for exchange should be hampered; and, therefore, instead of putting the burden upon the non-producers and the parasites they put the burdens of the extra cost of government upon industry, upon capital legitimately used, upon labour, upon factories, upon workshops, upon those who made things in order that others might use them.[32]

Labour therefore argued both that tariff reform would 'aggravate every social evil and inequality' – and that the 'rhetorical platitudes of free trade' did not offer a solution.[33] The meaning of free trade started to fracture in the days of its apparent triumph over tariff reform.

[31] *Report of the Fourth Annual Conference of the Labour Representation Committee, 1904* (London, 1904), p. 41; also the special conference on unemployed, 25 Jan. 1905, in *Report of the Fifth Annual Conference of the Labour Representation Committee, 1905* (London, 1905), p. 64.

[32] *The Labour Party. Ninth Annual Conference, 1909* (London, 1909), appendix II, 'The incidence of taxation', report of conference, p. 107.

[33] *Report of the Fourth Annual Conference of the Labour Representation Committee, 1904*, pp. 40–2, for speeches by Philip Snowden and Arthur Henderson.

* Philip Snowden (1864–1937) was born in the West Riding of Yorkshire, the son of a weaver; he grew up in a radical, methodist, *milieu* with strong admiration for Gladstone – attitudes which he never entirely lost. He became a pupil teacher and insurance clerk, before joining the civil service in the Excise service. An injury to his spine meant he was invalided out of the service, and he became active in the ILP, editing a socialist paper in Yorkshire and serving as chairman of the party 1903–6 and 1917–20. He was MP for Blackburn from 1906 to 1918; he opposed the war, and lost his seat in 1918. He returned to parliament in 1922, and served as chancellor of the Exchequer in the first two Labour governments, and as lord privy seal in the national government. He remained a committed free trader. (*DNB, 1931–40*, ed. Legg, pp. 822–5.)

† James Ramsay MacDonald (1866–1937) was born in Lossiemouth, the illegitimate son of a ploughman. He became a pupil teacher, moving to Bristol where he joined the SDF and then to London as a clerk. After a spell back in Scotland, he returned to London and became the private secretary to a Liberal candidate from 1888 to 1891. He continued to be involved with the SDF, but also joined the Fabians in 1886 and the ILP in 1894. His marriage to the daughter of a leading scientist and philanthropist gave him financial independence and contact with the upper middle class. He was secretary of the LRC from 1900, and treasurer from 1912 to 1924, and chairman of the ILP 1906–9. He was a Labour MP from 1906 to 1918, serving as leader of the parliamentary party from 1911. He opposed the war, and resigned as leader; he lost his seat in 1918. He returned to parliament in 1922 and became leader and first Labour prime minister in 1924 and 1929–31, before splitting the party over the formation of the national government. (*DNB, 1931–40*, ed. Legg, pp. 562–70.)

Free trade would not have reality until workers could trade with the only produce they had to sell – their labour. As J. R. Clynes* remarked in his presidential address to the Labour party conference in 1909, 'the service of every willing worker should be efficiently used', and it followed that free trade 'cannot have a literal meaning to the workman until he is really enabled to trade with the only product he has to sell – his labour. That is his only export, and the State should ensure him freedom to trade with his work instead of preserving conditions which prevent him from doing so.'[34] In the absence of measures to secure decent wages, free trade would not necessarily lead to prosperity, for it could simply mean increased competition and 'sweated' labour, a drop in wages and an inability of workers to buy what they produced.[35] In the opinion of Labour commentators, the emphasis on competition for foreign markets was misplaced and priority should be given to finding sufficient outlets for British goods at home in order to create employment. By removing the burden of parasites and the maldistribution of wealth, industry would be relieved of a dead-weight which limited its ability to compete in the capitalist world economy.[36] The greater competitiveness of foreign countries was *not* the result of protection, as Chamberlain claimed. Rather, it was the result of the costs imposed on Britain by 'landlordism' and 'the burdens which the non-producing sections impose on the industrious classes'. The state should therefore ensure freedom to work by a positive policy designed to give every worker an opportunity of earning an honest living.[37] A simple pursuit of free trade might mean competition with low wage countries and an outflow of capital; it might make consumers poor and starve producers of capital.

---

[34] *The Labour Party. Ninth Annual Conference, 1909*, p. 58; on the right to work, see J. Harris, *Unemployment and Politics: A Study in English Social Policy, 1886–1914* (Oxford, 1972), pp. 235–44; Hennock, *British Social Reform and German Precedents*, pp. 153–7.

[35] Trentmann,'Wealth versus welfare', 77–9, 82–5.

[36] D. Howell, *British Workers and the Independent Labour Party, 1888–1906* (Manchester, 1983), pp. 348–9; see Trentmann, 'Wealth versus welfare'.

[37] *Report of the Fourth Annual Conference of the Labour Representation Committee, 1904*, pp. 40–2; *Report of the Fifth Annual Conference of the Labour Representation Committee, 1905*, p. 64.

* J. R. Clynes (1869–1949) was born in Oldham, the son of an Irish grave digger. He became a cotton spinner, and in 1891 became an organiser of the Gasworkers Union. He was president of the Oldham Trades Council in 1892 and secretary from 1894 to 1912; he attended the meetings to form the ILP and LRC, and he was chairman of the LRC in 1908. He entered parliament in 1906, and served to 1945 with the exception of 1931–5. In 1917, he was private secretary to the food controller and chairman of the Consumers' Council; in 1918 he became food controller. He was leader of the party in 1921–2, until MacDonald returned. He held office as lord privy seal in the first Labour government and home secretary in the second government. He was president of his union – now the National Union of General and Municipal Workers – from 1912 to 1937. (*DNB, 1941–50*, ed. Legg and Williams, pp. 161–3.)

The mid-Victorian social contract of a 'neutral' free trade state was therefore under pressure from two directions, from neo-mercantilist industrialists and from socialists who were 'both reacting in different ways to the failure of Free Trade to respond effectively to the rise of foreign competition, unemployment and anxieties of "decline"'. Labour opposed tariff reform with its vision of an industrial mother country and agrarian colonies. But Labour's policies also set it apart from Liberal free trade. Labour stressed the development of a prosperous home economy through state action, and shared the tariff reformers' concern about the decline of Britain and the limits of trade.[38] This rhetoric could together bring industry and workers in alliance against the *rentiers* and financiers, against the burdens of mining royalties, rents and railway rates. Free trade could be redefined in order to create a prosperous, dynamic, domestic economy to the benefit of all active members of society. However, the rhetoric could also set workers against *all* property, defining industry and *rentiers* as equally exploitative. In 1909, one ILP MP adopted the labour theory of value, arguing that 'labour was the source of all wealth; and all the capital accumulated in private hands was the result of the unpaid labour of past generations of workmen and ought to be transferred to the National Exchequer'.[39] Party policy was therefore ambivalent.

The Labour party defined its policy on taxation at the annual conference in 1906. Taxation to cover the costs of social reform should be shifted away from 'the industrious classes' to 'socially created wealth such as rent and interest', in order to 'secure for the community all unearned incomes derived from what is in reality communal wealth'. So far, this followed new Liberal policies, but the ILP sponsor of the resolution went a stage further to suggest that taxation would help transfer capital and land to public ownership. A similar ambivalence appeared in January 1909 when Labour called a special conference to define tax policy more precisely. As Snowden argued,

Every question of reform was, at the bottom, a question of a more equitable and just distribution of wealth. What was meant by Social Reform, and what they who were Socialists meant by Socialism, was to secure for the wealth producers the use and enjoyment of the wealth which they produced. Our purpose, therefore, should be to see that social reforms were carried out in such a way that the people would receive the use and enjoyment of some part of that wealth which at the present time was unjustly taken from them; and . . . we had in the instrument of taxation a very potent means to that end.

[38] Trentmann, 'Wealth versus welfare', 85, 89, 97.
[39] *The Labour Party. Ninth Annual Conference, 1909*, appendix II, 'The incidence of taxation', report of conference, p. 109.

Poverty was the direct result of the 'idle rich', drawing unearned rent, interest and profit. Did this entail an attack on all private property and capitalism? Ramsay MacDonald was careful to remove any such concern, arguing that the fundamental aim of Labour taxation was to 'tax the parasite and not persons who gave service'. In his view, the problem was not riches as such – it was whether the money was earned, or acquired from the labour of others:

> We wanted to divide the non-producing parasite dependent upon society from the producer and the service giver; and we wanted to direct our attention to the pockets of the person who did nothing and had much, and direct it away from the pockets of the person who might possess something but gave much service ... [T]he Labour party stood for relieving as much as possible the financial burdens on industry.

Such an approach avoided a simple divide between workers and capital, and instead made a distinction between parasites who lived 'artificial lives' and producers, so converting the sectional interests of labour into the wider interests of the public at large. MacDonald adopted the same vocabulary as Hobhouse. However, the rhetoric of a producers' alliance against parasites was weakened by the fear that it was simply a device to destroy private ownership, so alienating producers and driving them into the arms of the Conservatives in defence of property in general. There was an unresolved tension within the party about its desire to reform or to destroy capitalism and private property.[40]

Despite these differences of emphases, the party was able to agree on four principles of taxation which provided an alternative to tariff reform and offered a means of financing social reform. First, taxation should be in proportion to ability to pay and to the amount of protection and benefit conferred on the individual by the state. Secondly, no taxation should be imposed which encroached on an individual's means of satisfying his physical and primary needs. Thirdly, taxation should aim at securing all unearned increment of wealth for the communal benefit. Finally, taxation should be levied on unearned incomes and should aim at preventing the retention of great fortunes in private hands. Specifically, the conference argued for the repeal of indirect taxes which fell 'oppressively on the industrious classes'. Rich *rentiers* and large incomes should pay for state protection and should cover the costs of social exploitation, paying for social reform by taxation of socially created wealth through a super-tax on large incomes, a special tax on state-conferred monopolies, an increase in death duties and taxation of land values. What

[40] *The Labour Party: Ninth Annual Conference, 1909*, appendix II, 'The incidence of taxation', report of conference, pp. 104–8.

was needed was more than retrenchment of military spending, as argued
by an earlier generation of radicals – it was 'better distribution of national
wealth' in order to transfer from 'the hands of the wealthy classes of this
country resources which are ample for carrying out immediately large
and long overdue schemes of social reform'.[41]

The 'people's budget' of 1909 went some way to meet the demands of
Labour by introducing a super-tax and taxation of land as well as increasing death duties. At the same time, it marked a limit of the fiscal policy of
the Liberal government, for it risked alienating middle-class voters with a
real danger of driving property into the hands of tariff reform.[42] The problem for the Liberal government was that it was becoming more dependent
on the support of Labour MPs after the general elections of 1910 – and
the party was now devising further demands for a legal right to work,
with labour exchanges, state insurance, regularisation of casual labour, a
forty-eight-hour maximum week and public works.[43] The issue was: how
to provide work for everyone, and so to give meaning to free trade in
the way suggested by Clynes? This approach posed serious problems for
the Liberal government, and also for Labour. In the minority report of the
Royal Commission on the poor laws, the Webbs had one solution: a state-
directed labour market. This solution did not appeal to trade unionists,
who wished to preserve free bargaining – and it certainly had no attraction
to new Liberals who wished to create an autonomous, self-reliant, worker.
And if the policy entailed high levels of social expenditure, and large-scale
redistribution of income from rich to poor, it would alienate middle-class
voters. Clearly, the Liberal government needed to find an alternative policy, which would provide social reform and preserve a free market, in
a way that contained the demands of Labour and secured middle-class
votes.[44]

Despite the differences of emphasis within the Labour party, there was
a basic assumption that publicly funded action was needed to remove
social evils, and to distribute rewards and opportunities in a fair way. As
Pat Thane has remarked, the assumption of most members of the party
was that the central state should provide general direction, with administration and control left to the localities in a democratic, decentralised,

[41] *The Labour Party. Ninth Annual Conference, 1909*, appendix II, 'The incidence of taxation',
report of conference, pp. 102–12; P. Snowden, *A Few Hints to Lloyd George: Where Is the
Money to Come From? The Question Answered* (ILP, London, 1909), pp. 1–7.

[42] For some indication that this was happening, see P. F. Clarke, 'The end of *laissez faire*
and the politics of cotton', *Historical Journal* 15 (1972), 493–512.

[43] *Report of the Eleventh Annual Conference of the Labour Party* (London, 1911), p. 101; the
same resolution was carried the previous year. See also Hennock, *British Social Reform
and German Precedents*, pp. 153–7.

[44] Harris, *Unemployment and Politics*; Gilbert, 'Winston Churchill versus the Webbs'.

system in order to create a 'community of active participatory citizens whose objective was to secure independence and a civilised life for all'. The earlier hostility of radicals to an intrusive central state was modified by a belief that the state could take positive action under the guidance of democratic institutions, which gave more weight to the role of local government, friendly societies and co-operatives than to state bureaucracy. The new approach has been well described by Thane as 'dynamic democratic radicalism'. Such an approach rejected Marxist notions of inevitable immiseration and denied that the state was an instrument of class control – a sign of the success of the project of Peel and Gladstone. The way forward was not through class struggle but rather by democratising the state so that it could be used to reinforce personal independence and stimulate character. Despite the resolution of 1901, the Labour party and ILP generally accepted that the state was neutral and under the control of parliament which could be used by Labour in the interests of all. Ramsay MacDonald rejected any notion of class warfare between a ruling and oppressed class, and even those who went a stage further largely accepted that parliament was the legitimate arena for social change through

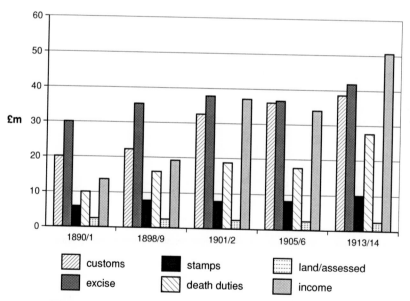

Figure 11.1 Principal categories of tax revenue, United Kingdom central government, 1890/1, 1898/9, 1901/2, 1905/6 and 1913/14
Sources: PP 1890–1 XLVIII, 1899 LI, 1902 LV, 1906 LXV, 1914 L, *Finance accounts of the United Kingdom, years ended 31 March*, pp. 16, 18, 20, 20, 20.

political action. The role of the state was to ensure the right to permanent, fairly paid, work or, failing that, public aid to maintain a sense of dignity. At the heart of Labour's rhetoric were notions of rights, justice, fairness, independence, self-respect, dignity and freedom, to be achieved through a relationship between the state and active, participating, citizens in an ethical commitment to a new social order. People should not become dependent on the state and sacrifice their autonomy; rather, the state should reinforce individual responsibility.[45]

At least before the First World War, the more 'mechanical' approach of the Webbs was less significant than a continued stress on ethical socialism and Idealism. Of course, the working class had most to gain in material terms and in control over their lives, but the usual argument put forward by Labour was that all members of society who were willing to make a positive contribution would benefit from stability and prosperity. Indeed, all social groups could support and foster change for the crucial issue was *ethical* commitment. Rights were not 'natural' as in the radical discourse of the early nineteenth century; they were *earned* through active involvement in state and society. The people who would lose, deservedly, were parasitical *rentiers* and idle workers, who took privileges without contributing to society. The blame for Britain's economic problems was firmly placed with the 'idle rich', who should be overturned by an alliance of the industrious classes. The ILP did not follow up the implications of the resolution of 1901 that society was riven by class warfare. Transformation to a socialist society would not come through revolution, but through state intervention and the rejection of *laissez faire*. As David Howell points out, their approach assumed that British industry could become more efficient and competitive, in a way that benefited workers, by removing the parasitical landowners and monopolists. A desire to create economic success for the British nation merged with a vision of a socialist commonwealth.[46]

Liberal fiscal policy

The Liberal government was in a difficult situation, facing challenge from the Conservatives on tariff reform and from Labour's attack on socially created wealth and demand for tax-funded welfare. The introduction of

[45] P. Thane, 'Labour and local politics: radicalism, democracy and social reform, 1880–1914', in Biagini and Reid (eds.), *Currents of Radicalism*, pp. 260–70, and D. Tanner, 'Ideological debate in Edwardian Labour politics: radicalism, revisionism and socialism', in Biagini and Reid (eds.), *Currents of Radicalism*, pp. 275–93. On Labour attitudes to parliament and patriotism, see Ward, *Red Flag and Union Jack* and on the continued importance of Idealism, Harris, 'Political thought and the welfare state'; R. MacDonald, *Socialism and Government* (2 vols., London, 1909).

[46] Howell, *British Workers*, p. 349.

Table 11.1 *Major fiscal changes of the Liberal government*

Budget of 1907

Income tax differentiated: rate remained at 1s on unearned income; lower rate of 9d on earned income up to £2,000.

Estate duty raised on large estates above £150,000; the rate was increased from 7.5 per cent to 10 per cent on estates of £1m. The amount in excess of £1m was then charged an additional 1 per cent on the first £500,000 to an additional 5 per cent above £3m.

The concession to earned incomes would be covered in a full year by the increased yield from the estate duty.

Budget of 1909

Graduation of income tax: earned income remained at 9d for incomes up to £2,000; 1s for incomes of £2,000 to £3,000; then 1s 2d. Unearned incomes up to £2,000 paid 1s, and then 1s 2d. Super-tax of 6d on all incomes over £5,000 on the amount by which the income exceeded £3,000.

On incomes under £500, abatement of £10 for every child under sixteen.

Death duty increased on estates above £5,000: the rate was now 4 per cent in place of 3 per cent on estates of £5,000 to £10,000, and reached 10 per cent in place of 7 per cent on estates of £150,000 to £200,000. The top rate of 15 per cent now applied from £1m, to the entire estate. The settlement estate duty was raised from 1 per cent to 2 per cent.

Land valuation and land duties: (1) tax on increment of value of 20 per cent whenever it changed hands by sale or death; (2) reversion duty of 10 per cent on the benefit to a lessor at the end of a lease; (3) annual tax of 0.5d in £ on site value of undeveloped land; (4) mineral rights duty of 1s in £ annually on rental value of the right to work minerals.

Source: B. Mallet, *British Budgets, 1887–88 to 1912–13* (London, 1913), chapters on budgets of 1907–8 and 1909–10, and p. 490 on estate duty.

differentiation and higher death duties on larger estates in 1907 went some way to meet the new Liberal and Labour hostility to 'unearned income' (see table 11.1). Lloyd George also launched a campaign against a specific form of socially created wealth which was compatible with the old radical traditions in the party: the land. The attempt to tax land did not accept the full implications of the attack on Rent in general, which would be a serious threat to the Liberal coalition by challenging a wide range of interests. Indeed, Lloyd George was less influenced by Hobson's view of the perils of under-consumption and overseas investment than by George Paish,* his unofficial economic adviser, who argued that overseas investment was beneficial for Britain so long as it remained within a free trade context.[47]

[47] Offer, 'Empire and social reform'.

* George Paish (1867–1957) was on the staff of the *Statist* from 1881, serving as joint editor from 1900 to 1916. He was a member of the departmental committee of the Board of Trade on railway accounts and statistics, 1906–8, and official adviser to the chancellor of the Exchequer from 1914 to 1916. (*Who Was Who*, vol. v: *1951–60* (London, 1961), pp. 843–4.)

Capital exports were at a low level in the decade or so up to 1905, and Paish argued that a lack of investment in world food production led to rising prices and constraints on productive industries. Chamberlain's case rested on the assumption that Britain's economic problems arose from tariffs imposed by foreigners; Paish countered that the fault lay with Britain and its timidity in developing the natural wealth of new countries. Consequently, Paish welcomed the revival of foreign investment from 1905 as a sign of a renewed spirit of enterprise. Cheap, abundant, food and raw materials would lead to an expansion of industrial output, and the British people would have a higher standard of living. Such arguments sustained a free trade, cosmopolitan, solution to Britain's economic future, based upon the investment of capital throughout the world, untrammelled by tariff barriers or by a desire to alter the domestic social structure in a fundamental way. Paish's optimistic account of British overseas investment as the guarantor of economic success led him to the conclusion that higher rates of taxation were not harmful:

have the British people not been told that the higher income tax, the heavier death duties and the land taxes would ruin the country and cause us to live upon our capital ... I have been looking for the proof of these predictions; but the evidence that we are accumulating wealth faster than we ever did before seems to me to be overwhelming, and I cannot but come to the conclusion that the new taxes have not had the disastrous consequences predicted. Indeed, they seem to show the truth of the proverb that 'the more you give the more you have'. Out of their great incomes the rich have given – somewhat reluctantly, no doubt – a part of the money needed for Old Age Pensions and for increasing the Navy, and this seems to have so stirred them to action that they have accumulated wealth faster than ever, and their incomes have grown as they never grew before.[48]

Taxation, it seemed, was a stimulus rather than a shock. In his view, economic prosperity was entirely compatible with higher taxation, despite the dire warnings of the City that the country would be ruined. He continued to accept the Gladstonian notion that accumulation and investment by the rich were beneficial, even when investment was overseas. Where he differed from Gladstone was in his rejection of the assumption that high taxes reduced private accumulation and investment. Lloyd George adopted this position in his Mansion House speech of 1912.[49]

Hobson's theories could be used by Liberal politicians without accepting their full implications, concentrating on the need to create a more active and dynamic economy in order to remove the worst social problems,

48 PRO, T171/18, paper on trade prospects by Sir George Paish.
49 PRO, T171/20, Mansion House speech, 1912.

increase economic efficiency and preserve a powerful empire. Winston Churchill commented in 1907 that

There are only two ways in which people can acquire wealth. There is production and there is plunder. Production is always beneficial. Plunder is always pernicious... We are here to range definitely on the side of production and so eliminate plunder as an element in our social system... We are resolved if we can to prevent any class from steadily absorbing under the shelter of the law the wealth in the creation of which they have borne no share, wealth which belongs not to them but to the community, wealth which they can only secure by vexatious obstruction of social and economic progress.[50]

Churchill was here defining 'plunder' in a narrow sense as the unearned increment in land, but he moved on to a wider attack on all accumulated wealth which was not active and enterprising. The burden of taxation should be shifted from wage-earners to those he termed 'income drawers', people who took from society more than they created – an approach similar to Hobhouse's concern for 'service'.[51] Churchill's ambition was to create a vigorous society in which the driving force was 'competitive selection'. Social reform was justified as a means of encouraging rather than replacing competition:

I do not want to see impaired the vigour of competition, but we can do much to mitigate the consequences of failure. We want to draw a line below which we will not allow persons to live and labour, yet above which they may compete with all the strength of their manhood. We want to have free competition upwards; we decline to allow free competition downwards. We do not want to pull down the structures of science and civilisation: but to spread a net over the abyss.[52]

As he remarked,

There is no chance of making people self-reliant by confronting them with problems and with trials beyond their capacity to surmount... Nothing in our plans will relieve people from the need of making every exertion to help themselves, but, on the contrary, we consider that we shall greatly stimulate their efforts by giving them for the first time a practical assurance that those efforts will be crowned with success.[53]

The result of these changes was a new fiscal policy based on the level and type of income, and the processes of acquisition.[54] In Churchill's view, the creation of a dynamic economy, and the use of socially created wealth to resolve problems of poverty and health, would produce a fit imperial race

[50] Speech of 20 Apr. 1907, quoted in M. Gilbert, *Churchill's Political Philosophy* (Oxford, 1981), p. 43.
[51] W. S. Churchill, *Liberalism and the Social Problem* (London, 1909), p. 234.
[52] Churchill, *Liberalism and the Social Problem*, pp. 82–3; see also pp. 279–80, 320, 335–6.
[53] Churchill, *Liberalism and the Social Problem*, p. 376.
[54] Churchill, *Liberalism and the Social Problem*, pp. 377–8.

and supply the resources for imperial defence. He was combining free trade finance and imperialism, and providing a defence against socialistic attacks on a competitive capitalist economy.

The appeal to Rent and 'socially created' or 'unearned' wealth was important in the rhetoric of the new Liberalism. Josiah Stamp suggested that the terms were used in different and confused ways, and merely offered *post hoc* justifications rather than the driving force for change. In his view, graduation arose from the application of marginal theories of value to different levels of income, and differentiation was no more than a refinement of 'ability to pay'.[55] He was surely right to suggest that acceptance of the marginal incidence of taxation was important in converting officials and politicians to graduation and differentiation. It was also clear to officials at the Inland Revenue and Treasury that the existing system of degression limited the yield of the income tax. However, the rhetoric of socially created wealth cannot simply be reduced to a simple matter of *post hoc* rationalisation – and confusion was part of its political attractions in a way that the lucid and logical Stamp failed to appreciate. It was crucial in creating electoral support for a reform in income tax and a major shift in the fiscal constitution, and its various meanings, from radical and socialist to prudential and imperial, helped in the task. Certainly, the Liberal government did not fully accept the definitions of Rent proposed by Hobson or the Webbs. It could appeal in different ways to critics of landed wealth and of empire, to socialist opponents of monopoly capital, and also to *supporters* of empire such as Churchill and the 'Limps', and to proponents of an active capitalist economy. The categories of 'parasite' and 'producer' were malleable, allowing Liberal politicians to claim that employers and workers were united as active producers versus passive *rentiers*, so blunting the appeal of a distinct Labour party and attempting to retain the support of middle-class voters. Fiscal politics did not simply reflect pre-existing interests; the rhetoric helped to define interests and identities.

The defining moment in the fiscal politics of the Liberal government was the budget of 1909. It was, as Lloyd George put it, 'a War Budget. It is for raising money to wage implacable warfare against poverty and squalidness.'[56] A less dramatic way of interpreting the budget is, in the words of B. K. Murray, an 'attempt to employ finance in the effort to hold the Liberal party's middle and working class support together in a "progressive" coalition for reform'. It introduced a graduated super-tax, which would appeal to Labour; yet at the same time, Lloyd George offered concessions to modest middle-class incomes, and especially to men with children. Most of the tax increase fell on the wealthy and on

[55] J. C. Stamp, 'The meaning of "unearned income"', *Economic Journal* 25 (1915), 165–72.
[56] The end of his budget speech, quoted in Murray, *People's Budget*, p. 172.

unearned incomes, and he could hope to retain the support of middle-
class taxpayers and prevent them from shifting their allegiance to the
Conservatives and tariff reform. The revenue could then finance welfare
for the working class, and retain – so it was hoped – their votes for the
Liberal party.[57] Further, he introduced an element of land taxation, so
appealing to Liberal criticism of landlordism and to Labour attacks on
Rent.

The result was to precipitate a constitutional crisis on a scale unknown
since 1832, for the House of Lords threatened to reject the budget.
Michael Hicks Beach had a shrewd understanding of the politics of taxation and advised the leader of the party, Arthur Balfour,* against allowing
the Lords to reject the budget. Not only was the constitutional case weak;
it would be counter-productive in terms of party politics:

> The 'interference of the Lords with taxation' will give the Government the very
> cry they want, and deprive us of the chance of success we should have had without
> it . . . the wisest policy would be, to let it [the budget] be tried. Let people suffer a
> bit by Radical legislation: then they will soon put an end to it. But I am convinced
> we *shall* be beaten on the issue that would now be presented: and to incur such
> a risk for the sake of what we might gain by the rejection of this Budget for a
> time, seems to me the worst gamble I have ever known in politics. What I cannot
> understand is, why the Tariff Reformers, of all people, should desire it. Their best
> chance is to let the 'only alternative' work, so as to convert people who suffer to
> their views.[58]

In fact, the Lords *did* oppose the budget and the ensuing constitutional
crisis was resolved by a general election in 1910. Although the Liberals
returned to office, they were more dependent on support from Labour
(as well as Irish) MPs. The Liberal government was uncomfortably aware
of the difficulties in which it now found itself. Election results in
Lancashire were already suggesting that Hicks Beach was right, and that
the 'only alternative' of high direct taxation was starting to drive middle-
class voters towards the Conservatives and tariff reform.[59] However, the
need for support from Labour members meant that the government had

[57] Murray, *People's Budget*, pp. 4–5.
[58] Gloucestershire Record Office, 2455, PCC/12, M. Hicks Beach to A. J. Balfour, 20 Sept.
1909.
[59] Clarke, 'The end of *laissez faire*'.
* Arthur James Balfour (1848–1930) was educated at Eton and Trinity College, Cambridge; he was a philosopher, and went into politics under the influence of his uncle,
Salisbury. He was Conservative MP 1874–1905 and 1906–22. He had great social prestige, and was a member of the 'Souls'. He was president of the Local Government Board
1885–6, secretary for Scotland 1886–7, chief secretary for Ireland in 1887–91, Conservative leader in the Commons 1891–2 and 1895–1902 and Prime Minister 1902–5.
He resigned as leader in 1911, and joined the War Cabinet as first lord of the Admiralty
1915, foreign secretary 1916–19 and lord president of the council, 1919–22 and 1925–9.
(*DNB, 1922–30*, ed. Weaver, pp. 41–56.)

to meet demands for social reform, with the danger of alienating middle-class taxpayers.

As we have noted, Labour was pressing for legislation to guarantee the right to work which would have serious financial implications. In the face of the loss of middle-class support, the Liberal government needed to devise a strategy of social reform funded in some other way than the income tax. The solution was contributory health and unemployment insurance in 1911, with weekly flat-rate payments from the employer and worker, and a small supplement from the government. The insurance schemes restricted sick and unemployment pay to limited periods, linked to the number of contributions paid into the scheme, so that there was not an open-ended commitment for tax-funding beyond a fixed and modest amount. Most of the cost fell on employers and workers, and there was very little redistribution of resources from the taxpaying class to the working class. Indeed, the finance of the scheme was regressive. The flat-rate contribution formed a larger proportion of the income of low-paid than of skilled workers; many well-paid men who were already members of friendly societies and trade unions now received a subsidy from the state. As F. W. Kolthammer pointed out in 1913, a family with an income of 18s a week paid 2.84 per cent in food taxes and 7.1 per cent if it consumed alcohol and tobacco; on incomes of 35s, the proportions were 1.46 per cent and 3.65 per cent. When health insurance was added, the taxation of a family with 18s rose to 9.1 per cent and with unemployment insurance to 10.25 per cent. The proportions were 4.68 per cent and 5.27 per cent for a family income of 35s.[60] For its part, the Treasury was concerned about the financial implications of the tax-funded pensions introduced in 1908, and argued for a shift to an insurance-based system with a strict limit to the calls on the government.[61] The Labour party was well aware that the Liberal welfare reforms and changes in the tax system were not redistributive, and passed a resolution attacking contributory insurance as 'unjust' to both employers and workers. The employers' contribution would drive up the costs of production, and therefore fall on 'the consuming public, who were, in the main, working people'.[62]

[60] F. W. Kolthammer, *The Ratan Tata Foundation. Memorandum on Problems of Poverty No. 1: Some Notes on the Incidence of Taxation on the Working Class Family* (London, n.d., 1913?), pp. 15–16.

[61] See Macnicol, *The Politics of Retirement,* p. 163 and Part II on the Treasury campaign against non-contributory pensions after the First World War.

[62] *Report of the Twelfth Annual Conference of the Labour Party, 1912* (London, 1912), pp. 96–7, and *Report of the Thirteenth Annual Conference of the Labour Party, 1913* (London, 1913), pp. 104–6; and see also A. Marwick, 'The Labour party and the welfare state in Britain, 1900–48', *American Historical Review* 73 (1978), 380–403.

The insurance schemes of 1911 marked one attempt to contain Labour pressure for more sweeping measures of social reform and taxation without alienating middle-class taxpayers. Another way of preserving middle-class electoral support was through tax allowances for family responsibilities. Lloyd George was following the strategy of Harcourt in 1894, of increasing taxation of larger incomes and reducing the rate on modest middle-class incomes by changes in thresholds and abatements. However, Lloyd George went a stage further: the budget of 1909 was not only the 'people's budget' with its populist attack on rich landowners, for it was also a 'family budget'. He introduced tax allowances according to family circumstances which outlived the immediate excitement of the onslaught on Rent. George Murray at the Treasury warned Asquith in 1909 that 'the supertax is a leap in the dark; and so is the concession to the "brats"'.[63] He was not entirely correct on the second point, for in 1799 Pitt allowed a deduction of 5 per cent tax for each child on incomes of £60 to £400, falling to 1 per cent on the largest incomes. In 1803, the concession was limited to third and subsequent children on a scale from 4 per cent to 1 per cent; it was abolished in 1806 and not restored in 1842.[64] When allowances were reintroduced in 1909, they took a different form: an allowance of £10 per child under the age of sixteen against gross incomes up to £500. In 1913/14, the cost of the allowance was estimated to be £240,000; in the budget of 1914, it was doubled to £20 at an additional cost of £210,000.[65] The income tax system from 1909 therefore introduced a concern for the family responsibilities of middle-class taxpayers, in striking contrast to the failure to introduce 'family allowances' – a cash benefit for children to help poorer families – until 1945.

The British welfare system was very different from the situation in France, where family allowances were paid to all families with dependent children, much earlier than unemployment and health insurance. In France, family allowances were associated with an anti-individualistic rhetoric of social Catholicism and pronatalism which argued that families with children should be supported as a patriotic measure. This rhetoric coincided with the interests of industrialists who established private funds (*caisses de compensation*) and used family allowances to tie workers to their firms and reduce pressure for wage increases. Family allowances were, therefore, part of a strategy of industrial discipline, which was only feasible

[63] Bod. Lib., MS Asquith 22, G. H. Murray to Asquith, 7 Apr. 1909, ff. 127–30.

[64] PRO, T171/388, Income Tax: child allowances. Inland Revenue, 31 Aug. 1945.

[65] PRO, IR63/46, Finance Bill, 1914, vol. 1, ff. 107–8, Income Tax: additional relief in respect of children; IR63/17, Finance Bills, 1907–9, ff. 139–40. Chiozza Money also wished to extend abatements to maintenance of poor relations, periods of extended illness and special misfortune.

because relatively weak male trade unionists were unable to resist inter-ference in collective wage bargaining. The private schemes provided the basis for subsequent state intervention, and France developed a 'parental welfare state'. In Britain, trade unions were stronger and the state was anxious to work with the organised working class in establishing formal collective bargaining. Family allowances were, in any case, supported by socialists and feminists as a way of liberating women from dependence on men, so that the rhetoric threatened dominant patriarchal assumptions rather than providing a patriotic measure of pronatalism. In Britain, so-cial insurance was paid to men as 'breadwinners', providing cover for sickness and unemployment when their earnings were disrupted. Noth-ing was offered to families where the male head of household was in work, and trade unions preferred to make a case for higher wages on the basis of family responsibilities. Tax allowances did not threaten patriarchy, for they were paid to the male head of household to set against his family commitments. Above all, there was a clear electoral calculation. Flat-rate cash family allowances would be of greatest assistance to the poor, and would lead to higher levels of taxation of the better-off. By contrast, tax allowances were of greatest benefit to the middle and upper income groups, and offered a tax concession to an important group of family men on modest middle-class incomes.[66]

One possible explanation for the payment of income tax allowances to the middle class was concern that a fall in middle-class birth rates would lead to a deterioration in the British race. In France, the drop in the birth rate throughout society led to support for pronatalist policies. Could it be that in Britain an emphasis on the faster fall in the birth rate of middle-class families led to income tax concessions? Certainly, Sidney Webb argued on these lines after the war, when he proposed tax breaks for middle-class families with incomes up to £1,500 or £2,000, and to continue while children were in full-time education. In Webb's opinion, a flat-rate relief did not assist middle-class families in the production of chil-dren, nor in their effective education in secondary schools, technical col-leges and universities.[67] The issue was also raised in 1939 by two eugeni-cists from Oxford who protested against a reduction in tax allowances, claiming that child-bearing would be discouraged 'among the higher

---

[66] Pedersen, *Family, Dependence and the Origins of the Welfare State*; A. M. Cartter, 'Income tax allowances and the family in Great Britain', *Population Studies* 6 (1952-3), 218-25, 227.

[67] PP 1919 XXIII pt 1, *Royal Commission on Income Tax, Third Instalment of Minutes of Evidence*, Qq. 6885-8. There was a link with his views on Rent achieved through closure of middle-class occupations.

intellectual levels of the population, represented on the average by the section of it which pays Income Tax'.[68] However, these eugenic concerns for the racial stock do not appear to have been central to Lloyd George's strategy in 1909. More significant was an immediate political or electoral consideration: the need of the Liberals to secure the loyalty of middle-class voters who were in danger of shifting to the Conservative party. Sir John Simon's* response to his eugenicist critics in 1939 is pertinent to the adoption of allowances in 1909. As he pointed out, the important issue was how to define the curve of the income tax. Changes in the level of surtax affected the rich, and adjustments in the standard rate affected middle incomes; for lower incomes, *allowances* were more important in determining their contribution.[69] This consideration helps to explain the introduction of children's allowances. The relative position of direct tax-payers had deteriorated. The real burden of indirect taxes tell by 17.5 per cent in the real burden of indirect taxes between 1861/2 and 1901/2, com-pared with a constant real burden of direct taxes.[70] Any further increase in direct taxes might alienate middle-class electors and drive them into the arms of the Conservatives and tariffs. The Liberal government had to show that free trade would not hit the lower levels of income through necessitating higher income tax, a point carefully considered by Harcourt in 1894 when he reduced the tax on smaller incomes; his approach was continued by Lloyd George in 1909. The tax rate on *earned* income did not rise under the Liberal governments: a man with two children and an earned income of £300 paid the same amount in income tax (£4 10s) in 1913/14 as in 1892/3.[71] Most additional taxation fell on a small num-ber of super-tax payers, unearned incomes and death duties on estates of £20,000 and above. Variations in children's allowances or 'brattage' be-came a central element in the tax system, reducing the liability of smaller incomes as tax rates rose during the First World War, and mitigating the impact of taxation on the large number of married men who were

---

[68] PRO, T172/1901, E. S. Goodrich, professor of zoology and comparative anatomy and E. B. Ford, reader in genetics, to Lord Horder, 5 Oct. 1939.

[69] PRO, T172/1901, Simon to Horder, 11 Oct. 1939.

[70] PRO, T168/62, 'Comparative burthen of taxation in 1861/2 and at the present day'.

[71] T. Balderston, 'War finance and inflation in Britain and Germany, 1914–18', *Economic History Review* 2nd ser. 42 (1989), 233.

* John Allsebrook Simon (1873–1954) was educated at Bath Grammar School, Fettes and Wadham College, Oxford; he was a fellow of All Souls in 1897 and called to the bar in 1899. He was a Liberal MP from 1906 to 1918 and 1922 to 1940. He served as solicitor-general 1910–13, attorney-general 1913–15, home secretary 1915–16 when he resigned on conscription. He formed the National Liberal Party in 1931 and served as foreign secretary 1931–5, home secretary 1935–7, chancellor of the Exchequer 1937–40 and lord chancellor 1940–5. (*DNB, 1951–60*, ed. Williams and Palmer, pp. 892–4.)

Table 11.2 *Taxation of married man with three children under sixteen as a percentage of income*

Income		Wholly earned			Half earned and half investment		
		Direct	Indirect	Total	Direct	Indirect	Total
£50	1903/4	nil	8.7	8.7	0.8	8.7	9.5
	1913/14	nil	8.0	8.0	0.8	8.0	8.8
£150	1903/4	0.2	4.3	4.5	1.4	4.3	5.7
	1913/14	0.2	4.2	4.4	1.4	4.2	5.6
£500	1903/4	3.5	1.8	5.3	4.7	1.8	6.5
	1913/14	2.6	1.8	4.4	5.3	1.8	7.1
£1,000	1903/4	4.9	1.2	6.1	6.6	1.2	7.8
	1913/14	4.0	1.2	5.2	7.1	1.2	8.3
£10,000	1903/4	4.7	0.3	5.0	7.3	0.3	7.6
	1913/4	7.7	0.3	8.0	11.5	6.3	11.8

Source: PP 1927 XI, *Report of the Committee on National Debt and Taxation*, pp. 472–3.

brought within the income tax for the first time.[72] Between the wars, the Conservatives used tax allowances to married middle-class men with children in order to define themselves as the party of the family and domesticity.[73]

Differentiation, graduation and allowances for children, allied to the attack on the landed interest, were intended to do two things. One was to produce revenue for social reform and defence by creating a more buoyant fiscal regime. The other was to construct an electoral alliance of the more prosperous working class (who were the main beneficiaries of welfare reforms) with the lower and middling reaches of the middle class, as producers whose enterprise contributed to the public good. In this rhetorical strategy, producers were defined against the parasitical owners of unearned or accumulated income who were widened from landowners to *rentiers* in general. It was a response of the Liberal government to the competing proposals of the tariff reformers and Labour, and dealt with the prospect of a deficit created by old age pensions and naval expansion. The additional revenue was raised by direct taxation, which avoided alienating working-class voters and limited the appeal of the Labour party. 'I have realised from the first', Asquith remarked in 1908, 'that if it could not be proved that social reform (not Socialism) can be financed on Free

[72] PRO, T171/134, McFadyean to N. F. W. Fisher, 11 Apr. 1916; Fisher to McFadyean, 18 Apr. 1916; T171/142, Board of Inland Revenue, relief in respect of children, n.d. [1917].
[73] M. J. Daunton, 'Churchill at the Treasury: rethinking Conservative taxation policy, 1924–29', *Revue Belge de Philologie et de Histoire* 75 (1997), 1063–83.

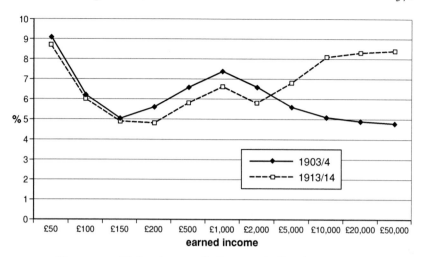

Figure 11.2 National taxes (indirect and direct) as a percentage of incomes of married men with two children
Source: H. Samuel, 'The taxation of the various classes of the people', *Journal of the Royal Statistical Society*, 82 (1919), 177–9.

Trade lines, a return to Protection is a moral certainty.'[74] The emphasis on taxation of unearned, *rentier*, income and the extremely rich meant that the majority of middle-class voters (small businessmen, salaried white-collar workers and many professionals) were reassured, and the appeal of tariffs as an alternative fiscal policy was contained. As Churchill remarked, the 1909 budget took food taxes to a minimum, and 'nothing in it touches the economy of the cottage home'. At the same time, most middle-class incomes of £300 to £2,000 were not affected except by death duties.[75] Indeed, most income taxpayers were less heavily taxed in 1914 than in 1905. The budget aimed to make the Liberals a party of social reform without alienating middle-class support. As Churchill argued,

The very rich are not singled out for peculiar, special, or invidious forms of imposition. The chief burden of the increase of taxation is placed upon the main body of the wealthy classes...; and that is a class which, in opportunities of pleasure, in all the amenities of life, and in freedom from penalties, obligations, and dangers, is more fortunate than any other equally numerous class of citizens in any age or in any country. That class has more to gain than any other class... from dwelling amid a healthy and contented people, and in a safely guarded land.[76]

[74] Quoted by Murray, *People's Budget*, p. 92, from House of Lords Record Office, Strachey papers SP S/11/6/5, Asquith to Strachey, 9 May 1908.
[75] Churchill, *Liberalism and the Social Problem*, pp. 290–1.
[76] Churchill, *Liberalism and the Social Problem*, pp. 90–1.

Churchill defended the trend away from indirect taxation, which the Conservatives threatened to reverse. 'We are resolved that it shall continue until in the end the entire change shall be defrayed from the profits of accumulated wealth and by the taxation of those proper indulgences which cannot be said in any way to affect the physical efficiency of labour.'[77] What Churchill was attempting to do was suggest that the fiscal policy of the Liberal government was in the national interest, that social reform was not a selfish class interest but a measure of social efficiency and justice in a balanced society.[78] There was a shift in the definition of ability to pay, by arguing that large incomes had a greater capacity to pay and by stressing that taxes designed to improve the efficiency and health of one group would benefit the entire community. As Herbert Samuel* argued, 'all expenditure which succeeds in improving the part benefits, not that part alone, but the whole of the community, and this is why all sections may justly be called upon to share the cost of measures which in their direct and immediate application touch only the well-being of the poorer'.[79] The Liberal budgets were therefore portrayed as producing greater equity, as well as a sense of shared responsibilities within an organic community.

The question was whether the attempt would succeed. The strategy posed electoral dangers, for it could be interpreted as marking the beginnings of an attack on property which would alarm many members of the middle class who defined themselves as property owners. After all, they might identify with property in general rather than with producers against parasites. For this reason, Lewis Harcourt, who had urged his father to accept graduation in 1894, feared that the budget might be counterproductive and 'will ensure the triumph of Tariff Reform'.[80] Of course, this was exactly what the advocates of tariff reform hoped *would* occur.[81]

---

[77] Churchill, *Liberalism and the Social Problem*, pp. 293–4.

[78] See Murray, *People's Budget*, p. 311.

[79] Samuel, *Liberalism* (1902), quoted in Murray, *People's Budget*, p. 35.

[80] Murray, *People's Budget*, p. 149, quoting University of Newcastle Library, Runciman Papers 28, Harcourt to Runciman, 24 Mar. 1909.

[81] University of Birmingham Library, AC 8/5/1, Austen Chamberlain to Balfour, 29 Jan. 1910.

* Herbert Louis Samuel (1870–1963) was born in Liverpool; his father was a partner of Samuel Montagu, the banking and foreign exchange firm. He was educated at University College School and Balliol, Oxford. He was a Liberal MP 1902–18, serving as under-secretary of state at the Home Office 1905–9, chancellor of the Duchy of Lancaster 1909–10, postmaster general 1910–14, president of the Local Government Board 1914–15, postmaster general 1915, chancellor of the Duchy of Lancaster 1915–16 and home secretary 1916, resigning when Lloyd George became prime minister. He was high commissioner in Palestine 1920–5, and chaired the Royal Commission on the Coal Industry 1925–6. He returned as a Liberal MP 1929–35, and was home secretary 1931–2. (*DNB, 1961–70*, ed. Williams and Nicholls, pp. 918–22.)

Balfour was well aware that Chamberlain's vision of imperial preference was divisive, but equally that protection, shorn of his full programme, was likely to become more appealing as a source of revenue.[82] The Liberal government needed to pay more attention to preserving the loyalty of its core supporters after 1910, and cautious voices in the government forced Lloyd George to retreat from his more ambitious proposals in the budget of 1914. The 'people's budget' marked the limits of Liberal fiscal reform, and Lloyd George's proposals for a further instalment of taxes on land and increases in direct taxation and progression were rejected by his colleagues in 1914. The threat of an increase in income tax alienated better-off voters; its removal annoyed the radicals. The extension of land taxes did not appeal to urban electors as Lloyd George hoped, and did not satisfy radical demands for a wider attack on unearned wealth.[83]

There were limits, but the budget of 1909 did mark an escape from Harcourt's prediction of 1895 that 'in the growth of the expenditure of the country you have very nearly reached the limits of tolerable taxation'.[84] Harcourt wrote before the demands of the Boer war put pressure on the fiscal system, at a time of growing demand for social reform and problems in local government finance. The ensuing debates led to a revision in the fiscal constitution rather than skirmishes at the margin. The disagreements over policy were more intense than at any time since the 1840s and 1850s, most of all over the land campaign. However, two points should be held distinct. The attack on land had greater rhetorical than financial importance, for the new taxes scarcely produced any revenue before they ran into problems of valuation and collection during the war. They faced resistance and non-compliance, and were abandoned after the war by Lloyd George's coalition government. More significantly, the revision of the income tax meant that Britain, unlike France and Germany, entered the First World War with an effective national tax regime. In Germany, the difficulties of introducing a Reich income tax created political tensions before the war: the alliance between social democrats and militarists in support of the tax was unstable and based on mutual resentment and the desire to use the revenue in different ways. In France, the income tax was only introduced at the very start of the war, and collection was seriously disrupted. At the end of the war, it proved much more difficult for

---

[82] University of Birmingham Library, AC 17/3/19, A. J. Balfour to A. Chamberlain, 23 Oct. 1907.

[83] Gilbert, 'David Lloyd George: the reform of British land-holding and the budget of 1914'. For a more cautious account, stressing procedural difficulties and lack of parliamentary time, see I. Packer, 'The Liberal cave and the 1914 budget', *English Historical Review* III (1996), 620–35. Packer argues that middle-class and business Liberals accepted the need for social reform and increased taxation.

[84] Murray, *People's Budget*, p. 21.

both Germany and France to impose taxes in order to cover the costs of debt and reconstruction; by contrast, the British government was more able to stabilise the financial system. In Britain, the debates in Edwardian Britain did not fundamentally weaken the legitimacy of the tax system and the state. By the outbreak of the war, the level of extraction had only returned to the level of the 1840s and 1850s, at around 12 per cent of GDP. During the war, the level doubled – and stayed there, without the threat to political stability apparent both after the Napoleonic wars in Britain and in other countries in Europe in the 1920s. Here was one of the achievements of the forging of the Gladstonian fiscal constitution: the state was trusted and legitimate, and the debates in Edwardian Britain did not fundamentally change that situation.[85]

---

[85] For two interesting and differing assessments of the comparative strengths of European fiscal regimes, see Hobson, 'The military-extraction gap and the wary Titan: the fiscal sociology of British defence policy, 1870–1913', *Journal of European Economic History* 22 (1993), 461–506 and N. Ferguson, 'Public finance and national security'.

This study ends as the British fiscal state was about to face its greatest challenge since the Napoleonic wars. The costs of the First World War soon eclipsed the strains of the Boer war and the naval race with Germany leading up to 1914, and spending returned to the peak of 1810. Government expenditure was displaced to a new level, for fiscal extraction did not fall to any great extent after the First World War (see figure 1.1). The British tax system was tested by the experience of war, and survived. Consent was preserved and the capacity of the state increased, despite strains in fiscal politics before the war. Lloyd George's budget of 1914 has been termed a 'debacle': the land campaign had run its course, pleasing neither the more cautious members of the Liberal party nor the radicals and Labour who wanted a more thorough attack on unearned wealth. Similarly, the proposal to increase the income tax alienated middle-class voters, while Lloyd George's retreat annoyed the radicals.[1] Lloyd George's difficulties in 1914 doubtless accounts for his caution in increasing taxes at the start of the war, and reliance on loans was to cause difficulties of inflation and postwar debt service.

Nevertheless, what stands out is not so much the existence of a fiscal crisis as success in negotiating the treacherous finances of a major war. When Britain entered the First World War, its fiscal system was more capable of sustaining the formidable demands of world-wide conflict than was the case in the other combatants. Treasury officials and politicians stressed that the steady repayment of the national debt over the nineteenth century merited confidence in the British government, so that loans would be forthcoming in times of emergency. By contrast, the German government failed to secure a loan in 1913 and was forced to introduce the *Wehrbeitrag* or defence levy on property and income.[2] The

---

[1] Gilbert, 'David Lloyd George: the reform of British land-holding and the budget of 1914', 138–9.
[2] Ferguson, 'Public finance and national security', 160; see the comments of the Treasury in PRO, T171/167, 'Paper prepared at the request of the chancellor of the Exchequer on the German defence levy of 1913'.

Reich did not have an income tax until 1913, and faced serious problems in reforming the fiscal constitution in order to meet the rising cost of defence. The Reichstag levied indirect taxes mainly for military purposes and had a wider franchise than the individual states which levied direct taxes for social expenditure and had restricted electorates. As a result, any attempt by the Reich to increase its revenues collided with two opposing forces. The states wished to protect their sources of direct taxation, and resented the incursion of the Reich. Within the Reichstag, the Social Democrats and centre left were powerful, and opposed the use of indirect taxes to finance militarism. Their support for direct taxes could only be secured by offering social reform, which cost more money and alienated the right. As a result, the government was destabilised and financial constraints were imposed on military spending. Not surprisingly, German commentators were envious of the ability of the British government to raise revenue from the income tax which was reformed before the First World War to provide a more efficient means of extraction.

Niall Ferguson has gone so far as to argue that the German government's consciousness of the greater fiscal resources of Britain contributed to the outbreak of war as a pre-emptive strike before too large a gap opened between the naval power of the two countries. The difference was apparent during the war, when 26.2 per cent of British central government expenditure was financed from current revenue compared with a mere 8.2 per cent in Germany.[3] His interpretation does not command universal assent, and this is not the place to enter into a discussion of the vexed subject of the origins of the First World War. Certainly, his interpretation of the fiscal history of the great powers at the onset of war should be modified. The comparative data of J. M. Hobson shows that British military spending was *lower* than other European countries as a proportion of the net national product: if Britain is expressed as 100 in 1913, Germany stood at 122, France at 149 and Russia at 160.[4] The conclusion drawn by Hobson is that *higher* spending by Britain would have acted as a deterrent to German aggression. Perhaps it was this point which created alarm in Germany: Britain had the capacity to spend money on warfare, its economy was less strained and political relations were less problematic. Similarly, France was experiencing difficulties in reforming its fiscal constitution prior to the war. The existing system of direct taxes was not

---

3 P.-C. Witt, *Die Finanzpolitik des Deutschen Reiches* (Lübeck, 1970); Ferguson, 'Public finance and national security', 156–8, 162; Kruedener, 'The Franckenstein paradox'; Schremmer, 'Taxation and public finance', p. 482; Balderston, 'War, finance and inflation', 226–8; R. Knauss, *Die deutsche, englische und französische Kriegsfinanzierung* (Berlin and Leipzig, 1925); Hobson, 'The tax-seeking state'.

4 Hobson, 'The military-extraction gap', 461–506.

easily reformed because of the range of different interests affected by specific rates. But sweeping away the existing system and replacing it with an income tax was scarcely any easier, for some groups would obviously lose their privileged position and the tax was associated with socialist campaigns for redistribution. The income tax was only introduced in 1914, and the yield was extremely low as a result of the problems of creating an effective administrative machinery during the war.[5]

Both in France and in Germany, the difficulties of war finance were brutally exposed after the war. In France, the costs of war pensions, reconstruction and interest payments forced the government to introduce a general sales tax in 1920, which was highly controversial.[6] Financial problems also contributed to the desire to impose heavy reparations on Germany. In Germany, political problems in passing the costs of debt service to industry meant that hyperinflation was used to reduce the burden of the debt at considerable costs of political and financial stability. Rampant inflation cut the government's debt and also destroyed the assets of institutions such as savings banks and voluntary associations, wiping out the savings of the middle classes, discrediting contracts and re-ordering wealth. As Ferguson comments, by sacrificing private savers as a corollary of liquidating the debts of the state, the political authority and legitimacy of the republic were brought into disrepute.[7]

Although Britain had its problems in dealing with the high levels of postwar debt and taxation, they were negotiated and the legitimacy of the state was preserved. Strains were apparent in the fiscal system, from at least four directions. Many workers came within the reach of the income tax, and complained that they were paying for massive transfers to the holders of national debt. The solution proposed by Labour was the conscription of wealth to complement the conscription of men to fight in the war, which was linked with the attack on unearned or socially created wealth. Such a policy threatened property owners, and the coalition and Conservative governments were anxious to contain support for the proposal. Any suggestion that the income tax should be cut or a new indirect tax imposed would simply play into the hands of Labour.

However, the coalition and Conservative government was faced by a second problem: a revolt by lower-middle-class taxpayers who suffered from inflation and resented 'waste'. The government was caught between Labour and the anti-waste movement, and had to strike a balance.

[5] Gross, 'Progressive taxation and social justice'.
[6] C. S. Shoup, *The Sales Tax in France* (New York, 1930); C. S. Maier, *Recasting Bourgeois Europe* (Princeton, 1975), pp. 466–506.
[7] N. Ferguson, *Paper and Iron: Hamburg Business and German Politics in the Era of Inflation, 1897–1927* (Cambridge, 1995).

Thirdly, the huge volume of short-term debt threatened the stability of financial markets. The City was anxious that this debt should be paid off, even at the expense of higher levels of taxation which would cause the government serious problems. Finally, industry was concerned that it was paying much higher levels of taxation than its competitors in Germany, so that it was being priced out of markets. In steering a way between these competing demands, the government was acutely aware of electoral considerations but was also concerned for the fiscal and financial stability of the country.

Above all, the permanent officials at the Treasury and Inland Revenue were adamant that the tax system should be seen as equitable, above class or sectional interests. The outcome was very different from Germany, where power was displaced from the elected representatives and bureaucrats to direct bargaining between organised interests. As Charles Maier remarks, the result was 'constant brokerage' of organised interests *outside* the legislature.[8] In Britain, parliamentary government continued to be accepted, and organised business was obliged to join rather than reject the party-political system.[9] Politicians and civil servants were anxious that the state and the fiscal system should not be seen to act in favour of one interest over another. Rather than a corporatist process of brokerage between organised interest groups, the Treasury officials advised politicians in some secrecy about the logic of the tax system and the needs for balance. Their concern was for the security of government revenues, the consent of taxpayers and the stability of the financial system. The state had its own interests, and the vital issue was its capacity to implement its goals in the face of opposition from powerful groups. This collective culture of administrators constrained what was feasible or permissible, and shaped the reaction to external pressures; contrary to Maier's analysis of continental Europe, the power of career bureaucrats remained considerable. The collective bureaucratic culture was peculiarly powerful in the case of taxation policy, resting on the development of budgetary orthodoxy since Peel and Gladstone and providing the basis for the high degree of consent achieved by the British state. Although Treasury views on fiscal rectitude can be seen as conservative, designed to preserve the *status quo* against radical challenge, the result was also to legitimate higher levels of taxation after the war. The Treasury was aware of the limits of consent and the need to sustain it. A much higher level of taxation, and of direct taxation in particular, was accepted

[8] Maier, *Recasting Bourgeois Europe*, pp. 4, 8–10, 580–1.
[9] J. Turner, 'The politics of "organised business" in the First World War', in J. Turner (ed.), *Businessmen and Politics: Studies of Business Activity in British Politics, 1900–45* (London, 1984), pp. 48–9.

between the wars without the resistance and even revolt found in other countries.

The restabilisation of the fiscal constitution at much higher levels of extraction forms the starting point of a second volume, with a new set of themes. This study has stressed the creation of legitimacy and trust in the Victorian state through the actions of the political elite and the creation of what has been called, for convenience, the Gladstonian fiscal constitution. Of course, Gladstone himself was always anxious that issues of taxation should not be allowed to set groups against each other, and he attempted to create a sense of an organic state based on fairness and equity between classes and interests. He was also concerned that money should fructify in the pockets of the people: government expenditure should be kept as low as possible in order to release private initiatives which would use funds more effectively. Adherents of Gladstonian orthodoxy were horrified by the levels of spending between the wars – the example of John Bradbury comes to mind, with his memorandum of dissent to the Macmillan committee of 1929–31 in which he called for 'strict economy in public expenditure'.[10] The Treasury view of the 1920s and 1930s adhered to many of the precepts of the Gladstonian fiscal constitution, with the belief that public spending would 'crowd out' private investment, and that the budget should be balanced.[11] Nevertheless, matters had changed for there was no real attempt to reduce spending to the level of 1913, and the long fall in public spending after the Napoleonic wars was not repeated. Rather, the problem was how to prevent its rising still higher. The proportions of direct and indirect taxation were also maintained up to the Second World War when the new indirect purchase tax was introduced. The implications of the Liberal reforms of the income tax before the First World War were now apparent, in large part through the budgets of Winston Churchill as Conservative chancellor between 1924 and 1929. The demands of war finance meant that the income tax became more progressive at the upper end, and remained high after the war; the reduction in tax was concentrated on more modest middle-class incomes with families to create a 'dip' in the incidence of taxation for a crucial electoral constituency. When the Second World War pushed taxes to a higher level, many middle-class voters continued to support higher taxes from which they benefited through spending on education and health.

---

[10] PP 1930–1 XIII, *Report of the Committee on Finance and Industry*, 'Memorandum of dissent by Lord Bradbury'.

[11] On the Treasury view, see G. C. Peden, 'The "Treasury view" on public works and employment in the interwar period', *Economic History Review* 2nd ser. 37 (1984), 167–81; P. F. Clarke, 'The Treasury's analytical model of the British economy between the wars', in Furner and Supple (eds.), *The State and Economic Knowledge*, pp. 171–207.

However, at some point the tax system was called into question. Was the pursuit of equality through redistributive taxation at the expense of incentives and efficiency? Although many Conservatives had a ready answer to that question in the 1950s, change to the tax system was not so easy. Institutional rigidities and distributional coalitions constrained action. A cut in the higher levels of income tax in order to create incentives might simply lead to demands from organised workers for higher wages, so leading to cost-push inflation and a loss of export markets, with a balance of payments crisis. The question facing politicians was how to break out of this vicious circle to a new, higher, level of growth. The theme in the next volume is the changing relationship between incentives and equality, and the shift in the way it was viewed between Winston Churchill and Margaret Thatcher, between Hugh Dalton and Gordon Brown.

The present study is open to the charge of adopting too benign a view of the British state in stressing the creation of legitimacy and trust. Was this merely a hegemonic rhetoric which masked deep divisions in society, limiting public spending on public health and welfare, and containing radical threats to existing structures of inequality? This interpretation owes much to Gramsci's realisation that the ruling class might maintain their position not only through force and coercion, but also by making the ruled interpret society through the eyes of their rulers. In other words, the process outlined in this book might be interpreted as the rulers' imposition on the ruled of a hegemonic discourse about taxation which might well have been against the 'real' interests of the majority of the population.[12] The sense of fairness and balance stressed by many Victorian politicians might therefore be merely a cover for a harsh and repressive reality. Hegemony expresses the interests of the dominant capitalist class, but Gramsci placed great importance on the role of intellectuals who articulate the ideas upon which it rested. A shift in the allegiance of intellectuals would be crucial for the replacement of one dominant class by another.

The interpretation of Foucault has influenced interpretations of British history, stimulating debate about a set of questions rather than acceptance of his particular interpretations. He moved away from any notion that intellectuals acted in the interest of a dominant social class, and instead emphasised the role of experts in disciplining and punishing, creating systems of classification and surveillance, both within the state apparatus and within charitable bodies. Expert power and knowledge rendered individuals as objects, whether through the state bureaucracy or within

---

[12] For discussions of Gramsci, see J. V. Femia, *Gramsci's Political Thought* (Oxford, 1981), and T. J. Lears, 'The concept of cultural hegemony: problems and possibilities', *American Historical Review* 90 (1985), 567–93; McKibbin, 'Why was there no Marxism in Great Britain?', is a Gramscian interpretation.

hospitals and schools. The issue becomes one of surveillance, of discipline and regulation.[13] The outcome was, in the opinion of Gatrell, a 'policeman state' which extended far beyond the creation of a professional police force and state control over the system of criminal justice. There was, he suggests, a more general process as 'experts' accumulated evidence that ever more bureaucratic control was needed to redress 'problems', and politicians and the public acquiesced in the creation of ever stricter social discipline. Gatrell admits that there was debate and resistance, and that some problems were real enough and generated their own response. Nevertheless, he argues that the British state in the nineteenth century acquired the 'technical and economic resources to underpin an evolving archipelago of centralised regulatory power'. Bureaucratic systems were established which took on their own life, a social power which was self-generating, creating data or social knowledge to justify further action as efficient and rational. As a result, discretionary procedures and individual or communal sanctions were eroded by discipline and surveillance. On this view, the state was not a progressive or benign agent reforming factories or sanitation: it was intrusive, engaged on surveillance and regulation of dissent, sexual norms, family life. Consent was constructed in a highly divided society by means of more or less concealed forms of coercion. The legitimacy of the state rested on cultural hegemony, but this was not always accepted voluntarily.[14]

Gatrell's main concern is with crime, with the definition of behaviour as socially unacceptable, which might be extended against political and industrial dissent. Thus measures adopted to deal with war-time emergencies or with fascist demonstrations in the 1930s might be used against unions or hunger marchers. This interpretation has support from David Vincent's study of secrecy and Charles Townshend's analysis of public order and security. In their view, the entrenchment of official secrecy means that definitions of public interest pass out of the sphere of public accountability: it was left to officials to define what the public should know, and what the public interest might be. The story is of 'blocked communications'. Trust, and the related notions of probity, confidentiality and integrity, become part of a process of closing off communication. The liberty of the citizen was eroded by lack of knowledge; and freedom to demonstrate and dissent was circumscribed by the use of arbitrary

[13] On Foucault, see his *Discipline and Punish: The Birth of the Prison* (English edn, London, 1977), and *Madness and Civilisation: A History of Insanity in the Age of Reason* (English edn, New York, 1973). Historians dissent from his interpretation but are provoked by his questions.

[14] V. A. C. Gatrell, 'Crime, authority and the policeman-state', in Thompson (ed.), *Cambridge Social History of Britain*, vol. III, pp. 243–310, especially pp. 244, 258–9, 265, 268.

power under the cover of public security. This view of the British state from the end of the nineteenth century suggests a desire by politicians and bureaucrats to distance themselves from repression and despotism, whether in the form practised in the past by the government of Lord Liverpool or in the rest of Europe – or indeed within the British empire. At the same time, they needed reserve powers to defend the government and propertied class. The solution was what may be termed 'honourable secrecy', the attempt to keep the existence of secrecy a secret, which gave great weight to trust, to the cultural and ethical values of self-discipline, honour and probity amongst the official elite and political class. This was possible in the late nineteenth century, when their social and educational background was relatively homogeneous. As Vincent points out, less self-confidence on the part of the political elite would lead to more blatant control of communication; more confidence would have made control unnecessary.[15]

These are powerful criticisms of fondly held beliefs about English liberty, suggesting that they were somewhat spurious. In a sense, the attack on secrecy and lack of knowledge connects with Quentin Skinner's recovery of the neo-Roman notion of liberty, with its belief that slavery and loss of freedom consists in the existence of even a *possibility* that others might constrain one's action.[16] The problem with the British state as it developed in the later nineteeth and twentieth centuries might be seen as the lack of any countervailing power on the executive and officials, who were their own self-authorising tribunal. The point stressed by Vincent and Townshend is that the system has stopped working in the present. Trust in 'honourable secrecy' now seems misplaced, and simply shields the state from scrutiny.[17] But as Vincent notes, for most of the period since 1832, secrecy 'has not been an exercise in pathology', for it delivered competence and morality through a public service combining gentlemanly self-restraint and professional self-discipline.[18] The present book deals with the construction of this sense of integrity and probity in state finances; it might become pathological in the later twentieth century, but in the mid-nineteenth century it offered a way of restabilising the state and recreating a sense of legitimacy.

The disciplining 'policeman state' was not all-powerful and the term might well be misplaced. The repeal of controls on contagious (that is,

---

[15] C. Townshend, *Making the Peace: Public Order and Public Security in Modern Britain* (Oxford, 1993), especially pp. 52–5; Vincent, *Culture of Secrecy*, especially pp. vii, ix, 314–16.

[16] Q. Skinner, *Liberty before Liberalism* (Cambridge, 1998).

[17] Vincent, *Culture of Secrecy*, pp. 316–20; Townshend, *Making the Peace*, pp. 190–1.

[18] Vincent, *Culture of Secrecy*, p. 315.

sexual) disease and the end of compulsory vaccination against small-pox suggest that the power of 'expert' bureaucrats and doctors could be countermanded; indeed, the self-confident bureaucrats in the British state were less likely to defer to medical expertise than in, for example, the United States. What stands out in Britain is the disinclination of civil servants in the Edwardian period to accept the nostrums of eugenicists; rather, they preferred investment in public health and preventive medicine.[19] In other words, the connection between types of expertise and authority varied and needs to be carefully considered in different states. Similarly, the location of power in the centre or localities was not a zero-sum game by which an accretion of power to one entailed a loss to the other. The attempt of the central state to impose more control over, for example, the poor law might result in a shift of local initiatives into the town council or voluntary hospitals. The negotiation of geographies of power was a continuous process, as new functions emerged or the economics of scale of different services changed. As we have seen, the politics of taxation was an important part of the geography of power, for the scope of local and central taxes varied over time and between countries. In Britain, local taxes rose more rapidly than central taxes for much of the nineteenth century and then reached a limit. The yield of local taxes stagnated from about 1900 and new sources of funding were in the hands of the central government. By contrast, in Germany local taxes were more buoyant, and the difficulty was in increasing the resources of the central state. Different fiscal regimes were therefore crucial to the form of the state.[20]

The geography of power also involved a complex negotiation between forms of authority rather than a simple matter of defeat or success. The example of inquests and coroners' juries is a case in point, which connects with the emergence of knowledge-based forms of governance. Again, this was not a zero-sum game in which experts win and the public or civic participation loses. It would be mistaken to reduce the history of the Victorian state to such simple binary oppositions. Ian Burney points out that these were 'highly permeable oppositions', which did not operate 'in pristine relationships of mutual exclusivity' so much as through continuing 'processes of interactive (and provisional) historical definition in which neither of the ostensible poles is in itself stable or complete'. In his study of the inquest, the medical profession wished to define it as a site of

---

[19] D. Porter, 'Enemies of the race: biologism, environmentalism and public health in Edwardian England', *Victorian Studies* 34 (1991); on the hostility to compulsory vaccination, see R. M. McLeod, 'Law, medicine and public opinion: the resistance to compulsory health legislation, 1870–1907', *Public Law* 12 (1967).

[20] See Driver, *Power and Paupers*, and Ogborn, 'Local power and state regulation'.

applied medical enquiry, which collided with notions of popular liberties in an open tribunal of lay people. The result was not a simple defeat of one monolithic rationale by another with a decline in participation and rise in expertise. Rather, the debate involved hybrids and ambiguities, of scientific democrats, popular bureaucrats, innovating traditionalists. The debate over the role of the inquest was framed by a discourse of 'English liberties' – the question was whether the inquest was seen as an expression of public opinion and freedom or a sign of the limits of participation, an irrelevance or even a barrier to knowledge.[21] Much the same point might be made about the relationship between lay commissioners and the government officials or surveyors. The commissioners (and the assessors and collectors) might be read as defenders of liberty against despotism, as protectors of the privacy of the citizen against inquisition. On the other hand, they could be criticised as bastions of privilege and barriers to accurate knowledge, so imposing additional taxes on other members of society who did not have power to manipulate the tax assessment to their own advantage. The bureaucrat could then be recast as the protector of liberty or equity, and of sound information. By the late nineteenth century, the liberty of the taxpayer was more likely to be protected by accountants who presented their clients' tax returns, and were accepted as trustworthy and reliable. The accountants and tax officials developed mutual respect for their professional expertise, reaching a *modus vivendi* over what was acceptable. And the change in the status of the commissioners to a court of appeal might be justified in terms of maintaining the ancient liberties of the citizen against bureaucracy. The danger was that the commissioners were seen as part of the tax system rather than independent arbitrators. The divisions between participation and expertise were blurred or ambiguous.

Similarly, secrecy was defined in different ways in different contexts. One of the main props of the Gladstonian financial constitution was the scrutiny of expenditure, the transparency of annual votes on each budget head. Gladstone interpreted any breach of this principle as an attack on English liberty. Citizens would behave with responsibility, pay their taxes and support the state, if the state itself spent the money it received in a responsible and open way. Minute scrutiny of spending differed from most other European countries, where the government had much greater discretion in its expenditure. The 'meanness' of British spending on public art collections, for example, may be seen as a sign of philistinism. More accurately, it was a sign of the greater power of the Commons to subject plans to criticism than in other European countries.

[21] Burney, *Bodies of Evidence*, pp. 1–3, 6–7.

Spending was therefore transparent. On the other hand, discussion of changes in the fiscal regime were increasingly carried on in secrecy, often limited to a small circle within the government. Secrecy in this case was justified as means of preventing 'corruption', of special pleading by interest groups which would subvert the political process. The cultural meanings of transparency and secrecy were therefore mediated through a discourse of probity and rectitude. Transparency in spending plans and secrecy in fiscal change were both justified by the same rhetoric, as leading to restraint and honesty, purging the state of corruption and making it 'knave proof'.

One result was to create a greater sense of trust in the way the state used the money provided by the public. However, trust might be misplaced, and the belief that the fiscal system was balanced and equitable might rest on cultural hegemony which sustained the *status quo* and the existing distribution of income and wealth as 'natural'. The interpretation put forward in this study of taxation is somewhat different. In the first place, the creation of a culture of fiscal rectitude was in many ways a response to the critics of the state, and adopted many elements of their language. After all, the radicals wished to purge the state and reduce its spending on militarism and sinecures; the task of the political class of mid-Victorian Britain was both to reduce spending and, just as significantly, to convince the public that they were taking effective steps to 'chain leviathan'. The assumption of radical critics was that government spending distorted social relations; the creation of equity and balance rested on *reduced* expenditure. The rhetoric of probity and trust created by politicians did not simply mean the imposition of cultural hegemony on the subordinate class. In the first place, it also constrained the ruling elite, for any attempt to use the fiscal system in a blatantly 'unfair' way would expose the rhetoric as no more than a sham. A central argument of this book is that politicians and, above all, Treasury officials, believed their own rhetoric – or acted as if they did, which is for all practical purposes the same thing. Secondly, the creation of a sense of probity and rectitude made it possible for radicals to turn to the state in a much more positive way than in the early nineteenth century. The organised working class in Britain was willing to work through the state and the fiscal system, and the cultural hegemony which established the sense of equity and fairness in one form might then be turned against the *status quo* by allowing the use of the state and taxation for redistribution.[22]

The language of taxation was central to defining relationships between citizens and the state, and to discursive construction of identities. As

---

[22] This follows McKibbin, 'Why was there no Marxism in Great Britain?'.

David Cannadine has argued in *Class in Britain*, one of the major tasks of politicians was to impose their vision *of* the people and the social structure *on* the people. He suggests that political history should be written less in terms of government administration and manoeuvrings for position than through an analysis of the use of political language and political culture 'in the creation and articulation of social identities'. The 'linguistic turn' has been a major theme in recent writing on British history. Cannadine suggests that politicians attempted to make people prefer one of three visions of society: as a hierarchy of finely layered and graded distinctions; as a three-fold division into collective groups of upper, middle and lower class; or as a binary divide between us and them.[23] Taxation was one of the most important sites of this attempt to impose one social vision in preference to another, and to marginalise alternative social descriptions. In many ways, Gladstone was articulating a vision of society as an organic, hierarchical, society against those who wished to describe it as divided between spontaneous and industrious incomes. In Gladstone's view, society should not be divided into two mutually exclusive categories, for spontaneous incomes might include morally deserving widows as well as the idle rich. One of the most important themes running through this study of taxation is the changing language of social description. It was more than simply a division between the hierarchical, triadic and binary perceptions of society, for there were contests within as well as between these social descriptions. The divisions between spontaneous and industrious incomes, and between earned and unearned income, were both based on a binary conception of society, yet the implications were somewhat different. The former suggested a need to relieve productive income of taxes in order to foster a dynamic capitalist society based on profit; the latter could be associated with a wider attack on the pursuit of profit as the basis of society and a desire to replace capitalism by socialism. And the binary divide might be used in order to define alliances within a triadic perception of society. The notion of a binary conflict between parasitical *rentiers* and active producers might be widely accepted, but related in different ways to other social groups. As we have seen, an attack on *rentier* property could be used to link workers and industrialists as active producers against idle parasites. On the other hand, it was possible to argue that *all* property was threatened by envious and selfish attacks from the property-less. The study of political language also needs to be extended from descriptions of the social structure to visions of the state and economy. The state and its relations with citizens were described through a rhetoric of fairness, equity and balance; and perceptions of

[23] D. Cannadine, *Class in Britain* (London and New Haven, 1998), pp. xi, 21–2, 164.

the national debt changed from a burden to a source of security and liberty.

A problem with the stress on the language of social description can be a neglect of institutional procedures and economic and social structures. The state and institutional structures should not be ignored. The widespread acceptance of the language of fairness, of the interpretation of the debt as beneficial rather than merely a burden, rested on the reshaping of the tax system, on the careful negotiation of compliance and the financial management of the debt. Historians should not simply study political language as an alternative to a careful analysis of administrative structures: they interact in complicated ways. The government of Lord Liverpool reduced taxes and introduced many of the administrative procedures to contain spending; they were not able to convince critics of their probity. The success of Peel and Gladstone was to create symmetry between administrative procedures and political language which *did* convince many Chartists and radicals. Further, the language of social description might be more than simply a way of perceiving society and giving it cultural meaning. Politicians might also use administrative measures and policies to change social structure to accord with their vision. This was most immediately apparent in the empire, where definitions of property rights or political authority were redefined to allow fiscal extraction. A similar point might be made at home, where taxes could be used to modify behaviour – whether through the imposition of taxes on forms of consumption, or the encouragement of life insurance, or the provision of tax breaks for family responsibilities.

The implication of the approach adopted here is that both political language and the form of the state matter. Compliance with taxation did not rest simply on the powerful rhetoric of equity and balance formulated by Gladstone and others; it depended on the systems of assessment and collection, on the role of the Commons in scrutinising spending plans and the exclusion of interest groups from shaping the fiscal regime. Different state systems might also create a greater or lesser degree of contestation and permeability. In the United States, for example, there was not a powerful career civil service with a well-developed ethos as in Britain; and there were competing centres of power and policy within the government. State institutions in the United States were therefore more open to new ideas, with greater diversity of official opinion within government. In Britain, institutions were designed to be 'knave proof' – difficult for politicians to turn to their own advantage, or to be exploited by particular interest groups. The last three or four decades of the nineteenth century saw the creation of the British state described by Furner and Supple: a more monolithic and impermeable system, with greater continuity and homogeneity of 'official' economic doctrine. On the other hand, Britain and the United States had common features compared with the more statist traditions of France or Prussia, with a greater willingness to delegate to other bodies and to respond to the concerns of interest groups.[24] One of the features of Britain in the later nineteenth century was the creation of extremely powerful normative assumptions in the Treasury about the fiscal constitution. This rested in part on the common social and education background of the officials, and their long-term careers within the civil service. But this is far from accepting the interpretation put forward by some historians that policy was determined, or at least heavily influenced, by the particular social grouping from which the officials and many politicians came – the so-called 'gentlemanly capitalists' of land and finance. On this view, the Treasury defined the national interest in terms of finance and largely ignored the demands of industry.[25] The interpretation adopted here is different. Policy did not reflect the dominance of one particular interest group, for that would threaten the assumption that the state was disinterested. 'Fairness' was more than a rhetorical device; it had to be seen to be done. Although this approach gives the state a large element of autonomy from interest groups, we should also admit that the state was susceptible to new ideas at particular times. States are not only about power; they are also about knowledge and thinking. State officials have access to data with which they think about social and economic issues. Interest groups put forward their demands and their own interpretations – yet the knowledge available within the state made it more than simply a broker between conflicting nostrums. It provided knowledge to assess the validity of competing claims which were judged against a definition of the public good or at least of the state's needs.[26]

These reflections are entering into highly complicated issues of the generation of economic knowledge and the relationship between ideas and action. In order to develop these reflections on the form of the British state and economic policies in the 'long nineteenth century', this study of taxation should be complemented by other studies of monetary and banking policy, free trade and consumption, regulation of monopolies and profits, and control of pollution and nuisances. We would need to consider the popularisation of political economy, the way it entered the political culture and institutional system; and the generation of economic

---

[24] See Furner and Supple, 'Ideas, institutions, and state', pp. 7–8, 35–6; and Skocpol, 'Bringing the state back in'.

[25] P. Cain and A. G. Hopkins, *British Imperialism: Innovation and Expansion, 1688–1914* (London, 1993).

[26] Furner and Supple, 'Ideas, institutions and state', p. 28.

and social knowledge. Certainly, it is time to jettison any simple notion that the Victorian state marked a simple shift from moral economy in the eighteenth century, with notions of fair prices and just wages, to a simple reliance on political economy and the invisible hand of the market. In reality, political economy and the market continued to be permeated with notions of morality – of the proper level of profit taken by railway or gas companies, of the rights of shopkeepers over their female customers who were using the credit of their husbands, of the freedom of polluters to pass social costs on to other members of society. Such issues of liberty and the relationship between the individual and the wider community were matters for political philosophy, for legal argument, for medical knowledge. Taxation was a central element in these wide-ranging debates over what it meant to live in a capitalist society, and informed many of the other debates. Monopolists had taxing powers over their customers; polluters imposed taxes on residents of towns who paid the costs of ill-health and dirt.[27] The language of taxation permeates the history of Britain in the 'long nineteenth century'.

[27] See M. J. Daunton, 'Taxation and representation in the Victorian city', in R. Rodger and R. Colls (eds.), *Cities of Ideas: Citizenship and Governance in Urban Britain* (Aldershot, forthcoming).

Appendix: chancellors of the Exchequer, 1841–1914

3 September 1841	Henry Goulburn
6 July 1846	Charles Wood
27 February 1852	Benjamin Disraeli
28 December 1852	William Gladstone
28 February 1855	George Cornewall Lewis
26 February 1858	Benjamin Disraeli
18 June 1859	William Gladstone
6 July 1866	Benjamin Disraeli
29 February 1868	George Ward Hunt
9 December 1868	Robert Lowe
30 August [?] 1873	William Gladstone
21 February 1874	Stafford Northcote
28 April 1880	William Gladstone
16 December 1882	H. C. E. Childers
24 June 1885	Michael Hicks Beach
6 February 1886	William Harcourt
3 August 1886	Randolph Churchill
14 January 1887	George Goschen
18 August 1892	William Harcourt
29 June 1895	Michael Hicks Beach
12 July 1902	Charles Ritchie
9 October 1902	Austen Chamberlain
11 December 1905	Herbert Asquith
16 April 1908	David Lloyd George

Bibliography

ARCHIVES

UNIVERSITY OF BIRMINGHAM LIBRARY

Austen Chamberlain Papers

BODLEIAN LIBRARY, OXFORD

Asquith Papers
Harcourt Papers

BRITISH LIBRARY

Gladstone Papers
E. W. Hamilton Papers

BRITISH LIBRARY OF POLITICAL AND ECONOMIC SCIENCE

Dalton Papers

GLOUCESTERSHIRE RECORD OFFICE

St Aldwyn Papers

LONDON METROPOLITAN ARCHIVE

Minutes and proceedings of London County Council

NATIONAL LIBRARY OF WALES, ABERYSTWYTH

Harpton Court Manuscripts

PUBLIC RECORD OFFICE, KEW

Cabinet Office
    CAB 37 Cabinet Papers

Boards of Stamps, Taxes, Excise, Stamps and Taxes, and Inland Revenue
    IR 40 Board of Inland Revenue: Stamps and Taxes Division
    IR 63 Board of Inland Revenue: Budget and Finance Bill Papers
    IR 74 Board of Inland Revenue: Private Office Papers: Memoranda
    IR 75 Board of Inland Revenue: Private Office Papers: Committee Papers
Treasury
    T168 Papers of Sir George Hamilton and Sir Edward Hamilton
    T170 Treasury: Papers of Sir John Bradbury
    T171 Chancellor of the Exchequer's Office: Budget and Finance Bill
    Papers
    T172 Chancellor of the Exchequer's Office: Miscellaneous Papers
    T176 Treasury: Papers of Sir Otto Niemeyer

PARLIAMENTARY PAPERS

PP 1828 V, *Second Report from the Select Committee on Public Income and Expenditure
of the United Kingdom. Ordnance Estimates.*

PP 1828 V, *Fourth Report from the Select Committee on Public Income and Expenditure
of the United Kingdom. Revenue Expenditure and Debt.*

PP 1837–8 XXI, *First Report from Select Committee on Rating of Tenements.*

PP 1847–8 XXI pt I, *Report from the Select Committee on Navy, Army and Ordnance
Estimates.*

PP 1849 IX, *First and Second Reports from the Select Committee on Army and Ordnance Expenditure (Ordnance).*

PP 1849 XIV, *Report from the Select Committee on the Friendly Societies Bill.*

PP 1850 X, *Report from the Select Committee on Army and Ordnance Expenditure
(Army).*

PP 1850 XIX, *Report from the Select Committee on Investments for the Middle and
Working Classes.*

PP 1851 VII, *Report from the Select Committee on Army and Ordnance Expenditure.*

PP 1852 IX, *First Report from the Select Committee on the Income and Property Tax
together with the proceedings of the committee, minutes of evidence, appendix and
index.*

PP 1852 IX, *Second Report from the Select Committee on the Income and Property
Tax.*

PP 1856 L, *Collectors' fines (Prescot divison): return of all persons with their names
and occupations in full, on whom fines have been levied from 1 Jan. 1850 to 23
June 1856 in the Prescot division in the county Palatine of Lancaster, for refusing
to act as collectors and assessors of government taxes....*

PP 1857 (1st session) IV, *First Report of the Commissioners of the Inland Revenue.*

PP 1857 (2nd session) IX, *Report from the Select Committee on Public Monies.*

PP 1859 session 1 XIX, *Copy of financial despatch to the government of India, 19
January 1859. Review of the finances of India as shown in the actual accounts of
1856–7 and as estimated for 1857–8 and 1858–9.*

PP 1859 session 1 XIX, *A copy of financial dispatches between the government of India
and the secretary of state for India respecting new loans required for India and of
all notifications of the government of India concerning the public debt.*

PP 1861 VII, *Report from the Select Committee on Income and Property Tax.*

PP 1862 XII, *Select Committee on Inland Revenue and Customs Establishments.*

PP 1863 VI, *Report from the Select Committee on Inland Revenue and Customs Establishments.*

PP 1865 XLI, *Copies of correspondence between the Treasury and the Board of Inland Revenue in August and September 1863 respecting the exemption from income tax of rents and dividends applied to charitable purposes and of correspondence between the Treasury, the Home Office and Charity Commissioners, respecting an inquiry into the management of certain charitable institutions, together with the reports of the Charity inspectors by whom such inquiry was conducted.*

PP 1867 L, *Copy of correspondence between the secretary of state for India in Council and the government of India in 1865, 1866 and 1867 on the subject of the permanent settlement of the land revenue in India.*

PP 1867–8 XIII, *Report from the Select Committee on Poor Rates Assessment together with proceedings of the Committee, Minutes of Evidence and Appendix.*

PP 1870 XX, *Report of the Commissioners of Inland Revenue on the duties under their management for the years 1856 to 1869 inclusive; with some retrospective history and complete tables of accounts of the duties from their first imposition*, vol. I.

PP 1870 XX, *Report of the Commissioners of Inland Revenue on the duties under their management for the years 1856 to 1869 inclusive*, vol. II.

PP 1871 XXXVII, *Copies of the circular letter addressed by the Board of Inland Revenue to the District Commissioners of Taxes in England and Wales, 16 May 1860.*

PP 1871 XXXVII, *Copy of a letter from the clerk to the commissioners of income tax for the City of London as to returns required from private employers of the salaries which they give to their clerks; also, of a memorandum from the Board of Inland Revenue thereupon.*

PP 1871 XXXVII, *Return of the amount of income tax collected in Great Britain together with the percentage of loss upon such amount.*

PP 1871 XLVIII, *Return of all taxes and imposts from which the revenues of the several colonies of the British empire are raised, together with the gross amount yielded by each tax or impost.*

PP 1873 XXXIX, *Return showing the number of persons charged to the income tax* . . . .

PP 1874 VIII, *Report from the Select Committee on East India Finance.*

PP 1874 XLVII, *Copy of a paper entitled 'Observations on some questions of Indian finance, by Sir John Strachey', 6 Feb. 1874.*

PP 1878–9 XLII, *Return of the number of persons charged to the income tax for the year ended . . . 5 April 1873 to 1878.*

PP 1878–9 LV, *Copy of a circular to all local governments and administrations in India, dated Simla, 16 June 1879, in explanation of the present financial position of the government of India, and of the recent orders issued regarding the reduction of expenditure and the revision of provincial assignments.*

PP 1881 XXIX, *Supplement to the 24th Report of the Commissioners of Inland Revenue on the Inland Revenue for the year ended 31 March 1881, being a continuation of the tables of accounts contained in Volume II of the report of 1870.*

PP 1886 XII, 1887 XIII, 1888 XXII, 1889 XV, 1890 XVIII, 1890–1 XVIII, 1892 XVIII, *Report and Proceedings, Select Committee on Town Holdings.*

PP 1890–1 XLVII, *National debt. Report by the secretary and comptroller general of the proceedings of the commissioners for the reduction of the national debt from 1786 to 31 March 1890.*

PP 1890–1 XLVIII, 1899 LI, 1902 LV, 1906 LXV, 1914 L, *Finance accounts of the United Kingdom, years ended 31 March.*

PP 1890–1 XLVIII, *Return showing ... the aggregate gross liabilities of the state ... at the close of each financial year from 1835–6 to 1890–1 ....*

PP 1898 LXXXV, *Customs tariff of the United Kingdom from 1800 to 1897, with some notes upon the history of the more important branches of receipt from the year 1660.*

PP 1900 XVIII, *43rd Report of the Commissioners of Her Majesty's Inland Revenue for the year ended 31 March 1900.*

PP 1900 XXIX, *Final Report of the Royal Commission on the Administration of the Expenditure of India.*

PP 1901 XXIV, *Final Report of Royal Commission on Local Taxation (England and Wales).*

PP 1905 XLIV, *Report of the Departmental Committee on Income Tax.*

PP 1905 LIII, *Return showing which of the colonies have established systems of graduated income tax levied at different rates on earned and unearned incomes, or both, with particulars in each case of the rate of tax and the system of assessment and collection.*

PP 1905 LXXXV, *Reports from HM representatives abroad respecting graduated income taxes in foreign states.*

PP 1906 IX *Report from the Select Committee on Income Tax.*

PP 1911 XLV, *Return showing for the year ended 31 March 1911 (1) the amount contributed by England, Scotland and Ireland respectively to the revenue collected by imperial officers (2) the expenditure of English, Scottish and Irish services met out of such revenue; and (3) the balances of revenue contributed by England, Scotland and Ireland respectively, which are available for imperial expenditure ....*

PP 1914 XXIV, *Final Report of the Royal Commission on Local Taxation (England and Wales).*

PP 1914 XL, *Final Report of the Departmental Committee on Local Taxation in England and Wales.*

PP 1918 III, *Select Committee on Gas Undertakings (Statutory Prices).*

PP 1919 XXIII pt 1, *Royal Commisssion on Income Tax, Third Instalment of Minutes of Evidence.*

PP 1920 XVIII, *Report of the Royal Commission on the Income Tax.*

PP 1927 XI, *Report of the Committee on National Debt and Taxation.*

PP 1930–1 XIII, *Report of the Committee on Finance and Industry.*

OTHER SERIALS

Annual conferences, Labour Party.

Dictionary of American Biography.

Dictionary of National Biography.

Labour Representation Committee and *Labour Party, Conference Reports.*

The Law Reports 1901. House of Lords, Judicial Committee of the Privy Council (London, 1901).

The Law Reports 1903. House of Lords, Judicial Committee of the Privy Council (London, 1903).

Reports of Tax Cases under the Act 37 Vict. cap 16 and under the Taxes Management Act.

Parliamentary Debates.
Parliamentary History of England from the Earliest Period to 1803.
Who Was Who.

PRIMARY PRINTED SOURCES

Alison, A., 'On the financial measures of the reformed parliament. No 1. The Whig budget', *Blackwood's Edinburgh Magazine* 29 (June 1831).
'Whig and Tory finance', *Blackwood's Edinburgh Magazine* 46 (Oct. 1839).
'Direct taxation', *Blackwood's Edinburgh Magazine* 61 (Feb. 1847).
Babbage, C., *Thoughts on the Principles of Taxation with Reference to a Property Tax and its Exceptions* (London, 1852).
Bentham, J., *Constitutional Code for the Use of All Nations and All Governments Professing Liberal Opinions* (London, 1830).
[Birmingham Income Tax Reform Association], *Address of the Birmingham Income Tax Reform Association to the Electors of Great Britain and Ireland* (Birmingham, 1857).
Blunden, G. H., 'The future of the income tax', *Economic Journal* 2 (1901).
Boyd, C. W. (ed.), *Mr Chamberlain's Speeches*, vol. 1 (London, 1914).
Boyd, W., *Observations on Lord Grenville's Essay on the Sinking Fund* (London, 1828).
Brooke, J. and Sorensen, M. (eds.), *The Prime Ministers' Papers. W. E. Gladstone*, vol. 1: *Autobiographica* (London, 1971).
The Prime Ministers' Papers Series. W. E. Gladstone, vol. III: *Autobiographical Memoranda, 1845–66* (London, 1978).
Brooks, D. (ed.), *The Destruction of Lord Rosebery: From the Diary of Sir Edward Hamilton, 1894–5* (London, 1986).
Burke, E., *Reflections on the Revolution in France* (London, 1790; Everyman edn, 1910).
The Writings and Speeches of Edmund Burke, vol. II: *Party, Parliament and the American Crisis*, ed. P. Langford (Oxford, 1981).
Buxton, S. C., *Finance and Politics: An Historical Study, 1789–1885* (2 vols., London, 1888).
Mr Gladstone as Chancellor of the Exchequer (London, 1901).
Buxton, S. C. and Barnes, G. S., *A Handbook to the Death Duties* (London, 1890).
Cairnes, J. E., *On the Best Means of Raising the Supplies of a War Expenditure* (London, 1854).
Campbell-Kelly, M. (ed.), *The Works of Charles Babbage*, vol. V: *Scientific and Miscellaneous Papers, II* (London, 1981).
Cannan, E., *The History of Local Rates in England* (London, 1896).
Chiozza Money, L. G., *Riches and Poverty* (London, 1905).
Churchill, W. S., *Liberalism and the Social Problem* (London, 1909).
Clayden, P. W., *England under the Coalition* (London, 1892).
Cobbett, W., *Noble Nonsense! Or Cobbett's Exhibition of the Stupid and Insolent Pamphlet of Lord Grenville* (London, 1828).
Cole, G. D. H. and Cole, M. (eds.), *The Opinions of William Cobbett* (London, 1944).
[Coode, J.], 'The income tax', *Edinburgh Review* 97 (1853).

[Croker, J. W.], 'Policy of Sir Robert Peel', *Quarterly Review* 120 (Sept. 1842).

Disraeli, B., *Sibyl, or the Two Nations* (London, 1845; Longman's edn, 1899).

Dowell, S., *A History of Taxation and Taxes in England from the Earliest Times to the Present Day*, vol. II: *Taxation from the Civil War to the Present Day* (London, 1884).

Edgeworth, F. Y., *Papers Relating to Political Economy*, vol. II (London, 1925).

Fabian Society, *Capital and Land* (Fabian Tract 7, London, 1888).

English Progress Towards Social Democracy (Fabian Tract 15, London, 1890).

The Unearned Increment (Fabian Tract 30, London, 1891).

The Difficulties of Individualism (Fabian Tract 69, London, 1896).

Socialism and Superior Brains (Fabian Tract 146, London, 1909).

Farrer, T. H., 'The imperial finance of the last four years, III', *Contemporary Review* 58 (1890).

'Sir William Harcourt's budget', *Contemporary Review* 66 (1894).

Financial Reform Association, *Financial Reform Tracts, 3, Taxation Part I* (London, 1848).

Financial Reform Tracts, Number 6, The National Budget for 1849 by Richard Cobden MP in a Letter to Robertson Gladstone, President of the Financial Reform Association of Liverpool, with a Report of the Public Meeting Held at the Concert Hall, Liverpool, December 20, 1848, at which the Budget was Announced to the Nation (London, 1848?).

Financial Reform Tracts, 15: Direct Taxation (London, 1850?).

Account of the Formation, Principles and Objects of the Liverpool Financial Reform Association as Embodied in the Speeches Delivered at a Public Meeting Held in Liverpool, Jan. 17, 1849 (London, 1849).

Address of the Council of the Liverpool Financial Reform Association to the Tax-payers of the United Kingdom, Showing how the Class for the Protection of Whose Property the National Debt Was Incurred, Changed the System of Taxation, so as to Remove the Burden from their Own Shoulders to Those of the People (Liverpool, 1849).

Report on Taxation. Direct and Indirect. Adopted by the Financial Reform Association, Liverpool, and Presented at the Annual Meeting of the National Association for the Promotion of Social Science, Held at Bradford, October 1859 (Liverpool, 1859).

Financial Reform Union, *Papers on Taxation and Expenditure Issued by the Financial Reform Union. Number 2. J. Noble, Suggestions for a Revision of Taxation* (London, 1868).

Papers on Taxation and Expenditure Issued by the Financial Reform Union: Number 3, A Budget for 1869 Based Upon Mr Cobden's 'National Budget' Proposed in 1849 (London, 1868).

Foot, M. R. D. and Matthew, H. C. G. (eds.), *The Gladstone Diaries*, vol. IV: *1848–1854* (Oxford, 1974).

Giffen, R., 'Some economic aspects of the war', *Economic Journal* 10 (1906).

Gladstone, W. E., *The Financial Statements of 1853, 1860–63* (London, 1863).

Speeches on Parliamentary Reform in 1866 (London, 1866).

'Free trade, railways and the growth of commerce', *Nineteenth Century* 7 (1880).

'Lecky's History of England in the eighteenth century', *Nineteenth Century* 21 (1887).

'Mr Lecky and political morality', *Nineteenth Century* 22 (1887).

[Greg, W. R.], 'The expected reform bill', *Edinburgh Review* 95 (1852).

'British taxation', *Edinburgh Review* 111 (1860).

Grenville, W., *Essay on the Supposed Advantages of a Sinking Fund* (London, 1827).

Haldane, R. B., 'The Liberal party and its prospects', *Contemporary Review* 53 (1888).

Hamilton, E. W., *Conversion and Redemption: An Account of the Operations under the National Debt Conversion Act, 1888 and the National Debt Redemption Act, 1889* (London, 1889).

Hamilton, R., *An Inquiry Concerning the Rise and Progress, the Redemption . . . and Management of the National Debt of Great Britain* (Edinburgh, 1813).

Hemming, G. W., *A Just Income Tax How Possible* (London, 1852).

Hobson, J.A., *The Evolution of Modern Capitalism: A Study of Machine Production* (London, 1894).

The Problem of the Unemployed: An Enquiry and An Economic Policy (London, 1896).

John Ruskin: Social Reformer (London, 1898).

The Economics of Distribution (London, 1900).

Imperialism: A Study (London, 1902; 2nd edn 1905).

The Industrial System: An Inquiry into Earned and Unearned Income (London, 1909).

Liberalism (London, 1911).

The Science of Wealth (London, 1911).

Richard Cobden: International Man (London 1918).

Taxation in the New State (London, 1919).

Confessions of an Economic Heretic (London, 1938).

Holland, G. C., *Suggestions towards Improving the Present System of Corn Laws* (London, 1841).

Hubbard, J. G., *How Should an Income Tax Be Levied? Considered in a Letter to the Rt. Hon. B. D'Israeli* (London, 1852).

Hume, D., *Political Essays*, ed. K. Haakossen (Cambridge, 1994).

Ingenbleek, J., *Impôts directs et indirects sur le revenue: la contribution personnelle en Belgique, l'Einkommensteurer en prusse, l'income tax en Angleterre* (Brussels and Leipzig, 1908).

Jennings, L. J. (ed.), *The Croker Papers: The Correspondence and Diaries of the late Rt Hon John Wilson Croker* (2nd edn, 3 vols., London, 1885).

Jevons, W. S., *The Coal Question: An Inquiry Concerning the Progress of the Nation, and the Probable Exhaustion of our Coal-mines* (London, 1865).

The Match Tax: A Problem in Finance (London, 1871).

Kennan, K. K., *Income Taxation: Methods and Results in Various Countries* (Milwaukee, 1910).

Keynes, J. M., *The Collected Writings of John Maynard Keynes*, vol. XXII: *Activities, 1939–45. Internal War Finance*, ed. D. Moggridge (London, 1978).

Kolthammer, F. W., *The Ratan Tata Foundation. Memorandum on Problems of Poverty No. 1: Some Notes on the Incidence of Taxation on the Working Class Family* (London, n.d., 1913?).

Lecky, W. E. H., *History of the Rise and Influence of the Spirit of Rationalism in Europe* (2 vols., London, 1865).

'Mr Gladstone and the income tax', *Nineteenth Century* 22 (1887).

[Lewis, G. C.], 'The late elections and free trade', *Edinburgh Review* 96 (1852).

'The fall of the Derby ministry', *Edinburgh Review* 97 (1853).

The Shade of Cocker and the Chancellor of the Exchequer: A Dialogue on the Income Tax (London, 1856?).

Lewis, G. F. (ed.), *Letters of the Rt Hon Sir George Cornewall Lewis to Various Friends* (London, 1870).

Lugard, F. J. D., *Political Memoranda: Revision of Instructions to Political Officers on Subjects Chiefly Political and Administrative, 1913–18* (3rd edn, reprinted London, 1970).

Macaulay, T. B., *The History of England from the Accession of James II*, vol. IV (1855; Folio Press edn, London, 1986).

[McCulloch, J. R.], 'Finance accounts of the United Kingdom for the year ended 5 Jan. 1823', *Edinburgh Review* 77 (1823).

McCulloch, J. R., *A Treatise on the Principles and Practical Influence of Taxation and the Funding System* (London, 1845).

MacDonald, R., *Socialism and Government* (2 vols., London, 1909).

Maitland, J. G., *Property and Income Tax: The Present State of the Question* (London, 1853).

Mallet, B., *British Budgets, 1887–88 to 1912–13* (London, 1913).

Malthus, T. R., *Principles of Political Economy*, vol. I, ed. J. Pullen (Cambridge, 1989).

Marshall, A., *Official Papers*, ed. J. M. Keynes (London 1926).

Matthew, H. C. G., *The Gladstone Diaries with Cabinet Minutes and Prime-Ministerial Correspondence. Introduction to Volumes XII and XIII, 1887–1896* (Oxford, 1994).

Matthew, H. C. G. (ed.), *The Gladstone Diaries*, vol. VI: *1861–68* (Oxford, 1978).

The Gladstone Diaries, vol. X: *1881–83* (Oxford, 1990).

[Merivale, H.], 'M'Culloch on taxation and funding', *Edinburgh Review* 82 (1845).

Mill, J. S., *Considerations on Representative Government* (London, 1861), in *Collected Works*, vol. XIX, *Essays on Politics and Society*, ed. J. M. Robson (London, 1977).

Principles of Political Economy, ed. W. J. Ashley (London, 1909).

Collected Works, vol. IV: *Essays on Economics and Society*, I, ed. J. M. Robson with an introduction by L. Robbins (London, 1967).

Collected Works, vol. II, *Autobiography and Literary Essays*, ed. J. M. Robson and J. Stillinger (London and Toronto, 1981).

Collected Works, vol. XXII: *Newspaper Writings*, I: *December 1822–July 1831*, ed. A. P. and J. M. Robson (London, 1986).

Morley, J., *The Life of William Ewart Gladstone* (3 vols., London, 1903).

Newmarch, W., 'On the loans raised by Mr Pitt during the first French War, 1793–1801', *Journal of the London Statistical Society* 18 (1855).

Norman, G. W., *An Examination of Some Prevailing Opinions as to the Pressure of Taxation in This and Other Countries* (4th edn, London, 1864).

Parnell, H., *On Financial Reform* (3rd edn, London, 1831).

Pigou, A. C., *Wealth and Welfare* (London, 1912).

A Study in Public Finance (London, 1928).

Pigou, A. C. (ed.), *Memorials of Alfred Marshall* (London, 1925).

Ricardo, D., *The Works and Correspondence of David Ricardo*, ed. P. Sraffa with the collaboration of M. H. Dodd (Cambridge, 1951–73).

Rickards, G. K., *The Financial Policy of War: Two Lectures on the Funding System and on the Different Modes of Raising Supplies* (London, 1855).

Ruskin, J., *Unto This Last: Four Essays on the First Principles of Political Economy* (London, 1862).

Works, ed. E. T. Cook and E. T. Wedderburn (London, 1903–12).

Samuel, H., *Liberalism* (London, 1902).

'The taxation of the various classes of the people', *Journal of the Royal Statistical Society* 82 (1919).

Sanger, C. P., 'Is the English system of taxation fair?', *Economic Journal* 9 (1899).

Seligman, E. R. A., *Progressive Taxation in Theory and Practice* (2nd edn, Princeton, 1908).

Sidgwick, H., *Principles of Political Economy* (2nd edn, London, 1887).

Smith, A., *An Inquiry into the Nature and Causes of the Wealth of Nations*, ed. R. H. Campbell, A. S. Skinner and W. B. Todd (2 vols., Oxford, 1976).

Snowden, P., *A Few Hints to Lloyd George: Where Is the Money to Come From? The Question Answered* (ILP, London, 1909).

Labour and National Finance (London, 1920).

[Spring-Rice, T.], 'Financial prospects, 1849', *Edinburgh Review* 89 (1849).

Stamp, J. C., 'The meaning of "unearned income"', *Economic Journal* 25 (1915).

British Incomes and Property: The Application of Official Statistics to Economic Problems (London, 1916).

[Tennant, C.], *The People's Blue Book: Taxation As It Is and As It Ought To Be* (London, 1856; 2nd edn 1857; 3rd edn 1862; 4th edn 1872).

Walker, F. A., 'The source of business profits', *Quarterly Journal of Economics* 1 (1886–7).

Webb, B., *Our Partnership*, ed. B. Drake and M. I. Cole (London, 1948).

Webb, S., 'The rate of interest', *Quarterly Journal of Economics* 2 (1887–8).

'The rate of interest and the laws of distribution', *Quarterly Journal of Economics* 2 (1887–8).

Webb, S. and B., *Problems of Modern Industry* (London, 1898).

A Constitution for the Socialist Commonwealth of Great Britain (London, 1920).

Whittaker, J. K. (ed.), *The Correspondence of Alfred Marshall, Economist*, vol. III: *Towards the Close, 1903–1924* (Cambridge, 1996).

Yonge, C. D., *The Life and Administration of Robert Banks, Second Earl Liverpool* (3 vols., London, 1868).

Young, A., *Travels in France during the Years 1787, 1788 and 1789 Undertaken More Particularly with a View to Ascertaining the Cultivation, Wealth, Resources and National Prosperity of the Kingdom of France* (Bury St Edmunds, 1792).

SECONDARY SOURCES

Alborn, T., *Conceiving Companies: Joint-Stock Politics in Victorian England* (London, 1998).

Anderson, O., 'Wage-earners and income tax: a mid-nineteenth century discussion', *Public Administration* 41 (1963).

'Loans versus taxes: British financial policy in the Crimean war', *Economic History Review* 2nd ser. 16 (1963–4).

A Liberal State at War: English Politics and Economics during the Crimean War (London, 1967).

Balderstone, T., 'War finance and inflation in Britain and Germany, 1914–18', *Economic History Review* 2nd ser. 42 (1989).

Bank, A., 'Losing faith in the civilizing mission: the premature decline of humanitarian liberalism at the Cape, 1840–60', in Daunton and Halpern (eds.), *Empire and Others*.

Barber, B., *The Logic and Limits of Trust* (New Brunswick, N. J., 1983).

Barker, T. C., *The Glassmakers. Pilkington: The Rise of an International Company, 1826–1976* (London, 1977).

Baugh, G. C., 'Government grants in aid of the rates in England and Wales, 1889–1900', *Historical Research* 65 (1992).

Bayly, C. A., 'The British military-fiscal state and indigenous resistance: India, 1750–1820', in Stone (ed.), *Imperial State at War*.

'Returning the British to south Asian history: the limits of colonial hegemony', *South Asia* n.s. 17 (1994).

Baysinger, B. and Tollison, R., 'Chaining leviathan: the case of Gladstonian finance', *History of Political Economy* 12 (1980).

Beckett, J. V., 'Land tax or excise: the levying of taxation in seventeenth- and eighteenth-century England', *English Historical Review* 100 (1985).

Beckett, J. V. and Turner, M. E., 'Taxation and economic growth in eighteenth-century England', *Economic History Review* 2nd ser. 43 (1990).

Bellamy, C., *Administering Central–Local Relations, 1871–1919: The Local Government Board in its Fiscal and Cultural Context* (Manchester, 1988).

Bentley, M. and Stevenson, J. (eds.), *High and Low Politics in Modern Britain* (Oxford, 1983).

Best, G. F. A., *Temporal Pillars: Queen Anne's Bounty, the Ecclesiastical Commissioners and the Church of England* (Cambridge, 1964).

Biagini, E. F., 'Popular Liberals, Gladstonian finance and the debate on taxation, 1860–74', in Biagini and Reid (ed.), *Currents of Radicalism*.

Liberty, Retrenchment and Reform: Popular Liberalism in the Age of Gladstone, 1860–80 (Cambridge, 1992).

'Liberalism and direct democracy: John Stuart Mill and the model of ancient Athens', in Biagini (ed.), *Citizenship and Community*.

Biagini, E. F. (ed.), *Citizenship and Community: Liberals, Radicals and Collective Identities in the British Isles, 1865–1931* (Cambridge, 1996).

Biagini, E. F. and Reid, A. J., 'Currents of radicalism, 1850–1914', in Biagini and Reid (eds.), *Currents of Radicalism*.

Biagini, E. F. and Reid, A. J. (eds.), *Currents of Radicalism: Popular Radicalism, 1850–1914* (Cambridge, 1991).

Binmore, K., *Game Theory and the Social Contract: Playing Fair* (Cambridge, Mass., and London, 1994).

Binney, J. E. D., *British Public Finances and Administration, 1774–1792* (Oxford, 1958).

Blake, R., *Disraeli* (London, 1966).

Bonney, R., 'The eighteenth century. II The struggle for great power status and the end of the old fiscal regime', in Bonney (ed.), *Economic Systems and State Finance*.

'Introduction: the rise of the fiscal state in Europe, c. 1200–1815', in Bonney (ed.), *Rise of the Fiscal State*.

'France, 1494–1815', in Bonney (ed.), *Rise of the Fiscal State*.

Bonney, R. (ed.), *The Origins of the Modern State in Europe, Thirteenth to Eighteenth Centuries: Economic Systems and State Finance* (Oxford, 1995).

The Rise of the Fiscal State in Europe, c. 1200–1815 (Oxford, 1999).

Bonney, R. and Ormrod, W. M., 'Introduction: crises, revolutions and self-sustained growth: towards a conceptual model of change in fiscal history', in Ormrod, Bonney and Bonney (eds.), *Crises, Revolution and Self-Sustained Growth*.

Bosher, J. F., *French Finances, 1770–95: From Business to Bureaucracy* (Cambridge, 1970).

Braddick, M. J., *The Nerves of State: Taxation and the Financing of the English State, 1558–1714* (Manchester, 1996).

Braithwaite, V. and Levi, M. (eds.), *Trust and Governance* (New York, 1998).

Brantlinger, P., *Fictions of State: Culture and Credit in Britain, 1694–1994* (Ithaca and London, 1996).

Brennan, G. and Buchanan, J. M., *The Power to Tax: Analytical Foundations of a Fiscal Constitution* (Cambridge, 1980).

Brennan, G. and Lomasky, L., *Democracy and Decision: The Pure Theory of Electoral Preference* (Cambridge, 1993).

Brenner, R., 'Agrarian class structure and economic development in pre-industrial Europe', *Past and Present* 70 (1976).

Brewer, J., *The Sinews of Power: War, Money and the English State, 1688–1783* (London, 1989).

Brown, J. and Rose, M. B. (eds.), *Entrepreneurship, Networks and Modern Business* (Manchester, 1993).

Brown, J. C., 'The condition of England and the standard of living: cotton textiles in the north-west, 1806–50', *Journal of Economic History* 50 (1990).

Brown, L., *The Board of Trade and the Free Trade Movement, 1830–42* (Oxford, 1958).

Brownlee, W. E., *Federal Taxation in America: A Short History* (Cambridge, 1996).

Buchanan, J. and Tullock, G., *The Calculus of Consent: Logical Foundations of Constitutional Democracy* (Ann Arbor, 1962).

Buenker, J. D., *The Income Tax and the Progressive Era* (New York and London, 1985).

Bulpitt, J., *Territory and Power in the United Kingdom: An Interpretation* (Manchester, 1983).

Burney, I. A., *Bodies of Evidence: Medicine and the Politics of the English Inquest, 1830–1926* (Baltimore, 2000).

Burrow, J. W., *A Liberal Descent: Victorian Historians and the English Past* (Cambridge, 1981).

Butler, D., Adonis, A. and Travers, T., *Failure in British Government: The Politics of the Poll Tax* (Oxford, 1994).

Cain, P. J. and Hopkins, A. G., *British Imperialism: Innovation and Expansion, 1688–1914* (London, 1993).

Calkins, W. N., 'A Victorian free trade lobby', *Economic History Review* 2nd ser 13 (1960–1).

Cannadine, D., *Class in Britain* (London and New Haven, 1998).

Cartter, A. M., 'Income tax allowances and the family in Great Britain', *Population Studies* 6 (1952–3).

Chatterton, D. A., 'State control of public utilities in the nineteenth century: the London gas industry', *Business History* 14 (1972).

Checkland, S. G., *The Gladstones: A Family Biography, 1764–1851* (Cambridge, 1971).

Clark, G., *Betting on Lives: The Culture of Life Insurance in England, 1695–1775* (Manchester, 1999).

Clark, P., *British Clubs and Societies, 1580–1800: The Origins of an Associational World* (Oxford, 2000).

Clarke, P. F., 'The end of *laissez faire* and the politics of cotton', *Historical Journal* 15 (1972).

Liberals and Social Democrats (Cambridge, 1978).

'The Treasury's analytical model of the British economy between the wars', in Furner and Supple (eds.), *The State and Economic Knowledge*.

Clinton, A. and Murray, P., 'Reassessing the vestries: London local government, 1855–1900', in O'Day (ed.), *Government and Institutions*.

Cocks, R., 'Victorian barristers, judges and taxation: a study in the expansion of legal work', in Rubin and Sugarman (eds.), *Law, Economy and Society*.

Coleman, J. S., 'Social capital in the creation of human capital', *American Journal of Sociology* 94 (1988), supplement.

Collini, S., 'Hobhouse, Bosanquet and the state: philosophical Idealism and political argument in England, 1880–1918', *Past and Present* 72 (1976).

Liberalism and Sociology: L. T. Hobhouse and Political Argument in England, 1880–1914 (Cambridge, 1979).

Public Moralists: Political Thought and Intellectual Life in Britain, 1850–1930 (Oxford, 1991).

Conway, S., *The British Isles and the War of American Independence* (Oxford, 2000).

Cookson, J. E., *The British Armed Nation, 1793–1815* (Oxford 1997).

Crafts, N. F. R., *British Economic Growth during the Industrial Revolution* (Oxford, 1985).

'Some dimensions of the "quality of life" during the British industrial revolution', *Economic History Review* 2nd ser 50 (1997).

Crew, M. A. and Kleindorfer, P. R. (eds.), *Competition and Innovation in Postal Services* (Boston, Dordrecht and London 1991).

Crowther, A., *British Social Policy, 1914–39* (Basingstoke, 1988).

Daunton, M. J., *House and Home in the Victorian City: Working-Class Housing, 1850–1914* (London, 1983).

Royal Mail: The Post Office since 1840 (London, 1985).

'Inheritance and succession in the City of London in the nineteenth century', *Business History* 30 (1988).

'Comments', in Crew and Kleindorfer (eds.), *Competition and Innovation*.

Progress and Poverty: An Economic and Social History of Britain, 1700–1850 (Oxford, 1995).

'How to pay for the war: state, society and taxation in Britain, 1917–24', *English Historical Review* 111 (1996).

'Payment and participation: welfare and state formation in Britain, 1900–51', *Past and Present* 150 (1996).

'The political economy of death duties: Harcourt's budget of 1894', in Harte and Quinault (eds.), *Land and Society*.

'Churchill at the Treasury: rethinking Conservative taxation policy, 1924–29', *Revue Belge de Phililogie et d'Histoire* 75 (1997).

'The material politics of natural monopoly: gas in Victorian Britain', in Daunton and Hilton (eds.), *The Politics of Consumption*.

Just Taxes: The Politics of Taxation in Britain, 1914–1979 (Cambridge, forthcoming).

'Taxation and representation in the Victorian city', in R. Rodger and R. Colls (eds.), *Cities of Ideas: Citizenship and Governance in Urban Britain* (Aldershot, forthcoming).

Daunton, M. J. (ed.), *Charity, Self-Interest and Welfare in the English Past* (London, 1996).

The Cambridge Urban History of Britain, vol. III, *1840–1950* (Cambridge, 2000).

Daunton, M. J. and Halpern, E. (eds.), *Empire and Others: British Encounters with Indigenous Peoples, 1600–1850* (London, 1999).

Daunton, M. J. and Hilton, M. (eds.), *The Politics of Consumption: Material Culture and Citizenship in Europe and America* (Oxford, 2001).

Davis, J., *Reforming London: The London Government Problem, 1855–1900* (Oxford, 1988).

'Central government and the towns, 1840–1950', in Daunton (ed.), *Cambridge Urban History*, vol. III.

Davis, J. and Tanner, D., 'The borough franchise after 1867', *Historical Research* 69 (1996).

Davis, L. E. and Huttenback, R. A., *Mammon and the Pursuit of Empire: The Economics of British Imperialism* (Cambridge, 1988).

Denzer, L. and Crowder, M., 'Bai Bureh and the Sierra Leone hut tax war of 1898', in Rotberg and Mazrui (eds.), *Protest and Power*.

Dewey, C., 'The end of the imperialism of free trade: the eclipse of the Lancashire lobby and the concession of fiscal autonomy to India', in Dewey and Hopkins (eds.), *The Imperial Impact*.

Dewey, C. and Hopkins, A. G. (eds.), *The Imperial Impact: Studies in the Economic History of Africa and India* (London, 1978).

Dickson, P. G. M., *The Financial Revolution in England: A Study in the Development of Public Credit, 1688–1756* (London, 1967).

Dobbin, F., *Forging Industrial Policy: The US, Britain and France in the Railway Age* (Cambridge, 1994).

Dome, T., 'Malthus on taxation and national debt', *History of Political Economy* 29 (1997).

Doyle, B. M., 'The changing functions of urban government: councillors, officials and pressure groups', in Daunton (ed.), *Cambridge Urban History*, vol. III.

Driver, F., *Power and Pauperism: The Workhouse System, 1834–1884* (Cambridge, 1993).

Duffy, A. E. P., 'New unionism in Britain, 1889–90: a reappraisal', *Economic History Review* 2nd ser 14 (1961–2).

Dupree, M., 'The provision of social services', in Daunton (ed.), *Cambridge Urban History*, vol. III.

Dyck, I., *William Cobbett and Rural Popular Culture* (Cambridge, 1992).

Eastwood, D., *Governing Rural England: Tradition and Transformation in Local Government, 1780–1840* (Oxford, 1994).

Edgerton, D., *England and the Aeroplane: An Essay on a Militant and Technological Nation* (Basingstoke, 1991).

Eley, G. and Blackbourn, D., *The Peculiarities of German History: Bourgeois Society and Politics in Nineteenth-Century Germany* (Oxford, 1984).

Eltis, W., *The Classical Theory of Economic Growth* (Oxford, 1984).

Englander, D., *Landlord and Tenant in Urban Britain, 1838–1918* (Oxford, 1983).

Evans, P. B., Rueschmeyer, D. and Skocpol, T. (eds.), *Bringing the State Back In* (Cambridge, 1985).

Falkus, M., 'The development of municipal trading in the nineteenth century', *Business History* 19 (1977).

Feinstein, C. H., *National Income, Expenditure and Output of the United Kingdom, 1855–1965* (Cambridge, 1972).

Feinstein, C. H. and Pollard, S. (eds.), *Studies in Capital Formation in the United Kingdom, 1750–1920* (Oxford, 1988).

Femia, J. V., *Gramsci's Political Thought* (Oxford, 1981).

Ferguson, N., 'Public finance and national security: the domestic origins of the First World War revisited', *Past and Present* 142 (1994).

Paper and Iron: Hamburg Business and German Politics in the Era of Inflation, 1897–1927 (Cambridge, 1995).

Fine, B., 'The developmental state is dead – long live social capital?', *Development and Change* 30 (1999).

Finlayson, G. B. A. M., 'The Municipal Corporation Commission and Report, 1833–35', *Bulletin of the Institute of Historical Research* 36 (1963).

'The politics of municipal reform, 1835', *English Historical Review* 81 (1966).

Finn, M., *After Chartism: Class and Nation in English Radical Politics, 1848–74* (Cambridge, 1993).

Flora, P. *et al.*, *State, Economy and Society in Western Europe, 1815–1975. A Data Handbook in Two Volumes*, vol. I: *The Growth of Mass Democracies and Welfare States* (Frankfurt, London and Chicago, 1983).

Foreman-Peck, J. (ed.), *New Perspectives on the Late Victorian Economy: Essays in Quantitative Economic History* (Cambridge, 1991).

Foreman-Peck, J. and Millward, R., *Public and Private Ownership of British Industry, 1820–1990* (Oxford, 1994).

Foucault, M., *Madness and Civilisation: A History of Insanity in the Age of Reason* (English edn, New York, 1973).

Discipline and Punish: The Birth of the Prison (English edn, London, 1977).

Fraser, D., *Urban Politics in Victorian England: The Structure of Politics in Victorian Cities* (Leicester, 1976).

Freeden, M., *The New Liberalism: An Ideology of Social Reform* (Oxford, 1978).

Freeden, M. (ed.), *Reappraising J. A. Hobson: Humanism and Welfare* (London, 1990).

Fukuyama, F., *Trust: The Social Virtues and the Creation of Prosperity* (New York, 1995).

Furner, M. O. and Supple, B., 'Ideas, institutions, and state in the United States and Britain: an introduction', in Furner and Supple (eds.), *The State and Economic Knowledge.*

Furner, M. O. and Supple, B. (eds.), *The State and Economic Knowledge: The American and British Experiences* (Cambridge, 1990).

Gambetta, D. (ed.), *Trust: Making and Breaking Co-operative Relations* (Oxford, 1988).

Gambles, A., 'Rethinking the politics of protection: Conservatism and the corn laws, 1830–52', *English Historical Review* 113 (1998).

Protection and Politics: Conservative Economic Discourse, 1815–52 (Woodbridge, 1999).

'Fishing for free trade? The political economy of fisheries policy in Britain and the UK, 1780–1850', *Journal of British Studies*, 39 (2000).

Gash, N., 'After Waterloo: British society and the legacy of the Napoleonic wars', *Transactions of the Royal Historical Society* 5th ser. 28 (1978).

Gatrell, V. A. C., 'Crime, authority and the policeman-state', in Thompson (ed.), *Cambridge Social History of Britain*, vol. III.

Gelabert, J., 'The fiscal burden', in Bonney (ed.), *Economic Systems and State Finance.*

Ghosh, P. R., 'Disraelian Conservatism: a financial approach', *English Historical Review* 99 (1984).

Gilbert, B. B., 'Winston Churchill versus the Webbs: the origins of British unemployment insurance', *American Historical Review* 71 (1966).

'David Lloyd George: land, the budget and social reform', *American Historical Review* 81 (1976).

'David Lloyd George: the reform of British land-holding and the budget of 1914', *Historical Journal* 21 (1978).

Gilbert, M., *Churchill's Political Philosophy* (Oxford, 1981).

Goldschied, R., 'Sociological approach to the problems of public finance', in R. A. Musgrave and A. T. Peacock (eds.), *Classics in the Theory of Public Finance* (London, 1967).

Gospel, H. F., *Firms and the Management of Labour in Modern Britain* (Cambridge, 1992).

Gospel, H. F. (ed.), *Industrial Training and Technological Innovation: A Comparative and Historical Study* (London, 1991).

Gray, P., *Famine, Land and Politics: British Government and Irish Society, 1843–50* (Dublin, 1999).

Green, E. H. H., 'Radical conservatism: the electoral genesis of tariff reform', *Historical Journal* 28 (1985).

'Rentiers versus producers? The political economy of the bimetallic controversy, c. 1880–1898', *English Historical Review* 103 (1988).

The Crisis of Conservatism: The Politics, Economics and Ideology of the British Conservative Party, 1880–1914 (London, 1995).

Grigg, P. J., *Prejudice and Judgement* (London, 1948).

Gross, J.-P., 'Progressive taxation and social justice in eighteenth-century France', *Past and Present* 140 (1993).

Hall, C., *White, Male and Middle Class: Explorations in Feminism and History* (Cambridge, 1992).

Hamlin, C., 'Muddling in Bumbledom: on the enormity of large sanitary improvements in four British towns, 1855–1885', *Victorian Studies* 32 (1988–9).

A Science of Impurity: Water Analysis in Nineteenth-Century Britain (Bristol, 1990).

Hanham, H. J., *Elections and Party Management: Politics in the Time of Disraeli and Gladstone* (London, 1959).

Hardin, R., *Collective Action* (Washington, 1982).

'Constitutional political economy: agreement on rules', *British Journal of Political Science* 18 (1988).

'Trusting persons, trusting institution', in Zeckhauser (ed.), *Strategy and Choice*.

Hardy, A., *The Epidemic Streets: Infectious Disease and the Rise of Preventive Medicine, 1856–1900* (Oxford, 1993).

Hargreaves, E. L., *The National Debt* (London, 1930).

Harling, P., 'Rethinking "old corruption" ', *Past and Present* 147 (1995).

The Waning of 'Old Corruption': The Politics of Economical Reform in Britain, 1779–1846 (Oxford, 1996).

Harling, P. and Mandler, P., 'From "fiscal-military" state to laissez-faire state, 1760–1850', *Journal of British Studies* 32 (1993).

Harris, J., *Unemployment and Politics: A Study in English Social Policy, 1886–1914* (Oxford, 1972).

'The transition to high politics in English social policy, 1889–1914', in Bentley and Stevenson (eds.), *High and Low Politics*.

'Political thought and the welfare state, 1870–1940: an intellectual framework for British social policy', *Past and Present* 135 (1992).

Private Lives, Public Spirit: A Social History of Britain, 1870–1914 (Oxford, 1993).

Harte, N. B., 'The rise of protection and the English linen trade, 1690–1790', in Harte and Ponting (eds.), *Textile History and Economic History*.

Harte, N. B. and Ponting, K. B. (eds.), *Textile History and Economic History* (Manchester, 1973).

Harte, N. B. and Quinault, R. (eds.), *Land and Society in Britain, 1700–1914* (Manchester, 1996).

Hasson, J. A., 'The growth and impact of the British water industry in the nineteenth century', *Economic History Review* 2nd ser. 38 (1985).

Hawkins, A. B., 'A forgotten crisis: Gladstone and the politics of finance during the 1850s', *Victorian Studies* 26 (1982–3).

' "Parliamentary government" and Victorian political parties, c. 1830–80', *English Historical Review* 104 (1989).

Hennock, E. P., 'Finance and politics in urban local government in England, 1835–1900', *Historical Journal* 6 (1963).

Fit and Proper Persons: Ideal and Reality in Nineteenth-Century Urban Government (London, 1973).

British Social Reform and German Precedents: The Case of Social Insurance, 1880–1914 (Oxford, 1987).

Hewitt, M., *The Emergence of Stability in the Industrial City: Manchester, 1832–67* (Aldershot, 1996).

Hilton, B., *Corn, Cash and Commerce: The Economic Policies of the Tory Government, 1815–30* (Oxford, 1977).

The Age of Atonement: The Influence of Evangelicalism on Social and Economic Thought, 1785–1865 (Oxford, 1988).

Hirst, F. W., *The Political Economy of War* (London, 1915).

Hobson, J. M., 'The military-extraction gap and the wary Titan: the fiscal sociology of British defence policy, 1870–1913', *Journal of European Economic History* 22 (1993).

The Wealth of States: A Comparative Sociology of International Economic and Political Change (Cambridge, 1997).

Hont, I., 'The rhapsody of public debt: David Hume and voluntary state bankruptcy', in Phillipson and Skinner (eds.), *Political Discourse in Early Modern Britain.*

Hope-Jones, A., *Income Tax in the Napoleonic Wars* (Cambridge, 1939).

Hoppit, J., 'Attitudes to credit in Britain, 1680–1790', *Historical Journal* 33 (1990).

Horne, H. O., *A History of Savings Banks* (London, 1947).

Howe, A. C., 'Bimetallism, c.1880–1898: a controversy re-opened?', *English Historical Review* 105 (1990).

Free Trade and Liberal England, 1846–1946 (Oxford, 1997).

Howell, D., *British Workers and the Independent Labour Party, 1888–1906* (Manchester, 1983).

Hudson, P., *The Genesis of Industrial Capital: A Study of the West Riding Wool Textile Industry, c. 1750–1850* (Cambridge, 1986).

Innes, J., 'The domestic face of the military-fiscal state: government and society in eighteenth-century Britain', in Stone (ed.), *An Imperial State at War.*

'Governing diverse societies', in Langford (ed.), *The Short Oxford History of Eighteenth-Century Britain.*

Isaacs, N., 'Principal: quantum or res', *Harvard Law Review* 46 (1932–3).

Johnson, P., 'Class law in Victorian England', *Past and Present* 141 (1993).

'Economic development and industrial dynamism in Victorian London', *London Journal* 21 (1996).

Jones, C. C., 'Split income and separate spheres: tax law and gender roles in the 1940s', *Law and History Review* 6 (1988).

Jones, L., 'Public pursuit of private profit? Liberal businessmen and municipal politics in Birmingham, 1865–1900', *Business History* 25 (1983).

Kay, J. A. and King, M. A., *The British Tax System* (Oxford, 1978).

Kellett, J., 'Municipal socialism, enterprise and trading in the Victorian city', *Urban History Yearbook* (1978).

King, S., 'Reconstructing lives: the poor, the poor law and welfare in Calverley, 1650–1820', *Social History* 22 (1997).

Klein, I., 'English free traders and Indian tariffs, 1874–96', *Modern Asian Studies* 5 (1971).

Knauss, R., *Die deutsche, englische und franzosische Kriegsfinanzierung* (Berlin and Liepzig, 1925).

Knox, B. A., 'The British government and the Governor Eyre controversy, 1865–75', *Historical Journal* 19 (1976).

Koepke, R. L., 'The *Loi des patentes* of 1844', *French Historical Studies* 11 (1979–80).

Kruedener, J. von, 'The Franckenstein paradox in the intergovernmental fiscal relations of imperial Germany', in Witt (ed.), *Wealth and Taxation*.

Krüger, K., 'Public finance and modernisation: the change from domain state to tax state in Hesse in the sixteenth and seventeenth centuries: a case study', in Witt (ed.), *Wealth and Taxation*.

Kumar, D., 'The fiscal system', in Kumar (ed.), *Cambridge Economic History of India*.

Kumar, D. (ed.), *The Cambridge Economic History of India*, vol. II: *c. 1757–c. 1970* (Cambridge, 1983).

Lachs, R., 'Income tax on capital profits', *Modern Law Review* 6 (1942–3).

Langford, P., *The Excise Crisis: Society and Politics in the Age of Walpole* (Oxford, 1975).

Public Life and the Propertied Englishman, 1689–1798 (Oxford, 1991).

Langford, P. (ed.), *The Short Oxford History of Eighteenth-Century Britain* (Oxford, forthcoming).

Lazonick, W., *Competitive Advantage on the Shop Floor* (Cambridge, Mass., 1990).

Lears, T. J., 'The concept of cultural hegemony: problems and possibilities', *American Historical Review* 90 (1985).

Leathers, C. G., 'Gladstonian finance and the Virginia school of public finance', *History of Political Economy* 18 (1986).

Lindert, P. H., 'The rise of social spending, 1880–1930', *Explorations in Economic History* 31 (1994).

'What limits social spending?', *Explorations in Economic History* 33 (1996).

'Poor relief before the welfare state: Britain versus the continent, 1780–1880', *European Review of Economic History* 2 (1998).

'Democracy, decentralization, and mass schooling before 1914', Agricultural History Center, University of California, Davis, Working Paper Series no. 104, Feb. 2001.

McBriar, A. M., *An Edwardian Mixed Doubles: The Bosanquets versus the Webbs: A Study in British Social Policy, 1890–1929* (Oxford, 1987).

McInnes, A., *Clanship, Commerce and the House of Stuart, 1603–1788* (East Linton, 1996).

McKay, J. P., *Tramways and Trolleys: The Rise of Urban Mass Transport in Europe* (Princeton, 1976).

McKibbin, R., 'Why was there no Marxism in Great Britain?', *English Historical Review* 99 (1984).

McLeod, R. M., 'Law, medicine and public opinion: the resistance to compulsory health legislation, 1870–1907', *Public Law* 12 (1967).

Macnicol, J., *The Politics of Retirement in Britain, 1878–1948* (Cambridge, 1998).

Magill, R. F., *Taxable Income* (New York, 1945).

Maier, C. S., *Recasting Bourgeois Europe* (Princeton, 1975).

Maloney, J., 'Gladstone and sound Victorian finance', in Maloney (ed.), *Debts and Deficits*.

Maloney, J. (ed.), *Debts and Deficits: An Historical Perspective* (Cheltenham, 1998).

Mandler, P., 'The making of the poor law *redivivus*', *Past and Present* 117 (1987). 'Art, death and taxes: the taxation of works of art in Britain, 1796–1914', *Historical Research* 74 (2001).

Mann, M., *The Sources of Social Power*, vol. II: *The Rise of Classes and Nation States, 1750–1914* (Cambridge, 1993).

Marks, S., 'The Zulu disturbances in Natal', in Rotberg and Mazrui (eds.), *Protest and Power*.

Marsh, P., *Joseph Chamberlain: Entrepreneur in Politics* (New Haven and London, 1994).

Marwick, A., 'The Labour party and the welfare state in Britain, 1900–48', *American Historical Review* 73 (1978).

Mathias, P. and O'Brien, P. K., 'Taxation in Britain and France, 1715–1810: a comparison of the social and economic incidence of taxes collected for the central governments', *Journal of European Economic History* 5 (1976).

Mathias, P. and Pollard, S. (eds.), *Cambridge Economic History of Europe*, vol. VIII: *The Industrial Economies: The Development of Economic and Social Policies* (Cambridge, 1989).

Matthew, H. C. G., *The Liberal Imperialists: The Ideas and Politics of a Post-Gladstonian Elite* (Oxford, 1973). 'Disraeli, Gladstone and the politics of mid-Victorian budgets', *Historical Journal* 22 (1979). *Gladstone, 1809–1874* (Oxford, 1986). 'Hobson, Ruskin and Cobden', in Freeden (ed.), *Reappraising J.A. Hobson*. *Gladstone, 1809–1898* (Oxford, 1997).

Matthews, D., 'Laissez-faire and the London gas industry in the nineteenth century: another look', *Economic History Review* 2nd ser. 39 (1986).

Melling, J., 'Welfare capitalism and the origins of welfare states: British industry, workplace welfare and social reform, c. 1870–1914', *Social History* 17 (1992).

Middleton, R., *Government versus the Market: The Growth of the Public Sector, Economic Management and British Economic Performance, c. 1890–1979* (Cheltenham, 1996).

Millward, R., 'The emergence of gas and water monopolies in nineteenth-century Britain: contested markets and public control', in Foreman-Peck (ed.), *New Perspectives on the Late Victorian Economy*.

'From private to public ownership of gas undertakings in England and Wales, 1851–1947: chronology, incidence and causes', *Business History* 35 (1993).

Millward, R. and Sheard, S., 'The urban fiscal problem 1870–1914: government expenditure and finances in England and Wales', *Economic History Review* 2nd ser. 48 (1995).

Millward, R. and Ward, R., 'The costs of public and private gas enterprises in late nineteenth-century Britain', *Oxford Economic Papers* 39 (1987).

Misra, B. B., *The Administrative History of India, 1834–1947: General Administration* (Bombay, 1970).

Mitchell, B. R. and Deane, P., *Abstract of British Historical Statistics* (Cambridge, 1962).

Mommsen, W. J. (ed.), *The Emergence of the Welfare State in Britain and Germany, 1850–1950* (London, 1981).

Morris, R. J., 'Structure, culture and society in British towns', in Daunton (ed.), *Cambridge Urban History*, vol. III.

Muldrew, C., *The Economy of Obligation: The Culture of Credit and Social Relations in Early Modern England* (Basingstoke and London, 1998).

Murray, B. K., 'The politics of the "people's budget"', *Historical Journal* 16 (1973).

The People's Budget, 1909/10: Lloyd George and Liberal Politics (Oxford, 1980).

Musgrave, R. A., *The Theory of Public Finance* (New York, 1959).

Fiscal Systems (New Haven, 1969).

Musgrave, R. A. and Peacock, A. T. (eds.), *Classics in the Theory of Public Finance* (London, 1967).

Nenadic, S., 'The small family firm in Victorian Britain', *Business History* 35 (1993).

Newcomer, M., *Central and Local Finance in Germany and England* (New York, 1937).

Nye, J. N., 'The myth of free trade Britain and fortress France: tariffs and trade in the nineteenth century', *Journal of Economic History* 51 (1991).

O'Brien, D. P., *J. R. McCulloch: A Study in Classic Economics* (London, 1970).

The Classical Economists (Oxford, 1975).

'The political economy of British taxation, 1660–1815', *Economic History Review* 2nd ser. 41 (1988).

Power with Profit: The State and the Economy, 1688–1815 (London, 1991).

'Taxation, 1688–1914', *History Review* Mar. 1997.

O'Brien, P. K. and Hunt, P. A., 'The rise of the fiscal state in England, 1485–1815', *Historical Research* 66 (1993).

'The emergence and consolidation of excises in the English fiscal system before the Glorious Revolution', *British Tax Review* (1997).

'England, 1485–1815', in Bonney (ed.), *Rise of the Fiscal State*.

O'Brien, P. K., Griffiths, T. and Hunt, P., 'Political components of the industrial revolution: parliament and the English cotton textile industry, 1660–1774', *Economic History Review* 2nd ser. 44 (1991).

O'Day, A. (ed.), *Government and Institutions in the Post-1832 United Kingdom* (Lampeter, 1995).

Offer, A., *Property and Politics, 1870–1914: Landownership, Law, Ideology and Urban Development in England* (Cambridge, 1981).
'Empire and social reform: British overseas investment and domestic politics, 1908–14', *Historical Journal* 26 (1983).
Ogborn, M., 'Local power and state regulation in nineteenth-century Britain', *Transactions of the Institute of British Geographers* n.s. 17 (1992).
Ormrod, W. M., Bonney, M. M., and Bonney, R. J. (eds.), *Crises, Revolutions and Self-Sustained Growth: Essays in European Fiscal History, 1130–1830* (Stamford, 1999).
Ostrom, E., *Governing the Commons: The Evolution of Institutions for Collective Action* (Cambridge, 1990).
Owen, D., *English Philanthropy, 1660–1960* (London, 1964).
Packer, I., 'The Liberal cave and the 1914 budget', *English Historical Review* 111 (1996).
Parker, G. N., *The Military Revolution: Military Innovation and the Rise of the West, 1500–1800* (Cambridge, 1988).
Parris, M., *Great Parliamentary Scandals: Four Centuries of Calumny, Smear and Innuendo* (London, 1995).
Peacock, A. T., Turvey, R., Stolper, W. F. and Henderson, E. (eds.), *International Economic Papers*, no. 4 (London and New York, 1954).
Peacock, A. T. and Wiseman, J., *The Growth of Public Expenditure in the United Kingdom* (2nd edn, London, 1961).
Peden, G. C., 'The "Treasury view" on public works and employment in the interwar period', *Economic History Review* 2nd ser. 37 (1984).
Pedersen, S., *Family, Dependence, and the Origins of the Welfare State: Britain and France, 1914–45* (Cambridge, 1993).
Perry, C. R., *The Victorian Post Office: The Growth of a Bureaucracy* (Woodbridge, 1992).
Petersen, E. L., 'From domain state to tax state: synthesis and interpretation', *Scandinavian Economic History Review* 23 (1975).
Phillipson, N. and Skinner, Q. (eds.), *Political Discourse in Early Modern Britain* (Cambridge, 1993).
Pocock, J. G. A., *Virtue, Commerce and History: Essays on Political Thought and History, Chiefly in the Eighteenth Century* (Cambridge, 1985).
Poovey, M., *A History of the Modern Fact: Problems of Knowledge in the Sciences of Wealth and Society* (Chicago, 1998).
Porter, D., 'Enemies of the race: biologism, environmentalism and public health in Edwardian England', *Victorian Studies* 34 (1991).
Prest, J., *Liberty and Locality: Parliament, Permissive Legislation and Ratepayers' Democracies in the Nineteenth Century* (Oxford, 1990).
Price, R., *Masters, Unions and Men: Work Control in Building and the Rise of Labour, 1830–1914* (Cambridge, 1980).
Prothero, I., *Artisans and Politics in Early Nineteenth-Century London: John Gast and his Times* (Folkestone, 1979).
Putnam, R. D., *Making Democracy Work: Civic Traditions in Modern Italy* (Princeton, 1993).
Bowling Alone: The Collapse and Revival of American Community Life (New York, 2000).

Read, D., *Peel and the Victorians* (Oxford, 1987).

Reeder, D. 'The politics of urban leaseholds in Late Victorian England', *International Review of Social History* 6 (1961).

Reeder, D. and Rodger, R., 'Industrialisation and the city economy', in Daunton (ed.), *Cambridge Urban History*, vol. III.

Ricci, D. M., 'Fabian socialism: a theory of rent as exploitation', *Journal of British Studies* 9 (1969–70).

Robb, P. G., *Ancient Rights and Future Comfort: Bihar, the Bengal Tenancy Act of 1885, and British Rule in India* (Richmond, 1997).

Roberts, R. O., 'Ricardo's theory of public debts', *Economica* n.s. 9 (1942).

Roberts, S., 'The direct taxation of Africans in the Nyasaland protectorate, 1892–1939: some determinants of revenue policy', *British Tax Revue* (1967).

Rodger, R. and Colls, R. (eds.), *Cities of Ideas: Citizenship and Governance in Urban Britain* (Aldershot, forthcoming).

Rose, M. B., 'Beyond Buddenbrooks: the family firm and the management of succession in nineteenth-century Britain', in Brown and Rose (eds.), *Entrepreneurship, Networks and Modern Business*.

Rose, M. E., 'The crisis of poor relief in England, 1850–90', in Mommsen (ed.), *Emergence of the Welfare State*.

Rose, M. E. (ed.), *The Poor and the City: The English Poor Law in its Urban Context, 1834–1914* (Leicester, 1985).

Rose, R. and Karran, T., *Taxation by Political Inertia: Financing the Growth of Government in Britain* (London, 1986).

Rotberg, R. I. and Mazrui, A. A. (eds.), *Protest and Power in Black Africa* (New York, 1970).

Rubin, G. R. and Sugarman, D. (eds.), *Law, Economy and Society, 1750–1914: Essays in the History of English Law* (Abingdon, 1984).

Rubinstein, W. D., 'The end of "old corruption" in Britain, 1780–1860', *Past and Present* 101 (1983).

Sabine, B. E. V., *A History of Income Tax* (London, 1966).

'The general commissioners', *British Tax Review* (1968).

'The abolition of income tax: a dream of 1873/4', *British Tax Review* (1973).

Sanderson, M., *Education, Economic Change and Society in England* (2nd edn, Cambridge 1991).

Schremmer, D. E., 'Taxation and public finance: Britain, France and Germany', in Mathias and Pollard (eds.), *Cambridge Economic History of Europe*, vol. III.

Schulze, W., 'The emergence and consolidation of the "tax state": the sixteenth century', in Bonney (ed.), *Economic Systems and State Finance*.

Schumpeter, J. A., 'The crisis of the tax state', in Peacock, Turvey, Stolper and Henderson (eds.), *International Economic Papers*, no. 4.

Seltzer, L. H., *The Nature and Tax Treatment of Capital Gains and Losses* (National Bureau of Economic Research, New York, 1951).

Semmel, B., *Imperialism and Social Reform: English Social-Imperial Thought, 1895–1914* (London, 1960).

Shoup, C. S., *The Sales Tax in France* (New York, 1930).

Ricardo on Taxation (New York, 1954).

Simon, C. J. and Nardinelli, C., 'The talk of the town: human capital, information and the growth of English cities, 1861–1961', *Explorations in Economic History* 33 (1996).

Skidelsky, R., *John Maynard Keynes*, vol. I: *Hopes Betrayed, 1883–1920* (London, 1983).

Skinner, Q., *Liberty before Liberalism* (Cambridge, 1998).

Skocpol, T., 'Bringing the state back in: strategies of analysis in current research', in Evans, Rueschmeyer and Skocpol (eds.), *Bringing the State Back In.*

Protecting Mothers and Soldiers: The Political Origins of Social Policy in the United States (Cambridge, Mass., 1992).

Smith, R., 'Charity, self-interest and welfare: reflections from demographic and family history' in Daunton (ed.), *Charity, Self-Interest and Welfare.*

Spaulding, H. B., *The Income Tax in Great Britain and the United States* (London, 1927).

Stebbings, C., 'Charity land: a mortmain confusion', *Journal of Legal History* 12 (1991).

' "A natural safeguard": the general commissioners of income tax', *British Tax Review* (1992).

'The general commissioners of income tax: assessors or adjudicators?', *British Tax Review* (1993).

'The clerk to the general commissioners of income tax', *British Tax Review* (1994).

'One hundred years ago: "official insolence" ', *British Tax Revue* (1996).

'One hundred years ago: works of art', *British Tax Review* (1996).

Stedman Jones, G., *Languages of Class: Studies in English Working-Class History, 1832–1982* (Cambridge, 1983).

Steinmo, S., 'Political institutions and tax policy in the United States, Sweden and Britain', *World Politics* 41 (1988–9).

Taxation and Democracy: Swedish, British, and American Approaches to Financing the Modern State (New Haven, 1993).

Stokes, E., *The Peasant and the Raj* (Cambridge, 1978).

Stone, L. (ed.), *An Imperial State at War: Britain from 1689 to 1815* (London, 1994).

Stopforth, D., 'Charitable covenants by individuals: a history of their tax treatment and their cost to the Exchequer', *British Tax Review* (1986).

Sugarman, D., 'Simple images and complex realities: English lawyers and their relationship to business and politics, 1750–1950', *Law and History Review* 11 (1993).

'Bourgeois collectivism, professional power, and the boundaries of the state: the private and public life of the Law Society, 1825–1914', *International Journal of the Legal Profession* 3 (1996).

Surridge, K. T., *Managing the South African War, 1899–1902: Politicians v Generals* (Woodbridge, 1998).

Sutherland, G., *Policy Making in Elementary Education, 1870–95* (Oxford, 1973).

Szreter, S., 'The importance of social intervention in Britain's mortality decline c. 1850–1914: a reinterpretation of the role of public health', *Social History of Medicine* 1 (1988).

'Economic growth, disruption, deprivation, disease and death: or the importance of the politics of public health for development', *Population and Development Review* 23 (1997).

Szreter, S. and Mooney, G., 'Urbanization, mortality, and the standard of living
debate: new estimates for the expectation of life at birth in nineteenth-century
British cities', *Economic History Review* 2nd ser. 51 (1998).

Tanner, D., 'Ideological debate in Edwardian Labour politics: radicalism, revisionism and socialism', in Biagini and Reid (eds.), *Currents of Radicalism.*

Taylor, M., *The Decline of British Radicalism, 1847–1860* (Oxford, 1995).

'The 1848 revolutions and the British empire', *Past and Present* 166 (2000).

Thane, P., 'Labour and local politics: radicalism, democracy and social reform,
1880–1914', in Biagini and Reid (eds.), *Currents of Radicalism.*

Thompson, E. P., *The Making of the English Working Class* (London, 1963).

Thompson, F. M. L., 'Town and city', in Thompson (ed.), *Cambridge Social
History of Britain,* vol. I.

Thompson, F. M. L. (ed.), *The Cambridge Social History of Britain, 1750–1950*
(3 vols., Cambridge, 1990).

Thompson, N., 'Hobson and the Fabians: two roads to socialism in the 1920s',
History of Political Economy 26 (1994).

Thompson, P., *Socialists, Liberals and Labour: The Struggle for London, 1885–1914*
(London, 1967).

Thorne, R. G. (ed.), *The History of Parliament: The House of Commons, 1790–1820*
(5 vols., London, 1986).

Tilly, C., *Coercion, Capital, and European States, AD 990–1990* (Oxford, 1992).

Townshend, C., *Making the Peace: Public Order and Public Security in Modern
Britain* (Oxford, 1993).

Trainor, R., 'The middle class', in Daunton (ed.), *Cambridge Urban History,*
vol. III.

Trentmann, F., 'The strange death of free trade: the erosion of "liberal consensus"
in Great Britain, c. 1903–1932', in Biagini (ed.), *Citizenship and Community.*

'The transformation of fiscal reform: reciprocity, modernization, and the fiscal
debate within the business community in early twentieth-century Britain',
Historical Journal 39 (1996).

'Civil society, commerce and the "citizen-consumer": popular meanings of
free trade in late nineteenth- and early twentieth-century Britain', *Center for
European Studies Working Paper* 66.

'Wealth versus welfare: the British left between free trade and national political
economy before the First World War', *Historical Research* 70 (1997).

'Political culture and political economy: interest, ideology and free trade',
Review of International Political Economy 5 (1998).

Turner, F., *Contesting Cultural Authority: Essays in Victorian Intellectual Life*
(Cambridge, 1993).

Turner, J., 'The politics of "organised business" in the First World War', in Turner
(ed.), *Businessmen and Politics.*

Turner, J. (ed.), *Businessmen and Politics: Studies of Business Activity in British
Politics, 1900–45* (London, 1984).

van Caenegem, R. C., *Judges, Legislators and Professors: Chapters in European Legal
History* (Cambridge, 1987).

Veseth, M., *Mountains of Debt: Crisis and Change in Renaissance Florence, Victorian Britain and Postwar America* (New York and Oxford, 1990).

Vincent, D., *The Culture of Secrecy: Britain, 1832–1998* (Oxford, 1998).

Wahrman, D., *Imagining the Middle Class: The Political Representation of Class in Britain c. 1780–1840* (Cambridge, 1995).

'The new political history: a review essay', *Social History* 21 (1996).

Waller, P. J., *Town, City and Nation: England, 1850–1914* (Oxford, 1983).

Ward, P., *Red Flag and Union Jack: Englishness, Patriotism and the British Left, 1881–1924* (Woodbridge, 1998).

Ward, W. R., *The English Land Tax in the Eighteenth Century* (Oxford, 1963).

White, J., *Central Administration in Nigeria, 1914–1948: The Problem of Polarity* (Dublin and London, 1981).

Whiting, R., 'Taxation and the working class, 1915–24', *Historical Journal* 33 (1990).

Williamson, J. G., *Coping with City Growth during the Industrial Revolution* (Cambridge, 1990).

Wilson, J. F., 'The finance of municipal capital expenditure in England and Wales, 1870–1914', *Financial History Review* 4 (1997).

Winch, D., *Riches and Poverty: An Intellectual History of Political Economy in Britain, 1750–1834* (Cambridge, 1996).

'The political economy of public finance in the "long" eighteenth century', in Maloney (ed.), *Debts and Deficits*

Witt, P.-C., *Die Finanzpolitik des Deutschen Reiches* (Lübeck, 1970).

Witt, P.-C. (ed.), *Wealth and Taxation in Central Europe: The History and Sociology of Public Finance* (Leamington Spa, 1987).

Wohl, A. S., *Endangered Lives: Public Health in Victorian Britain* (Cambridge, Mass., 1983).

Wolfe, W., *From Radicalism to Socialism: Men and Ideas in the Formation of Fabian Socialist Doctrine, 1881–89* (New Haven, 1975).

Wright, M., *Treasury Control of the Civil Service, 1854–74* (Oxford, 1969).

Wueller, P. H., 'Concepts of taxable income I. The German contribution', *Political Science Quarterly* 53 (1938).

'Concepts of taxable income, III: the American contribution', *Political Science Quarterly* 53 (1938).

Young, K., *Local Politics and the Rise of Party* (Leicester, 1975).

Zeckhauser, R. (ed.), *Strategy and Choice* (Cambridge, Mass., 1991).

Zeitlin, J. and Sabel, C., 'Historical alternatives to mass production: politics, markets and technology in nineteenth-century industrialisation', *Past and Present* 108 (1985).

Zimmeck, M., 'Gladstone holds his own: the origins of income tax relief for life insurance purposes', *Bulletin of the Institute of Historical Research* 58 (1985).

THESES

Ashbridge, P. M., 'The power and the purse: aspects of the genesis and implementation of the Metropolitan Poor Act, 1867', PhD thesis, University of London (1998).

Dawson, E. J., 'Finance and the unreformed borough: a critical appraisal of corporate finance, with special reference to the boroughs of Nottingham, York and Boston', PhD thesis, University of Hull (1978).

Dunn, L., 'A history of inheritance taxes in England', PhD thesis, University of London (1956).

Göschl, K. S. M., 'A comparative study of public health in Wakefield, Halifax and Doncaster, 1865–1914', PhD thesis, University of Cambridge (2000).

Halliday, S., 'Sir Joseph Bazalgette and the main drainage of London', PhD thesis, London Guildhall University (1998).

Hobson, J. M., 'The tax-seeking state: protectionism, taxation and state structures in Germany, Russia, Britain and America, 1870–1914', PhD thesis, University of London (1991).

Salmon, P., 'Electoral reform at work: local politics and national politics, 1832–41', DPhil thesis, University of Oxford (1997).

Index

Lightning Source UK Ltd.
Milton Keynes UK
22 December 2009

147827UK00001B/58/A